Philosophy in the Making

Philosophy in the Making

D.H.Th. Vollenhoven and the
Emergence of Reformed Philosophy

Anthony Tol

Dordt College Press

Cover design: Scott Vande Kraats
Layout: Carla Goslinga

© 2010 Anthony Tol

Fragmentary portions of this book may be freely used by those who are interested in sharing the author's insights and observations, so long as the material is not pirated for monetary gain and so long as proper credit is visibly given to the publisher and the author. Others, and those who wish to use larger sections of text, must seek written permission from the publisher.

Printed in the United State of America.

Dordt College Press   www.dordt.edu/dordt_press
498 Fourth Avenue NE
Sioux Center, Iowa 51250
United States of America

ISBN: 978-0-932914-86-6

Library of Congress Cataloging-in-Publication Data

Tol, Anthony.
Philosophy in the making : D.H.Th. Vollenhoven and the emergence of
    Reformed philosophy / Anthony Tol.
      p. cm.
Includes bibliographical references and index.
ISBN 978-0-932914-86-6 (pbk. : alk. paper)
1. Vollenhoven, D. H. Theodoor (Dirk Hendrik Theodoor), 1892-1978.
2. Philosophy and religion--Netherlands--History--20th century.
3. Reformed Church--Netherlands--Doctrines--History--20th century.
    I. Title.

B4095.V644T64 2010
199'.492--dc22
            2010047607

Know your desire.

TABLE OF CONTENTS

Acknowledgements 1

Preface 3

Chapter 1.
Vollenhoven's principled program

I. *Introduction* 17

II. *Isagôgè Philosophiae* 19
    A. Experience and method 21
    B. Clarity, method and textual layout of
       Isagôgè Philosophiae 25
    C. Methodical procedures: the thetical-critical method 30
    D. Methodical procedures:
       the method of knowledge organization 32
    E. Methodical procedures:
       the method of resolution and composition 37
    F. Lapses of method? 39
    G. To round off 41

III. *The academic context* 42
    A. The neo-Calvinist commitment 42
    B. "The way that leads to the knowledge of the
       Reformed principles" 46
    C. Kuyper on the "Reformed foundation" 50

IV. *Vollenhoven's program* 55
    A. Introduction 55
    B. Vollenhoven's procedure 56
    C. The reform of philosophy 61
       1. The religious relevance 63
       2. The worldview relevance 66
       3. The condition of cognition 69
    D. In summary 73

Chapter 2.
A BOLD BEGINNING: THEISTIC AND METALOGICAL INTUITIONISM

I.	*Introduction*	75
II.	*The early work*	76
III.	*The setting of the dissertation*	81
	A. Arithmetic	81
	B. Geometry	84
	C. A partial and qualified Kantianism	89
IV.	*The nodal points of (theistic) intuitionism*	92
	A. Intuition, formalism, empiricism	95
	B. Monism and dualism	98
V.	*"Knowledge is a relation"*	102
	A. The semantics of 'knowing'	103
	B. Relations, their nature	104
	C. Complexes	108
	D. Knowledge and appearance	110
	1. Getting to know	111
	2. The concomitant complex of the knowledge relation	113
	3. Monadism and the knowledge relation	115
	E. The nature of space	120
VI.	*Three-fold intuition and Gegenstände*	122
	A. Awareness versus knowledge	122
	B. Act, content and *Gegenstand*	125
	C. Analytical and metaphysical intuition	128
	D. *Gegenstandstheorie* and knowledge	131
	E. Summary	136
	F. Number	137
VII.	*Metaphysics*	139
	A. The principle of substance	142
	B. Individual substances	144
	C. Again: the metaphysical intuition	146
	D. A human being	154
	E. Microcosm and macrocosm	157

	F.	Self-knowledge and self-consciousness 160
	G.	Occasionalism 164

VIII.	*Theism* 166
	A. Actual infinity 167
	B. Divine transcendence and immanence 170
	1. The distinction of God and the world 171
	2. Transcendence and immanence with respect to the Self and the world 175
	3. Provisional summary 177
	C. Trinitarian theism 180
	1. God, the Father 181
	2. God, the Spirit 183
	3. God, the Logos 185
	a. Truth and knowledge 188
	b. Logos and acquaintance 189
	c. Logos and scientific knowledge 190
	d. Logos speculation? 197

IX.	*Metalogic* 201

X.	*The conception's characterization* 211

Chapter 3:
REFORMING REVISIONS: FROM MONADOLOGY TO LAW-SPHERES

I.	*Introduction* 217

II.	*The Janse contact: from self-centred subject to tasked subject* . 224
	A. Teaching elementary arithmetic 225
	B. Maria Montessori and child biology 226
	C. Janse's initiative, Vollenhoven's initial response 231
	D. Living soul and life-giving spirit 236
	1. Living soul and scientific explanation 237
	2. Worldview attitudes towards living souls 238
	3. Towards a biblical understanding of 'living soul' 239
	E. The acknowledged influence 241
	F. The Janse effect 244
	1. Living soul and scientific explanation 245
	2. Worldview attitudes towards living souls (subjectivity) .246

    a. 'Subject' as office 248
    b. Self-certainty undercut 250
  3. Towards a biblical understanding of 'living soul' ..253
    a. Logos-revelation vis-à-vis philosophy 253
    b. Biblical anthropology 257
 G. Conclusion...260
 H. Additional note 261

III. ***The Dooyeweerd contact: from adequate concept to modally qualified law*** 263
 A. Introduction 263
 B. The early contact 270
 C. Dooyeweerd in Vollenhoven's world of thought 275
  1. "The problem of municipal monopolies..." (October 1920) 276
  2. Letter to Vollenhoven, 17 December 1920 277
  3. Response to G. Scholten 281
  4. From the third of the three unpublished manuscripts 290
    a. *Gegenstand*-theorie and logic 299
    b. Cosmic Selfhood; 'modal relation' 302
    c. The system of the sciences 304
 D. Interlude 309
  1. Rudimentary conception and 'humanistic philosophy' 312
  2. Vollenhoven's due? 315
 E. Cosmos, logos and faith 320
  1. The introduction 320
  2. Logos as the realm of meaning 324
  3. Modality – Field of vision – Region category 328
  4. Logical thought 333
  5. Transition to cosmology 335
 F. Law-idea...341
  1. Law-idea as 'organon' 343
  2. Calvin's law-idea 346
  3. Calvinistic epistemology 348
  4. Sovereignty in its own sphere 350
  5. Discussion and assessment 351
    a. Law as boundary 353
    b. Law-idea as world-plan 355

		c. Law-idea and the 'central lookout tower' 358

    G. Overview: from critical realism to
transcendental criticism 361
        1. Vollenhoven's early thought in review 362
        2. Developments in 1922 364
        3. Developments in 1923 369
        4. Concept and idea 373

Chapter 4:
EMBARKING WITHIN BOUNDS OF LAW: THE INITIAL DEFINITE PLATFORM

I. *Introduction* 381

II. *Theism's "wavering glimmer"* 386
    A. Theism reconsidered 388
    B. 'Theos' and 'kosmos' 391
        1. A boundary problem 392
        2. Monism and dualism 393

III. *Boundary and law* 397
    A. The boundary properly determined 398
        1. Substance and antinomy 400
        2. The infinite and cosmic being 406
        3. The cosmic order 412
        4. Laws of being 416
        5. Qualities of subjection/functions of subjection ... 419
    B. The boundary threefold 422
        1. The Trinitarian theist position 423
        2. The work of the Spirit reviewed 425
        3. The work of the Logos and role of the
human logos reconsidered 428
            a. Why an intuition? 428
            b. The 'Logos-logos' difference 429
            c. Values and assessment 431
            d. Truth 'in itself' 434
            e. Truth known 435
            f. Truth acquired: thought 436
            g. Method 438
            h. Concluding summary 439
        4. Creator and creation 440

  a. The metaphysics of ideas 440
  b. 'Substance-phenomenon' philosophy 443
   i. The 'substance-phenomenon schema' deconstructed 444
   ii. Contra the dualist anthropology 448
  c. Order and law 450
  d. Creationism? 453

IV. *The cosmological 'intersection principle'* 454

V. *Review of Vollenhoven's initial definitive platform and new developments* 466
 A. Cosmic life and knowing 466
 B. Renewed anthropology 473
 C. Dualism overcome 479

VI. *Addendum. Vollenhoven's retrospective account of the early years* 491
 A. The early years in a nutshell 492
 B. The dissertation as remembered 495
 C. Dooyeweerd's 'modalization' of time 500
 D. From 'occasionalism' to 'ennoetism' 503
  1. The theory of priority 503
  2. Ennoetist metaphysic 505

Bibliography 513

Index 533

ACKNOWLEDGEMENTS

This book presents, with only minor changes, a part of my doctoral dissertation, submitted to the philosophy faculty of the Free University of Amsterdam. (The other part is the text-critical edition of D.H.Th. Vollenhoven's Isagôgè Philosophiae.) Prof. A.P. Bos guided the process of writing. His advice was, as always, prompt, to-the-point and helpful. I also benefitted greatly from discussions at various stages with K.A. Bril, John H. Kok, Jeremy G.A. Ive, and Henk E.S. Woldring. They helped me to diminish appreciably the number of deficiencies in the text, the remainder of which is solely my responsibility.

The Zonneweelde Foundation provided financial aid towards alleviating production costs, which I acknowledge with gratitude.

Special mention goes to my wife and family. They were supportive throughout the process of reflection and writing, allowing me to concentrate on the work and to forgo many a normal familial expectation. I look forward to relieving my debt to them.

Amsterdam/Bovenkarspel   Anthony Tol

PREFACE

"Those who cannot remember the past are
condemned to repeat it."

George Santayana

In the 1920s a distinct Reformed philosophy arose in the Netherlands. It was not specifically planned, in the sense that its appearing answered to a clearly defined goal. There was a melange of factors that accompanied its emergence, some personal and some related to the intellectual milieu. Two brothers-in-law, Dirk Hendrik Theodoor Vollenhoven (1892-1978) and Herman Dooyeweerd (1894-1977), entered into discussions with each other, with the intention of gaining a more 'Calvinist' understanding of matters intellectual, especially as concerns worldview and the foundations and methodology of the sciences. The aim of pursuing a Calvinist/Reformed understanding reflects their neo-Calvinist context, though they were critical of that context as well. Other influences, particularly those of the broader intellectual environment, relate to the dominance of neo-Idealism on the Dutch scene at the time. These influences were more problematic. The brothers-in-law never came to complete agreement as to the proper critical distance to take, nor how that distance was best formulated. This disagreement affected the understanding of Reformed philosophy itself. It resulted in its having two founders, as each acknowledged.[1] This entails, despite their agreement on many points of detail, that neither should be approached nor understood primarily through the other. We wish to take a close and critical look at the emergence of Reformed philosophy, with particular attention being given to the part played by Vollenhoven.

This study is not the first to turn to the decade of the 1920s and investigate Reformed philosophical thought in its burgeoning years. There is valuable and informative research available, though the overall

---

1   D.H.Th. Vollenhoven, in Vollenhoven 1953p: 112, speaks of "the fathers" of Calvinistic philosophy, in a context in which he discusses the differences between his own and Dooyeweerd's thought. H. Dooyeweerd refers to Vollenhoven as the "cofounder of the reformational philosophical trend of thought"; Dooyeweerd 1973: 5. Biographical information is provided throughout this study but in particular at the beginning of chapters 1, 2, 3 and section III of chapter 3. Vollenhoven was married to Dooyeweerd's older sister, Hermina Maria Dooyeweerd (1892-1973).

understanding is neither complete nor satisfactory. The early thought of Vollenhoven has been analysed by John H. Kok in his *Vollenhoven: His Early Development* (cf. Kok 1992) in detail. He was the first to subject early material to a thorough study. However, most of the attention went to the work that was prior to what Vollenhoven himself considered representative of his Reformed position, hence the recognition as to the connection—to whatever degree that there is one—between that early work and the Reformed position was left somewhat in abeyance. Also Kok explicitly refrained from bringing Dooyeweerd into his discussion.[2]

The early thought of Dooyeweerd received a prominent place in the Dooyeweerd biography of Marcel E. Verburg (cf. Verburg 1989). He included in his discussion essential and characteristic passages from unpublished work of the early Dooyeweerd, thereby showing that Dooyeweerd's thought definitely passed through a learning phase. But in his discussion of these early years there is no mention of Vollenhoven. The author brings him into the picture only at the point where the brothers-in-law accept their simultaneous appointments to their academic chairs at the *Vrije Universiteit* of Amsterdam in 1926;[3] Vollenhoven in the faculty of arts and philosophy and Dooyeweerd in the faculty of law. We will have something to say about this neglect in chapter 3 and how this affects Verburg's interpretation of Dooyeweerd's work prior to 1926. Then there is also Roger D. Henderson's dissertation study of Dooyeweerd's early thought, his *Illuminating Law: The Construction of Herman Dooyeweerd's Philosophy 1918-1928* (cf. Henderson 1994). Henderson focussed on Dooyeweerd's wrestling with the neo-Kantian context prevalent in the philosophy of law. He describes Dooyeweerd's development in the main in terms of the increasing distance he takes from that context, at the same time that the significance of Calvinism grows on him. Henderson recognizes the presence of Vollenhoven in this development, but he is not able to indicate its importance: "Vollenhoven played a role of some significance in the development of [Dooyeweerd's] early systematic thought. However, it is difficult to say exactly what role this was" (Henderson 1994: 27). We hope to be more successful in this respect through a close reading of the documentary evidence.

---

2   Cf. Kok 1992: 4, 292.

3   Cf. Verburg 1989: 87 ff. It is a longstanding practice, to which I shall adhere, to refer to this university in the context of English discourse as "Free University". We add that Vollenhoven's appointment to the chair of philosophy included lecturing on theoretical psychology and its history, taken at the time to be a branch of philosophy. In 1958 the main areas associated with his chair were specified as: philosophy, its history and philosophical anthropology. Cf. Klapwijk 1980: 559.

There are further informative and supplementing sources in the work of the late Johan Stellingwerff and in the volume, *The Legacy of Herman Dooyeweerd*, ed. by C.T. McIntire (cf. McIntire 1985). In his "History of Reformational Philosophy",[4] Stellingwerff offers a biographical description of the interaction between Vollenhoven and Dooyeweerd in the crucial formative years. But what must be counted as a lack is the failure to grasp the theistic context of Vollenhoven's initial thought, as laid down in his dissertation of 1918. Here, and in other work of Stellingwerff,[5] his emphasis is on the first appearance of characteristic features of the later position. Then, in the volume edited by McIntire, there is the opening chapter on Dooyeweerd's intellectual milieu by Albert M. Wolters (cf. Wolters 1985). This offers a very readable description of the neo-Idealist context in which the early Dooyeweerd moved. Wolters emphasized Vollenhoven's independent work in philosophy prior to Dooyeweerd's entrance into philosophy. He adds the intriguing remark that on the basis of Vollenhoven's early work, "a good case can be made for the thesis that he in some significant ways shaped the developing systematic philosophy of Dooyeweerd, especially in relation to the themes of the neo-Calvinist worldview" (Wolters 1985: 16). I don't know if Wolters has in the meantime himself substantiated the case. But I believe that the present work comes close to making the case in point, at least to the extent that this is feasible.

So we may conclude that, to date, it is not redundant to pay more attention to Vollenhoven's own systematic position, both within the context of his own development and in interaction with Dooyeweerd, as regards the emergence of Reformed philosophy. We should add that knowledge of Vollenhoven's historical work fares better, at least the work associated with the so-called "consequential problem-historical method" that he initiated in the mid-1940s. In this connection we call attention to the effort and works of K.A. Bril. He has made virtually all of Vollenhoven problem-historical material available, as well as offering an introduction to the method.[6] In the current study this problem-historical

---

4   Cf. Stellingwerff 2006: 32-45.
5   Cf. also Stellingwerff 1990 and 1992.
6   There is K.A. Bril's dissertation (in Dutch), *viz.* Bril 1986, and his introduction to Vollenhoven's problem-historical method (in English), cf. Bril 2005. Bril's edition of Vollenhoven's "Schematic charts" (cf. Vollenhoven 2000) includes a plethora of historical remarks related to western intellectual history. He has also edited Vollenhoven's articles for the *Oosthoeks Encyclopedie*, in which Vollenhoven makes full use of his method; cf. Vollenhoven 2005c. There is also the compilation of Vollenhoven's own articles on or related to this method, edited by Bril: Vollenhoven 2005a; and the English translation

work, being of later date, will not be addressed directly, though we will have occasion to refer to it when assessing Vollenhoven's own (late) characterization of his early work.

The present study wishes to fill in the stated gap in the understanding of the part played by Vollenhoven in the emergence of Reformed philosophy. It (the present study) started as the project of editing Vollenhoven's chief contribution to systematic philosophy, *viz.* the text that was used as syllabus for the introductory course in philosophy at the Free University. This introduction to philosophy, indicated as such with the classical title, *Isagôgè Philosophiae*, consists of carefully crafted notes that invite the reader to enter into doing philosophy. As it turned out, Vollenhoven kept returning to the text, from the time he was appointed to the chair of philosophy, in 1926, till 1945. In that time span, about a dozen different versions came into circulation, the first complete version stemming from 1930. The initial challenge was to select the most trustworthy version of the text.

Vollenhoven's own copy, and the notes and changes he wrote in the margins, as finalized in 1945, proved to be the 'best' copy. That copy was used for the bilingual edition of the text, that appeared in 2005.[7] The other versions were thereby definitely 'superseded'. But they still present an interesting window on Vollenhoven's work. The more significant differences between the versions could be traced to three important changes in the set-up of the text. In other words, between 1930 and 1945 there were four 'stages' in the development of the text. This reflects changes in Vollenhoven's own development. All these versions were subsequently edited and arranged in one text-critical edition. In that way the differences between the versions became more apparent, and the question as to their significance could now be addressed and studied. This text-critical edition is scheduled to appear simultaneously with the current study.[8]

In the general introduction to the text-critical edition of *Isagôgè Phi-*

---

of these articles: Vollenhoven 2005b. As to other relevant work, there is an introductory review by John H. Kok of the history and systematics of philosophy, in the spirit of Vollenhoven; cf. Kok 1998. Bennie Van der Walt has done much, over the years, to promote Vollenhoven's thought in South Africa; cf. Van der Walt 2006. In Tol 1993 there is a discussion of Vollenhoven's historiographical work against the background of his late systematic thought.

7   The bilingual edition is Vollenhoven 2005d, the separately published English only version is Vollenhoven 2005e.

8   Cf. Vollenhoven 2010. This text is entirely in Dutch, including the editor's general introduction, in which *inter alia* the 'stages' are discussed, and the account of the editing of the text.

losophiae, as initially planned, it seemed appropriate to include an indication of Vollenhoven's course of thought prior and up to the composition of the syllabus text. From the start it was not the intention merely to indicate when the main features of the text were selected or characteristic notions first appeared. That assumes that the final text, being the 'known outcome', is a sufficient end. In fact, this is not so. Vollenhoven's thought continued to evolve, and numerous important changes took place in the later years of his career. In other words, the text is 'provisional' (as he himself insists).[9] Thus, to understand it philosophically and not just verbally, one needs to understand the problems that sustain it. It is in connection with such problems that a change of thought signals a solution to, or at least a lessening of, a problem's urgency.

But Vollenhoven was not always inclined to do his thinking overtly, as readers of his work soon discover (though in the earlier work there tends to be more discussion). The problems that underlie the introduction to philosophy are not always evident. This is another reason why the option was pursued of tracing the context of Vollenhoven's thought, by including research of the earlier work, for this makes his choices more evident. Work that is, in a superficial sense, taken as having been surpassed, does not cease to have significance if it includes the more general schemata of problems that find continuation in a changed constellation of details. The significance towards understanding remains relevant, even though the implementation of such schemata involves critique of former use and changes of paths pursued. As this strategy was applied, the confirmation of its significance, and especially the manner in which this proved to be the case, led to surprising results.

The results were such as to invite and require proper discussion in their own right. This led to the introduction's expanding into a volume that could no longer answer to its subsidiary role, as originally planned. A more measured introduction was then written for the text-critical edition of *Isagôgè Philosophiae*, and this enabled the current text to become an independent volume.

---

9   Vollenhoven 2005d, **4**. References to the *Isagôgè Philosophiae* will in general be to the bilingual edition and its 224 sections, i.e. Vollenhoven 2005d, whereby the English half is identical to Vollenhoven 2005e. (A standard reference is then often combined: 'Vollenhoven 2005d/e', followed by a section number in bold.) References to specific versions will be through the test-critical edition, Vollenhoven 2010. (The section references in the text-critical edition and the bilingual edition are identical.) For Vollenhoven's late admission that *Isagôgè Philosophiae* needed reworking, cf. the foreword to the 1967 reprint; Vollenhoven 2010: 71. (Note that section numbers in bold are separated from the year code by a comma, page numbers are separated by a colon.)

In this independent study, due attention could be given to novel features disclosed through the research of the early material of both Vollenhoven and Dooyeweerd. The more significant of the novel features are the following.

i. In Vollenhoven's dissertation on the philosophy of mathematics from a theistic standpoint (cf. Vollenhoven 1918a), one is able to discern, at least in outline, a 'philosophical position'. The theistic standpoint, which is a variant of 'theistic intuitionism', is predicated on the scholastic theme of the harmony between two orders of rationality. One order is that of 'objective rationality', that holds of the nature of things, as secured in *ideas* of distinctive being, and the other order is that of 'subjective rationality' in the human being, who attempts to make its *conceptual* understanding more adequate by increasing the harmony of that conceptual understanding with the objective order. But Vollenhoven *qualifies* this scholastic use of concept and idea. He takes the criterion of the harmony between the two orders to be a necessary but not a sufficient condition of knowledge. As necessary criterion, the harmony is warranted by the (divine) Logos, which 'disposes' subject and object to come together. But this theistic criterion needs the supplement of the (human) intuition, rooted in the Self, in the sense that knowledge, as maintained, calls for a warranted conviction of certainty supporting fundamental 'synthetic a priori' judgments. The discussions on the foundations and methodology of mathematics, on epistemology and metaphysics and also the explication of theism, all hang together in Vollenhoven's initial 'qualified scholasticism'. This scholasticism will soon (in the course of 1923) be targeted as needing to be overcome. In the meantime there is the motive, expressed in late 1920, to be more consciously Reformed.

ii. Thus, evoking "Christian realism", Vollenhoven first underscores (in Vollenhoven 1921c) the dualistic use of 'concept and idea' so as to sharpen the opposition to the neo-Kantian use. In the latter, the idea is predominantly a directing or limiting concept, in being the regulative idea of the metalogical sphere, which harbours the growth of scientific knowledge. (The metalogical sphere is the '*Encyclopedia* of the sciences', i.e. methodologically organized domains of scientific knowledge.) Here concept and idea are *both* aligned to the metalogical sphere, the sphere in which scientific knowledge accrues as organized according to the idea (as limiting concept). But, for Vollenhoven, the growth of the metalogical sphere is controlled by the adequate concept, as 'sighted' by the metalogical intuition, leaving the idea free for its role as principle of distinctive being, with its own supporting metaphysical intuition. For, the metalogical intuition of an adequate conceptual ideal is distinct from the metaphysical intuition, which is aligned to the reality of the cosmos and its 'thought foreign' ideas of being. Hence, (adequate) *concept* and *idea* (of distinctive being) are distinct; *viz.* the adequate concept controls subjective rationality, in that it represents the ideal of the complete knowledge of the idea, which in turn secures the essence of objective rationality. Within the metalogical sphere there are distinct domains of validity. This latter point has similarities with Freiburg neo-Kantianism. The metalogical sphere and its distinct domains of validity together form the take-off point for the development of the modal order.

iii. Dooyeweerd who, since 1919, has been studying neo-Kantian works in the philosophy of law, accepts Vollenhoven's framework of Christian realism, calling it "critical realism" (sometimes "transcendental realism"). A close reading of his early work, especially of 1922, confirms the background in Vollenhoven. Metalogical notions, such as region category and modality, are appropriated from neo-Kantian writers and incorporated into the context of critical realism. At this time Vollenhoven and Dooyeweerd are in close contact in developing their realist position. But in October of 1922 Dooyeweerd becomes deputy director of the Kuyper Foundation. This, in turn, no longer allows the contact between Vollenhoven and Dooyeweerd to be as intense as it had been.

iv. In or about the summer of 1922 there is reportedly a "find" that would appear to revolve around the realization that *knowing resorts under being*. This has implications at various levels: metalogical, cosmological and theistic. The metalogical sphere of scientific knowledge, also called the *Gegenstand*-sphere, is now taken to be secured in how the cosmos is 'given for consciousness', as assessed in a 'modal viewing'. In line with this shift in how knowledge is secured, the Logos is looked on as the divine 'giver', in being the divine Word. In virtue of the Logos the cosmos is knowable. Thus the Logos is brought into closer rapport with the cosmos and its objective order of being. This 'find' evidences a tendency towards a more 'Christo-centric cosmism', that is now said to be an explicit motive (the Logos being 'in Christ'). The context here is still that of critical realism, but it is 'shifted'.

v. In November of 1922, the principal of an elementary school, Antheunis Janse, with whom Vollenhoven corresponded since 1919, quite suddenly criticises the notion of the immortality of the soul, the anthropological supplement to scholasticism. A main line of argument of Janse is that the notion of the immortality of the soul lacks proper biblical foundation. Vollenhoven is disconcerted and tries to 'correct' Janse. Vollenhoven, now in a very busy period, becomes overworked and in mid-January of 1923 spirals downward in a psycho-somatic crisis from which he does not fully recuperate until December 1923.

vi. With Vollenhoven out of reach, Janse proceeds to publish six (fairly short) articles in anthropology and on life attitude, in which he expresses his new ideas. These articles have never been referred to in Reformed circles. They invite careful scrutiny, all the more so since it is primarily this material that persuaded Vollenhoven, upon reading it after his recovery, that Janse is essentially right. However, Vollenhoven did have criticism, and he assimilated the main new ideas in his own way.

vii. At the same time—while Vollenhoven is still out of reach—Dooyeweerd advances, in about mid-1923, his notion of the 'law-idea'. It is, as cosmological principle, the 'organon' (instrument) by which a self-contained worldview is effectuated. The Christian law-idea is formally the boundary between the creator and the creature, materially it underscores a providential world-plan, that flows from God's wisdom and is known or accepted on faith. Dooyeweerd, moving intellectually in the context of (scholastic and shifted) critical realism, continues to use 'idea' in the metaphysical sense of principle of distinctive being. Thus, his law-idea here focuses on the predestined future as secured in the main structure of the cosmos. The human acknowledgement of this idea, through faith, provides the key to the subjective order of knowledge.

viii. After Vollenhoven's recovery, it is still about two years before he proceeds to publish. In correspondence at the time he indicates his rejection of the interpretation of the soul as being immortal, implying in fact a rejection of scholasticism as such. Between 1926 and 1931 his publications attest to a revised 'theistic position'. The notion of the law as boundary between God and the cosmos is in central position, and it is interpreted in such a way as to make the scholastic use of 'concept and idea' entirely ineffectual. The former 'subjective rationality' is now itself a creaturely condition subject to the logical law-sphere. It does not seek harmony with 'objective rationality', i.e. the structure of the cosmos, for it is itself already a part of that structure. Anything 'subjective' is divested of a basis in itself—the effect formerly thought of as warranted by the immortality of the soul on which the intuition is based. Subjectivity is now said to be 'tasked', i.e. to entail the human being's standing in subjection to the laws that evince cosmic boundaries. The impingement of law calls for a realism of the cosmos in its response to law. This impingement and the response assume an ontological *difference* between law and cosmic functioning. This understanding *contrasts* with Dooyeweerd's initial realist use of law-idea, *viz.* as cosmological principle—in its meaning as providential world-plan—for that use proceeds from the assumption of an ontological *agreement* between law and cosmos. For Vollenhoven, such an agreement undercuts the dynamics of standing in subjection—a dynamics on which the religious-moral struggle of good and evil (direction) is predicated—which is why Vollenhoven found the notion of 'law-idea' to be unsuitable from its first introduction.

ix. Dooyeweerd in turn, in about 1928 (cf. Dooyeweerd 1928b), begins to express himself in a way that is characteristic of *De Wijsbegeerte der Wetsidee* (1935-1936). He ontologizes meaning—"meaning is the being of all creaturely beings"[10]—making the acceptance of a reality that bears meaning redundant. This capitalizes on the (former) 'metalogical sphere' at the expense of the realism of the cosmos This calls for a reinterpretation of the understanding of 'law-idea', which now, as 'limiting concept', captures the presupposed coherence, totality and unity of meaning that is presupposed by thought. The Self is now taken as (transcendent) spiritual centre, that is focussed on the totality of meaning by means of its participation in the supra-temporal 'Archimedean point', a vantage point from which to view the diversity and coherence of cosmic meaning without predilection. When interpreting this 'move' against the background of the foregoing years, Dooyeweerd's new use of 'concept and idea' appears to be closer to a neo-Kantian use than ever before, and the themes he broaches in connection with the Self's spiritual centre—its intuitive experience and its involvement with time that is modalized in that experience—more than echo important traits of Vollenhoven's 'Self', as described in his dissertation but which in the meantime he had definitely abandoned (Vollenhoven 1918a).

Thus, by the end of the 1920s Vollenhoven and Dooyeweerd have each found a way of 'reforming' philosophy in a way that is critical of *traditional* scholasticism, as prevalent in their immediate environment. Vollenhoven reforms it from the perspective of a 'Trinitarian theistic position'. This position delineates the boundary within which philosophy is practised, guaranteeing philosophy's 'intra-cosmic' relevance and safeguarding it from speculation and antinomies. The Self, in Vollenhoven's definitive view, no longer proceeds from a prior self-certainty of self-consciousness. Dooyeweerd, in turn, goes from 'critical realism' to a 'transcendental criticism'. For him the Self, as transcendent spiritual principle of the human being, is the crucial factor. In its metalogical

---

10   Dooyeweerd 1935-1936 I: 6.

orientation regarding the diversity and coherence of meaning, as temporally experienced, the Self 'takes a critical stand' in the light of the supra-temporal totality and unity of meaning. The metaphysical intuition of cosmic reality is redundant. In the law-idea, as 'transcendental ground-idea' of philosophy, the Self accounts for its grasp of meaning in the face of the Origin of meaning.

Each of the brothers-in-law continued to develop his thinking, which naturally calls for description and study in its own right. But whichever 'final' formulation of the 'definitive' positions be deemed adequate, a difference remained between Vollenhoven and Dooyeweerd, a difference that cannot be assessed without taking serious stock of the early material this study attempts to elucidate and acknowledging Vollenhoven's role 'from the beginning'.

This study is organized in four chapters. The *first* chapter offers a discussion of Vollenhoven's program. Philosophy, being a practice, it cannot but be influenced by the main determinants of historical reality. By taking a standpoint in the light of an historical tradition one evinces consciousness of this participation as well as being alive to the need for revisions in light of historical change. Through his upbringing in the Netherlands and affiliation with the Reformed tradition of that country, Vollenhoven aligns himself to the Christian religion, in its Reformed expression, and supports a neo-Calvinist (or Kuyperian) world view. Upon his becoming the first full-time appointee in philosophy at the Free University in 1926, Vollenhoven develops an understanding of philosophy, as academic discipline, that is constrained, meta-philosophically, by religious and world-view features, and secured in an objective view of truth that presupposes a cosmic order of determinants of structural differences and connections.

Vollenhoven's introduction to philosophy, entitled *Isagôgè Philosophiae*, is his main expression of systematic philosophy. It is a set of carefully crafted notes in which he lays down his nuanced view of philosophy. A dominating thought is that scientific or academic disciplines need to proceed methodically. Vollenhoven needs no less than three methods to enable philosophy to be conducted responsibly: the thetical-critical method, the 'method of knowledge organization' (Vollenhoven himself nowhere names this method), and the method of resolution and composition. These three methods themselves determine the layout of the introductory text.

Understanding Vollenhoven also calls for attention to the context of the Free University and the Reformed tradition it wished to defend and promote. In that tradition there is an element of scholasticism, expressed in the assumption of a harmony between subjective and objective orders of rationality. By the time of his appointment to the chair of philosophy, Vollenhoven had rejected this assumption of scholasticism. He therefore felt challenged to set up a practice of Reformed philosophy in an alternative way. He underscored the distinct realities of the religious life, worldview engagement and structured cosmic creatures, and culled from these realities the main delimiting features (conditions) of philosophy, thereby accounting for what he took to be the important but limited task and place of philosophy.

The first chapter discusses these matters of text, context and principles in an exploratory way.

The *second* chapter discusses and analyses Vollenhoven's early thought. His dissertation (Vollenhoven 1918a) is the main object of attention here. It deals with the philosophy of mathematics from a theistic standpoint. Our discussion traces a path that begins with arithmetic and geometry, and ends with the theistic standpoint. On route the discussion touches on themes in the philosophy of science, on epistemology—especially the distinction between knowledge and intuition—, the use Vollenhoven made of Alexius Meinong's *Gegenstandstheorie* (which becomes the basis for the 'metalogical *Gegenstand* sphere' and thus the modal order) and matters metaphysical, especially the metaphysics of substance. The chapter also includes a section on 'metalogic', which emphasizes the 'realist' use of idea, with the (adequate) concept being linked to a 'metalogical intuition'. Finally, the whole discussion of the chapter is pulled together in a summarizing overview, which offers in outline the 'philosophical conception' Vollenhoven operates with in his early thought. Vollenhoven defends a qualified scholasticism at the time, whereby the assumption of a harmony between the subjective and objective orders of rationality is supplemented by the intuition, to warrant consciously experienced certainty.

The *third* chapter looks in detail at the two contacts Vollenhoven maintained, that were most consequential to him in the early years, namely with A. Janse and H. Dooyeweerd. The contact with Janse was instrumental in getting Vollenhoven to reconsider anthropology, in particular the theme of the immortality of the soul and its status as "*substantia incompleta*". Janse also emphasized the importance of the 'biblical understanding' of the human condition and what this presupposes about the human being and the world. Vollenhoven turned the latter into a constraint on philosophy that "reckons with Scripture". Vollenhoven's responses to Janse's challenges are discussed in the context of the ideas raised by Janse.

In the discussion of the contact with Dooyeweerd, all the attention is directed to describing the factual contact between Dooyeweerd and Vollenhoven, and analysing the evidence of Dooyeweerd's aligning himself to Vollenhoven as he (Dooyeweerd) works at the neo-Kantian writers in the philosophy of law. We then trace how Dooyeweerd begins to go his own way when he advanced the notion of 'law-idea' (in 1923) and transforms this from a critical realist notion into one of transcendental criticism.

The *fourth* and final chapter discusses and analyses Vollenhoven's initial definitive position, as evidenced by the writings of 1925 - 1931. We begin with a discussion of what Vollenhoven's criticisms are with regard to what he had called his earlier 'theistic position'. This puts the two notions of boundary and law in the limelight. Upon analysing their relevance, we come across Vollenhoven's revised Trinitarian theistic position, and how this leads to his cosmological 'intersection principle', a consequence of 'knowing's resorting under being'. This principle governs cosmology, understood realistically. The discussion is rounded off by a review of this initial definitive position and by looking ahead to important later developments, *viz.* in anthropology and the view of law. An addendum on Vollenhoven's own retrospective account of the early years ends the chapter.

The sources for this study are mainly in the Dutch language. Use is made of translations, when available; otherwise the translations are my own. References to sources are via their bibliographical code (author, year and page). I have tried to keep the references to unpublished material to a minimum. But there is important archival material that could not be passed by. All this archival material is in the "Historisch Documentatiecentrum voor het Nederlands Protestantisme (1800-heden)" of the Free University. Here one may find e.g. the archives of Dooyeweerd (collection no. 77), Janse (collection no. 157) and Vollenhoven (collection no. 405) referred to in this study.

I maintain a distinction in the use of single and double 'quotation marks'. The double are used for quotations and titles, the single serve to denote words that are merely mentioned.

In the course of my inquiry, important archival material came to light. Each new piece raised the spectre of possibly refuting what was thought to be known of the context. Luckily, during this research the newly found material tended to fall quite readily into place in a way that confirmed and nuanced my own prior understanding. This made it a joy to trace the contours of the emergence of Reformed philosophy, when subjected to a close reading. For the research seemed to go in the direction of illuminating a niche of cultural history that still has relevance and that we ought not to forget.

1

VOLLENHOVEN'S PRINCIPLED PROGRAM

> "[T]he norm [of philosophy is] that philosophy
> do justice to any diversity. . . ."
>
> D.H.Th. Vollenhoven (1959)

I. INTRODUCTION

The present work is a study of the emergence of Reformed philosophy in the Netherlands, with particular attention to the role and contribution of D.H.Th. Vollenhoven. The constraints on that emergence were, in part at least, connected with Vollenhoven's appointment to the chair of philosophy at the Free University of Amsterdam in 1926. His was the first full-time appointment in philosophy since the university was founded n 1880. This brought with it the task of setting up a full program of studies in philosophy. There was also the requirement that all incoming students be confronted with philosophy. This included both an introduction to systematic philosophy and a broad survey of philosophy's history. Vollenhoven seized on this requirement to develop his primary views in both areas in a way that reckoned with the Reformed tradition in which the Free University stood and which tradition the university wished to promote, as specified by its charter. This first chapter discusses the setting and the presuppositions of Vollenhoven's philosophical endeavours.

Vollenhoven held that the meaning of philosophy cannot be divorced from principles that illuminate our experience, underscore our responsibility and guide our endeavours. Such principles address the human condition and thus they figure in our awareness of it as we participate in it. In his or her own person, the philosopher provides the interface between the content of thought and the prevailing factors of the context, geographic-cultural, civic-societal, historical and religious. Through the fact of a human being's participation in that context, the philosopher's exercise of philosophy can never be neutral. He or she makes choices as to what is, what ought to be and what can be. For that very reason the fundamental choice of one's principles is a factor of importance and should be made explicit, open to critical discussion. Vollenhoven was aware of himself as a twentieth century Dutch-European, who held to a Protestant-historical world view and was committed to a Calvinist-Christian understanding of religion.[1] He developed an account of philosophy and its presuppositions and principles that reckons with the normative context of the human condition.

Vollenhoven developed his thought in close dialogue with his brother-in-law, Herman Dooyeweerd (1894-1977). Both occupied, simultaneously, chairs at the Free University of Amsterdam,[2] and from that base they initiated a movement, in the mid-1930s, that is now commonly referred to as 'reformational philosophy'.[3] Vollenhoven and Dooyeweerd shared the ideals that call for 'Christian philosophical thought'. But, while their respective contributions have many points of contact and overlap, the interpretation of their work cannot, and should not, ignore the distinct accounts each gave of their common ideals and the originality each invested in his written work.[4] Vollenhoven's work has, to date, not nearly had the exposure that Dooyeweerd's work enjoys.

One reason for the paucity of attention lies in the availability—namely the lack of it—of Vollenhoven's chief contribution to systematic philosophy: *Isagôgè Philosophiae*.[5] Prior to its publication in 2005 (cf. Vollenhoven 2005d and 2005e) it was only available as syllabus for pri-

---

[1] Vollenhoven distinguishes between religion and faith. He was critical of the most commonly accepted views as to 'the relation between faith and thought'. He held that faith and thought are, at bottom, part of a functional order, but that religion is a normative condition which, as religiously enjoined, is governed by the love command.

[2] Throughout their whole careers, Dooyeweerd occupied a chair in the faculty of law (1926-1965) while Vollenhoven held a chair in philosophy in the faculty of arts and philosophy (1926-1963). Philosophy was a section of the latter faculty. It became a faculty of its own in 1964, after a change, in 1963, in the Dutch Higher Education Act made this possible. In their inaugural addresses of 1926, each expressed with gratitude the other's simultaneous appointment, thereby ensuring continued "fruitful contact"; cf. Dooyeweerd 1926d: 75-76, and Vollenhoven 1926a: 67.

[3] This term includes Vollenhoven's preferred use of the expression "Calvinistic philosophy". Given the near equivalence of 'Calvinistic' and 'Reformed', I shall also speak of 'Reformed philosophy' in connection with Vollenhoven. Initially Dooyeweerd also spoke of "Calvinistic philosophy", together with his preferred phrase "Wijsbegeerte der Wetsidee" (Philosophy of the law-idea). Later Dooyeweerd dropped the term 'Calvinistic' in favour of 'Christian', used in an ecumenical sense; cf. Dooyeweerd 1966.

[4] For two recent discussions that acknowledge difference, cf. Stellingwerff 2006 and Friesen 2005.

[5] The category 'systematic philosophy' is not common in the English speaking world (as over against 'systematic theology'). Systematic philosophy is the study the general conditions that hold of philosophical inquiry, including the study of the connections between the chief disciplines of philosophy, *viz.* ontology, epistemology, anthropology, philosophy of science, etc.

vate study, in an unedited state. This text was itself revised many times. There is also a text-critical edition (cf. Vollenhoven 2010) in which all the prior versions that arose between 1930 and 1945 are now available. This edition provides a unique access to the development of Vollenhoven's thought in the indicated time span, for the more important changes attest to the general development of his philosophical views. Another source of Vollenhoven's writings, that has recently become available, are the articles Vollenhoven wrote for the *Oosthoeks Encyclopedie*, in particular the articles on important terms in philosophy.[6] This supplements the articles of Vollenhoven's later thought that were brought together in *Vollenhoven als wijsgeer* (Vollenhoven as philosopher).[7] Thus only recently has serious and representative study of Vollenhoven's thought become a distinct possibility, even in his own native language.

There is also a practical reason that accounts, at least initially, for Vollenhoven's lower profile. He was for many years the chairperson of the Association for Reformational Philosophy. He felt that a united front was in the best interest of the Association, an interest which he, as its chairman, had to promote and guard. Thus the discussion of internal differences was long kept under cover.[8]

In the broad spectrum of Vollenhoven's systematic work, the *Isagôgè Philosophiae* has pride of place. In our discussion below we will therefore focus on this text, though other titles will be referred to *en route*.

II. *Isagôgè Philosophiae*

Isagôgè Philosophiae arose (as we said) in the context of the author's teaching duties at the Free University of Amsterdam. Vollenhoven's appointment in philosophy at the Free University, in 1926, was as *ordinarius* (full professor) in philosophy. Others before him, such as Ph.J. Hoedemaker, Jan Woltjer, Wilhelm Geesink, Herman Bavinck and Hendrik J. Pos, had an interest in philosophy, and some of these men had assigned teaching tasks in philosophy. Hoedemaker and Geesink (both former clergymen) were responsible for the introduction to philosophy, the history of phi-

---

6   Cf. Vollenhoven 2005c.

7   Cf. Tol and Bril 1992. An internet search under "D.H.Th. Vollenhoven" reveals further possibilities of access to Vollenhoven's work.

8   This association was initially called "Association for Calvinistic Philosophy" (*Vereeniging voor Calvinistische Wijsbegeerte*). Vollenhoven was its first chairman from 1935 until 1963. In view of the importance of the unity of the Calvinistic movement, Vollenhoven never discussed his differing views with Dooyeweerd in public until after he had resigned as chairman of the Association. Cf. Tol and Bril 1992: 170-171; cf. also my introduction to Vollenhoven 1953p, in Tol and Bril 1992: 107-111.

losophy, logic and psychology (the latter being considered a philosophical discipline at the time). When Hoedemaker left the Free University in 1887, the teaching of philosophy was temporarily in the hands of Woltjer (in classical languages), until Geesink was given the main responsibility for philosophy in 1894. His lectures in philosophy never rose above an elementary level. Bavinck (in theology) broached philosophical themes to support his work in theology, though he never had an assigned task in philosophy. In 1926 Vollenhoven became Geesink's successor, and with his (full-time) appointment in philosophy a more integrated program of philosophy could be developed.[9]

Vollenhoven's teaching duties included the teaching of an introductory course in philosophy and a survey course in the history of philosophy, both of which were required courses for all first-year students.[10] For many years both courses were the chief staple of the Monday mornings, with history of philosophy being taught from 9 to 11 a.m. and systematic philosophy from 11 a.m. to 12 p.m. These courses were found to be difficult, particularly in the early years when there was no supporting material. Vollenhoven recognized the problem, and he agreed to make his notes of both courses available for student use, in stencilled form, in separate syllabi. The notes for the introduction to philosophy he named *Isagôgè Philosophiae*, which means 'Introduction to Philosophy';[11] those for the history of philosophy he called *Conspectus Historiae Philosophiae* (Survey of the history of philosophy). Because Vollenhoven kept revising the notes of these courses, two series of syllabi arose over the years. The

---

9   Cf. Klapwijk 1980 for a review of philosophy at the Free University from the university's inception in 1880. During its first fifty years (1880-1930) the Free University had only three faculties, namely, a Faculty of Theology, a Faculty of Law and a Faculty of Arts (and Philosophy). A medical faculty was begun in 1907 but had to be aborted in 1925. As to H.J. Pos, who was a linguist, he left the Free University in 1932 to accept an appointment in philosophy at the municipal University of Amsterdam. Cf. also Vollenhoven 1948h (the original Dutch text is Vollenhoven 1948k: 5-6); cf. also Van Deursen 2005: 105-115.

10   For more information, cf. Stellingwerff 1992, chapter 6: "Vollenhoven als hoogleraar" (Vollenhoven as chaired professor), especially pp. 74-80. Some course work in philosophy had been mandatory for all incoming students long before Vollenhoven's appointment; cf. Van Deursen 2005: 38. The Free University still requires that all students, of whatever faculty, be confronted with philosophy, in the context of a program called "Wijsgerige Vorming" (Philosophical education), for more on which, cf. Tol 2004.

11   The first complete set of these stencilled notes is dated "October 1930"; cf. Stellingwerff 1992: 75-76. The title of this work echoes Porphyry's famous *Eisagogè*, usually rendered in Latin as *Isagoge*, which is an introduction to Aristotle's treatise, *Categories*; cf. Spade 1994: 1-19. More than a terminological agreement with the title of Porphyry's work was not intended by Vollenhoven.

series of the *Isagoge*[12] texts is given attention in the current work. The historical series need not be specifically discussed here.[13] Suffice it to say at this point that he warns against confusing the study of the history of philosophy with the actual practice of philosophy (cf. Vollenhoven 2005d/e, **3**; comment 1).

A. Experience and method

In the course of study, of which the *Isagoge* is the text, Vollenhoven takes upon himself to introduce the actual practice of philosophy, at least its fundamental part. For him the practice is not geared beforehand to a distinct discipline of philosophy. Philosophy is fundamental inquiry. It has a motive, and its chief characteristics are related to the methodical procedure of the inquiry.

Philosophy is a fundamental inquiry, related, classically, to the striving for wisdom.[14] Vollenhoven has no quarrel with the classical view of philosophy proceeding from the experience of wonderment—"expectation, attuned to new surprises" (Vollenhoven 2005d/e, **15**)—as emphasized by Plato and Aristotle.[15] But he also allows for a more nuanced experience as well; e.g. he once listed in 1927: fascination upon perceiving the fine structure of a flower, curiosity as to what it means for someone to be colour blind, vexation over the question 'what is knowledge?', indignation at the injustice of social inequality, the affliction of sorrow, respect

---

12   Vollenhoven himself referred to his text as the "Isagogie", a word that may have been original with him. (However K.A. Bril informed me that the term was also in use within the university in Vollenhoven's student days.) In Dutch reference works, such as *De Kleine Oosthoek*, one finds the form '*Isagoge*' as available for Dutch use. However, that use is not common. *Webster's New Collegiate Dictionary* (1958) gives the same word as available in English, meaning "an introduction, as to a subject of research". We shall use this term—*Isagoge* (pronounced: isagoje)—as the abbreviated title of *Isagôgè Philosophiae*. References to the definitive version will be via its bibliographical code (i.e. Vollenhoven 2005d/e) and the relevant number (in bold) of the section; references to specific prior versions will be via the text-critical edition, Vollenhoven 2010.

13   Vollenhoven used this title for the historical series until 1948. From that date he switched to "Kort overzicht" (Short survey). The final text composed with this title is from 1956: "Kort Overzicht van de *Geschiedenis der Wijsbegeerte*" (Short survey of the history of philosophy), stencilled edition by THEJA (August 1956). This text has recently been reprinted in Vollenhoven 2005a: 27-93; English translation in Vollenhoven 2005b: 21-88. Vollenhoven's lecture notes in the history of philosophy are, apart from the published text cited here, still virgin soil in Vollenhoven studies.

14   Vollenhoven 2005d/e, 1.

15   Cf. Plato, *Theaetetus* 155d, in Plato 1961 and Aristotle, *Metaphysics* A 982b10 ff., in Aristotle 1941.

for God's majesty.[16] From such challenges, or others comparable, philosophical inquiry can *begin* for a person. But, whatever its beginning in human experience, the activity of inquiry that is set in motion would not be philosophical if it does not lead to insight, *viz.* to results capable of being expressed in a "complex of statements" (Vollenhoven 2005d/e, 1). The statements should be true, and the complex organized, based on the coherence between the statements. This means that the 'subjectivity' (or the contingency) of the beginning of inquiry—whether in wonder or bewilderment—needs to be controlled by constraints that answer to the required 'objectivity' of the results. For Vollenhoven the controlling efficacy is provided by *method*. To my knowledge Vollenhoven never defines 'method' in a formal sense, though he does work with a variety of methods. A method, roughly, is an orderly procedure of treatment of specific content or material, chosen for purposes of investigation or instruction. It is neither merely 'thought up' by the one who wields the method, nor simply externally applied arbitrarily, for it needs to be suitably linked with the material treated so as to meaningfully process the latter.

Vollenhoven finds the need of no less than *three methods* to do philosophy properly. Each method has its own order of procedure in connection with which a certain insight can be attained. It is only together that the methods yield what might be called, generically, "philosophical insight". But each has its own central feature. We first list them, and discuss them more thoroughly later.

The first method combines criticism and assertion. One takes a stand in connection with a topic at hand, but not without the explicit critical sense of one's choosing (or at least searching for) the best option, in the sense of the most *meaningful* one. At bottom, this method, which Vollenhoven calls "thetical-critical", is *intuitional*. For it takes place in the face of the historical context in which philosophy is practiced, that affects how the problems at hand are dealt with and how the preferences of tradition and the current approach influence the position provisionally taken.

The second method has no name, but it follows up on 'assertion' of the thetical-critical method. To assert is to underscore *truth*, in the sense that a predicate is attributed to something. That underscoring is justified—is knowingly in order—only if the something can indeed be determined as the predication indicates. Thus, grasping truth entails seizing on what is or exists and acknowledging it as knowable, *viz.* determinable in a way that is expressed in a *judgment*. Such judgments may be elicited by perception, but they can also be information statements, accepted truths

---

16   This is drawn from archived course notes, cf. Vollenhoven 1927ms; section 8d.

from others via news media, education, cultural tradition, etc. Very much of what we (claim to) know and act upon, is not specifically tested. That is the status of everyday knowledge (usually referred to as 'opinion'). It is practised in what might generically be called 'worldview'. Only when practice indicates that we go astray do we revise our opinion. Now assertions can be very determinate and detailed, but also very general. Philosophy involves the organization of our knowledge, thereby taking determinate and indeterminate being as the extremes of organization. For Vollenhoven, the main areas of determinate being are heaven and earth. The most indeterminate being is what holds of everything, in the sense that it can receive every predication. Every self-critical philosophy seeks to discern this and orientate its thought around this most basic of truths. This organization is methodical, for it involves passing from what is most determinate to what is indeterminate, and back. A candidate name for it (that I shall adopt) might be "the method of knowledge organization".

The third method of philosophy emphasizes the features of the logical or rational organization of philosophy as practiced in a *properly academic* sense. It is the method of resolution and composition. Here the challenge of *thought* is explicit, to the extent that this involves analysis (resolution) and synthesis (composition). For Vollenhoven academic (or 'scientific') thought operates within a context of knowledge organization, in other words, it operates with certain acknowledged determinants of reality. (Prominent in Vollenhoven are the *modal* determinant—of qualifications of being—and the *individual* determinant—of distinct individual existences.) Problems of thought are formulated in terms of determinants, and thought consists in elucidating ('bringing to light') a problem in terms of a careful indication of the factors involved (this is 'resolution'), and acknowledging the relational of combinational features that holds the indicated factors together (this is 'composition'). Each special science implements its own method(s) of resolution and composition. Philosophy applies this more generally—in other words, philosophy in the strict sense is also 'scientific'—in aiming to discover the status of determinants at the point where they defy further analysis, and how the connections between these 'rational primitives' contribute towards a better understanding of the whole.

The foci of the three methods can be pulled together in the following schema of 'knowing', that became standard in Vollenhoven (cf. Vollenhoven 2005d/e, **9**).

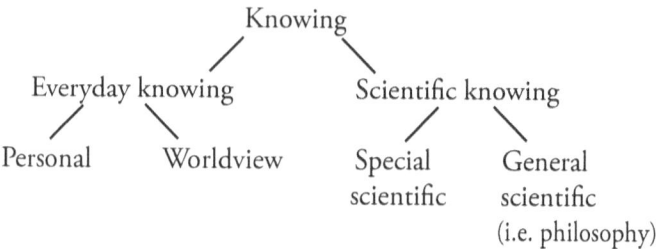

Knowing, as such, has an implicit intuitional feature, of meaningful awareness. In the thetical-critical method knowing is critically ascertained. When explicitly contextualized in the concrete personal and communal experience of *everyday knowing*, there is the added need for truth, extended as information. This gives the foothold for judgments that attest to the organization of our knowledge. *Scientific knowing*, in turn, calls for the additional function of distinguishing and connecting, when searching for truth via the method of resolution and composition. The determinants of reality provide the basis for this search. This scientific knowing takes place in a properly academic sense either in the context of the special sciences or as general inquiry, as in systematic philosophy.

Vollenhoven's practice of philosophy, to the extent that this is other than the critical appraisal of the thought of other thinkers, is doing 'systematic philosophy', understood as tracing the network of the determinants that are fundamental for any understanding and explicit knowledge of the structure, nature and dynamics of reality. This is performed against the background of a practical knowing and intuitional awareness, both of which embody conditions.

We can readily understand why Vollenhoven takes the norm of philosophy to be to "do justice to any diversity".[17] The awareness of diversity, of a difference that in some sense matters, is first of all intuited. It is known when a truth is ascertained with respect to it, in adducing relevant predications connected with the diversity. It is thought, i.e. understood, when placed in a relevant systematic context of determinants. Perhaps no trait is more characteristic of Vollenhoven's endeavour than his respect for the abundance of reality, as attested to by its diversity.[18] The role he allots to relationships does not undercut this; on the contrary, it allows diver-

---

17   Cf. Vollenhoven 2005b: 13. In Vollenhoven 2005d/e, **14**, Vollenhoven speaks of "the law ... for philosophical knowing".

18   One is reminded of William James' application of "the scholastic adage that whenever you meet a contradiction you must make a distinction". This adage was not lost on Vollenhoven, who found that most problems evidence a lack in making relevant distinctions or having improperly drawn distinctions. Cf. James 1992: 38.

sity to be entertained and understand. Unlike Hegel, he does not advance the dominating unity of a system. Vollenhoven's program is pluralist and fundamentally anti-reductionist.

B. Clarity, method and textual layout of *Isagôgè Philosophiae*

The reason for allotting *method* primary importance lies in philosophy's being, at heart, a *human practice*. If this practice is not haphazard—what Vollenhoven would never condone—then it is a practice guided and constrained by method, and thus also by the rules that determine a method. But in the teaching context, one cannot begin with the third method without appealing to the other methods. Thus Vollenhoven appeals specifically to intuitional support when he expresses his teaching aim to be: "to indicate with words, as clearly as I can, the most important determinants and diversity that I discern in the cosmos, so that others may also see them" (Vollenhoven 2005d/e, **18**).

Teaching others to discern what, in a fundamental sense, there is to discern — this calls for participation on the part of those learning from Vollenhoven. Vollenhoven expects this of the readers of the *Isagoge* as well. On his part, he tries to be as clear as possible in describing what he 'sees'.[19] Now clarity is sought not merely in the perspicuous style of the text but also through its organization. How clear is the *Isagoge* in these respects?

Vollenhoven sought clarity of expression by being *brief* and *succinct*, in fact characteristically so. We must admit that this did not always help him to achieve his aim. After all, brevity and succinctness don't always serve for clarity when there is need for explanation. (This naturally would have been provided orally in discussion sessions.) But on reading Vollenhoven, one soon realizes that his brevity of expression cloaks a complex

---

19 Reporting clearly what one 'sees'—i.e. discerns—has a general phenomenological ring to it. In 1920, in discussing the work of Hans Driesch, Vollenhoven says: "there is not any objection to the method of phenomenology, of objective logic (in Husserl's sense), as long as it proceeds in a purely descriptive way"; Vollenhoven 1920a: 12. Edmund Husserl, the father of 20th century phenomenology, claims in his last major work, *Die Krisis der europäischen Wissenschaften und die transzendentale Phänomenologie* (written 1935-1936): "I seek not to instruct but only to lead, to point out and describe what I see. I claim no other right than that of speaking according to my best lights [*nach bestem Wissen und Gewissen*], principally before myself but in the same manner also before others, as one who has lived in all its seriousness the fate of a philosophical existence"; Husserl 1970a: 18. The pathos of Husserl's self-description is striking. Vollenhoven is not lacking in pathos, but in him it concerns the richness of the being of creation, *viz.* "the presupposition that the wealth in that which is created will be much greater than has been ascertained to date"; Vollenhoven 2005d/e, **15**.

process of thought. Seldom is one privy to that process. Usually one has to make do with the results alone. On the other hand, Vollenhoven's succinctness evidences a talent for combining beguiling simplicity with deep subtlety, sweeping generalization with careful distinction. Here Vollenhoven is at his best. He has an impressive grasp of details, but always with a view to the framework in which they fit. He challenges the reader to exercise careful thought and to avoid ingrown confusing generalizations.

Brevity and succinctness can be a problem for someone expecting a 'full' account. Vollenhoven is aware of not giving a complete account (cf. Vollenhoven 2005d/e, **18**). But the lack of completeness, in turn, supports an experimental attitude, whereby results can be taken to be provisional, with room for improvement. Philosophy is, of course, no free-for-all. But in being the result of human effort, the insight gained, the interpretation accepted or the solution found is ineluctably subject to trial and error. Vollenhoven always took his results to be provisional, subject to possible improvement (Vollenhoven 2005d/e, **3**). The reader would misjudge Vollenhoven's guidance and his manner of providing this, if the context of his *own wrestling* is not given its due. But that context links his progress, which was not haphazard, to procedures that are methodical. This in fact leads to the second point about clarity, namely the clarity intended by means of the structure of the *Isagoge*. We find that the organization of the text is in step with the implementation of the three methods mentioned above.

At first sight, the *Isagoge* appears to have a perspicuous structure. The text develops at two levels. There is the overall organization of the text, with its divisions into parts and the progressive subdivisions of these parts. The main divisions of the text are: Preface, Introduction, three main Parts and an Appendix. It could hardly be simpler.

But there is also a second level, namely that of the content. The content unfolds in a sequence of consecutively numbered sections. Each section has its own numbered section head. These sections of the text are not aphorisms. Sometimes a section consists of no more than a short solitary assertive sentence. In fact most lack a complete expression of thought. They are more like 'planks in a platform', if by 'platform' we mean the whole philosophical context that undergirds Vollenhoven's work. Each plank (section) is a small contribution to the whole and offers its own egree of support.[20] In that sense each section calls for reflection, and each

---

20   The length of the sections varies from a short statement of six words to a disquisition of over 1700 words. On the whole, parts written later are longer than the earlier

needs to be understood in its own right. But its contribution to that whole depends on its link to the organized layout of the text. On more careful perusal, one finds that the above-mentioned methods play a leading role in the organization of the text, in that the main divisions are controlled by criteria of method.

The layout of the text is as follows (the numbers in bold refer to the 224 sections of the text). On the left we indicate in brackets where a method is introduced. The distinction to its right is the scope of text controlled by the method in question. The schema is followed up immediately with our commentary.

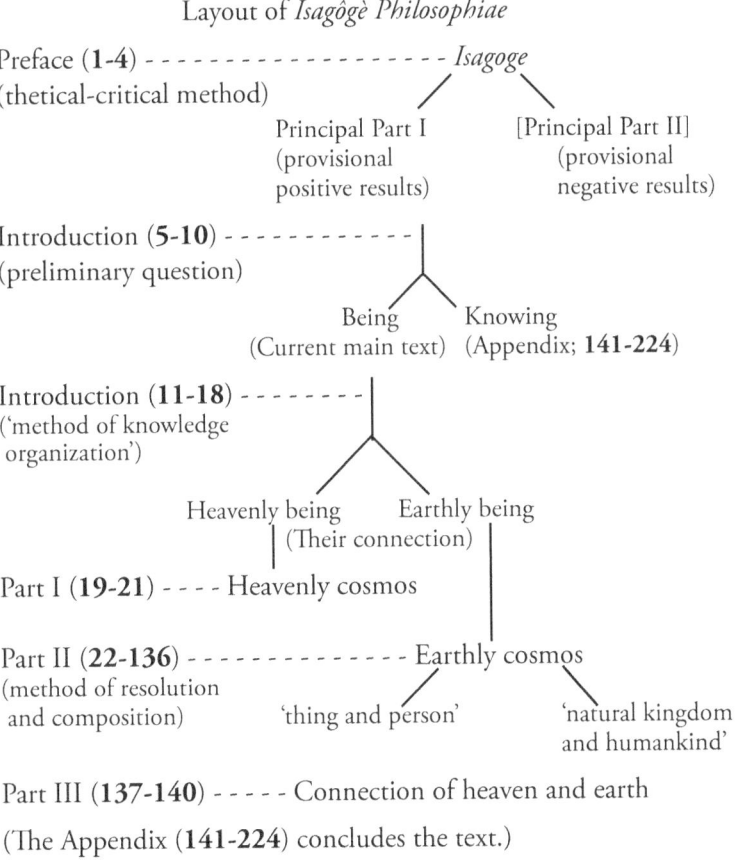

Layout of *Isagôgè Philosophiae*

Preface (**1-4**) ----------------- *Isagoge*
(thetical-critical method)
                          Principal Part I   [Principal Part II]
                          (provisional   (provisional
                          positive results)   negative results)

Introduction (**5-10**) -----------|
(preliminary question)
                   Being   Knowing
           (Current main text) (Appendix; **141-224**)

Introduction (**11-18**) --------|
('method of knowledge
organization')
          Heavenly being   Earthly being
                 (Their connection)

Part I (**19-21**) ---- Heavenly cosmos

Part II (**22-136**) ------------- Earthly cosmos
(method of resolution
and composition)   'thing and person'   'natural kingdom
                                                        and humankind'

Part III (**137-140**) ----- Connection of heaven and earth

(The Appendix (**141-224**) concludes the text.)

---

parts. E.g. the texts on the societal structures and on religion in the final version (of 1941/1945), the former of which is a newly composed text, while the latter is a rewritten text, come closest to having a degree of completeness that nearly makes them self-supporting.

In the Preface Vollenhoven motivates the study of philosophy and indicates the chief difference in the result of philosophy inquiry, *viz.* in that result being either positive or negative. This difference is controlled by the thetical-critical method. This distinction in positive and negative result governs the whole of the *Isagoge*, in fact more than the whole. The "negative result" was initially the second principal part of the *Isagoge* discussion. It offers discussion of the major philosophical alternatives that are criticized, as being incompatible with the accepted result, formulated as a connected account in the first principal part, the "positive result". That second principal part became redundant, as syllabus text, when it was published in Vollenhoven 1933.[21] From that point in time, the *Isagoge* text only contains the "positive result". But the thetical-critical method continues to mark the whole project of the *Isagoge*.

Next, the Introduction is announced as being about 'the place and task of philosophy'. It treats this topic after the discussion of a 'preliminary question' about the distinction of knowing and being. The latter is a major and characteristic distinction in Vollenhoven, being governed by the assertion that knowing resorts under being. (It is given full attention in chapters 3 and 4 of this study.) For now we wish to point out that the discussion of this preliminary question about being and knowing itself motivates the primary division of the text (the whole of the 'positive result') in a main text and an appendix. For, the central topic of the appendix is the *theory of knowledge*,[22] while that of the main text is *being*. In this setting, the nature (place and task) of philosophy is discussed in connection with philosophy's restriction to *cosmic* being. In the last two sections (**17** and **18**) of the Introduction we find the occurrence of terms

---

21   The "provisional negative result" was published as Chapter 3 of the systematic part of Vollenhoven's major work of 1933. The chapter is entitled "De grondmotieven der onschriftuurlijke wijsbegeerte" (The groundmotives of non-scriptural philosophy); Vollenhoven 1933a: 49-67. In the text-critical edition (Vollenhoven 2010) this text is reprinted in Appendix IIb. Vollenhoven continues to speak of positive and negative results in section **4**, but without the textual follow-up of the two principal parts, although traces of this earlier arrangement remain (cf. sections **6** and **141**); cf. also Vollenhoven 2005d/e.

22   The appendix is entitled "A number of the more complicated questions of philosophy", and lists three in particular, *viz.* theory of knowledge, the theory of technology and the theory of art. The length of treatment of this material is very disproportionate, with theory of knowledge discussed in 66 sections (namely **141-206**) and the other two in 9 sections each (**207-215** and **216-224** respectively). The first setup of the *Isagoge*, in 1930-1931, there was no appendix. The theory of knowledge is discussed as the main concluding *Part* of the 'positive result' (cf. Vollenhoven 2010, Appendix I). What justifies singling out theory of knowledge is its complete parallelism with the main distinctions of the main text. The discussion (as of 1932) of the theory of technology and theory of art is restricted to these theories' contexts in two 'law-spheres'.

with a methodical import, such as "orientation point" and "route", but without being given any leads as to how this works or proceeds. (The text is definitely too brief at this point!) However, we shall see that the second of the three methods is operational here. As we said, it lacks a name, but we shall refer to it as "the method of knowledge organization".

Finally, in the main body of the text we come across another, now third, discussion of method, one that is, in a textual sense, more explicit than the prior second method. This main body of the text is divided into three Parts, *viz.* on the heavenly cosmos, the earthly cosmos, and the connection between heaven and earth, respectively.[23] The first and third of these Parts are very brief texts, with all the attention being given to Part II, about the earthly cosmos. We notice that the third method pertains specifically to the second Part. In the description of this third method, there is mention of two characteristic routes: that of resolution (Vollenhoven 2005d/e, **23**) and that of proceeding to "ever-greater complexity" (*ibid.*; i.e. composition). Here, too, method motivates the organization of the text of this Part II. Its main division implements the distinction between on the one hand individual things and human beings, whereby individuality and modality have to be acknowledged insofar as these defy further analysis, *viz.* as being 'most resolved', and on the other hand the natural kingdoms and humankind that are, relevant to 'earthly existence', the greatest 'wholes' of complexity (*ibid.*, **26**).

So the step-wise introductions of the text touch on progressive restrictive divisions of the scope of the text.[24] The unwary reader is not likely to notice this, mainly because Vollenhoven's discussion of especially the second and the third methods is so casual, not to say nonchalant.

---

23   We need to be clear as to the meanings of the terms 'heaven' and 'earth'. 'Heaven' is not the starry sky but the abode of spiritual creatures; and 'earth' is not our home planet earth but, much broader, the created universe; cf. Vollenhoven 2005d/e, **20**. Naturally, as to the universe, the planet earth, and life on it, are known best.

24   Vollenhoven follows the same procedure in his "History of Philosophy", volume I (i.e. Vollenhoven 1950e). The entire historical project was planned to consist of nine volumes. The Preface addresses the whole project and introduces the problem of inquiry, the (problem-historical) method of approach and the main division of the field of study in three *Books, viz.* ancient, medieval and modern philosophy (or, in Vollenhoven's wording: prior to, during, and after the period of synthesis) (*op. cit.*: 11-21). The next introduction is that of the First Book, the period prior to synthesis philosophy, and motivates the division into two *Parts*: ancient Greek philosophy and Hellenistic philosophy (*op. cit.*: 23-29). The next introduction is directed to the First Part on ancient Greek philosophy and distinguishes two main *Divisions, viz.* the period prior to realism and the realist period (of Plato and Aristotle) (*op. cit.*: 31-34). Finally, there is the introduction to the First Main Division of ancient Greek philosophy prior to Plato. This last introduction is coterminous with the actual content of volume I (*op. cit.* : 35-39).

But the importance of method is undeniable. Thus we shall pause to give separate attention to each of the three methods, so as to supplement their cursory discussion in the *Isagoge*.[25]

C. Methodical procedures: the thetical-critical method

The thetical-critical method governs the entire practice of philosophy. It is predicated on the two main meanings of philosophy, mentioned in section **1**, *viz.* its being both a (subjective) activity and an (objective) acquired result. The activity of philosophy factually begins when a person is moved by some problem or something that fascinates. This reflection necessarily involves taking a "point of view", i.e. a certain understanding relevant to the context in which the reflection takes place. Vollenhoven stresses initiative and contingency. Two points are essential here. (i) However unique one's own 'beginning' of philosophy may be, one is not the first to philosophize. The whole history of philosophy attests to that. One should be prepared to learn from others, in taking stock of (relevant) results already available, but doing so critically and not in an attitude in which one lets others do one's thinking. (The latter takes place when one claims to be a 'Platonist', 'Aristotelian', 'Augustinian', 'Cartesian', 'Kantian', etc.) But (ii) however much one may be enamoured by one's 'own standpoint', it jeopardizes one's learning when that standpoint is turned into a privileged position and the acquired results shielded from self-criticism. Human activity is never beyond critique, hence one must be willing also to submit one's *own results*, and not just those of others, to criticism. A critical review of a result may, of course, reconfirm it, but it can also give rise to more explicit reasons to adjust or even reject it. (This assumes, of course, that the result is not merely a projection of the point of view, but also a reflection of data of reality considered.) Either way, the positive confirmation and the negative rejection remains *provi-*

---

25   It would appear that Vollenhoven in general eschewed procedural discussions in favour of the actual implementation of a procedure. E.g. he promoted his later "problem-historical method", not by dwelling on its setup but by pointing to the results obtained. "The utility of a method must be attested to by the results achieved with its help" (Vollenhoven 1950e: 6). In a later article on the problem-historical method, the positive meaning of the results achieved figures prominently. The article includes a (perhaps telling) memory of his student days: "the lectures at that time . . . included methodological introductions which were far too extensive, as least as far as we students were concerned" (Vollenhoven 1961c; reprinted in 2005b: 96). Albert M. Wolters' remark about Vollenhoven's work in connection with the problem-historical method may be generalized: "One of the exasperating things about that work is that Vollenhoven seems to have an aversion to discussing the methodological presuppositions implicit in his method" (Wolters 1979a: 231).

sional, for this embodies the attitude of always being prepared to learn, reconsider and reassess. So one ought to treat one's own results in a way that is no different from those of others (cf. Vollenhoven 2005d/e, **3**). In other words, Vollenhoven's proposal in this regard amounts to one's doing philosophy with an open historical mind. The thetical and the critical together warrant the expectation of philosophical advance. In a wording that was only superficially modified from 1930 on, Vollenhoven says:

> It is by maintaining that which is tenable in one's own position, by critically examining not only the result acquired by others but also the result of one's own thinking at an earlier time, and by having the courage to accept the implications of one's position, that one can make progress through struggle and attain a double profit: a reinforced *position* and a more definite *rejection* of whatever is inconsistent with it. (Vollenhoven 2005d/e, **3**)

The thetical-critical method brings systematic reflection and historical alternatives in direct contact with each other. It is true to say of Vollenhoven that he was always aware of the historical alternatives he rejected and those he accepted when making his decisions. (Regretfully, he did not always make these deliberations explicit.)[26] He operates from out of an overall historical consciousness that is intuitively tuned to what there is to know and to think. One might be inclined to suspect a specimen of the Hegelian dialectic operative here. The thetical and the critical results do have something of a 'thesis-antithesis' opposition about them. But the crucial step is what, in Hegel, is the follow-up of 'synthesis'. Whereas in Hegel's dialectic one relativizes and overcomes the difference of two terms in opposition, in reference to an 'identity in (the) difference' as seen from a higher standpoint,[27] Vollenhoven's method involves undergoing difference and ascertaining the relationships that are relevant to the difference in question. Thus Vollenhoven's 'relationships' are not

---

26   He did make these deliberations explicit in his first work, the dissertation on the philosophy of mathematics (cf. Vollenhoven 1918a). He favours mathematical intuitionism, and sets this off against formalism on the one hand and empiricism on the other. The discussion of his choices includes the 'lessons of history' regarding these three schools of mathematics. Cf. chapter 2, footnote 37 for an overview of the content of this work.

27   In Hegel, the 'thetical' is a posit of understanding, the 'antithetical' one of negative reason, the 'synthetical' that of positive reason. Because a synthesis involves a content that is more encompassing than that of the thetical and the antithetical alone, each step of synthesis yields a new posit of understanding, which in turn gets to be incorporated in a yet higher or more encompassing standpoint (of reason). In this way Hegel's dialectical method displays the advance of reason that ends in the (holistic) acquisition of 'absolute knowledge'. Cf. part VI "Logic further defined and divided" of "The science of logic" in Hegel's *Encyclopedia*; Hegel 1975: 113-122. We add that the terminology of "thesis-antithesis-synthesis" is what Fichte made popular, Hegel preferring "an sich – für sich – an-und-für sich".

like the syntheses of Hegel, that are (monistically) conceived to subjugate difference. Hegelian dialectics is one of dominance, Vollenhoven's is that of release – to "do justice to any diversity". Vollenhoven opposes a ubiquitous 'synthesis' of reason in favour of the 'a-synthetic' (i.e. 'analytic' or discerning) awareness of the richness of diversity.[28]

One final remark on the thetical-critical method. Vollenhoven nowhere specifies the kind of criticism he has in mind when applying the thetical-critical method. There is no mention, say, of 'transcendental criticism', 'epistemological criticism', 'ontological criticism', 'logical criticism', etc. I believe we can say that, for Vollenhoven, any criticism that enables us to learn from our mistakes or reconsiderations, that helps to see better what is the acceptable opinion over against the censurable one, what the better presupposition is, or what the real gist of a problem is, is welcome. The more important point is that criticism is not itself a viable 'point of view' or 'standpoint'. Such a standpoint would have to guard itself from the uncertainty of its own vulnerability, unless invulnerability is dogmatically maintained, which, either way, is to block the thetical-critical method. There is no human thought that unerringly thinks only itself, nor is there a knowledge, as humanly entertained, that is itself beyond criticism. For neither thought nor knowledge is an end in itself. Thought and knowledge entail activity, and activity cannot 'take place' without some place, and hence also something historically contingent, being taken in. Only in that way is there a result to be critical of. One takes a place (or a stand) through the intuition. This is not an unassailable certainty, but the awareness of the challenge of one's historical time and geographical place, which includes one's own existence, and engages us intellectually to accept what makes the best sense.

D. Methodical procedures: the method of knowledge organization

The *Isagoge*'s second method is more implicit than explicit. But by pulling all the evidence together, something of its relevance does come to view.

The focus of the second method is on knowledge. Here too there is a subjective and objective moment. Vollenhoven understands this in such a

---

28   For a typical example of this, cf. Vollenhoven 1942l. This text, which has three parts, discusses truth in the philosophy of religion (*godsdienst*, literally "worship"). The first part proceeds thetically in first discussing truth in religion (pp. 113-117). The second part discusses truth in philosophy (pp. 117-121), which is, in fact, a confrontational discussion of views that are present in the history of philosophy. Its third and last part (pp. 121-123) discusses the relation between truth in religion and truth in philosophy, with particular, critical attention to the 'synthesis' variants and how they *muddle* the unity of truth in religion and philosophy.

way as to oppose the 'split of subject and object' in two independent realities that Descartes saddles modern philosophy with. In chapters three and four Vollenhoven's epistemology is discussed directly. Here the mere mention of characteristic features will have to suffice.

The first characteristic feature is that the epistemological 'object' is not an independent reality, but is a feature of being to the extent that being is *knowable*. What there is to know is not present as ready knowledge (contrary to the copy theory of empiricism). But there are (knowable) data, that are knowingly gleaned and 'worked' into the possession that attests to 'having knowledge' (cf. Vollenhoven 2005d/e, **174**).

The second characteristic feature is that the human Self is not an intrinsic subject (contrary to idealism)—whether justified by appealing to the immortality of the soul or the evidence of a self-certain intuition— but has the *task* of being a subject. The Self has an *interest* in knowing, linked to a duty. Thus when the knowledge situation is said to involve 'knowing the knowable', the subjective and objective features implicit here are both contextualized, with the continued operational relevance of the thetical-critical method in the background. But this is not to deny the importance of distinguishing the two factors of the Self's knowing and being's being knowable; indeed, this importance is evinced by Vollenhoven's textual division of the main Parts of the *Isagoge* about '(cosmic) being' and the Appendix about 'human knowing'.

The third characteristic feature is that knowing and the knowable come together in the *ascertainment of truth*.[29] Meeting the duty of knowing involves an appropriation of truth, in which the knowable is represented. To come to know is to have knowledge, which is to enjoy a state of rest.[30] Such enjoyment contrasts with the opposite state of not knowing, which is in fact to stray. Truth is not come by merely through gaining content. Naturally, forming and gaining mental representations do take place. But this is psychical, or at least is psychically based. The factor of truth does not arise merely through representations.[31] Truth, when appropriated, and thus subsequently capable of being asserted, cannot be divorced from a normative factor in the epistemic situation. Truth cannot be asserted in a logical context when contradictions are not resolved (in accordance to logical norms). In a similar way, truth cannot be asserted

---

29   Cf. Vollenhoven 1926b: 381; also Vollenhoven 1926d: 54 ff.

30   Vollenhoven 2005d/e, **150**. Only in the sources of 1926 does Vollenhoven speak of the direct appropriation of truth. In the early 1930s he settles for the state of mind that truth brings with it, namely rest. This topic is discussed more thoroughly in chapter 4.

31   Cf. Vollenhoven 1926a: 20-21; also, for the distinction between truth and 'truth markers', cf. Vollenhoven 1926d: 149.

in a social context unless one reckons with the norms that adjudicate between what is socially in order and not in order, or in a legal context, what is just and unjust, or in an ethical sense, with good and bad. The factor of truth in human knowledge calls for an awareness of an 'ought'. Knowing entails responsibility.[32]

Now in the epistemic ascertaining of truth, Vollenhoven distinguishes between truth being conveyed as given and truth being acquired in being sought. The latter, *viz.* the truth acquired through being sought and attained, calls for an active logical-analytical functioning of distinguishing and connecting. That falls directly within the scope of the third method. In the current context we need to concentrate on the first alternative of truth conveyed. The case of truth conveyed is more typical of our everyday experience and knowing, and that falls within the scope of the second method. For when informed of events, or taught about situations, past and present, or when facts and norms are revealed, the recipient is in a position of acceptance. This is knowledge by communication, and there is something non-reductive about it. One cannot possibly doubt all communicated knowledge (as Descartes recommended) and rebuild it from self-asserted truth. But one may, of course, take any instance of knowledge that is conveyed and subject it to criticism. In that sense a 'procedure' can be set to work within the scope of conveyed knowledge.

One's personal beginning in philosophy will yield neither a full detailed knowledge nor a more abstract level of principles. This is itself telling. Our knowledge is in some sense always partial, capable of being made more determinate when considering details, or less determinate when taken generally. Pursuing these alternative courses is what makes for a methodical procedure in this connection. Vollenhoven takes determinacy to involve predication. Being has the feature of being knowable, hence in experiential practice, when having knowledge about something, or having knowledge conveyed about something, a predicate (experienced meaning) is attributed to something that is there, in such a way that this answers to truth. An important mark of truth is the effect of such knowledge. He speaks of 'enjoying rest' when knowledge proves in practice to be adequate, and of straying when not adequate (Vollenhoven 2005d/e, **150, 173** ff.). This is obviously relevant as everyday knowledge. The 'rest' is not primarily passivity but the ease of conscience, of having determined something in a way that is evidently in the 'right way'. In that

---

32   This responsibility is not incompatible with the "rest", spoken of above; cf. immediately below.

sense its accrual contributes significantly towards a more encompassing practice from a worldview standpoint.[33]

Predication conditions the being of something.[34] That being is not a bland feature. It is best to see it as a 'to be' of anything that exists. Every predication in this sense, adds a conditioning determination on the existent something. When investigated (according to the third method) the different sciences will distinguish different kinds and types of determination. But philosophy pursues a more general interest. At the level of the second method, philosophy's reflection can address the question as to what happens when 'letting go', so to speak, of determinations.

One might, in a formal sense, anticipate ending up, after all, with a completely bland notion of being, in its most indeterminate sense. But this 'formal sense' would not do justice to the situation at hand, as understood by Vollenhoven. Having knowledge involves taking a 'standpoint' (which is always already relevant in connection with the thetical-critical situation). As one courses on the route to greater indeterminacy, one does not form more abstract concepts—concept formation is relevant to the third method—but one's *predications* become more indeterminate, meaning that one's standpoint of insight becomes increasingly less specific. At the point where all determinations have been bracketed, one ends up with the minimal requirement of a *standpoint as such*, consistent with the conditions of knowledge (or being able to predicate what is).[35]

This 'point of greatest indeterminacy' is what Vollenhoven calls the "point of orientation" of philosophy (Vollenhoven 2005d/e, **17**). As standpoint, this still assumes a stance in reality. One does not transcend the cosmic conditions of existence that are relevant to the practice of philosophy. Thus, the relevance and need of orientation at this point follows from the feature of responsibility inherent in knowledge. This feature is now (at the orientation point) relevant in its most bare essence, *viz.* as implicating the validity of an 'ought' as centred in a norm or,

---

33   One might be inclined to take this view of knowledge as a specimen of pragmatism. It agrees with pragmatism in emphasizing the context of activity and the practice of life. But for Vollenhoven, activity and practice are subject to norms, which prevents the 'human interest', however real and relevant, from having the last word. Hence Vollenhoven does not share the pragmatists' 'instrumental view of knowledge'; cf. James 1992: 42 ff.

34   Archived lecture notes of 1927-1929 are an important source here. This material contains discussions not found elsewhere in Vollenhoven's *oeuvre*. On determinacy and indeterminacy, cf. Vollenhoven 1927ms, section 19, also 1928ms, sections 25-27.

35   These 'route descriptions' are in the archived lecture notes, mentioned in the previous footnote. Sections 22-24 of Vollenhoven 1927ms are on predication and determination.

stated more generically, in law. We need also to realize that, because all determinations are relinquished in this most indeterminate of 'positions', one cannot interpret this orientation point as involving (say) representations, which would be a determination of consciousness, or the privileged status of a social class, which would fundamentally bias the practice of philosophy, or a distinct spiritual condition, which would subject philosophy to a determination of prized value of a higher order, or whatever other option one's prejudice might fancy. There is the 'ought' of law, as principle of determination, that, at the point of orientation, can only be acknowledged in terms of its own primary obligating relevance.

At the orientation point, one is invited to make one's stand explicit. It calls for making explicit how 'determination' is understood, and how the things of existence (i.e. the cosmos) answer to determination. The very possibility of anything being knowable is at issue. The orientation point's being the most indeterminate portrayal of existence as cosmic being, nothing of the latter can be taken to effect a determining role. But then one needs to presuppose an origin of law that is *external* to cosmic being. This origin cannot be a species of cosmic being. Here we find, almost uniquely in Vollenhoven's work, an indication of why a divine being is called for. The divine being is the origin of law, and the divine being, in determining cosmic reality, has nothing in common with the latter.

> [W]hoever speaks of the being of God, without being conscious that this being is a being *above* the law and hence has nothing in common with being under the law [uses language lacking in meaning]. The one is the *archè* [= controlling principle] of the other, and whoever wants to subsume them under a common denominator will transgress, consciously or unconsciously, the boundary that God has posited upon him as creature. (Vollenhoven 1927ms, section *8)

Philosophy does not itself need to begin with the point of orientation. But philosophy that is self-critical cannot refrain from meeting the challenge of accounting for one's standpoint, that is exposed at the point of greatest indeterminacy. But what remains when all content of determination has been 'let go'? What is relevant here is the realization that one's standpoint is the substrate of one's philosophical practice, which entails regulation. Thus at the point of greatest indeterminacy there is the realization of 'standing in subjection' to rules or norms that regulate, without the latter being one or more quality or feature of the standing as such. Were the latter to be the case, then one will not have 'let go' completely to the point of greatest indeterminacy, and one would take as principle of *archè* whatever that feature implies; say, to be is to be conscious, or to be material, or to be extensive, or to be idea, or to be psychical, etc. In other words, one would be already 'on the move' in applying determinations (predications) without having considered the 'point from which one moves', or—in being properly accountable—taken stock of the regulation entailed by any move. The orientation point succeeds in orienting only when norms are given their due, not when a determined feature, however general, is granted the status of first principle. In other words, the orientation point, in being relevant to philosophy as practice or activity, is not a construal *of* philosophy but is an orienting condition *for* philosophy.

Philosophy that proceeds from the said orientation point has acquired for itself a meaning of 'origin', 'law' and 'cosmic reality'. It may now proceeds methodically towards the other pole of reality in its greatest determination. It will first formulate 'judgments of assessment or discerning' (cf. Vollenhoven 1926a: 10, 14), that express the most basic (modal) determinations of being of things, as intuited. From there, all further predication proceeds in an organized way, till it has included, knowingly and at the point of most complete determination, all things of heavenly and earthly cosmic reality. This suggests naming this (second) method the 'method of knowledge organization'. It is within the context of this method that Vollenhoven now formulate what he takes the 'place and task' of philosophy to be, in a way that is consonant with his use of the orientation point.

The 'place' of philosophy—in the sense of the scope of its discerning activity—is that of the whole cosmos (Vollenhoven 2005d/e, **16**). In its properly academic sense it is also *limited* to cosmic reality. The 'task' that philosophy accepts is, in a negative sense, "never deny or seek to push aside that which exists, not even to the smallest degree" (Vollenhoven 2005d/e, **15**a). The positive sense of the task is: to be sensitive to the richness of the cosmos (*ibid*, **15**b). Together this yields the imperative of philosophy, *viz.* of 'doing justice to every diversity' in connection with cosmic reality.

E. Methodical procedures: the method of resolution and composition.
The third method is specifically attuned to *thought*. The two prior methods are presupposed by it. The practice of philosophy is never in disjunction from the historical reality of philosophy, nor does philosophy take place in a mental vacuum, bereft of all knowledge and orientation. Of course one can always select and isolate. But then one still presupposes the knowledge that is relevant to the selecting and isolating. Philosophy

should not only not deny its ties to life, but also explicate such ties as one finds to be relevant conditions for doing philosophy. But when this is met, there is still need for a third method to characterize philosophy's properly academic status as a 'general scientific enterprise'.

This topic and the details of this third method are discussed more fully in the course of chapter 4, which focuses on Vollenhoven initial definitive position. At this point a summary indication will have to suffice.

For Vollenhoven, thought, in its primary sense, comes down to two very basic 'moves', *viz.* to *distinguish* what awareness reveals to be different and to *connect* what fits together in relationships. Vollenhoven turns this into a methodological rule that he applies throughout his work at every turn. "In every case where two things are different, we can ask about the relationship between the two" (Vollenhoven 2005d/e, **10**). The distinguishing and the connecting are 'subjective', in the sense that these need to be carried out (in terms of an 'analysing functioning'). Were there no difference and relationship, then the distinguishing and connecting would be wilful and imposed (which is not necessarily wrong, so long as this is adequately motivated). Objectivity is evident when the distinctions made and the connections laid are supported by difference and relationship *in the affairs*. Vollenhoven recognizes this at all levels: difference and relationship between subject and object, body and soul, good and evil, between this individual and that individual, between modes of being, etc.

There is also a systematic togetherness of difference and relationship.[36] Specific differences and relationship are relevant to states of affairs. But specific differences and relations can also be included in more complex expressions of difference and relationship. Vollenhoven speaks of a *determinant* (*bepaaldheid*) to indicate a fitting togetherness of difference and relationship. Determinants may be very minimal, e.g. the difference and relations between natural numbers, or very inclusive, as for example the difference and relationship between heaven and earth. Understanding the structure of reality results from distinguishing and connecting the relevant determinants of reality. The main part of the *Isagoge*—*viz.* Part II—describes this structure as a cosmology—Vollenhoven 2005d/e, **27-94**. This cosmology is outlined in section IV of chapter 4 of this study.

Vollenhoven uses the methodological terminology of 'resolution' and 'composition' in the context of reality's determinants. These terms denote the two 'routes' of thought, whereby the endpoint of the one is the beginning of the other (and vice versa). Vollenhoven speaks of "re-

---

36 Cf. chapter 4, where this is described as falling under the 'intersection principle'.

solving" and "proceeding in the direction of ever-greater complexity" (Vollenhoven 2005d/e, **24**).[37] But, here too, Vollenhoven is not set on terms. The important point is the identification of the 'endpoints' of the routes of resolution and composition. Resolution analyses until the determinate diversity is such as to defy further analysis. Within cosmology this diversity is of three kinds: modal difference, that of the diversity between individual beings, and the diversity of good and evil. The route in the direction of increasing complexity (i.e. making more concrete) begins with the (abstract) forms of diversity that are 'analytically simple'. When travelling along this route, the connections that can be posited in the diversity become explicit, in light of what fits in view of the determinants involved. On this route one accounts for progressively more encompassing 'wholes' (Vollenhoven 2005d/e, **23**). The endpoint of the route of composition places us in the area of the natural kingdoms and kinds (*ibid.*, **22**). In a complete treatment, both routes would need to be investigated. For practical reasons Vollenhoven chooses to trace only one of the two routes, namely the route of composition (*ibid.*, **24**). That is why the discussion in the *Isagoge* begins with the most basic diversity, in a cosmological sense, and ends with the context of greatest connection, found in religion. Naturally, the reader is expected to fill in the alternative route of resolution for him/herself, or at least to keep this in mind.

F. Lapses of method?

The *Isagoge* text is governed by method. The discerning reader will have noticed that this does not quite hold for the whole text. There are the (very brief) first and third Parts of the main account of the cosmos that fall outside of the scope of the third method (of resolution and composition). That method appears to be geared exclusively to the earthly cosmos. Because the first Part is about the heavenly cosmos, and the third Part about the connection of heaven and earth, these topics address a reality that mostly falls outside of our normal human experiential range. Either these Parts require their own method, or their inclusion in a text of philosophy is contestable. How do things stand?

---

[37] Vollenhoven does not actually use the term 'composition' in the *Isagoge*. He speaks of "gecompliceerdheid" i.e. 'complexity', or 'complicatedness'. But to speak of a method of resolution and complication seems strained. Vollenhoven must have felt a difficulty in choosing the right terms here. In work of 1926 he referred to the two directions as "simplicating" (*simplicerende*—which is a Dutch neologism) and "complicating" (Vollenhoven 1926d: 158 and 1926a: 58). This terminology is quite definitely strained. In the body of the *Isagoge* Vollenhoven uses the terms 'abstract' and 'concrete' in reference to the two routes, in expressions such as 'dispensing with abstraction' and 'making more concrete'; cf. Vollenhoven 2005d/e, **49, 64, 70, 95, 115**.

There can be no doubt that Vollenhoven meant to include these topics, judging by the method of knowledge organization. At one pole of this method, the point of orientation, one is led to understand, that the most general feature that may be asserted of the cosmos, is that it stands in subjection to a determination of law. At the opposite end there are the most specifically determined realities of the cosmos, these being the heavenly and the earthly realities. In virtue of determination, that reality is knowable, this must include earthly reality and heavenly reality. So how is the discussion of heavenly reality broached?

We need to reckon with a factor that has not been mentioned as yet. When speaking of something being knowable, one needs to take into account how that capacity (of being knowable) is actualized in confrontation with the knowing subject. In this connection Vollenhoven speaks of "means of knowing" (Vollenhoven 2005d/e, **173**), these being—he states this very traditionally—'Nature and Scripture' (*ibid.*). Nature as a means of knowing is the context of the awareness of ourselves and the realities around us, an awareness that is relevant in virtue of our being alive and living on the earth. This is our 'natural situation', the environment in which our awareness becomes specific in perception and conception. This mediation of nature—our natural habitat—aids in enabling us to conduct our inquiry of earthly reality according to the third method. The Scriptures, as means of knowing, serves a similar purpose, except that it operates in a different way. Scripture is a 'means that informs', i.e. conveys truths about realities, truths the human being would not have surmised without speculation or adequate control. This may be in connection with realities the human being is in touch with (e.g. earthly life, but in its 'fallen state') or realities beyond the scope of our 'natural' capacity to know, such as heaven (cf. Vollenhoven 2005d/e, **173**). In virtue of Scriptural revelation, God and the law are knowable, as are heaven and earth. Thus the first and third Parts of the main text of the *Isagoge* are 'constrained' after all, if not by an actual method, then nevertheless by a definite means of knowing.[38]

This 'double means approach' is not without its problems. We must at least be aware that Scripture serves in various capacities in Vollenhoven. As a religious document it is part of religious life, giving substance to life-attitudes and life-goals. The religious life, conducted biblically, involves covenant living, which address the human being in terms of responsi-

---

[38] There is, nevertheless, a certain reticence on Vollenhoven's part. His discussions of these two Parts hardly rises above brief notes. No doubt there is the motive to avoid speculation. But in the third Part he speaks of an influence of heavenly beings on earthly life, but he does not offer an analysis of this effect (Vollenhoven 2005d/e, **138**).

bilities and stewardship. This leads to the second role of Scripture, *viz.* namely with respect to worldview and the more specific neo-Calvinist Reformed tradition of 'sphere sovereignty'. While there is always something of an 'information side' to these religious and worldview roles, the import of Scripture here is not to inform but to enjoin, to warn, to realize the better sense, to pursue the good life. The role of the Scriptures in these two contexts (of religion and worldview) is, I believe, defensible.

But the third role, as means of knowing in that it provides information, is entirely focussed on informing about realities. One accepts the information 'on faith', but that cannot be the end of the matter. Even faith has need of opportunity and leeway for hermeneutical reflection, so as to come into focus with the intended and not the self-sought meaning. The question that Vollenhoven does not ask is whether the role of Scripture within the religious and worldview presuppositions of philosophy may not suffice (in the light of his aim) to delineate an understanding and practice of 'scriptural philosophy', without calling upon the Scripture as source of information.

Behind the Scripture stands the 'Logos revelation', an essential component of Vollenhoven's 'theistic position'. In his early work he pursues a 'theistic epistemic ideal' (cf. chapter 2), in which Logos revelation is the warrant of knowledge. Vollenhoven thoroughly criticizes and revises this in the second half of the 1920s. But in retaining an epistemic element of information conveyance, the 'theistic epistemic ideal' may not be entirely rejected. We will return to this when discussing 'Calvinistic philosophy'.

G. To round off

The *Isagoge* is a unique text. As collection of notes it leaves gaps that appear to fragment the text. Yet at the same time it evinces a unity of approach and conception that is subtle, nuanced and sweepingly broad. As an educational text, what it lacks in terms of being a finished product becomes a challenge to the interested reader. Vollenhoven guides without taking away all initiative from the student. The student and the reader need to think, and to think hard when following Vollenhoven.

In general, we can say that Vollenhoven turned the challenge of introducing philosophy to his own advantage. There is no simplification or popularization that merely pandered to the ignorance of a first-year student. For that reason the text serves as a valuable document in his own *oeuvre*. The handicap that remained for him was in having to decide what to include in an introductory text and what to pass over. That handicap needs to be seen in connection with the factor of obviousness. What was obvious to a first-year student at a Reformed bastion in the Dutch, ideologically divided society in the 1930s and 1940s, is easily lost in a different situation, certainly in that of the twenty-first century. Obviousness is not a stable trans-contextual factor. Vollenhoven and most of his students were at home in the Dutch situation, at least in the first two decades of his career.[39] In the *Isagoge* Vollenhoven made practically no comparisons with other traditions or assumptions in the practice of philosophy. In that sense, any reading of the *Isagoge* depends heavily, for its interpretation, on understanding the relevant internal connections between the main elements of the philosophical conception he elucidates and letting the attempted clarity of expression do the rest.

The emphasis of this study is on Vollenhoven's distinct philosophical contribution. To understand this, one needs to take careful stock of the presuppositions, and the themes associated with them, that Vollenhoven reckoned were relevant to philosophy, particularly those of religious and worldview character. However, the experience of these themes, in their actual religious and worldview settings, has a tendency to shift with time, as emphases change and interpretations are revised. We do not have to return to the 1930s and 1940s, or earlier, to appreciate whatever relevance these themes continue to have. But it is instructive to understand the past so as to be in the better position to responsibly filter out what inhibits and appreciate what is lasting for the future. We therefore first turn to take a closer look at the Dutch scene from about mid-nineteenth century on before looking more pointedly at Vollenhoven's program.

III. *The academic context*
A. The neo-Calvinist commitment

Vollenhoven's appointment in philosophy in 1926 had ideological constraints, besides meeting direct educational needs. The Free University of Amsterdam was founded by Abraham Kuyper (1837-1920) in 1880. It was for many years a privately funded institute of higher learning, finding its main support among the working class of Calvinist conviction. Kuyper had mobilized this group into a more active participation in Dutch national life. Sociologically this helped effect the emancipation

---

39   There were few foreign students at the Free University prior to the second World War. This changed after the war. One of Vollenhoven's first foreign students, the late Dr. Evan Runner, of Presbyterian background, from Philadelphia, U.S.A., remembered well the culture shock upon coming to the Netherlands in 1946. "As I went home and thought it all over, I began to realize that there was a broad spectrum of Reformed life, and that I had never experienced anything like this before. And I began to ask myself: Where did all this come from?" Van Dyke and Wolters 1979: 348.

of this class. But an ideological motive was no less relevant. Kuyper was adverse to the Enlightenment's liberalism and rationalism, which were dominant in modern Dutch life in the nineteenth century. He sought to develop an alternative standard for national life based on a *Reveil* of the Calvinist-Reformational consciousness. The model for this *Reveil* was the 'Calvinist conviction' that had accompanied the birth of the Dutch nation in the late sixteenth and early seventeenth century. The men of learning, who were in step with Kuyper and committed to the *Reveil*, were intent on educating their public to critically evaluate the Enlightenment's revolutionary and humanistic influence on society and culture, while at the same time they took the lead in blazing an alternative path. Kuyper's own voluminous writings, both popular and academic, had this dual purpose. Vollenhoven could identify with this striving. Educating students at the Free University was at the same time educating the future leaders of the church, the state and society.

When appointed, Vollenhoven was expected to develop a philosophy program that would accord with the spirit of the Free University as set down in its 'foundation' statement (or charter). (We look at this presently.) Vollenhoven, being of a critical and principled mind, could not align himself fully with any of the main schools of thought in his day—reinforced by what he judged to be the misguided influences upon his own initial work in philosophy (cf. chapter 2). Hence the conditions were ripe for him to strike out on his own. He took the opportunity presented by the compulsory philosophy introduction to formulate a 'philosophical conception' that would accord with the Calvinian-Kuyperian commitment of his community and meet the needs of the Free University's scientific endeavours.[40] This commitment was also of influence in Vollenhoven's choice of developing a systematic presentation of philosophy from out of its most basic presuppositions, in a way that would be enlightening to all students of the university of whatever faculty, without any prior choice of disciplines within philosophy.

---

40   The Free University, long a fledgeling institute of only three faculties, was required by law to expand into a full university according to a set time-table when receiving accreditation of its degrees in 1905. By 1930 there had to be a fourth faculty. This became the faculty of mathematics and the natural sciences. For the history of the mathematical side of this faculty, later to become a distinct faculty of its own, and Vollenhoven's influence on it in its early years, cf. Blauwendraat 2004; for Vollenhoven's influence cf. especially chapter two of Blauwendraat 2004. For a history of the natural sciences within this faculty, cf. Flipse 2005. During the planning stage of this fourth faculty, Vollenhoven addressed the problem of its 'foundation'; cf. Vollenhoven 1929d, in Rullmann 1929: 52-64. All the students of this new faculty were required to take Vollenhoven's introductory philosophy course once it opened its doors.

The Free University obviously had to meet academic standards from the start.[41] But it was more conscious, in the first half-century of its existence, of its place and importance in connection with Kuyper's neo-Calvinist movement. It was, as A. Th. van Deursen's recent history of the Free University describes it, the 'cornerstone' of Kuyper's national *Reveil* endeavour.[42] Kuyper's national reform program had already had success in an operational Calvinist-Christian press—a daily "De Standaard" and a weekly "De Heraut"—, in forming a Christian labour union and in establishing an "anti-revolutionary" political party with significant parliamentary representation. Kuyper had inherited the political ideal, along with the establishment of Christian schools free from State control, from his predecessor, Guillaume Groen van Prinsterer (1801-1876). Kuyper capped the Christian school movement with the establishment of the Free University.[43]

In appealing to the Calvinistic roots of national life, the *Reveil* could be looked upon as a reactionary movement, which to some extent it no doubt was. But Kuyper had more than simply conservative-restorative motives. He accounted for his practical endeavours in terms of a worldview that was relevant for, and that could meet the challenges of, contemporary life. This worldview account is that of 'sphere sovereignty', which is a religiously motivated view of society in which the 'societal spheres' of family, business, school, jurisprudence, state, church, and so on are each seen as divinely endowed with the responsibility of regulating its own affairs, without one sphere encroaching upon another. This fits in with the Christian-Calvinist confession of *divine sovereignty* having authority over all of life and calling for *human responsibility* in all of its walks. In its being relevant for its time, in fact in even being innovative in calling for democratic participation of the people in whatever sector of society,

---

41   If necessary, prior to its accreditation (granted in 1905), students could be re-examined at a state university, which never presented problems for the students; cf. Van Deursen 2005: 39.

42   The term occurs in the title of Van Deursen 2005.

43   Establishing the Free University was not the last of Kuyper's achievements. In 1886 Kuyper mobilized the so-called 'complainers' within the State Reformed Church (Nederlandse Hervormde Kerk), in the movement called "de Doleantie". This movement merged with the main sector of another group that had seceded from the State Reformed Church in 1834, to form the 'Reformed Churches' (Gereformeerde Kerken) in 1892. This new wing of Calvinistic churches was organized along congregationalist lines (hence the plural form). There was a very close practical affinity between it (the new wing) and the Free University; cf. Algra 1966, especially chap. 25, pp. 317-332. J. Koch's recent biography of Kuyper gives a very full discussion and evaluation of Kuyper's ideals and activities; cf. Koch 2006.

it is progressive and not reactionary, hence it may with good reason be considered '*neo*-Calvinist'.[44]

Kuyper's advocacy of this neo-Calvinism agreed with the modernistic notion of the human subject having the right to regulate and improve its practical affairs. However, there was disagreement as to the provenance of this right—delegated or inborn?—and what form this origination takes—through embracing responsibility as a religious duty or discovered in the free use of reason? For Kuyper, sovereignty is the primary prerogative of divinity, but a partial sovereignty is delegated to the human being in the context of Christian freedom.[45] Humanism honours sovereignty as state sovereignty which, though secured in the rights of the state's free citizens, dominates over all other human institutions. In practical terms this means that neo-Calvinism opposes all forms of totalitarianism on point of principle, while humanism could stem state totalitarianism only by counterbalancing it with liberalistic autonomous individual freedom. There is an uneasy, not to say conflicting, tension between individual freedom and state control, a tension that encouraged rather than hindered the occurrence of the deep tragedies of the twentieth century.

The opposition between neo-Calvinism and humanism was not just shadow boxing. Kuyper's advocacy of sphere sovereignty was of practical effect in being instrumental in turning Dutch society into a "verzuilde

---

[44] The matter of Kuyper's conservatism is discussed by George Harinck in the introduction to the recent Dutch republication of Kuyper's "Stone lectures" on Calvinism. The conservatism is due to the link between Kuyper's worldview of sphere sovereignty and its late 16th and early 17th century Protestant-Reformed religious signature. It is in virtue of that signature that the worldview of sphere sovereignty opposes primary features of modernity as expressed in the latter's humanism. But in the practical implementation of sphere sovereignty, Kuyper was innovative, for example in being among the first to implement the system of political parties in Dutch politics. In its practical outreach Kuyper's program was in step and vied with modernity's late phase of modernism. The term modernism, as used in this study, denotes the effectuation of practical progress in science, morality and art. This progress is motivated within modernism by the ideal of constructive rational perfectibility. As a late phase of modernity, modernism is clearly recognizable from the second half of the nineteenth century on. Modernism would appear to have exhausted itself—at least the uncritical acceptance of its own worth—in the last quarter of the twentieth century, as signalled by 'post-modernism'. This is not to say that *modernity* has come to an end. Now, while modernism's practical humanism puts it at odds with the outreach of neo-Calvinism, there are nevertheless significant influences in the latter's method and goal of meaning conferment. Kuyper, we wish to add, used the term 'modernism' as synonym for 'modernity', hence he lacks the distinction assumed here in the phases of modernity, phases that Vollenhoven referred to as "early and late rationalism"; cf. Kuyper 2002. For the view of modernity and its phases assumed here, cf. Tol 2005a.

[45] Cf. Kuyper 1930: 32.

maatschappij"—society as a columniation—i.e. a society in which different worldview orientations affect the operation of segments of society, such as education, labour, press, politics, etc., leading to distinct 'parties', not just in politics, but also in all the other areas of society. Thus each worldview orientation defines its own 'column' (or 'pillar'; *zuil*), as a cross-section of society. By the end of the nineteenth century, Dutch national life had four main orientations: Anti-Revolutionary (i.e. Protestant-Reformed), Roman Catholic, Social-democrat and that of Liberalism.[46] This remained in effect till deep into the twentieth century.

Hence, the rise of the Free University has to be understood within the context of a neo-Calvinist worldview and a Calvinist-Christian life orientation within Dutch society. This placed this academic institution under an obligation. As an alternative to State controlled institutions, it had to demonstrate that it was able to function as a mature university, capable of legitimating its practice. To that end, Kuyper had taken up into the charter of the Association, under whose auspices the Free University operated, a 'foundation' statement. The second article of the regulations of the Association read:

> For all the education given in its schools, the Association is based entirely and exclusively on the foundation of the reformed principles, and it also acknowledges as foundation for education in Theology the three Forms of unity....[47]

It comes as something of a surprise to find that these "reformed principles" were never spelled out. After all, the Christian-(neo-)Calvinist character of the education offered at the university was to be safeguarded through them. Initially there was, as is often attested, an intuitive consensus as to what was meant. But towards the end of the nineteenth century questions were raised as to the nature and identity of the intended reformed principles. Because the role that philosophy was expected to play at the university is intimately connected with this whole problem, and would affect Vollenhoven when he was appointed in 1926, this matter of the reformed principles calls for some discussion.

---

46   Koch 2006: 574-575.

47   Quoted in Van Deursen 2005: 23. For completeness sake, we add that "the three Forms of unity", normative for theology besides the Reformed principles, are the ecclesiastical documents: *Heidelberg Catechism* (1563), *Belgic Confession* (*Nederlandse Geloofsbelijdenis*) (1566) and *Canons of Dort* (1619). In 1968 an ecumenical mission statement was proposed and it soon came to replace the reference to the "foundation of the reformed principles" in Article 2. Cf. Van Deursen 2005: 272.

B. "The way that leads to the knowledge of the Reformed principles"

In 1895 a practical conflict brought the problem of the reformed principles to a head. A.F. de Savorin-Lohman, active in politics for Kuyper's Anti-Revolutionary party, and also a professor of the Free University, had clashed with Kuyper and was discharged from the university. A point of issue concerned the reformed principles. Everyone was agreed that the principles in question stood (in some sense) in relation to Scripture and the (Reformed) confessions. Lohman implemented this by adding that he could not be forced "to accept other principles as being Reformed than such as he could himself acknowledge."[48] In other words, he made it a sole matter of conscience as to what he could identify as being properly Reformed. Herman Bavinck, who advised the board of the university in connection with this conflict, deemed Lohman to be mistaken. Conscience cannot be the last word. Between the time of the Scriptures and our own endeavours lies history. Calvinism arose in that period of history. Calvinism is more than just the work of John Calvin, for Calvin was engaged in a cause that was greater than himself, a cause believed to be led by the Holy Spirit. It is through historical study, in particular the study of the historical course of Calvinism, that one should be able to come to an identification and acknowledgement of the Reformed principles.[49]

The Senate of the Free University (i.e. the body of its professors) decided to seriously confront the issue. Kuyper, Woltjer and Fabius (representatives of the three faculties of which the university consisted at the time: theology, classical languages and law respectively) put together a document, published in 1895, on the topic of the Reformed principles, entitled "Publication of the Senate of the Free University regarding the Investigation towards Determining the Way that Leads to the Knowledge of the Reformed Principles."[50] The circumspect title is explained in the Foreword (signed by Woltjer and Kuyper). The cardinal question concerns the proper identification of the reformed principles. But this proper identification needs to be properly researched. Thus there is a prior methodological question concerning the route that is to lead to the identification of the said principles. The document only broaches this preliminary question, hoping that by helping to set the research in mo-

---

48   Van Deursen 2005: 63.

49   Van Deursen 2005: 65.

50   Woltjer and Kuyper 1895, i.e. *Publicatie van den Senaat der Vrije Universiteit, in zake het onderzoek ter bepaling van den weg die tot de kennis der Gereformeerde beginselen leidt*, with a foreword by J. Woltjer (Rector) and A. Kuyper (Abactis) (Amsterdam: Wormser, 1895), 16 pgs. It consists of 18 sections. For more about this document, cf. Van Deursen 2005: 64-65.

tion, the proper identification—the Senate report speaks of a "scientific truth"—of the principles would eventually be confirmed some time in the future (Woltjer and Kuyper 1895: 6).

A number of features stand out in this report. After stipulating that under "Reformed principles" is to be understood "principles of Calvinism", in virtue of the near synonymy of "Calvinism" and "Reformed" (section 1), we come to the gist of the matter in the second section. A distinction is make in the use of the term 'principles': "under 'principles' is *not* to be understood those starting points [*uitgangspunten*] which lie in the facts and in the essence of things, but such principles which, in consciousness, control the world of thought" (Woltjer and Kuyper 1895: 8). This is not to say that the starting points in *the facts and the essence of things* are irrelevant for thought, but that they can "function in the foundation of education only after being expressed in the form of thoughts" (*ibid.*).

The distinction in question comes down to recognizing two forms of rationality: *objective rationality*, which is the order inherent in the facts and the essence of things, and *subjective rationality*, the conscious order of thoughts. This distinction will play a leading (but problematic) role in the unfolding of Vollenhoven's early work and in the emergence of Reformed philosophy. The distinction is a classical one of *scholasticism*, which furthermore postulates the *harmony* between the two orders. The 'harmony' is implicit in the above statement of the Senate report, in that the investigation of the world of conscious thought is expected to lead to insight in, and formulations of, the thoughts that represent the principles in the facts and the essence of things. But—the Senate report is cautious—the confirmation of the representation of the principles of the objective order can take place only when the time is right, after proper preparation. In the meantime the research is to be historical and directed to the 'subjective thoughts'. This calls for researching historical Calvinism, in its relevance for and control of the whole of human life (section 3 and 4), so as to discover the leading thoughts. These leading thoughts are not the 'product' of persons, i.e. are not identical to what, say, John Calvin actually thought. But they are the thoughts that inspired him and transcend him in their fecundity (section 5). We get close to the heart of neo-Calvinism when the text asserts the divinely privileged status of Calvinism, at least in its (aggrandized) self-assessment, *viz.* as "proceeding from God and not the human being, who [God] granted to a part of Christianity the higher life form, which is embodied in Calvinism" (Woltjer and Kuyper 1895: 9). Thus, the historical research of Calvinism is to lead to the identification of what are ultimately the divinely determined thoughts and order of life God granted Calvinism to know. We add, though the Senate report does not say so explicitly, that these divinely determined thoughts will be the sought for Reformed principles, for they will also accord with, or be operative in, "the facts and the essence of things".

Towards its end, the Senate report includes a section that touches on philosophy (section 16). In looking for reformed principles for our time—proceeding from out of the subjective order—there may be candidate principles which, so the report suggests, might be of help in providing answers to questions raised in our time and not in the 16th century; e.g. questions first raised by Kant about *the knowing subject*. The report lists: questions "about the nature and essence of knowledge, how the knowing faculty operates, the relation between the knowing faculty and the knowable object, the boundaries of our knowledge, the method of acquiring knowledge in the distinct ways of the natural and human sciences" (Woltjer and Kuyper 1895: 13).

But it would be a mistake, the report warns, to interpret such candidate principles about the knowing subject as belonging to the reformed principles directly. Their candidacy, in turn, needs itself to be assessed in terms of the reformed principles. In a statement that would appear to express which principles (or the sort of principles) to expect as present "in the facts and the essence of things", the candidate principles that help to understand the epistemic situation need to reckon with certain data, as laid down from Calvinistic side, in connection with "the human being's being created according to God's image",[51] *viz.* data:

"- about the essence of the human being and its faculties,
- about the relation of our knowledge to God's knowledge,
- about the relation of the human being to the cosmos,
- about the eclipse of our understanding and the darkening of our wisdom through sin,
- about the relation between natural knowledge and specifically re-

---

51   This anthropological-religious assumption appears to be the fulcrum for the reformed principles. Naturally, it needs to be metaphysically interpreted for it to be revealing for the objective order of rationality. In the *Isagoge* Vollenhoven does not offer it his support. He makes a specific point of advancing a relational, over against an ontological, interpretation of this 'imaging'. "The formulation *being (created) in the image of God*, indicating a relational state, is to be preferred over *the image of God*, because the latter is an abstraction, a usage that has proven historically to have its dangers. This danger became particularly acute when some who laid the emphasis on "image" then also lost sight of its being related to God, subsequently began to ask what that image might be and sometimes ended up identifying it with a specific group of functions or even with a supposedly innate understanding." (Vollenhoven 2005d/e, **117**)

vealed knowledge,
- about the consequences of *palingenesis* (regeneration) and of *illuminatio* (enlightenment),
- about the forms that creaturely knowledge has in angels and the blessed;
- and to collect this data in such a way as to be able to erect the theory of knowledge" (Woltjer and Kuyper 1895: 14).

This much is clear: philosophy is thought to lie very close to where the investigation into the epistemic situation—i.e. the subjective order—discloses the contours of the order of the essence of the human being—i.e. the (main?) lead into the objective order—that centres in the confession that the human being is created in the image of God. Vollenhoven's appointment to the chair of philosophy is still some 30 years in the future. But something of the level of the themes broached here is recognizable in his approach to philosophy, though he did not accept the scholastic *duplex ordo* of rationality. Initially, in his dissertation of 1918 (cf. chapter 2), he held to a qualified scholasticism, but when appointed to the Free University in 1926 he had rejected the scholastic framework altogether.

The report on the reformed principles had a certain stimulating effect at the turn of the century. Woltjer gave the problem of the reformed principles considerable attention, which he interwove with his theory of the divine Logos.[52] Woltjer was Vollenhoven's mentor, but mention of his influence on Vollenhoven is better touched on later (cf. chapter 4, section III.B.4.a.). Kuyper also gave the topic his attention, in a more popular way, particularly in the *Lectures on Calvinism* held in 1898. It is instructive to trace Kuyper's more independent line on this score.[53]

C. Kuyper on the "Reformed foundation"

Kuyper, as is to be expected, had fairly definite thoughts on the matter. To start with, he held that the reformed foundation could not be hon-

---

[52] Cf. Kok 2007: esp. 52-59. For an overview of Woltjer's work, and the interactions of Woltjer with Vollenhoven as student, cf. Van der Laan 2000. Woltjer himself discussed "the nature and task of philology in the light of the reformed principles" in Woltjer 1891: 2-20. In Woltjer 1896: 179 he states: "our university, which proceeds in its education from determined principles, principles that touch the root of all things".

[53] For a much fuller sketch of the 'philosophical situation' prior to Vollenhoven's appointment at the Free University, cf. J. Klapwijk's discussion of "the period of philosophical reconnaissance", in his "Hundred years of philosophy at the Free University", in Klapwijk 1980: 528-553, which, besides Kuyper, also includes discussions of Woltjer, Geesink, Bavinck and Pos.

oured when a person's Christian beliefs remain external to the exercise of his or her academic talent. For the Free University it was not to be a matter of appointing academically talented persons, who were Christians to boot. The sciences and the academic subject matter, as taught and studied at the Free University, had to be Christian "as to principle, method and result".[54] The latter were essential to, or at least implied by, the "Reformed foundation". For, as Kuyper explained in his Stone Lectures at Princeton University in 1898, "the birth of the Free University [had been] for [the sake of] the general cultivation of the sciences on the foundation of the Calvinistic principle".[55]

In that same lecture series Kuyper explains more fully what this Reformed "foundation of the Calvinistic principle" involves. To begin with, science is never separated from nor opposed to faith, at least for science properly understood. Science, Kuyper holds, is possible only "when you discover in the specific phenomena, perceived by empiricism, a universal *law*, and thereby reach *the thought* which governs the whole constellation of phenomena."[56] In governing phenomena, such a thought cannot be without an intention and an interest, determining self-consciousness. Science that is self-consciously aware of what guides it, acknowledges many presuppositions. It is here that Kuyper speaks generically of 'faith':

> Every science presupposes faith in self, in our self-consciousness; presupposes faith in the accurate working of our senses; presupposes faith in the correctness of the laws of thought; presupposes faith in something universal hidden behind the special phenomena; presupposes faith in life; and especially presupposes faith in the principles, from which we proceed; which signifies that all these indispensable axioms, needed in a productive scientific investigation, do not come to us by proof, but are established in our judgment by our inner conception and *given with our self-consciousness*.[57]

The presuppositions that Kuyper here lists are, of course, not specific or unique to (neo-)Calvinism, and Kuyper did not mean to imply this. Furthermore, the man of science of Kuyper's day (the vast majority being in fact men) would not contest *grosso modo* the presuppositions as such. Ever since Auguste Comte had formulated, in his *Cours de philosophie positive*,[58] his "positive philosophy", as philosophy of (experimental)

---

54   Van Deursen 2005: 63, who here paraphrases the university's annual report of 1897.
55   Quotations are from the English translation of the Stone lectures, Kuyper 1931: 140.
56   Kuyper 1931: 112-113.
57   Kuyper 1931: 131.
58   Comte published this work, in six volumes, between 1830 and 1842. It constituted the first statement of what was to become the philosophy of science. He advanced

science, there is a growing recognition that science does indeed have presuppositions. What the 'man of science' could object to is Kuyper's attributing these presuppositions to faith. He would be more inclined to see them as held to and affirmed by reason. There might be discussion about what, exactly, is "behind the special phenomena"—and perhaps here one could speak of faith—or which axioms are indispensable for "productive scientific investigation"—but this is surely a matter for reason to discern! Does this important point about presuppositions then merely come down to a discussion as to what to *call* it: 'faith' or 'reason'?[59]

In the meantime, when compared to the Senate report, discussed above, and its distinction between the subjective and the objective orders, I believe we can recognize that the 'thought', on which Kuyper now predicates 'faith', is that of the objective order. In the cited passage, the 'thought' is, among other things, the law governing phenomena, thus is part of the 'essence of things'. Its being "given with our self-consciousness" would appear to mean, not that this thought arises in and through consciousness, as something of a subjective order, but given with the fact of self-consciousness, thus itself presupposed by self-consciousness and the subjective order. At least Kuyper gives to the 'thought' in this context a cosmic significance, as we see more clearly in the sequel.[60]

---

the important idea of the "encyclopaedia of the sciences", which holds that the mutual relations between the (basic or primary) sciences provide a window on understanding the structure of the world. This notion of the encyclopaedia of the sciences was very influential in the twentieth century. The influence on Vollenhoven (and on Dooyeweerd, for that matter) was, as will become clear in the sequel, marked. Cf. Comte 1975, especially the section on "Positive philosophy as philosophy of science" in the Introduction, pp. xlviii-lxiii.

59   A discussion such as this suffers readily, among other things, from a lack of distinction in the use of the terms and from differences in options between languages. The Dutch language has only the one word 'geloof'—the term which Kuyper used in his Dutch text—for what in English is denoted either as 'belief' (classically defined as "thinking with assent", having a wide application) or as 'faith' (what might be termed "trusting confidence" or "accepted on trust"). The English use of 'science' is modelled on, if not actually restricted to, the natural sciences, while the Dutch term 'wetenschap', like the German 'Wissenschaft', has a much broader application, meaning any context of expertise that requires learning and is advanced by learning. A fruitful discussion of the relations of these terms would of course need to take these distinct meanings into account.

60   It is, I believe, of secondary importance whether the objective order be taken dualistically, as terrains of the natural (nature) and the supra-natural (grace), or more monistically, as a higher/inner idea controlling lower/outer phenomena. The primary point of contention is the postulated difference between the objective order and the subjective order as such, and that difference concerns (cf. chapter 3) the metaphysical versus the metalogical order respectively. Kuyper clearly has a more monistic approach to the objective order, which was (still) metaphysical. The difficulties in this connection will be

For Kuyper, more is at stake than the semantics of what to name it. There is the deeper question as to how the conjunction of science and faith is put to use. There is a serious conflict, Kuyper held, concerning the view of the cosmos, in the light of which the scientific investigation of the cosmos takes place. There are, what Kuyper calls, the 'Normalists', who consider the cosmos to be the panorama of a natural evolutionary process "from its potencies to its ideals".[61] Opposed to them are the 'Abnormalists', who believe that the cosmos is *not* a natural process. They believe that the cosmos is created, that a fall disturbed whatever natural processes there are, whereby these processes are turned into abnormal ones, and that regeneration is required to counter the abnormality. The norm for understanding this "creation, fall and regeneration" cannot be found in natural processes themselves, but only in "the Triune God", in whom the Abnormalists find the ideal norm. In comparison with the Abnormalists, the Normalists, in making the natural cosmos the source of norms or ideals, maintain a worldview of Naturalism, if not Pantheism or Deism. So there is a real conflict between the "two scientific systems of the Normalists and the Abnormalists", which is a serious difference in worldview—namely between the "faiths" (or presuppositions) of each of these scientific systems to the degree that they are tapped into a worldview—that affects "the whole domain of life".[62]

It will be readily understood that the single 'Calvinistic principle' Kuyper has in mind is that of the 'Abnormalists'. Their understanding of "creation, fall and regeneration", which is fed by their Christian convictions—and, we should add, in theology is to be interpreted in the light of the content of the ecclesiastical "Forms of unity"—enjoins them to accept certain deep seated views about the world, such as its not being a self-supporting system, the presence of distinct divine activity in it, the possibility of occurrences contrary to natural regularity, and the like. The whole becomes a view of a highly furnished world, which neo-Calvinism was prone to take as (biblically endorsed) objective reality.

This is probably about as close to a formulation of the intended 'Calvinistic principle' that Kuyper comes. The principle embodies a view, *believed* to be fundamentally true of the world, and thus its *thought* acts as presupposition in the scientific inquiry and academic understanding of the world. This double role is both an asset and a liability. It was able,

---

discussed more thoroughly in chapter 3 below, in the context of the 'critical realism' of the early Vollenhoven and Dooyeweerd.

61   Kuyper 1931: 132.
62   Kuyper 1931: 133.

on the one hand, to reach and mobilize a large sector of the populace of Calvinist conviction, many of whom lacked advanced education, into providing practical support in maintaining the Free University in virtue of their being able to identify with the 'worldview' in question. On the other hand, its relevance as foundation for an academic institution of teaching and research is not immediately clear. Is it a 'meta-statement', representing a 'meta-truth', harbouring (to use Kuyper's words already quoted) the "indispensable axioms, needed in a productive scientific investigation", without need of interpretation in their own right? In that case the Free University could be seen as endorsing a scholastic 'metaphysical order', whereby 'supra-natural truth' (or 'ideal truth') informs 'natural truth' ('reasoned truth') with dogmatic correctness. Or is the principle a statement of orientation, meant to provide a normative context for the university's teaching and research? This could serve to motivate the university's operations and provide a practical goal, leaving to the research itself the task of discovering the principles relevant to a science. I believe that the former, 'meta-truth' interpretation—also implicit in the Senate report—was long predominant. The theological faculty gave this extra emphasis and support. The chair of theological dogmatics was, after all, the prized position of the university. Certainly its third occupant, after Abraham Kuyper and Herman Bavinck, *viz.* Valentijn Hepp (occupant 1922-1950), held that theological dogmatics dictates to all the sciences.[63]

We can at least pinpoint what Kuyper, in his discussion as conducted in his *Lectures on Calvinism*, did not succeed in answering. Given the parameters of his thought, Kuyper did not explain how one proceeds from the 'Abnormalist' position, via the self-consciousness that lies at the root of 'science and its faith', to the selection of those principles, methods and results of science that attest to a Christian scientific practice.[64] Only

---

63   In the words of J. Stellingwerff, Hepp maintained that "science is subject to Scripture, which we know through exegesis; [but] the exegete must proceed from dogmatics; accordingly the dogmatic theologian has the final say"; cf. Stellingwerff 1990: 83. One finds this corroborated in Hepp 1937b, from which we cite the following statements: "The God of truth, being Himself one, is the warrant for the unity of the truth, which He destined in analogical manner for the human being to praise Him, and that all genuine judgments of truth constitute a unity. The unity of science stands firm beyond all doubt" (p. 16). To that end Hepp notes that "all a priori judgments, whose acceptance is the *conditio sine qua non* for true science, have their source in revelation" (p. 25). All revelation, whether the general (i.e. in Nature) or the special (i.e. in Scripture), "is divine truth revelation" (p. 25). Finally, "special revelation must never be interpreted according to general revelation, but rather general revelation needs special revelation as hermeneutical key" (p. 25). (Translation mine)

64   In this formulation one readily recognizes the chief concern of Dooyeweerd's

via some such derivation could a Calvinist framework be formulated, on Kuyper's terms, that would be normative for the faculties and the sciences. In 1900 Kuyper declared that making such a formulation perspicuous is the task of Christian philosophy. "And that is what we urgently need, 'a philosophical system, erected according to our own principles'."[65] It would take another quarter of a century before the first full-time philosopher could be appointed. The expectations within the Free University community were high. After all, all incoming students of the university are confronted with philosophy.[66]

IV. Vollenhoven's program
A. Introduction

In developing his philosophy program for the Free University, Vollenhoven was expected to throw light on the matter of basic principles; at least, philosophy at the Free University would have to rest on the foundation of Reformed principles and be a 'Calvinistic philosophy'. Vollenhoven openly chose the latter term as label for his philosophical endeavour, even though it invites misunderstandings. He meant to indicate his allegiance to the historical tradition in which the university community stood, the tradition which that community wished to advance in a way that is relevant to university life. In this tradition, the Reformed religious life-attitude stands central, and in its neo-Calvinist setting it also addressed problems of society and culture, as is clear from Kuyper's program of sphere sovereignty.[67]

---

later "transcendental critique of theoretical thought", which aims to demonstrate the inner connection between scientific thought and religion. This connection is mediated in Dooyeweerd by a self-consciousness that is 'supra-temporal', initially viewed as transcendent ego, later reformulated in terms of transcendental subjectivity. Vollenhoven never endorsed this concern in this form. Vollenhoven (as will become clear) sees knowledge as contextualized: "knowing resorts under being". It is in specifying this "resorting" that the constraints upon "theoretical thought" come to the fore, as attested by his distinct use of the methods discussed above.

65   Van Deursen 2005: 63; the inner quote is from Kuyper in the university's annual report of 1900.

66   Stellingwerff 1992: 74.

67   Practically speaking the term 'Reformed' is a synonym for 'Calvinistic', as is also emphasized in the Senate report (Woltjer and Kuyper 1895: 7-8). Initially the term 'Reformed' was applied to Huldrych Zwingli's attempt at community-centred reform based in Zürich, in distinction from Martin Luther's work, which was called 'Evangelical' from the start. Through Heinrich Bullinger, who continued to develop Zwingli's ideas, in particular the idea of Covenant, this 'reformed' branch of the Reformation in Switzerland was absorbed into John Calvin's later consolidation. Cf. MacCulloch 2003: 132, 174-179.

Vollenhoven's main aim is to indicate that philosophy can comport with this tradition. This does not mean that he wishes to establish a specific religious philosophy, nor a philosophy of a worldview. He limits philosophy, in the strict sense of the word, to academic philosophy, to philosophy with a general academic—'scientific' as he called it—character. Only at this level can argument be effective. Here one is expected to seek clarity and understanding, to respond to indications of contradictions or of antinomies between approaches. One is expected to review the facts without explicit bias and to acknowledge the relevance of material one might have overlooked when pointed out. This is what belongs to the craftsmanship and erudition of being a philosopher. The sounding board for academic philosophy is cosmology insofar as this concerns the referent of the realities in connection with which distinctions are made, connections are laid, and a general understanding is pursued of 'how things are and develop' in a network of determinants. In other words academic philosophy is practised according to the method of resolution and composition, and its worth is to be able to contribute to a better understanding of life, easing "the confusing diversity between philosophical theories" (Vollenhoven 1933a: 48).

Now what guides this practice of philosophy is the reflection conducted according to the other two methods that are discussed above, the 'method of knowledge organization' and the thetical-critical method. In speaking of methods here, Vollenhoven means to say that the reflection taking place at this level has its own rules. It is not a haphazard 'what I happen to think' or 'what I happen to prefer by way of philosophy', but a serious pursuit that concerns the presuppositions of philosophy. The discourse in which philosophy reflects upon itself is not of the same nature as the discourse of philosophical practice as such. Over against the latter, there is the reflection on presuppositions, which is meta-philosophical. We need to ask what the connection is between the meta-philosophical and philosophical discourses.

B. Vollenhoven's procedure

If we turn to the main work of 1933, "Calvinism and the reformation of philosophy", we find Vollenhoven's program in action in a specific way. The introduction—the first discussion of content—pleads that the execution of philosophy needs two things: systematic insight and historical overview. This places the practice of philosophy squarely within the thetical-critical method, although this term does not occur here. The systematic insight needed "before all else" is "a clear view of the diversity" in the chaos of opinions (Vollenhoven 1933a: 9). An appeal to some sort of a 'philosophical common denominator' closes the door on systematic insight. The historical overview, in turn, is to aid the systematic insight. "Nothing is so refreshing as a good bath in history" (*ibid.*). It discloses data that have become lost to memory, and also lays bare connections one had not suspected. Both systematic insight and historical overview are needed, without merging one under the other. Clearly, insight and overview are not ends in themselves; they are ever going concerns. They involve reflection that helps to come to grips with the relevant data of the themes and problems one is interested in as philosopher. The reflection calls for an intuitive discernment of what is relevant, as contributing to the insight and the overview sought.

A second introduction (this one for specifically the systematic part) poses the meta-philosophical question as to what philosophical thought is (*op. cit.*: 13). The question is posed in the interest of a preliminary explanation of the use of the term 'Calvinistic philosophy'. Vollenhoven now argues in line with 'the method of knowledge organization', though again without being methodologically explicit. The central thought is that, philosophy being a general science, philosophical thought must lay great stress on guarding against excluding anything that is knowable (*op. cit.*: 14). Things are not merely known in themselves but also in relation to other things. Knowable is not only the cosmos as such—to which philosophy proper is directed—but also what concerns the whole, and thus what transcends it. The knowable *reveals* itself to the knowing subject, and this enables knowledge to arise. Thus a 'revelatory faith' is not at all a strange component of everyday knowing. In other words, the effect of religion and worldview make themselves felt here, of whatever kind, thus not necessarily specifically 'Calvinistic'. But a Calvinist will take a position that is informed by the Christian religion and a Reformed worldview. This puts a premium on the meanings of the words he/she uses, as well as on the general orientation that that specific mode of everyday knowing represents.

The discussion then turns to philosophy proper. Vollenhoven now lays great stress on the confusion in 'current philosophy', which for him is philosophy in the 1920s and 1930s. This can cause people to turn away from philosophy. For some, the confusion of philosophy puts it at too great a distance from real life, for others it makes progress hopeless, if not dangerous (*op. cit.*: 15). In Vollenhoven's inaugural address (1926a) he voices a similar critique in connection with the relation of 'current philosophy' and science. The Free University needs to go its own way, he says, in light of the problematic nature of 'current philosophy', which is "either life philosophy, which becomes alienated from every reflection on questions regarding science, or it progresses in logicistic one-sidedness, that exaggerates the meaning of science and forbids every voyage beyond the pillars of Hercules of the formalistic passage" (Vollenhoven 1926a: 5-6). Thus he sketches the current situation as a dilemma that, either way, does not do justice to science.

What Vollenhoven particularly rejects is interpreting the religious and worldview moments of knowing as a species of philosophy, say 'idealism', which in turn induces a misleading meaning on philosophical idealism as being a 'Christian philosophy'. This wreaks havoc with the dynamics of one's "faith life" (meaning one's religious and worldview participation). One needs to recognize that "the terminology of most philosophers is so saturated with humanism [itself, obviously, of religious and worldview signature (A.T.)] that one cannot begin to filter this out and bring it in agreement with . . . the language of [Reformed] faith" (*op. cit.*: 16). Thus Vollenhoven concludes: "Synthesis between the Christian faith on the one hand and the current philosophy on the other hand is impossible" (*ibid.*; emphasis of the whole statement deleted).

This important statement needs to be interpreted carefully. The 'impossibility' of the synthesis is not a theoretical impossibility, perhaps thought to involve a problematic version of the relation between faith and thought, but an impossibility in the light of the (then) current situation. Also, Vollenhoven does not mean to say that the "Christian faith" cannot be in step with non-Christian thought. The latter is simply not in the picture here. It is the humanism of current philosophy that spoils things. His formulation leaves the door wide open for the possibility of a synthesis between 'non-current philosophy' and the Christian faith. *It is not for the sake of the Christian faith that a reformation of philosophy is sought, but it is for the sake of 'current philosophy', in light of its confusions.* A philosophy that comports with the Christian faith—a so-called Calvinistic or Scriptural philosophy—is not derived from (hence is also not rooted in) the Christian faith, as if there is a template for the 'Idea' (in the weighted sense to be met with in this study) of a Christian philosophy. That would in fact be either a scholastic way or an idealist way of posing the problem.[68] The philosophical discourse is—as Vollenhoven said

---

68   In the inaugural address Vollenhoven mentions and argues against "the power of the double tradition" of scholasticism and humanism (1926a: 64). On the one hand scholasticism Christianizes, in the sense of adding a supra-natural reality to, the natural realm, while on the other hand humanism's linking up with Christianity tends to reduce the opposition between Christianity and humanism to "a skirmish between conserva-

of the task of science in his inaugural address—"elevated but limited" (1926a: 65; philosophy being a general science, this qualification holds for it too). Hence it is of primary importance that philosophy remains within the bounds of its 'place and task', in line with its method. The philosophical discourse presupposes meta-philosophical discourse, but it is not a derivation or species of it.

Finally, what about the positive effect of the meta-philosophical discourse on the philosophical? At the end of his systematic discussion (chapter 2 of Part I of 1933a) Vollenhoven gives an example. The focus is on the continuity of meaning. There are terms, such as 'nature', 'death', 'spirit', etc. that have a meaning in the religious context, but which often clashes with the use in different philosophical theories. Unless one is clear about this difference, the result is likely to be very confusing all around. For example, in the Christian religion, humanity is said to be fallen in Adam, which is a failure in answering to the right direction of the good life divinely commanded. Outside of the religious context one comes across other interpretations, e.g. that humanity has a 'corruptible human nature', which is quite a different thing, or other more recondite meanings, depending on the definition of 'nature', say: the lower bodily functions, or the human essence as in neo-Platonism, which locates this essence between the divine One and the level of individuation (*op. cit.*: 48). The fact that there are many philosophical theories is one thing—the erudite scholar should be able to keep these apart and help others to do so—but when there is a feedback to the everyday and the religious level, one easily becomes disoriented and confused in what one believes or knows (or thought one knew). One has "placed too much confidence in current philosophy" (*ibid*).

The ending of the sentence containing the last quoted phrase adds an important point: besides the overconfidence in current philosophy, "one does not see the deep chasm which separates it [current philosophy], in virtue of principle and history, from childlike faith" (*ibid.*). The phrase "in virtue of principle and history" means that the expressions of current philosophy can be identified as to its principle(s) and located as to its arising in history. These are the very features that the thetical-critical method seizes on. Thus, via this method it should be possible to

---

tive and progressive rationalism" (*ibid.*). Vollenhoven argues for an alternative to both traditions. At this point in his address he also quotes from the Senate report of 1895 (cf. Woltjer and Kuyper 1895: 13-14), *viz.* the part about the importance of including questions concerning the knowing subject in relation to Reformed principles. But he bypasses—I tend to think intentionally—the scholastic formulation of the problem of the reformed principles that we found in that report.

clarify the differences (the deep chasm) and *confront* them consciously.

We have stayed close to Vollenhoven's text in the above, so as to be adequately justified in asserting that "Christian / Scriptural / Calvinistic philosophy" is not itself a recondite view of things, as reflected on or understood in terms of a prior system of belief.[69] A Reformed philosophy is a philosophy reduced to the sober proportions of a cosmic context, liberated (ideally) from ambiguities, contradictions and antinomies that beset thought when speculative and dogmatic moments are left to have their hindering effect. It does not aim to offer an apology for the Reformed faith, but it attempts to be in accordance with the meanings of key terms of religion and worldview, making it possible, in meta-philosophical discourse, to delineate the 'place and task' of philosophy (1933a: 22). But the substance of philosophy, its main themes and determinants (structures) are of a general nature and accessible to all who think philosophically.[70] Vollenhoven gives a specimen of this understanding of philosophy in the systematic discussion of chapter 2 in Part 1 of "Calvinism and the reformation of philosophy", along with a critical sketch of an understanding of the main motives of philosophy that does not comport with a Reformed understanding (chapter 3 in Part I of 1933a). The proof of the better result does not lie in any transcendental argument, but in a down-to-earth comparison of what is achieved. Vollenhoven expressed his conviction that his own results were conducive to greater clarity than what is offered in symbolic logic and in phenomenology (cf. 1933a: 67). One could, of course, question this, for Vollenhoven's thought is for many not an easy nut to crack. But the position he takes is clear. A standpoint with

---

69   Earlier we made reference to the one exception, *viz.* the effect of biblical revelation in connection with the heavenly cosmos. Vollenhoven advocated this as the only way of knowing this part of the cosmos. Thus it is meant to inform at the philosophical, and not merely at the meta-philosophical level. It does not fall within a scholastic pattern of nature and grace, for the heavenly realm is not a realm of grace but a realm of spiritual nature. But Vollenhoven's discussion of this is too brief to allow a full understanding as to why he thought he needed this at the philosophical level.

70   In the Preface to Vollenhoven's *History of Philosophy I* (1950e) the author states that he "ventures to study this part of human cultural history [i.e. the history of philosophy] in the light of the Word revelation, which also here cannot be excluded without detriment to the inquiry" (1950e: 5); thereby, he adds, the first volume of this history of philosophy begins the execution of "the program that I unfolded in *Het Calvinisme en de reformatie van de wijsbegeerte* (1933)" (*ibid.*). The 'light of the Word revelation' is *not that it adds content* to the philosophical concepts investigated, *but removes factors* that hinder seeing the philosophical themes in the conceptions of ancient philosophy. The focus is therefore on the problems within the main *cosmic themes, viz.* (i) genesis vs. static structure, (ii) monism vs. dualism (the order of cosmic being), and (iii) 'wholes vs. things', either as universalism, individualism or partial universalism.

respect to philosophy is essential, but it is taken always on condition that its results remain open to possible improvement. The latter keeps one's thought in direct contact with alternative, and possibly important, insight not yet realized.[71]

C. The reform of philosophy

Vollenhoven's goal was a 'reformation' of philosophy. The term 'reformation' is intentionally ambiguous. Vollenhoven wanted on the one hand to point to the tradition of the historical Reformation as forming the religious and worldview background of his philosophical thought, and on the other hand to signal the internal difference in philosophy itself that would accrue when philosophy is informed by this tradition. In appealing to the Reformed tradition, in its Calvinian-Kuyperian strand,[72] Vollenhoven was able to put a Reformed stance to work, not by apologetically assigning philosophy the task of routing up 'Reformed principles' and coming to their defence, but by showing how the historical tradition of the Reformation itself, in its essential aspects, places *limitations* on philosophy, in part to avoid speculative misunderstandings, in which philosophy overreaches itself, in part to be clear as to philosophy's own delimitation of 'place and task'. How are we to understand this?

Vollenhoven's tactic might be surprising. Is this not side-stepping the issue? What he side-steps is the scholastic option of the issue involved. The relation of the Reformed principles to philosophy is not that of axioms to derived theorems, but more like orienting directive and being directed (or, more abstractly, that of rule to rule-following activity). Those partial to the first option require that the statements of religion and the worldview in question be themselves treated as a cognitively acceptable

---

71   In a comparison of Vollenhoven's approach to that of Dooyeweerd, J. Klapwijk asks whether for Vollenhoven "there is a basis or point of application for dialogue with those who think differently, as Dooyeweerd intends in his transcendental critique" (Klapwijk 1980: 559). This question is posed from Dooyeweerd's viewpoint. From Vollenhoven's side one can say that, in virtue of the thetical-critical method, there is never a cessation of contact, whether positive or negative. As to Dooyeweerd's transcendental critique, it presupposes an ontology of meaning, in terms of which a format for dialogue is posited. One may question how 'open' the dialogue then remains (cf. the discussion of Dooyeweerd in chapter 3).

72   N. Wolterstorff distinguishes "two perspectives that have been prominent in the Calvinist tradition": the common-sense philosophy stemming from Thomas Reid in Scotland, and neo-Calvinism in the Netherlands. Within the former a 'reformed epistemology' has been developed in which notions, such as 'warrant' and 'proper function', are set to work to show that certain statements of faith are, in a cognitive sense, 'properly basic'. Needless to say, Vollenhoven is a distinct representative of the second perspective. Cf. Wolterstorff 1983: vii. For 'Reformed epistemology' cf. Van Woudenberg and Cusveller 1998, and for a critical discussion of 'warrant', cf. Tol 1998.

'basic statements'. What is then accepted on faith as relevant to live by, is at the same time taken to be acceptable to reason as a cognitive belief in virtue of the fact that other beliefs can be derived from it (or with its help). In that way the belief is 'asserted' as basic statement within reason's use. But there is a step from faith to reason here that remains entirely inconspicuous, and an important feature of its inconspicuousness is the step from the specific and concrete character of the non-philosophical (or meta-philosophical) context that clings to statements of faith (accepted in trust), to the general validity of reason's use as belief (and asserted as true belief) in the philosophical context.

Now if the relation of historical tradition and philosophy is taken to be more like that of rule to rule-following activity, what does this say? Well, one ought to start by taking a tradition seriously, which is to say that its significance and effect in life's practice have to be discerned and acknowledged. Clearly, Reformed religion and the Kuyperian worldview are such a practical reality. Each is of distinct character. Reformed religion is experienced in the pronounced form of biblical covenant religion. The existential condition of life is that the human being is aware of standing in relation to God, of being addressed to avoid evil and seek the good, of having the freedom to accept responsibility for oneself and for others and stewardship for the non-human world. Biblical religion advances a basic stance in life. The Kuyperian worldview, in turn, is that of sphere-sovereignty. It meshes with Reformed religion, in particular in seizing on freedom and responsibility and implementing these in a diversity of offices and forms of life, in such a way as to define an harmonious societal intercourse. There is divided power and delimited responsibilities. The reality of religion and worldview is not, as such, dependent on intellectual or philosophical defence. They are maintained as prized, historically grown realities as practices, at the same time being in competition with other (world) religions and (western) worldviews of different makeup. Their reality in life does not call up questions of truth, at least not immediately, but it sets *problems*. For any context of activity is constantly confronted with challenges and changed through achievements. An indirect effect of life practice on philosophy is that the latter finds its own practice to revolve around problems as well. For Vollenhoven, philosophy is basically an activity aimed at acquiring results (Vollenhoven 2005d/e, 1). Thus, in understanding and in coming to practice philosophy, one ought to follow more the line of problems seeking solution than of testing derived truth from an axiomatic basis.

What the Reformed tradition can mean for philosophy—at least that is the lesson one learns from Vollenhoven's example, the explanation of which I shall take responsibility for—involves a certain approach to philosophy. Philosophy is to *cease* from addressing matters that cannot be resolved within the range of human understanding, but at the same time to *acknowledge* certain 'synthetic a priori' elements, called up by Reformed religion and worldview, that serve as setting limits to philosophy in virtue of its being a practice. Three specific matters are broached in this connection from out of the Reformed tradition. They are culled from religion, worldview and the theme of knowledge.

1. The religious relevance

To start with, philosophy is not a panacea for all human ills. Much traditional philosophy has overt, but also covert, redemptive aims to advance the human race, not least of all in even down-to-earth philosophies as Marxism and Positivism. Such philosophies evince not only an alliance of philosophy with worldview matters, such as social struggle or technological innovation, but also bring secular religious motives into play.[73] These are broached in the context of a specifically formulated philosophical outlook. They are on that account often abstract, artificial or one-sided, and more often than not, dictatorial and dominating to boot. Philosophy is pressed into the role of being a redemptive surrogate, either in covering over a religious lack or in being a secular substitute.

Philosophy can be sensitive to such a role only if there is something in its makeup that seduces it, even when the actual outreach is misguided. From its earliest beginning there is the notion of *archè*, meaning 'controlling beginning', that denotes a primal situation of determination that affects everything else. In time, more refined notions take its place, such as 'first cause', 'highest good', 'final end', 'absolute idea', etc. When notions such as these are entertained and applied, they cannot but introduce deep incisions into how reality is understood. Oppositions are introduced so as to indicate what part of reality has the said capacity and what part lacks it; or, stated more generally, what part of reality is intrinsically *sovereign* — with respect to which everything else stands in *subservience*. This puts one part of reality in a position of dominance over another part of reality. Matters are made worse when such chasms are used to secure the difference of good and evil. All this leads to tension-ridden views.[74] These

---

73 For secular religious notions in Marx, cf. Van der Hoeven 1976, especially "Eschatology and Utopia", pp. 103-106. As for positivism, in volume IV of his *Système de politique positive*, Comte discusses "worship". Here he formulates projects that are to lead to the realization of the "Religion of Humanity". Cf. Comte 1975: 459-476.

74 Vollenhoven goes out of his way to show that a proper understanding of the

views may be interesting to consider aesthetically, but they are hardly convincing as ways to live by—there are just too many alternatives—though some do present themselves as being specifically religiously relevant (e.g. Gnosticism, higher Platonism, absolute Idealism, etc.).

But when philosophy becomes the channel of religious meaning, cognition is expected to be the modus that answers to religious need. This can only give rise to confusion. When religion is presented in the mode of philosophy, deity must in some sense be intra-cosmic, for the categories of dominance and subjection are used to present this religious meaning. But religion, in its own meaning (certainly in the biblical tradition), sees divinity as transcending the world in virtue of being its creator. Here the world still has oppositions and differences, but not understood to be of such a fundamental kind as to put one part over against another part *as the fundamental fact*. A transcendent creator is beyond the polarities of philosophical understanding, for the relation of God and the creation cannot be understood in terms of cosmic categories as such. But then this suggests a different understanding of the cosmos, *viz.* one in which fundamental tensions and polarities are not expected to be present in the world; hence one that assigns a task: should antinomies, contradictions, paradoxes, etc. occur, then they are to be taken as marking errors in understanding, which need to be resolved through the discovery of a better understanding.

Thus, if sovereignty and subservience are taken in the biblical meaning, this suggests for philosophy a view of the cosmos that lacks anything that is intrinsically self-sufficient. Religious belief does proceed from a transcendent deity, but there are no uniform categories that do justice to the religious relation of God and the world. From out of religion's own meaning, there is no urgent need for 'proofs of the existence of deity', for intuition (or religious sensitivity) is more relevant here than cognition. But then, 'subservience' too, when not understood as marked by a deity of dominance, undergoes a shift in its meaning. For 'standing in subjection' is then more readily evidenced by features such as: dependence, relativity, relatedness, vulnerability, etc. The specific choice for the biblical religion and the intuitive way in which the meaning of the word 'world' functions in the biblical context, throw a light on the understanding of cosmic reality, and thereby philosophy is challenged to pursue an alternative understanding as compared to a more traditional, non-biblical understanding of the world with its deep divisions. The promise

---

cosmos should never give occasion to secure the antithesis of good and evil in it; cf. Vollenhoven 2005d/e, **88-90**.

of this biblical option is an understanding that is free from antinomies and paradoxes.

Vollenhoven's first proposal towards reforming philosophy, as motivated by the Reformed tradition, is to bring to bear an intuition of the cosmos that invites and stimulates study and understanding of its richness of diversity, of interconnections, of multiplicity of modes, of its possibilities, etc. (cf. Vollenhoven 1933a: 312-313; as over against, say, the cosmos taken as 'vale of tears', 'non-being', 'domain for exploitation', 'self-regulating system', etc.). The 'point of contact' with traditional philosophy lies in the theme of sovereignty and subservience, hence he is not bringing in anything foreign, rather he removes a source of continual unrest. It then remains to be seen whether the fuller understanding of the biblical deity and its relations to the world can be of service in philosophy; one can explore not only the notions of transcendence and immanence, but also the Christian understanding of divinity as Triune.

So if sovereignty and subservience are different in their being, not interlinked in a common categorial system, then the question of their connection is of distinct importance. Were one to deny this difference, as occurs in the traditional context of western thought, then there are two extremes between which other views might be placed. Either everything is taken to have a source in itself, to be sovereign in being self-creative; — but then subservience is only an effect of the confrontation with a greater source. (Nietzsche, with his 'will to power', has explored this option in the context of aesthetic modernism, though motivated by ancient culture and thought.) Or, everything is 'purely structural', lacking initiative—as in a Parmenidean 'block universe'—and life is determined by what can only be called fate. These ('analytical') alternatives are extreme and call up antinomies and paradoxes.[75] In a 'synthetical' understanding, both notions are respected in their distinct meaning, and a 'third factor' is required to mark their (non-categorial) 'belonging together'. Applying this to the biblically inspired approach to sovereignty and subservience, this 'third factor' can only be 'law'. Then sovereignty is the reigning through law in a normative way, and subservience is recognition of standing in subjection as supported by law. Vollenhoven's understanding of the cosmic whole is that of a domain standing in subjection to normative law. Law then signals the boundary of this whole. Philosophy has the task of understanding

---

75   E.g. in Nietzsche there is the antinomy that successful sovereignty can only take place through domination of the environment and at the cost of others' sovereignty; no sovereignty without subservience, and vice versa (cf. Nietzsche 1969: 215-217, the application to slave morality). The paradoxes of Zeno are the classical illustrations of difficulties with the 'block universe'.

the cosmos, and to limit itself to the cosmos in doing so. The motive to accept this task derives from biblical, meta-philosophical reflections.

2. The worldview relevance

Philosophy can have an important effect on society and on the attitude human beings have towards their environment. Utopias recommend different constructions of society, and in modern times there have been various templates of society devised towards implementing a radical social reform. The extremes are the stifling governmental control of socialism over against the minimal government interference of liberalism, and each brings with it its own misery. Often there is a specific philosophy whose wisdom recommends the societal form in question. Now if philosophy were indeed the universal wisdom it aims to be, then it ought to display more uniformity than it in fact does, and its promise of beneficence be more relevant than is the case.

When philosophy turns to real life it does not speak with one voice. Of course, philosophy, as such, builds no world except that of its own concepts and statements. It needs to assume and be able to *appeal* to a world of activity and experience that we acknowledge as being our societal, cultural and natural world, in short, our life-world. The prima facie diversity of the life-world is not an irremediable chaos. Rather than brushing it aside in favour of some chosen order enforced on society, it should be elucidated and reflected upon in terms of its own focal points, its own 'forms of life' (to use Wittgenstein's term).[76] This calls for the kind of reflection that is typical of worldview consideration which, in Vollenhoven, takes place in terms of its own method. Worldview reflection calls attention to the life-world and elicits from it a primary interpretation.[77] It

---

76   Cf. Wittgenstein 1976: 8e, remark 19.
77   In 'Levenseenheid' (The unity of life) (1955), Vollenhoven speaks of 'enframing concepts' (*omramingsbegrippen*) in this regard, i.e. concepts that specify a hermeneutical context of practical understanding; cf. Tol and Bril 1992: 131. I believe that a closely similar problem, though stated in a different idiom, is broached by Bertrand Russell, when he speaks of "the hierarchy of our beliefs". For him this hierarchy is based on spontaneous or instinctive beliefs that are obvious, on which rest derivative beliefs that are less obvious to us. But since obviousness varies, a hierarchy such as Russell proposes cannot be stable in itself, thus he also calls for the inclusion of "that feeling for reality which ought to be preserved even in the most abstract studies." Russell 1919: 169; cf. also Russell 1966: 127 ff. and Russell 1959: 25-26. Questions of obviousness or common sense introduce a factor of 'outlook', which is to say 'worldview', and is no less 'worldviewy' when it concerns 'the scientific outlook'. The latter is a choice as to the preferred "conduct of life" as prevailed upon by science; cf. Russell 2001: 74-77. The problem of determining "the hierarchy of our beliefs" would appear to be a positivistic way of posing a hermeneutical problem.

is within that context that different worldview systems and options ought to be discussed. In that sense, the Kuyperian view of sphere-sovereignty is one worldview option among others, that can be reviewed for its potential as a worldview system.[78] Philosophy, in the academic sense, ought to respect the right and good sense of worldview reflection, and refrain from imposing its more general categories on real life.

Now, though Vollenhoven places this limitation on philosophy, there is nevertheless, as with religion, a need for philosophy to take stock of worldview reality. The problem concerns pluralism. There is an obvious diversity of existence. Short of the question how that can be, there is the matter of understanding it and being able to deal with it. Only on assuming a world of activity, humanly experienced, can philosophy apply itself to the world, which it needs to do in order to name, describe, explain, affirm, criticize or deny things of it. The most general way to state this 'dealing with the world' is in terms of *freedom and responsibility*. Without freedom no activity can be meaningful; and without responsibility results lack substance. But freedom without responsibility—i.e. absolute freedom—turns activity into wanton conduct, when lacking context and restraints; then too, responsibility without freedom (i.e. absolute duty) predetermines results in a way that cancels moral obligation. How can freedom and responsibility be 'taken together'.

Vollenhoven avails himself of Kuyper's worldview teaching of sphere sovereignty. He brings this Reformed influence to bear, not in urning philosophy into a species of worldview thought, say, along lines recommended by Wilhelm Dilthey,[79] but by acknowledging, as relevant for scientific understanding, the kind of diversity that sphere sovereignty entails at the practical level (Vollenhoven 1953I: 102-103). What brings freedom and responsibility together, in a way that is also delimiting for philosophical thought, is the insight that activity is rule-bound.

Activity becomes intelligible when seen in the light of a rule being followed in the execution of activity.[80] Now different rules can illu-

---

78   This is of course what Kuyper did in his *Lectures on Calvinism*, when speaking of Calvinism as a 'life-system'; cf. Kuyper 2002.

79   In his *Weltanschauungslehre* (worldview doctrine) Dilthey divides worldviews into artistic, religious and philosophical types. Philosophy is thereby taken to be a kind of worldview. The Dutch tend to see all worldviews as basically implying a religious or faith stance, which is probably why they long preferred the broader phrase 'world and life view'. However, this puts religion in a too direct connection to culture, causing confusion between the distinct relevance of both religious discourse and worldview reflection. Cf. Goheen and Bartholomew 2008 for a current defence of a close-wedded relationship.

80 Cf. Miller and Wright 2002 for a cross-section of the current discussions of this and related topics.

minate the 'same activity'—i.e. one and the same sequence of events—in different ways. (Think of the different meanings that a simple handshake can have.) Rule-following is meaning-determining without being deterministic or exclusive. Meaning is multiple to the extent that this is warranted by the relevant rules. A rule gains in relevance when it links a motive to a purpose, i.e. directs what one in *freedom* chooses to achieve. At the same time such a rule makes the reference to and assessment of achievement possible, which is to say that *responsibility* with regard to what takes place in the activity is not a vacuous matter. Because most activity is in fact interactive, the responsibility is not only to oneself, as the executing agent, but it involves other beings as well. Thus when taking freedom and responsibility seriously in the context of rule-bound activity, the problem of their connection—their 'belonging together'—is not simply a matter of a 'moral state',[81] but it concerns a diverse texture of freedom and responsibility, in the light of the diverse kinds of activity and the diversity of the rules to which they are subject. In other words, taking cognizance of a *diversity of law-spheres* is an intellectual requisite for dealing with the problem of the human being and the life-world. Vollenhoven opts for this kind of diversity of power and delimitation of responsibility in securing a philosophically relevant pluralism.

The diversity of law-spheres fits in with the religious relevance, in that it presents the 'law as boundary' in an application of 'cases of law'. Each sphere, in being rule-bound, becomes the domain of a 'kind of functioning' in accordance with its (main) rule (Vollenhoven speaks of 'ordinance'). The rule has the effect of *empowering* (as an 'ought') the activity that is relevant in that sphere, granting a 'right' to the initiation (in freedom) of the activity in question, but also upholding that the activity be directed to fulfilling a 'duty' (of responsibility).

So, in both the case of the religious relevance and that of the worldview relevance, Vollenhoven takes a specific stand in the Reformed tradition. It is a stand of one among many possible stands. He makes his choices for 'Reformed' reasons, and understands his choices in terms of the best meaning he can give to matters of religion (covenant religion) and worldview (sphere sovereignty).[82] To the extent that this is meta-phil-

---

81   One is reminded of Kant's practical reason, whereby freedom is the transcendental condition of activity, revealed by the a priori validity of the moral law (which says to act in such a way as to permit the individual's maxim of the will to be always and at the same time the principle of a general legislation). Freedom and the moral law together define a 'causality of freedom'. This specifies an ethic of intentions. Here responsibilities tends to reduce to austere instances of duty. Cf. Kant 1997: xiii, 28.

82   Sphere sovereignty is for Vollenhoven an adequate, indeed normative, view for

osophical, the reflection that takes place is controlled by the thetical-critical method and the 'method of knowledge organization'. The application to philosophy is not a wilful imposition. There is the recognition of a 'need' in philosophy itself, a need called up by philosophy's being an activity itself and aims to achieve a cognitive result. The application is not a matter of turning the religious and worldview presuppositions into direct philosophical concepts, prior to any choice, assimilation or rejection in philosophical discourse (that way philosophy overreaches itself as evinced by antinomies); rather, the import of religious meaning (as focussed in law) and that of worldview (empowering law-spheres) have the effect of defining the parameters that delineate the 'place and task' of philosophy as (cognitive) activity. In this way, meta-philosophical presuppositions of philosophy entail conditions for philosophy. The result in Vollenhoven is 'Reformed philosophy'. Vollenhoven nowhere claims an exclusive or privileged right to this philosophy, only that it has a right to be identified as a specimen of (general) philosophy. "Every philosophy proceeds from a worldview basis," he says, "but not every philosophy accounts for this fact" (Vollenhoven 1953l/Tol and Bril 1992: 103). Its strengths and weaknesses—assuming it is formally consistent and materially consequential—can only be ascertained in comparison with philosophies of different standpoint.

3. The condition of cognition
There is one further condition to consider. Philosophy is a cognitive enterprise, hence its cognitive character needs to be specified and warranted. Vollenhoven holds that philosophy is for the most part concerned with the theory of knowing and its ontological underpinnings (cf. Vollenhoven 2005d/e, **6**) It is through the condition of knowledge that this third condition, of cognition, is specified.

There are several reasons for this choice of the problem of knowledge as delimiting philosophy. First of all, there is a concern from out of the Reformed tradition itself. A tenacious feature of that tradition (especially the conservative wing of Protestant scholasticism) is the occurrence of

---

understanding and participating in societal life. This is not to say that he was entirely happy with the term. In Kuyper's use the delegated sovereignty relevant to a sphere is too easily confused with the sovereignty that belongs to God alone. "He [Kuyper], in his use of 'sovereignty', did not think exclusively of the sovereignty of God, but—influenced by Romanticism—also included the authority of office-holders within a societal sphere" (Vollenhoven 1950n, Tol and Bril 1992: 44). In another place he says that the term "can perhaps sometime be replaced by a better one" (Vollenhoven 1968b, Tol and Bril 1992: 204). The term 'sphere responsibility' or 'delimited responsibility' would at least accord better with Vollenhoven's interpretation.

'*logos* speculation'. It holds that to think truly is to think God's thoughts after him. Now all truth may be God's truth, but that does not cancel the need to reckon with the human condition when the human being is cognitively active. The human mind has no direct link with the Divine mind. This speculative theory deserves to be critiqued.[83]

Secondly, there is the influence of the time of Vollenhoven's formative years. He showed special interest in philosophical schools that practised philosophy with academic rigour and favoured philosophy itself as a '*strenge Wissenschaft*' (rigorous science), as Husserl maintained in defence of his phenomenology early in the twentieth century (cf. Husserl 1911). This in fact involves taking a stand over against the main alternatives, *viz.* either in conceiving of philosophy as a fundamental form of 'social engagement', as in socialist philosophy (of Marxism and neo-Marxism), or practising philosophy as 'worldview interpretation', in the spirit of, say, the hermeneutical historicism of Dilthey. The aesthetic interest of the latter and the societal interest of socialist philosophy were less relevant for someone of the Reformed tradition, as over against the cognitive interest of philosophy as a 'general science'.[84] In the guise of a general science philosophy would stay in the close proximity of the special sciences. An important facet of its task would involve philosophical inquiry into the methodological problems of the sciences. The young Vollenhoven made a definite choice. A statement from the opening discussion in his dissertation is telling in this regard: "Every topic in philosophy derives its importance from questions as to values, boundaries and relations of the distinct sciences mutually" (Vollenhoven 1918a: 2).[85]

---

83   The equivocation of human thought and divine Logos is explicitly countered in Vollenhoven 1932b, and in fact it is an important factor in his argument for an alternative "Christian logic" (that recognizes limitations). Vollenhoven's understanding of the human being "in God's image" does not contradict with this (cf. Vollenhoven 2005d/e, 117). See chapter 2, for Vollenhoven's own early reference to the (divine) *Logos*, and chapter 4 for his more definitive view.

84   Cf. Vollenhoven 2005d/e, **9**; also Vollenhoven 1953l in Tol and Bril 1992: 96. Also, the opening sentence of the article on 'Calvinistic philosophy' in the *Oosthoeks Encyclopedie*, states: "Calvinistic philosophy is the correlate, in science, of the Calvinistic view of world and life, which is non-scientific in character." Reprinted in Vollenhoven 2005c: 76. The three main philosophical interests mentioned here are characteristic of modernism. From about mid-nineteenth century on, these began to 'pull apart'—which is really a decentralization of the human subject in the context of modernism—and be the topic of heated methodological conflict. For a discussion of this 'pulling apart' cf. Tol 2005a, where this trait of modernism is placed in the context of the whole 'modern period' of philosophy.

85   In this light we can understand why Vollenhoven, early in his career, was open to the influence, as he later admitted, of the Marburg school of neo-Kantianism and

A third argument for choosing for the knowledge condition is to catch in the bud the possibility of knowledge being applied to underscore either an undesired religious influence of philosophy or an uncritical worldview importance. Knowledge presupposes an *agent* capable of *knowing* and a *referent* that is *knowable*. But how does one deal with this duality? There are examples in the history of philosophy—some being historically very prominent and influential—in which this distinction in knowledge is interwoven with the sovereignty-subjection distinction and others with that of freedom-responsibility. Spiritualism, Gnosticism, Neo-Platonism, etc. tend to interpret the experience of knowing as indicative of an illumination by divinity, or at least an involving of deity. (This is behind the 'logos' speculation as well.) Naturally, that experience of knowing tends to underscore a privileged position of the knower, taken as revealing its elevated relevance or even a right to rule. As to freedom and responsibility, a striking example is the application of science, in the form of the scientific outlook as privileged modern worldview. Facts, when known, are able to be controlled. The subject-object split, on which much of modern science is based, allows the knowing subject to subject the object to his own aims, within the margins that the knowledge of the object technically allows. The scientific outlook can then take on ideological forms of advancing programs of construction, their only check being the technological means of execution. There is no responsibility for the object, nor for the context of the life-world, for the fascination lies with what scientific power can achieve, rather than satisfying the wonderment of knowing the object. The 'substantive reason' of the latter, that ought to accompany actual worldview choices with a view to context and human ends, is replaced by an instrumental reason that reckons only with possibilities in the object as means.[86] As worldview, the scientific outlook is one-sided, and on that score, as dominating force, detrimental.

Vollenhoven grants to knowledge its own importance, that also warrants its distinct status with respect to the religious condition and that of worldview. Not that there is no religious knowing. Vollenhoven claims

---

Husserlian phenomenology. Both schools take philosophy as primarily serving a basic scientific-cognitive interest. Cf. Vollenhoven 1953p in Tol and Bril 1992: 112.

86   In Russell 2001, on the scientific outlook, Russell sketches the development of science from contemplation to manipulation. The former is based on the impulse of love, the latter on the impulse of power. In contemplation the love impulse is satisfied through the (Gnostic) ecstasy in the knowing agent, in manipulation the impulse of power is satisfied through technical control over the object. He hopes that the instrumental reason of scientific technique "will not outweigh the ends which it should serve" (*op. cit.* : 219). Remarkably, Russell, in assessing knowledge, points to either its divine-like quality for the knower or the world-view practical use of the object.

that God is knowable (Vollenhoven 2005d/e, **173**), but the achievement of religious knowledge depends on revelation as means. And there is knowledge at a worldview level as well, this being mainly in the form of contextualized or communicated knowledge (involving the organization of knowledge). There still remains the important category of scientific knowledge. Here one inquires and thus seeks knowledge, and this involves searching out the *truth*. When truth is sought there needs to be a *knowing agent*, who seeks to know, and a *knowable referent* in relation to which knowledge is sought. There is the overriding importance, here too, as to their 'synthesis', the warrant of their 'belonging together'. For Vollenhoven this warrant is truth.

Vollenhoven maintains that between the knowing agent and knowable referent there is a "direct connection" (Vollenhoven 2005d/e, **174**) that is itself not mediated by knowledge. When truth is the warrant of this 'direct connection' of knowing agent and the knowable referent, then—a negative implication—neither pole should have priority over the other. This is what occurs in either subjectivistic or objectivistic tendencies. When the agent is preferred over the referent, that invites forms of psychologism or aprioristic (formalistic) constructions that go proxy for the truth. Cognition is either a psychic state or belongs to the level of language. But when the referent rises above the agent, the latter tends to be seen as passive, performing the role of receptacle for the data of the referent. This is empiricism, the epistemology of which is based on a copy theory. Knowledge is the copy of the referent as represented in the mind. But truth cannot arise merely through data being copied. The agent needs to grasp something rightly. Thus 'analytic' solutions are not convincing.[87]

When Vollenhoven takes truth to be an independent condition of knowledge, *viz.* the warrant of agent and referent to be together, then each is gauged in relation to truth, not vice versa. The knowing agent has a task or duty, epistemologically, to seek the truth as challenged by a referent, not represent it, make a copy of it, control it or whatever. The seeking of the agent takes place in law-spheres, subject to modal norms. The referent, in turn, has the epistemological value of being knowable, meaning that it has an intrinsic diversity that can be grasped or understood rightly or wrongly. Here a feature of structure is present. Truth moderates the togetherness of the knowing agent's rule-bound seeking

---

[87] Already in his dissertation Vollenhoven took a stand against formalism and empiricism, in favour of a view in which the subjective and the objective sides are in balance, held together by a synthetic a priori, the certainty of which is intuitively grasped; cf. chapter 2 of this study.

and the knowable referent's structured complexity of features and qualities. There is knowledge when the discerning agent has rightly grasped some complex feature of the referent.

When generalizing this to maximal scope, one can see that, when philosophy seeks to know the cosmos in a general way, the knowing agent is humankind in its subjection to the order of normative law. At the same time the knowable referent is the cosmos in its intrinsic complexity, the broadest expression of which is the structured or gradated order of the cosmic law-spheres. Truth is the warrant that grasping cosmic structure in accordance with the normative law-order is not futile, i.e. that it makes cognitive sense. In that sense, truth is not subsidiary to philosophy but one of its conditions.[88]

D. In summary

In Vollenhoven's Reformed understanding of philosophy, as an activity that seeks results, philosophy is delimited by a three-fold problematic: the sovereignty-subservience duality, the freedom-responsibility duality and the knowing agent-knowable referent duality. Philosophy as practice is conditioned by these polarities. The philosophical habitat, its 'consciousness', is limited to the cosmos, but the 'form' of that consciousness involves ineluctable features that link philosophy to religious, worldview and human reflective realities.

Vollenhoven made historically contingent choices in coming to practice philosophy. But what counts for him is that "by their fruits you shall know them" (cf. Matthew 7:16). The results of philosophical activity are insights, understanding, statements, that are marked and constrained by the three-fold problematic, but constrained in the specific way that the three dualities focus thought on what holds each together, *viz.* normative law, the order of law-spheres and truth. Any philosophical result is in some sense a reflection of these three foci. One would not be far amiss—we are now interpreting Vollenhoven's *oeuvre*—if one takes normative law to be the principle of cosmic *being* (*est*), looks on the order of the law-spheres as the context of the cases of an *ought* (*debet*), and considers truth—that entails a normative handling of cosmic structure—as the principle of ability, of the *can* (*potest*), the principle of response to law.[89]

---

88   In chapter 4 Vollenhoven's systematic position is subject to a broader discussion.

89   This would link Vollenhoven, though probably entirely unintentionally, to John Bisterfeld (1605-1655), one of the encyclopaedists of the Protestant university of Herborn, where also Caspar Olevian and John Althusius taught. Bisterfeld chose these three 'transcendentals', *est*, *debet*, and *potest*, in his *Philosophiae Primae Seminarium* (1641)—a

One could—though Vollenhoven nowhere does this—pull the three-fold problematic of philosophy together, including the three-fold result of normative law, order of law-spheres and truth, in what might be called philosophy's 'fundamental ground schema'. No doubt, *prima facie*, the term 'schema' sounds formal and empty. But, upon taking a closer look at Vollenhoven's work, one finds plentiful use of the term 'schema'. To my knowledge, it is never defined formally, but in its occurrences it has a kind of (pre-)structuralist use of indicating important effective polarities. Thus Vollenhoven speaks of "the schema 'this-that'" (2005d/e, **88**), meaning the diversity or contrast between two particular things; the "schema" of good and evil (*op. cit.*, **91**), here too meaning the contrast between these; similarly in "schema means-ends" (*op. cit.*, **60**); "schema nature-grace" (*op. cit.*, **130**); and there are other examples. This use is certainly not formal and empty but constructive, even constitutive. If the word is taken in that sense, then the only oddity in using it in reference to 'ground schema' above is that this ground schema involves three poles, whereas the examples are all bi-polar. But surely this is peripheral. The important point is to understand that the three terms are taken together in a way that preserves their mutual effective contrast. If this is acceptable, then the phrase "fundamental ground schema" can be interpreted as denoting the delimiting problematic of philosophy in Vollenhoven, in its cosmonomic focus. It is this schema that underlies Vollenhoven's program of philosophy.

---

work much admired by the young Leibniz—as mutually convertible conjugates of thought. As applied to Vollenhoven, and interpreted from his standpoint, these notions signal the primary (but non-convertible!) differences of stature. In Vollenhoven they are non-convertible, for est is most primary, with *debet* in secondary place, followed by *potest*; cf. Loemker 1972: 143.

2

A Bold Beginning: Theistic and Metalogical Intuitionism

"Whoever allows truth to exist as abstraction,
kills its efficacy as norm."

D.H.Th. Vollenhoven (1918)

I. INTRODUCTION

Vollenhoven's initial choices in philosophy were made in connection with his dissertation project in the philosophy of mathematics. The dissertation, entitled *The Philosophy of Mathematics from a Theistic Standpoint*, was published and defended (in that order) at the Free University of Amsterdam in 1918.[1] In the ensuing eight years Vollenhoven combined the further study of philosophy with the pastoral duties of a minister of the "Gereformeerde Kerken" (Reformed churches).[2] In the fall of 1926 he became the first full-time professor of philosophy of the Free University, a position he held until his retirement in 1963.

The time between 1918 and 1926 was, both philosophically and personally, eventful for Vollenhoven. The main contours of the philosophical position, which he had developed in the dissertation, remained essentially constant until 1922. (In 1921, a 'metalogical' moment came more to the fore; cf. section IX below.) Vollenhoven described his position as 'theistic intuitionism' (1918a: 438). His theism was, from the

---

1   D.H.Th. Vollenhoven, *De Wijsbegeerte der Wiskunde van Theïstisch Standpunt* (Amsterdam: Van Soest, 1918). Hereafter in this chapter referred to by its bibliographical code: 1918a.

2   He first served in Oostkapelle, in the province of Zeeland, 1918-1921, then in The Hague 1921-1926. In Zeeland he became acquainted with Antheunis Janse (1890-1960), the head of a local Christian grade school, who posed stimulating anthropological questions. The period in The Hague enabled Vollenhoven to have close and more personal contact with his friend and (as of October 1918) brother-in-law, Herman Dooyeweerd (1894-1977), who lived in The Hague. Cf. the brochure, Van der Walt 1989, on Antheunis Janse, also the Vollenhoven biography, Stellingwerff 1992. Cf. chapter 3 for our own discussion of these important contacts.

start, critical of what Vollenhoven later called 'logos speculation'—a view which postulates a close connection between human thought and the divine Logos[3]—but it did include features of traditional scholasticism, namely the view of the harmony of subjective and objective rationality. But even at the time this scholasticism was subject to definite constraints, particularly in connection with the intuition. Discussions with Antheunis Janse and Herman Dooyeweerd, and renewed reflection on Kuyper's thought, helped Vollenhoven to reform his thought and strike out on new paths that he, together with Dooyeweerd, called "Calvinistic". In Vollenhoven's use of this term it implied opposition to, and criticism of, much traditional thought.[4]

However, the change that the new developments of 1922 initiated is difficult to trace in Vollenhoven's case. For he suffered a breakdown in his health, that incapacitated him for most of 1923. It took some time—his pastoral duties were after all his first priority—before he resumed to publish in philosophy. Published documentation of his changed position is not found prior to 1925. So the period of illness and recovery forms a natural watershed between his initial theistic intuitionism and the subsequent, more focussed Calvinistic understanding of his philosophical endeavours. But the period of illness also hides the transformation that took place. In view of the paucity of documentation, we need to resort to a comparison of his thought before and after the breakdown in order to ascertain and assess the change. The present chapter focuses entirely on the position of 1918-1922. Subsequent chapters look at what the contacts with Janse and Dooyeweerd brought to bear (chapter 3) and how Vollenhoven redrew the lines of his thought (chapter 4) up to the early 1930's, when the first version of *Isagôgè Philosophiae* is completed.

II. *The early work*

What is the importance of Vollenhoven's early thought towards understanding his mature position, or, more specifically, *Isagôgè Philosophiae*? To the extent that this early thought is focussed on the philosophy of mathematics, the importance is indirect. While Vollenhoven did retain an interest in mathematics (and the natural sciences), he published very little that concerned mathematics directly later in life.[5] What *Isagôgè Phi-*

3 Cf. Vollenhoven 1932b: 1-2; also Vollenhoven 1948p: 27.

4 Vollenhoven continued to speak of 'Calvinistic philosophy' in later years. As of 1923 Dooyeweerd also used the term 'law-idea' to characterize his position, though he too spoke of Calvinistic thought. In his later years he preferred 'ecumenical'. Cf. chapter 1, footnote 3.

5 The main articles are Vollenhoven 1936hh, i.e. "Problemen en richtingen in de wijs-

losophiae contains as to mathematics does not require any explicit knowledge of the earlier work, except that comparison with that early work reveals implicit differences and connections. Vollenhoven never developed his interest in the exact sciences to the point of having a workable command of the basics of these sciences. So his references to mathematics and the sciences dwindled as his career in philosophy progressed.

Vollenhoven's initial focus was not on mathematics and the natural sciences as such but on their philosophy. In the dissertation, in which he limits himself to mathematics,[5a] he states that his explicit aim is to show that three main 'directions' (or schools) in mathematics, namely, empiricism, formalism and intuitionism, are 'offshoots' (*uitlopers*) of three "directions in metaphysics", namely materialism, psycho-monism and dualism (1918a: 3). These details will be discussed in their proper place below. At this point we want to emphasize that it is hardly illuminating to connect an approach in a specific science, i.e. mathematics, to metaphysics, without the mediating role of the philosophy of science, along with essential epistemological considerations and ontological reflections. This is indeed as we find it in Vollenhoven. The outcome in metaphysics, whereby materialism and psycho-monism are each criticised for being one-sidedly monistic, while dualism is embraced as being a viable view—this outcome is achieved only upon bringing to bear considerations of methodology of science, views as to what knowing and knowledge is, what the role of intuition and of certain 'mental objects' is, and, most important, how the polarity of thought and being sets the stage. These 'mediating philosophical topics' are not all discussed separately by Vollenhoven. One finds their relevant features strewn throughout the text. This makes understanding the thought of the young Vollenhoven something of a challenge.

It is in connection with metaphysics, in the guise of cosmology, that Vollenhoven takes a specific stand. The stand is motivated by theism. Thus Vollenhoven's preference for intuitionism, as direction in mathematics, is secured in the philosophical position that he called 'theistic intuitionism' (1918a: 438). This position combines a 'dualistic metaphys-

---

begeerte der wiskunde" (Problems and approaches in the philosophy of mathematics) and Vollenhoven 1938m, i.e. "Is de ruimte euclidisch of niet-euclidisch?" (Is space Euclidean or non-Euclidean?).

5a Initially Vollenhoven's aim was broader, *viz.* to study "the influence of philosophy on the latest representatives of mathematics and the natural sciences" (Stellingwerff 1992: 25), whereby the two forms of monism (materialism and psycho-monism/idealism) and Vollenhoven's own preferred dualism were to be discussed as directions not only in mathematics but also in physics, biology and psychology. Cf. *op. cit.* : 25-27.

ics' with theistic considerations. The dissertation provides by far the most important documentation of this position in the time frame of 1918-1922.[6] Because Vollenhoven's later work is decidedly in philosophy and not in the sciences nor in the philosophy of science, it is important towards understanding Vollenhoven's mature work to raise the question as to how his theistic intuitionism influenced and affected his later thought. My own conclusion is that, without an adequate understanding of this early phase, important features of Vollenhoven's later thought remain in the dark. Also, as our discussion of Dooyeweerd's early work will reveal in chapter 3, there is importance for him too, though to date this has never been pointed out convincingly.

The aim of this chapter is to bring Vollenhoven's theistic intuitionism into focus. We will not be satisfied with a mere description of this position. Understanding the effect of earlier thought on later thought is not so much a matter of confirming or deleting distinct features of a position as coming to grips with the very course of that thought itself. To that end we cannot ignore the 'mediating philosophical topics' that contribute towards delineating the course of Vollenhoven's thought. But that requires 'collecting' the relevant fragmented statements in theory of science, in epistemology, in ontology, in the philosophy of mind (i.e. Alexius Meinong's *Gegenstandstheorie*) etc., so as to discover, at least in outline, how these topics are understood and what relevance they have in the defence of 'theistic intuitionism'. This more general understanding should also provide a more favourable opportunity towards recognizing what it is that changes when Vollenhoven's initial definitive position comes into view in the second half of the 1920s. The 'route of discovery' dictates the main course of discussion of this chapter. Beginning with arithmetic and geometry, we pass through the stations of philosophy of science, epistemology, theory of mind and metaphysics, ending with an integrated, theistic view. (The final section is a discussion of a 'metalogical' shift within Vollenhoven's early period of thought.)

---

6   Vollenhoven's dissertation is a 'young man's book', displaying the qualities that such books generally have: courageous and innovative, but also overambitious. (Cf. footnote 37 below for a summary indication of the content.) In the report of mathematical theories Vollenhoven's discussions are at times vulnerable—examples of which the Amsterdam mathematician, Gerrit Mannoury, did not fail to point out in his reviews (cf. Mannoury 1918, 1919a and 1919b)—but the historical parts are impressively rich in details. The sense of working in view of an ideal gives the work its unique value. He is daring in his criticisms and assertive as regards his own standpoint. As biographical fact, it is, I think, correct to say that Vollenhoven's talent lay decidedly more with philosophy than with mathematics. But he had an aptitude, especially noticeable in later writings, for concise formulation that made the reading of the philosophy of mathematics congenial.

A Bold Beginning: Theistic and Metalogical Intuitionism

Vollenhoven's earliest work has long been neglected. Admittedly, he did little to encourage others to take notice. Once he had become convinced that 'Christian philosophy' was better served by a reassessment in line with Kuyperian neo-Calvinism, he came to think his early work as misguided. We shall discuss this in chapter 4. Preferring to look ahead rather than back, he invested more effort into developing a more adequate approach to philosophy than in repairing what he took to be ill conceived. In fact, he never mentions or refers to his dissertation, except late in life in (mostly brief) autobiographical reflections. In these reflections he 'explains' his early orientation as having been influenced in a decisive way by Henri Poincaré.[7] The long silence regarding his earliest work and the self-critical autobiographical references strongly suggest that Vollenhoven held his early work to have been unredeemably surpassed in his post-1922 work. There is also very little evidence of interest in Vollenhoven's dissertation after its initial appearing during his lifetime,[8] except on Dooyeweerd's part.[9] But the latter's relation to Vol-

---

7   These reflections are cited and discussed in section VI of chapter 4; cf. footnote 183 of chapter 4 for the titles of the sources, which are Vollenhoven 1953p, 1953o, 1963c, 1968b.

8   There were a number of reviews when the work appeared; cf. the separate listing in the bibliography, which mentions, among others, 'G. Mannoury', 'H.J. Pos', and 'H.W. van der Vaart Smit'. Cf. chapter 1, footnote 40 for references to Vollenhoven's influence in the early years of the department of mathematics and natural science of the Free University. However, there are also late references to the dissertation in E.W. Beth's work; e.g. it is listed in Beth 1940: 267, and Beth 1950: 144. In later years, A.M. Wolters briefly discusses the historical parts of Vollenhoven's dissertation as an example of a 'proto-problem-historical' approach in his master's thesis, written at the Free University in 1970. The main part of this thesis was published (after Vollenhoven's death) as Wolters 1979a: 231-262. Hendrik Blauwendraat's recent interest in Vollenhoven's intuitionism (cf. footnote 11 below) motivated Van der Heiden and Muis 2003, which elicited the response Tol 2003. For the work of John H. Kok, cf. below.

9   In Dooyeweerd 1973, i.e. Dooyeweerd's "tribute to the 80 years old cofounder of the reformational philosophical trend of thought", he praised Vollenhoven's dissertation as "an enormous achievement", in which the latter "presented an extremely penetrating critique of the philosophic foundations of the main directions taken in modern mathematics; especially his critique of Cantor's theory of transfinite numbers and of Brouwer's intuitionism." Though this work, Dooyeweerd continues, "proved to be quite bound to the traditional metaphysics of realist scholasticism", nevertheless this phase of pre-reformational thought "remains very important since its critique of the dominant trends in modern mathematics contains numerous worthwhile considerations meriting our attention even today." This statement evidences Dooyeweerd's more than passing acquaintance with, or at least renewed memory of, the text. This praise after 55 years—which for the 80 year old Vollenhoven was quite misplaced!—may also be indicative of an influence which the work had on Dooyeweerd. We will see that there is rather firm evidence that some key notions in Dooyeweerd, such as time and intuition, have a striking similarity to

lenhoven's early work is a topic that requires its own discussion, and will be broached in chapters three and four.

Yet the neglect of the dissertation, and in its wake the neglect of the period 1918-1922, has in turn seriously handicapped a fuller understanding of Vollenhoven's thought. Even without internal evidence, one does not expect, on psychological grounds, for someone to merely wipe the slate of one's mind clean and start again afresh. Topics come and go, but methods, orientations, assumptions and fundamental beliefs are more stubborn. We hope to show that in terms of methodology, epistemology and ontology, there is considerable continuity between the early and late 20s, and lingering influence in later years. And where changes are evident, these often occur within 'schemata' that provide orientation for changes without themselves being directly affected. One set of terms in particular, namely 'monism and dualism', which are crucial for Vollenhoven's ontology, retain much of their 1918 meanings until the late 30s. It is only in the last revision of *Isagôgè Philosophiae*, in 1941, that Vollenhoven's later understanding of monism and dualism becomes definitive.[10] All this is not to say that Vollenhoven's thought lacks unity, or that the unity of his thought did not shift. But the unity of a 'philosophical conception' (not to be confused with its worldview background) is complex, permitting a latitude of realization within its defining parameters.

The important exception to the neglect of Vollenhoven's early work is John H. Kok's *Vollenhoven His Early Development* (Kok 1992). This book length study greatly eases the task of finding one's way in the rather intricate thicket of themes of Vollenhoven's early thought. The work also provides translations of important parts of the early work, particularly the dissertation. Kok focuses on the development of Vollenhoven's thought prior to the work that began after his accepting the chair of philosophy in 1926. However, little is said about the connection of this earlier work with Vollenhoven's later development. We, in turn, will direct the discussion of Vollenhoven's early work to highlighting its main features with a view to uncovering the *philosophical conception* of Vollenhoven's theistic intuitionism. This should help trace the path that led to *Isagôgè Philosophiae* and Vollenhoven's later work.[11]

Vollenhoven's early use. Cf. section VI.C. of chapter 4.

10   It was S.U. Zuidema (cf. especially Zuidema 1963: 138) who first discussed this difference, thereby implying the continuous self-critical reformation that Vollenhoven applied to his own thought.

11   Blauwendraat 2004 discusses Vollenhoven's early work. In chapter two, "Mathematics and philosophy" there is a summary discussion of Vollenhoven's mathematical intuitionism, pp. 49-66. However the philosophical interpretation given calls for discus-

III. *The setting of the dissertation*

An important determining factor of the setting of Vollenhoven's early work is its theism. He claims that philosophy ought not only to reckon with God's presence, but also to conform to God's will as norm for thought and action. Were we to emphasize this at the beginning of our discussion we might immediately elicit the response that Vollenhoven subjects the philosophy of mathematics to an influence that is foreign to it. Such a response would be unfortunate. For, while Vollenhoven does maintain the relevance of theism for the philosophy of mathematics—or for philosophy in general—he counters the charge that this lacks proper motivation. Our strategy, as explained above, will be to begin our discussion from the other end, from the side of mathematics. That will enable us to see more clearly why Vollenhoven deemed theism to be relevant, and what his theism amounts to, as we include discussion of the said 'mediating philosophical topics', ending with the metaphysics of substance. But when beginning with mathematics, we need to discuss arithmetic and geometry in at least such detail as will enable us to discover the turn-of-the-twentieth-century features Vollenhoven took to be philosophically relevant.

A. Arithmetic

Vollenhoven accepted the traditional division of mathematics in two main scientific disciplines: arithmetic and geometry.[12] Each has a number of sub-disciplines. But arithmetic is basically the science of number. While there are various kinds of number systems—rational, real, complex, and the like (1918a: 223)—all are based on the natural numbers. The principle on which arithmetic rests is "the principle of complete induction" (1918a: 427). This principle is based on the series of the natural numbers, *viz.* the numbers 1, 2, 3, and so on. The principle of complete induction is a basic principle of proof in arithmetic. It states that if an arithmetical formula holds for the number 1 and also holds for the number n when it holds for the number $n-1$, then the formula holds for all the natural numbers. In virtue of this principle Vollenhoven distinguishes the *science* of arithmetic from the *account* of the natural numbers, calling the latter "arithmetic of the first order" and the former "arithmetic of

---

sion. In Stellingwerff 2006: 28-31 there is a summary discussion of selected features of Vollenhoven's early thought.

12   Vollenhoven does not discuss the adequacy of this division. In view of 19th century developments in mathematics, one might expect separate mention of algebra and analysis. The latter includes the differential and integral calculus. The relations of these disciplines to arithmetic and geometry will not be discussed here.

the second order". Arithmetic of the second order involves arithmetical statements and this constitutes arithmetic as scientific discipline. One might mention in this connection, though Vollenhoven passes it by, G. Peano's account of (scientific) arithmetic, with its five axioms, the fifth of which (in the usual order of presentation) is the principle of complete induction.[13] This arithmetic of the second order is also subject, as is any science, to logical principles, especially the principle of contradiction and that of excluded middle.

On the other hand, "arithmetic of the first order", as Vollenhoven calls it, seeks to account for the natural numbers themselves. This is not a science, for the account of the natural numbers is not a matter of statements but of the (intra-mental) construction of terms. It concerns the mental process in terms of which the natural numbers arise.[14] This is the process that lies at the basis of counting.[15] This process is not subject to the principle of contradiction. However, logic is still relevant here, for numbers are subject to the principle of identity, a principle that holds of terms generally.

In this account of arithmetic, Vollenhoven is indebted to the intuitionistic mathematicians, Henri Poincaré (1854-1912) and L.E.J. Brouwer (1881-1966). Each is discussed in a separate section of the dissertation.[16] These men defended the idea that mathematics is at bottom a matter of human mental construction. Accordingly, their point of view

---

13 Not that Vollenhoven was unacquainted with Peano's work. He criticises him for his 'formalism', namely holding deduction to be the only suitable method of mathematics, and not seeking an explanation for the notion of number (cf. 1918a: 229-230). The five axioms are: (i) 1 is a number; (ii) the successor of any number is a number; (iii) no two numbers have the same successor; (iv) 1 is not the successor of any number; (v) the principle of complete induction. There are three 'primitive terms' here: 'one', 'successor (of)', and 'number'. For an introductory discussion of this system, cf. Chapter 1, "The Series of Natural Numbers", of Russell 1919.

14 Apposite is: "[n]umber is not a thing or a symbol but a series creation of the mind [*geest*], which as such has no determinate scope, but [which series] is determined only comprehensively by the principle of complete induction" (1918a: 157).

15 Vollenhoven states: "We also distinguish mathematics of second and first order and apply this in arithmetic. That of the second order is the science of numbers, the theory of their properties, etc. That of the first [order] is not a science, but it is what is given in the second [order], namely the act of counting" (1918a: 413). Counting is described psychologically (cf. footnote 20 below), but, in the interest of anti-psychologism, counting is in turn accounted for in a way that grounds the three primitive notions of arithmetic in a metaphysical and objective intuitionist context (à la a *Gegenstandstheorie*).

16 Both sections are in chapter IV, "The critical part"; section 15 is on Henri Poincaré (pp. 352-384) and section 16 on L.E.J. Brouwer (pp. 385-402). Cf. footnote 37 for an overview of the dissertation.

is finitistic, allowing only the so-called 'potential infinite'—the infinite as an unending series of finite objects—a place in mathematics, not the notion of the 'actual (or completed) infinite'. Georg Cantor (1845-1918) had incorporated the notion of the actual infinite in his theory of transfinite numbers, a theory much contested at the beginning of the twentieth century by both mathematicians and philosophers.[17] The unending series of the natural numbers, each member of which is finite, is an exemplary basis for mathematical construction. The series of the natural numbers itself is accounted for in terms of repetition or successive recurrence. By the repeated addition of 1, after having begun with 1, every natural number can be reached. The principle of complete induction seizes on this possibility. For Poincaré and Brouwer the principle is intuitively compelling, and in fact this motivates the appeal to an intuition. The principle of induction, says Poincaré,

> is only the affirmation of the power of the mind which knows it can conceive of the indefinite repetition of the same act, when the act is once possible. The mind has a direct intuition of this power, and experiment can only be for it an opportunity of using it, and thereby of becoming conscious of it.[18]

Brouwer, somewhat more nuanced, includes the notion of time and synthesis (two-oneness). He states:

> This neo-intuitionism [of Brouwer's own approach; A.T.] considers the falling apart of moments of life into qualitatively different parts, to be reunited only while remaining separated by time, as the fundamental phenomenon of the human intellect, passing by abstracting from its emotional content into the fundamental phenomenon of mathematical thinking, the intuition of the bare two-oneness. This intuition of two-oneness, the basal intuition of mathematics, creates not only the numbers one and two, but also all finite ordinal numbers, inasmuch as one of the elements of the two-oneness may be thought of as a new two-oneness, which process may be repeated indefinitely. . . .[19]

Vollenhoven accepts these statements insofar as they legitimately belong to the foundation of mathematics, legitimately, in the sense that these statements indicate what 'first order arithmetic' is about. But what is the intuition? What about the synthesis of this intuitive bi-unity? And

---

17   Vollenhoven also devotes a section to the discussion of Cantor's work; cf. Section 8. "The revival of the doctrine of the actual infinite", pp. 175-188.

18   Cf. Poincaré 1902: 13.

19   From L.E.J. Brouwer's inaugural address, Brouwer 1912: 69. Brouwer developed his ideas against the background of western mysticism. He gives a sampling of this in Brouwer 1905. Vollenhoven quotes a closely similar statement of Brouwer from the latter's dissertation, Brouwer 1907; cf. Vollenhoven 1918a: 387. Cf. also footnote 103 below.

how is the intra-mental act of repetition and its temporal character to be understood? The intuition is a priori and synthetic.[20] Immanuel Kant (1724-1804), who himself initiated intuitionism in mathematics, spoke of (mathematical) *judgments* as being synthetic a priori; but for both Poincaré and Brouwer it is the *intra-mental act* itself that is said to be synthetic and a priori. Can Kant still be called upon as a proponent of early twentieth century intuitionism? Vollenhoven brings the full weight of philosophical analysis to bear upon these sorts of questions, delving deep into epistemology and metaphysics. But before we follow suit, there is also geometry to consider.

B. Geometry

Geometry was long identified with the famous work of Euclid, and his view—Euclidean geometry—was long held to be the science that revealed the exclusive truth about space. But from about the mid-nineteenth century, alternative geometries were found to be possible. Typical of Euclidean geometry is the parallel postulate, which says (in one of its versions) that, given a line and a point not on the line, one and only one line can be drawn through the point that is parallel to the given line. Non-Euclidean geometries replace the parallel postulate either with the postulate of there not being any such line, for every line through the given point intersects the given line, or the postulate of there being more than one distinct line parallel to the given line. In these alternative cases, space is said either to shrink or to stretch respectively as one moves away from a given position. In the first case space is convex-like, having a 'positive constant measure of curvature', while in the second case space is concave-like, with a 'negative constant measure of curvature'. Euclidean space has zero measure of curvature, thus it is said to be 'flat'. These different 'measures of curvature', being constant and mutually exclusive, ensure that the respective geometries are also mutually exclusive. But, besides these geometries, there are also geometries that are more general than either Euclidean or non-Euclidean geometries, in that they have no quantitative notions, thus 'measure of curvature' is not a relevant

---

20   Vollenhoven formulates counting as follows: "Accordingly counting takes place through the analytical intuition; [the fact] that we count we *know* by means of the concrete intuition which makes us aware of this *possession* of the analysing intuition. Also the certainty we have that this distinction can be repeated continually by treating every duality as unity (Brouwer) and that this *possibility* is unending; this [certainty] we have through being aware of the human spirit's power it possesses in this matter (Poincaré), hence in virtue of concrete intuition" (1918a: 414). Vollenhoven here mentions two forms of intuition, the concrete and analytical, of what turns out to be a total of three, the third being the metaphysical intuition. This is discussed below.

notion here. These non-quantitative geometries, for example projective and descriptive geometry, lack a 'metric function'. The most qualitative geometry of all is topology, known at the beginning of the 20th century as '*analysis situs*' (analysis of situation) (cf. 1918a: 146).[21]

The unifying idea of geometry that arose in the late nineteenth century is that of 'the group of transformations'. A geometry does not study space sec, as if it were an object in its own right, but it studies the behaviour of figures in space when 'moved about'.[22] Depending on the permitted movement—the technical term is 'transformation'[23]—a specific geometry studies those properties of spatial figures that remain invariant under the application of the transformation rules in question. In Euclidean geometry the size and shape of figures remain unchanged when subject to change of position, rotation or reflection, while in projective geometry shape and angles change but the straightness of a line remains unaffected. In topology nothing related to size or shape remains invariant, but features such as the interior of a figure, connectedness, dimensionality, and the like do remain invariant. Each geometry elucidates certain select features of space, but no geometry has a privileged position regarding the study of space as such.

Vollenhoven is aware of and assumes these developments in geometry. In order to specify his interest in these matters one other development must be mentioned. The question as to the 'truth of space' was

---

21   Vollenhoven refers, incorrectly, to descriptive geometry and *analysis situs* as cases of non-Euclidean geometry (1918a: 143). Mathematicians speak of Euclidean and non-Euclidean geometry only when geometry includes a metric (or distance) function. It is on account of the metric function being chosen differently for Euclidean and non-Euclidean geometries mutually that these geometries exclude each other. Descriptive geometry, projective geometry and topology are more general geometries, in the sense that they study properties that are logically prior to metrical properties, hence they are neither Euclidean nor non-Euclidean and treat of features common to both Euclidean and non-Euclidean geometry alike.

22   When in Euclidean geometry a proof of the congruence of two figures, say two triangles, is given, the net effect is as if one had moved one of the triangles and laid it on top of the other to demonstrate their fit. Geometries with 'constant measure of curvature' (positive, negative or zero) are the only ones in which figures can be 'moved about' without distortion. Cf. the work of D. O'Shea, O'Shea 2007, which contains a very accessible account of Euclidean and non-Euclidean geometries.

23   The transformations in question must form a 'group'. This is an algebraic term that limits the kind of transformations permitted. The group structure requires that (i) if two transformations are executed in sequence, there is a transformation that performs both in one, (ii) the order in which transformations are applied is irrelevant, (iii) there is an identity transformation, which leaves everything as is, and (iv) every transformation has an inverse. Under these rules a set of elements (transformations) is said to form a group.

made more problematic through the development of the arithmetization of geometry. Descartes had initiated analytic geometry, in which he showed how a geometrical structure could be expressed in terms of algebraic equations, which could be solved numerically. As long as there was no sufficiently developed number concept that could do justice to 'irrational numbers', such as $\sqrt{2}$ (which represents the length of the hypotenuse of a right-angled triangle with sides of unit length) the truth of geometry could not be considered supplanted by its arithmetization. But the late nineteenth century also saw the development of the real number concept (Richard Dedekind, Karl Weierstrass, Leopold Kronecker), which essentially removed this last barrier. The net effect is that one does not need to accept a distinctly geometrical truth, for every geometrical statement can be 'translated' into the discourse of algebra and the fully developed real number concept (including set theory). Geometry is no more true or consistent than algebra and number theory. In other words, this arithmetization of geometry obviates the need to postulate something like an intuition of space, at least for mathematical purposes.

In this question of space and geometry Vollenhoven took a stand that was also informed by the intuitionists, Poincaré and Brouwer. Brouwer essentially accepted the arithmetization of geometry, except that the real number concept (along with much of higher analysis) had to be reformulated in terms of constructive procedures. Vollenhoven in turn accepts this too. He states that the *general validity* of geometrical statements is offered indirectly by arithmetical statements (1918a: 19, 386-387). But this does not pre-empt for him the philosophical importance of the discussion of the nature of space in its own right, for which Poincaré provides the lead.

Poincaré discussed space and geometry in a way that applied and illustrated the idea of a group to the movements of solid bodies in conjunction with the human body. We all learn to compensate for the movement of objects by a bodily movement that restores the original relative position of the object and our body. If a body is deformed, we learn to analyse this into partial deformations, each of which we could compensate for in terms of our own body. "*If, then, there were no solid bodies in nature there would be no geometry*",[24] and the laws that we set-up to account for the phenomena of displacements are the object of geometry.[25] If there were beings with a different bodily structure, say, their bodies

---

24   Poincaré 1902: 61. Poincaré is here referring to the empirical origin of geometry, where geometrical figures are identified as properties of more or less unchanging bodies.
25   *Ibid.*, p. 63.

changed in certain ways as they moved, then they would formulate a different geometry, for the account of these displacement phenomena would call for other laws than we (human beings) draw up in accordance with our experience. No one geometry in its own right is to be preferred above another. What decides our preference is convenience and convention in the face of our factual or biological make-up. Our bodily make-up in its psycho-physical organization makes three-dimensional Euclidean geometry convenient for us. This convenience is for Poincaré a contingent result of human evolution (cf. 1918a: 378).

Vollenhoven accepts the link of space and geometry to the human psycho-physical organization. But he feels strongly obliged to differ from Poincaré's interpretation of it. First of all, if the arithmetization of geometry allows us to confer *general validity* to geometry in virtue of the general a priori validity of arithmetical systems, then there must be something a priori to geometry as well. Of course, Poincaré never denied this. Experience may play a role in the genesis of geometry, he said, but its validity is not dependent on there being natural solids as facts. Scientific geometry works with abstract and ideal figures, therefore the idea of a 'group' is also a general concept.[26]

But secondly, the combination of this a priori validity with the psycho-physical account of the genesis of geometry is not without its problems. If, in virtue of our psycho-physical organization, three-dimensional Euclidean geometry is convenient, that convenience must have a basis. We need to appeal to a more fixed—for Vollenhoven even principled—connection between *psyche* and *soma* that explains how our sensibility is integral to our bodily make-up. Evolution offers no explanation here. It merely points to the outcome of the organization as the interplay of many environmental factors. Poincaré's acknowledgement that the concept of group is a priori does not solve the problem. For this notion, he says, "is imposed on us not as a form of our sensitiveness [*sic*], but as a form of our understanding; only, from among all possible groups, we must choose one that will be the *standard*, so to speak, to which we shall refer natural phenomena".[27] Poincaré does not see an intimate connection between the group notion and the human psycho-physical organization as such, hence the standard geometry we choose in application to the study of nature remains entirely arbitrary.

---

26   Poincaré states: "The concept of these ideal bodies is entirely mental, and experiment is but the opportunity which enables us to reach the idea. The object of geometry is the study of a particular 'group'; but the general concept of group pre-exists in our minds, at least potentially"; *op. cit.* , p. 70.

27   *Ibid.*, p. 70.

The reference to 'form of sensitiveness' brings the Kantian notion of space, as 'form of sensibility', into the picture (presumably that is what is meant here). Space, according to Kant, is the side-by-side integrative factor of phenomenal givens (sense-data), a factor that is intrinsic to the human receptive capacity. In that sense space is part and parcel of the human psycho-physical organization. Vollenhoven is more Kantian than Poincaré in this regard, for he (Vollenhoven) *does* regard space as a form of sensibility. For him this warrants the acceptance of an a priori feature in the region of the psycho-physical, quite apart from any geometrical determination. For space, in this sense, allows us to *localize* sense-data within a spatial continuum. But human bodies are themselves included in this continuum and participate in it. If we abstract the body from it, the very possibility of receptivity to sense-data is eliminated. So if, with Poincaré, one agrees that the three-dimensional Euclidean characterization of this localization continuum is (most) convenient, then this convenience must say something about the character of the psycho-physical connection itself. The convenience must be an effect of the nature of the psycho-physical connection, allowing us to maintain that our preferred standard is necessarily three-dimensional and Euclidean.[28]

So, as in arithmetic, there is also a synthetic a priori relevant to geometry that Vollenhoven appeals to. The two are distinguished as a priori of *first and second rank*, respectively. The difference in rank marks the intra-mental provenance of the a priori of arithmetic over against the

---

28 Cf. 1918a: 378-379. It is important to keep in mind that this standard concerns 'first order mathematics' (a term Brouwer used), which is the domain of construction, not that of the scientific development of geometry which, like second order arithmetic, concerns statements and proofs. Vollenhoven agrees that there is no preferred second order geometry, for each geometry operates in terms of its own 'group of transformations'. Kant, who preceded the development of non-Euclidean geometries, held that Euclidean geometry reveals the real structure of space, of which the human form of sensibility is a condition. Vollenhoven acknowledges that this view is superseded by nineteenth century developments. But he retains the Euclidean characterization of the (first order) human spatial operations (1918a: 394). Its focus concerns localization. This has both spatial and temporal features, hence the temporal as well as the spatial forms of sensibility are brought to bear. Despite this apology on my part, I still think that there is something very dogmatic in Vollenhoven's preference for Euclid. Vollenhoven maintains that it is theistic to interpret the human psycho-physical organization as Euclidean, this being a general feature of the synthesis of body and soul, holding in virtue of creation (1918a: 379). In the mid-1920s, he revises his view of body and soul, in consequence of which sensibility becomes a psychological notion, based on the 'psychical function' of a human being, while 'soul' is taken to be a holistic directional notion, relevant to the whole human Self. The 'psycho-physical' is then understood to be a subsidiary feature of the human being, and space is no longer dependent on this feature.

psycho-somatic context of that of geometry.[29] Thus, though Poincaré and Brouwer help Vollenhoven define the problem of space, he feels compelled to seek an alternative solution, a solution, as we shall see, that calls for the distinction between phenomena and metaphysical substances.

C. A partial and qualified Kantianism

Vollenhoven avails himself of Kant's account of "forms of sensibility" to formulate his views as to space and geometry. But there are also certain differences. In his appeal to Kant there is an immediate occasion for confusion. Kant speaks of intuition when he appeals to space and time as forms of sensibility, while Vollenhoven uses 'intuition' in *contradistinction* to forms of sensibility. Forms of sensibility in Kant are peculiar in that, as forms, they have an organizing or determining role in connection with the human reception of sense-data. Their non-empirical status attests to their a priori character, and their determining or conditioning role gives them a transcendental meaning relevant for the phenomenal order. Thus the representation of a form of sensibility involves a peculiar awareness (as concerning something not empirical but transcendental), and it is this awareness that Kant calls 'pure intuition'.[30] For him intuitions, including the pure ones, always pertain to the phenomenal order of sensibility. Kant appeals to the intuition of time to justify the synthetic a priori validity of statements of arithmetic—the intuition of time justifies the mental operation of successive addition / subtraction as indicated by the arithmetic statement—while the intuition of space similarly justifies the synthetic a priori validity of geometrical statements—which attribute simultaneous (spatially represented) properties to geometrical figures. This double intuition serves as the backdrop for the 'mental work' involved in understanding mathematical validity transcendentally, indeed, it provides the *de jure* validity of mathematical statements. The close analogy between arithmetical and geometrical statements in this regard in Kant allows the account of their validity to be included in one doctrine of the transcendental aesthetic.

Vollenhoven's distinction of rank between the a priori of arithmetic and that of geometry does not fit this Kantian mould. The difference between the intra-mental and the psycho-physical is too pronounced to see them in correlation. On several counts the difference with Kant is

---

29 Consider: "[T]he apriority of arithmetic is of a higher rank than that of geometry and kinematics; we can distinguish them as intuition and form of sensibility" (1918a: 417).

30 Cf. Kant 1998: 156 (A21/B35).

reinforced. In the first place, though Vollenhoven does speak of *Anschauungsformen* and their two kinds, time and space, he does not link arithmetic to time taken in this sense. In fact he says little about time as form of sensibility, but from what he does say it is clear that it is *kinematics* that he deems appropriate here (1918a: 433-434). Time as form of sensibility—it too is seated in the human psycho-physical organization—is for him a condition of motion.[31]

In the second place, Kant's linking of time to arithmetic (this would be Vollenhoven's second order arithmetic) is modified in important ways by Vollenhoven. Arithmetical statements must, as do all judgments, comply with the principle of contradiction. Their synthetic character derives from their including, as given data, the sequence of the natural numbers, i.e. first order arithmetic. To *this* (first order) arithmetic Vollenhoven links a much more intimate sense of time than that of time as form of sensibility, namely the time of *endurance in successive, currently undergoing moments of experience*. (The echo of Henri Bergson's *durée* here is not coincidental.) Vollenhoven takes intuitionists, such as Augustine and Kant, to task for failing to distinguish properly between 'time as succession' and 'time as form of sensibility'. Augustine failed to recognize the latter and Kant merged succession with form of sensibility (1918a: 134).[32]

Then, thirdly, Vollenhoven makes the explicit choice of reserving the term 'intuition' to describe the most primal facets of intra-mental awareness, which is the locus of succession and number (first order arithmetic).

---

31 Space and time are the kinematic conditions of motion in Vollenhoven. Given the transcendental roles of time and space as forms of sensibility in Kant, these forms also represent space and time as absolute. Newton spoke of absolute space and absolute time as if they are the *sensorium Dei*, which in Kant become the *sensorium humanum*. But because Vollenhoven does not argue transcendentally, he can separate the role of space and time, as forms of sensibility, from that of their stature as absolutes. The result is that he sees absolute space and time as limits that science approaches in its attempts to localize things spatially and temporally. The forms of sensibility are conditions of localization, namely conditions of the cognitive act (*kendaad*) of localization, relative to the human body, in which "the human being strives in the direction of the limit of absolute space [and time]" (1918a: 131). Absolute space and time in themselves, and when not taken to be limitative but as absolute boundaries, entail the self-contradictory notion of 'completed infinity' (as completed endlessness). An 'absolute boundary' is in this context also self-contradictory. By taking absolute space and time to be limitative notions, and in correlation with space and time as conditions of sensibility, the impending contradictions are averted (cf. 1918a: 300, also p. 135).

32 Consider the following summary statement: "But the connection of arithmetic and time is not parallel to that of geometry and space. Geometry and kinematics are the sciences of space and time, respectively. However arithmetic is the science of *succession*" (1918a: 348).

With this use of 'intuition' it follows that there is a deep difference between the number sequence of first order arithmetic and spatio-temporal localization. The former is based on inner perception. Here we are aware of intra-mental change. But the locus of localization is in the psycho-physical organization, which can at best only be sensed. Accordingly, he deems it unsuitable to speak of an intuition of space, and he criticises Pascal for having defended the relevance of such an intuition (cf. 1918a: 104). (By implication he also does not accept an intuition of the time factor at this level, relevant for kinematics.) In connection with space we must make do with the outer perception of bodies, to which the human body also belongs. This is why Vollenhoven also speaks of a difference in rank of the two kinds of a priori: "the apriority of arithmetic is of a higher rank than that of geometry and kinematics; we can distinguish them as intuition and form of sensibility" (1918a: 417).[33]

So the two kinds of a priori, pertaining to mentality and sensibility, respectively, have little in common. However, what they do have in common is that both have a subjective and an objective moment. Inner perception reveals the presence of mental acts and content, which shift and change to be sure, but the presence of which is confirmed by self-consciousness (1918a: 72). Outer perception reveals phenomena as the appearing of things. But this involves a given objectivity in correlation with the forms of sensibility on the side of the sensible subject. The mathematical synthetic a priori finds its direct application in these two kinds of perception.

The cardinal importance of the mathematical synthetic a priori is that it is the most primal indication of the subjective and the objective 'coming together'. Knowledge, in Vollenhoven, involves the subjective 'working over' of the objective given. To that end the subjective moment must realize an integration—a 'two-oneness'—with respect to the objective data. Its possibility with respect to mentality is attested to by the synthetic a priori of arithmetic, the intuition of number; the synthetic a priori of geometry lies in the psycho-physically sensed possibility of spatial-temporal localization.

The two sides of the subjective and the objective are reflected in every judgment. That is to say, Vollenhoven maintains that every scientific statement has a formal and a material moment. The formal reflects

---

33   In order to avoid confusion between Vollenhoven's and Kant's uses, I use "forms of sensibility" as translation of *Anschauungsformen*, not "forms of intuition". Clearly, both are appropriate in light of Kant's meaning. Vollenhoven avails himself of the Dutch "aanschouwingsvormen", which leaves the relationship to the use of "intuition" (the Dutch is "intuïtie") linguistically undecided, hence capable of distinct use.

the moment of the human ordering of thought, the material reflects the given (1918a: 434-437). The most empirical of statements is never without the human touch, just as the most abstract statements of arithmetic are not without the content of intuition (1918a: 72). Even first order arithmetic, which 'constructs' prior to making any statements, has its objectivity, *viz.* the 'reality of succession', of which we are intuitively aware in inner perception. Hence mathematical knowledge is not only important in its own right, but its own possibility also provides the foundation of the possibility of (natural) scientific knowledge generally.

But this clarification of the mathematical a priori appeals to a pronounced view of science, which is not universally accepted in all traditions of science. This topic needs to be discussed in its own right, as one belonging to the philosophy of science. In doing so, new features will be broached in Vollenhoven's account and defence of intuitionism. A definitive statement regarding Vollenhoven's account of number and space depends on the elucidation of knowledge and intuition respectively, and hence needs to be provisionally tabled. We resume the discussion by focussing first on prime features of the philosophy of science. That discussion will also introduce one of the props of Vollenhoven's theism.

IV. THE NODAL POINTS OF (THEISTIC) INTUITIONISM

Vollenhoven's early understanding of philosophy itself already had strong leanings towards philosophy of science. Philosophy for the young Vollenhoven comports with that species of modernism that limits philosophy to the topic and interest of knowledge. Its primary focus lies with problems concerning the demarcation and the relations between the sciences. Thus Vollenhoven takes the importance of a philosophical problem to lie in "questions as to values, boundaries and relations between the distinct sciences mutually" (1918a: 2). This is in line with positivism's 'encyclopaedia of the sciences' and neo-Kantianism's 'derivation of the sciences', though Vollenhoven has his own view as to the place of the sciences in philosophy.

Be that as it may, it was as philosopher that Vollenhoven chose to formulate the nature of his investigations. He expresses the problem of his investigations in terms of two primary relations that mathematics has to other disciplines, namely to logic and to physics. Mathematics has a *rigorously logical* structure. This means that the main principles of logic (identity, contradiction and excluded middle) are relevant for mathematics. On the other hand, mathematics is also *generally applicable*, which makes it an ideal instrument for physics. "In this way the chief questions posed themselves: what is the relation of mathematics to logic and what is the relation to physics?" (1918a: 2).

Throughout the dissertation, there are three terms that constantly recur in the discussion of these two main questions: *norm*, '*ratio*' and '*empirie*'. These terms signal the relevance of the "normative, rational and empirical elements" (1918a: 410), respectively, of scientific knowledge. In their interplay these terms together delineate a very important facet of intuitionism, and their schema also provides critical edge to the opposition of alternative views. The three terms are best seen in the following arrangement:

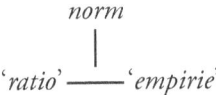

The *normative* element (*norm*) appeals to objective logical norms. Logic is indeed formal for Vollenhoven, but this needs to be taken in a sense that is over and above the factual concern of consistency of discourse, the latter being a rational feature. He takes the said logical principles to be norms that regulate and guide the knowing subject in its treatment of content of thought.[34] The *rational* element (*ratio*) pertains to the activity of thinking as such. This activity takes place in 'mental acts'— Vollenhoven speaks of "psychical acts"—and it yields content appropriate to these acts. This cognition and its content are basically of three kinds: (sense-)awareness, recollection and representation. Cognition is only properly cognitive when norms regulate the psychical acts on which cognition is based. In this sense Vollenhoven *combats* psychologism, which has no place for norms. Finally there is the *empirical* element (*empirie*). This is "the given" that stands in opposition to thought and to mental acts in general. It is what is other than thought, foreign to thought (*het denkvreemde*). In a generic sense, Vollenhoven speaks of 'being' in this regard, but more often it is just *the given*. The given consists of 'things' in

---

34 In light of the subject matter of the dissertation, the norms in question are for the most part limited to logical norms required for the sciences. But Vollenhoven's view at the time was broader. In a 1919 manuscript on pedagogy, he speaks of norms for "the areas of science, morality and art". Quoted in Kok 1992: 17. Also, in a letter to the theologian, F.W. Grosheide, dated 16 November 1921, Vollenhoven states: "logic is, together with ethics, aesthetics etc., precisely as science of norms distinguished from the explicative [i.e. descriptive; A.T.] sciences . . ."; cf. Vollenhoven 16-11-1921. Norms may be said to pertain to a 'domain of validity'. In another manuscript of 1921 Vollenhoven asserts: "But the norm as such differs from all that exists. Norms have their own mode of being. They hold ["gelden"; i.e. have validity]"; cf. Kok 1992: 21. Viewing norms—often taken as objective values—as populating a distinct realm is typical of the Baden or Southwest German school of neo-Kantianism.

interaction, or in 'relations' in which things stand through their interactions. Though foreign to thought, things are knowable in virtue of the self-revelation by which they 'give' themselves as real phenomena. So in a summarizing nutshell: *knowledge* of the given arises when thought (the rational element) succeeds in *knowing* the given (the empirical element) under the *guidance* of norms and ideals (the normative element).[35]

In the course of our subsequent discussion various distinct epistemological features of this view of knowledge will come to light. At this point we limit our discussion to mathematics and its general intuitionistic form. The characteristic feature of mathematical intuitionism is its acknowledgement of the *synthetic a priori*. Mathematics as such has no direct truck with anything empirical. In that sense the application of mathematics to physics, or to material content in general, is a secondary problem. As to the formal side, the a priori feature of mathematics focuses on synthesis, not analysis. If it were only a matter of analysis, the a priori would limit mathematics to (logically) formal statements (tautologies and contradictions), as in logical positivism. So Vollenhoven denies a unity of mathematics and physics on the one hand and also of mathematics and logic on the other (cf. 1918a: 9).

Returning to the general characterization of knowledge and its three features, there is a characteristic a priori feature here, when Vollenhoven's insists that the rational feature of thought needs norms in order to adjudicate between a successful coming to know and a possible failure (error). In other words the "intra-mental" quality of knowing, in which thought in its striving to come to know operates, would leave the *sense of legitimacy* cliff-hanging if divorced from any subjection to norms. So there is a 'synthesis' here between the knowing subject and the norms that are sensed as being 'necessary', not necessary in a formal sense, but as indispensable to warrant the legitimacy and the need of thought to be rightly directed. It is a matter of grounding certainty. "[Apodictic certainty] exists in one's awareness, and to declare this awareness to be *legitimate* one needs to accept the possibility of *synthetic* judgments *a priori*. If they are to be worthy of the name [of "synthetic a priori"] . . . then their certainty must be immediate, intuitive, which is why we refer to this approach [*richting*] as *intuitionism*" (1918a: 9).

We add here two points, to be discussed more thoroughly later. First, the more specific qualification of *theistic* intuitionism is motivated

---

35   Consider: "the subject of knowing is a function [i.e. activity of thought; A.T.] of the Self that strives to know and to that end subjects itself to the norms of logic; the object of knowing is a function of the thing outside of me, its appearing, its revelation to me or effect on me" (1918a: 228-229).

by the question as to the source of norms. The answer is that all norms, ideals, and the like have a divine origin: "there are no norms other than divine ones" (1918a: 175).

Secondly, only after highlighting some of the inner workings of the intra-mental can we be more specific about the synthetic a priori that Vollenhoven accepts for mathematics. At this point it is important to realize that the appeal to an intuition arises from a general epistemological consideration, or, as we will come to call it, a 'metalogical' feature of validity, not a need that is relevant only to mathematics, as in Kant. Every judgment, for Vollenhoven, is a synthesis, for each has a formal and a material element, whereby the material element is absorbed by the formal element in a way that is normative. It is in reckoning with normative validity that "*all* forms of judgment are modifications of the synthetic a priori" (1918a: 435). Hence the appeal to an intuition here is a general one. The synthetic a priori that is specific to mathematics has more distinct features in connection with the difference between first and second order mathematics (construction versus statement) and the difference in rank between arithmetic and geometry.

Returning now to the specific discussion of the methodology of mathematics in Vollenhoven, that discussion branches out in two directions. On the one hand he proceeds with a critical discussion in which he confronts his understanding of mathematical intuitionism with alternative approaches; on the other hand, he sounds out his own intuitionism for its epistemological and metaphysical assumptions. An important motive for this latter 'sounding out' lies in the fact that fellow intuitionists—Poincaré and Brouwer—are not *theistic* intuitionists (in the sense that they do not appeal to norms). Thus theistic intuitionism needs to be discussed in a way that will reveal its foundations in epistemology and metaphysics. It is only in this intrinsic 'sounding out' that the notion of the intuition becomes fully explicit. We shall discuss each of these two branches in turn and continue first with the methodological discussion.

A. Intuitionism, formalism, empiricism

The understanding of intuitionism in the theistic perspective on the interplay of the three elements—the normative, the rational and the empirical—has a critical edge in the confrontation with alternative, in particular with non-theistic views. No doubt the appeal to the normative element is most vulnerable here. Not that non-theists would reject it outright, but its *separate* position as a third element, beside the rational and the empirical, is perhaps most readily contestable, certainly for the 'modern mind'. When this is indeed contested, several consequences result.

(i) When the normative element is *denied* its distinct position, its role of regulating the synthesis between the rational and the empirical is, practically speaking, annulled. This calls for a different view of knowledge, in the sense of requiring an alternative view as to the connection of the subjective and the objective. Either knowledge is taken to be realized when (in a primarily subjective orientation) thought is said to *picture the facts* or when (in case the objective predominates) thought merely *reacts to stimuli*. "Two theories of knowledge stand in opposition here: picture theory or reaction" (1918a: 282). The former view is that of *rationalism* (or *conceptualism*; Vollenhoven also speaks of *parallelism* in this regard), the latter view is *empiricism*.

(ii) Presumably the normative element—or whatever the compulsive moment is that is retained—could also be *merged* with either the rational or the empirical elements. The resulting view of logic will then no longer be distinctly normative. When the rational element is central to logic, logic will be primarily *deductive* and its contribution to knowledge limited to the *analytic a priori*. But when the empirical element dominates, logic will be *inductive* and its contribution to knowledge primarily *synthetic a posteriori* (1918a: 8).

(iii) Furthermore, an uneven polarity is set up between the two poles of the rational and the empirical. The merging of the normative element with either pole can be taken as justifying the *dominance* of the chosen pole over the other pole (1918a: 72). This results in reductionisms. Rationalism will tend to see the given as a construction of its own making. Vollenhoven calls this view *psycho-monism*. Empiricism tends to regard the mind as an epiphenomenon. Vollenhoven calls this view *materialism*. Generically, each view is *monistic*. In contrast, theism is said to be *dualistic* (1918a: 8).

In the above discussion the methodological context of Vollenhoven's early thought comes clearly into view. Theism is a 'dualistic standpoint' in which the normative element is recognized and acknowledged to be distinct from the rational and the empirical elements. This calls for a factor—the intuition—that justifies the possibility of the synthesis of the rational and empirical elements.[36] The implication of this for mathematics is that it should exemplify the connection of the rational and the empirical, without identification with either, and of course remaining distinct from (normative) logic as well. The essence of mathematics is seated in

---

36 Consider: "If however intuitionism cannot bind *ratio* and *empirie*, then it has lost its birthright and right to exist" (1918a: 52).

the *synthetic a priori*, which calls for an intuitive certainty, such as mathematical intuitionism banks on. But, as already stated, not all mathematical intuitionists are theists in the sense of being properly dualistic, as indeed neither Poincaré nor Brouwer was. Their intuitionistic mathematics is not at fault—Vollenhoven accepts their mathematical work as basically adequate, also in its relation to logic and physics—rather it is the philosophical underpinning and understanding of their work that calls for critical revision.

It is the 'monistic standpoints', in which the normative element is reduced to and merged with either the rational or the empirical element, represented in psycho-monism and materialism respectively, that call for more thorough criticism. The implications for mathematics is that any functional intuition will be denied as irrelevant. For psycho-monism mathematics is merged with logic, a logic itself reduced to matters of consistency and deduction. Vollenhoven calls this mathematical orientation *formalism*, and it is a distinct historical tradition in mathematics. On the other hand materialism identifies mathematics with the empirical given and inductive research. This is represented by the school of *empiricism* in mathematics. Vollenhoven wishes to demonstrate that these three approaches to mathematics, *viz.* intuitionism, formalism and empiricism, are "direct offshoots" of theism, psycho-monism and materialism, respectively, taken as metaphysical systems (1918a: 3). To that end, history is called upon—the history of philosophy and of mathematics—to "lead" the demonstration (1918a: 3). However, we must leave these historical discussions, often impressively rich in conceptual detail, for what they are and concentrate on the thematic side of Vollenhoven's work.[37]

---

37 It is instructive at this point to report on the structure of Vollenhoven's dissertation. The text consists of a short introduction and five chapters. The *first chapter* is "The constructive part". Here Vollenhoven previews the solutions of the four major problems: (i) mathematics' relation to logic as concerns necessity; (ii) mathematics' relation to physics as concerns generality; (iii) number and the relevance of time, and (iv) space. The *second chapter* is called "The historical part". In its three sections he discusses empiricism, formalism and intuitionism, respectively, from early classical times till the middle of the nineteenth century. In the section on empiricism there are discussions on Democritus, Epicurus, P. Gassendi, F. Bacon, J. Locke, J. d'Alembert, A. Comte and J.S. Mill; in that of formalism: Pythagorians, Heraclitus, Eleatics, Zeno, Sophists, Stoa, Indian and Arabian thought, Scholasticism, R. Lullus, F. Toletus, T. Hobbes, B. Spinoza, N. Malebranche, G. Berkeley, (the earlier) G.W. Leibniz, D. Hume; and in intuitionism we find: Socrates, Plato, Aristotle, Euclid, A. Augustine, Thomism and the Victorines, G. Galilei, R. Descartes, B. Pascal, (the later) G.W. Leibniz, I. Newton and I. Kant. The *third chapter* is entitled "The referential part" and discusses, in five sections, innovations that affected mathematics in the second half of the nineteenth century: non-Euclidean geometry, the logic of relations, "*Gegenstandstheorie*", the revival of the doctrine of actual

B. Monism and dualism

The terms monism and dualism play an important role in Vollenhoven's entire thinking. We need to be clear as to their use in his early thought.

The context of their introduction in the early work is methodological. Dualistic thought, in its theistic expression or as "Christian philosophy", distinguishes between "moral freedom" and "natural necessity" (1918a: 3). In other words, it accepts the possibility of freedom without which deference to anything normative would be meaningless, over against natural necessity, which in itself is not to be denied.[38] Monistic thought seeks to make do with only the natural realm. Monism, as here understood, is essentially reductionist, in virtue of which monism is also one-sided in most of the polarities it confronts, as indicated above.[39] Dualism is not reductionist. But Vollenhoven throws interesting light on his methodological dualism in a summary statement with which his final chapter begins. He states:

> *Monism* denies the unique nature of mathematical knowledge and includes it either with the natural sciences or with logic. Dualism, too, strives for unity. But it considers the opposition *ratio-empirie* to be too sharp to reduce the one to the other. Hence, it must look for unity in a common root: namely, in the synthetic a priori – this term taken in its broadest sense. (1918a: 403)

This 'common root' of the rational and the empirical elements is intriguing. It suggests a prior unity, not merely a unity in virtue of the rational

---

infinity, and the arithmetization of geometry. The *fourth chapter* is "The critical part". Empiricism, formalism and intuitionism are again discussed, but now in connection with (early twentieth century) contemporary authors. Its sections are "the newer empiricism": C.F. Gauss, P.I. Lobachevski, G.F.B. Riemann and M. Pasch; "the newer formalism": H. von Helmholtz, E. Schröder, G. Frege, logicism and the Marburg school, and separate sections on G. Mannoury and B. Russell; finally "the newer intuitionism": B. Bolzano, H. Lotze and H. Bergson, and separate sections on H. Poincaré and L.E.J. Brouwer. The *fifth* and *final* chapter is "The thetical part". Here Vollenhoven ties together the loose ends that have accrued in the previous discussions in a statement of his 'theistic intuitionism'. John H. Kok reprinted the original text of this final chapter, along with a translation, in Appendix I of Kok 1992: 308-353.

38   I believe that this essentially Kantian characteristic of theism's dualism is central to it, since it pertains to norms directly. Other features of dualism, such as "the principled distinguishing between human sciences and natural sciences, between rule of thought and natural law, between norm and fact" (1918a: 2) are more subsidiary.

39   This leads among other things to unsatisfactory responses to error. For empiricism error is simply a mistake in need of correction. Error in formalism is an infelicitous portrayal of facts, which a revised formulation can ease, in the sense of being more useful in a biological sense. The critical theist, distinguishing as he/she does between norm and (natural) law, will distinguish between error as anti-normative and error as mistake. Cf. 1918a: 10-11.

and the empirical elements coming into a synthesis, which is effectuated in knowledge, but a prior unity making knowledge possible. Let us look at other statements.

In speaking of dualism, a Cartesian dualism—of body and soul, matter and consciousness (in their usual interpretation)—comes readily to mind. But Vollenhoven rejects this dualism as being an unsuitable illustration of the dualism he means. In Cartesian dualism, the elements in polarity are mutually incompatible. His statement of rejection is instructive in connection with the problem at hand.

> Descartes is a dualist and accepts the interaction [of body and soul]. But this [interaction] becomes impossible if body and soul are related as space [is] to thought. However much the interaction may be a *conditio sine qua non* for intuitionism, it cannot be accepted in this way. For, if the intuition is to offer its reconciliation, then the two [elements] that are to be reconciled may not stand so far apart from each other as in Descartes, because then one only achieves that the intuition is foisted with two mutually incompatible predicates. (1918a: 99)

Leaving the specific reference to Descartes for what it is, there is in this quote a more general statement about dualism en passant. The polarity, that specifies a dualism, is said to stand in need of reconciliation, and the intuition is looked upon as providing this. To that end the polarity must not be so great as to forfeit the possibility of reconciliation. One must be able to relativize the difference. In this vein Vollenhoven states: "The fundamental thought of intuitionism proceeds from the currently experienced (*beleefde*) synthesis" (1918a: 104); and: "The point of the intuition is the occurrent experience of multiplicity-unity (*het beleven van veelheid-eenheid*), and where this is impossible . . . it is better not to speak of intuition" (1918a: 105). So, whatever dualities there be, it must be possible to encompass the duality involved in an occasion of experience; or stated otherwise, the possibility of unity, as required for reconciliation, must be real. In that sense, the interaction, being a necessary condition for intuitionism, must entail some feature that keeps the inter-acting together.

When we apply this interpretation to specific dualities we get a more precise picture of what Vollenhoven has in mind. At the point where he first introduces dualism he adds in a footnote: "When we speak of dualism we continually mean the approach that distinguishes matter and mind [*stof en geest*] *qualitatively*; monism denies every qualitative difference."[40] No doubt monism, in its reductionist sense, at bottom al-

---

40   1918a: 3, note 1. We add that the qualitative difference between matter and mind involves that of being spatial and non-spatial, respectively. But this is not a fundamental difference for Vollenhoven, for space itself calls for a connection with the human

lows only quantitative differences. But when Vollenhoven speaks of a qualitative difference I take him to mean the same sort of difference that is relevant to interaction, namely there being a polarity or duality that falls within the range of the *mutual compatibility* of the difference in quality—difference of contrast, not of contradiction. Thus some 'common category'—or at least the possibility of a unity of contrast within an occurrent experience—is presupposed.

If we turn to more specifically anthropological statements we find that the Self—Vollenhoven speaks consistently of the I (*het Ik*)—exemplifies such a point of unity of differences. "Our Self perceives spatially, but *in* the Self we distinguish soul and body" (1918a: 423; emphasis added). Here the Self is represented as containing or at least involving both soul and body. The dualism of soul and body remains intact, but it is clearly not the kind of dualism that Vollenhoven balked at in Descartes (as quoted above). "If we now take the Self as a higher synthesis in virtue of a *determined* connection between one soul and one body, then the Self is accordingly a synthesis of two substances" (1918a: 423-424). When we come to discuss Vollenhoven's metaphysics, we will find him referring to the Self as itself being a substance. In *this* substance we find the "determined connection" between soul and body. Thus, though soul and body are themselves substances—usually referred to as 'incomplete substances', for neither is complete as regards the full human being—they do not forfeit the existence of the unity of the Self, taken as 'complete substance'. This Self, so it turns out, is an invariant principle for all psychical synthesis, whether taking place in the 'soul' (as intra-mental experience) or in the 'body', i.e. in our bodily psycho-physical organization (cf. 1918a: 429-432). The duality, which is real, still reckons with unification, the possibility of which must be provided by some principle or feature that includes whatever it is that counts as duality.

The dualism of thought and being, the basis of epistemology in Vollenhoven, is also an example of a reconcilable dualism. "Dualism acknowledges the distinct character of both *psyche* and *physis*, and it connects the contribution of each in the coming to be of knowledge. Thought and what is foreign to thought [*het denkvreemde*], [namely] being, lie reconciled together in the life tension of the Self" (1918a: 72). The epistemological problem is related to the anthropological one. That which is foreign to thought is 'brought to mind', so to speak, via the

---

agent. In order to speak meaningfully of space one needs to accept both (non-spatial) things that interact and a receptive subject with a spatial form of sensibility (cf. 1918a: 418). Thus there is a common, non-spatial ground in every encounter of mind and matter.

forms of sensibility of the bodily organization and the intuition of intra-mentality. Every judgment, that itself embodies a reconciliation of the subjective and the objective, attests to the effort of the Self that connects these. The anthropological and the epistemological moments are voiced together in the statement: "Intuitionism in its entirety has lost its right of being if soul and body are not distinguished qualitatively. But equally its bottom gives way if both stand in contradictory mutual opposition, interaction is impossible and accordingly the intuition includes incompatible predicates" (1918a: 102).

Intuition's bi-unity can give the impression that the unity is an effect resulting from a subsequent synthesis. That unification is not excluded, indeed that is the aim, and in the currently experienced synthesis this is what takes place as 'psychical growth'.[41] But the diversity that is synthesized requires a factor that guarantees that the synthesis is possible. In that sense a condition of unity precedes the diversity and its interaction. The anthropological statements strongly suggest that the Self is an *essence* controlling through psychical synthesis two 'species', namely on the one hand that of the intra-mental life of intuition, including time as succession in occurrent experience, and on the other hand that of the psycho-physical organization and its two forms of sensibility, space and time.[42] In other words the soul transcends the body in its inner mental life, but there is also a connection to the body's psycho-physical organisation.

Vollenhoven's later use of the term monism and dualism in the context of his problem-historical method—initiated in the early 1940s—is more restricted to cosmological and ontological features. In reflecting on his former use, Vollenhoven, in his later years, considered his former "normative dualism" (as I shall call it) of the early theistic intuitionism to be a variant of *genetic or dynamic monism*. The anthropological state-

---

41 Psychical synthesis is the whole point of intuition's reconciliation. It is "a growth of consciousness such that it preserves and takes up into itself in the further process of development what has gone on before, retaining the unique nature of the components. To that end what is needed is not development in the sense of unfolding what is present in preformation, but in the sense of *gathering up*, that is, reality of succession" (1918a: 413).

42 We can add that with regard to the three primary psychical acts: recollection, sense-awareness and representation, the first is a requisite of intra-mental life, the other two are bound to the psycho-physical organization of the body (1918a: 420). Thought is more than just an intra-mental function, as will be clarified below, for it requires recollection and psychical synthesis as substratum (1918a: 413). The a priori of intra-mental life, it being of 'first rank' as compared to the second rank of that of the psycho-physical organization, suggests that a higher value is attributed to the intra-mental than is attributed to the psycho-physical body.

ments, quoted above, bear this out.[43] We shall have more to say about Vollenhoven's self-characterization of his early work in the addendum to chapter four.

The above discussion of dualism has focussed in the main on the human being and epistemology, as rooted in the human being. This will continue to be the general locus of our interest in this chapter. But we here append the note that Vollenhoven also allows for a broader use of 'intuition'. "But also religion . . . can only be approached as an intuitive connection. . . . Accordingly theism acknowledges in its religious mystical intuition, that the duality of God and his creature continues to exist, for religion is bi-unity and, as with every synthesis of oppositions, can only be currently experienced" (1918a: 73). Here Vollenhoven's dualistic notion of intuition, as applied to religion, gives the relation between God and mankind a dynamic experiential and unity-in-difference character.

V. "*KNOWLEDGE IS A RELATION*"

We shall now delve more deeply into Vollenhoven's thought. The discussion of the intuition so far has not exhausted the main points of Vollenhoven's epistemology, in fact not even that of the intuition itself. He distinguishes knowledge and intuition, the focus of knowledge is on how it arises in the presentation of anything that is foreign to thought, while that of intuition is on the intra-mental and concerned with validity. In connection with the intuition Vollenhoven incorporates Meinong's *Gegenstandstheorie*. Both topics have characteristic features that are important to take into consideration when reviewing Vollenhoven's development. In this section we shall discuss knowledge, in the next the systematics of the intuition will be elucidated along with the place that *Gegenstandstheorie* occupies.

Knowledge is characterized as being a relation: "All knowledge assumes a connection laid between our thought and the other [i.e. being]" (1918a: 130; cf. also pp. 186, 208, 412, 420). The characterization of knowledge as a relation places this theme squarely in the polarity of thought and being, i.e. the relation between the rational element and the empirical given. In connection with knowledge, in contradistinction to intuition, we can even say that being had priority over thought: "But the

---

43   A statement of 1921 emphasizes unity in difference in another way. "'A body and a soul are two' and 'a body and a soul are one' cannot both be true in the same respect, but by introducing different points of view (e.g. *substantia incompleta* and *completa*) they can be connected: they are both true in a different respect"; Vollenhoven 1921c: 104. Cf. also chapter two, "Dualism", of Kok 1992, for a more expansive discussion of Vollenhoven's early dualism.

supposition of knowing is existence and hence being is logically prior to thought. . . . Knowledge is a relation between the Self and the given; if one deletes the given, then knowledge is no more" (1918a: 382); "being is always richer than thought" (1918a: 437). The prominent example of this knowledge is that of perception. Vollenhoven distinguishes between outer and inner perception. Intuition, being peculiar to inner perception, will be discussed later. Outer or regular perception calls into play conditions of sensibility of the psycho-physical organization, which thereby delineates what may be called the phenomenal order. But first we should pause to sort out the terminology involving 'knowing' and also say something about the word 'relation'.

A. The semantics of 'knowing'

An important difference for Vollenhoven between knowledge and intuition lies in the characterization of knowledge as being a *possession*, while intuition is a *consciousness* or a *mental state* (1918a: 440). Terminologically, the difference is caught in Dutch in the distinction between "*kennen*" en "*weten*". The latter term is usually followed by a pronoun, often 'that' (*weten dat*). English lacks a similar terminological distinction. Both meanings fall under the use of 'knowing'. However, there is a distinction in the use of 'knowing' in connection with the presence or absence of a pronoun. When 'knowing' occurs without a pronoun, as in 'I know my way about' or 'she knows the president personally', the word 'know' puts the subject in direct relation to the object. In such cases one can speak of 'knowledge by acquaintance'. But when 'knowing' is followed by a pronoun, as in 'knowing that', 'knowing which', 'knowing how', 'knowing when', 'knowing where', etc., then the grammatical object of the sentence indicates a state ('I know that it was wrong') or a capacity ('He knows how to play a guitar') or simply consciousness ('She knows when to leave the party'; 'You know which bike is yours'). When knowledge is said to be a relation, we shall take it that Vollenhoven means 'knowledge by acquaintance'. This at least fits in well with Vollenhoven's use. (The given examples of acquaintance only require "*kennen*" in Dutch, the cases of 'knowing + pronoun' require '*weten* + pronoun'.)[44]

---

44   We should also clarify our rendition of Vollenhoven's distinct uses of "*ervaren*" and "*beleven*". The former is 'experience', but the latter has no direct equivalent in English. (There is the German "Erleben".) It is experience actually taking place and (at the same time) one's being sensitive to its taking place, so that one is directly affected by it. One is usually aware or is directly conscious of the experience (as a state of consciousness). But Vollenhoven also allows for an affect that is unconscious, such as when asleep or unaware of being influenced (cf. 1918a: 440). I shall render the noun form "het *beleven*"

It was Bertrand Russell who made the phrase 'knowledge by acquaintance' popular at the beginning of the twentieth century. He meant by acquaintance a 'direct cognitive relation' between a subject and an object, whereby the converse of this relation is that of presentation. "That is, to say that *S* has acquaintance with *O* is essentially the same thing as to say that *O* is present to *S*."[45] Two kinds of objects were especially favoured by Russell as being the objects with which we are acquainted in a primal sense: universals and sense-data. But this is acquaintance within a reductionist program, which Vollenhoven did not endorse. Normally we would not hesitate to say that we are acquainted with things and persons ('I know/am acquainted with just the person you mean'), for we know these complex objects (or persons)—to the extent that we know anything—in virtue of their presentation. In interpreting Vollenhoven (and leaving Russell aside here) one can say that acquaintance takes place at the common sense level, the level at which an object presents or gives itself, by standing in relation to us,[46] in order for it to be known. In this sense, presentation involves an order of appearing secured by the objects presented.

B. Relations, their nature

The word 'relation' too requires some preliminary discussion. The topic of relations is complicated and open to various choices. Vollenhoven made a number of choices in his early thought, and others later. Though the reasons are not always clear, we need to signal the choices and also to be aware of the alternatives.

For Vollenhoven in his early years, relations are always *dual*. A relation involves two terms and only two terms.[47] There is little said by way

---

as 'the occurrent experience', the verb itself "te *beleven*" as 'to currently experience' and the adjectival use, as in "beleefde synthese", as 'currently experienced synthesis'. It would appear that A.N. Whitehead's "occasion of experience" expresses a closely similar meaning, though Vollenhoven's use precedes that of Whitehead. There is a disjunction between "*kennen*" (to know, to be acquainted with) and "*beleven*" (to currently experience or be aware of). The former is oriented to a given object that the Self comes to know, the latter to an effect upon the Self, usually one that one is aware of (cf. 1918a: 431).

45   Russell 1911: 148.

46   The term 'relation' is used here as a feature that binds or connects things and/or persons together. When used to indicate a thing or person in a descriptive sense, as when an uncle is a relation or a friend an acquaintance, the use is derivative.

47   Vollenhoven would appear to insist on this point. A footnote reads: "In order to prevent all misunderstanding, one is reminded here that, for intuitionism, a relation always consists of *[steeds bestaat in]* two predicates" (1918a: 66, footnote 2; cf. also p. 12). The note is appended to a statement about knowledge being a relation, which, in

of argument to support this limitation to binary relations. There is nothing implausible in accepting relations with more than two terms, e.g. 'between' requires at least three terms, as does 'give', in order to satisfy their meaning. Vollenhoven will acknowledge this later, when the early specific emphasis on binary relations has changed.

Relations being limited to binary relations, their two terms can be generally described as referent and relatum. The *referent* of a relation is the *a quo*, the term from which the relation proceeds, and the *relatum* is the *ad quem*, the term to which it proceeds (1918a: 86, 406). This also allows for specification of the *sense* (or *direction*) of a relation, it being always *from* the referent and *to* the relatum. This sense of a relation makes it important to distinguish a relation ('*aRb*', short for '*a* stands in the relation R to *b*') and its converse ('*bRa*'). When the difference of sense is essential to a relation, '*aRb*' excludes '*bRa*'.[48]

But the most important facet by far is (what might be called) the 'make-up' of a relation. Relations, so Vollenhoven insists, presuppose suitable predicates in each of its terms (1918a: 12). It is in virtue of these predicates of terms that a connection or relation can be laid between the terms. The relation, as a "laid connection" (*gelegd verband*), elicits a feature of the relational situation that is not itself constitutional (so to speak); only the predicates of the related terms are constitutional. The truth-content of a relational statement, namely what one comes to possess when knowing what is stated, is itself warranted only in light of relevant predicates of the terms of the relation. This view of a relation—or rather of its justification—is consonant with the (so-called) 'monadic' view of relations, which, as it turns out, is consistent with monadological features of Vollenhoven's metaphysics.[49]

Vollenhoven's reading of, for example, Leibniz, Kant, Lotze, Mei-

---

combination with Leibniz's view of the inherence of a predicate in a subject, enforces that "knowledge of extra-mental reality is dependent equally on both the [knowing] subject as referent and the [given] object as relatum" (1918a: 66). So this understanding of a relation finds a prime illustration in epistemology.

48   For specific relations the difference in direction may not be relevant, as when a relation is symmetrical (such as 'equal to') or non-symmetrical ('brother of'). For asymmetrical relations the difference is always relevant, for then the relation implies the negation of the converse (such as 'east' vs. 'west', 'left' vs. 'right', etc.).

49   At one point Vollenhoven makes a distinction between "real relations" and "ideal relations", in a discussion about the difference between synthesis in music and in mathematics. The distinction seems to be one of characterization, *viz.* factual over against ideal, not one of kind: monadic versus non-monadic (1918a: 168-169). The distinction between factually real and ideal is important, it being analogous to that between physics and metaphysics.

nong and Russell made him aware of the problem of relations. Relational facts have tended to be discredited. Statements that involve relations have often been analysed in such a way as to try to circumvent them. A relational statement is then replaced with one or more statements with a (supposedly more trustworthy) subject-predicate structure. Russell has given an explicit account of three different views as to the nature of relations.[50] We call brief attention to each of these.

(i) There is, to start with, the *monistic* (or holistic) view, which holds that a relation is a property of the whole formed by the terms that the relational statement is about. Take 'aRb', say, 'a loves b', this statement is about a and b. Consider the terms as forming a whole, say denoted as 'a and b', then the relation is taken to be a property that is attributed to the whole (in our example: 'a and b are in love'). This view reduces a relation to a (unitary) property. An evident liability of this reduction is that the view does not preserve the distinction between a and b. The whole formed by the terms taken together does not preserve an order, and also the diversity of the terms is effaced. The emphasis on 'wholes' generally signals an attitude of disdain towards plurality or diversity. The model monist/holist in this regard is F.H. Bradley. In his *Appearance and Reality* (1893), reality is the Absolute, considered to be the whole, while plurality and diversity are relegated to appearances, at most attributable to the Absolute as aspects. Here relations are explained away as being ephemeral.

(ii) The second view Russell distinguishes is the *monadistic* view. Here too relational statements are supplanted by predicative statements. In this case a relational statement is replaced by two subject-predicate statements. The meaning of the relational term is apportioned over properties attributed to each of the terms. Thus the statement 'aRb' is interpreted as being equivalent to the conjunction of '$(a)r^1b$' and '$(b)r^2a$'. If, say, 'aRb' is 'a exceeds b', then 'r^1b' denotes the predicate 'is greater than b', and it is attributed to a, while 'r^2a' denotes the predicate 'is less than a', and it is attributed to b. The two predicative statements together are taken to be equivalent to the original relational statement. In this case too, as with monism, there is a problem with the order of the terms, i.e. the directional sense of a relation. This order is not preserved, unless the order of the two predicative statements in the conjunction is to account

---

50   Cf. Russell 1903, especially "Chapter XXVI. Asymmetrical relations", pp. 218-226. Vollenhoven was well acquainted with Russell's work. His 98 page discussion of Russell's thought (up to about 1915) in 1918a is critical in tone on account of Russell's 'formalism'. But Russell's anti-psychologism and his appreciation of Meinong, made him (at least technical facets of his work) more congenial than Vollenhoven explicitly admits.

for this. But the conjunctive connection between statements is in itself symmetrical, so this is not the way to preserve intrinsic order.

A different sort of objection can also be raised against the monadistic interpretation of relations. Concerning the two predicates, each expresses in its *meaning* one of the terms of the relation as relational factor, not however as a term receiving a predicate but as part of what is predicated (such as in the example above: the predicate attributed to a, namely 'r^1b', involves the meaning of b and the relational feature, 'r^1', as a specific feature; likewise the predicate attributed to b, 'r^2a', involves the meaning of a and the relational feature, 'r^2', also as specific feature). This tends, to say the least, to undercut the intended reduction. The 'reduction' achieved is not the elimination of a relation—indeed, it is implicitly replaced by *two* other relations—but rather the re-interpretation of a relation as the work of the mind that deals with meaning or representations, for only their meaning figures in the expression of the predicates. The arch-monadist is Leibniz. He held that the relations a thing has to all other things are programmed into the 'perceptions' of that thing and are intrinsic to it. This is an ontology that supports monadic relations.[51] Relations here are not ephemeral, as in the monistic view, but their being 'laid' in the things, as work of the mind on the basis of predicates of the related terms, makes a relation *specific* to the terms.

(iii) Russell's third view is the one he himself advocates. He calls it the view of 'external relations'. Relations are just as real and general as properties, and if a property can be attributed to a thing or subject, without requiring inhering predicates, then there is nothing objectionable to attributing a relation to two or more subjects. Upon accepting relations, the full 'logic of relations' can be developed that does justice to the properties of symmetry, asymmetry and non-symmetry and transitivity, intransitivity and non-transitivity. In virtue of these properties, one needs to accept that the terms that enter a relation are not affected by the relation (though of course the terms gain relational properties in virtue of their standing in relation). They must retain their self-identity within the application of this logic. Also the relations themselves retain a general (or universal) meaning, and are not particularized into specific relations by the terms. That would create havoc with general logical rules, e.g. transitivity, for in the rule of transitivity: '(x,y,z) if xRy and yRz then xRz', the three occurrences of the R must be identical, i.e. not affected by the nature of the (pairs of) terms related in each occurrence of the relation. Thus relations are here said to be 'external' to the terms they relate.

---

51   Cf. Leibniz 1976a.

Vollenhoven's insistence that intuitionism treats relations as consisting of two predicates puts his intuitionism within the monadistic camp, though in a way that does not make relations, in their own epistemic sense, merely the work of the mind. Later, in *Isagoge Philosophiae* there is distinct evidence that Vollenhoven allowed for external relations at a very fundamental level. Vollenhoven was never partial to monism, in the holistic sense of the word. However, in his early work (here in discussion), though he does not advocate an 'external view' of relations, his use of relations is nevertheless nuanced. At the epistemological level one proceeds from 'the given', in the way it gives itself, i.e. in the 'appearance' of relations, and one knows relations accordingly. Hence, here one can allow and make full use of a 'logic of relations', without needing to keep their monadic 'make-up' in mind. But at the metaphysical level, the 'monadic make-up' is essential. "[D]ualism acknowledges substances and relations in which they stand, hence it can accept this logic of relations as method for the sciences that occupy themselves with relations, but not for metaphysics, which after all also speaks of substances [with inherent predicates]" (1918a: 157-158). The 'monadic reduction' of relations has important consequences for the interpretation of the knowledge situation. Stated in a nutshell: if 'knowledge is a relation', *viz.* knowledge that relates the knower (thought) and the given (being), then that relation, which is attested to by the truth-content one possesses, must presuppose certain features of the knower and other features of the given without which knowledge, as possessed, would not be justified.[52] But before developing this further, there is another feature of relations that needs attention, namely what Alexius Meinong calls 'the partial coincidence' of relations and complexes.

C. Complexes

The problem often raised in connection with relations is how one is to understand a relation's relating. Quite irrespective of the view of relations one adopts, though the external view makes the problem particularly noticeable, there is the question: if a relation is to relate (two) terms, doesn't one need new relations to relate the relation to the terms? If this be accepted as a genuine problem, we can see that an infinite regress threatens. Why should the new relations introduced to relate the original relation

---

52   Cf. "For if our Self wants to acquire knowledge of something else, then revelation of this other is necessary, as well as the reception [*opneming*] of this other by the Self. Hence knowledge is itself a relation. . ." (1918a: 186; cf. also pp. 66, 228-229). As will become clear, the "revelation" required on the side of the object is met with 'forms of sensibility' on the side of the subject.

to the two terms be able to do the job if the original relation requires this assistance. Would not the new relations in turn require relations so as to be able to relate? But then every appeal to relations requires additional relations to make the prior relations work. This clearly yields an infinite regress that ends either in having to accept that any relational situation is infinitely complex, or to reject as self-defeating any serious entertainment of relations. The acceptance of an actual infinity places the problem 'at infinity', but without aiding the understanding in any way. (Vollenhoven would add that its concept, interpreted as completed endlessness, is contradictory.) Thus the rejection of relations seems to be the only acceptable outcome. F.H. Bradley, the most renowned British neo-Idealist of his day and who initially inspired Russell, developed a host of arguments that aimed to demonstrate the incoherence of any notion of relations.

But Meinong, and later Russell, did not accept this undercutting of relations. At least, irrespective of the possible value of a reduction, one still has to face up to the relevance of a relational statement in connection with its truth-value. A relation is nothing if it does not relate. This requires, in the first place, that we treat relations as being of a different category than the terms related by the relation. If one's asking how a relation relates implies the positioning of a relation as term 'between' the terms it is to relate, then one has implicitly reified or hypostatized the relation, treating it as a thing. We end up with a set of three things, namely the two terms of the relation and the relation itself, which together do not yield a related whole. This is not the way to understand relations. Secondly, one also needs to take into account that the truth-value of a relational statement is affected, generally, by the order of the terms of the relation. When A loves B, this does not imply that B, in turn, loves A. The directional 'sense' of a relation comes into play here.

To facilitate meaningful discussion of relations, Meinong proposed that every relation is pared to a *concomitant complex* of the terms as related by the relation. Meinong spoke of a "partial coincidence" here, i.e. "where there is a complex, there is a relation, and vice versa".[53] Complexes require parts, while relations require terms. One may specify the partial coincidence, in its double formulation, as follows: (i) Given a complex C, this must have parts, and these parts, say a and b, must stand in some relation R to each other. (But R cannot be taken to be an additional element forming a class with a and b, for that would undercut the

---

[53] Grossmann 1974: 66. Vollenhoven quotes Meinong directly: "The law: 'Where there is a complex, there is a relation, and vice versa' [is what Meinong] calls 'the principle of partial coincidence'"; 1918a: 168; cf. also pp. 167, 228, 319).

relation, which must actually relate.) (ii) Given a relation R, there must be terms, and these terms, say *a* and *b*, must form the parts of a complex C. (But C cannot be the unity of the complex as whole, for that would cancel or supersede the parts *a* and *b*.) The partial coincidence between considering *a* and *b* as parts of a complex whole on the one hand and as terms of relating relation on the other hand, reminds one that the parts of a complex have relational relevance, and that terms of a relation contribute to a complex unity. Partial coincidence does not privilege one view of relations. It defers hypostatization, either of the unity of the whole or of the relation as element.

Now what is the relevance of these systematic distinctions in connection with Vollenhoven?

D. Knowledge and appearance

When Vollenhoven characterizes knowledge as a relation, several things are entailed. I first list these and then discuss each in turn.

In the first place there is the acquaintance on the part of the human agent with whatever it is that presents itself as given. This is not a static 'here is the human agent' (situated on the pole of thought) and 'there is the presented object' (the pole of being). "Knowledge arises through inter*action*" (1918a: 283), the action being something that the human agent must initiate with respect to the given object in order to come to a knowledge of it. Knowing has its own dynamics, and the knowledge gained is formulated in judgments and concepts.

In the second place, there is the principle of partial coincidence between a relation and a complex. Knowledge as relation that is laid knowingly calls up the companion statement about the knowledge situation as complex. Vollenhoven identifies these 'parts' of the concomitant complex as *referent* and *relatum*. "So now too knowledge is a relation between a rational being and a given something, hence is dependent on both subject and object. But no relation without a complex, without order in the referent and relatum, and without a non-parallel connection between these orders" (1918a: 412). The referent is the knowing subject, while the relatum is the given object. But neither is simple. Each introduces a thematic complexity that calls for discussion.

Finally, in the third place, there is the consequence of Vollenhoven's specific monadic view of a relation. If a relation "always consists of" two predicates, this seems to say that knowledge, in being a relation between the knowing subject and the given object, itself reduces to certain characteristics of the knowing subject and certain other characteristics of the given object respectively. The question is what this 'reduction' consists of and what its status is. Is the dynamics of knowledge 'dissolved' into subjective and objective characteristics? We find that the discussion here shifts from a discussion of the *origin* of knowledge, *viz.* coming to know, to the *legitimacy* of knowledge, *viz.* how knowledge can be justified. This last (or third) point requires us to make explicit our states of consciousness or awareness that accompany our knowing, as 'predicates' of the Self. States of consciousness or awareness involve thought turned reflectively towards the Self's own states. In other words it requires us to turn to the intuition. And there is also the question: in what sense are 'predicates' of the non-Self relevant?

But first, a fuller discussion of these three points in question is in order.

1. Getting to know
As to acquaintance (the first point), the simplest example of the dynamics of knowledge acquisition is extra-mental perception. A human being perceives an object, such as a book or a tree. Perception as relation presupposes the contrast of thought and being. In perception the object is given. It exists independently of our thought. It "reveals itself to us through its relations to us" (1918a: 418) of presentation. The perceiver, in turn, also has states of awareness that can play a role in perception. But when we say that we see a book, we don't see our relations to the book (1918a: 418, 431). (Often we are not even aware of our states as perceiver.) Thus, the acquisition of knowledge is oriented to the object perceived. This remains a primal situation, whatever the attendant awareness and the means are that accompany this primal given.

Now the simplest specimen of knowledge, gained through perception, is expressed as a *judgment* in subject-predicate form: 'A is *b*', say: 'The book is thick' (cf. 1918a: 276). The knowledge gained itself attests to thought's processing or working over or assimilating (*verwerken*) of the given in its being receptive to it. Through this 'working over' of the given by the Self, as knowing agent, a predicate is formed, in our case '(is) thick'. Of all that the book 'presents', this feature is noticed, selected and specifically attributed to it *knowingly*.

But one can also gain a *concept* of the object. Not only can we perceive the book to be thick, but also its having well-thumbed pages, heavy covers, faded colours, an out-dated font, etc. In a concept one brings together features noticed of the object, and keeps these together in reference to the object. A concept of the object progressively becomes more complete, in the sense of becoming more adequate to what the object reveals of its being, as we become more and more acquainted with it. At the same time one realizes that the richness of the thing's being, precludes the practical possibility of ever attaining a fully adequate concept of it. Any actual, less-than-adequate concept of a thing acts as a proleptic concept (*begripsrepresentant*), in the sense that it, factually, does deputy duty for the adequate conceptual knowledge one is striving to achieve in the process of becoming more fully acquainted.[54] The knowing agent has a role in both judgment and proleptic concept, but the focus is on the thing known. And, between judgment and proleptic concept mutually, proleptic concepts are formed on judgments.[55]

The focus on the object needs, it would seem, its own warrant to secure the formation of judgments and concepts. For the object is *selected* in order to serve as referent or subject of the judgment and the recipient of predicates. And in a concept, too, though no actual concept of the object is adequate to its complexity, there needs to be the *acknowledgement* of the distinct being that one is coming to know (to some degree), quite apart from the degree to which this is private to the knower. (Vollenhoven quotes Russell, in evident agreement, who states "different people *see* the *same* object as different shapes according to their point of view"; 1918a: 329). Vollenhoven is actually somewhat cavalier here, to the extent that he does not press the point. But he holds that anything has distinct being in virtue of an *idea*. An idea is an extra-mental archetype, or "thing-law", of a given object, which has a limitative relevance for every attempt at knowing the object. A full understanding would count as an adequate concept of the idea or thing-law, but no actual concept can fully measure up to it, though may approach it in an on-going, limitative sense. In his own words: "If one understands an adequate concept to be the complete expression of the thing-law, then this has limitative value. But the given, that is, the archetype of the [adequate] concept that

---

54 Essential to a concept is its reference to an object or its extension. In concrete concepts (as in our discussion) the object is named or described, but in the case of general concepts this will be replaced by a variable, this being the placeholder for reference. In other words, concepts generally have a feature that is indeterminate or variable (cf. 1918a: 163). This also distinguishes a concept from the mere grasp of features or characteristics (i.e. intensions). Concepts are not formed arbitrarily by mere thought; rather "things and thing-relations enter into our subjective forms, [hence] the interaction of things is a necessary condition for forming thing-concepts" (1918a: 229).

55 In discussion, John H. Kok referred me to the manuscript on Bergson, written in 1921, in which Vollenhoven states that, in knowledge acquisition, as judgments accrue, (proleptic) concepts, which are based on these, are able to become more adequate. Vollenhoven 1921ms.

exists only as limit, does enter into a synthesis with the *Gegenstände* [i.e. objective meanings, occurring as predicates; A.T.]. That synthesis is to be found in the judgment in which a proleptic concept is the subject of a predicate, . . ." (1918a: 411; cf. also p. 440). Clearly, this broaching of ideas is metaphysical. Ideas do not figure in an explicit sense in the perceptive getting-to-know, but they are called upon to account for knowledge, in warranting the recognition of the distinctive being one becomes acquainted with. Epistemology cannot be adequate without metaphysics, which is why it is recounted at this point. When we discuss Vollenhoven's metaphysics, we will return to this use of ideas.

2. The concomitant complex of the knowledge relation.
But—now turning to the second point—every relation or laid connection has a concomitant complex, in this case that of referent and relatum.[56] In turning to the concomitant complex of the knowledge relation, one finds features that occasion the dynamics of knowing. The referent and the relatum are each part of larger 'orders'. There can be no knowledge as relation "without order in the referent and relatum, and without a nonparallel connection between these orders" (1918a: 412). Vollenhoven gives various formulations of the relation of referent and relatum, such as "the relation between subject and object, between the Self as subject of knowing and the non-Self as object of knowing, between the Self and the *Ding an sich*" (1918a: 335). At one point he simply speaks of "a Self and a non-Self" (1918a: 427). These are partial descriptions, for we find a fuller description in the following: "If you don't exercise your thinking you will not be able to follow a scientific presentation, and if your eyes are defective you will have difficulty with experimentation. With that it is granted that *ideals* should lead us in the use of understanding and sense-organ. Knowing, then, is not a correspondence of being and thinking, but a working over of the given by the Self in its psycho-physical organization in subjection to the norms and ideals set for human knowing" (1918a: 410).

The emphasis here is on the occasion of knowing. But this is not to deny the 'order of the object'. In fact, our discussion of ideas in the previous section, whereby ideas, as thing-laws, govern things in their appearing and their interacting, has broached a very essential feature of the order of the object. Objects belong to a metaphysical order. There is more

---

56   In a summarizing discussion Vollenhoven states that "[e]very relation assumes a relatum and a referent" (1918a: 437). Hence, for any relation one can consider its concomitant complex, not just the epistemological 'knowing relation'. We return to this below.

to be said, but let us first return to the Self and the order of the knowing subject, that initiates knowing through interaction.

The interaction through which knowledge (judgments and concepts) arises, is contextual. Undeniably the given, though acknowledged to involve a reality that is foreign to thought, only gets to be known in terms of conditions of sensibility, which involves spatial and temporal coordination and the 'point of view' of the knower. The factual mediation in the active interaction of coming to know something does not forfeit the object's being given, though this 'giving' or appearing will be different from different points of view. The appearance, as revealed by a thing, calls up a representation in the mind of the person viewing, in correlation with the psycho-physical organization of that person. Vollenhoven states: "the mind [*geest*] is structured in such a way that a specific colour-awareness in the psychical [series] corresponds with a certain frequency of vibrations in the physical series (*causa occasionalis*)" (1918a: 328). This distinction between appearance and representation would collapse if there were no identity conditions relevant to the thing and its appearances. (Here the acknowledgement of the idea of the object is implicit.) Thus the object known is not of our making, though our representations of it (which come to expression in judgments about it) are limited, being as they are in virtue of our own psycho-physical limitations in interaction with the mind, a limitation that makes every conceptualization of the object proleptic. If the given were not acknowledged as given, there would be little sense in attending more carefully in perception, or attempt to diminish handicaps in our sensory system, or to sharpen our concepts to be less inadequate in the face of the object than they already are. All this attests to there being ideals towards optimizing our bodily sensibility, operative in the occasion of knowing.

Beside the mediating role of the psycho-physical organization, as relevant to the object's being given, there is also mediation that concerns the knowing subject. The 'working over' (assimilation or processing) executed by the knowing subject needs to be guided. The knowing subject is not a mere copy machine, providing a copy of the object in terms of the subject's own awareness (à la formalism), nor is it a behavioural reaction pattern induced by the given's functioning as stimulus (as empiricism would have it). The Self seeks to know, and to that end relevant norms are called upon by which to *adjudicate* between a result (whether as judgment or as concept) that is acceptable as knowledge and one that s unacceptable, as being erroneous.[57] The norms are a distinct partici-

---

57 Accordingly, the human Self is not in itself a knowing subject, but needs a norm

pant in the game of knowledge, alongside of the two other elements, the rational element of thought and the given object (of being). The norms Vollenhoven singles out in particular are the two logical principles of contradiction and excluded middle.[58] Naturally, there must also be a 'will to know', meaning that there must be a willingness on the part of the Self to come to know in a way that avoids error. To that end there needs to be a willingness to submit to norms.

We note in passing that Vollenhoven is not very explicit about this 'will to know' in its own right. It seems to be implied in any striving to know. In any case, the Self is not on its own accord a 'knowing subject', apart from the recognition of and submission to norms. And, of course, the relevance of norms and ideals indicates that thought is embedded in a thinking (rational) being, who exercises its (subjective) rationality in the dynamics of knowing. So there is a *subjective rational order* that is governed by norms and ideals, as well as an *objective rational order*—the metaphysical order—of things and relations, as determined by ideas. (The topic of the two rational orders will return in the discussion of theism below.)

3. Monadism and the knowledge relation

The monadistic view of relations—the third of the three points listed above—is most evident in accounting for the relation of acquaintance. The Self that comes to know or to be acquainted with a given object is capable of doing so in virtue of (what might be called) conditions of mentality. We see with our eyes and, when we think, there is cognitive awareness. But in the factual dynamics of coming to know, i.e. in forming judgments of perception and concepts of things discerned, we are usually not explicitly aware of the role of our eyes or the procedure of

---

to attune the Self in an appropriate way. This norm—or any norm—is not in the Self as such; norms are extra-mental (cf. 1918a: 430). They have a domain of validity that calls for recognition. In summary, Vollenhoven's view of receptivity is (in the main) Kantian, his view of mind, decidedly not. For Kant, cognition proceeds from a spontaneity of mind.

58 "[L]ogic must remain formal, hence it can never offer a content . . .; for without a content to process not a single judgment can ever be deduced from the logical norms" (1918a: 407; I believe Vollenhoven means to say "in accordance with", instead of "from" [*uit*]). The relevance of the principle of excluded middle—in virtue of which the denial of a falsehood yields a truth (cf. 1918a: 313, 407)—is not elaborated on in Vollenhoven's early work. Treating logical principles as norms has some affinity with what has come to be known as 'natural deduction'. In systems of natural deduction one does not proceed from axioms, i.e. statements taken to be true, but from rules that are instructions for doing or permission to do something. Cf. Alexander 1971: 246 ff.

our thought, for the focus is on the object perceived. But it cannot be denied that there are conditions, both on the side of the Self (knowing subject) and on the side of the object (given thing), which, when not complied with, would undercut any 'laying of a connection' that knowledge attests to. Thus certain 'predicates' need to hold with respect to, on the one hand, the Self, as knowing subject, so as to be able to know the object, and on the other hand the given object, the non-Self, for it to be knowable by the Self, before there can be any (legitimate) knowledge acquisition.

But if one applies the formal wording as to what a relation is—in a 'monadic view' a relation "always consists of" (1918a: 66, note 2) two predicates of the related terms—in a direct way to knowledge as relation, confusion may result. Does this mean that what we have described with respect to this relation, i.e. the coming to know an object through working it over mentally, is actually (really!) to be seen as consisting of factors that are predicable of the Self on the one hand and the given object on the other? When knowledge is said to arise in a process of interaction of thought and being, must we count this as illusory, or at most a first guess (or a construct of the mind) in the face of what knowledge 'actually' is, namely the confluence of certain features ('predicates') of the Self and the object? I believe this would be a wrong interpretation of what Vollenhoven means. For that would mean that in the order of knowledge, where the relation is grasped in its own 'truth-content' (so to speak), there is no 'reality in the knowing'. Knowledge is of a phenomenal order, but the phenomena nevertheless are real. The difference between knowing and straying (being in error) are important and real. We will see that, when discussing science, Vollenhoven attributes to knowledge its own kind of reality, *viz.* a 'metalogical' reality that is distinct from the psychical reality of the Self and the objective reality of the world—a reality that grows through the interaction of the Self and the world in the process of increasing our knowing. Hence I take the formal wording of a relation, in its application to knowledge, as expressing the conditions to which any case (occasion) of knowledge must comply. The conditions that hold for knowledge acquisition are not themselves knowledge components—as if one will now deal with the 'real' knowing that makes the acquired knowing second best. They are the conditions that *validate* or *legitimate* the possession of knowledge. These conditions do not replace the genesis of knowledge with an alternative procedure. (The distinction, quoted above, between epistemology, which makes use of relations, and metaphysics, which reduces relations to substances with inherent predicates, is crucial here.) It is like driving a car. The conditions for driving are having a vehicle in good working order and a driver who is capable, careful and licensed to drive. But this says nothing about an actual drive from A to B, although the conditions hold throughout any actual drive taken. Knowledge acquisition is likewise a way of getting from A (ignorance) to B (knowledge possession). But the conditions for coming to know do not prefigure but certify the possession as such. So what conditions hold here?

Vollenhoven introduces the distinction between knowledge and intuition, i.e. between knowing and (occurrent) awareness (*beleven*), between what is *mentally possessed* (knowledge) and what counts as a *mental state* (consciousness), as requisite for knowledge possession. The intuition gets at what actually affects the Self, of which the Self becomes aware in self-reflection (or self-consciousness). Here we find the Self to have a certain make-up that conditions knowledge possession. In other words, here are the 'predicates' of the Self by which the Self participates in the relation of knowledge. This topic, which is that of the intuition, is so important and central to Vollenhoven's early work that it requires its own discussion, which we will turn to very shortly below.

But there is also the 'object side' to consider. Here too there must be something that helps 'validate' knowledge. The object needs to be 'knowable'. But what is the 'knowability' of the non-Self?

We quoted Vollenhoven (at the beginning of section D.2.) as saying that every relation, not just knowledge as relation, consists of relatum and referent (cf. 1918a: 437). That means: "We distinguish in the given, *thing* and *relation* (first-order relations, forces that things exert on each other)" (1918a: 418). These 'first-order relations', also called 'thing-relations', attest to a pluralism in the given. We don't just come to know solitary things, but also the interrelations between them. But these interrelations are indicative of their own mutual interactions, hence in an ultimate formulation Vollenhoven speaks of things and their forces—in another context we find him *proceeding* from this assumption: "For if the essence of things is law [i.e. idea] and their relations force [*kracht*]..." (1918a: 346). In speaking of force here we have the monadological (Leibnizian)[59] reduc-

---

59 Leibniz spoke of the monads of bodies as centres of force. A question that is closer to home is whether Vollenhoven is influenced here by his mentor, Jan Woltjer, in particular the latter's paper "Het wezen der materie" (The essence of matter). Woltjer here defends the view that material bodies consist of forces, without there being a substratum or *Ding an sich* that bears or exerts these forces. Prima facie Vollenhoven seems to contradict this, when he insists that one must accept the notion of substance as the warrant of constancy in change (or application of force). But (as we will see below), when that

tion of the thing-relations to 'predicates' (discernable features) of the related terms. A force is a capacity of a thing, a prerequisite for any activity or effect that a thing exerts on any other thing. This being 'in the given', it is itself foreign to thought. It belongs to the ontology of beings.

But epistemologically, the relational situation is dominated by the relation of knowing, between the knowing subject (perceiver) and the given (complex) object. We see the book lying on the table; so we speak of the relation of 'lying on', but we are not aware of this in terms of the 'forces' operative in the book (gravitational effect/weight) or the table (resistance due to its atomic structure). When selecting and concentrating on the relational feature, when expressing what one sees (comes to know), one in fact "hypothetically substantializes" the relational feature (1918a: 431). This does not cancel or contradict the monadic understanding of thing-relations. It is a hypothetical strategy that is epistemologically useful, but unsuitable in metaphysics.

We have said that Vollenhoven speaks of the given as 'revealing' itself to the knowing Self, as in: "the object of knowing is a function of the thing external to me, its appearing, its revelation to me or its effect on me" (1918a: 228-229; cf. also the quote in footnote 52). This is apposite, for it suggests something about the object's being knowable, though its meaning remains vague. In the meantime we have come to distinguish two forms of knowledge, namely that of *concepts* and of *judgments*. A concept always focuses on 'a thing', in the sense of having an objective reference (whereby an adequate concept—could it be had—would constitute the complete knowledge of the thing's idea, i.e. the thing in its entire make-up). A judgment attributes a predicate to a subject, whereby one asserts a property or quality as holding for a thing or (which is also a distinct possibility) a relation as holding between things (e.g. 'the book is thick' and 'the book is lying on the table', respectively). In the (phenomenal) given there is *thing* and (thing-)*relation*, and in Vollenhoven's ultimate (metaphysical) terminology, this is *thing* and *force*. The given's being at all *knowable* depends on this distinction between thing and (thing-) relation, i.e. between thing and force, for without that distinction concept and judgment would collapse. There would be no complexity in any essential sense. What is revealed phenomenally as 'thing-relations' would not be indicative of a supporting 'thing', but only the data for the knowing subject. There would be no intrinsic structure of properties or quali-

---

constancy is found to lie in the idea or thing-law, there is a possible compatibility with Woltjer's view, all the more so since Woltjer grants ideas a phenomena determining role. Cf. Woltjer 1914; also chapter 4, section III.B.4.a.

ties for a concept to conceptualize, and judgment would have nothing to assert, and would thereby devolve into a mere mental categorization. Thus the knowing Self can only acquire knowledge in the form of a judgment, and also a subsequent conceptualization, on condition that the Self 'picks up' this difference between a thing and an interrelated complex as facet of the given's revelation of itself. This facet is what constitutes the non-Self's capacity to be known (its being knowable). It is not merely a distinction of mind to distinguish an object (referent) and a concomitant complex of a judgment; there is an analogous difference in the object (of thing and force) that induces the distinction in knowing, though the analogy is not a one-to-one correlation. Without this distinction in the object there would be no extra-mental touchstone to differentiate between meaning and truth. To both judgments and concepts the principle of contradiction applies, thus truth must have a bearing on both. Meaning can be attributed to anything that affects the mind, in the sense of being psychically enjoyed. But truth needs to answer to validating conditions.

In summary, Vollenhoven's monadism would appear to be epistemologically motivated. His view of "knowledge as relation" ("between a rational being and a given something, hence dependent on both subject and object"; 1918a: 412) brings together several features of his thought. First, there are the two orders between which the knowledge relation is laid: a *subjective order* in which thought takes place on the part of the knowing subject, and an *objective order* in which (as Vollenhoven also calls it) the 'being' and 'so-being' of the given object are revealed. In the second place, each order must have certain 'predicates' enabling the knowledge relation (as exemplified by judgment and concept) to be laid. There is a certain analogy between the orders: on the side of the object there is the difference between thing and thing-relation in virtue of which the object is knowable; on the side of the subject there is the mental grasp of 'intra-mental meaning', involving a unitary term or a term with a relation. The latter is essential to the knowing subject. Vollenhoven formulates this 'intra-mental meaning' in terms of a *Gegenstandstheorie*, which is annexed to his understanding of the intuition.

We now need to discuss the intuition head-on. But before turning to that, there is a mathematical topic, the discussion of which can now be completed, for it is directly linked to the understanding of knowledge as relation. That topic is the nature of space.

E. The nature of space

In discussing the nature of space Vollenhoven is prima facie Kantian though not without certain differences. In his introductory discussion he states: "In any case, space is not parallel to time as succession, only with time as form of sensibility" (1918a: 19). If Vollenhoven were Kantian, he would have accepted *as an intuition* the representation of this form of sensibility as the capacity of our receptivity to organize sense-data side-by-side. In other words space (as form of sensibility) would be the direct object of an intuition. Since time as form of sensibility is analogous to space, the same holds for time. (This is time as sequence, not time as succession.)

But Vollenhoven does not treat forms of sensibility as transcendental conditions but as conditions for factual relations, more specifically for the relation of acquaintance. We don't see space but we perceive spatial relations, in the sense of difference of positions. This presupposes, as given, things standing in mutual relations, and *revealed* as such in that which is the *given* in the relation of spatial perception. But this *given* in the relation of spatial perception is itself very complex, it being a thing-relation of thing-relations. Say, I see a book. It consists of pages and covers. Any two pages stand in a (thing-)relation (r_1), so there are many relations at this level. But these relations themselves form the structure (involving relations of parts, r_2, between pages and covers) we call a book. And it is that structured object, the complex of the relations of relations, that we perceive as spatial object in the (knowing-)relation of perception (r_3). Space is relevant to this relation of perception, and, as any knowing-relation, it has a subjective and objective element, of perceiver and perceived. In that sense spatial perception is a species of acquaintance. "Thus there is also something subjective in the awareness of space and this element may safely be called form of sensibility" (1918a: 130-131).

This view of space is at least consistent with the assumption of space as required by geometry as the study of groups of transformations. Geometry works with figures and studies their variant and invariant properties when moved about (transformed). The structure of a figure is a composition of relations of relations, *viz.* an organization of elements (points, lines, planes, etc.) any two of which stand in specific relations. Geometry is an idealization of what is concretely relevant in perception. Space is the ambiance within which figures and things, including the human body, move about.

This embedding of space in the existent relation of acquaintance does not detract from its unique character. At least Vollenhoven insists that space is still *sui generis* (1918a: 421, 422). Its unique character lies in the fact that it permits us to *localize* our perceptions and sense-data. Localization is something humans do in determining direction and position, but it also assumes a context in which localization takes place. In this connection we must distinguish relative and absolute space. Relative space involves localization relative to our bodies and the given. "The existence of relative space must *depend* on both our thinking as well as on the given" (1918a: 419). "Relative space is determined *in part* by the knowing subject, *in part by the object*" (1918a: 420). On the other hand, absolute space sets the limit to every attempt at localization. It is a limitative concept, but not a normative one. It is a supra-individual ideal of construction. It is "that picture in which the ideal human being would arrange all individual space-impressions with and next to each other" (1918a: 426). But just as the limit of a sequence is not to be found in the sequence, so the *ideal* for knowledge is not to be found in the empirically given, no more than an *ideal* for the natural *sciences* is found in nature. Of absolute space nothing is to be found in nature (cf. 1918a: 427). In other words, absolute space depends on the idea of the world (discussed below).

Because time as form of sensibility—time as sequence—is on an equal footing with space, it too is to be interpreted in its relevance for localization. The study of time in this sense does not belong to mathematics. Time as sequence is relevant for motion, hence the study of time, as form of sensibility, belongs, as stated earlier, to kinematics.

Here we see how basic geometry is for the natural sciences. Geometry presupposes space as the relation between the human body and the world about the body, the locus of location. This can be reinforced with the science of arithmetic, when geometry is arithmetized. When time, as one-dimensional sequence, is included one is able to study motion. The sciences of kinematics, mechanics and physics follow suit.[60] In each of these sciences, there is the presupposition of a synthesis between thought and the given. Not that each science has its own synthetic a priori that accounts for this. Every basic judgment of these sciences is a modification of the synthetic a priori (of second rank), namely that of localization, this being the (constructive) synthetic a priori of the three-dimensional

---

60 The science of arithmetic (second order arithmetic) does not itself originate in the phenomenal order of thought and being, but is a product of thought alone, with only *Gegenstände* as content/being. Hence arithmetic does not introduce the order of the sciences, although it is a factor in the organism of the sciences. Through the arithmetization of geometry, which also affects the natural sciences' use of geometry, the science of arithmetic has a relevance prior to geometry.

Euclidean character of space (and time). The basis of this synthesis lies rooted in the human psycho-physical organization, which influences how the data of the world are thought. Thus, though each natural science turns some part of the data of nature into the object of study, there is also the anthropological influence of the ineluctable human working over of the data, within the limitative character of absolute space and time. This induces an organization of the sciences mutually, according to the ratio, distinct for each science, between the subjective or formal side of the judgments of a science and the correlative objective or empirical side. In this way the organization of the sciences makes way for the organism of the sciences (cf. 1918a: 417, 433-436)[61] and for the "reality" of the sciences—what I called the "truth-content"—being that of the actually acquired synthesis, as knowledge, of the objective (the given) and the subjective (the knowing subject) (cf. 1918a: 12, 96, 381). The topic of the organism of science will occupy us again in section IX on metalogic.

VI. THE THREE-FOLD INTUITION AND *GEGENSTÄNDE*
A. Awareness versus knowledge

Besides knowledge by acquaintance there is intuition. Intuition is an awareness that is very relevant for epistemology, which Vollenhoven associates with a conscious state of the human Self. This is the 'knowing + pronoun' form that involves experience in that direct sense that we have called *occurrent* (*beleven*). It is typically a kind of inner perception, an intra-mental awareness that in turn gives rise to a unique kind of objectivity, namely of *Gegenstände*. At the same time this inner perception lays bare the very essence of intuition as intra-mental two-oneness or bi-unity. The fundamentals elucidated by this inner perception reach to a metaphysical level, in that intuitive awareness also allows for Self-awareness, or the awareness of my own existence or presence. In elucidating this complex problematic we approach the essentials of Vollenhoven's intuitionistic conception.

It all begins with self-consciousness. This should not be confused with self-knowledge. Self-knowledge is a species of acquaintance: the Self as knowing subject (hence in willing conformity to the norms of truth)

---

61   We add that, though the sciences of this organism are epistemologically situated in the thought-given polarity of acquaintance, this does not sufficiently explain their nature. Science is more and other than enhanced perception. One needs to include scientific 'rigour'. This will be acquired through the application of the *Gegenstandstheorie*. The organism of the natural sciences and mathematics—in the order: formal arithmetic, geometry, kinematics, mechanics and physics—will play a heuristic role in determining the 'lower law-spheres' when Vollenhoven revises his thought.

seeks to gain knowledge of the Self as given reality ('thing'). That given Self is the full human being. One's acquired knowledge of the Self is formulated in judgments and concepts, which means that the Self, as knowing subject, has worked over something of what the Self reveals of itself, as it would any other given object, in striving to achieve an adequate concept of it. But this is necessarily partial and incomplete, hence the knowing subject must make do with proleptic concepts concerning its own Self. This self-knowledge takes place in a *Self-approaching process* in which we gradually acquire more and more truths (judgments) about ourselves, expressed as true statements about our Self, and as represented in proleptic concepts (cf. 1918a: 429-432).

But besides this progressive, factual getting to know ourselves, there is also the direct self-awareness in self-consciousness. As such this is not anything esoteric. We have quoted Vollenhoven as saying that we can only get to know a given thing in virtue of the relations we have to the thing, and the thing to us. But it is the thing that we become acquainted with, not the relations we have to the given thing (cf. 1918a: 418). It is this "in virtue of the relations" that now receives attention by way of 'self-awareness'. E.g. when I see a book, I get to know an object. But in or through self-awareness I am able to add the awareness of my seeing. Then I can say that I *know* the object, but that I am *aware* of the state in which I get to know it. The knowing (*kennen*) and the being aware (occurrent experience, *beleven*) are distinct; I *know* the object in virtue of seeing it, and I *know that* I see it in self-awareness.

This 'additional' consciousness is directly linked to the relations that are so prominent here. We need to bear in mind the monadic interpretation Vollenhoven gives to relations. Relations require predicates in the related terms. Thus the relation of my seeing an object involves some feature(s) of myself as perceiver that accounts for my participation in the relation of perception. The object perceived also has certain predicates that account for its participation in the relation of seeing, namely in its being seen. But we need to add immediately that no one can apperceive how this operates or what that state is *in the object*. This is a consequence of things being external to consciousness, hence foreign to thought: "if one acknowledges . . . the difference between knowing and occurrent experience [or awareness], then one realizes immediately that the experience of things apart from the Self as substance is an impossibility" (1918a: 431). That is to say, one cannot participate in the thing-relations of the knowable given; e.g. we do not experience the lying on the table of the book that lies on a table, but we can of course experience our own lying on a table.⁶²

So what we *can* do is 'look in ourselves' to apperceive what goes on in us. That is what self-awareness is all about, and it is distinctly intuitional. Self-awareness yields to an inner viewing of the Self to the extent that self-consciousness *adds consciousness to* the relations of the Self to the given. In other words, in self-consciousness or self-awareness, I am aware of those features in my Self whereby I participate in the relations in which the Self stands to other things and persons. This view of consciousness is attested to by Hans Driesch, and also Henri Bergson is of influence here.⁶³

Self-consciousness, then, offers a unique disclosure. It enables us to become aware of our states of consciousness that are intrinsically relevant to our mental life. It is an experiencing of our inner life not as static state of (mental) affairs, but an experiencing of its dynamic presence to the Self and conditioning the Self in its many kinds of activity. It is a 'being aware as I undergo', and this is essentially *occasional*, for the awareness that arises in me as state of consciousness is dependent on the occasion of experience. Its importance for epistemology is that the awareness of the 'knowing that the Self undergoes something when experiencing something' is impossible to deny, hence it has a conditioning and delimiting effect on what the Self actually comes to know. There is a certainty intrinsic to this awareness that needs no further foundation, for it is indeed self-awareness. Note: this does not mean to make the Self an immediate object one can reach for—that would turn it into a knowing-relation.

---

62   The strategy of the hypothetical substantialization of thing-relations, mentioned earlier, helps to nevertheless get to know this relation, as over against attempts to be aware of it, by artificially turning it into an object of knowing (cf. 1918a: 431-432).

63   Vollenhoven avails himself of Driesch's formulation at this point: "I *am aware* that I *exist* as substance, i.e. stand in relations". (The quotation is from Driesch 1917: 1.) (1918a: 439-440). As to Bergson, Vollenhoven declares of Bergson that "in his system, if that term is applicable in his case, many points of agreement are to be found with the views advocated in this study" (1918a: 348). But it is only when discussing the kinds of intuition that Vollenhoven becomes specific. He follows the lead of the Danish philosopher, H. Höffding, who distinguished four kinds of intuition in Bergson: concrete, practical, analytical and metaphysical. There is something of a merry freedom here of pick and choose. Vollenhoven finds little use for the practical intuition in the present context, so he only retains the remaining three (as we shall see immediately). Bergson responded to Höffding's four meanings by saying: "I should be inclined to say that there are more!" Bergson 1983: 34; also Höffding 1916. P.S. About the "practical intuition", Vollenhoven says (in his own review of his dissertation): "The [practical intuition] concerns what is obvious in life and, over against pragmatism, it has value only in discovering and stating problems, not in solving them, as Bergson often appears to maintain" (Vollenhoven 1918c: 210-211).

Nor can we intuit another human being's awareness, like feeling someone else's toothache. One can know oneself and others only in the self-approaching process described above. What concerns us now is the immediacy to the Self of what the Self in its current presence undergoes, this being a *state of consciousness*. This is a 'two-oneness', the essential schema of intuition. Hence, in virtue of its certainty, self-consciousness offers prospects of *legitimating* the results of our mental life, in particular our knowing activity, by appealing to this intra-mental fund of certainty that human beings have an immediate access to. But we should also add that the monadic interpretation of relations makes every relation in which a human being participates, specific to that person. Thus Vollenhoven's self-awareness or method of intuition is also ineluctably *solipsistic*.[64]

In working out this view of intuition we need to introduce distinctions not yet broached, in particular the distinctions of act, content and *Gegenstand*.

B. Act, content and *Gegenstand*

The introduction of act, content and *Gegenstand* would seem to place Vollenhoven's work in a phenomenological setting. But we ought not to proceed from phenomenological presuppositions without discussion, for that would introduce confusion. We do best to follow Vollenhoven in his own descriptions and analyses first, though there is a general sort of compliance on Vollenhoven's part to his (early twentieth century) time.

The introduction of mental acts and content in the course of the nineteenth century served to replace a rather static view of mentality with a more dynamic model. The mind does not merely have the static capacities of intelligence, will, feeling, etc., that first need to be activated before their effect is recognized, but mentality, when taken to be of a psychical nature, has a dynamics of its own, which can be analysed and sorted in a variety of acts, each of which has its own sort of effect or content. For Vollenhoven *acts* are the mental pole of the relations in which the Self can stand with respect to other things, and the *content*, appropriate to an act, is what is effected through these relations as content of the state of consciousness of the Self. In light of his epistemological aims, Vollenhoven singles out three acts in particular, namely those of sensing, representing and remembering. *Sensing* is required in connection with the interaction of mind and body. The body's forms of sensibility, temporal and spatial,

---

64 Whether he felt this to be a liability *at the time* (as he did later) is difficult to say for lack of evidence. But this feature of subjectivity went by the board in the shift in the mid-1920 towards his definitive "Calvinistic thought" (cf. chapter 3).

are the main means a human being (or Self) has towards becoming aware of the body and of what the psycho-physical organization of the body effects. *Representing* is quite typical of mentality itself. Thinking is nothing if not a dealing with representations. *Remembering*, in turn, lies at the heart of the Self's ability of attaining psychical growth. Without the accrual of memory, knowledge and awareness could serve no ends or ideals of achievement.

In self-consciousness one can be aware of the mental acts and their content. The prime form of this is of course in occurrent experience. Hence in its immediacy this involves "a *distinct* sensation, a remembering of a *distinct* event or a *distinct* representation" (1918a: 349), which, as distinct content, is psychically enjoyed to the extent that the mind undergoes it. But the mind's enjoying it allows it to be distinctly aware that content is present to mind through acts. There is an intimate contact between the Self and the activated content, which is constitutive for the Self's state of consciousness. The awareness of this contact is intuitional, and it occasions a certainty of the act's effect, namely "I am *immediately conscious that* I sense something, [*that* I] remember something, and [*that* I] represent something" (1918a: 349; emphases in brackets added). This intuitive immediacy of consciousness Vollenhoven calls, à la Bergson, the *concrete intuition*. This intuition is essentially a bi-unity, involving a mental presence of act / content to my Self. The factor of act qualifies the Self's own participation, while the content, enjoyed in the undergoing of the relevant act, is held to or retained as 'mental material' of inner consciousness. This 'mental material', when objectively acknowledged, Vollenhoven calls, following Meinong, a *Gegenstand* (a German word for 'object', which Vollenhoven retains in German, as has become common practice, in order to retain its peculiar character). "Thus the *content* is what is *specific of the Gegenstand*, while *it itself* is the [mental] *material* in the *representation* (1918a: 163).[65] Vollenhoven adds that a *Gegenstand* is "foreign to thought", which is not to say that it is not mental, but that a *Gegenstand* involves a mental presence of its own accord and is not simply 'thought up'. It is capable of being apperceived in inner perception. *Gegenstände* (the plural of *Gegenstand*) may be looked upon as being

---

65   Vollenhoven's discussion of *Gegenstände* is generally limited to representations, though the act-content distinction is also applied to remembering and sensation, including the positing of their content. At one point he does speak of "*Gegenstände* of sensation, representation and remembering" (1918a: 404). At another point he also includes, besides 'knowing that', 'feeling' and 'desire'. But this variety does not require or define differences in distinct kinds of *Gegenstände*. It is the immediacy of what is perceived by inner perception that takes precedence (cf. 1918a: 172-173).

objective meanings, but in the guise of *immanent objects* (1918a: 162). The mind grasps them with certainty in virtue of their immediacy to the active Self. Nothing can be more certain than this intuited bi-unity, intuited in occurrent experience (or in an occasion of experience).

The step from content to *Gegenstand* may seem somewhat arbitrary—indeed, an important factor is still missing from our account. In incorporating the basics of this theory of Meinong into his own intuitionistic framework, Vollenhoven adds a feature lacking in Meinong. Eager to avoid psychologism, here too, Vollenhoven felt that the objectivity of a *Gegenstand* needs to be explicitly warranted, over against what could otherwise be considered a grasping at changing, and perhaps only fleetingly enjoyed, psychical content. He therefore stipulated that a *Gegenstand* needs to comply to the principle of identity, this principle being "the norm for all *Gegenstand* forming" (1918a: 433). When one posits what is experienced in direct awareness, one turns the (experienced) content into a fixed meaning with an unchanging intrinsic identity, under the aegis of the norm of identity. In that way the mind can subsequently operate with it as a *term of thought* with a stable meaning.[66]

Vollenhoven also (following Meinong) allowed for complex *Gegenstände*—Meinong called these '*Gegenstände* of higher order—by combining given *Gegenstände*. Thus 'haunted castle', 'the man next door', 'the square root of 10', etc. are *Gegenstände* of higher order (complex terms), but so are 'square circles', 'wooden irons' and the like, despite their 'impossibility'. What is impossible about them only becomes evident when *Gegenstände* are used as concepts to characterize essences (things), or in judgments. Concepts and judgments are subject to the norm of truth and logical consistency. But *Gegenstände* as such are only subject to the principle (norm) of identity. This gives *Gegenstände* a very wide range of mental use, as terms wielded by thought (1918a: 411).[67] As we shall see,

---

66   Vollenhoven refers to C. Sigwart, *Logic*, 4th edition, ed. by H. Maier (1911), for this understanding of the principle of identity: "it brings to consciousness identity and difference of distinct acts of representation, which as such are the same, but not identical" (1918a: 14). In Sigwart's own words, as quoted (in German) by Vollenhoven: "the principles of logic [among which the principle of identity]... are...*imperatives* that command that each object of our representation be strictly held to be the same and to prevent all changes, all unnoticed shifts of our representations, . . ." (1918a: 15; translation mine). Vollenhoven says furthermore about Sigwart, that "it was first with Sigwart that finally a new logic dawned for intuitionism" (1918a: 161). We add that the novelty relates to taking logical principles as norms or imperatives governing active mental functionings.

67   In "De activiteit der ziel in het rekenonderwijs" (The activity of the soul in learning arithmetic), Vollenhoven repeats the conditions for counting, mentioned in 1918a: 433. Only now he is more explicit when he states: "the acknowledgment of the principle

they are put to special metalogical use in the philosophy of science.

C. Analytical and metaphysical intuition

But the intuition is not limited to this concrete intuition. The introduction of *Gegenstände* has of itself already strained the appeal to the concrete intuition, calling for the recognition of other features of the intuition. Thus, there is also the immediate awareness in which one "grasps the equality or difference between two concrete intuitive givens" (1918a: 350). This facet of the intuition Vollenhoven calls the *analytical intuition*. For example there is the difference between act and content in the mind itself that is immediately evident (e.g. the difference between remembering and the remembered), and also one's positing the *Gegenstände*, in light of the principle of identity, cannot take place without 'analytical awareness' (1918a: 416). Of *Gegenstände* and their differences we are also immediately aware, and it is in virtue of this objectivity, and by means of the analytical intuition, that it is possible to formulate a theory of *Gegenstände*, distinguishing different kinds and different orders among them.[68] The notion of number also "finds its sole explanation [here] for the true intuitionism" (1918a: 350; cf. below). Through the concrete intuition, 'inner perception' is possible, but once it takes place the analytical intuition is needed to find one's way among these mental objects and in

---

of identity by this Self [is required] so as to become, in obedience to the logical norm (not law of nature), subject of distinguishing" (Vollenhoven and Janse 1919a: 102-103). In other words, the content that results from the Self's experience of something given can be posited as a *Gegenstand* only when the Self is constrained by or is attuned to the logical norm of identity in virtue of which the Self takes on the quality of distinguishing subject. In other words the positing 'identifies' objective meanings on condition that it is your will to turn representations into terms, in the context of inner perception. In this way the norm of identity links the Self (as distinguishing subject) to content (as distinguished in its own identity). In his discussion of Brouwer, Vollenhoven had stated that the Self's submission to the law of identity is a role of the Self as "knowing subject" (1918a: 401). This would appear to imply, confusingly, that the appeal to the principle of identity presupposes submission to the principle of contradiction. In 1918a: 431, Vollenhoven states: "The question now arises what the norm is for the truth of judgments. It can hardly be other than the principle of contradiction (which includes the principle of identity, without being deducible from it) and its deductions." He probably means to say that the principle of contradiction includes the demand of having objective and self-identical terms. The principle of identity as such is the norm for objective terms, *Gegenstände*, and if they were subject to truth, Vollenhoven would, *inter alia*, not be able to accept the so-called "impossible *Gegenstände*" (wooden iron, square circle, etc.), which he does accept; cf. his explicit statement 1918a: 411.

68   Vollenhoven ends the section on Meinong's *Gegenstandstheorie* by declaring that "his system is very well structured from a dualistic viewpoint and excellently suited for theistic and intuitionistic exposition" (1918a: 175).

dealing with them. Conversely, distinguishing and comparing is so primitive—Vollenhoven sometimes even speaks of "the comparing and connecting Self" (1918a: 416)—that its occurring takes place unbeknown, were it not that the concrete intuition signals its occurrence and brings what the analytical intuition effects to our consciousness (1918a: 414).

Then there is also the *metaphysical intuition*. It's most complete description is: "the immediate insight into identity in *difference* of spatial and temporal localization with respect to both the continuity of motion (real succession in continuous spatial and temporal discerning [*aanschouwing*]) and the ideas of species in distinguishing individuals" (1918a: 351). This description is not itself immediately self-evident. It seems better first to take a more indirect route to get to the metaphysical intuition. Then, when discussing Vollenhoven's metaphysics in a following section, we can return to this statement. For now we can approach the intention of the metaphysical intuition from the point of view of the connection between the three kinds of intuition.

The three kinds of intuition are said to hang together. Beginning with self-consciousness, the concrete intuition reveals this to be nothing but the occurrent experience of the different relations in which the Self stands to the given. The analytical intuition gives the Self a handle on this participation by distinguishing mental act and content and by positing that the awareness of the content is present through acts. But there is a feature that is still not sufficiently accounted for, namely, the differences in the contents of acts and, accordingly, also the differences in *Gegenstände*. For example, the mere capacity or act of sense-awareness, i.e. my sensing, does not explain why I might be (say) first aware of red, then blue and then green. Any act of sensing does not of itself produce difference in content. This difference must be due to (some feature of) the given to which the Self stands in the relations that one becomes conscious of in self-consciousness. There must be—in virtue of the monadic nature of relations assumed all along—an immediate awareness of the *reference to a given* that is other than the Self *in virtue of which* the content of the acts of consciousness gain their differences of contents. This intuition of reference to a given something is the *metaphysical intuition*.

We need to emphasize that this intuition is not a direct contact with the given as given. That is what the acquaintance relation of knowing is all about. The metaphysical intuition is, as is anything intuitional, 'intramental' and is predicated on the Self's participation in the relations to the given. The metaphysical intuition takes into account the feature of receptivity or the feature of being influenced or affected by what is extra-mental. However this is not to say that the being of the extra-mental, as given in its appearance, is carried over unchanged into the intra-mental effect.[69] The metaphysical intuition is the awareness of being thus affected: *that* I am affected that way. It induces a distinctness of thinking as an effect of a distinctness of being. So this 'reference to the object' is not a 'looking the object in the face', but it is the awareness of an act's being affected by something that effects difference in the mental content. It too is an undergoing, the taking place of which yields a certainty.

Although Vollenhoven does not say so, one could consider, as the corollary of the metaphysical intuition, the certainty of there being an external world. But to the extent that this certainty of fact does not imply an effect upon mentality, it could not replace the metaphysical intuition. In the more expansive formulation of the metaphysical intuition (yet to be discussed) we will find that Vollenhoven includes two prime features of *identity* relevant to this external effect.

At this point we can summarize that sameness of acts (whether of sensation, of representation or of remembering) but difference in the content of these acts, as discerned by the concrete and the analytical intuitions, calls for the metaphysical intuition to account for this difference. Thus the analytical intuition is the binding factor between the concrete and the metaphysical intuition. "This distinction between knowing act and content is already analytical intuition and so, the analytical intuition's assimilation of the concrete [intuition] postulates the metaphysical [intuition]" (1918a: 404).[70]

---

69   Recall the earlier quote: "the mind [*geest*] is structured in such a way that a specific colour-awareness in the psychical [series] corresponds with a certain frequency of vibrations in the physical series (*causa occasionalis*)" (1918a: 328). The metaphysical intuition is a kind of general 'appeal to externality' on the part of awareness, without preempting what that externality might be in detail (though a basic difference of thing and thing-relation is 'picked up' so to speak). Should one ask how the appearing of the given can be discerned if it is not carried over or supplanted by the characteristics of the intuited representations, then Vollenhoven could again point to the difference between knowing and being currently aware. Knowing *is* a dealing with appearances of the given, but this is such that it does *not require us* to realize that we are being appeared to. Also when we realize *that* we are being appeared to, we may be mistaken as to what appears.

70   This correlation of act and content might suggest a phenomenological connection. But this would be incorrect. Vollenhoven nowhere hints, let alone states, that this correlation evidences a relation of intentionality between act and content, even though for phenomenology, this relation of intention secures the principle of intuition. In the bi-unity of intuition, as maintained by Vollenhoven, one pole of the duality is always the currently experiencing Self. This reflects the Bergsonian provenance of Vollenhoven's understanding of the intuition and the context of life-philosophy.

D. *Gegenstandstheorie* and knowledge

When bringing *Gegenstandstheorie* into closer proximity to epistemology—after all, the former serves to provide thought with objective terms that are accounted for through conditions of intuition—we can compare *Gegenstände*, judgments and concepts and also inquire as to how they interrelate.

Each of these three attests to a 'synthesis of thought and being', as controlled by a principle. The synthesis characteristic of *Gegenstände* is intra-mental, being that of the 'mental material' of immanent objects and the Self as *distinguishing* subject. The norm that holds here is the principle of identity. The realm of *Gegenstände* may be said to 'subsist' intra-mentally. Their intuitive availability makes them ideal material of thought, serving as objective terms or meanings, irrespective of whether there is any relevant 'transcendent object', although the metaphysical intuition makes one aware that there is an effect of something external.

Judgments and concepts also attest to the synthesis of thought and being, in the sense that the *knowing* subject interacts with given data. This is the synthesis of knowing, and in both cases this synthesis is subject to the norm of truth, i.e. the logical principles of contradiction and excluded middle. Judgments are the most direct form of this synthesis in terms of their subject-predicate structure: the subject-term denotes the given, while the predicate is the chosen meaning of thought. With concepts the emphasis shifts towards the given thing, which forms the focus of conceptual knowledge. The "reality of scientific knowledge" is based on judgments, but this knowledge seeks to increase the understanding by coming, through the accrual of judgments, to increasingly more adequate concepts.

Now if *Gegenstände* and their intuitive certainty are to benefit epistemology in general, it must be possible to use them in connection with judgments and concepts. Under what conditions can this take place? First of all, there is the difference between concept and judgment to reckon with. In his *Gegenstandstheorie* Meinong had introduced the distinction between an *Objekt* and an *Objektiv*. The former, 'Object', is the *Gegenstand* as (simple or complex) term, such as a *Gegenstand* of representation. Now *Gegenstände* of representation are applicable to concepts, though a (proleptic) concept is not a representation (1918a: 163). For Vollenhoven a concept signals the grasp (understanding) of something given or concerning the given, but always incompletely. For in conceptual understanding, something is left out or is lacking. A musical tone is always produced somehow (voice, instrument, the wind, etc.), has a volume (loud or soft), falls within one of the octaves audible to the human ear, etc. The concept 'tone c' is *about* a given (or producible) sound but with features left out (or left variable). In this sense, the content of a concept is determined by choice of attention in the face of the given, and this distinguishes the concept from a *Gegenstand* (of representation), which is merely a term posited by (the analytic) intuition. But such a *Gegenstand* can serve as the intension of the concept. In becoming the intension of a concept, the *Gegenstand* brings a fixed meaning of the understanding to bear on discerned data, on the condition that the term does not contain contradictory predicates (which is why the principle of contradiction must hold here, for concepts). Vollenhoven does not settle for a concept as a statically held intension, with an extension of data falling under it; a concept takes part in a striving to understand, and in that sense there is the drive towards making concepts more adequate to the given than they represent at any one point. A (proleptic) concept acts as a series principle governing the functional variability of the intensions, as they are added or changed in the concept's becoming more adequate. A *Gegenstand* determines an intension, but a concept has an extension as well (1918a: 412). In summary, a concept is said to *possess* a *Gegenstand* while not *being* a *Gegenstand* (cf. 1918a: 163).[71]

Now as to judgments, a judgment is not a concept, though a concept can occur in a judgment as the subject-term. In Vollenhoven's use, a judgment is the most typical case of knowledge being a relation, namely the relation of thought and being. The relation is "laid" when the knowing subject's choice of predicate is attributed to a discerned object that is in some sense given. Contrary to the situation of conceptual understanding, in the relational situation there is the relation that has to be respected. This is achieved in being aware of the concomitant complex of the judgment, namely the complex of subject (referent) and predicate (relatum) as related ("the president is ill"), as over against a summation of these terms and an added relation term ("president", "ill[ness]" + "is"). When grasping the content of the judgment, there is a unity of thought, a unity that is required so as to be able to ascertain the truth or falsehood of that content. In virtue of this unity, the content has the feature of 'truth-value', i.e. the feature making it relevant to consider the content as being true or false. Now this thought, which is unique to the relational complex—not to be confused with complex terms that lack the relational

---

71   This does not prevent Vollenhoven from speaking of a *Gegenstand* "becoming" a (proleptic) concept (1918a: 412). The condition here is that the "becoming" is governed by the principle of contradiction, which must be adduced if there is to be any concept at all.

moment, such as 'tall hunter', 'wooden iron', 'ill president', for these lack 'truth-value'—is a distinct kind of *Gegenstand* that Meinong called an *Objektiv* (which term is usually translated directly as "Objective" to retain its technical meaning). A judgment, then, is not itself a *Gegenstand*, but it *has* a *Gegenstand*, namely an Objective, this being an immanent object intuited when the knowing subject judges. (G.E. Moore and Russell introduced the term 'proposition' in this respect.)[72]

The difference between a judgment and the *Gegenstand* that a judgment is said to have, is evidenced by two peculiar features: "conviction" and "the qualification of 'yes' and 'no'" (1918a: 163). In more current terminology, this is *assertion* and the *choice of true or false*. Assertion (and also denial) pertain to the act of judgment. The choice of true or false pertains to the content, a choice that is also relevant when judging. The Objective, as *Gegenstand*, is merely the thought, without assertion or denial, and also without choice as to actual truth-value, though the possibility of this choice is left open in virtue of the peculiar 'complex unity' that an Objective is. Besides the Objective of the judgment as such, there is also the possibility of thinking the parts of the concomitant complex of a judgment in terms of their own *Gegenstände*. In that case, the subject term is an Object, but the predicate is said to be an Objective (1918a: 163-164). This tends to confuse. Does the objective of the predicate differ from that of the whole judgment? Presumably (though some doubt remains) we need to see this in terms of the thought-being connection as relevant to *Gegenstände*, namely as intra-mental subsisting being. In that case a *Gegenstand* of representation, i.e. an Object, has being in the sense that it is simply the term (possibly complex) that it is, while the *Gegenstand* of a predicate is said to be a 'so-being' (1918a: 163). The latter term refers to a qualification, reminding one, in the case of predicates, to take into account a predicate's feature of being (truly or falsely) predicable of something.

I believe the following example illustrates Vollenhoven's meaning. The judgment "the president is ill" itself has as Objective 'that the president is ill', which expression preserves truth-value (but without choice

---

72   Cf. especially B. Russell, "Meinong's theory of complexes and assumptions", i.e. Russell 1904. On p. 457 Russell states: "This Objective of the judgment is what (following Mr. G.E. Moore) I have called a proposition: it is to the Objective that such words as true and false, evident, probable, necessary, etc., apply". The *Gegenstände* 'Object' and 'Objective' will be written with a capital 'O', to distinguish these *intra*-mental entities from the extra-mental (or transcendent) entities: 'object', as synonym for 'thing', and 'given complex' for 'things in relations / things in interaction' (i.e. facts/events), respectively. The term 'Object' occurs seldom, being implicit in the use of *Gegenstand* when not further qualified.

as to which value holds). But the parts of the judgment have their own *Gegenstände*. For the subject term this is the Object 'the president' (as determinate intra-mental meaning), but it could also be expanded into the complex term 'the ill president', for this does not involve a relation. The predicate has an Objective, referred to as: 'illness had by x'. Here there is a relational feature in the *Gegenstand* itself, which is why this *Gegenstand* is an Objective and not an Object. This illustration also makes evident the *monadic approach* to a judgment. A judgment, being a case of knowledge as relation, presupposes features in the terms which allow the relation to be 'laid'. Intuitive awareness picks up on the certainty of the *Gegenstände* here. But there is knowledge only when a choice in truth-value is actually asserted in the face of the given.

So, relevant to the epistemological context is the distinction of *Gegenstände* in Objects and Objectives, both involve a certitude of mind, the former as relevant for the content of concepts, the latter for that of judgments. What about this distinction itself? It involves a difference in content that cannot be adequately accounted for in terms of the knowing or distinguishing subject alone. (There is a subjective difference of course between wielding a concept, as when understanding, and formulating a judging, but this is a difference between the acts, and it does not characterize the difference between an Object and an Objective.) So Vollenhoven concludes that, here too, there must be a "corresponding distinction in the given" (1918a: 404). Hence, our intuiting this distinction is by means of the metaphysical intuition, in combination with the analytical intuition that is always present to perform the distinguishing. This distinction in the given that is relevant here (as Vollenhoven immediately clarifies) is the one previously mentioned about things and relations. "Thus metaphysical intuitionism acknowledges that *things* and *relations between these* are given, independently of our knowing" (*ibid.*). Note that Vollenhoven here speaks of "metaphysical intuitionism". The metaphysical intuition is an attitude of mind respecting the given, it cannot actually warrant (it only surmises) a metaphysical difference. But if we take into account the distinction within knowledge between concept and judgment, these being oriented to the given, then we can say that a concept concerns a thing, namely a particular *being*, while a judgment concerns the qualification of a thing or numerous things via their relations, which involves *so-being*. One may then say that concepts and judgments have metaphysical intent in that they get us to know *being* and *so-being*, respectively. This is based on the order of the (thought alien) world, when acknowledging the difference between things and their relations, and this acknowledgment at the same time suggests the distinction entertained in the mental order of thought, *viz.* between the Object and the Objective.[73] Hence the distinction of immanent Object and Objective in the order of thought attests to a very basic structural feature in the order of the existent world of transcendent objects, namely things and the relations between things, though the reflecting is not such as to be a mere copy of it. The difficulty in pinpointing this 'non-copy difference' does not diminish the importance of the distinction of being and so-being in the intra-mental and the extra-mental orders. Without it, on the human side the distinction in knowing between understanding and judging would collapse, while on the object side one could not proceed from the difference between thing and relational structure. The metaphysical intuition involves the awareness that this distinction of being and so-being is not of our making. In that sense, the difference between being and so-being is a condition of reality's being knowable.

Now why skim this analytical realist landscape? The obvious answer is that it has an intrinsic relevance for the early Vollenhoven. In that sense it needs to be mentioned and seriously considered in any overview of that early work. But it also has consequences for the future. In the early

---

73   Vollenhoven says at one point that being and so-being belong to *Gegenstände*. "Hence the *Gegenstand* of a judgment qua talis is the affirming or denying *relation*, the *so-being*, not the *being*, which is *Gegenstand* of the representation" (1918a: 164). He is paraphrasing Meinong at this point and emphasizing that the ontological status of *Gegenstände* is intra-mental. This should not be confused with being that is "foreign to thought" in an extra-mental (transcendent) sense. But I believe there is (another kind of) confusion in Vollenhoven, when he attributes assertion to the *Gegenstand*, while this is more appropriate to the judgment to which the *Gegenstand* belongs (*ibid.*). This is implicitly corrected in his own discussion in the next paragraph when he speaks of assumptions and compares these to judgments. Also, Vollenhoven no doubt means to say that, concerning a judgment—this being a connection of being and thought—the *Gegenstand* of the judgment is not the relation inherent in the judgment but the concomitant complex of this relation. The sloppiness seems to be influenced by the difficulty of insisting on the one hand that, via the metaphysical intuition, the mind (thought) attests to being affected by the outer world (being), on the other hand that this influence is not a mere copying. So in some sense there is similarity between the extra-mental and the intra-mental, but at the same time a difference. The following statement shares (I believe) in this confusion: "The *Gegenstand* is ... the immanent object whose occurrence [*ontstaan*] is accounted for in part by a transcendent object, in the event that it exists, in cooperation with the human mind" (1918a: 162). This seems to distinguish between *Gegenstände* that arise through the effect of something existing in the outer world and those lacking such an effect. But *Gegenstände* constitute the order of thought, of which the principle of identity is the norm, so whatever 'impulse' derives from the outer world, this is necessarily channelled through mental acts. It requires subsequent attention to discern which *Gegenstände* have corresponding transcendent objects and which do not.

1920s these two orders define the problem of the relation between *logos* and *cosmos*. When Dooyeweerd enters into discussion with Vollenhoven, this problem is prominently present. Also, the role of the intuition and *Gegenstandstheorie*—the latter being then referred to as the *Gegenstand-sphere*—are reflected on in a way that leads to the modal order. The mature reflections of both Vollenhoven and Dooyeweerd cannot be properly appreciated without reckoning with the provenance of these reflections in the early work of Vollenhoven. The subsequent discussions of chapters 3 and 4 should bear this out.

E. Summary

In summary, the mental world of immanent things and the extra-mental world of transcendent beings are the terrains of the two main philosophical disciplines: *Gegenstandstheorie* en metaphysics (1918a: 166) respectively. The immanent things of the mental world come to consciousness through the intuitive awareness of inner perception. These things 'exist in the mind' to the extent that the mind can posit a distinct awareness of thought-content. Two kinds of *Gegenstände* stand out: those of representation (or memory or sensation), called simply Objects, and those of judgment, Objectives. The posited content need in no way have any truck with the transcendent world of empirical things or the extra-mental world of validity of norms, ideals and ideas, though something in the posited content, that determines a *Gegenstand*, may have been suggested by an effect of the transcendent world. Such an effect is thought to be relevant for the difference in kind between Objects and Objectives, this being a reflection of the distinction between things and their relations in the transcendent world. We can say, as has become usual, that *Gegenstände subsist* in the mental world as objective terms, not as subjective notions merely enjoyed. Important for Vollenhoven's understanding of this mental world of thought and its *Gegenstände* is that it stands under the aegis of the principle of identity.

The metaphysical world is the transcendent world. Because Vollenhoven uses the term 'transcendent' in the sense of 'transcendent to consciousness', this world is not merely a super-sensible world, but it also includes the empirical world as given to thought, independently of our knowing. It is the world of outer perception, the world that we attempt to get to know in concepts and judgments. This world stands under the aegis of ideas. Ideas are not (Lockean) representations, but determinations of *distinct beings*.[74] In the section on metaphysics (see below) this

---

74 Cf. Vollenhoven 1921c: 79. Vollenhoven speaks of "een anders-gedacht-*zijn*", i.e.

world will be explored in more detail. But for now we can state that a very basic feature of this world is that of things with their own inner complexity and standing in mutual (thing-)relations. The 'revealing' of the things of this world, which allows it to be known, is not of our making. There is, however, the effect of the thing's orientation with respect to our bodily presence. E.g., for the longest time mankind only knew the moon from the side that constantly faces the earth. The fact that that is how the moon 'reveals itself' to the inhabitants on earth does not make this appearing 'subjective'. There is a physical limitation, which has consequences for our sensibility. But it is such limitations that one attempts to lessen—ideally attempt to completely overcome—in a continuing process of conceptually getting to know better, as we try to make our (proleptic) concepts more adequate to the reality that they are about.

We need to deepen this topic of metaphysics. But now that all the intuitional prerequisites are in place, we can first complete the discussion of Vollenhoven's account of numbers.

F. Number

Space, we found, finds its explanation within the order of knowledge. Number, i.e. the first order arithmetic of the natural numbers—this concerns counting as knowing act (*kendaad*)—is accounted for within the 'order of intuition' (if we may call it that). Because the intuition is the occurrent experience of multiplicity-in-unity, it is deemed to be capable of providing the suitable—indeed, the only suitable—account of the notion of number (1918a: 105).

Now, first of all, we can only count *Gegenstände* (1918a: 124), at least in an original sense. The terms that enter into the count must obviously retain their distinct character. Outer objects can also be counted, but their identity condition (via forms of sensibility) is complicated. *Gegenstände* comply directly to this condition in virtue of the principle of identity. As objective meanings, *Gegenstände* are posits of mentality and capable of being perceived by inner perception and known intuitively. In other words they form a *kind of (mental) being* in their own right (1918a: 72), a 'mental material'. This gives the notion of numbers—the successive grouping of more and more units of *Gegenstände*—its objectivity, and even its unique character *sui generis* (1918a: 229). In Meinong's terminology, a number is a *Gegenstand* of a "higher order". Higher order

---

"a *being* [which is] thought distinctly". Thus, an idea is not the thought, but the incentive calling for distinct thought with respect to a being, itself foreign to thought, that 'gives' itself to be thought.

Gegenstände are 'superiora' in virtue of being composed of other *Gegenstände*, namely the 'inferiora' that function as their constituent elements. Each number beyond the number one, has constituent units that are the inferiora to the number in question. As *Gegenstand* of higher order, a number forms a plurality, and that constitutes a distinct kind of superiora. Numbers are a distinct kind of *Gegenstände*, they are not concepts (1918a: 416). (As concepts, numbers would have to be features of something.) Our awareness of numbers is in virtue of the analytical intuition that seizes the (higher order) difference between the numbers as *Gegenstände* (1918a: 416). It is all intra-mental.

But something more is called for in connection with the natural numbers. "*Numbers* are not *things*, but *members* of a series, that can be created by means of the principle of that series" (1918a: 380). The principle in question is of course the principle of complete induction, recounted earlier (section III.A.). This principle appeals to the power of the mind of being able to repeat indefinitely the addition of units (*Gegenstände*) and of our being conscious of that power. The latter consciousness is in virtue of concrete intuition (1918a: 384). This is the clue that permits Vollenhoven to look deeper.

The indefinite repetition that one is aware of in concrete intuition is traceable to the succession that is characteristic of any occurrent experience. Every experience has its moments, and in their succession—their passing by—'psychical growth' takes place. This calls for memory to prevent the moments from slipping away, for only then can there be the development of psychical growth in virtue of the gathering together of moments. But this succession can only be real or objective if, here too, the principle of identity is brought to bear upon the experienced moments: "without the norm of identity there is no awareness of the occurrent experience of succession [*geen weet van de beleving van successie*]. But the converse is also true: without succession the norm [of identity] has no meaning and it becomes a vain tautology" (1918a: 401, 416). The Self that undergoes experience needs to subject itself to the norm of identity—and hence ought to!—if the occurrent experience is to yield an enriching enjoyment rather than a confusing diversion. And "without it [namely real succession] our own psychical existence becomes impossible" (1918a: 417).[75] So the presence of succession serves as condition to define a series principle that is relevant for the series of the natural num-

---

75 The requirement that the Self subjects itself to the norm of identity is similar to the Self having to subject itself to the norm of truth to be knowing subject in the case of knowledge by acquaintance. Cf. footnote 67 above.

bers. The awareness of this presence of succession is in virtue of the concrete and analytical intuition, which 'sees' that the mind has the power to indefinitely continue this putting-in-succession. This is the synthetic a priori of (first order) arithmetic, and it is the basis for accepting the principle of complete induction.

Accordingly, the notion of number and that of the series of the natural numbers are based on (intra-mental) *real succession*, which is itself an indispensable prerequisite of psychical synthesis. Thus it is in the locus of the concrete intuition that the meaning of numbers arise, whereby the succession of experienced moments forms the raw material, as it were. When, through the analytical intuition, these moments of real succession become a sequence of *Gegenstände*, the meaning of number becomes definite (1918a: 417).[76] But prior to acknowledging the role of the principle of identity here, we realize that succession must actually take place. But for succession to take place, *time* must be presupposed, without which succession cannot be. Time here is the succession of moments of an occurrent experience intuited concretely. Here is the link, deep in mental psychical synthesis, between *time, number and the concrete intuition*. But this is decidedly not time as form of sensibility, that organizes sequentially data of (outer and inner) sensibility. The time of occurrent succession is more like the very form of reflective consciousness itself, or in any case a condition for it.

VII. METAPHYSICS

The topic of metaphysics enables us to begin to round off the discussion of Vollenhoven's philosophical standpoint. The discussion of theism, which is to follow, will complete this.

In his report of Meinong's work Vollenhoven states that Meinong's juxtaposing of *Gegenstandstheorie* and metaphysics is analogous to what he (Vollenhoven) calls *ratio* (the rational element) and *empirie* (the empirical element), respectively (1918a: 166). Meinong holds that the two disciplines of *Gegenstandstheorie* and metaphysics together cover the whole domain of philosophy (1918a: 173). Vollenhoven agrees, but only on condition that the link between these disciplines be included. That

---

76 Reverting to the three terms that are undefined in the Peano system of arithmetic, namely 'one', 'number' and 'successor of', Vollenhoven's intuitionistic determination of these terms are: 'one' can be any *Gegenstand* (Object), 'number' is the series principle of complete induction, and 'successor of' is real succession, whereby succession does not forfeit unity. The latter is best exemplified in the Self, in which succession takes place, but controlled by the invariance of the Self. "Hence the Self should be marked as the ideal principle of succession and this law is the invariant" (1918a: 429).

link is mathematics, for it harbours the synthetic a priori, required to link the rational and the empirical elements, in its most original form (1918a: 166, 173).

In this summary statement we find again the three nodal points—the empirical, the rational and the normative—of Vollenhoven's standpoint, but now in an embellished form. *Gegenstandstheorie* is the amplification of thought in the sense of being a very liberal exposition of 'the thinkable' (including such odd 'thinkables' as 'square circle', 'wooden iron', etc.).[77] The empirical is linked to metaphysics. This is at first blush a strange combination. But Vollenhoven often expresses the juxtaposition of *ratio* and *empirie* as that of thought and being. Whatever the precise meaning of 'being' is, it is in any case used in connection with whatever is foreign to thought and capable of being cognitively assimilated by thought—at least in an on-going attempt—in (proleptic) concepts. Hence, being includes the things and the interactions between things of the outer world. These are material beings. But there is also soul or psychical being. This is of particular importance in the case of a human being and its Self. The Self is basically of a psychical nature, and while this involves material or bodily existence, it also includes higher mental life. This Self is not something constituted by thought. It is the reality standing (so to speak) 'behind' thought, with access to thought. So metaphysics, as study of being, occupies itself with that which *transcends conscious thought* in the sense of being foreign to thought or presupposed by thought, such as the existence of physical things and the Self.

Then there is the normative element. This is implicit in mentioning mathematics as the link between the rational and the empirical elements. Mathematics embodies the synthetic a priori, the proto-typical form of the synthesis of thought and being. In mathematics there are the a priori of space at the psycho-physical level (localization) and the a priori of number at the intra-mental level (succession). But the latter is of first rank over against the second rank of the former. Only with respect to the synthetic a priori of number can one speak of an *intuitive* certainty,

---

77 Vollenhoven does not address the question whether his norm of identity, to which the 'distinguishing subject' appeals when positing *Gegenstände*, would not in fact preclude such 'unthinkable' *Gegenstände* as 'round squares' and the like. These 'impossible *Gegenstände*', which Vollenhoven explicitly accepts (cf. 1918a: 411), are (so one would think) uncertain as to their identity, and accordingly the distinguishing subject should experience difficulty when applying the norm of identity. Vollenhoven could have cited such 'unthinkables' as indicative of the 'pre-norm' situation and as examples of psychical confusion. Meinong, who did not appeal to norms, did not feel an objection here. For him 'impossible *Gegenstände*' also subsist, which he took to be commendable, so that sentences, such as "a square circle does not exist", would have a referent.

namely the certainty of the analytical intuition.[78] Through this intuition, the Self is able to take on the qualities of distinguishing subject (in the context of which *Gegenstände* are posited) and of knowing subject, for in the analytical intuition's distinguishing and comparing of content, identity is posited in light of the norm of identity, and judgments are formed knowingly in the light of the norm of truth. So behind the intra-mental synthetic a priori there is intuition and there is the cognitive need for norms.

Knowledge and intuition—or judgment and awareness, respectively—are reconcilers of thought and being. Knowledge reconciles the knowing subject with the given object in outer perception. There must be something given as knowable, otherwise knowledge falls away. "The presupposition of knowing however is existence and thus being has logical precedence over thought" (1918a: 382). Awareness, in turn, reconciles the identity awareness with (intra-mental) occurrent experience. Here the focus is not on being but on self-consciousness (although, as we shall see, self-consciousness is ultimately linked to the Self in a metaphysical sense). But since every reconciliation involves relations and every relation consists of predicates attributed to the terms of the relation, we need also to consider the nature of the terms. In an ultimate sense the terms are *substances*. So the discussion can now turn to metaphysics in a specific sense: "dualism acknowledges substances and relations in which they stand, accordingly it can accept this logic of relations as method for those sciences that occupy themselves with relations, but not for metaphysics which also speaks of substances" (1918a: 158).

We can depict the place of metaphysics with an embellished portrayal of the triadic scheme of the normative (Norm), the rational (thought) and the empirical (being) elements.

---

78 Every judgment, being a synthesis of thought and being, is at bottom a variation of the synthetic a priori (1918a: 435). But the difference in rank between the two synthetic a priori's of mathematics indicates a difference in their evidence. That of number is intuitively certain, but that of space is marked by the context of sensibility. Although nothing is 'logically prior' to the synthetic a priori of localization, in the sense that the latter cannot be deduced from more primitive givens, that is not to say we have a 'dead certainty' about it. There is a factor of acceptance on faith here in the sense that localization involves our psycho-physical organization, a structure we cannot apperceive but only 'sense'.

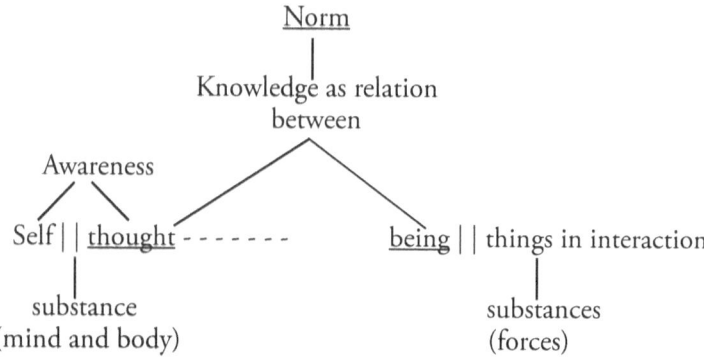

Knowledge is dependent on the appearing of the given, and in that sense can be said to be linked to the phenomenal order of appearances. The intuitive order concerns self-awareness, an important part of which is positing thought (as *Gegenstände*). Now we must look 'behind the phenomena', so to speak, to discover their substratum, and also attempt to discern the substratum of thought, i.e. the metaphysical Self. These are the two major examples of substance.[79]

A. The principle of substance

Vollenhoven's metaphysics of substances is entirely dogmatic in its use. The metaphysics of substance proceeds from the principle "acknowledged by *all*, [namely] that every operation (*werking*) requires a subject of operation" (1918a: 405; cf. also p. 438). The claim that this principle is accepted by all is of course entirely gratuitous.[80] But a motive for choosing this metaphysics is to be found in Vollenhoven's theistic viewpoint, as will become clear in the next section. The principle itself states that every change is a change of something, and that this something must remain recognizably itself or invariant despite the change. Besides speaking of 'subject' of change or operation, Vollenhoven also speaks of 'substratum' (1918a: 429). Thus the subject here is what undergirds or bears the

---

79   Consider: "if thought is a connection then there must be things between which thought is the connection: the subject and object of acquaintance [*kennen*], but these are themselves but qualities of things that exist metaphysically: the subject of acquaintance is a function of the Self that wants to know and to that end subjects itself to the norms of logic; the object of knowing is a function of the things outside of me, their appearing, their revealing to or their action upon me" (1918a: 228-229).

80   Vollenhoven was no doubt aware that he was on thin ice. In a lecture on Bergson, he criticized him for not accepting this principle. For him "everything changes without there being anything that changes"; Vollenhoven 1919b. Bergson is a clear counter-example to Vollenhoven's 'all'. While Vollenhoven acknowledged Bergson's influence, as we saw, this influence did not extend into the area of metaphysics.

change, what in Greek thought is referred to as the *hypokeimenon*. An important corollary of the principle of substance is the logical principle that Leibniz made popular: *praedicatum inest subjecto*, the predicate inheres in the subject (1918a: 66, 270ff). However, Vollenhoven does not apply this principle in epistemology, contrary to Leibniz. If this were applied in epistemology, it would enjoin that, in an ultimate sense, a judgment is analytic. Such a judgment would not attest to a knowing assimilation of an object, but merely be an image of it, which induces formalism. Instead, Vollenhoven links this inherence principle to his view of relations, which we can now see as having metaphysical relevance: "*praedicatum inest subjecto*, thus knowledge of extra-mental reality depends on both the subject as referent and the object as relatum" (1918a: 66), because every relation depends on predicates in the terms said to stand in relation. "*Praedicatum inest subjecto*" is the shibboleth of monadology, and Vollenhoven concurs to the extent that his substance with inherent predicates resembles a monad. "The monad is supposed to distinguish the substance from the aggregate. But precisely for that reason the subject-predicate theory is valid only in metaphysics. In metaphysics relations do not have an independent existence, but they are reduced to real predicates of referent and relatum" (1918a: 275).[81] The view of 'knowledge as relation' has been discussed in the foregoing. We now come to its foundation in the metaphysics of substance, namely the Self and the extra-mental reality.

From Vollenhoven's use of the inherence principle, one can get a clearer view of its meaning for him. In a wording taken from Russell's discussion of Leibniz, Vollenhoven states that the metaphysical interpre-

---

81 Though Vollenhoven is clearly positive about the monadology, he does not use this term in the exposition of his own position, not even the term 'monad'. One can only guess at the reason for his reticence. There may be the general problem of the association with Leibniz, for whom monads were 'windowless'. Vollenhoven defends a "*causa occasionalis*" (1918a: 328) which, however much this leaves the correlation of an appearance and the representation it causes in the dark, is not compatible with the notion of a monad that is windowless. John Kok therefore speaks of a "mitigated monadology" at this point, mitigated "because the monads are not windowless—there is interaction"; Kok 1992: 222, also (same page) footnote 157. There are also at least two points of criticism that Vollenhoven directs against the monadology, as traditionally conceived: (i) it views a body as an aggregate of monads, and (ii) the body as aggregate is not sufficiently determined. Vollenhoven maintains that a body is itself a substance (i.e. a monad, not an aggregate) and that "the monadology needs to be supplemented with the Platonic doctrine of ideas" (1918a: 272 note 2; cf. the ensuing discussion for this reference to ideas). Perhaps the overall differences between this use in Leibniz and Vollenhoven's qualified approval were still such as to constrain him to avoid this terminology in the formulation of his own thoughts.

tation of the principle implies that "nothing is absolutely real but indivisible substances and their variable [*sic*] states" (1918a: 269).[82] From Vollenhoven's comment about Russell being reluctant to admit this, we can imply that Vollenhoven agrees with it. A logical consequence of the principle is that "the sum of the predicates is to be slightly less than the substance" (1918a: 274). In other words the substance is not a kind of sum total or mere collection of the predicates that inhere in it—if that were true all basic judgments would be analytic—but the substance is a reality over and above that sum. In that sense Vollenhoven rejects Leibniz's principle of the identity of indiscernibles, which holds that every difference must be discernible in terms of predicates. Vollenhoven sees in it a truncated form of the norm of identity. If every difference between two things (substances) needs to be grounded in a difference of predicates, then the substances themselves have no reality over and above the predicates. The implication of Vollenhoven's view is that any two things are, as such, numerically distinct, without having to presuppose a difference in predicates (1918a: 274, 285).

A general question that arises in connection with substances is: what is the status or nature of a substance? The terminology of 'subject' (in the sense of 'sub-jectum', something 'thrown under') and 'substratum' suggests a kind of hidden or primary matter. But this would raise an insoluble problem. Going back to the basic principle of "change but not without a substratum that does not change" Vollenhoven explains: "All the same, something cannot stay the same *and* change, unless this something is the *fixed law* that expresses the rule of change" (1918a: 429). So there is a category difference between the changing predicates, or the appearances of things, and that which remains constant in their variability. The constancy is that of law, *viz.* the rule which itself determines change and variability. The substance, it turns out, is the ideational principle of that rule—an 'idea'—the essence of a thing. "We too admit, that the essence of things, retaining thereby the qualitative difference between spirit and matter [*geest en stof*], is ideational, but *extra-mental* ideational" (1918a: 229). This essence is not someone's idea or cogitation; its seat is beyond human mentality. It concerns "the Platonic doctrine of ideas" (1918a: 272 note 2). We need to look at this more closely.

B. Individual substances

Let us first review individual things and then turn to human beings.

---

[82] Russell's own wording is: "Nothing is absolutely real but indivisible substances and their various states"; Russell 1900: 114.

When he defends Lotze against negative criticisms of Russell, Vollenhoven approvingly explains his (Lotze's) meaning to be: "the essence of things is 'Geistigkeit' [spiritual/intellectual], the existence is relation. . . . [T]wo *things* are the same if their idea, their law, is the same; they can then differ in relations; e.g. two dogs of the same breed are the *same* and yet not identical; the *essence* is the same, [while] the objective and subjective relations differ. Only in this way can individuality be maintained" (1918a: 281-282). Vollenhoven seems to be saying that the substantial essence of things is the kind or species they represent. Their existence in relations, i.e. their origination, their interaction with other things and the like, is responsible for their mutual differences. But since relations are reducible to predicates, we can say that a German shepherd dog does things in a German shepherd dog-like way; i.e. its 'predicates', namely its characteristics, hang together in a way that is characteristic to that breed. But these predicates also induce differences in the interactions any German shepherd dog is involved in, and that accounts for the individual differences.

But this is not entirely satisfactory.[83] Individuality seems to be maintained only through the differences of existence. But the notion of substance as law means that the substance is a fixed law expressing a rule of change (1918a: 429). In this connection, ideas are 'thing-laws', i.e. "ideas regulate functional development as fixed laws" (1918a: 228). So the idea of a thing is not just a constant pattern of coherence between the characteristics, properties, states and what not of an individual thing, but the idea regulates the coherence in a way that keeps the individual, in all its changes and development, in line with its species identity. Ideas regulate both simultaneous coherence and successive change, and in that way keep the dynamics of an individual within the bounds of its essence. Within those bounds the exemplars of a species can have all the individual difference they in fact have, because for each there is an idea.[84]

One might express the notion of individual substance in the following way. The thing is a distinct mental and/or physical existence, with fitting properties, features, etc. The idea is an extra-mental essence. The two, the thing and the idea, maintain a very basic relation. But the thing is individual and the general idea is an extra-mental essence. To maintain

---

83 John Kok helped me to see that the formulated view is indeed unsatisfactory.

84 Thus Vollenhoven says that in the case of identical twins, "there is in an objective sense distinction of ideas"; Vollenhoven 1921c: 80. Also, in his letter to the theologian F.W. Grosheide, 16 November 1921, he states: "if God observes an animal he immediately knows both the species connection (also which species) and the individual distinctness."

a relation, there have to be basic features on each side on which the relation is based (monadism). The (general) idea needs to have a specific relevance of 'holding for' the individual, while the thing requires a 'conforming to' the idea as a general feature. That means on the one hand that the idea needs to be individuated, something that only God can do, and which in fact he does—in connection with the human being: "God constantly realizes the *general* idea 'human being' in a *particular* way" (1918a: 72-73). On the other hand, the deepest metaphysical feature of things is that they are dynamic. A thing has the capacity of force to influence and affect other things, which is to say that they can enter into thing-relations and interact mutually. But this is not just chaotic happening; there is a coherence and continuity that guarantees that the changing features conform to a *development* evincing a species identity. There is a regularity or a 'succession' in the features, which is to say that things are structured temporally and spatially. In that way the idea, when individuated, serves as an individual regulator, while the individual thing regulated maintains a coherence and continuity in its dynamic space-time existence, conformal to its species identity, in a way that expresses 'real succession'. One expects a distinct term here, representing the individual and its controlled states, such as 'monad'. But Vollenhoven seems consciously to refrain from using this term (cf. footnote 81 above).

There is also a larger context, defined by the limitative nature of absolute space and time, which is supra-individual. That will be addressed when discussing the structure of the world.

C. Again: the metaphysical intuition

It is appropriate now to pick up on a matter we had to leave unfinished earlier, and that is Vollenhoven's more specific formulation of the metaphysical intuition. It is described as the "immediate insight into identity in *difference* of spatial and temporal localization with respect to both the continuity of motion (real succession in continuous spatial and temporal discerning [*aanschouwing*]) and the ideas of species in distinguishing individuals [*soortideeën in de onderscheiding der individuen*]" (1918a: 351). Being an intuition, it concerns a fundamental awareness or state of consciousness, but being the metaphysical intuition, the awareness concerns the mind's content being affected by the presence of the outer world, though the effect is not that of a one-to-one copy or picture of the world.

The metaphysical intuition has been mentioned twice already. The first time was in connection with the differences in the contents of representations, memories and sense-data, that could only be accounted for as the consequence of being affected by the outer world. Via the analytical intuition this awareness of differences can be grasped in their own right, and in light of the principle of identity, turned into *Gegenstände*. The second reference to the metaphysical intuition was in connection with the distinction, among *Gegenstände*, between 'Objects' and 'Objectives'. Objects are distinct (intra-mental) meanings (terms), representing things, or features, properties or aspects of things. They may be simple or complex, and entertained through the imagination or through the experiential awareness of things. Objectives are relational complexes, the awareness of which we bring to bear when understanding things in their own (thing-)relations (say, head resting on hand) or the (thing-)relations to other things (say, hand picking up a book). This awareness, whether of terms or of relational complexes, is important in that it conditions what the knowing subject recognizes as 'the given', i.e. what things reveal of themselves as data for knowing. The data is grasped 'term-wise' and/or 'relational complex-wise'. The metaphysical intuition acknowledges that this distinction is not itself merely 'thought up', but that it reflects a difference of being. Not surprisingly, this distinction is important for epistemology as well, in that concepts 'have' Objects (as their intensions) and judgments 'have' Objectives (on which propositional truth-value is based).[85]

Now, in the third, more specific, reference to the metaphysical intuition, the focus is on localization. Localization assumes the larger context of space and time. Space, we found, has both a subjective and an objective determination. It calls for a perceiver with a spatial 'form of sensibility', who cannot but see what he/she sees in a spatial, side-by-side way. On the other hand, the thing perceived also has intrinsic complexity, of parts in relations, that sustains an extensional viewing. Time, as sequence, here falls in the same category, except that it involves a one-dimensional sequential viewing, supported by a succession relation in the object seen.

Vollenhoven now calls the 'objective side' of space and time, *abso-*

---

85   Many *Gegenstände*, whether as Objects or Objectives, can be 'thought up' and are constructed intra-mentally, as higher order *Gegenstände*, without having a motivation in terms of the given. These lack correlative transcendent objects. In the case of Objectives, the judgments that possess Objectives that lack a correlation to the given are considered false, those that do have such a correlation, true (cf. 1918a: 165, 306, 319). In a more current terminology, an Objective can be considered to be a proposition (as did Moore and Russell, in interpreting Meinong), and the transcendent correlate, when it exists, a fact. Then propositions have truth-value (true or false), while a fact could be called a 'truth-maker'. The presence or lack of presence of a fact motivates the choice as to the truth-value of a proposition that is accepted. So are fictions 'false-makers'? For Vollenhoven there is no such species of transcendent reality.

lute space and time. We cannot speak of space and time being 'things', in the sense of completed wholes, for that would disregard the subjective component required when referring to space and time. Space and time not being completed wholes, they cannot have boundaries, for then they would need to be absolute. For, if space (or time) stops 'here' ('now'), what about the 'there' ('then') beyond the boundary? Every boundary assumes the context of space and time, hence the concept of an 'absolute spatial or temporal limit' is self-contradictory (cf. 1918a: 135). So space and time are absolute in the sense that they provide the *context* for the drawing of limits. This is not to accept Newton's notions of absolute space and time (which are an independent block expanse and an eternal flowing, respectively[86]). But one needs to recognize that any locating or ordering of sensations by the human subject assumes a limitative context in which there is always a 'beyond' with respect to the localization in question.[87]

Thus localization assumes the larger context of a limitative absolute—an 'ever beyond'—in space and time, which is in step with the psycho-physical organization of the sensing (human) subject, for which space and time are forms of sensibility.[88] I believe we can say that each of the two references to the metaphysical intuition, described earlier (*viz.*

---

86   I. Newton, *Mathematical Principles of Natural Philosophy*, trans. by F. Cajori (New York: Greenwood, 1969), vol. I, p. 6. It is only with the advent of Einstein's general theory of relativity that the question of the 'shape' of the universe affects the notion of the boundary of the universe. It is now clear that travelling within the universe never meets up with a boundary. This is analogous to not meeting a boundary when travelling on the earth. But this does not require the universe to be (spatially) infinite, no more than that the surface of the earth is infinite. The term 'absolute' needs to be carefully defined if it is to be useful. Cf. O'Shea 2007: esp. 32-35.

87   "Absolute time is the limit for the infinite possibility of constantly locating processes, to the extent that they are discerned . . . , more completely" (1918a: 382). As to absolute space: "Not that we take it to be a thing, but it does need to exist outside of our thinking of the empirical given, if one is to speak of relative localizations" (1918a: 382-383). In summary: "Limitative absolute space and time are on an equal footing. To these answer in the Self, in its striving to attain complete knowledge, the ordering attempt to arrange sensations in this absolute space and processes in this absolute time" (1918a: 347-348).

88   This bare and formal condition of localization of the space-time continuum is evidently able to take on more human meaning as context of signification. Vollenhoven formulates a curious task for Christian psychology: "the possibility of localization is not unexplainable; one needs only to have recourse to the theory of local *signs* (or 'placemarks' (Land)). When every point in our spatial picture corresponds to a determined psychical sign, a *distinct* impression, the problem is solved. The empirical realization of this postulate in the near future must be set as the first requirement for Christian psychology" (1918a: 422-423).

the substrate for mental content and the basis for the distinction between Object and Objectives), assume or imply the *differences* involved in spatial and temporal localization. The first reference simply calls for an awareness of an outer source that induces differences of content. In the second reference, one can readily place the 'thing-relations' among spatial and temporal relations. Now, in the third reference to the metaphysical intuition, Vollenhoven appeals to the immediate insight into *identity* in the difference of spatial and temporal localization. 'Identity', in this context, is new.

For this awareness of identity, Vollenhoven points to two features within the domain of spatial and temporal localization: the continuity of motion and the ideas of species in the distinguishing of individuals. In referring to these as identity conditions, Vollenhoven is indicating what is basically constant within the domain of localization or the outer world vis-à-vis human awareness.

The first identity condition is the (basic) feature that pulls the spatial and the temporal dimensions together, namely (continuous) motion. This continuous motion is said to be a "real succession in spatial and temporal discerning". For the human being, the spatial limit of localization is three-dimensional Euclidean space, taken as 'absolute space', while the temporal limit of localization is one-dimensional time, taken to be "one-dimensional real succession" (1918a: 434). So it is the temporal dimension of motion that induces 'real succession' to continuous motion.[89] This real succession prevents change from being haphazard. The 'real succession' that is relevant here cannot be the subjective undergoing of experience in self-consciousness, as revealed in the concrete intuition. For that takes place intra-mentally, in explicit disjunction from sensibility and *its* spatial and temporal dimensions. The 'real succession' here is the objective counterpart (as it were), which concerns the given world to the extent that the given is organized and thus capable of being discerned as the most basic feature of identity that the spatial and temporal dimensions permit, namely in (the trace of) continuous motion. So this feature of identity is the outer expression of real succession, and we are now said to be immediately aware of such an identity. (This factor of objective real

---

89   This appeals to the situation of our human psycho-physical being structured so as to make three-dimensional Euclidean space a synthetic a priori for localization, now expanded to include time. "[F]or us the connection of Euclidean three-dimensional space with one-dimensional real succession is the only one possible, this being for the same reason on which the preference for this particular space construction is based. Other beings [*viz.* other than the human beings we are] could have a different mechanics, but real succession would always be one of the dimensions" (1918a: 434).

succession will recur in the discussion of theism.)[90]

The second immediate awareness of identity at the level of spatial and temporal localization is that of the ideas of species (*soortideeën*) in the discerning of individuals. This is not a matter of an awareness of relational change, but of an awareness of (species) identity of the things that are subject to change. However much individual things can be distinguished—this thing over against that thing, as governed by individualized ideas—there is over and above this an immediate awareness of species identity between individuals that are genetically related. Species too are governed by ideas, only they retain the generality of the species concerned, controlling the development that can take place within the limitations of species identity. Thus this immediate insight into species identity is an intuitive recognition of the general idea of a thing in its spatial and temporal development, which is why Vollenhoven places this intuition among differences of spatial and temporal localization.

Taking these two instances of metaphysical awareness as concerning identity-in-difference together, we can see at once that, as compared to the earlier, less specific indications of the metaphysical intuition, Vollenhoven has now given a more specific formulation to the intuition of what was previously simply called "things and (thing-)relations". He has now pointed to the intuitive identity involved in each of the two components. In building on this simpler expression there is, we admit, a certain plausibility in speaking of a 'metaphysical intuition'. The plausibility lies is its ontological roots. The categories of thing and thing relations are so fundamental and basic to thought, that it is difficult to express any knowledge of reality without appealing to these categories as necessary conditions. In an earlier context we pointed to Vollenhoven's speaking of 'being' and 'so-being' in connection with 'things' and 'thing-relations'. The metaphysical intuition is the immediate insight into the ontological conditions of the world as given to thought.

Now, what of the unity of intuition, *viz.* the unity of the concrete, analytical and metaphysical intuitions? In an earlier context it was pointed out that the unity is a complex unity. In its grasping of sameness and difference, the analytical intuition fulfils a bridge-function between the concrete intuition and the metaphysical intuition. In a summary expression of the three intuitions, already quoted, Vollenhoven speaks of the metaphysical intuition being *postulated* (in the sense of 'acknowledged',

---

90 In a summary statement about the reality of succession, to which we return below, Vollenhoven indicates its two applications: (i) it is important as distinguishing feature between divine and the human existence and (ii) to distinguish between things metaphysical and physical (cf. 1918a: 428).

not as 'posited to be such') by analytical intuition, in virtue of the latter's working over of the concrete intuition.[91] The content of mentality cannot be sufficiently accounted for without acknowledging an effect of the given world on that content, especially to the extent that this concerns identity. But in *postulating* this metaphysical intuition, Vollenhoven is, I believe, saying that this intuition cannot be informed by (let alone derived from) the concrete and the analytical intuitions, singly or combined. In other words, each of the three forms of intuition is a distinct fund of insight: (i) concrete intuition: awareness of what one undergoes in concrete occurrent experience, (ii) analytical intuition: awareness of sameness and difference, and (iii) metaphysical intuition: awareness of identity in differences regarding the given world (identity in differences of space-time localization as concerns motion and species identity of different individuals). These three together, in the given order, delineate the basic contours of consciousness as 'state of awareness', as revealed in self-consciousness. Though each form of intuition is immediate, there is nevertheless a difference in how the different forms interlock. Concrete intuition must be first, or else awareness simply does not take place. Only when there is awareness can there be awareness of similarity and difference (the analytical intuition), and on the basis of this, awareness of identity in difference (the metaphysical intuition).

Our discussion of the metaphysical intuition has focussed on the world, as do Vollenhoven's discussions generally. But we need to add that the Self too, being a metaphysical reality according to the principle of substance, falls within the 'reach' of the metaphysical intuition. The same sequence of concrete, analytical and metaphysical intuition holds here. Only now we need to take into account that the succession of moments one is aware of in concrete intuition and distinctly noted in their similarity and difference by the analytical intuition, (also) calls for a 'subjective' reality that is relevant to this intra-mental awareness and which does the comparing and relating (cf. 1918a: 350). Vollenhoven claims, as immediate awareness, that there must be something given in this respect, and that this must be what we call 'the Self'. This is (as will be argued further below) not to know the Self, for then the Self is taken as object of knowledge. We cannot even say that this Self presents itself in self-consciousness, for self-consciousness is the awareness of the states *of* my Self, being the indicators of the relations in which the Self stands to other

---

91 The quotation in question is: "This distinction between knowing act and content is already analytical intuition and so, the analytical intuition's assimilation of the concrete [intuition] postulates the metaphysical [intuition]" (1918a: 404).

things. The metaphysical intuition only claims the certainty that, in the light of concrete experience and analytical awareness, there is the effect of a reality underlying this. But one must leave to the principle of substance the characterization of this reality as being that of a Self.[92]

And what, also, of the connection between intuition and knowledge? We emphasized that intuitions serve as conditions for knowledge. Knowledge (acquaintance) focuses on the object, and judgment and concept result from thought's working over of the object as given. The intuition has its own focus in self-awareness. We did also say that concepts and judgments have *Gegenstände*, which are themselves the result of the concrete and analytical intuition. But in the context of discussing the connections between the three forms of intuition that Vollenhoven accepts, he states: "if the connection [between these forms of intuition] is lacking, then the first [i.e. the concrete] and the fourth [i.e. the metaphysical] will exist without connection and hence self-consciousness and world knowledge, [the latter] being impossible without concepts of species, will remain unconnected" (1918a: 351).[93] Vollenhoven here says

---

92 At this point my reading of Vollenhoven diverges somewhat from that of John Kok. I believe he does not sufficiently distinguish the different roles assigned to the metaphysical intuition on the one hand and the metaphysical principle of substance on the other. The intuition is an immediate awareness, and it is metaphysical when that awareness concerns the certainty of identity-in-difference of what affects mentality without being attributable to anything within mentality. The metaphysical principle of substance proceeds from the self-identical reality underlying change, a (constant) reality that needs to be posited by the metaphysical principle if change (and hence also succession) is to be deemed real, as intuition enjoins. There is a passage in Vollenhoven that would appear to support Kok's reading. In a summarizing formulation of the three intuitions Vollenhoven adds: "from self-consciousness through the activity of the mind to postulating a Self and a non-Self that stand in connection with each other through relations"(1918a: 427). So here the role of intuition is said to end 'metaphysically' in 'postulating' a Self and a non-Self. Kok accepts this reading at face value, while I take the use of "postulating" here to be unfortunate, but perhaps explainable in light of the context of its being a summary formulation. If one keeps the distinct meanings of the metaphysical intuition and the principle of substance in mind, one can point to the ambiguity of this 'postulating' here and avoid a 'Self-centred reading' that makes Vollenhoven's thought more idealistic than it appears to have been. Cf. Kok 1992: 75, 80-81, etc.; cf. also the comment at the end of section VII.F.

93 In this context Vollenhoven also mentions the "practical intuition", which is the second one in his listing of the (four) forms of intuition in Bergson. But he states that "true intuitionism" only accepts a practical intuition for the purpose of stating problems, hence he does not include it in his discussion of the three forms of intuition he does accept as being fundamental. In his own review of his dissertation Vollenhoven describes the practical intuition as focussing on "what is obvious in life, and, over against pragmatism, it has value only in discovering and stating problems, not in solving them, as Bergson often appears to maintain"; cf. Vollenhoven 1918c: 210-211.

that a consequence of the lack of connection between the concrete and the metaphysical intuition is that self-consciousness, which is the concrete intuition, and world knowledge, which is embodied in judgments and concepts, will be disconnected. We need to discuss two things here: the connection between the metaphysical intuition and world knowledge, and the connection between concrete intuition and world knowledge.

As to the metaphysical intuition and world knowledge, one does not, of course, intuit the world. But if world knowledge involves, necessarily, the concept of species, then Vollenhoven does allow this concept to have its own Object as *Gegenstand*, which, as intension of the concept, at the same time, grasps the essence of the species, i.e. the species identity—and that brings in the metaphysical intuition. But we need to look at this more closely. The concept of species, as example of world knowledge, is empirically gained. If A looks like a German shepherd dog, and B looks like a German shepherd dog, and so does C, then one can form the concept of this kind (or species) of dog. Now this concept is proleptic, for it cannot pretend to be a complete knowledge of the species, which would be a knowledge of the (general) idea of this species. But however incomplete this knowledge is, the (proleptic) concept can be entertained in such a way that one becomes aware of the concept's *Gegenstand*. This awareness is intuitive, as is everything that concerns *Gegenstände*. But then this intuition is metaphysical, for, though it arose in a conceptual context, the awareness involved is that of the (species) identity of spatially and temporally different individual dogs. The connecting of the empirically defined concept of the German shepherd dog species and the metaphysical intuition of the identity of the idea of this species only works if one, somehow, links the identity-in-difference of the empirical German shepherds and the fixed, or self-identical, meaning of the mental Object 'German shepherd'. This is not trivial. The self-identical meaning of the *Gegenstand* is governed by the principle of identity (identity of meaning; intuition), while the species identity of the different dogs is governed by the idea (identity of essence; substance). Here we have the two orders, the mental (subjective) order and the extra-mental (objective) order, coming together. Vollenhoven was very hesitant about the connection of these orders, but he did speak of a 'harmony'. The discussion of this point will be resumed below in the context of discussing theism.

Then there is the connection between the concrete intuition and world knowledge. The fact that this is linked to the analytical intuition's connecting role of the metaphysical intuition and the concrete intuition must assume the connection between the metaphysical intuition and world knowledge, just discussed. Now we have explained earlier, quite explicitly, that Vollenhoven denies that there can be direct (occurrent) awareness of a state of being outside of the psychical subject. So his reference to the concrete intuition cannot be meant as a case in which self-consciousness somehow 'feels' the world. The inclusion of the analytical intuition makes it more likely that the concrete intuition is meant *together* with the analytical intuition. In that case the whole domain of *Gegenstände* opens to us. The awareness of identity-in-difference (metaphysical intuition) is connected to the concrete intuition via the analytical intuition through the mediation of *Gegenstände*. The awareness of an identity-in-difference is grasped in terms of *Gegenstände*, and this provides the connection with the concrete intuition, without having to assume any recondite 'experience' that is outside of the psychical subject. So, to the extent that world knowledge is had in concepts, these concepts have in turn *Gegenstände*, and these *Gegenstände* provide a fixed point for the concrete intuition's awareness here.

The topic of knowledge and intuition will return when discussing the 'metalogical' situation of scientific knowledge. In that context too the connection between intuition and knowledge is essential.

D. A human being

A human being too is an existent creature. "The metaphysical existence of the Self is accepted in virtue of the principle that for every change there is something that changes" (1918a: 438). This is the original principle of substance, applicable to a human being as well as to things, to which Vollenhoven again adds, ingenuously: "accepted and applied by all [philosophers?] without reserve" (1918a: 438; cf. also p. 405). The Self is an ideal unity of changing states and qualities. The Self as substance is therefore understood as law or controlling principle of change (1918a: 433). If we apply the distinction made earlier between individuated idea and dynamic reality in coherence and continuity, then we find that the use of the word 'Self' shifts between these two meanings. On the one hand the Self is the individuated idea or 'thing-law' of a distinct human being, on the other hand the Self is the individual that stands in relations to other individuals and things, but always within a personal coherence and continuity of 'psychical synthesis'. This double use does not attest to confusion, but it delineates the Self as 'complete substance', calling for the synthesis of change and the constancy that regulates change.

Prominent in this regard is the difference between body and soul, found in the Self, the Self as their "higher synthesis" (1918a: 423). But the exact nature of body and soul is difficult to grasp clearly. For, there is another duality that plays a more prominent role. When speaking of the body, Vollenhoven always speaks of the psycho-physical organization. This presumably is the 'body as substance'. It has a 'psychical dimension' interwoven into it. Through this bodily organization a human being stands in relations with other beings and with the world in general. This is the basis for knowledge by acquaintance, which proceeds from the given object as sensed. But, besides the psycho-physical, there is also self-consciousness, in which an individual is intuitively aware of its own states and qualities. This awareness of our acts and their different contents—an awareness that is intuitional, the content of which may be posited as intra-mental *Gegenstände*—is said to be a "primal psychical event" (1918a: 416). In its being intra-mental, its operation is not a bodily or physical event, though human mentality in fact is never disconnected from the body. Also the intra-mental should not be identified with full conscious life. For, as we found, the mind can be affected in its states subconsciously and even unconsciously, as when in sleep (cf. 1918a: 440). This complex mental life is (presumably) the 'soul as substance'. It is distinct from the body in that the body is the terrain of sensibility, while the mind is the region of intuition. But the term 'psychical', being relevant to both, bridges the difference—and this difference is, I believe, the fundamental one here—between the psycho-physical body on the one hand and the intra-mental awareness of (predominantly self-)consciousness on the other. The two are attributable to the Self in light of the reality of what Vollenhoven calls 'psychical synthesis', which binds body and mind together.

Psychical synthesis is characterized as being "a unity with retention of the distinct character of the [constituent] elements" (1918a: 421). The three capacities of memory, sense-awareness and representation are essential here. Vollenhoven says little about their exact roles, except to suggest that if the body were to fall away, sense-awareness and representation would not be available (1918a: 420). But clearly, the empirical input of data takes place via sense-awareness and representation as acts of the psycho-physical body, whose acts in turn align mental content. This content, and the acts to which they are correlated, must be present in order for the upper psychical capacity of self-awareness to be able to grasp these intuitively and currently. All this can only be meaningful, in the constructive sense of a growth of consciousness, provided there are acts and contents of recollection on the basis of which psychical synthesis can take place (1918a: 413). So the third capacity of memory would appear to be essential to intra-mental life. The acts together are an important factor in bridging the difference between the psycho-physical body and the mind.

Growth of consciousness has need of bodily input, but as such it is not a determinate (or natural) process. It also calls for effort from the side of intra-mental awareness. We found that at the intra-mental level the knowing subject must comply to norms if its effort to acquire knowledge is to be successful and not end in error. In that sense the knowing subject involves its own *will to know*, for to be a knowing subject the Self must submit, in the sense of subject itself, to the norm of truth.[94] Here a peculiar tension can arise within the life scope of the Self in connection with the Self as "subject of willing" (1918a: 430). Our personal and factual life is, as such, not normative, dominated as it is among other things by the feeling of pleasure and pain and a factually existent 'subject of willing'. If emotion and will oppose the norm, then the knowing subject must "eliminate" this; "thus the norm demands that the truth be acknowledged, separated from pleasure and pain, *sine ira et studio* ['without positive and negative prejudice'; Tacitus], even if the factually existent Self as subject of willing does not want this" (1918a: 430). Thus, by implication, feeling and willing can influence the mind adversely, and when such occurs the mind is required to deal 'forcefully' with this anti-normative situation, setting matters aright in disregard of one's own feeling and willing! This dominance of the cognitive over feeling and willing is justified by the norm to which cognition is subjected. But Vollenhoven does not say how to implement this in practice.

In short, the body in its psycho-physical organization affects the mind in the sense that it provides the input of data, but it may also hinder its submission to norms. The mind, in turn, absorbs the input of acquaintance as intra-mental possession and in reflection enriches its own state of awareness, but only if it wills to submit to norms. Thus the disruptive anti-normative tendencies can be of body or of mind. Vollenhoven often speaks of the interaction between body and soul. No doubt this involves the factual exchange that takes place between the psycho-physical body and the mind. But more important is perhaps the opportunity that interaction presents for the Self to undercut anti-normative tendencies in the continuous struggle to submit to norms. In that submission lies the priority.

---

94   Similarly, the distinguishing or thinking subject, another quality of the Self, must comply to the norm of identity in positing *Gegenstände*. Cf. also footnote 67 above.

E. Microcosm and macrocosm

In the course of Vollenhoven's own summarizing discussion we find the statement: "The human being is a microcosm" (1918a: 442). The phrase occurs in a passage that critiques the mystical notion of the human being as 'micro*theos*', a 'god in the small'. Mysticism lets God and the world merge, says Vollenhoven, in consequence of which a human being too is thought to partake directly of divinity. But when God and the world are properly distinguished—the proper distinguishing of which is part and parcel of Vollenhoven's theism, as we shall see—then norms, ideals and ideas are *called for* to secure the difference of God and the world. Likewise these factors of difference help delineate the human being's place vis-à-vis the cosmos. A human being, as a 'world in the small', can never really merge with the world in the large, let alone God. A human being has its own place, secured by its essence. But in the security of that essence we can compare the structure of a human being with that of the 'world in the large'.

This 'theme of macrocosm and microcosm', as Vollenhoven will later call this problematic,[95] goes unmentioned here. So the solitary occurrence of "microcosm" is of course far from being a sufficient indication of Vollenhoven's adhering to this theme. But when seeking an overview of the numerous, philosophically basic polarities in Vollenhoven's early work, there is a 'coming together' that suggests an ordering that is consistent with this theme in one of its historically viable renderings. Our emphasis will be on the 'coming together', but it helps heuristically to keep a 'micro- and macrocosm schema' in mind.

---

95   We note that John Calvin found the human being "not ineptly" characterised as "man a microcosm"; cf. Calvin 1960: 54. This may be in the background of Vollenhoven's use here. It was only while developing his consequental problem-historic method for the study of the history of philosophy in the late 40s that this theme came into full prominence in Vollenhoven's work *as problem*. In his prior work the theme is initially fully present, as will be argued here, but it was soon tempered considerably, though traces of it are evident in the *Isagoge*, left untouched in the last revision in 1945. (Cf. in chapter 1, section II.E., in the context of the discussion of the 'method of resolution and composition'.) The theme, which has deep roots extending to Presocratic thought, involves the cosmic expression of universality and individuality, placed side by side. This horizontal positioning of man (and perhaps animal varieties as well, there are numerous ways in which it can be operative) and the world implies the presence of a number of basic analogical similarities in their structure. A popular though speculative illustration of this horizontal positioning is the view that ontogenesis (in this case of humans and animals) passes through all the stages of phylogenesis. This application however is not traceable in Vollenhoven. Cf. D.H.Th. Vollenhoven, *Schematische Kaarten: Filosofische concepties in probleemhistorisch verband* (Schematic charts: Philosophical conceptions in a problem-historical lattice), i.e. Vollenhoven 2000: 354-355.

The most insistent philosophical polarity in Vollenhoven's early work is that of thought and being. This duality is first broached as an epistemological subject-object distinction. But even as epistemological distinction, being (or the object) is that which needs to give or reveal itself to thought in a process of coming-to-know. Being is external to thought, and every bridging of the difference in a concept *of* something does not annihilate the difference but presupposes it. Even as adequate concept (could it be had), the difference between the concept, as belonging to the *order* of thought, and that which the concept is about, being of the *order* of being, remains intact (cf. 1918a: 443). The very fact that there is an order of thought *and* a metaphysical order of being is telling. We see at once that this difference is the basis for the distinct focus of "self-consciousness", which is intuitional, on the one hand, and that of "world knowledge", which is dependent on the given, on the other. The distinction of Self and World is the thought-being distinction in cosmological dress. Could this be a distinction of microcosm and macrocosm? Yes, it could, but only if there is a significant analogy of structure in each.

When we now look at each order, we find, first, that thought calls for foundation in the Self. But "thought as function of the Self is empty" (1918a: 229). We need to include a larger context of body and mind. Thus, through the psycho-physical organization of the body, thought gains its data through sensibility in the two forms of space and time, while through the 'psycho-mental' capacities, consciousness and self-consciousness can take place. When we now look at the metaphysical order, we see that there is a basic distinction between the 'real' and the 'ideal', i.e. between what is factually present (nature) and the region of ideas: "the essence of things, thereby preserving the qualitative distinction of matter and spirit [*stof en geest*], is ideal [*ideëel*], but *extra-mental* ideal" (1918a: 229). But we also see at once, on the one hand, that the factual is enclosed within the limitative notions of absolute space and time, which are *correlated* to the human forms of sensibility of space and time, and, on the other hand, that the region of ideas is, as the *extra*-mental domain of validity, at a level with the norms and ideals that have validity for the mental life of the Self. So thought and being, when taken in their own contexts of the Self and the World respectively, appear to have basic analogies or a similarity in their make-up, suggesting a side-by-side positioning. This brings a micro- and macrocosm schema into the picture.

By adjusting our previous schema to highlight the two sides of the Self and the World, we can depict the basic distinctions, in a provisional simple version, as follows.

A Bold Beginning: Theistic and Metalogical Intuitionism

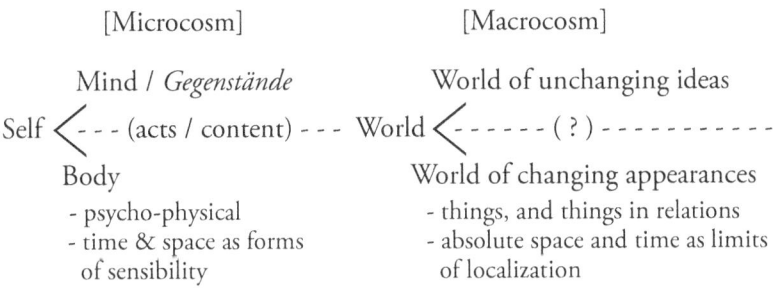

The usefulness of this schema is that it helps to convey a basic moment of organization of a philosophical conception. Texts that are exclusively devoted to a single area of philosophy will generally offer little by way of indicating a basic philosophical position. But a text such as Vollenhoven's dissertation itself keeps reaching down to fundamentals. It does not stay at the level of the philosophy of mathematics. So one's understanding of the text calls for attention as to how basic themes come together. The schema of micro- and macrocosm offers a heuristic aid towards capturing ontological, anthropological and cosmological matters which, certainly in their intersection, touch on basics.

We will find that this schema is also very useful towards depicting Vollenhoven's understanding of theism, when coming to that. For now, I wish to add two remarks in relation to the schema as it stands. In the first place, space and time, as relevant for the factual world of changing appearances, are not themselves distinct 'things' in the world. Only in the context of the human perception of the world can one speak of time and space, meaning that there, time and space are dependent on the one hand on things and their forces (in the macrocosm) and on the other hand on the human forms of sensibility (in the microcosm). Space and time are relational, and they are predicated on the relevant features of the World and of the Self. In that sense, the Self and the World 'belong together' and 'come together' in every reconciliation of thought and being, but never so as to annihilate the distinction between these. The natural sciences make essential use of the space and time structures (in kinematics, mechanics and physics). They too are predicated on the subjective and the objective, at the natural or factual (real, as over against ideal) areas of the body's forms of sensibility and world of changing appearance. It is in not belonging to either the world in the large or the human psycho-physical structure that the sciences constitute a 'reality' of their own, a reality 'in between' that of the Self and the World at the bodily-factual level. The "reality of science [is] itself a synthesis of the given, the object, and subjective factors" (1918a: 12, cf. also pp. 96, 106, 381, 434-437). The above schema of the Self and the World help to put this in perspective.

The second remark is to point to a further analogy between the 'mind' on the part of the Self and 'ideas' on the part of the unchanging ideal world. When the Self wants to know, it must 'become' a knowing subject, which implies a submission to the norm of truth.[96] In other words, mentality threatens to be psychically anarchic unless such submission takes place. Norms have general validity, holding for individual mentality that becomes normatively correct only on condition of such 'holding'. Now there is an analogous arrangement of generality and individuality on the part of ideas. There are general ideas of species (essences), but they need to be individualized in order to hold for distinct things and human beings. Without such 'holding for', the dynamics of individual things or human beings would be chaotic, lacking the constraint of the species characterization. Taken together, *viz.* ideas and norms, it becomes clear that they both belong to the 'region of validity', which involves both the mental on the human side and the extra-mental on the part of ideas (on the side of the world).[97] This will prove to be of particular significance in the discussion of theism.

Other illustrations add to the plausibility of the micro- and macrocosm schema. There are the obvious dual foci of self-consciousness and world knowledge. Also the two forms of 'the reality of succession', one with respect to the Self and the other as regards the world, give added support. But the schema is not an end in itself. Its usefulness is to help offer an adequate analysis of Vollenhoven's themes and thoughts.

F. Self-knowledge and self-consciousness

We can now again pick up the topic of self-consciousness and discuss it in connection with the specific relevance of the metaphysical intuition for it. Self-consciousness is not to be confused with self-knowledge. The latter, we saw, requires the quality of knowing subject seeking to become more and more acquainted with the Self to the extent that the Self reveals itself. Self-knowledge is a species of 'world-knowledge' or acquaintance with beings, for this approach is not different from that of knowing any other thing. The approach is outward, via the appearances, and its re-

---

96 A relevant citation is: "the subject of knowing is a function of the Self that wants to know and accordingly subjects itself to the norms of logic" (1918a: 228).

97 To complete the picture, the 'realm' of *Gegenstände* is intra-mental, and they may be said to subsist. This distinguishes the realm of *Gegenstände* from both the real (existence) and the 'region of validity' (norms and ideas). Cf. the more explicit diagram below.

sult is always incomplete. For we become acquainted with our selves, as creatures with body and soul, through the avenues of what we reveal of ourselves and how we interact with other human beings and things. This 'Self-knowledge' involves a *Self-approaching consciousness* (*Ik-benaderend bewustzijn*; 1918a: 433), via the world as it were. In other words, in this approach we would become acquainted with the 'appearances' to ourselves, whereby the diversity of 'bodily appearances' and 'mental appearances' (in the sense of attestations of mentality) would be quite evident. In relating this to the Self, the body and the mind will each be treated as a unity of substance, but as *substantiae incompletae*, for neither is congruent with the complete Self.

But, there is also a direct self-consciousness of the Self, in which the Self is grasped intuitively (from within itself). Vollenhoven emphasizes that this is entirely different from Self-knowledge. "The Self-approaching consciousness differs *toto caelo* from self-consciousness" (1918a: 439). Grasping the Self intuitively does not take place in the guise of the quality of knowing subject. Self-consciousness is prior to, and a condition for, Self-knowledge. Actually the metaphor of 'grasping' is misleading. The Self is not a 'kernel' of some primal reality, capable of being grasped. The Self is an ideal law—the complete substance—that harmonizes the basic states of mind and body in continuity, coherence and development. Unless we could retreat into the mind of God, where we might expect to 'find' this law (as idea), an alternative interpretation of the use of 'Self' needs to be sought. Self-consciousness, as we found earlier, involves the awareness of our states in the experience of undergoing them. These states, like the 'perceptions' of Leibniz's monads, signal the relations in which the Self stands.

So self-consciousness involves a complex and peculiar awareness. It answers to *concrete intuition* to the extent that the Self currently experiences its specific states. But because the experiences actually take place, there is also a passage from one state to another state, similar to what Leibniz called 'appetition'.[98] This is the temporal succession of states. The Self is able to be aware of this through the *analytical intuition*, which brings the differences between these states to consciousness, provided memory retains them. (Here too awareness of number is made possible in the groupings of distinct moments.) But finally the *metaphysical intuition* contributes its share in connection with the reality of the Self. The Self as substance is the (human) essence that is individuated into the idea or thing-law of an individual human being. At the same time

---

98 Cf. Leibniz 1976a, section 2: 636, or Leibniz 1976b, section 15: 644.

the deepest orderliness of a human being is the movement of the succession of its (psychical) states (in psychic growth). Now the metaphysical intuition is the immediate insight into the identity in difference of space and time as regards continuous motion—now to be applied as coherence and continuity in the succession of states—and as regards the idea of species of differing individuals—now relevant as the unique Self that I am. This metaphysical intuition signals the awareness of myself as having a constant identity, in virtue of my Self as idea, in the succession of my changing states, that is coherent in virtue of my Self as 'thing-law'. In other words, the Self as idea or law manifests itself as the *law of succession of my states* (in the context of psychical growth). A human being cannot fix onto that law apart from actually experiencing succession. Thus the metaphysical intuition of the Self is the awareness, acting as warrant, that the currently experienced *succession is real*. My Self is the warrant of the identity that remains constant in this succession. The moments of this succession can be subjected to the principle of identity and thus be turned into *Gegenstände*. But the reality of succession is prior to this, the awareness of which is not subject to any norm. "The succession is currently experienced by that Self even without the acknowledgement of these norms; however the moments are only distinguished again in subjection to the principle of identity, the norm for all *Gegenstand* formation" (1918a: 432-433). (It is as if the Self itself, as law or idea, is the 'norm' of the awareness of succession, but then the human being would have to subject itself to its Self, which is humanistic *and* distinctly paradoxical.) But a human being can never divorce itself from the succession of its occurrent experience, thus it can do no better than acknowledge that the *temporal* factor of succession is the determining form of this awareness of succession.[99] And of course psychical synthesis acts on the moments and prevents them from remaining detached units.[100] This is

---

99 In the section devoted to Brouwer, when discussing Brouwer's intuition of time, Vollenhoven states: "We immediately recognize here the connection with the metaphysical intuition and the awareness of the occurrent experience of succession: the intuition of time is currently experienced as succession of moments, but this is only possible with a unity as basis (metaphysical intuition). The latter [is] the principle of the unity of personality. . . . Only succession is currently experienced immediately; the unity of the Self must be presupposed. . ." (1918a: 394).

100 This psychical synthesis does not enable one to reach the unity via the moments. Vollenhoven does claim that the unity of the Self can, while the unity of extra-mental things cannot, be currently experienced, "but not consciously, for consciousness always splits" (1918a: 440-441). Read in context, one will understand that Vollenhoven does not mean to say that consciousness splits apart into two parts (perhaps suggested by the difference between knowledge and intuition), but rather that consciousness is a divider.

as basic as we can get in understanding the metaphysical existence of the Self as substance.

We can now see why self-consciousness is so important to Vollenhoven. It focuses the attention on the states of the Self, these being indicative of the relations in which the Self stands. In that sense, self-consciousness is consciousness of one's standing in relations to what exists, to the extent that these relations depend on the states in the Self. The deepest intuition of this self-consciousness is that of the awareness of the reality of succession of one's states. Thus, in a way that is completely open to our awareness, we have an intra-mental indication of the unity of being and thought. Here 'being' refers to the reality of succession (and the presupposed unity of the Self), and 'thought' denotes the (self-)awareness of undergoing that succession. It is through the play of the three forms of intuition, concrete, analytical and metaphysical, that this synthesis was achieved. Thus intuitionism is a viable foundation of knowledge, taking knowledge to be a reconciler of thought and being. The success in achieving this in the Self, i.e. 'the world in the small', gives confidence when seeking reconciliation with the 'world in the large' outside of the Self. "Philosophy ought to proceed from self-consciousness" (1918a: 404).

P.S. A textual *aporie* recurs in the above, in connection with the metaphysical intuition, and relates to what is raised in footnote 92 above. The metaphysical intuition is engaged in a way that would appear to be more correctly attributed to the metaphysical principle of substance. When 'intuiting the Self', there is the self-consciousness of the occurrent experience of succession of moments (concrete intuition), which moments the analytical intuition distinguishes and keeps apart. The metaphysical intuition, in turn, is the awareness that this succession of moments is real, i.e. actually occurs in the Self. One can understand Vollenhoven's insisting that "this is only possible with a unity as basis", that basis being "the principle of the unity of personality" (1918a: 394; cf. also footnote 99). That 'unity of personality' can be none other than the Self. In its having to be presupposed (*ibid.*) one is immediately inclined to think of the relevance of the principle of substance, the Self being a substance and the basis of all its changing facets. But Vollenhoven adds, after "unity as basis", in brackets: "metaphysical intuition" (cf. the quote in footnote

---

Conscious awareness always involves the awareness of distinct moments. This is probably why one does not come across Bergson's '*durée*' in this connection (as undivided duration of experience), despite the Bergsonian provenance of Vollenhoven's 'intuition'. Vollenhoven's repugnance towards anything suggesting a holistic consciousness relates to its pantheistic overtones. The latter is incompatible with Christian theism.

99), which is puzzling. If this were counted as a slip of the pen, reading "metaphysical principle" for "metaphysical intuition", then this passage could be considered amended. For there would then also be restored consistency with the statement that "only succession is currently experienced immediately; the unity of the Self must be presupposed" (*ibid.*).

But elsewhere—cf. the quote in footnote 100—Vollenhoven states that, whereas "the unity of things external to us cannot be currently experienced, that of the Self can [be currently experienced]" (1918a: 440-441)—however, he adds that this is not a conscious experience! Vollenhoven, as noted earlier, also states that the mind can be affected unconsciously, such as when asleep (1918a: 440). But how is the unconscious awareness of the unity of the Self affected? Perhaps Vollenhoven means to suggest that this is religious, e.g. regeneration. But then it is of a different order. I am not acquainted with any passage in Vollenhoven's early work where this is broached. Therefore it is not at all certain that a 'self-(un)consciousness' would make for a redundancy of the principle of substance.

I believe we should retain the distinction between the roles of the (metaphysical) principle of substance and the (epistemological) principle of intuition, including the metaphysical intuition. Where, in the text, the metaphysical intuition seems to usurp the role of the metaphysical principle, I prefer to take this as confusion rather than taking it at face value. The havoc that results from permitting the confusion of things metaphysical and epistemological would threaten to undermine a consistent interpretation of Vollenhoven's early thought.

G. Occasionalism

The schema of micro- and macrocosm helps draw diverse facets of Vollenhoven's thought together. But this does not characterize the 'coming together' itself. If we attempt provisionally to characterize Vollenhoven's conception (we return to this later), then we can do no better than begin with Vollenhoven's own characterization as "theistic intuitionism" (1918a: 338). The qualification 'theistic' will be discussed below. The noun 'intuitionism' is a programmatic term of seeking to reconcile any duality in a normative way. Intuitionism's "right to exist" (1918a: 52) depends on its being able to bind the rational and the empirical elements of knowledge. This is the main epistemological duality, and it is reconciled by means of the synthetic a priori. Other dualities are also brought together. The Self binds soul and body through psychical growth, and, in the religious experience, God and creature are brought together. There is always a duality or multiplicity *becoming* a complex unity. There is a dynamism at work that constantly seeks to relativize difference by turning it into a workable togetherness. The main function of norms, ideals, ideas, thing-laws and the like—elements of constancy in the 'domain of validity' that must be brought to bear in the dynamism of reconciliation—is to guide, orientate or direct the many in their becoming one.[101]

At the same time the term 'dualism' can mislead. We made note of the fact that Vollenhoven also speaks of a 'common root' (1918a: 403) as precondition for the possibility of synthesis. The duality must not be taken as a static or principled difference. It is here that experience plays its crucial role, as fundamental for intuitionism. "The fundamental thought of intuitionism proceeds from the currently experienced synthesis" (1918a: 104). Here Vollenhoven prescribes that the diversity must come within the range of an *occasion of experience*, the effect of which is that, through the experiential undergoing of the diversity or multiplicity (Dutch: "het *beleven*"), a merging (or coming together) can take place through psychical synthesis. Here the occasion itself is the precondition for the possibility of unification. Thus the term 'occasionalism' suggests itself as characterization of Vollenhoven's intuitionism.

Occasionalism, as here used, involves an object-subject relation. The object comes first in the sense that it must present itself as initiating the occasion in which the subject proceeds with its work of assimilating the object. (We quoted earlier: "being has logical precedence over thought"; 1918a: 382.) This occurs at the bodily level, where physical stimuli occasion the experience of sense-data (here Vollenhoven himself speaks, as we saw, of *causa occasionalis*; cf. 1918a: 328, also p. 330). Knowledge by acquaintance also proceeds from the presentation of the object to the Self. And at the intra-mental level of the intuition itself, there is the Self's being in touch with mental content that triggers the intuitive certainty of intuitive consciousness.[102]

In the addendum to chapter 4 we discuss Vollenhoven's own char-

---

101 In 1921, Vollenhoven characterizes his position epistemologically as "epistemological dualism", on account of the importance of the distinction between idea and concept; cf. the further discussion below; Vollenhoven 1921c: 79.

102 Considerable and important points of agreement can be found with the 'occasionalism' of A.N. Whitehead, as found in his writings from the mid-1920s. This is a typological agreement, not a causal-interactive one. (There is no evidence that Whitehead was ever aware of Vollenhoven's existence.) However an important difference is that there is less of a microcosm-macrocosm arrangement and more of a universalism (holism) to Whitehead's occasionalism. (Holism does not cede independent reality to a microcosm.) An accessible introduction to Whitehead's thought are his two lectures "Nature lifeless" and "Nature alive" (1934), reprinted in Whitehead 1938, chap. 7 and 8.

acterization of his earliest conception when looking back at it more than 30 years later. We will find that the term 'occasionalism' has in the meantime taken on a technical meaning, as the descriptive term for a 'type' of thought, in the context of his later problem-historical method. But that characterization will appear to accord remarkably well with the analysis of his thought offered in this chapter, even though, when looking back, Vollenhoven came to a different self-characterization. He himself spoke of 'ennoetism', which is a term that emphasizes a contemplative mind that absorbs the object in the process of its contemplation ('ennoetism' means: in the mind). Clearly, this introduces a problem, the discussion of which we leave until the end of chapter 4. There are different strands that come together in this problem, and to unravel them we need to be able to refer, among other things, to Dooyeweerd's early thought as well. The discussion of his early work is in chapter 3.

VIII. *Theism*

Vollenhoven's theism appeals to divinity both as a fundamental motivational factor of his philosophical endeavour and to cap, topically, the philosophical understanding that he achieves. In the combination of these two appeals to divinity there is a restless tension. After all, aims can be realized in different ways. Vollenhoven was a 'theistic thinker' all his life, in the fundamental motivational sense, but his formulation as to what this entails in terms of philosophical understanding varied over the years.

Vollenhoven held that it is possible to combine being a Christian and a thinker (1918a: 2). He accepted this not as a fact of faith, to be defended by reason, but as a mission to execute in the deployment of thought. It is *as mission* or *ideal* that Vollenhoven introduces theism. It is defined at the beginning of *De Wijsbegeerte der Wiskunde* as "the philosophy that God wills that we should have" (1918a: 2). In that opening text nothing is said as to how we can know what God wants, or also why, whatever this will is, it should commend itself to the thinker, Christian or otherwise. At the end of the book Vollenhoven is more explicit. There he says that theism is not an existing system; "in an absolute sense it is the epistemic system [*kensysteem*] that God wants that we form concerning all the given" (1918a: 443). Theism in this sense is an ideal that we can never completely realize. Here the phrase 'all the given' refers of course to the reality that is knowable for human beings. And what God's wanting implies is that we form our knowledge in accordance with the logical principles, used as *norms*, which is more than merely as rules of deduction, as formalism would have it, nor as generalization of data-experience, as empiricism teaches. In concluding his discussion of Meinong, Vollenhoven had said: "There are no norms other than divine norms" (1918a: 175). And, in criticism of Malebranche's "We see the things in God", Vollenhoven says that it is not our task to see what God sees, for, were this the case, then "that eradicates the distinction between God as norm giver, also for our thought, and the human being who is subject to his norms" (1918a: 53). Truth, says Vollenhoven, is "the view of facts the way God wants us to view them" (*ibid.*). To illustrate this negatively (for a positive interpretation, cf. below), a view of the facts that is *im*permissible is any view that (for example) engenders contradictions (the principle of contradiction being viewed as a norm). Thus thought is bounded by norms, acting as injunctions that are to be abided by in willing submission, not (supra-)natural facts we cognitively accept on faith. In short, theism, as here described, does not call upon a human being to think God's *thoughts* after him, but to think as God *wills* that we *ought* to think, namely according to norms.

A. Actual infinity

But the appeal to divinity also has a more specific theological and metaphysical content, with relevance for mathematics. The relevance for mathematics lies in the problem of infinity. Mathematical intuitionism was attractive to Vollenhoven on account of its rejection of the actual infinite in the constructive parts of mathematics. But this was not the end of the matter. In the discussion of Poincaré's work, Vollenhoven indicates that Poincaré argues for the denial of the actual infinite in mathematics by the radical tendency of treating everything related to science, including its object, as a construction. Theistic intuitionism disagrees, says Vollenhoven, for it acknowledges the given (object of science) as prior to construction (or assimilation), and it distinguishes the given from that which the human mind is able to create (1918a: 380). Therefore Poincaré, who, in his idealistic humanism, did not make this distinction, denied the actual infinite completely. But theism "discounts the actual infinite [only] *to the extent that* human creativity reaches, hence within science, within that 'reality' in which, in distinction from the given, this latter and the [knowing] subject enter into a synthesis" (1918a: 381). In other words, the given is a reality that, in a metaphysical sense, allows for the existence of the actual infinite.

In introducing the problem of infinity, Vollenhoven had, from the start of his project, immediately stated its connection with "the position taken in the conflict over the possibility of metaphysics" (1918a: 2). Within (mathematical) intuitionism there is no consensus, for Poincaré denied the actual infinite out of hand, while Brouwer, who had pantheistic and mystical leanings, had his own thoughts on the matter.[103] For Vollenhoven, the given depends upon an existent infinite being, who controls existence by means of (extra-mental) ideas. Ideas have an intrinsic possibility of including infinite complexity. That is why the given, taken metaphysically, does not as such discount the notion of infinity. In the metaphysical order of reality, divine (objective) rationality is operative. But we must be careful in relating this to human understanding. The notion of 'completed infinity' is indeed a possible *Gegenstand*. But it cannot be taken up in a (proleptic) concept—i.e. taken up into the context of knowledge—for, in virtue of the principle of contradiction, which holds for concepts, this *concept* must be rejected as being self-contradictory (cf. 1918a: 413).[104] What is given to know is richer than what one actually gets to know.

---

103   Even before completing his doctorate on the intuitionistic foundation of mathematics in 1907, Brouwer published a work entitled *Leven, Kunst en Mystiek* (Life, art and mysticism); Brouwer 1905. In this work he expresses sentiments that centre on the retreat into one's Self, as a "dying unto the old world of sensibility, of time and space and all other diversity, and the eyes, no longer bound, open to a joyful silence" (Brouwer 1905: 14). This is how the soul "finds the naked formless essence of the divine unity" (*ibid.*; Brouwer here quotes Meister Eckhart). This divine unity would appear to be the actual infinite. It is reflected in Brouwer's mathematics, in his acceptance of the "intuitive continuum". In his dissertation he states: "The continuum as a whole was intuitively given to us; a construction of it, an act which would create as individualized 'all' points of it by means of mathematical intuition, is unthinkable, and impossible"; Brouwer 1907: 62. In the biography of Brouwer, the biographer, Dirk van Dalen, comments: "Brouwer's view of the continuum shows a suggestive similarity to the mystic experience of the initial chaotic state of the individual. . . . So the continuum, being traditionally the flowing, continuous medium, must from Brouwer's point of view, have been the structure *par excellence* created by a human faculty analogous to the original mystical state"; Van Dalen 1999: 114-115.

104   This argument involves the assumption that 'infinite'= 'not finite'/'unending', for only then is 'completed infinity' contradictory. Also, the fact that Vollenhoven now speaks of "complete", rather than "actual", suggests the (impossible) process of passing completely through an unending series. The recognition of the actual infinite in metaphysics does not endorse Cantor's theory of transfinite numbers. This theory falls within the constructive part of mathematics, and statements of existence within the domain of the theory can only be proven, according to mathematical intuitionism, by an appeal to finite procedures (including the potential infinite of the principle of complete induction). We can also mention here, as K.A. Bril pointed out to me, the fourth of the twenty-five theses Vollenhoven appended to his dissertation for the occasion of its defence, which reads: "The denial of the existence of an actual infinity is correct for epistemology, not for metaphysics."

What one "gets to know" mathematically is what Vollenhoven calls, following Brouwer, mathematics of the second order. This is mathematics as a system of judgments and concepts, in arithmetic or geometry, as the case may be. But this appeals to, and presupposes, a 'first order' mathematics. For arithmetic, this involves the wherewithal of the natural numbers, accounted for through the act of counting; for geometry it concerns the context of space, which is the context of localization, orientation, measure and the like. First order mathematics focuses on construction or synthesis. But it is not a matter of practical or empirical construction. It is construction that is geared to and exploits the possibilities of the *human constitution* of mind and psycho-physical body. Mind and body are the foci of the synthetic a priori in mathematics. In the case of the mind, the Self is able to intuit this directly in the self-conscious discovery of the reality of (psychically experienced) succession and the analytical realization that the mind has the power of *unending* repetition, once an act is possible (e.g. of turning an experienced moment into a *Gegenstand*, which can be successively added, giving rise to numbers). The principle of complete induction is based in this unending a priori synthesizing capacity. In the case of the body, the mind can do no more than 'sense' the body, by means of the body's forms of sensibility of time and space. These forms, in turn, are the subjective conditions for the human being to localize itself and other bodies and things about it. The 'convenience' of three-dimensional Euclidean space for localization, and the attempt of ever more complete localizations (outward and inward continuity) in absolute space and time, are indicative of the constitutional connection of the human mind and body. Thus three-dimensional Euclidean space is the form of this a priori synthesis of localization. Behind each of these unending a priori synthesizing capacities is the reality of succession.[105]

But these anthropologically founded mathematical 'principles', in their being concerned with the human constitution, are also metaphysical, in the sense of pertaining to the human being in its capacity as creature. As with any creature, there is an idea involved that controls a crea-

---

[105] On the last page of the dissertation Vollenhoven himself states his conclusion. "Our conclusion is that given metaphysically are things [both material and mental] and relations [i.e. their forces] both of which must be thought, as to their *form of existence*, in real succession. First order arithmetic is then based on the activity of the human mind *in se*, the localization attempts in space and time as forms of sensibility are based on the activity of *mind* and *body together*, absolute space and time are the supra-individual limits posed as ideal on our capacity to order" (1918a: 444). Here we see, what has not been emphasized as yet, the role of succession as that of 'a common root' of both arithmetic and geometry. Naturally, this does not merge time as occurrent succession with time as sequence (form of sensibility).

ture's existence. I believe that this is in the background of Vollenhoven's statement: "three-dimensional space can be maintained as being an a priori synthetic thought of God" (1918a: 379). This 'thought of God' concerns the psycho-physical organization, in so far as this is determinative for the human capacity to localize. The "divine thought" concerns a constructive creaturely capacity, and it is not a statement or divine truth in its own right. This "thought" fits the context of first order mathematics, not second order mathematics. The "thought" involves an infinity of being, capable of synthesis, as is normally controlled by an idea.[106]

Important towards grasping Vollenhoven's theism is the question how one is to understand Vollenhoven's use of the term 'God' (as the actual infinite). Then, the matter of the relation between God and the world calls for more thorough elucidation. Finally, because Vollenhoven appeals and adheres to the Christian faith, we expect a relevant reference to the understanding of 'God' as seen from that perspective. We turn now to a discussion of these matters.

B. Divine transcendence and immanence

Vollenhoven accepts theism, but he is also critical of some of its implications. In the realist setting of Vollenhoven's thought, God is most readily referred to in the context of the duality of 'God and the world', a phraseology that Vollenhoven also uses (1918a: 438). The metaphysical property of God as being actually infinite, sets God off against the finite, or at most potential infinite, context of the world, finite in temporal duration and in spatial extent, and secured in that finitude as set in absolute space and absolute time (which, being limitative in lacking fixed boundaries, are potentially infinite). God transcends the world. But if this were one's primary focus, theism could not be adequately distinguished from deism, the view which, indeed, also emphasizes God's transcendence but limits his relevance to being the 'First Cause' of the world. One misses a sense of God's continuous presence here. But were one to offset this with an emphasis of God's immanence, then the balance might be tipped towards pantheism, which makes the status of the world, in its difference from God, problematic (cf. 1918a: 443).

The terms 'transcendence' and 'immanence' need a reference to the world to give them meaning. This reference is part of the problem of deism and pantheism, for both adjust God's presence or absence, his relevance or irrelevance, by taking the world as referent. But the Jewish-

---

106   Discussion with John H. Kok helped clarify my understanding of Vollenhoven's use of 'thought' here.

Christian tradition sees the world as a *creation* of God. This, of course, is also a statement about God vis-à-vis the world, but it also invites a focussing on God without such a reference. After all, one cannot apply the categories of the world to God, at least not without further ado. The world in space and time is a poor model for understanding the deity. Vollenhoven agrees with Augustine in the latter's view that space, time and change were themselves created with the creation of the world. According to the human measure, this puts the time of creation at the beginning of time, and by implication—Augustine does not seem to have addressed this question—the place of creation from where all positioning proceeds. But since time and place themselves arise in and through creation, the creation act of God cannot itself be defined or located temporally and spatially. In the "excellency of an ever-present eternity" (Augustine) God in his essence is non-temporal and non-spatial, hence is thereby also all-present with respect to time and space but without determination of *when* and *where* (cf. 1918a: 133-134).[107] This way of speaking about God retains its validity with or without the world, for the temporal and spatial dimensions do not affect it either way. "God is neither discrete, nor temporal nor spatial; whereas he is active" (1918a: 284, n. 1). This 'activity' of God, being non-temporal and non-spatial in character, would appear to suggest that this feature of God is the very principle of the dynamics of reality, an activity that makes present in space and time, a source of empowerment. Because ideas arise in virtue of this activity (cf. below), it cannot be taken to be an activity of thought as such, but would appear to be deeper or more primary than thought, on a par with Vollenhoven's later cherished characterization of God as "the Sovereign One".

But how is the difference between God and the world then to be introduced? And how is one able to acknowledge God's transcendence and immanence?

1. The distinction of God and the world
The distinction between God and the world—to raise this point first—comes to pointed expression in the following passage. Vollenhoven's study of Rudolf Hermann Lotze raised the following consideration:

> Hence he [Lotze] distinguishes here unending time, as a subjective way of viewing, and the succession of the activity itself, which makes this putting-in-a-series possible, and of which holds that it is "die eigenste Natur" [the most characteristic nature] of what is real. This distinction appears to us to be of the greatest importance for theism and hence also for true intuition-

---

107 Vollenhoven quotes from Augustine, *The Confessions*, Book XI, chapter 13; cf. Augustine 1994: 167-168.

ism. For when the essence of things is law, and their relations force [*kracht*], then it is self-evident that space is a form of sensibility and also absolute time construed spatially; but if succession, too, is a [mere] subjective form, as Lotze maintains prior to 1878, then the essence of things is intellectual [*geestelijk*] and eternal: the distinction between presence [*bestaan*] in the Counsel of God and in reality falls away and with it the creation, which [in that case] is merely the name for the transition of the one into the other. But when, in contrast, the reality of succession is acknowledged, as Lotze does after 1878, then created things have a characteristic existence of successive self-development [*een eigen, successief zich ontwikkelend bestaan*], sufficiently distinguished from that of God; this existence [*bestaan*] is no longer a modification of the one substance, and God must have more attributes than personality and unity. He also possesses the incommunicable [attribute] of eternity. (1918a: 346)

Lotze is here said to distinguish between time as form of sensibility, which is a subjective condition, and as succession, the latter being the characteristic that makes 'putting in a series' possible, as objective condition. It is Lotze's characterization of succession, as being the most characteristic feature of what is real, that is the focus of attention here, especially in view of the possibility of being able to make a clear distinction between God and created reality when succession is taken to be objective.

Now Vollenhoven does not question his own ontology. The essence of things is law, meaning that this essence is secured in the (intellectual/ spiritual) "Counsel of God". And the relations of things are forces. From the foregoing it is clear that Vollenhoven means to say that things influence each other, *viz.* enter into mutual interactions. And that means that things lay between themselves spatial and temporal relations, calling for forms of sensibility so as to be able to be viewed as such. But Vollenhoven then seems to cut corners. He only mentions space as form of sensibility, and time is explicit only as absolute time, said to be construed spatially. I believe he means to say, when fully expressed, that absolute time and space delineate the context of spatial and temporal viewing. These are, as he says elsewhere, ideals. Hence unless there is another feature that guarantees objectivity, absolute time and space are nothing without the viewing subject and its striving. In other words, they reduce to subjective notions. And furthermore, since time is usually thought of as a dimension, time is then actually construed spatially. This emphasis on space at the cost of time, when objectivity is lacking, is what seems to be involved in Vollenhoven's formulation in which he short-changes time.

But then the feature of succession is brought to bear. If this is taken to be subjective, then it does no more than underscore the merely sequential schema of time as form of sensibility. In connection with change, this merely underscores the before and the after, but it does not give a handle on temporal development. Now the essence of a thing, as idea, is as such eternal. Thus, if at the level of factual reality there is no way of accounting for the temporal feature of things, *viz.* in their developmental change (coming to be and passing away), then the distinction between things as they exist in the world and in the counsel of God becomes blurred ("falls away"). To talk of creation then amounts to no more than to pass from the idea of things to a viewing of things in terms of subjective forms of space and time. Things are then no more than a modification in the divine mind. They never take on an extra-mental status. This amounts to a monistic view with pantheistic overtones, for one is unable to draw a clear distinction in this modification. For Vollenhoven these consequences are sufficient to condemn the whole view.[108]

But everything changes when succession is taken to be objective, or, as Vollenhoven says, taken as real. Then there is a factor over and above that of the forms of sensibility, especially as regards the feature of time. Real succession is not merely a matter of passing along a series of moments of time, arranged as earlier and later, but real succession says that change involves real states of development. Succession allows for a disclosure of things in terms of their own intrinsic possibilities, as governed by a law. If the idea of a thing is its law—Vollenhoven's own statement is: "ideas regulate the functional development as fixed laws" (1918a: 228)— then it is the law of change of this self-disclosure in its real succession of states. We now have a *sufficient distinction* between things, existing in their self-development, and things as present (or represented) by their ideas in the divine mind. The reality of succession enforces that existent things are temporal as opposed to being eternal. Things are finite, but especially finite in time. Eternity is an attribute of God, not of creatures.[109]

We can supplement this account with several considerations. In the first place, we previously pointed to the two contexts of 'real succession' in Vollenhoven. The long quote makes no reference to real succession in the human Self, deep in the psyche. But it seems evident that the char-

---

108   Vollenhoven definitely rejects such a monistic metaphysics when he appeals to the reality of succession. In his discussion of Russell, Vollenhoven states: "if there is [only] one substance, then our consciousness is a part of the self-consciousness of the one, but then we could not design a system of the All (monism)", for such a system (so we add) would require recognition of diversity. Thus "a monistic logic is absurd" (1918a: 318).

109   In the discussion about God's essence being non-temporal and non-spatial, Vollenhoven adds: "[God's] being non-temporal does not only include the negation of objective temporality, which holds of *everything*, but also that of succession, whereby He distinguishes himself from creation" (1918a: 134). In a footnote here (no. 2) he refers to the scholastic distinction: "*creatio in successionem et in tempore.*"

acterization of succession, as "the most characteristic nature" of what is empirically or factually real in connection with the things of the world, holds without change for the human Self as well. The heart of the Self is psychical growth or synthesis, controlled by the Self as idea. This is a succession at the heart of human experience. The important difference between the two contexts is that the succession intrinsic to experience can be intuited in self-consciousness, that of the world needs to be accepted as a metaphysical truth (illumined or conditioned by the metaphysical intuition), over and above space and time as forms of sensibility.

Secondly, the distinction between God and the world is here discussed in terms of ideas in the Counsel of God and succession in the world. But this can be broadened. Nothing is changed or discounted if we think of the ideas as belonging to the 'realm of validity'. But then, besides ideas, one can include norms and ideals. They too are a factor in determining the distinction between God and the world, *viz.* the human world. "The normativity of logic can only be maintained by distinguishing God and world, for otherwise the logical 'laws' [i.e. the logical principles of identity, contradiction, excluded middle] are merely empirical discoveries or arbitrarily posed rules" (1918a: 438). (Recall, logical laws are norms, and norms are "(syn)theses of God" (1918a: 407).) And as to ideals, "the Spirit [of God] posits and maintains the norms and ideals" (1918a: 410). Clearly, the way the distinction between God and the (non-human) world is drawn in terms of ideas (and succession) also holds for the distinction between God and human beings. The latter, besides being structurally controlled by their own individual idea or law, are also subject to norms and ideals in their mental life.

Then, thirdly, there is the understanding of 'world'. Vollenhoven sides completely with Kant in taking world to be an idea.[110] The world is not a thing. We cannot point to it with distinction, but at best only approach it in an empirical synthesis. It is a whole of appearances, of which it is impossible to say whether it is finite or infinite. Every boundary would have to be absolute, but we cannot think what is not bounded, i.e. what is beyond the boundary. Hence the world can never be taken as being complete in itself. It is not self-conditioned. The world does have cosmic features that support viewing it as spatial and temporal. But this does not make the world a mere object of consciousness. "For every appearance poses problems, *inter alia* of thing and relation" (1918a: 135) – meaning that behind the appearances there is interaction of real things. But with real things come ideas. Also, the world as a whole is not the sum-

---

110   This paragraph is based on 1918a: 134-135.

A Bold Beginning: Theistic and Metalogical Intuitionism

total of things in relations (which would make it an 'analytical' notion). That whole needs its own condition of organization, met with in its own idea. Though Vollenhoven does not say so in this particular discussion, it would appear to follow that the idea of the world especially serves to regulate its development, in the sense of its being in succession or process. So the factual world cannot be understood apart from what might be called the 'world order' of the factual world and its ideational condition.

2. Transcendence and immanence with respect to the Self and the world
Now finally something can be said about the divine transcendence and immanence. In discussing the distinction of God and the world, Vollenhoven, we found, points to the presence of a 'realm' on which a human being, or anything of the world, has no influence. Also it cannot be identified with anything of the human being or the world. It is a 'realm' of objective validity, relevant for ideas, norms and ideals. Is this realm divine? I don't believe Vollenhoven thinks of this realm as being itself divine, at least *not independently* divine. It can be considered to be a realm that God has devised and uses as means. Then ideas have a "presence [*bestaan*] in the Counsel of God" (1918a: 346) and norms are "posited by God the Holy Spirit" (1918a: 391), more or less (so I tend to think) the way sensations have existence in human receptivity and *Gegenstände* are posits of human mentality. If sensations and *Gegenstände* 'are' human, then (roughly similarly) ideas and norms can be considered to be divine in their distinct way, and so norms are said to be "divine (syn)theses" (1918a: 407). But the important point is there being a realm of validity, and this attests to the presence of divinity in positing it in a way that transcends the factual, changing world.

Now, when considered in itself, this realm of validity might remind one of Plato's ideal world. It is important to realize that Vollenhoven does *not* endorse considering this realm merely 'in itself'. There is an immanence that matches transcendence. On Vollenhoven's view: "Without some content to be worked over, not a single judgment can ever be deduced from [i.e. be in accordance with] logical norms. Even the principle of identity assumes *Gegenstände*, and the principles of contradiction and excluded middle require judgments for which they hold. Without thoughts there is no norm for thought" (1918a: 407). This correlation of norms to what they norm has everything to do with divine immanence. Having stated above that the logical norms attest to God's transcendent presence—for, we now add, the norm-character of logical principles derives from the divine will—Vollenhoven continues: "but [this normativity] also requires God's immanence in maintaining these laws *for our knowing*" (1918a: 438; emphasis added). Thus the character of validity of norms, their 'holding', calls for a correlate, *viz.* that which answers to the norm. But the latter—at least as regards logical norms—involves human thoughts, judgments and concepts. The *impingement* of norms for our mental life is what attests to God's immanence. Or, stated from the side of the human being, thought cannot be broached without being obligated to reckon with truth as norm. To wilfully disregard norms is at the same time to disfavour God's immanence. The Self has the quality of knowing or distinguishing subject only on condition that the Self subjects itself to logical norms.[111]

God's immanence is attested to in our willing compliance to norms. No doubt the same holds for human action in the light of ethical norms of right and wrong. But is God's immanence thereby solely of human relevance? I believe there is a metaphysical relevance too, though Vollenhoven does not (to my knowledge) say so explicitly. The realm of validity not only includes norms and ideals, it also concerns ideas. Now ideas fix the essence of things, which is their species characteristic. These are general ideas. But, as discussed earlier (cf. the section VII.B. on individual substances), Vollenhoven accounts for individuality in terms of God's individuating the general idea of human being. In this way particular ideas of individuals function as thing-laws, controlling their functional development. In other words, a thing-law is an individualized idea that controls the actions and appearances of that thing in a way that is in step with its development within the bounds of its species.

Quite apart from how we ought to evaluate this view of individual creation, it seems difficult to discount its being additional evidence of God's immanence, in Vollenhoven's view of things. General ideas "in God's Counsel" are individuated, and as individuated ideas control, delineate, 'hold for' a factually real (space-time-genetic) creature. If a norm's holding for distinct (human) thoughts evidences God's immanence, then an individuated idea's being a thing-law for a (human or non-human) creature—which is of God's doing in letting a creature be—can hardly be counted as something of a different order. There can be no individual without its own controlling idea, hence I take this to evidence God's immanence with respect to the creation of each individual.

When we accept this additional case of God's immanence, we get

---

111   The theist is therefore very aware of his or her attitude. "For the Self that strives for knowledge[,] to acknowledge the normativity of logic is . . . for theism a theonomic urge. . . . [T]heism willingly subjects itself in the conviction that also these norms of God are good" (1918a: 439).

a more integrated understanding of Vollenhoven's metaphysics. The key notion here is the principle of substance. Every substance has a unity that is more than the sum of its features. This unity has the character of a law, controlling the changing features, illustrative of the 'predicates that inhere in a subject'. Such a complex unity, with an inner dynamics of changing features ('perceptions', 'states'), is the *monad* of Vollenhoven's monadology. Though, as we said earlier, Vollenhoven eschews the term 'monad' (but not 'monadology'), one cannot fail to recognize the monadic view of substances in this metaphysics. But now we can see that each substance is a 'spiritual' entity, in terms of its individual law-thing, maintained by God, which controls the factual existence of a thing in its temporal and spatial features in a genetic-species context.

There is a passage in Vollenhoven's discussion of Brouwer in which the two 'evidences of divine immanence'—norms holding for human thought and ideas holding for things—appear together. "Our fundamental thought of metaphysical (spiritual) substances, whose appearances are the object of physics, is in complete harmony with our view of truth as norm, posited by God the Holy Spirit as law-giver with regard to the striving of the supra-individual subject of science" (1918a: 390-391). The "complete harmony" between the two justifies our having taken them as analogous. In the World-order, these "metaphysical (spiritual) substances" are the monads, the appearances of which are the phenomena studied by physics. On the human side are the norms, to which human beings are subject in their quality as knowing (or distinguishing) subject. The context of the discussion (in the quote), which is about science, accounts for the fact that the human subject is here taken to be the scientific community, not an individual subject. But this does not affect the argument at this point.

3. Provisional summary
Although *Christian* theism still needs to be discussed, we can attempt a provisional summary on the basis of our discussion so far.

In Vollenhoven's approach, the distinction between thought and being forms the basic polarity. On this distinction is predicated the difference between intuition and its context in self-conscious awareness on the one hand and world-knowledge and its striving to attain adequate concepts on the other. Awareness and knowledge themselves are always a synthesis or reconciliation of thought and being, hence they 'bridge', so to speak, the polarity of thought and being. The distinction of thought and being is also dressed up cosmologically in terms of the human Self and the World in the large. The analogy between the setup of each—the Self with body and mind, and the World-order with its physical reality of things in relations that appear and the ideal reality of metaphysics—suggests the schema of microcosm and macrocosm, a philosophical theme with deep roots in the western history of thought.

In mentioning this schema, certain misconceptions should be warned against immediately. We need to say at once that a popular use of this schema, one in which the physical world is in some sense taken to be the body of God, is, in Vollenhoven's case, entirely unserviceable. God's reality is an "Excellence" that is prior to and beyond any world, it being itself the fundamental condition of any world. It is only in connection with our given world and our human reality that we can discern a transcendence and immanence of God, in that there is a transcendent ideal realm of validity that impinges immanently upon the human subject and holds for the given things of the world. This is the central nerve of Vollenhoven's theism.[112]

We may hazard to complete our previous 'cosmic' overview diagram, hoping for a positive heuristic effect.

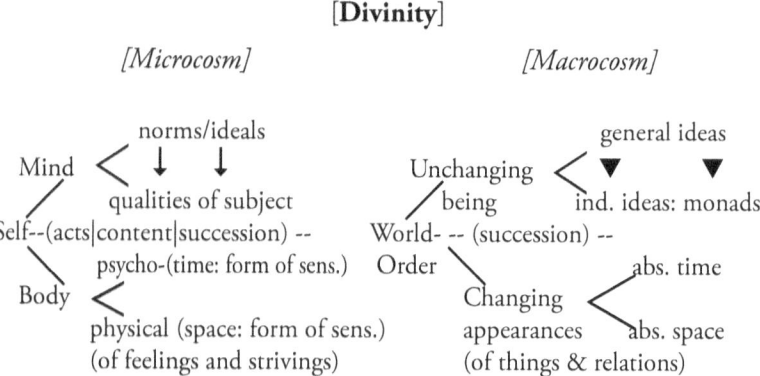

['↓': impinge upon; '▼': hold for through individuation]

The 'World order' (the term itself is not in the early Vollenhoven) is

112   The limited usefulness of this schema of micro- and macrocosm was clarified in discussions with John H. Kok and Jeremy G.A. Ive. As to the phrase 'God and the world', when this is meant to state something ultimate with respect to reality, the expression is unsatisfactory. For it leaves untouched both the difference by which the two are distinguished and the connection that justifies the use of 'and'. God's being 'original' (the Excellent or Sovereign One) ought to cancel any discussion of the (supposed) framework in which God and the world are held together, assuming this to be distinct from God. For a discussion in defence of such a framework, whereby God is taken to be "the first being of the universe", cf. Plantinga 1980.

the factual world of things and relations, with a capacity of self-development, as controlled ideationally. The 'things' include plants and animals. This 'genetic' development is of particular importance in its attesting to the reality of succession in the empirical world. It is itself psychical in nature, being the reality behind organic phenomena which, in their outward appearance, are spatial and temporal.[113] The factual world is a whole of appearances, whose boundary cannot be conclusively drawn. For, while every boundary calls attention to what is beyond, the unbounded cannot be thought by a human being (1918a: 135). The relations between things, which act as forces through which things position or affect each other, are a condition for being able to be aware of space and time. They are absolute in that they form unending parameters for the localization of appearances.

This factually real world is however 'incomplete'. Its structure is an open structure, in the sense that its controlling principles are not intrinsic to it. There is a realm of validity, an ideational world that transcends the factual world, in which general ideas are the essences of species, in the context of which individualized ideas control the appearances and development of individuals belonging to a species. An individualized idea is a thing-law for the individual it holds for, being its unchanging substance of changing appearances, or the subject of inhering qualities, which appearances and qualities are themselves in real succession. The net result is a monadology of substances (monads) that interact through their intrinsic striving or states to which outer appearances attest.

Roughly in tandem with the World order is the 'world' of the Self. It is itself a substance, thus outwardly it is part of the world order. In a self-approaching process it can get to know itself as an existing Self in contradistinction from other human beings and non-human things.

The *Self* is a psychical synthesis, controlled by the idea of the Self. The Self is itself a metaphysical entity, a principle of invariance controlling the 'states' of body and mind. The psychical qualities of the body are interwoven with physical matter to form a psycho-physical organization. These states of the body can be sensed, allowing the reception of data that the body itself arranges in temporal and spatial patterns. Besides

---

113   This is of course a new argument. In discussion with Hans Driesch Vollenhoven expressed his preference for studying living organism using the methods of physical and chemical science *and that of psychology*, rather than postulate a vitalistic entelechy, such as Driesch did. This means that the early Vollenhoven allows for a 'plant psychology'. He distinguished human psychology, which is personalized, from that of animals and plant, which is not personalized. We return to this in the discussion of A. Janse in the next chapter.

the act of sense-awareness, there are also the acts of representation and of remembering. Through these acts there is a reservoir of content that forms the basis of mental life. The Self, being intuitively aware of both acts and content, is able to posit these as self-certain states of the Self on the basis of actually undergoing their presence (in concrete intuition) and distinguishing them in their self-identity as *Gegenstände* (through the analytical intuition). The reality of succession in self-conscious experience makes intuition possible. The Self discovers that, as mind, to cogitate what is psychically enjoyed, requires compliance to the norm of identity.[114] This is indicative of the general situation of mind: without compliance to norms, the psychical synthesis lacks orientation and aim. The Self is a subject in the context of science, morality and art only when subjecting itself to norms and ideals.

Vollenhoven also speaks of another "reality", *viz.* the reality in which thought and being, or the Self and the World are reconciled. This is the reality of knowledge and science. In reference to our schema, it needs to be situated *between* the Self and the World, for each contributes to it, with space as its foundational feature. It is a reality that grows through human effort. It calls for a Self that subjects itself to norms, especially the norm of truth (logical principles), but also requires ideals to pursue. The primary ideal of science is the supra-individual ideal of forming a continually more adequate concept or understanding of the World. The World, as acknowledged in its Idea, calls up the ideal of an adequate understanding of it. This basic aim of science is important in connection with Vollenhoven's Trinitarian theism and certain metalogical reflections of the early 1920s, yet to be reviewed.

C. Trinitarian theism

The discussion of Vollenhoven's theism has focussed on divinity in a generic sense, though we discovered distinction in the difference between ideas and norms. A central, not to say characteristic, doctrine of Christianity is that of the divine Trinity. Vollenhoven's own Christian theism takes this into account. God is a Godhead of three Persons: God the Father, the Creator, God the Son, the *Logos*-revelation, and God the Holy

---

114   My guess is that the 'immortality of the soul', which is a feature of the mind as '*substantia incompleta*', relates to the impingement of norms on the mind, interpreted as evincing divine immanence. Could a 'mortal mind' answer to the divine call? Vollenhoven nowhere indicates his defence of this characteristic in his early work. But after 1923 this immortality is contested. Given the importance of this theme, one tries to see how it might have been defended, apart from a general 'scholastic-theological' understanding. Anthropological remarks recur in chapters 3 and 4.

Spirit, the Guide. Vollenhoven offers no apology for this doctrine, but he does integrate the roles of these divine Persons in a way that pulls his entire conception together into a close-knit unity. In view of the possibility of 'Logos speculation', which has not been discussed as yet, we shall need to take a careful look at the distinct uses of the Persons of the deity, though we also state at once that there is nothing like a 'full theological account' to be found in Vollenhoven's early writings.

1. God, the Father

To start with the first Person, God the Creator, the references to this Person are rather meagre, but the relevance of this Person is difficult to miss. In an aside in the discussion of Poincaré's thought, Vollenhoven states: "there is no evolution unless God creates new ideas" (1918a: 379). Knowing that for Vollenhoven the substance of a thing is an idea, acting as the thing's thing-law, it follows that the very possibility of any new reality requires the creation of the appropriate ideas of that reality. This primary condition is traditionally met by God, the Father.[115]

The first Person of the Trinity is also broached, implicitly at least, in the long quote above about Lotze (cf. section VIII.B.1. above) where Vollenhoven speaks of "the Counsel of God". In the Reformed confessions this phrase occurs in the teaching about God the Father, who, by his "eternal counsel and foresight", preserves and rules over the creation (world).[116] Kuyper discusses the term in his commentary on the *Heidelberg Catechism*. He attributes to it a very broad meaning. God's Counsel means "his *goodwill*, or also his *predestination*, his *decision*, his *prior decree*, and also, if you will, it can be expressed more simple yet as his *order* (*bestel*), his *will*, his *law*, his *ordinance*."[117] In drawing his conclusion Kuyper summarizes: "First there is a *thought*, then there is a *word*,

---

115   For lack of textual evidence we need to leave unmentioned what, if any, the means of creation are for Vollenhoven here. Vollenhoven is silent about (say) the Pauline doctrine of the mediating role of the Son, i.e. the Logos, "by whom and for whom" all things were created (Col. 1: 16). Thematically there is the individuation of ideas in Vollenhoven, which suggests mediation. But he nowhere discusses this in his early work.

116   Cf. *Heidelberg Catechism*, Sunday 9, Question/Answer 26. The term also occurs in Sunday 12, Question/Answer 31, in which Christ is said "to reveal the hidden counsel decisions and will of God [the Father]". In the *Belgic Confession* the term occurs in Article 16, about the divine election. The term (counsel /boulé), as used in reference to God, occurs only once in the Gospels (Luke 7: 30), several times in Acts (cf. 2: 23; 13: 36; 20: 27) and in the Pauline letter to the Ephesians 1: 11. The New International Version edition of the Bible translates this as 'purpose' or 'will'. For these confessional documents, cf. Zwanepol 2004.

117   Kuyper 1892: 189.

and only then an *affair* arises. . . . The thought, the thinking through, the planning [*beraming*] of God's Counsel is accordingly prior to all creation" (*op. cit.*: 193-194). We cannot be sure that Vollenhoven endorses this broad meaning of 'Counsel of God' in its entirety. But in the quote about Lotze the term is used to indicate the presence of "the essence of things" in God's Counsel, as idea or thing-law, in contradistinction to the existence of the thing in creation, which is the existence of successive self-development. Seen in that light, ideas are an ingredient of God's planning and rule over all things. We may take this to mean that, for Vollenhoven, God the Father is the warrant for the metaphysical order that sustains things and their interactions, including the essence of the human Self.[118]

Now, if we take a slightly closer look at Kuyper's view of creation, there is the possibility of an influence that only became explicit in Vollenhoven later, though there would appear to be an immediate relevance as well. In Kuyper's view, the Persons of the Trinity convene in the work of creation.[119] The Father is the "principal actor" here, for he has priority over everything, from whom the thought proceeds. (The Father chooses the best thought among the alternatives of "possible worlds"; *op. cit.*: 194.) Then, secondly, there is the eternal Counsel, "which disposes over all things" (*op. cit.*: 202). Here, however, the Son has a role. "That Son is the eternal Word, in which the content of the Counsel of the Lord lies expressed" (*op. cit.*: 200). This divine speaking now is: "God's calling forth [*in het aanzijn roepen*] of things that are outside of himself, of which the plans and representations lie hidden in his eternal Counsel" (*op. cit.*: 207). Then, thirdly, it is only on the basis of this Counsel that Creation takes place, "which realizes this Counsel of the Lord in its [the Creation's] origination and development" (*op. cit.*: 202). Here the Holy Spirit is of influence. "And now where these creatures are not only called forth but also receive an *existence* [*een zijn*], having breath and life and animation, there it is the Holy Spirit that hovers over all that is created and ignites and makes it laden with life" (*op. cit.*: 207). Accordingly, the triune God created our universe in a completely self-sufficient way, without requiring

---

118 One accepts this, of course, on faith. But comparison and choice between options of faith are still relevant. Vollenhoven opts that for dualism it seems better to end "in the Counsel of a God who has wise reasons for everything, than in fate" (1918a: 408).

119 This convening holds in Kuyper for the other two main divine activities as well, namely salvation and sanctification. Only, in the case of salvation, it is the Son who takes the lead as "principal actor" (*hoofdwerker*), with the Father and the Holy Spirit cooperating, and in the work of sanctification the Holy Spirit is the principal actor, with the Father and Son cooperating; cf. Kuyper 1892: 168.

anything outside of itself. "First this universe was only in God's thought. Then he expressed it through the Word and it stepped outside [of Him]. And having been called forth outside of Him, it is guided to its goal by the Holy Spirit" (*op. cit.*: 207).[120]

In a summarizing statement, late in his career, entitled "Life-unity" (*Levenseenheid*),[121] Vollenhoven is explicit in his view of the Persons of the Trinity as also convening in the work of creation, though his wording is more directly biblical and less theologically laden than Kuyper's wording; e.g. he does not adduce the work of the Son/Logos there in terms of 'God's Counsel' but merely refers to 'God's speaking' in the Genesis 1 creation account.[122] But, upon realizing that Vollenhoven is definitely familiar with this view of creation, one suspects that all along this is in the background of numerous summary wordings of creation in Vollenhoven, when he speaks of the creation of things, the imposition of the law (or God's creational speaking) and the development of creatures.[123] Certainly the last point about the development is explicitly said to be guided by the Holy Spirit already in the first version of the *Isagoge* in 1930 (§19). This is not the place to discuss this further. But we will see in chapter 4 that Vollenhoven's shift to the more definitive 'Calvinistic philosophy' made him question and reject the interpretation of the confession of God's creation work in terms of a doctrine of ideas. But Vollenhoven was less reticent about the work of the Spirit, probably because its effect is more 'empirical'. At least there is a peculiarity in connection with the work of the Spirit, already in 1918, to which we now turn.

2. God, the Spirit
Turning first to the third Person, namely God the Holy Spirit, rather than

---

120 This summary statement is complete only if we add that creation in Kuyper is not limited to what took place "in the beginning" (Genesis 1:1), but includes the goal of creation, namely the Completion (*voleinding*) at the end of time. God's Counsel holds sway over creation, right up to this completion (Kuyper 1892: 194). Providence is God's *foreseeing* what creatures need and *providing* for that need, hence it assumes the creation but considers it from the perspective of time. But because everything has been laid down from eternity in God's Counsel, this providence, as foresight, is attributable to God only in a figurative sense (cf. Kuyper 1892: 216).

121 Vollenhoven 1955i: 118-133, esp. pp. 123, 124 en 126.

122 When one keeps this in mind, then there is a mediating creation role of the Son in Vollenhoven, capable of accounting for the Pauline "by whom and for whom" all things were created (Col. 1: 16).

123 Cf. Vollenhoven 1926d: 190; also Vollenhoven 1930d, §§ 74, 75 and 76. In Vollenhoven 2005d/e, **117**, Vollenhoven states explicitly that "the activity of Logos and Spirit play a special role in [God's creating activity]". This statement stems from 1941.

the second Person, there is a fairly explicit description of his work. We already quoted, but repeat in this context: "Our fundamental thought of metaphysical (spiritual) substances, whose appearances are the object of physics, is in complete harmony with our view of truth as norm, posited by God the Holy Spirit as law-giver with regard to the striving of the supra-individual subject of science: practising science is to approach the adequate concept as ideal" (1918a: 390-391). "[T]he Spirit posits and maintains the norms and ideals . . ." (1918a: 410).

The work of the Spirit, as formulated in these quotes, is directed specifically to human beings in their higher mental life.[124] Norms and ideals require submission and enjoin human deference, hence the very possibility for the Self's taking on the quality of knowing subject (and distinguishing subject) involves the human response to this 'law-giving' role of the Spirit. This law-giving is not to be confused with the thing-laws (the ideas) of things in general. The latter are related to essence, and that is a determination of being, limiting variability of factual response. Norms and ideals however are primarily relevant for mental activity: norms orientate and ideals are goal-guiding. Thus the law of contradiction, as a norm of truth, enjoins that contradictory statements be excluded from our system of knowing, while adequate concepts serve as ideals to strive for in the process of which use is made of proleptic concepts.

The 'law-giving' role, so explicitly apportioned to the Spirit, is perhaps unexpected. One is more inclined to think of law solely in connection with ideas, or at least with that expression of divine will that organizes and maintains the world. But the context of knowledge acquisition (as species of higher mental life) is essential here. In a lecture on Bergson, first given in 1919, but written out only in 1921, Vollenhoven repeats this same thought. The act of knowing needs to be executed "in obedience to God's norms. He is Law-giver here."[125] There can be little doubt about the Spirit's 'Law-giving' role as linked to 'norms', and this connection is in direct rapport with human activity and response.

---

124   The norms and ideals relevant here are those with respect to the pursuit of knowledge in science. There are also norms for morality and art, though these are not mentioned in the dissertation. Vollenhoven broaches this in an unpublished manuscript: "Paedagogiek en Paedagogie"; Vollenhoven 1919ms. In the letter to the theologian, F.W. Grosheide, dated 16 November 1921 (quoted earlier), Vollenhoven writes (we repeat the quote): "logic is, together with ethics, aesthetics, etc., precisely as science of norms distinguished from the explicative [i.e. descriptive; A.T.] sciences . . . ."; Vollenhoven 16-11-1921. So the work of the Spirit in the dissertation is especially directed to scientific knowledge acquisition.

125   Vollenhoven 1921ms: 12-13. There is also a press report of the lecture, as given in 1919; cf. Vollenhoven 1919b.

It will not have escaped notice that, when the Father-Creator is the warrant for the metaphysical order of substances and their appearances, and the Spirit is the 'law-giver' for human mental activity, we in fact have an apportioning of the relevance of these divine Persons over the difference between the World-order ('macrocosm') and the Self ('microcosm') respectively in their own internal operation, metaphysical and epistemological, respectively. We can add that the indications of divine transcendence and the matching immanence, discussed above, also agrees with these Persons, for we had to distinguish this relevance in connection with the World-order on the one hand and the Self on the other. This helps us in understanding the work of the second Person of divinity, namely God as *Logos*, to which we now turn. His position 'between' the first and third Persons suggests a relevance 'between' the World-order and the Self. The *Logos* puts us in touch with the conditions of knowledge, and knowledge has everything to do with the 'reality of science', the achieved reconciliation of being and thought.

3. God, the Logos
Knowledge as relation, we said, bridges the difference between thought (reinforced with *Gegenstände*) and being (the given in appearances). In a generic sense, *thought* has its locus in the human Self, while *being*, which is that which is foreign to thought, has its focus in the World-order. (Of course, the Self too is a being. It is its distinctive psychical nature, of body and mind and our intuitive ability to be aware of it in self-consciousness, which sets it apart.) If the relation between *Gegenstand* (thought) and the given (being) is to be worthy of the name, it must be more than a mere one-to-one side-by-side arrangement of *ratio* and *empirie*. (This is why the schema of micro- and macrocosm cannot be the end-all and be-all in itself, and also why knowledge itself is a distinct reality as 'reality of science'.) Knowing involves thought's (*ratio*) working over the given (*empirie* / being) according to norms and ideals. In the larger context of theism, this calls for a mutual arrangement of the order of the Self and the order of the World, whereby each secures a 'rationality': the Self a 'subjective rationality' (of norms and the epistemic qualities of a subject), the World an 'objective rationality' (of ideas and monadology). But Vollenhoven prefers to conduct his discussion using the terms '*ratio*' and '*empirie*'. In any case, the important point is that God has a role at this level. There is a connection between *ratio* and *empirie* that is relevant for knowledge and is warranted by the divine Logos. "Likewise, the divine Logos may not be inserted in the theory of knowledge as an *unknown third* [factor],

to which *ratio* and *empirie* would stand in the same one-to-one relation" (1918a: 409) for that resolves nothing in the correspondence itself. But:

> proceeding from the *judgment* we see in it the synthesis enacted by the *cooperation* of norm, *ratio* and *empirie* and hence we can only find the normative, rational and empirical elements through analysis. In other words, operations are *taking place*, more or less in obedience to the norms, there is connection, an interaction between *ratio* and *empirie*. The Logos, then, is not an unknown third [factor], but in him rests on the one hand the disposition of two distinct things, namely as subject and object of knowledge, respectively, to enter into a synthesis; on the other hand, the Spirit sets and maintains the norms and ideals to which the actualization of this disposition from our side must subject itself, lest it result in invalid [i.e. anti-normative] or not completely valid [i.e. not ideal] knowledge respectively. (1918a: 409-410)

The subject-object relation of knowledge, said to be grounded "in two distinct things", is of course secured in the Self as knowing subject and the given as knowable (or appearing) object. The judgment attests to the synthesis. The divine Logos *predisposes* the synthesis to take place. But the disposition as such is not easy to grasp. No doubt there is a motivational element (e.g. in connection with the will to know in the qualities of distinguishing subject and knowing subject) on the side of the human subject.[126] But the object too must be involved in the disposition, at least that is as Vollenhoven would have it.

Now it would appear that rationality is involved here. At least that is present in both subject and object. The "logical order of our thought" (*viz.* subjective rationality) *harmonizes* with "the order in the given that is independent of thought" (*viz.* objective rationality), for both "stem from the same Logos" (1918a: 409). This common source in the Logos may invite 'Logos-speculation', so Vollenhoven proceeds cautiously. He declares that he does not contest the harmony of these two rational orders; on the contrary, he claims that it can be found directly in special revelation (cf. 1918a: 409). "The ultimate ground of things—we gladly admit it—is *rational* and not blind, but the danger in this statement lies

---

126   We should probably also include the forms of sensibility in this regard. In his critique of Brouwer, Vollenhoven states: "In our opinion theism offers a considerably more stable basis for geometry, in taking space to be a form of appearance and form of sensibility, which God himself does not possess, for he determines the *essence* of things, but donated to the creature to be able to know certain *objects* appearing in a determined way" (1918a: 399). In a note Vollenhoven refers to page 410, the page we quoted from above (the main quote about the Logos). The uncertainty regarding the form of sensibility being dispositional pertains to the question as to whether human receptivity, which makes us sensitive to 'being appeared to', follows from our psychical essence or is a trait of our rationality.

in equating human and divine reason" (1918a: 408). A popular version of this equating is 'thinking God's thoughts after him', which is speculative, for one does not reckon with the difference between divine thinking and human thinking. In considering this to be 'dangerous', Vollenhoven clearly rejects it.

Apart from signalling this danger, Vollenhoven also takes the extra step in contesting, what most forms of Scholasticism would probably accept, namely that the harmony of the two orders is a *sufficient* foundation of knowledge. Knowledge is a relation, as every judgment evidences. But harmonization is for Vollenhoven not itself a connection or a relation. A judgment attests to the assimilation of a given object by the knowing subject. The predisposition of the Logos is, in part, to stimulate the knowing subject's assimilation, it is not to secure (though it does warrant) harmony. For one cannot let the order of our thought simply dictate to the object. There are elements of the order of our thought—*Gegenstände* such as a wooden iron, a round square, etc.—that are not met with in reality (the given) and hence have nothing with which to harmonize. Then, from the side of the object, one also needs to recognize or acknowledge features of the object in the course of the knowing subject's working over the object. Such recognition or acknowledgement (of the idea) would also appear to be part of the Logos' disposing. But if we merely 'take' the object and grasp its representation, we only 'copy' it—and thus, true enough, to be in harmony with it!—but we then do not as yet know it, for there is no predication. In sum, we cannot merely proceed from either the subject or the object, and then construct a harmonious synthesis, when accounting for knowledge. (That would be, in view of Vollenhoven's philosophy of science, a variant of formalism or of empiricism, depending on which side is predominant.) This view of the relevance of the Logos could also invite speculation. Vollenhoven opts for an alternative approach of analysis. The *human task* lies in the *analysis* of the cooperation of the normative, rational and empirical elements implicit in the acceptance of judgments (cf. 1918a: 409-410), rather than in offering an account for (or a justification of) their synthesis.[127] It is in emphasizing analysis and the human task that Vollenhoven here distances himself from a speculative use of, or appeal to, the Logos.[128]

---

127   By opting for analysis Vollenhoven accepts that some knowledge is always given or at least already present when analysis proceeds. This would appear to be primary knowledge by acquaintance or of presentations as grasped by outer perception, and the concrete intuitive givens of inner perception. In terms of science, this prior knowledge relates to the synthetic a priori of geometry and of arithmetic, respectively.

128   Though Vollenhoven uses the notions of 'Logos speculation' and 'scholasticism'

a. Truth and knowledge

So Vollenhoven seems to sidestep rather than undercut scholasticism and Logos-speculation. The scholastic harmony between the logical order and the metaphysical order does remain in place, but it is not available directly. Also the Logos is quite evidently present. What does this imply? Let us canvas Vollenhoven's epistemology to pin-point more carefully the relevance of the Logos.

Wouldn't truth be considered to have a direct link with the Logos? Perhaps surprisingly, Vollenhoven's understanding and use of truth in this his earliest thought do not have direct rapport with the Logos, at least in a constitutive sense. Truth is (as already quoted) "the opinion of the facts as God wishes that we have" (1918a: 53), whereby we need to distinguish between "God as norm-giver also for our thinking and the human being, subject to his norms" (*ibid.*). In being subject to norms, the human being is subject to God the Holy Spirit, and truth is integral to this. Truth is not an effect of, or warranted by, the Logos. Indeed, as already quoted, "truth is a norm, posited by God the Holy Spirit as law-giver" (1918a: 391). Also, through the immanent impingement of norms, truth is "self-guaranteeing", as Vollenhoven notes appreciatively in connection with Lotze (1918a: 160-161), for no human being can abrogate a divine norm nor ignore its obligating effect.[129] At best we can say that knowledge possession, of which every judgment is a case, is availing over truth-content, such as the Logos would dispose the human being to have.

Now how does this understanding of truth work in the actual acquisition of knowledge? Let us consider the primary form of knowledge, namely that of acquaintance. An object 'gives itself' by its entering into relations and interacting with other things, all the while being controlled

---

with care, he is not very explicit in what he takes them to be. But his later criticisms of these notions give a kind of hindsight into at least relevant features of his former use. Logos speculation ignores the boundary between God and the World/Self (cf. Vollenhoven 1926a: 18, 21) as attested by "thinking God's thoughts after him", likewise with the absence of 'transcendent and immanent' conditions for the Logos. Scholasticism, in turn, evinces an uncritical appeal to rationality. In emphasizing the harmony between subjective and objective rationality, there is an equivocation of the general feature of a concept (formed by the subject) with the analogical similarity discernible in different methods of science (scientific order of the world), thereby confusing a *conceptual* synthesis with a *methodological* synthesis (cf. Vollenhoven 1926a: 62). This enables the harmony of the two orders to be considered a sufficient criterion for knowledge.

129   This property of truth is not merely founded in the contradiction of scepticism, which must assume the truth of its denial of truth, but is also supported by a positive view, such as in Plato, where God is the measure of all things, or in Lotze, where norms continue to hold even while searching for norms. (Cf. 1918a: 75, 87, 160-161, 312, 405.)

by the *idea* of the object in question. This 'giving' allows it to be noticed as real phenomenon or appearance. The knowing subject's noticing of the given phenomenon gives rise to representations in the knowing subject through psychical acts. The knowing subject in turn must submit to *norms* if the content of the representation is to be more than fleeting experience, and to be involved in predication. The idea is part of the *order of things*, while the norms are correlated to the *order of thought*. But acquaintance is more than a harmony between these orders. For a representation is a result of my noticing, which may be (and usually is) very limited, while the given phenomenon is an expression of a thing that exists, which is extremely complex. ("[B]eing is always richer than thought. . ."; 1918a: 437). But in acquaintance we do relate these, and this takes place in judgment when the representation is *attributed* to something real, as justified by my noticing. Vollenhoven's example: "the tree in my garden" is a representation, which is neither true nor false as such. In the judgement "the tree in my garden exists", the representation is attributed to an object, truly if the object exists, falsely if there is no such object. Truth is a norm here in that the attribution that gives rise to the judgment in knowledge by acquaintance involves the activity of the knowing subject, who *ought* to base the attribution on what is *noticeably* given.[130]

The role of the divine Logos is indeed not sufficient to account for acquaintance. The attribution of a representation (as predicate) to a thing (as subject of judgment, formulated as a proleptic concept) signals the assimilation of the given by the knowing subject. Ideally, this assimilation is predisposed by the Logos, though of course often very practical motives are operative too. But be that as it may, there is no need—at least not an obvious one—to refer to any harmony between the order of things and the order of thoughts, such as is warranted by the divine Logos. But Vollenhoven had said that he does agree with the notion of harmony. How relevant is this? And is it put to use anywhere?

b. Logos and acquaintance

Now the *Logos* is not entirely absent from knowledge by acquaintance.

---

130 Vollenhoven outlines this way of dealing with truth in the 1919 manuscript, "Paedagogiek en Paedagogie" (Vollenhoven 1919ms). In 1918a Vollenhoven tends to equate the norm of truth with logical principles: "The question now arises, what the norm is for the truth of judgments. It can hardly be other than the principle of contradiction (which absorbs the principle of identity, without being derivable from it) with its derivations" (1918a: 431). The discussion of the 1919 manuscript is a welcome 'synthetic' addition to the 'analytic' understanding of 1918a. "Logic must be viewed as purely formal. . . . Logic evaluates the correctness of judgments according to norms"; 1918a: 407.

Because knowledge is a relation, with every judgment is associated a concomitant complex of referent and relatum. The judgment cannot be apportioned exclusively to either the human subject (who determines the predicate or relatum) or the given (which provides the judgment's subject or referent). It signals their 'interaction', the subject's 'assimilation' of the given. Thought and being have entered into a synthesis. But the result, as concomitant complex, also calls for a *raison d'être*. There is more than just the interacting of subject and object, as predisposed by the Logos. For "both subject and object would not lend themselves for such a synthesis in case it was not in the nature of both. For each relation assumes a predicate in both terms, and hence a laid connection" (1918a: 12). A subject's submission to norms (of the Spirit) and an object's revealing something according to its idea (maintained by the Father) may be, and no doubt are, in harmony, but that is not the connection laid on their basis. (A disharmony between the order of thought and the order of things would, of course, forfeit the very possibility of such a connection that constitutes knowledge.) The knowledge that is gained, signals the *laid connection*, a case of *achieved reconciliation* of subject and object, and this requires a *warrant distinct* from either the Spirit or the Father, though both are presupposed. Knowledge comes to be possessed, hence truth-content is had knowingly. This is what the Logos warrants, for this would appear to be in virtue of the Logos' being the 'common source' of the order of thought and the order of being (cf. 1918a: 409).

But knowledge by acquaintance is not the only kind of knowledge. Acquaintance is knowledge gained through outer perception in everyday experience. The accumulation of judgments allows the knowing subject to formulate concepts, which afford a closer understanding of reality. This brings us to scientific knowledge which, while not in opposition to everyday experience, has an added depth to it. It turns out that the Logos has a more prominent role here.

c. Logos and scientific knowledge
Scientific knowledge is predicated on the human striving to know the human environment (cf. 1918a: 413) in a (self-)conscious effort to know. This requires not only memory and psychical growth of the content of memory, hence succession is presupposed (1918a: 413), but also stable terms and invariant laws (1918a: 429). In other words, in scientific knowledge one strives for the certainty (in the psychical growth) that is only available when conditioned by intuition and intra-mental awareness. How is this certainty brought to bear upon our initial acquaintance

of the environment?

In the first place, *Gegenstände* are applied to provide stability of meaning. *Gegenstände* are "posited as the substrate of the phenomena" (1918a: 429), i.e. phenomena, perceived as sensory content, are placed in a web of meanings that provides terminological clarity, an "immutability of thought" (*ibid.*). Without such immutability, any scientific exchange of thought would be impossible (1918a: 429). Thus this is essential for inter-subjectivity at the scientific level. Also, the discerning of phenomena and their features, when formulated in the light of *Gegenstände*—hence formulated in terms of the representations and their interconnections one is aware of—is more rigorous and objective than when formulated merely as sensed in perception. The discerned too now forms more clearly the challenge of thought. The clearer one discerns the given object and its interactions by means of *Gegenstände* (Objects/entities and Objectives/propositions), the more objective (*gegenständlich*) is the content discerned, and the more intensely does one apperceive its objection (its being *gegenständig*) to assimilation. In other words, the 'given' is consciously placed in an intra-mental light (of cognized entities and propositions).[131] (One almost wants to say: the given is placed in a consciously prepared 'field of inquiry', adjusted to the relevant inter-subjective investigation taking place. But this is to anticipate a near future development.)

One needs to keep in mind that the added focus on awareness, which the more systematic use of *Gegenstände* encourages, should not be seen as cancelling the reference to the given, intrinsic to the use of concepts. (Such a cancelling threatens when '*Gegenstand*' and 'concept' are not distinguished.) It is helpful to repeat here that a concept may 'have' a *Gegenstand* as its intension, but it has an extension too, which provides the extra-mental reference. Concepts are derived from judgments through abstraction (1918a: 161, 275), and on that account proceed from a situ-

---

131   In accounting for *Gegenstände* Vollenhoven assigns (as pointed out) a role to the metaphysical intuition to account for the differences in content between different *Gegenstände*. It is therefore not counterintuitive, in a scientific context, to use *Gegenstände* as substrate for phenomena. (A phenomenon harbours problems, *inter alia* that of thing and relation, hence the intra-mental reflection of this in terms of Objects and Objectives is fitting; cf. 1918a: 135.) To be relevant, some of the *Gegenstände* of representation must agree with transcendent objects in the phenomena. (This may tend to blur the difference between the appearance of the given or transcendent things and the corresponding representations, suggestive of an uncritical scientific idealism.) But because (presumably) a whole web of *Gegenstände* is applied as substrate, one is then in a position to be able to discover new phenomena, as suggested by the web of *Gegenstände*, namely when searching for further fitting transcendent objects of the *Gegenstände* so used.

ation of the assimilation of the given by thought (1918a: 130, 412), as signalled by prior acquaintance. Thus, like judgments, the principles of contradiction and excluded middle are applicable to them (which means that they have truth-value[132]). Concepts can also be used to indicate *connections*. Though examples are regrettably lacking, one may take (so I presume, say) the statement of a formal implication (e.g. 'all humans are mortal') as expressing (as Objective) a lawful connection between concepts. When instantiated, such an expression of lawfulness represents an essential connection. Such a connection is a very select instance of grasping how the inherence of qualities in a substance is itself structured, as governed by the idea.[133] The long and the short of all this is that, when, in a scientific context, *Gegenstände* are applied to undergird phenomena, the distinction in *Gegenstände* between Objects and Objectives brings to the fore an emphasis on conceptual entities and connections between them, respectively, in a way that provides for a scientific analysis of the phenomena being studied.

Methodology is also essential to science. There are methodological differences between the sciences mutually. But the sciences also belong together, in being part of the vast activity called the scientific enterprise.[134] The sciences that Vollenhoven mentions explicitly are (second

---

132   I believe we may reconstruct this as follows. A *Gegenstand* can be associated with a concept, i.e. be the *Gegenstand* had by a concept, only in such cases as when the principle of contradiction is applicable. Take, say, 'large ball', which is a complex *Gegenstand*. It can be the intension of a concept, say, 'x is a large ball', which is abstracted from the judgment 'this is a large ball'. The latter has truth-value, which is preserved in the abstracted concept so long as there is an implicit scope to the variable expression. In other words, Vollenhoven's concepts suggest a context of use in first order predicate logic. This is reinforced by his insisting that a concept is also the principle of a series, the series being formed by the values of the variable occurring in the expression of the concept. The variable here must preserve the extra-mental reference, thus be interpreted in realist fashion.

133   When interpreted in terms of the first order logical idiom, the formal implication is '(x).A(x)→B(x)'. Here the 'A(x)' and 'B(x)' are concepts, in Vollenhoven's sense. When instantiating this universal generalization by substituting a definite value, say 'c', for the variable, we get 'A(c)→B(c)', which expresses an essential connection between features applicable to c, for example, take 'A(x)' to be 'x is human' and 'B(x)' 'x is mortal', then the instantiation says: if c is human then c is mortal. The universal generalization expressed the 'connection' that mortality cannot be divorced from humanity, the instantiation states this in application to c.

134   The discussion of the sciences is here limited to mathematics and the natural sciences. Vollenhoven also speaks of 'normative science', e.g. he states that for theism theoretical logic is a normative science (cf. 1918a: 401-402). Cf. also the letter to F.W. Grosheide, quoted in footnote 124 above (Vollenhoven 16-11-1921), where logic, along with ethics and aesthetics, is said to be a "science of norms". It is difficult to ascertain, from Vollenhoven's early writings, what the precise nature of a normative science is. But

order) arithmetic, geometry, kinematics, mechanics and physics (1918a: 417, 433-434). This order is not random. Taken methodologically, the sciences form an *organism* (1918a: 417). It is in the guise of this metaphor that Vollenhoven speaks of 'the reality of science' (also known as the 'encyclopaedia of the sciences').

The heart of the 'reality' of science is that it constitutes a reconciliation of thought and being. Though science is complex, and taking into account the 'enhancement' of the factor of thought through the emphasis on *Gegenstände* and the understanding of things and their connections via concepts on the side of the object (being), the bottom line is still— this also is and remains characteristic of knowledge as such, *viz.*—"being enters into the judgment via the (*purely formal*) forms of our thought" (1918a: 434). Judgment is reconciliation of thought and being, which says that '*all* judgments are synthetic and all have a formal and a material element" (1918a: 435). This holds for arithmetic which, though intramental, has the 'mental material' provided by the intuition of number. In geometry, there is the notion of space that is itself in part subjective (the spatial form of sensibility), in part objective (relations between and in things). The natural sciences all appeal to space, and these sciences develop and advance by making increasing use of mathematics. In that sense, the synthetic a priori that holds in mathematics, is also valid in the sciences that build on mathematics. Thus "*all* judgment forms are modification of the synthetic a priori" (1918a: 435).

If the judgments of every science consist of a formal (a priori) and material (ideal or real) element, what distinguishes the sciences mutually? Vollenhoven's immediate answer is short-lived, at least in 1921 he suggests an important revision (cf. the section on 'metalogic' below). But he did hold—"as his opinion", he says with some uncertainty (1918a: 435)—that the distinction between the sciences can be accounted for *quantitatively*, merely in terms of the different ratios between the formal and the material elements (1918a: 435). Arithmetic is largely formal, but it does have intuitive content. Each science adds some content, in the form of *Gegenstand* representing phenomena, that is lacking in the science it is directly based on. Vollenhoven makes no effort to distinguish kinds or categories of *Gegenstand* at this point.[135] Geometry is not

---

see the discussion of Dooyeweerd in chapter three, where this question returns and a provisional statement is made.

135   One senses an indirect influence of the Marburg neo-Kantians here in the pronounced unity of method of all the sciences. Although this school developed the sciences entirely from out of the self-development of thought, Vollenhoven takes thought and being together. But the common method he favours on this basis does not do justice (as he

just (arithmetized) analytic geometry, but has in addition the notion of a group (of transformations), and within the range of possibilities of the group concept, different geometrical systems can be defined and studied (1918a: 433). Kinematics, in turn, adds the notion of one-dimensional real succession, representing the factor of time. So there are as many systems of kinematics as there are geometries (1918a: 433-434). Vollenhoven does not state the additions unique to mechanics and physics, but we may conjecture that these involve the addition of the notions of kinds of forces and energy forms, respectively. From arithmetic upwards, there is a (quantitative) increase in the encumbrance of content through the 'amount' of *Gegenstand*, in the range of its terms, that the science in question studies.

Hence, the organism of the sciences has, as principle of unity, the *one common method* of knowing, a material-formal and a formal-material method in one (cf. 1918a: 436). Every science reconciles thought and what is strange to thought. At the same time, the ratio between the formal and the material allows for "uncountable modifications". The organism of the sciences is not nearly full-grown.[136] (We here leave the statement of method for what it is. Features of it return in the section on 'metalogic' below; and in chapter three there is a fuller discussion.)

Returning now to the Logos, whereas we previously had difficulty pointing to a relevant role for the Logos, this now comes into full view. The very formulation of the aim of science, *viz.* "human striving to know the human environment in the most general way" (1918a: 413), is in direct step with the disposition, provided by the Logos, of subject and object coming into a synthesis. In short, the Logos motivates science. To know the environment is for a human being to be at home in it, reconciled to it. But couldn't this just be a pious or innocent way of affirming human dominance over nature, through science, now justified by appealing to the Logos, much as Descartes foresaw when he states that, via the natural sciences, human beings could "render themselves the masters and possessors of nature"?[137]—not if one *disallows* an interpretation of science

---

will soon come to see) to the *qualitative* differences between the sciences, when referring, as he does in 1918a, only to differences in ratio of the formal and the material. There is also a 'scholastic' feature here of taking conceptual synthesis as having direct methodological implications (cf. footnote 128 above).

136 The three features discussed above in connection with scientific knowledge, namely phenomena expressed by *Gegenstände*, reference of concepts and connections, recur in Vollenhoven's revised thought in 1926, though the notion of the 'organism' of science is revised quite drastically; cf. chapter three.

137 Descartes 1972: 119.

that gives priority to subjective rationality. The Logos' being the common source of the rationality of the subjective order and the objective order guards against such an interpretation.

But the subjective order and the objective order do have to be adapted to the context of science. The subjective order has gained significance through the intra-mental interpretation of the appearances, dealt with by a science, in its upholding these in a web of *Gegenstände*. At the same time the reference to the objective order, which is that of the world order, is supplemented in that the (proleptic) concepts through which (something of) reality is understood, have well-chosen *Gegenstände* as their intensions, and also put connections between things into sharper relief. But however much the synthesis of these two orders of rationality may be achieved in science, the world order itself still far exceeds the knowledge and understanding actually gained of it to date. So an appeal to the harmony of the subjective order and the objective order cannot be a license for the subject to dominate the object. The harmony is never complete, always partial, with the insufficiency on the side of the subject, hence in this sense too it can never be a "sufficient basis" for knowledge as such. (The certainty of the synthetic a priori's of arithmetic and geometry is a bare minimum of sufficiency.)

So the striving to know continues unabated, though there is gratitude in any progress made. Science, for Vollenhoven, must be seen as something that essentially needs to be practiced, like a project that is never completed.[138] This makes it to be a human enterprise of striving, *viz.* to come into a better rapport—more reconciled—with the environment.

The following statement, already cited, but very relevant in our present context, sheds confirming light. "Our fundamental thought of metaphysical (spiritual) substances, whose appearances are the object of physics, is in complete harmony with our view of truth as norm, posited by God the Holy Spirit as law-giver with regard to the striving of the supra-individual subject of science. Practicing science is approaching the adequate concept as ideal" (1918a: 390-391). If "the object of physics" can be read as "the object of the natural sciences"—after all Vollenhoven is here speaking generally of appearances of metaphysical substances—then this "fundamental thought" concerns the philosophy of science directly.

---

138   This is in step with, though Vollenhoven does not endorse its humanistic overtone, the prevailing modernistic and neo-Idealist sentiment of the time, of European culture having the spiritual *Gestalt* of shaping its historical life according to (infinite) ideas of reason and unending tasks. The scientific enterprise itself unfolds unending possibilities of rational knowledge. Cf. Husserl 1970b: esp. 274.

Science is practiced by the community of scientists (= the supra-individual subject of science). That community is subject to the logical norm of truth. Its position is characterized in relations to norms, as standing in subjection to these, not in relation to the world, as dominating over it. The "adequate concept" which this community strives to achieve as ideal, must be—to use details from previous discussions—the complete knowledge of the world as complex whole, as determined metaphysically by its idea. This 'idea of the world' is that of the monadology of substances, their "thing-laws" intermeshing to form the rational order of the world. In mentioning the "complete harmony" between (his fundamental thought of) the metaphysical order and the order of the scientific community, Vollenhoven is implicitly referring to the Logos, all the more so since there is a reference to divinity here (the Holy Spirit, who guides through ideals *inter alia* of the adequate concept), and the connection laid by the Logos is based on that of the Spirit (normatively guiding thought) and the Creator (maintaining metaphysical ideas).[139]

So the organism of science is hemmed in and supported by the subjective order and the metaphysical order of the world. The Spirit guides in positing the ideal of the adequate concept, the Father maintains the world and its phenomena through the order of ideas. The unity of the sciences is the unity of method, and this makes the organism of science a whole and a reality in its own right, in need of its own warrant, which is the Logos. Thus, there is a 'dualism' here too, between the fact of science and its principled guarantor, the Logos. If such a guarantor of scientific rationality were lacking, then the knowledge-seeking human being would seek a point of attachment or implementation of rationality elsewhere. In Vollenhoven's early thought, the most likely alternatives to reconciliation would be the monistic variants of formalism and empiricism.[140] Formal-

---

139   The aim of science being to understand (in continuously more adequate concepts, as governed by logical norms) the given reality (as governed by ideas), the *duality of concept* and idea is characteristic here. The idea, fully known, is the adequate concept, which serves as the limit (never reached) in the actual process of scientific understanding. In 1921 Vollenhoven used this "dualism of concept and idea" as characteristic epistemological feature of his standpoint. Cf. the discussion of metalogic in the next section.

140   In Vollenhoven's case, the theme of a common scientific method, in its formalistic variant, was particularly pressing on account of its prevalence in the Marburg School of neo-Kantianism. There the idea of the unity of method was used to derive the diversity of the sciences. Proceeding from the *autonomy of thought*, thought advances, through its own activity of posing problems, and creates the content and the categories relevant to science. This has a spin-off that informs culture with rationality. One of the earliest critical comments on the Marburgers is in Vollenhoven 1921c: 83, 86. As to the variant of empiricism, in this same article Vollenhoven confronts Hegel, whose "romantic meta-

ism encourages maintaining rationality as (subjective) principle of dominance in light of an absolute spiritual freedom, while empiricism sees in rationality a(n objective) structure that leaves no leeway for responsibility in its favouring deterministic bodily behaviour. So a 'Logos understanding' of the scientific enterprise undercuts these problematic alternatives, in relating the rationality of scientific knowledge to the reconciliation of the human being and the environment. Not that the environment is as such hostile to the human being. The analogy of cultivation is perhaps useful here. Cultivation is taking care of nature, while at the same time being of cultural benefit to the human being. Knowledge is what the human being enjoys when 'cultivating' the world-order, in accordance with the conditions, means and ideals the human being has to achieve this. In that sense, whatever doubts one might have about Vollenhoven's appeal to the divine Logos, he does favour, practically, a distinct and worthy understanding of science.

d. Logos speculation?
Vollenhoven endorses a Logos-doctrine as an integral part of his Trinitarian theism. The doctrine itself concerns rationality. Seen in operation and as implementing Vollenhoven's understanding of theism—*viz.* thinking as God would have us think, hence always in subjection to norms and ideals—I believe Vollenhoven is not guilty of Logos speculation. There is no "thinking God's thoughts after him", which leaves the question of human viability entirely unanswered.[141] There is also no appeal to a harmony between the subjective human rational order and the objective rational order of the world as settled principle that could encourage dogmatism of thought. The world embodies an infinite complexity that the human being can, at best, only approach serially and potentially, and always with a sense of overcoming inadequacy in understanding. Thus the order of knowledge, as achieved understanding, is a finite 'reality of science'. The human being exerts effort when coming to know the world, and what results always bears the human stamp.[142] The Logos is the war-

---

physics" he takes to be "empiricistic", in the sense that "thought is sacrificed to being". The dialectical method is the method of the self-moving notion, as part of the world process, through which the world becomes rational; *op. cit.* : 83, 84, 87.

141   There is also the problem of what exactly divine thinking is. Vollenhoven took any reference to divine *discursive* thinking to be meaningless. He stated this in reply to the theologian, F.W. Grosheide, who had written that "Divine logic is richer than ours" (Grosheide 30-10-1921, and Vollenhoven 16-11-1921).

142   This is in line with the discovery of Thomas Kuhn, decades later, of the paradigm dependence of scientific knowledge. The fact that this had a 'bombshell' effect when

rant that this achieved result is intrinsically meaningful, in the sense that it does, however partially, contribute to a reconciliation between the human being and the world. The human being experiences the evidence of that warrant in the certainty of the anthropologically founded synthetic a priori's of arithmetic and geometry.

But what are we to think of this appeal to the Logos? Is it entirely without its speculative moments? Vollenhoven himself soon came to object to a number of its features. Without anticipating these here, let us instead try to get an overview of Vollenhoven's Logos-doctrine as it was.

In summary, the role of the Logos in the early Vollenhoven is threefold. (1) The Logos is motivational in that it is the disposition for subject and object to enter into a synthesis. This makes it the prime condition for knowledge, which is always an achieved synthesis. (2) The Logos is the source of rationality. For the synthesis between subject and object to be possible, they must lend themselves in their nature to such a synthesis (cf. 1918a: 12). The subjective rational order in the human being and the objective rational order in the world are in harmony in virtue of their source in the Logos. (3) In consequence of this harmony, the Logos is the principled assurance that the (subject's) ideal of the adequate concept does represent a complete knowledge of the idea of the world. It is in this third sense that Vollenhoven speaks of theism as ideal, *viz.* "the epistemic system that God wants that we form concerning all the given" (1918a: 443).

Vollenhoven's view of reason, implicit in this use of the Logos, is in line with the classical view of rational understanding promoting wisdom.[143] When stating this in broad strokes and in the spirit of the mindset of the early Vollenhoven, the following picture emerges. In the classical view, reason is linked to the 'spiritual realm', where the principles of wisdom reside. In Vollenhoven this is divinity insofar as this transcends the world and the human being. But divinity is also immanent, in that the world and the human being are subject to the control of ideas, the impingement of norms and the beckoning of ideals. Here the Logos makes itself felt in bringing being and thought, the world and the Self, ideas and norms/ideals together as knowledge. Rationality is grounded

---

launched in the early 1960s evidences the naïve view of 'harmony' between thought and fact within neo-positivism then dominant. Cf. Kuhn 1970.

143   This motive recurs also in the work of the renowned Dutch logician, E.W. Beth (1908-1964), especially in his last work, *Door wetenschap tot wijsheid* (Through science to wisdom); Beth 1964. He was acquainted with Vollenhoven's work (cf. footnote 8 above), but regretted Vollenhoven's being a "confessional thinker", and how that influenced his protest against Cantor's work; *op. cit.* : 19-20.

in the spiritual realm, not as a factor of reason in relation to faith (as a web of belief), but as itself a factor of assurance in the context of religion. Here religion is the relation of the human being, in his/her environment, to the spiritual realm, in the active sense of complying to or hindering what divine immanence enjoins. Reason is the 'good sense' that says that complying is conducive to promoting the right relation of the human being to his/her world, as evidenced by knowledge in its reconciliatory effect.

Though reason's link to the spiritual realm is not without its ambiguity—especially as to what empowers reason—it cannot be denied that the Logos' motivating subject and object to enter a synthesis is positive and indispensable. For if, instead, knowledge finds its motivation in mundane gain or control, it tends to become a factor legitimating violence, rather than contribute to wisdom, as intellectual developments in the twentieth century illustrate only too clearly.[144]

More problematic is the defence of rationality in subjective and objective guise. The conviction that they are in basic harmony is gratuitous, short of an explanation of what the subject-object distinction entails. We found that subjective rationality belongs to the Self, that embodies the pole of thought, while objective rationality belongs to the World-order. Here we came upon the suggestion of a micro- and macrocosm schema, a classical but also speculative structure. It would appear that the analogy of structure between the Self and the World-order is itself the ground for harmony. To his credit, Vollenhoven soon rejected the bald opposition of this schema, when realizing that thought itself *belongs to* being and *resorts under* it. The problem that arose out of this reconsideration is that of understanding how the 'logical function' of the human being itself fits in with, and is conditioned by, the structure of the cosmos.

The third feature of the Logos causes the greatest discomfort. Vollenhoven's 'realism of science', seeing in science a reality beside that of the Self and that of the World-order, on the one hand underscores the distinct realities of the Self and the World-order, on the other hand makes for a very ethereal implementation of the reconciliation that achieved

---

144   In the course of the 20th century a transformation of rationality took place (in the context of modernism in science, morality and art) *viz.* from substantive reason to instrumental reason. This transformation has replaced whatever higher motive of reason there was with the desire for control within the life-world. In modernism the life-world (of science, morality and art) is constantly in the making, and understanding it is geared to improving and exploiting the making. 'Post-modernism', I believe, is modernism in process of questioning this process, while at the same time applying it in deconstructive ways. Cf. Tol 2005a.

knowledge embodies. Whatever the personal and institutional prerequisites of science are, they go largely unmentioned. (Though Vollenhoven did mention a healthy psycho-physical organization, a keen mind and a willing striving to achieve ideals; cf. 1918a: 430.) With the emphasis on the unity of scientific method, the Logos comes into full focus, as methodological warrant, but without any discussion of the intrinsic complexity of scientific methodology and the different kinds of science (mathematical, descriptive, human, social, information, technical, etc.). Perhaps one can turn this around—though one cannot be sure that Vollenhoven would agree—and ask whether the emphasis on the encyclopaedic nature of the methodology of science is itself not *meant* to focus on the (divine) Logos, as warranting faith and confidence in light of it being the condition of knowledge's reconciliation. That would put the scientific enterprise in touch with the Christian faith, as centred in the Logos, but in a way that leaves untouched the inner complexity of the scientific enterprise. In other words, we then have an understanding of science that, in a broad sense, is neo-Idealist and that accommodates Christian dogma.

In the early Vollenhoven there is, in any case, a narrow fit between the divine Logos and human scientific knowledge, which soon became very uncomfortable. When he revised his position he attributed to the Logos a much broader revelatory significance, without retaining the direct lineage to scientific knowledge (cf. chapter 4).

Be that as it may, Vollenhoven's early thought proceeds from three realities: that of the Self, Scientific knowledge and the World. The first and the third are conditioned, in part transcendentally, in terms of what each needs to be itself, *viz.* the impingement of norms and the control of individual ideas, respectively; and in part dogmatically, in how the needed conditions are provided for by a feature of divinity, *viz.* norms and ideals posed by the Holy Spirit and general ideas of essence maintained by the Father. The transcendental factors form the boundary between divinity on the one hand, and the Self and the World on the other. The dogmatic factors of divinity fall within the transcendent essence of divinity (of will and thought respectively) in its Excellence. When we include the role of the Logos as motivating the synthesis of which knowledge consists, then Trinitarian theism provides the fundamental context of Vollenhoven's conception. And because Trinitarian theism is per definition Christian, the early Vollenhoven has succeeded in formulation a 'Christian understanding' of reality. In illustration, capping our former diagram, we get:

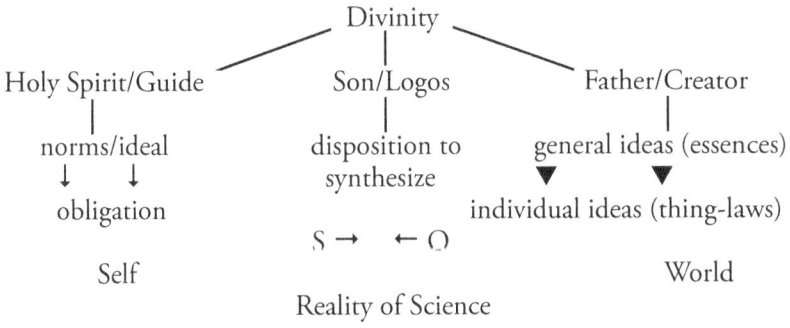

['↓': impinge upon; '▼': individuation]

IX. METALOGIC

The position of the Logos, as indicated in the diagram, is 'central', and also distinct in that it is not presented in terms of its own conditions of transcendence and immanence. At least Vollenhoven gives no explicit indication as to how that might be understood. What he emphasizes is the Logos as condition for science and thus also as the warrant of the validity of scientific knowledge. This *theme of validity* is not made explicit in the work of 1918 (except in connection with the synthetic a priori's of mathematics).[145] But in 1921 Vollenhoven writes more explicitly about validity in the context of what he calls "the meta-logical world". This requires attention in its own right to see how it fits in with Vollenhoven's early thought generally. Also there are several features of it which, in hindsight, act as stepping stones towards new developments. For that reason we want to include a discussion of this is a separate section.

By way of introduction, the following citation from Vollenhoven's letter to the theologian of the Free University, F.W. Grosheide (Vollenhoven 16-11-1921), states the provenance of validity, taken as *posited synthesis*, that implicates the domain of the Logos.

> Proceeding from God, Reformed-wise, we must say that His thought is ... *syntheticizing*, and now with that positing (also via His thought, not just via His will) is also the positing of all contents (included their relation and distinction) in the *meta*-logical domain. In addition [there is] the positing of the norm that we ought to image this meta-logical world, to see it

---

145 The relation of truth to validity is conspicuously lacking in this discussion of validity. In 1918 truth is a logical norm, warranted by the Spirit, and is identified with the logical principles of contradiction and excluded middle. Every judgment of knowing that is a properly normed reconciliation of thought and being may be accepted as true. But scientific validity depends, for an important part, also on the mathematical a priori's and their application in the natural sciences.

and read from it relation and distinction.[146]

This statement, though not a shining example of clarity, does suggest with the reference to divinity, "Reformed-wise", a Trinitarian context. This is borne out by the three "posits": *thoughts*—otherwise said to be 'ideas' of the Father—*content* "in the meta-logical domain"—which, as we shall see, must concern the Logos—and the *norm* or injunction to represent this content of the "meta-logical world", which we may assume proceeds, as does all norm-giving in the early Vollenhoven, from the Spirit. In referring now to a metalogical domain or world, where before he merely referred to the Logos—at least he now speaks of "the sphere of pure epistemological 'validity'" (see below)—Vollenhoven indicates a more realist approach to the Logos, with its focus on validity. In being located between the Self and the World, or rather between the rational order of human thought and the rational order of the world, one may expect this meta-logical domain to have a mediating role.

Vollenhoven's addressing a metalogical concern becomes evident in 1921 in his use of a more metalogical terminology. It is a shift of emphasis towards epistemic concerns. There is no essential change discernible in Vollenhoven's metaphysics, but more weight is placed on the epistemic structure that is built around it, and in that sense there is an increased appeal to matters related to the Logos.

Soon after completing his dissertation Vollenhoven took a more careful look at the epistemological context of his thought. Why he did this is difficult to say for sure. But the emphasis on 'extra-mental' norms and ideas was *inter alia* motivated by 'anti-psychologism',[147] perhaps unexpected for someone for whom intuition is so important. Then there was the urge to carve out a distinct niche in the predominantly neo-Kantian context of the time. It was through Heinrich Rickert, a member of the Southwest German school of neo-Kantianism, that both matters were advanced. We know that Vollenhoven read Rickert shortly after 1918, and that he took some 'metalogical' terminology over from

---

146   Vollenhoven 16-11-1921. Grosheide had written Vollenhoven after reading the latter's "Hegel op onze lagere scholen?" (Hegel in our elementary schools?); cf. Vollenhoven 1921c. He inquired as to whether Vollenhoven saw the possibility of applying the metalogical distinctions he makes in this article to questions of biblical exegesis. Vollenhoven replied in a carefully worded nine page letter, that is in fact a valuable statement of aspects of his thought at that time.

147   Vollenhoven's single-term characterization of Meinong's *Gegenstandstheorie* had been that it is "anti-psychologistic". We have already mentioned Vollenhoven's positive assessment of this theory in the service of theism and intuitionism; cf. 1918a: 161, 175.

him.[148] The term 'metalogic' was current in Vollenhoven's day, especially in neo-Kantian circles, though it does not occur in Vollenhoven's dissertation. The term pertains to what is assumed or needed in connection with grasping logic and its truth, whether formulated or unformulated: the unformulated is what is intuitively grasped, the formulated is what is circumspectly apportioned over requisite categories. There is a realist tendency in its use, so metalogic tends to emphasize the ontological or realist features of knowledge.[149]

Vollenhoven's most explicit statement on metalogic is in "Hegel in our elementary schools?" (1921).[150] Here he contrasts 'hetero-thesis', as subjective opinion, with 'hetero-logic', as objective state of affairs, and also 'synthesis', as a subjective relating, with 'systasis', as acknowledged objective connection. These terms are Rickert's.[151] They are said to mark 'spheres', which is a way of emphasizing irreducibility of validity. For example, Rickert took generalizing thought to be proper to the natural sciences, but not to history which calls for particularizing thought. 'Heterologic' marks objective validity, over against the subjective preference of heterothesis. The second contrast, between synthesis and 'systasis', concerns the difference between judgment as synthesis of opinion on the one hand and the judgment's structure as concomitant complex on the other. That structure is now called a *systasis*,[152] which literally means 'standing

---

148   In a letter to Felix Krüger, dated 19 May 1920, Vollenhoven says that, while writing his dissertation, he was not closely acquainted with the Baden (= Southwest German) School (of W. Windelband, H. Rickert, E. Lask). But, in the meantime, having read Heinrich Rickert's *Der Gegenstand der Erkenntnis* (1892), he finds multiple points of agreement (*vielfach in Einklang*). Cf. Vollenhoven to Krüger 19-05-1920. Rickert was initially at the University of Freiburg (1891-1916) before becoming Windelband's successor at the University of Heidelberg. Besides 'Baden School' the Southwest German School of neo-Kantianism is also referred to as the 'Freiburg School'.

149   The article "Metalogik" in the *Historisches Wörterbuch der Philosophie* does not contain a general definition of the term on account of the diversity of its use. In a very brief report of the term metalogic in Ed. von Hartmann, B. Erdmann, H. Rickert, G. Ralfs and N. Hartmann, the author, Th. Rentsch, remarks that "the 'transcendental ontology', developed in metalogic, represents the terminal point of the development of neo-Kantianism towards a transcendental Platonism"; Rentsch 1980 (translation mine). Vollenhoven's own metalogical views themselves take on a more realist turn when, in 1926, he expresses affinity with Bolzano's use of "Wahrheiten an sich", etc.; Vollenhoven 1926a: 51-52; cf. also chapter 4.

150   Vollenhoven 1921c; the article is in two parts, both dated July 1921.

151   Cf. Krijnen 2001: 256 ff.

152   I shall treat 'systasis' as a foreign term and italicize it when not occurring in a quote or single quotation marks. Vollenhoven retained the term *systasis* into the early 30s until it became redundant for him.

together' (of referent/subject and relatum/predicate).

Vollenhoven now asserts the following about 'heterology' and 'systasis':

> The way one distinguishes nature or *physis* from the metaphysical, in like manner one can *distinguish* in epistemology (first the psychical, then) the logical, that norms the psychical, and behind that the 'world' of the objective hetero-logy and systasis, the metalogical sphere or also the sphere of pure epistemologicall 'validity'. (*Ibid.*, p. 80)

We see immediately that this is stated against the background of the distinction between the World and the Self. The World displays the order of metaphysical substances, the appearances of which are the concern of physics, while the Self, itself psychical in nature, is controlled or regulated by logical norms. The 'world' of objective heterology and systasis is "behind" this. In being concerned with "pure epistemological 'validity'", it is directly relevant for (the organism of) science. In other words, this "metalogical sphere" is hard to place other than in conjunction with the Logos.

This metalogical or objective sphere is then placed in a broader context of constancy and change. Vollenhoven states:

> Hence in the objective sphere *rest* dominates, in the subjective sphere motion, change, transition. . . . In other words, thinking approaches being; better put—so as to avoid all confusion of knowing and occurrent awareness [*beleven*]—thinking approaches being in the way it processes this in its own way; thinking approaches the adequate concept, the complete knowledge of the idea. (*Ibid.*, p. 80)[153]

The theme of "thinking approaches being" is all too familiar. Thinking proceeds from the Self (subject to logical norms) and involves processing what is given to it from the side of the World to think. It is a case of the subject thinking the object, i.e. of subject and object undergoing a synthesis, such as the Logos motivates. Vollenhoven now introduces here the contrast of change and rest. Knowing involves the process of getting

---

153 I wish to point out that the phrase "thinking approaches being in the way it processes this in its own way; thinking approaches the adequate concept, the complete knowledge of the idea" repeats precisely the relation of thinking and being that Vollenhoven had maintained in 1918. In his valedictory lecture, given 26 October 1963, Vollenhoven claims to remember that, during a conference in Hardenbroek on epistemology, in 1919, he pointed to "the necessity of advancing beyond knowing to being, of which knowing is a part." The above quote, which is from 1921, is not consistent with this report of memory, at least its last phrase. Vollenhoven had from the start emphasized the priority of being over thinking (cf. 1918a: 382, 437). But that is not to make it a part of being. Knowing's 'resorting under' or taken to be a part of being is first explicit in 1926. Vollenhoven 1963a: 97. Stellingwerff, who takes Vollenhoven at his word here, without any verification, draws conclusions that are in fact unfounded; cf. Stellingwerff 1992: 40-41.

to know. In and through knowing one approaches the adequate concept, as factor of 'rest', though never actually acquiring it. But it is there as beckoning ideal. Vollenhoven now underscores this role of the adequate concept more explicitly than had previously been the case. The adequate concept, which, as ideal, *stems* from the Spirit, has a pronounced relevance (as factor of rest) in the process of knowledge. This being a metalogical feature, it is something that is warranted by the Logos. The Logos too is now etched out more distinctly than before. We need to look at this more carefully, especially the tandem: (adequate) concept and idea.

Now two things are relevant in connection with an idea. First, there is our being aware of it. Awareness of an idea, says Vollenhoven, is the grasping of a being distinctly thought (*een anders-gedacht*-zijn; Vollenhoven 1921c: 79). An individual thing is grasped in its idea, which is its warrant and controlling principle. This 'grasping' is an acknowledgment, the awareness of which is provided by the metaphysical intuition. The latter (we repeat) is the "immediate insight into identity in difference", which includes the insight into "the ideas of species in different individuals" (1918a: 351). The metaphysical intuition involves our ability to grasp the distinctive identity of an individual, put into effect on the occasion of an acknowledgment.

But secondly, there is also the epistemological implication of the idea, in the sense that, were it actually known, that would involve a complete knowledge of the individual or reality so characterized, in all of its relations. Such knowledge constitutes an *adequate concept* of the idea, but not, of course, practically to be had on account of its unending possibilities and features. Human beings make do with stand-ins or proleptic concepts, whereby the adequate concept serves as validating *ideal* in the use of proleptic concepts, that is, within the scope of thought in the process of coming to know. As ideal it serves as a *goal* that is also direction determining for the coming to know process (Vollenhoven 1921c: 81, note 1). Such a role is said to be 'metalogical' (and so pertains to the Logos). But can this be distinguished from the metaphysical intuition?

As validating ideal, the adequate concept has the two features, *viz.* being an endpoint or goal of thought and being direction determining for the process of coming to know. How can this be metalogically described? In this connection Vollenhoven speaks of "schouwen", which is literally 'to behold' or 'to view': "in supposition we already behold intuitively this endpoint [of the adequate concept as ideal]" (*vermoedend schouwen we reeds intuïtief dit eindpunt*; Vollenhoven 1921c: 85). This description of sighting the ideal is already sufficient to realize that this 'metalogical intuition' is not the same as the metaphysical intuition. The metalogical intuition is a 'suppositional viewing' or 'taking stock of' a goal, an effect of which is to orientate the knowing process; the metaphysical intuition is the ability to grasp, or is the state of grasping, the controlling identity of something as distinctive being—the *that* we grasp something when we acknowledge the idea. But in 'transcendental realism', as advanced by Vollenhoven,[154] there is, behind every ideal (or adequate concept), the idea (as thing-law). When ideal and idea are taken together, this gives a 'fuller' use of intuition than would be the case when only one of these two is respected. Within neo-Idealism, with its 'autonomy of thought', one tries to make-do with *only* the validating (epistemic) ideal. For Vollenhoven goes on to say that Husserl's intuition is limited to being aware of essence—his '*Wesensschau*', in which any content of consciousness is a goal (object of intention) in itself—while in Bergson's use there is no acknowledged goal, whereby in his case the intuition takes on the gliding feature of the life stream (*ibid.*) We understand Vollenhoven to be saying here, against neo-Idealism, that *either* the ontic focus of an idea is taken up into the ideal (as in Husserl), but then the "taking stock" becomes that of intuiting (mental) entities, *or* the ideal delineates a direction of motion without a distinctive being behind its (relative) goal (Bergson). Either way there is only a metalogical intuition, not a metaphysical one. Vollenhoven makes the further statement that neo-Kantians generally tend to use the term 'idea' exclusively for the ideal. "Monism [that characterizes neo-Kantianism] has no word for what I called, in realist fashion, 'idea', for it cannot admit the existence of this idea (the thought of God)" (Vollenhoven 1921c: 86, note 4 from previous page). Hence, for Vollenhoven, the use of 'idea' remains distinctly theistic and distinct from metalogical use.

Now why did Vollenhoven come to emphasize this 'metalogical' feature of his thought? There are, I believe, two reasons. In the first place, validity is the 'sort of thing' that can only be sighted in acknowledgement. Something is or is not valid. There is no change or development here. This secures the 'rest' that Vollenhoven speaks of in the statement

---

154   Vollenhoven speaks of "the Christian realism" that "acknowledges mind and matter to be metaphysically real" (Vollenhoven 1921c: 81, note 1), which, of course, means that they are governed by ideas. The same was said by Vollenhoven in his 1918 dissertation. The self-characterization he there gives as 'theistic intuitionism' is best taken to be a 'transcendental realism', for there are determining conditions, both epistemological and metaphysical, for the Self and the World. In 1918a: 220 Vollenhoven speaks of surmounting rationalism (typical of formalism in mathematics) and embracing "transcendental realism". When Dooyeweerd joins in, the term 'critical realism' also occurs (cf. chapter 3).

quoted above. This rest gives stability to thought when ideals are accepted. To be sure, it is linked to a metaphysical reality. But, in the epistemic context of actual thinking, it is not the grasping of essence that satisfies thought—that might, at best, link a *Gegenstand* to the identity of a corresponding transcendent object—what satisfies is the sighting of a goal that directs thought towards gaining and increasing validity (as knowledge).[155]

The second reason is to give the process of thought, which has an unavoidably subjective feature, more clearly objective support. At the same time thought needs to recognize the objective and not rule over it: "it is not thought that, in its pride, imposes the law on the object, but it needs to acknowledge the objective by taking into account [objective] heterology in the [subjective] heterothesis, *systasis* in the synthesis" (Vollenhoven 1921c: 80). However, when the objective is duly acknowledged, one may nevertheless speak of a "certain autonomy of thought in its own sphere" (*ibid*.). The content of thought does not come from (subjective) thought itself (this over against the Marburg neo-Kantians), but thought does have to proceed *methodically* in the assimilation of content. The emphasis here is on the procedure within the organism of the sciences. To that end it needs "norms and ideals that do not hold elsewhere" (*ibid*.). The heteronomy appealed to here "can well be combined with an autonomy, the 'sovereignty (of regulation, not of creation) in its own sphere'" (*ibid*.).[156]

This emphasis on the metalogical can also be seen as high-light-

---

155   It is perhaps possible to interpret the 'rest' of the adequate concept (as epistemic goal) and its direction-giving relevance for the process of thinking in terms of proleptic concepts as attesting to divine transcendence and immanence, respectively, with respect to the Logos as second Person of the Trinity. There is too little explicit textual support either for or against this interpretation of the two features of the adequate concept. But I tend to regard it as correct, for it forecloses on Logos speculation, hence enables Vollenhoven all the better to circumvent this "danger". At least by 1926 there is a 'full boundary', involving the whole Trinity, between God as three Persons and all of creation.

156   This is the first occurrence of the Kuyperian phrase in Vollenhoven's work found to date. The fact that it is put in quotation marks sets it off and makes it an intended choice. This 'sphere sovereignty' should not be confused with Vollenhoven's rather loose use (in the pattern of the Freiburg neo-Kantians) of 'sphere', 'world', 'circle', 'terrain' or 'area' for things objective, subjective, qualitative, metaphysical, metalogical, logical, psychical-logical, psychological-logical, etc., all of which occur in "Hegel op onze lagere scholen?" (Vollenhoven 1921c). It is only in connection with the one occurrence of 'sphere sovereignty' that he speaks of "norms and ideals that do not hold elsewhere", thereby thinking especially of the methodology of science, when properly controlled by the metalogical intuition. The given characterization is, I take it, sufficient to distinguish it from the other uses of sphere, circle, etc. And it puts "sovereignty in its own sphere" within the direct range of influence of the Logos.

ing features of the fundamentals of science. We note in passing that, whereas the principles of logic are extra-mental norms (given by God the Spirit), the use of logic, when thinking, is something that is carried out in a psychical process. In that sense "logic is the ethics of psychical thought" (Vollenhoven 1921c: 82). But knowledge arises through the use of thought in the assimilation of the Given, and this knowledge needs its own criteria of validity, apart from conforming to the logical norms governing the psychical thought process. Here is where the metalogical quest arises, a quest that is of particular importance for the philosophy of science. How can objectivity be guaranteed if the thinking taking place is necessarily subjective?

Vollenhoven had of course introduced the *Gegenstandstheorie* to counter psychologism. A *Gegenstand* is an objective meaning, discerned by the analytical intuition, the objectivity of which is secured in the conformity to the principle of identity. A *Gegenstand* is nothing if not a self-identical term. It would appear that the very terminology of 'heterologic' versus 'heterothesis', and '*systasis*' versus 'synthesis', and especially the statement: "to acknowledge the objective by taking into account [objective] heterology in the [subjective] heterothesis, *systasis* in the synthesis" (Vollenhoven 1921c: 80), expresses the roles otherwise attributed to the *Gegenstand*, as Object and Objective respectively—"would appear" (I say), for Vollenhoven does not say so in so many words in "Hegel op onze lagere scholen?". But the Object is the meaning [a heterological one?] one holds in thought when fixing the intension of a (proleptic) concept [heterothetic?], and the Objective is the relational complex [the *systasis*] one has in mind when assessing and asserting a judgment [the synthesis]. The conspicuous absence of such a relevant term as '*Gegenstand*', relevant in this metalogical context, is difficult to explain unless it is in fact redundant here. I believe we can safely assume this to be the case.[157] At the same

---

157 Supporting evidence is in C. Krijnen's study of Rickert, referred to earlier. He speaks of Rickert's '*Prinzip der Heterothesis*' as essential to his '*Gegenstandsmodell*'; Krijnen 2001: 256. The absence of the term *Gegenstand* may relate to the absence of another term, *viz.* 'concrete intuition'. The metalogical intuition of the ideal of the adequate concept is aligned to the metaphysical intuition. The role of the analytical intuition—immediate awareness of difference and similarity—which in Vollenhoven's prior work was linked to the concrete intuition, would appear to have shifted. I believe the metalogical intuition is simply the analytical intuition. Its being more in tandem with the metaphysical intuition than with the concrete intuition, justifies reassessing its role and hence also renaming it. In Vollenhoven 1921c the emphasis is not on norms (impinging on the Self) but on the adequate concept as ideal (directing the growth of scientific knowledge). This may be a formal reason for not mentioning the cluster of notions relevant to norms (Self, distinguishing subject, concrete intuition, analytical intuition, etc.). A material reason may be

time we can lament Vollenhoven's using these contrived terms of Rickert, even though this use was short-lived. They hinder seeing the continuity of Vollenhoven's thought at this point.[158]

There is a point in the discussion of science here that seems to suggest a new element. In a footnote Vollenhoven makes a remark in the context of a discussion of contradictions, that will become crucial for his later thought. When one is confronted with contradictions, one needs to consider the 'respect in which' to foreclose contradictions, i.e. one cannot (may not) attribute two contradictory predicates to one and the same subject at the same time and *in the same respect* (cf. Vollenhoven 1921c: 101; emphasis added). Can this question of 'respect in which' be linked to another metalogical notion here introduced for the first time, namely that of "diverse domains of validity of logical norms" (*verschillende geldingsgebieden der logische normen*; Vollenhoven 1921c: 85, note 3)? Interpreted in the context of Vollenhoven's thought at the time, he must be referring here to the various domains of the sciences. These domains were formerly distinguished exclusively by the *quantitative* characteristic of the ratio of the formal (form of sensibility) and the material (range of phenomena represented by *Gegenstände*) in each science. In view of Vollenhoven's metalogical interest, would it not be fitting to include a criterion for the 'respect in which' the categories of a science are relevant, to pinpoint the use of the principle of contradiction? After all, he had not spoken of "domains of validity" with respect to logical norms before. The most natural way to realize this would be to introduce an 'ideal' for each science, which would also guide the growth of knowledge in a science. There would then be a 'metalogical intuition' for each domain of science, a 'viewing' of the domain's qualifying characteristic in the light of its adequate concept as validating ideal. We know that Vollenhoven will very soon (in the mid-1920s) make just these moves. (More telling is also their occurrence in early work of Dooyeweerd, discussed in the next chapter.)

---

that 'self-consciousness', 'concrete intuition' and the like now sound too subjective and thus are left out of the discussion here. But if one distinguishes between norms and ideals, there is no reason to assume that Vollenhoven might at this point have dropped the cluster of terms related to norms.

158 In *Logos en Ratio*, Vollenhoven comments on this "heteronomic" terminology in Rickert. The latter's "heteronomy of values", Vollenhoven says, does not signal a break with humanism. It must be seen in the context of Rickert's characterization of the sciences of value as individualizing (over against that of the natural sciences as generalizing). The individual encounters norms or values as "the other". But this is not to say that their provenance lies outside human beings: "the values stand above the individual as social norms, but the philosopher is still called upon to 'ground' the former in the 'reine Ich'. . ."; Vollenhoven 1926a: 59.

We cannot be certain that the preparations found in this article, are not in fact steps already taken, here presented in rudimentary form, awaiting explication.[159] In any case, the previous strong sway of the (Marburg-like) unity of scientific method is definitely disrupted in favour of a more (Freiburg-like) pluralistic approach. In 1926 the organism of the sciences is said to consist of 'fields of inquiry of distinct modality'.[160]

So while the three heterological features of *Gegenstände* (Objects and Objectives), concepts (with external reference) and fixed connection were already present in Vollenhoven's thought, that of 'domains of validity' is new. Such domains give a pluralist allocation to the said heterological features. He needs the notion of an ideal—which is that which orientates thought and guides it in a sure way, "restfully", in the advance in knowledge—to give substance to this feature. He had, of course, also spoken of ideals before, and certainly of the adequate concept as ideal, but not in terms of a 'metalogical intuition'. In amplifying his use of intuition—the redubbed analytical intuition—as inclusive of viewing or sighting, the additional emphasis on ideals of knowledge is made more evident.

The introduction of these epistemic notions was motivated, in part by the drive to increase his own insight and to clarify his theistic standpoint, in part to differentiate his standpoint from that of prevalent non-theistic thought. In his response to the letter from F.W. Grosheide, referred to earlier, he spoke of the hetero-thesis/hetero-logy and synthesis/*systasis* distinctions as "the discovery that was so liberating over against the trap [*klem*] of [neo-]Kantianism"[161] According to Vollenhoven, neo-Kantianism in general cannot accept the notion of an idea as acknowledged distinctive being, distinct also from a distinctively thought epistemic goal

---

159   The article is a criticism of a work in elementary arithmetic by two Hegelian inspired authors (P.J. Bouman and J.C. van Zelm). Vollenhoven confronts these authors with his intuitionist position. The fact that Vollenhoven brings his former philosophical discussion up-to-date in long footnotes, points, I believe, to the desire to announce the newer views publically and to confirm their authorship. Cf. also chapter 3, section II.A.

160   I don't think there is sufficient evidence to hold that Vollenhoven here links these "diverse domains of validity of logical norms" to the notion of sphere sovereignty, also mentioned in this article. At best he thinks of the entire scientific enterprise, the 'organism of the sciences', as a 'sphere' that stands subject to its own logical norms of methodological procedure. The domains that are associated with the fundamental sciences belong to the metalogical realm, as we find in Dooyeweerd's early work at the time. The more Kuyperian understanding of 'sphere sovereignty' only appears when the notion of 'law as boundary' is underscored in a cosmological setting (cf. chapter 3).

161   Vollenhoven to Grosheide, 16-11-1921. Presumably Vollenhoven was especially thinking of the Marburg neo-Kantians.

and direction-giving ideal. (An important motive of neo-Kantianism was to avoid Kant's appeal to the "*Ding an sich*", which is the reality behind the appearances, interpreted by Vollenhoven as consisting of Ideas. Here Vollenhoven is more Kantian than the neo-Kantians!) Without the idea behind the ideal, the ideal itself becomes a mere projection of thought, and so the autonomous character and creative function of thought is held to be immune to critique. But when the idea is acknowledged, there is a characteristic duality of idea and ideal, the latter being the adequate concept one approached in thought. This gives added reason for Vollenhoven to emphasize and concentrate on the role of the Logos in connection with his theistic standpoint. The Logos after all disposes subject and object to merge in the pursuit of knowledge. Thus, through the Logos there is a coming into rapport of human rationality—thought guided by adequate concepts as ideals—with the structure of the world, as grounded in ideas, that attests to divine (i.e. objective) rationality. The advance of scientific knowledge, however much this calls for human effort, is divinely prepared and conditioned. For,

> thinking is ... a function of the soul, which gains its high value through the inner affinity of subjective reason in the human being with the objective rationality, assumed to be in the world (because God has laid it there) .... (Vollenhoven 1921c: 86)[162]

The 'inner affinity' is exactly what the Logos guarantees. And because "practising science is to approach the adequate concept as ideal" (cf. 1918a: 390-391) it seems that the divine Logos has to be acknowledged in order to understand the most fundamental condition of scientific thought. At the same time, an essentially scholastic feature—*viz.* the supposition of the harmony between the subjective and objective orders of rationality—has been made more secure and more nuanced through this emphatic metalogical elucidation. In effect this makes a break-away from scholasticism more difficult to achieve.

X. *The conception's characterization*

The thought of the 'early Vollenhoven' we have canvassed in this chapter—in the time period 1918-1922—is given two characterizations. Vollenhoven first spoke of "theistic intuitionism" (1918a: 338). Then in 1921 he referred to his position as "epistemological dualism" of (adequate) concept and idea (of being) (Vollenhoven 1921c: 81). Common

---

162 In the same vein: "consciousness is more than a fact, namely [it is also] a function that organizes the given according to an organizing principle that is also operative in the world" (Vollenhoven 1921c: 87).

in this period is the presupposition of "Christian realism", which attributes metaphysical reality to mind and matter (*geest en stof*) (1918a: 3; Vollenhoven 1921c: 81, note 1).

The take-off point of theistic intuitionism is in the philosophy of mathematics, in particular the mathematical intuitionism of the intuitionist mathematicians, Henri Poincaré and L.E.J. Brouwer. Vollenhoven sounds out the philosophical role of the intuition. He tackled this by first positioning his analysis in a methodological context. Mathematical intuitionism is, broadly speaking, an alternative to two other approaches: formalism and empiricism. Upon comparison, including a historical review of their developments, intuitionism is found to be more satisfactory than formalism and empiricism. But Vollenhoven finds his fellow intuitionists to be wanting in their specific 'intuitionist standpoints'. Poincaré placed too much emphasis on construction, as motivated by pragmatic humanism; Brouwer gave the mental constructions of mathematics too little status of their own, this being a consequence of his pantheistic and spiritualist leanings. Vollenhoven's own intuitionism calls for finitude in mathematics and science proper. But the 'theistic' qualification allows accepting the given (metaphysical) reality as being an infinite reality. This theism has been interpreted above as a 'Trinitarian' theism, a theism culled from the Reformed tradition of Dutch Calvinism.

For Vollenhoven, theism endorses a 'dualism', the primary exemplar of which is that of norm and fact, or freedom and necessity. Norms derive from God, and they condition subjective or 'psychical' processes. Facts are governed by natural laws, and this is a matter of internal structure, of being created that way, as maintained by ideas in the mind of God. While the norms and ideas are posited dogmatically, norms also have a transcendental obligatory effect upon the human being as knowing subject, while ideas condition things as substances (in being their 'thing-laws') with inhering qualities. The structure of metaphysics is a monadology of substances, whose inhering qualities appear as phenomena. This gives the human being two epistemic options of outer and inner perception. Outer perception is a 'coming to know' that proceeds from the given phenomena and is channelled in the human being via the psycho-physical body and its capacity of sensibility. Here norms guide the 'working over' of the phenomenal givens as sensed, which results in judgments and concepts. Inner perception is immediate (intuitive) awareness on the part of a human being as substance (Self) of its own inhering qualities in relation to itself (self-consciousness) and in relation to other human beings and things. Intuition is the certitude *that* the inhering qualities are present and, as present, that they condition. There are three kinds of intuition: *concrete*, which is awareness of self-conscious experience in the undergoing, *analytical*, the immediate awareness of sameness and difference in the acts and contents of experience, and *metaphysical*, which is the awareness of identity in difference, as effect of either outer or inner being. Judgments and concepts are to outer perception what *Gegenstände* (Objects and Objectives) are to inner perception.

The two kinds of perception are predicated on the peculiar distinction between the Self and the World, as inner and outer being, respectively. This suggests an analogy of structure, indicative of a micro- and macrocosm schema. This is borne out in that the psycho-physical organization of the Self, and its forms of sensibility of space time, is in step with the World of facts, plants and animals, set in the context of absolute space and time localization. Besides this factual (or real) level there is also the 'ideal' level of the intra-mental within the Self and the extra-mental as regards the World. This level is also the 'domain of validity'. Here the Self takes on mental qualities in virtue of the impingement of norms (and ideals), while on the part of the World there are the ideas, the essences of species, that are individuated to be the (intellectual) thing-laws or substances that control the appearances and development of things and their interrelations. There is a priority of the ideal over the real. The real is alive and becomes, but it is intrinsically geared to being managed by the ideal. Intersecting the polarity of Self and World there is the 'dualism' of ideal and real, unchanging and changing being, norm and fact.

The dualities and polarities are seen as qualitative differences with a workable effect. They are contrasts capable of and requiring reconciliation, achievable in virtue of a deeper unity controlling the oppositions. Hence the dualities and polarities presuppose a dynamic unity making reconciliation possible.

The 'workings' of this reconciliation is basically of an occasionalist nature. Something is given or felt, and this in turn activates or occasions an operation that does something with what is given or felt by way of enhancing, guiding or controlling it. Hence knowing proceeds from given phenomena, which occasion representations in human receptivity. These representations are the material for the Self's forming judgments and concepts, as knowing subject when orientated by norms. Judgments and concepts are a "reality of science", also a reality of reconciliation, signalling the satisfactory working over or assimilation of the initial given phenomena (of the World) by the knowing subject (Self).

A prime example of occasionalism is the intuition. Intuition is the certitude of the Self's being affected on the occasion of its undergoing experience. This certainty allows the Self to posit the effect as condition of consciousness, which, in light of the impingement of the principle of identity, gives rise to *Gegenstände*. The latter are self-identical meanings, being simple or relationally complex mental objects (*viz.* so-called Objects and Objectives, respectively). When this 'intra-mental material' is judiciously brought to bear in judgments and concepts, expressive of the knowledge of things and their relations, there is the deepening of insight that makes scientific knowledge possible.

Vollenhoven's theism is presented as the ultimate warrant of the interaction of the Self and the World. The World's structure is in virtue of ideas that are thoughts in the mind of God the Father. The Self's cognitive, ethical and aesthetic thought takes place in qualities of subjection to ideals and norms, which find their source in God the Holy Spirit. God as Logos is the disposition needed for Self and World to undergo the synthesis resulting in knowledge as reconciliation. The Logos also embodies the basic conditions for maintaining the 'reality of science' as 'organism'.

In 1921 Vollenhoven introduced a new way of characterizing his standpoint. He now speaks of "epistemological dualism", the characteristic feature of which is the duality of concept and idea. The terms as such are not new for him. The term 'idea' denotes the essence or the 'thing-law' of anything existent, while the notion of a concept is that of 'adequate concept', which is the complete knowledge of an idea. Because a complete knowledge of anything can never be had, the adequate concept serves as ideal of knowledge to strive for. In tandem with the metaphysical intuition, which is the awareness of identity in difference of ideas, there is now also metalogical intuition, that sights the ideal as beckoning goal of knowledge. This metalogical intuition has validating import against the background of the idea. In other words, epistemic ideals, formerly attributed to the Spirit—the warrant for all ideals—is now brought into a more direct rapport with the Logos.

There is no discernible difference in the metaphysics nor an essential change in the structure of knowledge implied in this new characterization. But Vollenhoven is now able to emphasize different features. The metalogical intuition emphasizes a realist view of validity, for the validity provided by the ideal of knowledge calls for a background of ideas (being). There is a shift also in the consciousness of knowledge. Vollenhoven's emphasis on the validity of the metalogical intuition seems to supplant the need for philosophy to begin with self-consciousness. This helps alleviate the possible misunderstanding of Vollenhoven's having embraced a kind of 'psychologism'. Also it avoids the solipsism of self-consciousness. There is also the suggestion of a shift in the view of the organism of science. There is mention of "diverse domains of validity of logical norms", whereas formerly the distinction between the sciences mutually was a quantitative matter of differing ratios between the material and the formal elements of a science.

The change in characterization also attests to a more insistent "Christian realism" over against neo-Kantian practice. Marburg neo-Kantians propagated the notion that thought produces the very facts and content it itself works over when realising scientific knowledge (Vollenhoven 1921c: 83). This denies an order of reality that is God-given. The neo-Kantians of the Southwest German school, while they differed with the Marburgers on important points, do not differ, in Vollenhoven's assessment, on this principled point. They too "failed to break with the one-sided interest in thought: they only concern themselves with forms of thought in disregard of the object" (*op. cit.*: 83). Neo-Kantians only have an eye for the ideal of thought (*op. cit.*: 86, footnote 4), not the idea behind the ideal that gives it importance in reality.[163] In that light one can understand Vollenhoven's concern for realism: the heteronomy of thought calls for a recognition of being that is given and which thought approaches. However, this is to endorse neither a naïve nor an empirical realism, for, in approaching the given, thought operates according to its own method, which is critical and requires respect for transcendental conditions. In that sense there is a certain 'sovereignty of thought' that is consistent with heteronomy.

Throughout these early years Vollenhoven maintained the distinction between thought and being. This distinction is operative both in his intuitionism and in the metalogical re-emphasis of his standpoint. It is on this polarity that the duality of Self and World is also predicated. We recognize in this polarity the schema of microcosm and macrocosm, for both Self and World are cosmic, though Vollenhoven did not specifically name this schema. But it does not need to be named in order for him to come to a point of critical reassessment, *viz.* if thought itself has being, then, strictly speaking, the distinction between thought and being is not only unclear, it is in fact impossible to draw. (It is like trying to distinguish boys from humankind to which they necessarily belong.) But this calls for deep reflection on the nature of the Self and its thought on the one hand and the metaphysics of being and its structure on the other, for

---

163   Thus Vollenhoven can claim that neo-Kantians limit the whole use of 'idea' to what he calls the ideal (Vollenhoven 1921c: 85, note 4).

these topics tended to make the distinction between thought and being operational. Only when Vollenhoven saw an alternative solution for this problem was 'Calvinistic philosophy' on the way to be born.

3

REFORMING REVISIONS:
FROM MONADOLOGY TO LAW-SPHERES

> "But that with sufficient effort and available time one can achieve the goal of a Calvinistic [understanding of] science that can withstand [neo-]Kantianism and not [merely] avoid it—of that I am no longer in doubt. . . . I now see more [clearly] its possibility."
>
> D.H.Th. Vollenhoven to A. Janse (21 March 1924)

I. INTRODUCTION

In this chapter we look at two contacts Vollenhoven kept in his early years, namely in the period 1918-1926, that were of special significance to him at the time. The first contact is Antheunis Janse (1890-1960), the second Herman Dooyeweerd (1894-1977). This is the period in which Vollenhoven served as minister of the *Gereformeerde Kerken* (Reformed churches), first in Oostkapelle, in the province of Zeeland (1918-1921), then in The Hague (1921-1926). From there he returned to Amsterdam, when he accepted the appointment to the chair of philosophy at the Free University, as its first full-time philosopher.

In the period in question, in particular the years in The Hague, Vollenhoven executed an important overhaul of his thought. He becomes more self-consciously Calvinistic in his thinking. For him this meant placing the difference between God and the creature centre stage, with the difference characterized as 'law', i.e. law as the boundary between them. Not that he had been insufficiently aware of the difference between God and World in his early work. But he had contextualized this difference in a specific metaphysics, namely a monadology, by means of a realism of ideas. Ideas in that context are 'thoughts of God', by which beings are maintained in their distinct individuality. Each being is, monad-like, a creature governed by its idea or 'thing-law', which controls all its properties, qualities and changing appearances and relations to all other things. Thus the monads together constitute a vast network of changing and (seemingly) interacting beings, the whole of which is our cosmos.

There is a 'logic' to this whole, a 'monadology', in that all the monads act in harmony with each other, controlled by God's predestining Counsel. At some point Vollenhoven began to feel the liability of the speculative character of this metaphysics and theology. After 1923 ideas are no longer on his philosophical palette. The human being cannot read God's mind. In this respect God is 'above the law', beyond the range of human ability.

The rejection of the monadology as speculative metaphysics had implications for the understanding of the cosmos 'under the law boundary'. In what sense does the cosmos deserve unstinted respect? It deserves respect in the evidences of its being ineluctably law-bounded. Kuyper had spoken of 'sphere-sovereignty', which denotes a view of society in which officeholders have delegated authority (or limited sovereignty) in distributed domains (or distinct societal spheres of efficacy). Each sphere has its own focus of responsibility, meaning that each sphere is differently marked or conditioned as to how power exercised within it can be good, wise and God glorifying. The 'boundary' of a sphere is a law-condition that is part of the difference between God, who imposes law, and the human creature, who stands in subjection to law. This Kuyperian teaching in turn suggested a teaching on which a cosmology could be based, but only after Vollenhoven, now accompanied by Dooyeweerd, had worked out the outlines of an epistemology and philosophy of science that recognizes domains requiring acknowledgement by intuition before logic and scientific method can meaningfully be set to work. When the domains were clarified as to their conditions, cosmological presuppositions could be pointed to that embody these conditions. Only then could Kuyper's societal teaching of 'sphere sovereignty' be re-gauged to serve as cosmological theory of 'law-spheres'.

Vollenhoven's transition from a monadology to the theory of the law-spheres is the main theme of this chapter. It took place at two levels. There was first of all the speculative side that needed considerable trimming. A favoured haunt of speculation is metaphysics and theology. In the early Vollenhoven these disciplines harboured his realism of ideas and an associated Trinitarian theism. At the time, these topics were formulated in a way that was in agreement with a widely supported Christian-intellectual understanding. But he came to a more Calvinist-Kuyperian standpoint, in the light of which former work no longer satisfied. So he sought reform and an understanding of philosophy that comported in a more satisfactory way with his standpoint.

The problem comes to a head in *scholasticism*, itself an inextricable mix of the philosophical and the theological, a term much overworked in Vollenhoven's Reformed milieu. One peg of this tradition is anthropological, in that it maintains a duality in the human being, of an immortal soul and a mortal body held together in a complex unity. The early Vollenhoven gave his support to this view. The body is clearly mortal, being part of changing empirical reality that unfolds and develops. But mentality, despite its own changing states, is sensitive to the impingement of norms and is able to acknowledge ideas of distinctive being. That attests to an unchanging basis of mentality, an 'immortal soul' in the human being.

It was Antheunis Janse who openly questioned this view of an immortal soul in discussions with Vollenhoven. Janse read widely—authors such as Hans Driesch, Max Scheler, Maria Montessori, etc.—but the result was at first somewhat eclectic. Vollenhoven provided critical comment to Janse's reading in philosophy. More decisive was Janse's reading of the Bible. This he read as a religiously sensitive person. The anthropological content in the Bible, he found, addresses 'existential' questions of living human beings. Rather than confirming the view of an immortal soul in the human being, the term 'soul' in biblical discourse is, so he took it, short for the whole living person. The so-called biblical support for an immortal soul view does violence to the text. Vollenhoven was initially taken aback, but he soon came around in acknowledging Janse to be essentially correct.

Vollenhoven became more aware of how thoughtlessly philosophy is read into the biblical text in the tradition of scholasticism, turning that text into a source of speculation. With Janse, Vollenhoven came to see that the Bible, as word-revelation, in the first place offers redemptive orientation in terms of the religious life, this being itself, a *this-worldly* life-with-God, in recognition of the divine will. A biblically inspired religious life stands on its own feet. It enjoins a life attitude of love, of doing justice to every diversity. The philosophical challenge is to stop doing philosophy in the accommodating categories of scholasticism, do philosophy without speculative intent and be guided by the love command.

The most visible, because vital, consequence of this 'reformation' of philosophy is perhaps the notion of 'standing-in-subjection'. It draws attention to the notion of subject, but now in its passive connotation of *sub-jectum*, 'thrown under', not in its active connotation of *subjecting*, the Self in autonomous control. If we may generalize, the Janse effect led Vollenhoven to reconsider his initially more self-centred understanding of subjectivity, particularly as evidenced in his appeal to what he called the concrete intuition (what one learns in and of oneself, monadically or solipsistically), and reformulate it as a subjectivity of responsibility, a subject standing under law in law-spheres, a tasked subject. We take this transformation, from self-centred subject to tasked subject, as the guiding thread in the discussion of the early Vollenhoven-Janse contact.

The second level of Vollenhoven's transition from a monadology to the theory of the law-spheres took place at the more grass roots level of methodology. Here too there is an element of scholasticism that needed to be overcome.

Vollenhoven had initially upheld a qualified scholasticism in his view of rationality, in the sense that he maintained a harmony between the subjective rationality of human thought, as guided by logic, and the objective rationality that is inherent in the structure of reality. Ideas capture that objective structure as 'thoughts of God', and human rationality is set on the course of gaining knowledge of the ideas through adequate concepts (i.e. limitative notions of the complete knowledge of ideas). Traditional scholasticism takes this harmony of subjective and objective rationality to be a *sufficient* basis for knowledge, provided that objective rationality is somehow available or revealed in the *idea* and subjective rationality is motivated to match it in the *adequate concept*. But here, as we found in chapter 2, Vollenhoven disagreed. To be sufficient for knowledge, the scholastic harmony needs the supplement of the *intuition* as well. Knowledge needs not only to be rationally understood but also to be confirmed in the certainty of its validity. Here an intuitive moment is essential, supporting 'synthetic a priori's', so as to warrant the concept's becoming more adequate to the idea it seeks to know.

To repeat an essential strand of chapter 2, Vollenhoven's study of mathematical foundations had emphasized the need for a synthetic a priori for (first order) arithmetic and a synthetic a priori for geometry. For these a priori's he sought an *anthropological* justification. The arithmetical a priori is the principle of recurrence, which, as Poincaré had averred, is nothing but the *power of the mind* to repeat indefinitely an act once that act is possible, and that the mind has a direct intuition of this power (cf. chapter 2, section III.A.). On the other hand, the a priori of geometry focuses on localization, the unlimited continuum of positions far and near (in three-dimensional Euclidean geometry + one-dimensional time), as gauged by our *bodies in their psycho-physical organization*. The certainty in geometry cannot be as great as in the case of arithmetic, for bodily self-awareness is limited to sensibility, with time and space as forms of sensibility (cf. chapter 2, section V.E.).

There was progress when, in July 1921, Vollenhoven formulated a metalogical variant of his intuitionism (cf. Vollenhoven 1921c). He now accepts the more pluralistic notion of different scientific domains of logical validity, in each of which scientific knowledge is sought. Logical thought is in methodical progress, advancing insight to become more adequate to the adequate concept of a domain, which itself represents the full truth of that domain. The full truth is the complete knowledge of the idea governing the being of the domain in question. A distinct intuition of certainty is now specified, one that 'sights' the adequate concept of a domain, as 'intuitively viewed' goal. This 'metalogical intuitionism' is no longer linked to an anthropological feature, though the Self must, of course, acknowledge what it intuitively sights on. But, as such, this variant of intuitionism still falls squarely within the scholastic context of the harmony between subjective and objective rationality. Objective rationality is still warranted by the metaphysical presence of ideas of distinctive being. The metalogical intuition has only reinforced and re-organized Vollenhoven's qualification of the scholastic harmony as to how the concept becomes adequate to the idea.

A main topic of discussion between Vollenhoven and Dooyeweerd, according to the document evidence to be reviewed in this chapter, concerns the methodology of 'critical realism' (as Vollenhoven's early position now comes to be called). The aim of their contact was to promote a more distinctive Calvinistic metaphysics, or life- and worldview as Dooyeweerd called it. Dooyeweerd wrote up their burgeoning views. A characteristic trait of their development becomes particularly noticeable in the treatment of the 'content of knowledge' and its metalogical warrant. The earlier anchorage of synthetic a priori's in anthropology no longer served, once different scientific 'domains of validity' are distinguished. Together, these domains of knowledge form the '*Gegenstand*-sphere', an important feature of which is its 'region categories' or 'modalities'. A modality is initially merely the notion of the highest factual unity of the *Gegenstand* (= objective meaning content) within a science, as intuitively viewed by the Self. A modality is therefore closely allied to a science's adequate concept, i.e. the anticipated complete knowledge of what is studied in a science, for the modality is the intuition of the highest unity of the adequate concept. In its context of intuiting the highest factual unity, 'connections' relevant for the region in question are discerned and catalogued as 'synthetic apriori's' in their own right.

Then, in late 1922, there is evidence of an provisional reorientation of the *Gegenstand*-sphere. In critical realism the *Gegenstand*-sphere is warranted by the divine Logos and accordingly not directly linked to either the Self or the World. This 'sphere of the content of knowledge' is now described as the 'created logos' (consciousness, act-content correlation) using a phenomenologically spiced terminology. To 'modality' (as region category) is added the notion of 'modally distinct mode of viewing'. The tandem 'modal viewing and modality viewed' now serves as context in which the essential connections, expressed as 'synthetic a priori's', come to view. As our discussion will show, this methodological shift has novel consequences for the theism of critical realism.

Retaining the realist mode of thought, a new step of progress is evident, in the latter half of 1923. On Dooyeweerd's side this step is the easiest to follow. He advances the notion of a 'law-idea' to capture how the cosmos is itself law-bounded in spheres of law, but at the same time organized in a way that evidences God's providential upholding of the cosmos. This law-idea is presented as the cosmological *organon* of the Calvinistic life- and worldview, and in that role as providing a foundation for epistemology. On Vollenhoven's side there is a lack of direct documentation. But we *can* say that he now too works with the notion of the law as boundary between God and the cosmos, as evidenced in spheres of subjection to law. He saw this as organized in what can be called 'the intersection principle' (of thing and law-sphere). The intuition of (modal) law is determinative for the qualities of subjection on the part of the Self. Vollenhoven's side of this development is the main topic of chapter 4. What this step towards a 'Calvinistic standpoint' implies with respect to the 'qualified scholasticism' of the harmony of subjective and objective rationality needs to be addressed in its own right.

The 'discussion' with Dooyeweerd is actually a bit of a misnomer, at least to the extent that this can be reconstructed. It is only from one extant letter that Dooyeweerd wrote to Vollenhoven, and from later reports, that we know that it took place. Between 1921 and 1923 Dooyeweerd's research papers work towards conceptual clarity in terms of the standpoint of critical realism. In 1923 Dooyeweerd begins to publish his findings. His writings during the 1920s have never been read against the background of Vollenhoven's early thought. My detailed discussion of Vollenhoven's early work in chapter two sheds light on Dooyeweerd's writings of the early 1920s. A careful analysis of the characteristic traits in Dooyeweerd's texts documents the emergence of notions that will find their way into the settled positions of these brothers-in-law. But my discussion will seek to emphasize the context that was valid at that time. My analysis also puts us in a position to test their statements about their contacts and what these contacts entailed. I have found it to be expedient to bracket all statements about that contact, or the lack of it, in favour of letting the evidence guide us. My conclusion will be that Vollenhoven's presence in the emergence of Reformed philosophy is far more prominent than has been recognized or at least admitted to date. Hopefully this discussion will contribute to setting the historical record straight. What is most impressive in the cooperative enterprise of the brothers-in-law, apart from the actual path followed in their research, is the intensity of their search for new ways and avenues. This is too easily overlooked or its importance smothered in the smugness of 'knowing the outcome'. However, that outcome in the late 1920s and early 1930s turns out to be less homogeneous than it is commonly assumed.

The guiding thread of the discussion of the Dooyeweerd texts is: from adequate concept to modally qualified law. As stated above, we leave for chapter four a more integrated account of Vollenhoven's formulation of philosophy as based on the cosmology of law-spheres.

An unexpected turn of events of a more personal nature also played a role of some significance at the time. Just as the need for critical changes began to be felt, Vollenhoven suffered a collapse in mid-January of 1923. This kept him out of the running for most of that year. In the meantime both Janse and Dooyeweerd made 'moves' (so to speak) that Vollenhoven could take cognizance of only after or in the late stage of his recovery. In both cases, Vollenhoven could not give his full approval. In Janse's case this concerns anthropology—Janse's two 'sides' of body and soul. With respect to Dooyeweerd there is the problem of the interpretation of the notion of law in terms of what Dooyeweerd called the 'law-idea'. It was not until 1925, and especially 1926, that Vollenhoven again turned to publishing in philosophy. By that time he had been able to integrate the efforts of both Janse and Dooyeweerd into a review of his options.

In the following account, we are able to indicate the essentials of Vollenhoven's response to Janse's new ideas. But in Dooyeweerd's case this is not feasible to the same degree. Part of the reason is the lack of material from Vollenhoven's side. We know very little as to what actually transpired between the brothers-in-law, when discussion was resumed after Vollenhoven's illness. Another reason is that Dooyeweerd initially shared Vollenhoven's position, so that the continuity was more pronounced than the discontinuity. When a discontinuity becomes evident in late 1923, we need the context of Vollenhoven's publications of 1925-1926 (and later)—which attest to Vollenhoven's own overhaul of his position—to be able to give the Dooyeweerd effect (whether positive or negative) its full due. That is why we leave that overhaul to the next chapter.

II. *The Janse contact: from self-centred subject to tasked subject*[1]
Antheunis Janse was a school teacher, whose formal training was limited to elementary and normal school. Through concentrated self-study of the Bible, philosophy, theology and politics, he developed his talent and became the author of many books, brochures and articles. He was one of the initiators of the Association for Calvinistic philosophy when this was formed in December 1935. During the second World War, he personally suffered at the hands of the Germans. Yet, on religious grounds, he openly opposed resisting the German occupation. This estranged him from many of his friends and associates, including Vollenhoven.[2] After the war, there was renewed contact. But he was soon diagnosed as having Parkinson's disease, which slowly incapacitated him.

Janse was headmaster of the Christian elementary school in Biggekerke, a small village within ten kilometres (as the crow flies) of Oostkapelle, where Vollenhoven was pastor of a congregation from 1918 till 1921. Janse studied Vollenhoven's dissertation. Their contact grew out of the correspondence, started by Janse, that was initially about the dissertation. Vollenhoven took an interest in him, and this led to an exchange that lasted until 1950.[3] Though Janse was more than two years Vollenhoven's senior, he looked up to Vollenhoven as to a mentor, who in turn responded in kind. Janse's lack of academic credentials prevented the relation with Vollenhoven from becoming one of equals,[4] but this did not

---

1   This discussion of Janse's early work attempts to give a full account of what Janse brought to bear in his contact with Vollenhoven during the early 1920s, but also the limitations of his influence. As for the later dispute about the human soul that took place in the mid 30s, which involved Janse as well as Dooyeweerd, one may consult J. Glenn Friesen's website: www.members.shaw.ca/hermandooyeweerd/Curators.html.

2   For details about Vollenhoven's response to Janse's stance regarding the war, see Stellingwerff 1992: 155-157.

3   The *Janse Archives*, long in private hands, are now in the Historical Documentation Centre at the Free University of Amsterdam (Archive number 157). (J. Glenn Friesen first drew my attention to its presence in the HDC.) The extant Vollenhoven-Janse correspondence is very extensive, with several hundred letters on both sides. This correspondence is to date largely virgin terrain. There are also remarks in a personal diary for the years 1929-1946. For more on Janse, cf. Janse, W. 2001: 285-288; also Van der Walt 2008.

4   Vollenhoven says, in an aside that reveals implicit class distinction, that Janse was always called "Mister Janse by us". (This is "meneer/mijnheer Janse", not "meester Janse", the latter being how he would be addressed as teacher.) Given the context of this statement, which is a discussion between Vollenhoven and Dooyeweerd, the "us" includes Dooyeweerd as well. It may also be interpreted as referring to the circle of the Association

restrain Janse from taking an independent stance on topics he was well read on, guided by a trained sense of spiritual discernment. Vollenhoven acknowledged that Janse's stimulating questions influenced him, especially in the early years of their contact. It set him to thinking certain matters through anew. We shall try to discover what the stimulation was and the nature and extent of Janse's influence.

A. Teaching elementary arithmetic

Their first contact focussed on arithmetic and Janse's experience of teaching it at the grade school level. Janse found practical confirmation of some of the basic matters Vollenhoven had defended about the status of numbers in his dissertation. The intuitionistic view, that number is based on an activity of the mind, namely counting, and that this activity is prior to the formation of the number concept, made sense to Janse. He observed that a child does not grasp numbers via the empiricist's way of viewing collections, nor by way of the formalist's preference of a conceptual-representational approach via symbols. The quantity of a collection, whether perceived or represented, cannot be directly ascertained when the amount is more than four or five.[5] Our only recourse is to counting. This also affects the way a child learns to perform arithmetical calculations. For example, it takes greater effort to calculate what '2 + 6' is than '6 + 2'. Janse could appeal to the results of German practical psychological studies of learning arithmetic based on counting, which turned out to be comparable to Vollenhoven's intuitionistic ideas. So Vollenhoven and Janse published a joint paper on the topic, entitled "The activity of the soul in learning arithmetic".[6]

Arithmetic continued to hold their attention. A work of P.J. Bouman and J.C. van Zelm, entitled "Arithmetical thinkables in logical coherence, with – as specimen of applied logic – a method of arithmetic for elementary schools", published in 1918,[7] turned out to be popular. The work bore the stamp of the Hegelian philosopher, G.J.P.J. Bolland (1854-1922), a leading Dutch thinker at the time. The work pleased neither Vollenhoven nor Janse, for neither had Hegelian leanings. Each

---

for Calvinistic philosophy, of which Janse was a board member. Cf. Vollenhoven 1968b: 207.
5   Cf. Vollenhoven 1918a: 27.
6   Vollenhoven and Janse 1919. Janse's primary source was Ranschburg 1916.
7   P.J. Bouman en J.C. van Zelm, *De rekenkundige denkbaarheden in logische samenhang, met – als proeve van toegepaste logica – een rekenmethode voor de lagere school* (Amsterdam: W. Versluis, 1918).

published a critical discussion of this work.[8]

Vollenhoven took the opportunity that this publication presented to argue that it does not suffice to merely oppose standpoint to standpoint—i.e. a non-Hegelian ideology over against the Hegelian ideology of the authors—the difference needs to be made explicit in consequences at the level of insights and method.[9] Thereupon Vollenhoven gives a summary account of his intuitionistic views, and their opposition to formalistic and empiricistic views, though now in the terminology of a more direct *metalogical* discourse (of concept and idea; 'worlds' of rest and empirical change; etc., as discussed in chapter 2). Janse took the more practical side and discussed the inadequacies of the Hegelian method. Though it was refreshing, he said, to be shown an alternative either to a rote mechanical approach or to an approach that burdens every step with a justifying reason, this Hegelian alternative does not reckon with the psychology of the child. For Bouman and Van Zelm attempted to combine thinking and doing in one by focussing on what they call "the self-organizing capacity of thinkables".[10] By continuously distinguishing and combining numbers (as 'thinkables'; e.g. '4' can be 'disunited' by thought into 1, 1, 1, 1, while the later can, in turn, be 'reunited' by thought into '4'), there is an arithmetical 'growth' from one thinkable to another that is not arbitrary, but such that "the one thinkable can be thought as a seed of another thinkable".[11] A mainstay of Vollenhoven's philosophical critique levelled at this work is that the Hegelian approach—the dialectical method at work in the self-organization of 'thinkables'—introduces change in the (meta)logical sphere, i.e. mixes and confuses empirical change with eternal truth.[12] Janse's practical critique focussed on emphasizing that this method is not in tune with the mind of the child. The "self-development of arithmetical thinkables" does not reckon with how a child thinks.[13]

B. Maria Montessori and child biology

The psychology of the child – there lies the immediate crux of Janse's concern. As teacher his task is to guide a child's development. This involves stimulating the child's mind and correcting errors in understand-

---

8   Cf. Vollenhoven 1921c and Janse 1921a. Each paper is dated July 1921. Vollenhoven's title is eyebrow raising: "Hegel in our elementary schools?"

9   Vollenhoven 1921c: 79.

10   Janse 1921a: 139.

11   *Ibid.*

12   Vollenhoven 1921c: 84; Janse 1921a: 140-141.

13   Janse 1921a: 141 ff.

ing. But Janse also wished to understand which conditions are conducive for learning and which occasion errors.[14] He wished to understand what makes a child tick. This led him to read up on pedagogical developments and new insights that would help him to understand 'the soul' of a child. The novel pedagogical method of Maria Montessori (1870-1952) was making waves at the time, and Janse reviewed her work extensively. In a paper, dated 26 November 1921,[15] he discussed her work and underscored its importance for education, and for Christian education in particular. At the same time he emphasized that the ideological context of Christian education requires that certain limitations be imposed on, or alternatives taken into account with respect to, Montessori's more general worldview position. Janse's own frame of reference in this paper is still, broadly speaking, in line with Vollenhoven's substantialist anthropology. But in the following year we find him radicalizing his thought to the point of proposing an anthropological view that would bring about serious revisionary reflections on Vollenhoven's part. But in Janse's own anthropological view certain Montessori features continued to play a significant role.

We need to see in some detail what Janse's reaction is to Montessori's approach and position, for he finds her work on the one hand to be helpful and challenging for Christian education, while on the other hand to contain certain ideological features that are unacceptable. What Janse admires most about Montessori is her sharp eye for what he calls "child biology" in her work (1921b1: 336). In her pedagogical approach she fully respects the *living child*, which implies that the child must be given every opportunity for growth and development. The child learns most naturally when stimulated at a time when the child is most ready for it. The living child in the classroom also requires freedom to enable it to develop in a way that answers to its needs and stage of development (1921b1: 330). The requisite freedom must be protected from unwelcome intrusions from without by maintaining a carefully structured context of learning. It must be clear what is and is not permitted, and these rules must be strictly maintained (1921b2: 375; 1921b3: 19, 24). Also, by conducting "exact experiments", it must become clear which

---

14 Janse investigated the main causes leading to spelling errors, reckoning it to be more important for the child to recognize these causes than merely to learn to spell correctly by rote; cf. Janse 1923a.

15 He published this paper—"Sketches . . . for self study"—for the sake of pedagogical study clubs that were active at the time. It appeared in three instalments. Cf. Janse 1921b. I shall distinguish the instalments, *in this section*, as 1921b1, 1921b2 and 1921b3 respectively without mention of the author.

pedagogical means are conducive to the child's development and which less so (1921b1: 339). The focus on this "biological activity and freedom" (1921b3: 25) was for Janse a pedagogically sensible way of getting to understand the child better in its learning situation and of advancing that learning. "Montessori's great merit is perceiving the child from a biological standpoint and never losing sight of *the living child* in her methodology" (1921b1: 338). There was a pedagogical challenge here that the Christian school movement could not and should not ignore.[16] "Montessori," so Janse concluded, "opened our eyes for God's natural laws of child life" (1921b2: 371, 375)

But Janse's positive response is not the whole of his response. He also finds influences in Montessori's work, especially ideological ones, that are less welcome. For example, he sees a "personalism of the child" that makes the child an end in itself (1921b1: 333; 1921b3: 24). This is fostered in terms of a life-philosophy that exaggerates respect for *life*. Life itself is an end-all and be-all—he quotes her statement: "'Life' is the source, creator and goal of our existence" (1921b1: 333)—thus her view is a variant of monism (1921b2: 373; 1921b3: 24). Janse's Christian standpoint, as informed by the theism at the time (cf. below, also 1921b1: 332; 1921b2: 371), advances a dualism of natural law and norm, and thus was by definition at odds with monism, which, in Montessori's case, comes down to neglecting the norm in favour of natural law.

Janse gives two telling consequences of this neglect. In the first place, the controls that are to guarantee the free growth and development of the child are chosen with a view to making "exact experiments" of the life-situation possible. This limits and restricts the insight into the lawfulness of the pedagogical situation to that of natural biological lawfulness.[17]

---

16 "In the area of the *biology* of the child Christian pedagogy must reckon with her [Montessori's] work and respect her labour, for she shows us the child from a side from which we are not used to seeing it" (1921b3: 24). Also: "In our opinion, our Christian education would neglect its *Christian calling*, if it does not apply itself with full force to the theoretical and practical application of the *biological* principle of the *activity of the child in the school*" (1921b3: 19).

17 Janse quotes Montessori: "Life *reveals itself—creates, offers its gifts*—but all within limits and laws *that are unchangeable*" (1921b1: 333; emphases presumably Janse's). The quote is from chapter two of Montessori 1916. Hélène Leenders, in a careful study of Montessori's work, finds that Montessori's extolling life leads to three *questionable* assumptions: "that children are by nature prone towards realizing a good development, that the development of different children is in principle uniform, and that her [educational] material is the only material that is possible [because determined by scientific experiment]". Leenders 1999b; cf. also her dissertation, on Montessori and fascistic Italy, Leenders 1999a.

The controls that constrain the pedagogical situation ought also to be of a moral and more generally of a spiritual character (1921b1: 331, 335, 339-340; 1921b2: 377). The latter are not given sufficient latitude in Montessori's approach.

In the second place, psychology is limited to a role that is subservient to biology. Montessori's psychology, Janse claims, is 'mechanistic', for it operates within the unchanging laws of life (1921b1: 333; 1921b3: 24).[18] There is no fixed inward reality, only the physiology of capacities that develop into perceptual, cognitive and practical unities. Life itself is such that she sees it (as Janse says graphically) as "souling and bodying" in the child according to natural laws (*het leven dat 'zielt' en 'lichaamt' volgens natuurwetten*, 1921b1: 334; also 1921b3: 24). This hampers the exercise of the higher functions of the soul. The role of psychology is to help stimulate the learning instinct. But what Montessori attempts to activate is always outwardly directed, lying in the extension of the sense organs, and this lacks an inner spiritual resonance. Consciousness operates through the sense-organs, and the aim is to connect inward life to them. "The entire psychological side of her method consists not in tracing the activation of the *functions of the soul* as such [Janse has just mentioned 'thinking, willing and feeling'; A.T.], but in *the activation of the sense-organs through 'the inward life'* and in providing material [i.e. appearances] for the sense-organs so as to satisfy the creative drive of 'life'" (1921b1: 335).[19]

Thus praise *and* blame flow energetically from Janse's pen. The praise for the clear emphasis on the biology of the living child as subject of pedagogy is unstinted.[20] In fact Janse's concluding statement is that

18   I think that the term 'mechanistic' is ill-chosen. In Janse's own discussion he recognizes that the unchanging laws are biological laws, and that they are such as regulate the response of the human organism to the stimulation of the sense-organs. However, it may be that Janse held that such life response could be clarified (to a limited degree at least) mechanistically, as did Vollenhoven at the time; cf. footnote 21 below.

19   In this sense, Montessori's method has traits of behaviourism, in the sense of operant conditioning (B.F. Skinner). The environment of the life context has a stimulating effect on behaviour. In that sense Montessori's method is amenable to practical or political forms of indoctrination. In the 1920s and 1930s she sought to integrate 'fascistic culture' in her approach. This attempt was evidently subsequent to the time that Janse studied her work. It is not mentioned in his Montessori paper, nor have I found any mention of this in Janse's later writings. Cf. the dissertation of H. Leenders, mentioned above, Leenders 1999a.

20   Expressions, such as: "splendid criticism" (1921b1: 332), "very great merit" (1921b1: 336; 1921b2: 370), "splendid contribution" (1921b1: 336), "heartfelt esteem" (1921b1: 336), "very powerful attack" (1921b1: 337), she "opened our eyes" (1921b2: 371), etc., occur throughout this paper.

"*Montessori's biological view* of the child in school and her *adjusting* of the school and the [pedagogical] method *to the biological laws* of life have the right to be *fully appreciated, powerfully propagated, scientifically elaborated, and practically applied* on the part of Christian Pedagogy" (1921b3: 22). To be negligent here is to "slight God's laws of nature of child life" (1921b3: 22). At the same time the errors in her philosophy, worldview and psychology (1921b1: 337), discussed above, make it impossible for Janse to endorse her overall position.

If the reader has difficulties reconciling the praise and the blame, Janse had no problem here, for he assimilated Montessori's work in the framework of a dualistic view. In his words: "we reject Montessori's Monism and we stick to Dualism. (Object and subject are *two*, and not to be united in the idea 'life')" (1921b1: 373). Christian Pedagogy, Janse claims, had too long failed to appreciate the life of a child in terms of its own (bodily) expression of its life, its capabilities and its needs, i.e. biological laws which ought to be respected as divine laws (cf. 1921b2: 371). Here Montessori offers a fitting antidote, which is timely and necessary. But Montessori, in turn, did not sufficiently sound out the personality and spiritual side of the living child, i.e. its 'soul', her monism and the limitation of psychology to biology being the handicaps in this regard. Thus Christian Pedagogy ought to continue to point out "that the rational and moral and especially the religious norms for human life have in themselves infinitely more importance [*gewicht*] than the biological laws" (1921b2: 371).

The dualism between laws of nature and norms for the mind and spirit reflect Vollenhoven's own dualism directly. This induces Janse to reinterpret Montessori's anthropology. Where she sees body and soul to be two sides of life as unity—life as actively 'souling' and 'bodying' from within itself—enabling the body to grow and the mind to develop, including the multiplicity of its functions, the Christian pedagogue discovers, with respect to the "functions of the soul", that it is "in reality nothing other than the Self, the person, the living-soul-as-substance, the '*Zentralbezogenheit*' [central involvement], the bearer of 'life', that which remains itself in the flood of appearances" (1921b1: 334). This is the human being, hence also the child, as spiritual being, as person who responds to rational, moral and religious norms in and through its functioning as living being. Janse formulates here, as he will later acknowledge, the scholastic view of the human soul as 'immortal substance' or '*substantia incompleta*', and it is in the main in step with Vollenhoven's own anthropological view at the time. The only important recognizable difference with Vollenhoven's view is that Vollenhoven tended at the time, as is evident from his discussion of Driesch, to see biology as a secondary science, dependent on psychology on the one hand and chemistry and physics (or physiology) on the other.[21] Janse places biology more in the centre of the human psycho-physical bodily organization. But there is complete accord in the overall view: "We [Dualists] do not see, in the background of the functions of the soul, 'Life' that 'develops itself according to fixed laws', rather [we see] the living *soul* as spiritual substance, which ought to obey the *norms* that are imposed on it, but is *not dominated* by *laws* of nature" (1921b2: 376). Janse could accept, and in fact heartily recommended, Montessori's "biology of the child", as governed by natural laws of growth and development, but only on condition that this be supplemented by a recognition of the deeper dimension of the spiritual substance and its compliance to norms.

C. Janse's initiative, Vollenhoven's initial response

The next significant step in the contact between Janse and Vollenhoven is a letter of Janse to Vollenhoven, dated 1 November 1922. The letter is abundant evidence that the anthropological problem continued to hold Janse's attention. But he now indicates a shift in his view.[22] He has continued his reading on the topic, in particular authors such as Max Scheler, Hans Driesch, Herman Bavinck, and the dissertation of The Rev. S.O. Los on the topic of feeling in the Holy Scriptures. Janse is now

> inclined to assume a dualism: spiritual world (= heaven or of the heaven) and earthly world (matter and living soul). Our spirit returns to God [in heaven], who gave it—but we *are* living soul = be-souled-body and then 'of the earth', as such 'dust and [ashes (Job 42:6)]', not only our body (*Körper*). In Scheler I found a beautiful view of Spirit as the subject of the '*Akte*'

---

21   Following Driesch, in his early work Vollenhoven took the essential concept of biology to be that of organic form. This is applicable to plants and animals and also to human beings. Organic form attests to the synthesis of matter and instinct, the matter being physical-chemical in nature and the instinct psychical (note the monad-like structure here). Vollenhoven criticizes Driesch for accepting a distinct organic entelechy (an inner goal directing force), before having seriously entertained the possibility of a uniform explanation of organic form as the expression of the *interaction* of psyche and physical matter. On the latter assumption biology, as science, makes use of the methods of the physical sciences *and psychology*. (Hence psychology is relevant for anthropology, zoology and also botany. This may suggest an Aristotelian psychology, but the context of Vollenhoven's early thought does not support a psychology of three faculties.) Cf. Vollenhoven 1920a: 23-24; cf. further discussion below.

22   Janse's Montessori paper, we repeat, was dated 26 November 1921, but since it appeared in three instalments, it was fully public only in the course of 1922. The novelty of this letter of 1 November of that year is quite unexpected.

[acts] and in Driesch a beautiful view of be-souled body as one '*Leib*' [i.e. living body]. For body [*Leib*] is more than Körper— . . . it includes the soul that belongs to a body (*Körper*). Isn't soul, flesh, in the Holy Scriptures always of the earth? In the Holy Scriptures, soul = life. And spirit is from above. And spirit works in on living beings, as we perceive daily. In this way I make a clear distinction between soul and spirit.[23]

Janse's distinction between spirit and (living) body cuts through the traditional body-soul distinction in a quite radical way. According to the view he now proposes, the soul is no longer an (incomplete) substance,[24] for its role is replaced by two different factors. On the one hand, the soul as warrant of life is now seen as being inherent to a living being itself. The living being is *Leib*, i.e. 'be-souled body', versus *Körper*, which is body not intrinsically alive. On the other hand, the factor that served to distinguish the (substantial) soul from the body—its constancy and its intrinsic focus on norms over against the vicissitudes of the body and its dependency on natural laws—is now apportioned to the spirit. This spirit is an animating factor, a gift of God, not an inherent mental faculty (or cluster of faculties). One can be strong in spirit, i.e. have the courage to do what needs doing, while at the same time tremble in the execution. (Janse mentions the Dutch King William III in this regard.) The soul's unity with the body makes it incapable of being immortal. Though Janse continues to speak of 'soul', the soul that 'be-souls' a body is in fact now more like a function of the living being than a substantial component within it. And though the name of Maria Montessori does not occur here, Janse has now implicitly come closer to her idea of a living being than had previously been the case (though still retaining the distinction between factual and normative psychology). Also, Janse's understanding of living being, of soul that 'be-souls' the body, is now distinctly holistic, as in Montessori.

Vollenhoven's reply is dated 7 November 1922, hence he replied quickly, within a week.[25] Vollenhoven admits that the distinction between

---

23   J.H. Kok quotes a large part of this letter in his Kok 1992: 41, footnote 46 in Dutch. The above translation is mine.
24   As to the use of 'incomplete', it is not the soul as substance that is incomplete. The substantial (or immortal) soul is itself only a part of the human being. There is also the body, itself a mortal substance, which is also an incomplete substance in comparison to the (full) human being. The connection of the two substances in the Self ('Self' as the "higher synthesis"; Vollenhoven 1918a: 423), which is a "complete substance", is in virtue of creation (as over against experiential accrual), hence difficult for a human being to fathom.
25   The entire letter (in Dutch) is in Stellingwerff 1992: 61-62. John Kok incorporated a key passage in Kok 1992: 42. I quote this passage (slightly adapted) in the next paragraph.

spirit and soul has more about it than is commonly thought. But this admission is rather perfunctory. For Vollenhoven focuses on the (more or less) Aristotelian background of the authors mentioned by Janse, which authors, so the letter seems to imply, are leading Janse astray in his writing. (Janse has prepared an article as well.)[26] Vollenhoven proceeds to list his objections to the Aristotelian three-faculty psychology as current in the scholastic tradition. The key part of this letter is Vollenhoven's "tentative solution" to the problem of the Aristotelian psychology, which solution he asks Janse to consider and respond to. The problem was never Vollenhoven's own problem in a direct sense. Vollenhoven's proposed "solution" is *for Janse's consideration* (it is also "not yet ripe for publication", Vollenhoven adds). It retains the view of the immortality of the soul, but in its formulation Vollenhoven makes more use of metalogical terminology (of 1921) that was his wont in 1918. In any case, the tentative solution defends the notion of the immortal soul, which is implicitly under threat in Janse's letter and probably explicitly so in Janse's draft article.

The "tentative solution" reads as follows.

> The tentative solution as far as I see it is this. There is an ideal world of validity [*van het gelden*], neither psychic nor rational, but 'holding' [*geldend*]. Then a world of values: ethical, juridical, and religious values, and so forth. Also a world of physical beings; probably also one of that which is biological to which I begin to attribute more independence than I did earlier. The faculties are not layers, but relations of the one soul to those diverse terrains. The soul of plants, animals and humans is distinguished not by the *number* of faculties, 1, 2 and 3 respectively, but by the nature of the relations between the respectively distinguished souls on the one hand and these worlds [on the other]. In this way the soul remains a unity.
>
> The whole human soul, as unique new project of the Divine Artist, is immortal; psychology continues to have one *Gegenstand* and one method, namely, that of inner perception. Physiological psychology is not psychology, but physiology; which can inform us at most about the relation of soul and body, probably only about the latter and its reactions and so forth, that accompany psychical acts. And we have nothing that requires conceiving re-birth as a *donum superadditum*.[27]

Much of this "solution" fits the early Vollenhovian mould, though there is some novelty. There are three (perhaps four) 'worlds'. The "ideal world of validity" might be thought to be the metalogical domain of the

---

26   In the same letter Vollenhoven asks Janse to withhold publishing an article on the living soul and the life-giving spirit, "for I would regret it if the confusion in this area in our psychology continues unabated"; Stellingwerff 1992: 62. Presumably a copy of this manuscript was included in Janse's letter to Vollenhoven. I shall refer to this article as 'the draft article'.

27   Cf. Kok 1992: 42.

Logos, though in stating that it is "neither psychic nor rational", he seems to have in mind the extra-mental world of ideas apart from the human Self and the Logos. The second world of values can be accounted for if we recall that Vollenhoven spoke not only of science but also of morality and art.[28] There are norms for (scientific) thought, but also ideals and values for human action (all of which are warranted by the Spirit). Then, the world of physical beings is the domain of changing things, characterized by force and relations. The possibility of a fourth world, as domain of biology, is something new, for Vollenhoven had tended to treat biology as secondary to psychology and the physical sciences.[29] It is difficult to say what the incentive is that is making Vollenhoven reconsider biology (an influence of Janse's Montessori paper?), but in 1926 the status of biology as independent science is definitely accepted.

The three-fold faculty psychology of Aristotle is now explained in terms of the various relations the soul can have to the domains distinguished, without needing to actually divide the soul into three faculties (of cognition, animation and nutrition). The soul's relation to the ideal world is, clearly, the ground of cognition, its relation to the world of values serves to animate activity, and its relation to 'things' is nutritional (or vegetative) to the extent that living tissue and water, minerals, etc. are required to sustain life. But the fact that this 'relational approach' is said *not* to require diversity in the psyche, the latter being the common term of these three relations, suggests a possible change in Vollenhoven's 'logic of relations'. A consistent 'monadic view of relations'—"a relation always consists of two predicates"[30] of the related terms—*would* require such a diversity in the psyche. Vollenhoven now appeals to differences in the "nature of the relations [themselves]", as relevant for the souls of plants, animals and humans, on the one hand, and the 'worlds' on the other. That is to say, plants have only the one 'vegetative' relation (to the physical [life-]world), animals stand in both 'vegetative and animal' relations (to the physical world and world of values, respectively—assuming that

28   Cf. chapter 2, footnote 124.
29   Cf. footnote 21 above.
30   Vollenhoven 1918a: 66, note 2; cf. the discussion of 'relation' in chapter 2 above. In a monadic view, the relations in which a human being stands make use of the qualities of or states in the human being, on the basis of which the relations can be 'laid' (on the human side). The Self, as law of the individual, regulates the mutual coherence and continuity of these qualities. At this point in time (end of 1922) it is more likely that Vollenhoven has modified his understanding of a relation, rather than that his anthropological view has changed significantly. In a text of Dooyeweerd at that time (1923a2; cf. section III.E. below) there is talk of 'essential connections', which would appear to imply 'external relations'.

animals can be said to relate to values to the extent that they sense instinctively what is good for them and act accordingly) and human beings stand in these two relations as well as the third, the 'cognitive relation' (to the extra-mental world). Because the unity of the psychic moment in the human being is preserved, psychology's method of inner perception is not hampered, and its *Gegenstand*, i.e. the objective meaning that characterizes it (which is probably something like 'the dynamics of psychical growth'?) also holds across the (psychological) board. The only threat to this unity is physiological psychology. But Vollenhoven decides that this is essentially physiological, and thus is psychological only in an indirect sense. Finally, if in human beings this soul is immortal—in the study of Driesch Vollenhoven spoke of the personalized soul in human beings over against the non-personalized souls of animals and plants[31]—then there is no need for any *donum superadditum*, a superadded gift of grace.

Janse responded immediately with a draft letter of 23 pages, dated 8 November 1922, but this was never sent, according to Stellingwerff. He let his response simmer and a partially rewritten letter (even longer than the draft letter), dated 30 December 1922, was sent in reply to Vollenhoven's letter of 7 November. Janse felt that Vollenhoven had misunderstood what he took 'living soul' and 'life-giving spirit' to be. Vollenhoven, in fact, had not really addressed his ideas (as contained in his letter, the content of the 'draft article' is unknown). From later correspondence (see footnote 41 below) we know that Vollenhoven did not set this letter of Janse aside. Despite his very busy schedule, in mid-January he was working on his response. But on Sunday morning, 14 January 1923, Vollenhoven collapsed on the pulpit from overwork and mental exhaustion. This triggered a serious psychosomatic breakdown of his health. It wasn't until November of that year that he resumed his pastoral tasks, and in December he preached again for the first time after his recovery. But his first philosophical publication posterior to his illness is dated March 1925. There is a definite gap in the Janse-Vollenhoven contact at a very crucial moment.[32]

31   Cf. Vollenhoven 1920a: 24. The distinction between the personalized and non-personalized soul is one reason why Vollenhoven's early psychological view did not support a three-faculty psychology, when his monadic theory of relations was in full force. Implicitly Vollenhoven had a 'two-faculty' psychology. The unity of the Self was taken to be the psychical synthesis of (at least) memory, representational and perceptual input of the psycho-physical body, and the (personalized) data of inner (mental) perception. But Vollenhoven says so little about the body and sensibility—after all, the body can only be accessed indirectly via the forms of sensibility—that it is difficult to know how he considered the workings of the non-personalized psyche.
32   Cf. Stellingwerff 1992: 63-64. Part of the pressure on Vollenhoven was his hav-

D. Living soul and life-giving spirit

Janse keenly felt the importance of his ideas about living soul and spirit. When it became apparent that Vollenhoven would be 'out of reach' for some time, Janse proceeded to publish his own ideas without awaiting further consultation with Vollenhoven. The ideas he raised in his letter of 1 November 1922 are given a more thorough discussion, and one is able to surmise after the fact the extent of the influence of this material on Vollenhoven.

Janse published six (fairly short) articles, during Vollenhoven's sick-leave, on the theme of the living soul in *Paedagogisch Tijdschrift*.[33] These articles have gone unmentioned, I presume because unnoticed. Stellingwerff makes no reference to them,[34] and Kok also passes them by in his study of the early Vollenhoven. Yet here we find the first published critique of the notion of the 'immortal soul' as *substantia incompleta*, and also the first initiative towards what became "Calvinistic philoso-

---

ing to fill in for a colleague pastor for some time. He was also under contract to write a popular volume on French philosophy for the *Volksuniversiteitsbibliotheek* [Open/Home University Library], with February 1923 as expected date of completion. Cf. letter of J. de Zwaan, chairman of this series, 9/10 February 1922 to Vollenhoven. What also cannot be discounted, given the timing, is a possible added effect of intellectual anxiety about the problem of the immortal soul, as raised by Janse. Stellingwerff reports that Mrs. Vollenhoven returned Janse's letter of 30 December to him at the end of January, 1923, along with a note in which she states that her husband has been institutionalized. Roger Henderson mistakenly reports that Mrs. Vollenhoven's note was dated 8 November 1922; cf. Henderson 1994: 28, note 65. In fact, her note, which is in the *Janse Archives,* is undated.

33   I have not been able to ascertain whether the draft article of Janse, that Vollenhoven refers to in his letter of 7 November 1922, is identical to one or more of the articles Janse published in 1923. But in light of the agreement between the content of Janse's letter to Vollenhoven of 1 November 1922 and these published articles, there could hardly have been significant differences, if any. The six articles are:
- Janse 1923b, "Levende wezens" [Living beings] (dated 20 February 1923);
- Janse 1923c, "Tweeërlei levenshouding tegenover 'de levende ziel'" [Two kinds of life attitudes towards 'the living soul'] (dated 27 February 1923);
- Janse 1923d, "Oostersche opvattingen over het levende wezen" [Eastern views about living beings] (dated March 1923);
- Janse 1923e, "Indo-Germanen contra Semieten over de levende ziel" [Indo-Germans and Semites on the living soul] (dated March 1923);
- Janse 1923f, "Liefde voor – of heerschappij over de levende zielen (Indo-Germanen contra Semieten)" [Love for or dominion over living souls (Indo-Germans contra Semites)] (dated March 1923);
- Janse 1923g, "Waar gaat het om in de artikelen over 'de levende ziel'?" [What is the point of the articles about 'the living soul'?] (dated 3 December 1923).

34   There is no reference in Stellingwerff's Vollenhoven biography, i.e. Stellingwerff 1992, nor in his history of Reformed philosophy, i.e. Stellingwerff 2006, nor in his chapter six on "The rise of Calvinistic philosophy", Stellingwerff 1990: 107-127.

phy'. From the correspondence with Janse, that was resumed after Vollenhoven's recovery, we get some idea as to Vollenhoven's response. But it is only in the light of what Vollenhoven comes to publish after his illness that one can surmise (cf. below) the actual effect though, as we shall see, Vollenhoven did not approve of everything in these articles. Of course, Janse and Vollenhoven each had their own emphases. The educational context of Janse as teacher, in interaction with young, but very concrete 'human living souls', placed a stamp on his work. Vollenhoven, in turn, sought a methodologically responsible philosophical formulation of the anthropological problem. He came to put particular weight on the term 'direction' (as we shall see). But Vollenhoven later did admit that he was influenced by Janse. The nature and extent of it needs to be discussed.[35]

Janse's new ideas, to state them briefly, can be placed under three heads: (1) living soul and scientific explanation; (2) world-view attitudes towards living souls; and (3) biblical understanding of living souls.

1. Living soul and scientific explanation
Living beings are characteristically different from dead matter, in the sense that non-living matter may be divided into parts, and these parts recombined to form a whole, while a living being is an indivisible whole (cf. Janse 1923b: 118). This (in itself obvious) fact needs to be taken more seriously in scientific explanations than is usually done. A living being cannot be explained in terms of a conglomeration of given elements or parts, rather, such components of a living being can only be explained by accepting the living being as given whole (cf. *ibid.*). In biology one must keep life intact if one is to come to knowledge of the living being as such (cf. *op. cit.*: 119). There is an analogous problem in psychology. If one treats an animal or human being as a body + soul, or consciousness

---

35   In the end, the anthropological problem was never really resolved. An intangible feeling of dissatisfaction continued to haunt it even in Vollenhoven's old age. Vollenhoven's chosen term 'direction' is first explicitly used in an anthropological context in Vollenhoven 1930b: 24, i.e. *De eerste vragen der psychologie* [The first questions of psychology]. Cf. also Vollenhoven's extensive reflections in his lecture "Problemen rondom de tijd" [Problems in connection with time]; Vollenhoven 1963: esp. pp. 184-194. Dooyeweerd too did not come to full clarity in his anthropological views, which in themselves display considerable differences with Vollenhoven's. In 1942 he published 32 theses on "De leer van den mensch in de wijsbegeerte der wetsidee" [Anthropology in the philosophy of the law-idea]; Dooyeweerd 1942: 134-143. Anthropology was to be discussed *in extenso* in the third volume of Dooyeweerd's planned trilogy, *Reformatie en Scholastiek in de Wijsbegeerte* [Reformation and scholasticism in philosophy]. The first volume, on Greek philosophy, was published in 1949, but the remaining volumes were not published, in fact the manuscript of the third volume remained a torso. Cf. Verburg 1989: 264-269.

as thinking + willing + feeling, then psychology has lost its object, namely the living being as "living soul", according to Janse (cf. *op. cit.*: 119). Metaphysics too needs to reconsider this. Explanation is not advanced one stitch if, in the face of the failure of mechanistic explanations of life, one introduces a vitalistic principle (such as Driesch proposes), for one then continues to proceed from 'parts' without being able to reckon with the whole in its unity. "Whether one reduces the living being to the living cell (materialism), or to a 'life-force' (vitalism), or to two '*substantiae incompletae*' (soul as spiritual substance in a body as material substance) (scholasticism), *as a whole* it remains a mystery, which resists all further scientific 'explanation'" (*op. cit.*: 120-121).[36]

Janse wishes to exclude all dualism in the approach to factual living being or living souls. They are not "souls or vitalities in a body"—one is reminded of what Gilbert Ryle would later call "the dogma of the Ghost in the Machine"[37]—but "be-souled bodies", intrinsically living or animated bodies. There can be no soul without a body, no thought without brains; no thinking, feeling or willing can be perceived in disjunction from the body (cf. Janse 1923c: 142). This is as we *experience* plants, animals and human beings. But Janse also emphasizes that living beings and living souls, as *given wholes*, are the objects of the sciences, biology and psychology, respectively (cf. Janse 1923d: 145).

2. Worldview attitudes towards living souls

One finds two attitudes in the approach to living beings: vanity and humility. The attitude of vanity is evident from the scientific approach that wishes to explain at all costs. This natural scientific approach proceeds through analysis and synthesis and is applied at the cost of having to deny the given whole of living beings. Philosophers and psychologists then end up wrestling with abstractions, and natural scientists study dead matter in the hope of being able to understand the living being better (cf. Janse 1923c: 142). When one's attitude is that of humility, one readily accepts the mystery of life as given, and one avoids reductions or the introduc-

---

36 This is probably the first time that someone spiritually akin to Vollenhoven raised objections against this anthropology. That Janse does indeed have Vollenhoven in mind in this first of his six articles of 1923 is evident from the last of the six. There he says: "Hence most of the difficulties stem from the *division of the subject itself* in the sense of: the human being *is* body *and* soul (scholasticism), or it is only soul (psycho-monism) or it is only 'body' (materialism)"; Janse 1923g: 226. The formulation of this criticism uses the main distinctions and terminology of Vollenhoven's dissertation, that Janse had studied carefully.

37 Ryle 1949: esp. chapter 1, "Descartes' myth", pp. 13-25.

tion of special explanatory principles.

These attitudes, especially that of humility towards life, have given rise to various world-views. The man in the street never thinks of an animal as a machine. Also Eastern thought has always respected the unique character of living beings. Then too in early Greek thought one finds the acceptance of soul-stuff or world-soul (cf. Janse 1923d: 146). Today life-philosophy is re-emphasizing Eastern traits. Generically one may group this with Indian philosophy, that tends to project one's own life onto the world, onto the universe and on God. German Idealism has a similar trend. This results in the Indo-German attempt to look for life itself, the "*Ding an sich*", as a higher reality. This stands in contrast to Semitic thought, which is also 'Eastern', but with a different focus. It is not anthropo-centric but theo-centric (cf. Janse 1923e: 150), and it is on the whole realistic and not idealistic (cf. *op. cit.*: 151). In "Semitic realism", as found in the Bible, the human being is not portrayed as emotionally bonded to life and in love with nature, but as having dominion over nature (cf. Janse 1923f: 178). Thus, it is Semitic to maintain that psychology studies living beings only from their factual side, not their normative side. Psychology can posit no norms (cf. Janse 1923c: 144). Norms relate to 'spiritual substances', which in turn belong to the spiritual world. Only the effects of the spiritual world in the living soul are perceptible and fall within the domain of psychology, not spiritual substances as such (cf. *ibid.*).

3. Towards a biblical understanding of 'living soul'
Semitic realism calls for a more specific review of the use of 'living soul' in the Bible. Janse discovers that the use of 'soul' is intimately tied to the concrete living being. It is associated with 'breath'. In the Bible God is portrayed as "the Giver of all life-breath in living creatures" (cf. Janse 1923d:147). Texts, such as, "And God breathed into his [man's / Adam's] nostrils the breath of life and man became a living being [lit. 'living soul']" (Genesis 2: 7) are read by Janse as conveying insight and specific information.[38] This breath is life-giving spirit, given to animals and hu-

[38] Janse warns against the 'naive realism' "that wishes to proclaim directly as *the truth* our view concerning facts and Holy Scripture." He allows that parts of *his view* (as he emphasizes) may be subjected to criticism, but "in essentials we proceed safely when we trust Holy Scripture and experience *as they come to us*" (cf. Janse 1923g: 226, note 1). I interpret Janse as claiming that the data of Scripture and experience, when acquired in trust, reveal their true meaning, and may then be appealed to without further interpretation. Janse would appear to maintain that trust, or what is accepted in good faith, makes further hermeneutics redundant. (But this, I believe, is still hermeneutically naive so long as the 'history of revelation' in the context of human history is not taken into account.) In

man beings alike. In virtue of this life-giving spirit, animals and human beings are active and animated creatures. This makes it possible to consider beings in their full activity, which, for human beings, calls for a reckoning with norms—the good, the true and the beautiful (cf. Janse 1923f: 229)—but also with their factual presence and perceptual appearance. In this given factual presence one deals with 'living souls', be-souled bodies. Janse speaks in this regard of an inner side and an outer side. These inner and outer sides can never, of course, be separated from each other, thus there can be no soul without a body, nor living body without soul. They form a whole. But the be-souled body is alive in virtue of the spirit operative in it. The spirit is as such imperceptible, and only its effects in the living soul can be observed.

The spirit enters the human being but also departs. "The human being is flesh and bone, dust and ash, just as animals are. Except, when it dies—'like the beasts' [Psalm 49: 12]—its breath (spirit) returns to God, who gave it spirit, and the breath of animals (the life) goes into the earth" (Janse 1923f: 178-179). To return to God is to return to the spiritual world, where spiritual substances belong (cf. Janse 1923c: 144).

Psychology ought "to accept 'the living soul' as given datum and to study the living being in question according to its inner and outer side, according to the spirit operative within, the life that lives in it, etc." (Janse 1923c: 141, note 1). The two sides of the living being may be approached by means of outer and inner perception (cf. *op. cit.*: 143).[39]

Janse's inchoate ideas are a bit of a mixed bag, with practical, scientific, philosophical and religious implications that are not all clear. Janse later brought more organization to his ideas.[40] In the meantime Vollen-

---

practice it comes down to a close reading of the Bible, against the background of—taking stock of Janse's standing in the Reformed tradition—Reformed theology. As to experience, Montessori had of course emphasized "seeing the child" as a *given* living being, a direct object of psychology and pedagogy, and accepting that datum.

39 In reply to criticisms, raised by W.H. Vermooten (cf. Vermooten 1923, which motivated the writing of the sixth article of 3 December 1923), Janse states what he takes to be the aim of psychology as science. It is probably the first statement of the ideal that, generalized, came to be known as 'the reformation of science'. It is in any case close to what Vollenhoven came to consider a Christian practice of science. Janse says he "*attempts to occasion the laying of a foundation, out of which in time a distinct [eigen] psychology may possibly blossom, which connects with the Holy Scriptures' understanding of 'soul'* ". He also "attempts to find a distinct position in the contemporary currents [of psychology]". The "distinct position", Janse further explains, in no way "ignores history" nor "lacks connection with current science" (Janse 1923g: 225). The criticisms of W.H. Vermooten were raised in the latter's "Letter to the Editor", dated 20 October 1923.

40 In the foreword to his *Om 'de levende ziel'* [Concerning 'the living soul'], i.e. Janse 1940, Janse mentions his publications related to the 'living soul'. After referring to the

hoven, when sufficiently convalescent, read Janse's work after having received the printed articles from him shortly after 1 November 1923 (Vollenhoven's birthday).[41] Not everything that he found here was acceptable, but Janse did stimulate him to come to greater clarity on a number of important issues.

E. The acknowledged influence

Before discussing the direct effect of Janse's ideas on Vollenhoven, let us first see what Vollenhoven, late in his life, acknowledged as to Janse's influence on him. It concerned in the main questions related to anthropology, but it was also broader. Vollenhoven nonetheless remains elusive about the points involved. From what Vollenhoven says, the influence would appear to have been liberating rather than (re)constructive. It is only proper to look at the nature of this influence more closely. There are two sources.

The first source is a short commemorative article on the occasion of Janse's death in 1960 (cf. Vollenhoven 1960d). In it Vollenhoven states that he felt Janse's influence most strongly when he was minister in The Hague. Janse, he says, had by then "come to a more biblical view of 'the living soul', which liberated me from a considerable amount of unfruitful traditional speculation" (*op. cit.*: 1). Vollenhoven does not go into more detail. Instead, he relates Janse's emphasis on the Bible's language being concrete and not scientific, which in turn is said to have dusted the Word-revelation of a layer of scholasticism. A consequence that at least touches

---

articles of 1923 in *Paedagogisch Tijdschrift* he mentions *De mensch als levende ziel* [The human being as living soul], i.e. Janse 1934a (46 pgs); *Ikke* [My Self], i.e. Janse 1934b (16 pgs.); and *Van idolen en schepselen* [On idols and creatures], i.e. Janse 1938 (147 pgs.). In the decade between the initial articles and the titles of 1934 Janse came to accept the main contours of Vollenhoven's Calvinistic thought. In 50 short articles he introduced "Calvinistic philosophy", based in the main on Vollenhoven 1933a. These articles were later republished in Janse 1982. Janse's brochure, *De mensch als levende ziel*, was one of the targets of V. Hepp's criticism in the (rather bitter) dispute that raged at the Free University and in the Gereformeerde Kerken in the mid-30s about the status of the human soul. Cf. Hepp 1937a.

41   In Vollenhoven's first letter to Janse after his recovery, dated 19 February 1924, Vollenhoven mentions the receipt, among other things, of the articles. "Of course the articles attracted my attention the most, all the more so since I found much that was known to me from your writing at the end of 1922. You asked me then for my assessment and I was busy with that when I could not go on." The last phrase, "toen 'k niet verder kon", is ambiguous. Vollenhoven could not go on either because Janse's letter stumped him or because the collapse intervened. I believe he means the latter, for he is describing his situation when working on Janse's letter, not specifically referring to that letter as the cause of his breaking off the writing.

on anthropology is Vollenhoven's appreciation of Janse's "warning against substituting childlike faith with inner experience" (*ibid.*). Inner experience—or "innerlijke ervaring", a term that for Vollenhoven and Janse has overtones of mystical experience—is related to Vollenhoven's use of 'intuition' in the early years of this contact, so here we have at least a clue.

A second reference to Janse, which is in Vollenhoven's autobiographical remarks in "Problems of time in our circle" (cf. Vollenhoven 1968b), largely confirms what he had stated earlier. Janse, Vollenhoven claims, helped him to see that in the Bible the living soul is the full human being (*op. cit.*: 206). When he was in The Hague, Vollenhoven continues, it was through Janse's influence that he had come to the point of being able to remark from the pulpit "that the term 'immortal soul' is definitely to be rejected" (*dat de term 'onsterfelijke ziel' er beslist niet mee door kon*) (*op. cit.*: 207). Here, too, the reader is told what to avoid, but not given a tangible replacement, except to abide by the concrete language of Scripture.

Some of the information in the above remarks can be pinpointed more closely, some other features require discussion. The first point, namely as to when the influence of Janse was felt most strongly, must refer to the period in The Hague *after* Vollenhoven's collapse in January 1923. In his letter of 7 November 1922 Vollenhoven had tried to dissuade Janse from pursuing the novel path he was then taking. Also, Janse's having "come to a more biblical view of 'the living soul'" points in the same direction. Janse had come to this view, which Vollenhoven at first frowned upon, in the course of 1922, *after* completing the Montessori paper, in which paper, Janse, as we saw, still held to a dualism of body and soul. The pulpit remark about the term 'immortal soul' also most likely dates from *after* Vollenhoven's collapse and recovery. The term is still cherished in the said letter of 7 November 1922.[42] It is unlikely

---

42 There is somewhat confusing evidence here. Stellingwerff reports: "When K.A. Bril asked Vollenhoven on 13 December 1968 when the theory of the functions first arose, he replied that it was in 1921. He had changed the word 'soul' in the offprints of the German article on Driesch to 'the psychical [function]', and he received these offprints in August 1921"; Stellingwerff 1992: 53 (my translation). Stellingwerff dates the beginning of the development of reformational philosophy from this point. Stellingwerff implies that Vollenhoven made the said change very soon after receiving the offprints (at least in the same year) and that presumably the change was made in all the offprints. The latter is certainly not true. Of the numerous offprints I have been able to consult, I have not found any switch of 'soul' to 'psychical'. There is one offprint of the German text in the Vollenhoven Archives (405, Box 4, folder 1921) which has evidence of having been reread by Vollenhoven, in virtue of two markings in the margins (on pp. 349, 354), and the addition of a bibliographical title (namely Görland 1921) in footnote 43, p. 357. But

that Janse's draft article, that Vollenhoven referred to in that letter, and Janse's lengthy epistle in response to this letter, dated 30 December (the text Mrs. Vollenhoven later returned to Janse), could have swayed Vollenhoven away from his view of the immortal soul prior to his collapse two weeks later. (We don't know which way he was swayed while working on his initial response at the time of his collapse; cf. the quote from the letter of 19 February 1924 in footnote 41 above.) But the term 'immortal soul' is so intimately connected to deeply lying convictions, that Vollenhoven could probably only think the matter through over a longer period of time, e.g., in the later stage of his recovery, and when he could read what Janse had in the meantime published after receiving his articles in November 1923.

So if the period in which the Janse influence was felt most strongly marks the transition from Vollenhoven's initial 'theistic intuitionism' (including the more metalogical characterization as 'concept-idea dualism' in 1921, or the alternative of 'critical realism') to what he considered a more 'Calvinistic' turn of thought—I believe that this is indeed the case—then that turn began in the course of 1923, during his recovery, in the wake of Janse's critical proddings. (Presumably the draft article of Janse, that Vollenhoven asked him to hold back, was the first prod in that direction.) How the rethinking took place is difficult to surmise, for Vollenhoven's publishing in philosophy only resumed, as already mentioned, in 1925. But the chief evidence for the change are two letters to Janse in

---

it does not have the change in question. One cannot be sure when Vollenhoven reread this offprint. But in the top-right corner of the cover page Vollenhoven placed the date "Aug. '21" and the remark "Geschreven Dec. '20" (Written December 1920). On the basis of this data, this offprint could possibly be the first one Vollenhoven received. He would then have read it to check the printed content and dated it before filing it away. Be that as it may, it is safe to say that the evidence adduced does not support the date of "August 1921" as marking the beginning of the development of reformational philosophy. In fact the correspondence with Janse contradicts this. More to the point is the question where in the said article the change might be expected. There is one sentence (constituting a distinct paragraph) that would certainly have gone by the board once soul and psyche were more carefully reviewed and distinguished. In view of the terminology used, it is also of interest for Vollenhoven's later development. The sentence is: "Hence the entelechy in Driesch is another name for the immanent teleology, it is *direction*, not *thing*, also not an impersonal thing, but conflicts with the most primary supposition of comparative biology and certainly with the substantialistic view of the soul, one of the characteristics of Christian psychology"; Vollenhoven 1921b: 345-346 (translation mine), also Vollenhoven 1920a; offprint p. 20. As compared to the original Dutch article, some of the content was reworked in the German translation, but this passage was not affected.

February and March of 1924.[43] In his rethinking, Vollenhoven integrated into his new view the novelty that is evident prior to 1923 (especially the letter of 7 November 1922), namely the inclination to grant biology a more independent status as science,[44] and what appears to be the release of monadism, so characteristic in his early thought. In themselves these two points cannot be placed in a direct correlation to the Janse influence concerning anthropology, for they were prior to it.[45] In other words, there are more things on Vollenhoven's mind in late 1922 than Janse's prodding alone. To see the broader scope we need to include Dooyeweerd's presence in Vollenhoven's early development, which is given separate attention below (cf. in particular section III.G.2).

F. The Janse effect

So what was the effect of Janse's novel work of 1923 on Vollenhoven? I summarized Janse's work of that year under three heads: (1) living soul and scientific explanation; (2) worldview attitudes towards living souls (subjectivity); and (3) towards a biblical understanding of living souls. Let us review Vollenhoven's reactions under the same heads.

---

43   The resumed correspondence between Janse and Vollenhoven after Vollenhoven's recovery is not revealing as regards the question of the soul. In the letter to Janse of 19 February 1924 Vollenhoven does say: "As to your critique against the dualistic metaphysics I completely agree with the result, not the argumentation used." I believe we may interpret this as stating that Vollenhoven had come to his own rejection of the immortal soul as *substantia incompleta,* though he does not give his own reasons for this rejection here. He goes on to argue that Scripture is of no help here, for it has at least three 'notions' of the soul, none of which is completely satisfactory. As to the term 'Calvinistic', in a following letter to Janse, dated 21 March 1924, Vollenhoven writes: "with sufficient effort and available time one can achieve the goal of a Calvinistic [understanding of] science that can withstand [neo-]Kantianism and not avoid it–of that I am no longer in doubt. And while it used to be more [a matter of] hoping and praying that it might succeed, I now see more [clearly] its possibility." (Both letters are in the *Janse Archives* 157, Box 8, Folder 32.)

44   In that same letter to Janse of 19 February 1924, Vollenhoven reports: "Having worked on mathematics and physics, I am now especially occupied with the logical foundations of biology and must get this behind me before I can tackle psychology." Vollenhoven did not publish the results of this work in biology, though he came to a more 'biological' characterization of the relation between the individual and the environment (cf. below). He did make his later work in psychology available, *viz.* the privately published lecture given on 9 November 1929, "De eerste vragen der psychologie" [The first questions of psychology]; cf. Vollenhoven 1930b.

45   As already stated, there is the possibility that Janse's Montessori paper played a role in getting Vollenhoven to reconsider the question of biology's status as science. But even if this were the case, Vollenhoven did not come to a Montessori-like understanding of biology; cf. below.

1. Living soul and scientific explanation

Janse's view that psychology and pedagogy need to take a living being as given datum in scientific explanation combines different points. In Janse's new view, body and soul are two sides of a single whole being, and he appealed to this body-soul holism to block reductionism in scientific explanation. Vollenhoven concurs in criticising reductionism, but for a different reason. For Vollenhoven "[e]ach science has its *distinct* [*eigen*] primary method, its distinct differentiation" (Vollenhoven 1926d: 59). Scientific understanding takes place within a pluralism of methods. A physicalistic approach, say to psychology, or a mathematical approach to economics, must necessarily leave aside matters of psychological relevance in the first approach or economic relevance in the second simply because the method used is itself devised in relation to other kinds of states of affairs. The scientific concern for method, calling for discussion in the philosophy of science, is not directly met by appealing to a holistic anthropology.

In fact, for Vollenhoven the criticism of scientific reductionism is *independent* of the holism of a living being, as Janse has it. Vollenhoven has no place for 'wholes' or 'things' in the special sciences at all. E.g., physics does not investigate things, but energy interactions (cf. *op. cit.*: 193). "The *cancellation* of a 'thing', an object of perception, is prior to all science" (*op. cit.*: 188; emphasis added). Things are present in fields of inquiry only to the extent that they functionally participate therein, i.e. one investigates a relevant function of a thing in connection with the relevant functions of other things, in their mutual lawfulness, after having discerned the distinct character of such a field.[46] In that sense the holism of body and soul, or the presence of an entire 'living being', is *not* a datum of *any* special science.

There is a source of confusion here in the use of 'wholes'. Experience confronts us with living beings and human 'living souls'. Also one addressed wholes in philosophy—in connection with the 'thing con-

---

46   In direct response to Janse, Vollenhoven states, in his letter of 19 February 1924: "That the soul is an other side of the biological I deem incorrect. At least, if psychology is to remain an independent science, it needs as foundation not another manner of viewing an object that it shares with another science, in this case biology, but [it needs] its own discerned [*geschouwd*] field–away with the *Ding an sich*, etc.–which it shares with no other science." He adds the metalogically important remark, that attests to a direct development of the view of 1921: "For only in this way can we investigate what its categories and synthetic a priori judgments are. In this way each science can be integrated in the whole, in the framework of logic and epistemology." In the meantime, Dooyeweerd referred to this 'framework' as the "metalogical *Gegenstand*-sphere"; cf. the discussion of Dooyeweerd below.

cept'—and in pedagogy, which is concerned with the development of a (whole) human being. Also 'caring for the soul' (*zielkunde*) involves the whole human being when in distress, or in need of pastoral counselling, or psychiatric aid or whatever the appropriate attention might be. In all such cases Vollenhoven agrees that it is entirely inappropriate to approach wholes in terms of constituent parts, e.g., the human being as body + soul, consciousness as thinking + willing + feeling, etc. But such references to wholes needs to be distinguished from the specific object of a special science, in particular psychology. (The latter focuses on 'psychical functioning', and it studies states of affairs, such as suggestion, awareness, sensibility, pain, emotion, etc., as he states in Vollenhoven 1930b: 16.) In 1926 Vollenhoven distinguishes, in his philosophy of science, different 'fields of inquiry' in light of different 'law-spheres' (to be discussed below), whereby 'things' or 'wholes' are not the primary data but rather the functioning that becomes discernible when considering the 'intersection' of law-spheres and wholes/things. Janse, it would appear, evinces the influence of Montessori in his emphasis on given wholes as object of psychology. On the other hand, Janse's urging that psychology treats only of matters of fact and does not touch on norms, fits well in Vollenhoven's own revised view. However, all told, there is more for Vollenhoven to criticise than to endorse with regard to this first topic.

2. Worldview attitudes towards living souls (subjectivity)
The question of the attitude in which science is conducted stimulated a development in Vollenhoven that was far-reaching. The point of endorsing humility as opposed to scientific hubris is entirely well taken. Scientific understanding is possible only when conditions of knowledge and the world are accepted. Whatever transcends these conditions is speculative. Vollenhoven could only agree. He had himself rejected the scientific 'study of God' already in his dissertation (cf. the discussion of theism at the beginning of chapter 4). But Janse took a further step in distinguishing between Indo-German worldviews and Semitic realism.

Janse gleaned the distinction itself from Paul Deussen, a German expert in Indian philosophy and an enthusiastic follower of Schopenhauer.[47] While Deussen sought to combine the Indo-German and Semitic (or biblical) views, Janse seizes on the distinction to emphasize their differences, in preference of 'Semitic realism'. The latter's biblical 'dominion over nature' is incompatible with the former's bonding with nature. Janse takes dominion as involving a *task*, stewardship—naturally, 'dominion' is

---
47   Cf. Janse 1932g: 228; on Paul Deussen, cf. Loemker 1967.

not to be confused with 'domination'—while bonding involves participatory understanding through *feeling*. In the latter approach one looks for meaning and substance in "life itself" as felt, leading to the speculative construal of idealistic philosophy. In Semitic realism, on the other hand, attention is placed on the execution of a task, and this elicits questions as to what needs to be effected, by what means and which results accrue. The two 'worldviews' have entirely different mind-sets.[48]

We cannot say for certain whether this distinction between Indo-German and Semitic had a direct effect upon Vollenhoven, but a significant change in his thinking is remarkably consistent with it.[49] The distinction also seems to reflect (as already quoted) what Vollenhoven later referred to as Janse's "warning against substituting childlike faith with inner experience". For, after his recovery, Vollenhoven attests to a revised understanding of mentality or subjectivity. He undoes it of its independent, inner worldly status that had characterized it as (incomplete) substance. Let us look at this more carefully.

Mentality (in Vollenhoven's early work, which we here review briefly) had been deemed to have an inner independence—which was consonant with its foundation in an immortal soul—in virtue of the intuitive certainty of experiencing what goes on in the mind on the occasion when that activity takes place. The Self is not only certain that the mental activity occurs, when it occurs, but also that there is a mental result—the *content* that stands in correlation with an *act* of occurring—which that activity achieves. This certitude is, of course, characteristic of what Vollenhoven had called the 'concrete intuition', and the immediate awareness of the distinction of act and content justifies the extension to the analytical intuition. This Self, active in this sense and when *once mentally sure of itself*—after all, the intuition is a mental awareness involving an immediate Self-certainty, without the guidance of any norm—is then able to determine the *attitude of mind* in terms of which it (freely) chooses to obey norms, such as the logical norms and also norms of ethics and

---

48   Thus Janse summarizes (Janse 1923f: 179): "The Creation does not stand between the human being and God—a typical Indo-Germanic thought—but the human being stands directly over against God, . . . hiding himself . . . or praising Him. . . . He [/she] stands in between God and the other creatures on earth."

49   Vollenhoven did keep the terms "Indo-German" and "Semitic" in mind for a number of years. The term "Indo-German" occurs in Vollenhoven's lecture notes of 1926-1927 (Vollenhoven 1926msA; Epistemology; section 22.d) at the point where he criticizes mysticism and refers to naturalistic mysticism as "Indo-German mysticism". John Kok referred me to the lecture notes of 1927-28 (Vollenhoven 1927ms) where, in several places (cf. pp. 55, 106-108, 118, 120), the term "semitic" is used. The terms are not retained in later writings.

aesthetics. The Self acquires 'qualities of being a subject' when submitting to norms. One may, of course, also choose to disregard norms, though one then forfeits the safeguards against confusion and error provided by the norms. In these "qualities of being a subject", two things are presupposed: norms, posed by the Spirit, and a Self that it is mentally certain of its inner awareness through the concrete and analytical intuitions. The norms and the Self's mentality are mutually independent, for the Self's mental state may be epistemically submissive or dismissive with respect to norms.[50] The will has an autonomous effect here.

a. 'Subject' as office
But in 1926, seemingly out of the blue, Vollenhoven formulates a revised use of the term 'subject'. He now insists that when speaking of a subject (in the sense of a human agent) of knowledge or knowing subject, the term 'subject' should be taken as denoting an *office* [*ambt*] or a post, which calls for an operating practice. Being a subject is a matter of being 'called' to execute a *task*, of being 'instated' [*ingesteld-zijn*] in an office. This calling or being instated is not selective as to the person actually instated in a post, as in society, say, that of a judge in a court of law, or a country's president when elected, or a professor to his/her chair. *Every human being is instated in the office of 'being a subject'.* Vollenhoven links this 'call' of all human beings to basic human mental conditions, an important class of which are epistemic conditions. For he now states the view that the human being is a knowing subject in virtue of being instated in "the domain of truth". 'Acquiring knowledge' or 'getting to know' involves performing a task 'set by truth' (as it were). Knowledge is only had when the human being has acquired the state of 'possessing truth', upon having exercised or actualized this 'office'.[51]

Now how are we to understand this? To keep the explication brief at

---

50   We take it that the same would hold for aesthetic or ethical norms, in which case the qualification is not typically epistemic but evaluative or prescriptive, as the case may be. On the whole Vollenhoven limits his discussion to epistemology, as has been the case since 1918, but he often intimates the possibility of a wider application (e.g. in correspondence).

51   Consider: "acquiring knowledge presupposes that the human being is instated in the domain of truth [*'n ingesteld-zijn van den mensch op het gebied der waarheid*], whereby it is possible, by actualizing this being instated into an actual attunement/attitude [*actualiseren tot instelling*]—thus by exercising its office [*ambt*] of being subject—it comes to possess truth, to have knowledge." "Truth . . . is completely independent of anything psychical, which can get to be possessed by some human being when it fulfils its task in this regard." Mankind has "a task to fulfil: exercising the office of being subject"; Vollenhoven 1926b: 381-382.

this point (the theme returns in chapter 4), there is a religious motivation here. Vollenhoven speaks explicitly of thinking and knowing as being exercised in the context of the human being's 'prophetic office' (Vollenhoven 1926d: 55)—in passing he adds: "both of the other offices" (*op. cit.*: 62), without being specific. There is no doubt that what he has in mind here are, as the Reformed view has it, the three offices of a human being in his/her response to God, namely as prophet, priest and king. In 1930 Vollenhoven expresses this as follows: "In its highest function the human being, as priest, answers the divine claim through praise and prayer; he [/she] is prophet in speaking with fellow human beings about God's glory; and on the basis of his [/her] superiority in all functions he [/she] is king over the non-human creature" (Vollenhoven 1930d, §80; or 2010, Appendix I). In spirit we have here what Janse expressed as the 'Semitic' life-view. Janse does not mention these offices in his writings of 1923, but on the basis of the Reformed tradition Vollenhoven would certainly have more readily recalled these three offices, when reading of Janse's 'Semitic' appeal, than letting himself be taught by Paul Deussen's uncritical syncretism.

But motivation is not sufficient to account for a change of view. We need to pick up on what these offices suggest. The offices focus on and emphasize the 'place' of the human being in life, or rather, they characterize human living in its actual religious response (priestly office), in its interaction between human beings (prophetic office),[52] and in the human dominion over all non-human creatures (kingly office). They point to general responsibilities. It is in this sense that these 'offices' indicate factors that human life is involved in, not by choice but by being *already situated* in life. At the same time, depending on how we respond in this situation and accept or ignore our responsibility, we make a heaven or a hell of life in how activity within these offices is carried out.

---

52   It is not immediately obvious that knowing and thinking can be associated with the prophetic office. But the clue lies in the phrase "God's glory" that occurs here (cf. the prior quote). The world that surrounds us witnesses to God's power (as the Psalmist of Psalm 19 attests). But those who fail to see this, says Vollenhoven, turn it into a revelation of something else. In that way they offer instead a theory of essences (Plato) or forms of subsistence (Aristotle); cf. Vollenhoven 1926msA, §7. Vollenhoven's own early metaphysics was of the same order, being predicated on the distinction between substance/essence and appearance. God's 'glory' or 'power' became a more explicit presupposition of Vollenhoven's revised theory of knowledge, it being the basis of reality's being 'know-able' or 'intuit-able' (cf. chapter 4). In Vollenhoven 1926a: 10-15, the metaphysics of Plato and that of Aristotle are discussed along these lines.

b. Self-certainty undercut
We get closer to Vollenhoven's actual change of view in noting a confusion with respect to these offices. In the Calvinist tradition itself they are not always distinguished from the roles attributed to thinking, willing and feeling. "Were not even recently the three offices identified with thinking, willing and feeling, and an attempt hazarded to subsume under this humanistic triad faith as understood by Calvin?" (Vollenhoven 1926d: 61-62). Vollenhoven must have had a special case in mind that would be known to his immediate readers. But, on looking back, his concern has a note of autobiography as well. Thinking, willing and feeling have a certain autonomy in his early thought. Thinking stands in polarity to being. It is the thinking pole that makes consciousness and the concrete intuition possible. Feeling is generally related to the psychophysical body and the latter's sensibility, from which the will must distinguish itself so as to avoid becoming too attached (cf. chapter 2, VII.D.). The will is also present as determining factor with respect to the attitude taken towards norms.

In other words, on consideration, Vollenhoven may be implicating himself—at least this would not be self-contradictory—in being self-critical of his former 'occasionalism' and of the self-certain intuition that the occasion of an occurrence of consciousness affords. Naturally, this attests to allowing a degree of psychologism, even though he had expressed the need to curb this. (Recall, Meinong's *Gegenstandstheorie* was attractive for its anti-psychologism.)[53] So Vollenhoven would have been inclined towards criticism. Part of his current criticism stems from the realization that certainty is not a substitute, not even a criterion, for truth. The intuitive certainty of being in the know, no matter how irresistible or convincing that certainty is, does not as such guarantee that the Self cannot be wrong. (The 'that I sense something', however undeniable when concretely intuited, is no guarantee that what I sense is as I take it to be; say: the stick, though straight when out of water, is quite certainly(!) seen to be bent when partially in water). Hence Vollenhoven's former 'concrete intuition', and the self-consciousness that it makes possible, needs to be reviewed. In his now placing knowledge squarely on truth, the concrete intuition's epistemic relevance diminishes. At best, it has undeniable psy-

---
53 Such an intention is apt to take on its own momentum of radicalization. When *Logos en Ratio* was in press, Vollenhoven wrote to Janse and explained: "In my inaugural [i.e. *Logos en Ratio*] . . . you will find a more keen struggle against rationalism, a total break with all psychologism." (Vollenhoven to Janse, 25-10-1926). In Vollenhoven's case, the momentum stems from avoiding subjectivism, the avoidance of which helps to undercut the religious humanism that is based on inner experience.

chological features, and so it is best relegated to psychology. (The truth that I sense what I sense is properly speaking a psychological truth, even when the judgment based on this is quite erroneous.)

In line with the above, we now find Vollenhoven drawing a clear distinction between perception and knowing, between on the one hand what I learn through experience, and on the other what I know in virtue of grasping truth; "to perceive is not [yet] to know".[54] Vollenhoven's former 'knowledge by acquaintance' as well as the effects of the concrete intuition are also now relegated to psychology. The knowing he retains is the knowing of truth. It is in the 'domain of truth' that the knowing subject is assumed to be instated. The 'office of being a subject' is presupposed by the knowing subject. To get into a better rapport with this point we need to see more clearly what other considerations (besides anti-psychologism) are relevant to Vollenhoven's change of position, especially as pertains to norms.

Vollenhoven's early position has a certain analogy to that of (Southwest German/Baden/Freiburg) neo-Kantianism. We noted earlier how, in the 'qualities of being a subject', two things are presupposed: norms as posed by the Spirit and a Self that is mentally certain of its inner awareness. The latter is predicated on the pole of thought. What Vollenhoven takes to be 'posits of the Spirit', neo-Kantianism takes to be simply *objective values*, and the latter act as the objects that are investigated in the value sciences by the thinking Self. It is through reflecting on values that evaluation takes place, i.e. values are 'valued' in relation to the valuing subject. The values that are valued in this way come to act as norms. Hence, in neo-Kantianism, norms have their normative efficacy *in virtue of* the evaluating subject. Now in the early Vollenhoven, the duality of 'posits of the Spirit' (i.e. norms) and the Self is not itself defined as a relation of object to subject. The Self is a substance, and its mentality has a substantial basis that is 'addressed' by norms through the Spirit. Norms originate with the Spirit, not the evaluating Self. But that said, the Self is still in an independent position as compared to norms, capable of being either submissive or dismissive, which is also to regulate, or at least influence, a norm's 'normative efficacy'. The intuitive self-certainties provide their own context here. They are not themselves regulated by norms, be-

---

54 Vollenhoven 1926a: 10. In this same work he no longer speaks of "*kennen*" (acquaintance) and "weten" (knowing that), but of "weten van", which is 'knowing about', and "weten dat", i.e. 'knowing that'. The 'knowing about' is primarily psychological, for it concerns a psychological situation of being 'in the know' (cf. *op. cit.* : 20, 39, 64). The second form, "knowing that", implies the awareness of truth (irrespective of the sense of certainty).

ing simply based on 'the reality of succession' in the Self.

Everything comes into focus when we reckon with the possibility that the basis of mentality in the Self is no longer a basic given. Janse's questioning of the 'immortal soul' would appear to have had critical effect here in that, without that substantial soul, the independence (self-certainty) of subjectivity totters. For, without a basis in a mental/spiritual (incomplete) substance, the certainty would be psychological at best. However if subjectivity now (as revised) attests to being 'instated' in offices or general tasks, we can also expect the 'norms of the Spirit' to be readjusted as well. That is indeed the case. Vollenhoven retains the notion of norms that hold for subjectivity, but he generalizes and relocates them. Norm are reinterpreted to be part of the 'creation or cosmic order', which order is an order of cosmic law. Vollenhoven retains the theistic origination of laws and norms, only we no longer hear that this is in virtue of the Spirit, specifically directed to the human being. The law-order holds with respect to everything creaturely, and only in the specific human creaturely situation does Vollenhoven retain the term 'norm'. This means that the 'qualities of being a subject', which signal the submission to norms by a human being, now too is generalized. Everything creaturely 'stands in subjection' to the law-order. It is the way everything creaturely is 'instated'. It is only in virtue of a basic pluralism in the law-order that there is differentiation in the qualities of standing in subjection. In chapter 4 we will return to this theme of norm and subject.

All told, the influence of Janse, as this pertains to his advancing a 'semitic worldview' and the human being's having a task of stewardship with respect to the world, was much like a prod with surprising effect. In his letter to Janse, 19 February 1924 Vollenhoven expressed his agreement with the criticism directed to the body-soul problem, but he found fault with Janse's alternative. But that was not the (negative) end of the matter. Vollenhoven felt the evident immediate need to first revise the notion of subjectivity before discussing, at the end of the 1920s, the anthropological problem head-on (cf. our discussion below). We find that by that time Vollenhoven has come to a closer agreement with Janse than he could admit to in 1924. That facet of the influence had had to grow. The more immediate effect was re-interpreting subjectivity as a 'tasked' subjectivity. The self-security of 'inner experience' is reworked in a way that calls for response on the part of the human being—response to norms—without assuming an fixed basis of subjectivity. Janse had not envisaged this as such, but he did influence Vollenhoven to pursue this path.

3. Towards a biblical understanding of 'living soul'
The implications of "Semitic realism" for anthropology and the appeal to Scriptures were to be a definite influence on Vollenhoven, though these took a little while to 'take'. We quoted Vollenhoven as having said that Janse had "come to a more biblical view of 'the living soul', which liberated me from a considerable amount of unfruitful traditional speculation." This admission gains in significance against the background of Vollenhoven's mind-set at the time. In his letter of 7 November 1922 Vollenhoven had been quite dismissive about the relevance of an appeal to Scripture in discussions pertaining to soul and spirit. "Calling upon Holy Scriptures to decide in such questions must be challenged [*gewraakt*]. The Holy Scriptures speak in the language of daily experience. Otherwise we return to Ptolemaeus on the basis of Judges or Joshua (Joshua 10: 12)".[55]

Vollenhoven's first letter to Janse after his recovery (19 February 1924) continues in the same vein. "If the Scriptures had a definitive notion of the soul throughout, then it could be analysed and formulated, however without being binding. For in these things the Scriptures have no authority other than a historic-ethnological one." In fact, continues Vollenhoven, there are at least three notions of the soul in Scripture. In a scientific sense, only a single meaning can satisfy [note the 'one word one meaning' principle here], but at the moment of writing, Vollenhoven says, no one option does completely satisfy, so he is unable to decide. He agrees that the "current dualistic view" of body and soul should be opposed, including the "dualistic metaphysics", but he also expresses disagreement with the view (of Janse) of "the soul [as being] the other side of the biological" body. Vollenhoven says that he prefers to defer the matter until he has come to consider psychology, after first finishing his research of the foundations of biology.

a. Logos-revelation vis-à-vis philosophy
But Vollenhoven soon took a position that displays considerable agreement with that of Janse. In the first place he modified his dismissive attitude towards the relevance of the Scriptures for our understanding. To be sure, the Scriptures make use of everyday language, as he had emphasized, and the Scriptures should never cancel or replace scientific inquiry. But in 1926 he insists that the Scriptures are irreplaceable when it comes to conveyed truth about "the whole", i.e. about creation in general and the general situation of humankind, that transcends science (Vol-

---
55 Vollenhoven to Janse, 7 November 1922, in Stellingwerff 1992: 62.

lenhoven 1926b: 388).

Vollenhoven was able to come to a rapprochement with Janse on the basis of a shift in his own basic position. He has come to realize that "knowing resorts under being" (*ibid.*). This realization undercuts a basic distinction of Vollenhoven's early work. He had assumed the polarity of thought and being. On *thought* is predicated the Self and the intuitive awareness that takes place in the Self; the world or cosmos is predicated on *being*. This distinction is also a key factor in the scholastic formulation of the problem of knowledge. The Self's continual striving to know is an attempt to come to an adequate concept of reality, which, if achieved, would constitute a "complete knowledge" of the object of knowledge in question. For the subjective order of thought and the objective order of being are assumed to be in harmony.

But Vollenhoven has come to see this to be basically flawed. If thought constitutes the basis of the order of the Self and of consciousness, then surely this is to acknowledge its being. True, it is a being as changing subject or consciousness, but its being assumes the "reality of succession" (cf. chapter 2). Thus thought certainly involves a form of being. But then it is illicit to draw a distinction of being and thought, for thought, being a form (species) of being, cannot formally be distinguished from it. (E.g. one cannot distinguish mothers and humankind, for mothers necessarily belong to humankind.)[56] So if thought is separated from the cosmos, what remains of the cosmos is fractured and not capable of being treated as a whole.

Vollenhoven comes to a basic reorientation of his standpoint. If thought is of necessity a part of being, then so is knowing, for knowing is what thought drives. But then one needs to presuppose an intrinsic connection of thought and knowing on the one hand and the cosmos as a whole on the other. These connections cannot be knowingly investigated by thought, for they are evidently presupposed in any exercise of thought. The problem is one of contextualization: whatever is part of a greater whole, and dependent on it, cannot be entertained in separation from that whole.

Now where is this leading to? It introduces Vollenhoven's 'layered' account of philosophy and science. Thought is possible only when conducted within the 'essential connections' that link thought to the cosmos. These essential connections are worked into general scientific procedures,

---

56   Vollenhoven argues this in connection with the terms 'being' and 'validity' (1926b: 388), as illustrating the situation of 'cosmos' and '(created) logos', the latter being the term for '(human) thought' (*op. cit.* : 389). The 'created logos' is part of the cosmos.

hence thought takes place in a structured context of either a general, procedural pursuit of knowledge in philosophy (sec) or a specific, procedural pursuit of a special science. The essential connections concern on the one hand the link of the Self, as knowing subject, to the knowledge enterprise (human logos)—this is a *participatory* link of executing a task—and on the other hand the connection by which the reality of the cosmos is *represented* in this enterprise. (We return to this in chapter 4.)

At this 'level of thought' (or procedural activity executed in the context of the 'created logos') knowledge and truth are sought through the procedure of thought (which, as described earlier, involves resolution and composition). One cannot, it appears, come to know the whole in this way, for a connection to the whole is always already assumed. Now two things are important here. On the one hand the notion of 'the whole' is certainly one that is entertained in the mind. It is like what Kant said of metaphysics, the "need for completeness of insight" is ineradicable, but it cannot be satisfied through the concepts of the understanding.[57] On the other hand, the procedured pursuit of thought and knowledge is itself *actually carried out* by the human being in the context of the world, which calls for its own guiding truths. The latter relate to the 'layer of worldview', in that here many truths (and falsehoods) are brought to bear that have been conveyed through upbringing, education, tradition and group interests, which *de facto* pertain to 'the whole' of the human being living in the world. This is no less a level at which reflection takes place, but not a specimen of 'scientific resolution and composition'. It is a reflection of practice, where means are linked to ends, where knowledge is taken in its role of leading to results that satisfy or raise discontent. Life experience is on the one hand informed and confirmed by tradition and successful practice, on the other hand, that very experience also sifts out 'supposed truths' that turn out to be erroneous in leading astray. Hence, there is a 'determination of knowledge' at this level, involving truth, but in a way that is geared to life-practice.

But we need to reckon with yet a third 'layer'. What is it that gives for satisfaction and what for discontent? Here deep-seated attitudes and interests are at work. Whatever one might think as to their accessibility and the relevance of addressing them—peacefully or (all too often) violently—this topic concerns 'the whole' in its *meaning* as implemented and striven for. There is an intuition of 'the good life' as longed for, that is

---

57 In Kant, this calls for the ideas of pure reason. "Pure reason does not in its ideas point to particular objects which lie beyond the field of experience, but only requires completeness of the use of the understanding in the complex of experience." (Kant 1977: §44, p. 73)

not decided on the basis of a determination of knowledge, although that can be brought to bear in support of basic convictions. This third level is ineluctably religious. This is not to be understood as raising the human being beyond the cosmos, but as implementing the ideal of the good life that is hoped for by the human being in living in the world. The religious factor is not of the world but for the world. In other words, at this level, the 'good life' is intuitively marked by what effects redemption and fulfilment.

The situation of philosophy, as sketched, might be described as philosophy being 'fed' by worldview (life-experience) and religious attitude (life-fulfilment), but that philosophy 'digests' these in terms of its own limited possibilities. Philosophy's food is meta-philosophical, but what it stomachs is philosophical. At the meta-philosophical levels of worldview and religion there is much diversity in what constitutes these, including prized writings of wisdom and guidance. A human being makes religious choices and has worldview preferences in view of what each involves, without first reasoning this out in (legitimating) philosophical argument. (Could all conveyed truth be reconstructed? Can the intuited sense of redemption and guidance be conceptualized?) Vollenhoven had a firm choice in the Christian religion and had a definite worldview preference in the tradition of neo-Calvinism. This brings with it an acceptance of the factor of Revelation, of Word/Logos revelation. The Scriptures and the main Reformed documents serve to *orientate* a life-practice that is part of the Reformed tradition. In orientating a life-practice, it is not in competition with philosophy—except when philosophy itself is thought to offer orientation and life-fulfilment, basing it all on 'thought' in denial of any accepted knowledge and the intuitive sense of importance. Whatever is seriously held to meta-philosophically, implements the whole of Self and World in a way that serves as background for the basic notions of philosophy; for example, this gives relevance to the notion of *archè*, the unity or source of reality, and to the necessitation factor (*deon*) that effects or warrants the order of the world.

Thus philosophy is not to merge with religion nor with worldview. It operates, i.e. conceptualizes, in terms of its own method, but does so in a practice that is linked to life. Every philosophy, so Vollenhoven claims, proceeds from a "a non-scientific basis"; "but not every philosophy accounts for that fact" (Vollenhoven 1953I: 103). Naturally, it is important to philosophy to meta-philosophically reflect on its own basis. The differences in method that this involves prevents the philosophical discourse from merging with that of life-view and religious experience. But in being narrower than these methods, philosophy can still benefit from the encompassing effect of these discourses. Vollenhoven included an appeal to the Scriptures and the Reformed tradition in his religious and worldview choices, in the hope that this basis would have a beneficent—he spoke of 'reforming'—effect on philosophy.

So Vollenhoven came to practice philosophy in a way that comports with the Scriptures, *viz.* a way that accepts the orientating truth to be found there. The Scriptures are interpreted by Vollenhoven against the background of the Reformed tradition, which he took as providing their best interpretation, namely the Calvinian interpretation. Hence he characterizes his thought as "Calvinistic philosophy". (The right way to read this is: 'philosophy as practised in the light of Calvinistic presuppositions but according to the 'scientific'/academic method of thought'.) Vollenhoven nowhere simply quotes Scripture in his practice of philosophy, as circumscribed within the limits to which he restricts proper philosophy. But as regards meta-philosophical reflection, he feels that it is clarifying to be open about one's worldview and religious sources. Naturally, when speaking and writing for his 'home base', he avidly practiced that openness.

Science that proceeds from a view of reality as illuminated by the Reformed presuppositions and outlined in Reformed philosophy is described as "Christian scholarship". A different meta-philosophical context influences a different qualification of scholarship. To insist on the importance of Scriptures in Christian scholarship is not to take it as a source of data for a particular science, but to reckon with its meaning-orientating role (cf. Vollenhoven 2005d/e, **173**; 2010, **173**). Here we are back to Janse, though now generalized. In connection with psychology, Janse had spoken of the laying of foundations that are also in rapport with "the Holy Scriptures' understanding of 'soul'" (cf. footnote 39 above). This is in line with what Vollenhoven came to see as correct and desirable, from his standpoint. Here a consonance with Janse's more detailed statements is noticeable.[58]

b. Biblical anthropology
So the spirit of Janse's appeal to Scripture is recognizable in Vollenhoven's

---

[58] We should not overlook the fact that Vollenhoven places the Scriptures against the background of the Logos: the Scriptures are a result of Logos-revelation. Janse did not make this distinction. Janse lies more open to the charge of maintaining a 'naïve hermeneutics' with respect to biblical statements. In Vollenhoven's case there is always the 'history of revelation' to take into account when he appeals to Scripture. Admittedly, Vollenhoven's 'child-like faith practice' tended to minimize this difference with Janse.

own reformulation of his position after 1923. Vollenhoven no longer has the dismissive attitude he first had, once he could tie the appeal to Scripture in to his revised view of the Logos: not Logos as principle of rationality but as source of life-direction. When he could define for himself the role that does justice to the Scriptures, he was more than willing to seriously consider basic features of Janse's biblically inspired anthropology. Vollenhoven expressed himself in this vein for the first time in the lecture "The first questions of psychology" (Vollenhoven 1930b).[59] It would appear that, in the first place, he simply came to agree with Janse's interpretation of the biblical use of "living soul", namely that this denoted a human being (or an animal) as concrete, living, breathing body (or flesh). In the Bible, he says, "'soul' denotes the breath-through-the-nose of animal and human being ... and in that sense they stand in relation to the earth's atmosphere... [and] the word 'body' denotes in the Holy Scriptures things as such, hence *inter alia* also souls (= animals and human beings), although the use of 'body'—other than the word 'soul'—lacks the emphasis on breathing. Hence the words 'soul' and 'body', while not being precisely equivalent, can still be used for the same thing. . . . Accordingly, the Holy Scriptures can attribute eating, drinking and dying to the soul."[60]

In tandem with this admission Vollenhoven emphasizes that this is *concrete language* use, in line with everyday speech—such as when we speak of "that poor soul", meaning a concrete person who suffers some serious setback.[61] What Janse had failed to do adequately, in Vollenhoven's view, was to distinguish this use from that of the object of psychology as science, which investigates "pain, awareness, memory, etc. and hence does not analyse the whole human being" (Vollenhoven 1930b:

---

59   Janse was present when Vollenhoven gave the lecture on 9 November 1929. Although he is not mentioned by name, Janse readily recognized the effect of his own earlier writings. In his dairy he noted for that day: "Fortifying — what has[n't] all happened since my writing of 8 November 1922. The Lord has worked *wonders*." Cf. Janse 1929-1946.

60   Vollenhoven 1930b: 13. This 'nose breath', which contrasts with the breath through the mouth, is meant to emphasize the difference between breath or air as life function and breath as bearer of speech, the latter being indicative of distinct mental activity. Vollenhoven notes that the Greek word "psyche" originally meant "breathing, by which we are related to the atmosphere" (*op. cit.* : 11). Notice that, despite the near equivalence of 'body' and 'soul', Vollenhoven does not (at this point) resort to Janse's terminology of inner and outer sides of a whole.

61   In daily speech, says Vollenhoven, "'soul' is approximately the same as 'human being', and there is not only nothing against this but everything in its favour"; Vollenhoven 1930b: 11.

11). When one fails to make this distinction in language use—between everyday language use and scientific discourse—the aim of doing good scientific or theoretical work in psychology would appear to require that one advance a theory about the total makeup of psychic creatures, human or animal. The unity of an animal or human being is then analysed as composed of basic parts: organism + animality or psycho-physical body + soul/mind/rationality, respectively. But if the scientific practice of psychology is directed towards "the psychical function" of an animal or human being, rather than to the whole object or being, then there is no scientific requirement to split an animal or human being up into basic components beforehand. In the context of science, such an anthropological or zoological theory would even be speculative, and such speculation is best not introduced into the practice of science. Here we see something of the "liberation" from "unfruitful traditional speculation" that Vollenhoven spoke of in this connection.

Vollenhoven also went along with Janse in distinguishing an earthly and a spiritual or heavenly world. In many ways this remained a torso, never worked out in a way that makes the reader sit up and take notice. He claims that our main source for speaking of the heavenly world is, again, the Scriptures. Heaven is the abode of angels and spirits, of both the good and the evil ones (cf. the brief account in *Isagoge*, par. 19-21, also 137-140). They influence conduct on earth, but, in not specifying, let alone analysing, this effect, he failed to indicate how this illuminates the human condition or gives insight into understanding our cosmos. Perhaps part of the problem was the tension that would result from taking data of Scriptures and apply them in a scientific context.

However there is a feature that at least locks this doctrine in with the mainstays of Vollenhoven's thought generally. In the heavenly realm the distinction between good and evil seems to be an accomplished fact. Its effect on human life makes itself felt in the necessity for a human being to choose between good and evil. Thus the problem of *direction*, so prominent in human life, acquires added importance upon realizing that the struggle between good and evil is influenced, according to Vollenhoven, by the effect of good or evil spirits in the heavenly realm. There was only a partial agreement with Janse here. Janse thought of spirit as an animating factor in the human being, *over and above* the unity of body and soul and distinct from both, which returns to the heavenly realm at death. Vollenhoven never added a distinct factor of spirit to the duality of body and soul.

G. Conclusion

As we overview the 'Janse effect' on Vollenhoven, we can only conclude that it was more effective for what it initiated than conclusive in what was posited. Thus the extent and specific format of the influence in Vollenhoven were due more to his own professional grasp of philosophy than to Janse's enthusiastic but somewhat inchoate initiatives of 1922-1923. Janse did not adequately distinguish between the living soul and the psychical function, and this created extra confusion in connection with the sciences of biology and psychology. Vollenhoven brought clarity here by continuing in the line of his metalogical reflections of 1921.[62]

Janse got a better hearing with his emphasis on the difference between 'Indo-German and Semitic worldviews'. It was not the 'biblical view' of the latter, as such, that first attracted Vollenhoven, rather the different human attitudes towards the world and the human being's place. He saw that his own 'concrete intuition' was at least like the Indo-German view of participation, which has deeper moorings in the substance-phenomenon metaphysics. Vollenhoven accepted the Semitic view of the subject's dominion, in answering to a task, as making more sense than mentality as substance, founding the self-certainty of inner experience.[63] This required an overhaul of the metaphysics of the Self and its *"substantiae incompletae"*. (In its extension came revisions in the understanding of perception and knowing.) A 'tasked subjectivity' became a hallmark of Vollenhoven's thought, what he referred to as the subjectivity of 'standing in subjection'.

Janse's most effective influence was in anthropology and his insistence that there is a distinct biblical view of 'living soul'. Vollenhoven came to an almost total agreement, but only after having settled for himself the relevance of the Logos-revelation, of which Scripture is a result,

---

62 In Vollenhoven's discussion of "psychology as a science", in Vollenhoven 1930b: esp. 10-17, he seems to have (implicitly at least) Janse in mind. The confusion of 'soul' and '*psyche*' is central to his discussion (p. 11, 16), and he specifically mentions the "Western-Eastern" bedding of our anthropological thoughts (p. 15), a reminder of Janse's use of "Indo-German worldviews", for the reference to "Eastern thought" is in itself quite unexpected here. In line with Janse, Vollenhoven is very dismissive with respect to any "*substantia incompleta*" construction. This is of course in self-criticism of his own prior position.

63 It is not coincidental that Vollenhoven reconstructs the substance-phenomenon metaphysics in his *Logos en Ratio* (1926a), pointing to Plato as an important actor here, with his distinction between essence and appearance, and the analogy he introduced between a thing and its (eternal) essence and a human being and its (immortal) soul; cf. *op. cit.*: 10-11. In "The first questions of psychology" he states it to be "a first demand of Christian thought to break totally with this substance-phenomenon metaphysics" (Vollenhoven 1930b: 15), this metaphysics being indicative of what the Apostle Paul speaks of as the "natural human being" who "does not understand the things of the Spirit of God".

for philosophy. Here the problem of 'the whole' demanded attention in a way that got Vollenhoven to reject his own prior 'qualified scholasticism' of the harmony between subjective and objective rationality. What the Logos reveals must be understood in the context of the love command, which is direction determining and aims to reveal and to guide, it does not reveal, or appeal to, a realm of ideas by which reality is structured ('objective rationality'). The structure of reality is noticeable, but cannot be fathomed, let alone understood. In the context of that structure one must recognize a 'created logos', enabling distinctions to be made and connections to be laid by the human being in its 'logical quality of subjection' ('subjective rationality'). The need for a scholastic 'harmony' is now completely redundant.

The metaphysics of Vollenhoven's view of the world/cosmos needs a more careful scrutiny than has been given so far. But the clarification of the Logos, as itself the source of conditions that enjoin a trusted faith in the text of Scripture, removed whatever scruples there were—such as Vollenhoven had had in the early 1920s—in accepting the relevance of Scripture's authority. Apart from the specific point about 'spirit', Vollenhoven was, practically speaking, in agreement with Janse's formulation of a Scriptural anthropology.

The revision of 'inner experience', the removal of a 'layer of scholasticism', and the acceptance of a 'biblical anthropology', these being the main points Vollenhoven recalled in later years of Janse's influence, can indeed be given a place in Vollenhoven's development in the early and mid-1920s. Janse deserves mention here, even though at that time he lacked Vollenhoven's level of sophistication. Through Janse's prodding, Vollenhoven came to creatively formulate the basics of a 'Calvinistic philosophy'.

H. Additional note

When Janse reformulated his anthropological ideas a decade later in the brochure, "The human being as 'living soul'" (1934)[64]—a work that was aggressively criticized by Valentijn Hepp (1879-1950) in the heated dispute in the mid-1930's in the Reformed Churches in the Netherlands, along with the views of Vollenhoven and Dooyeweerd[65]—he expressed essentially the same ideas, except that some points are made more explicit.

His main point is that the Scripture proceeds from an understand-

---

64   Janse 1934a.
65   In 1936-1937 Hepp published four brochures under the general title, *Dreigende deformatie* [Threatening deformation], the second of which is *Het voortbestaan, de onsterfelijkheid en de substantialiteit van de ziel* [The continued existence, the immortality, and the substantiality of the soul]; cf. Hepp 1937a.

ing of the human being that is essentially different from that of Greek philosophy (Janse 1934a: 5). In the latter the predominant anthropological view is that of an immortal soul within a mortal body. To the soul are attributed spiritual and typically human values and personality, to the body physical corruptibility (*op. cit.*: 14). Janse challenges the understanding of anthropological terms that occur in the Scriptures, that makes explicit use of this schema of Greek anthropology. (The first and longest of the two chapters is devoted to this challenge; *op.cit.*: 7-29.)

In the Scriptures the use of 'living soul' refers to the whole concrete person as a living, active being. The presence of soul and body is so intimate, that the soul can be said to hunger and thirst, and when dead, the 'dead person' is a 'dead soul' (*op. cit.*: 13). Janse ventures to be more exact in his biblical explication. He opts for three terms: 'body', 'soul', and 'spirit'. The spirit is an animating factor, a 'wind' (*op. cit.*: 45), which comes from God, and returns to God at death (*ibid.*). Spirit is what a human being has. But soul and body are the two sides of the human being, *viz.* the human being as *outward* and *inward*, respectively. The chief characteristics of soul in the living human being are breath, blood and consciousness (*op. cit.*: 41). An animal has the same make-up, but God has introduced a difference, namely that the human being accords with the image of God, which the animal lacks. The difference involves the much greater complexity of functioning of a human being as compared to an animal, and also the human being's having dominion (*op. cit.*: 38-39).

Janse's view is that at death, when the spirit returns to God, the inward and outward presence of the human being comes apart. Dying is a loosening from all of the life-spheres (*op. cit.* : 43), but it also involves the living being. The inward presence leaves the outward via the last exhalation or the flowing blood when mortally wounded. The outward presence that is buried is to us not 'the remains' but still the person, only now inanimate; slowly it returns to dust and bones and is forgotten (*ibid.*). The inward presence is said to be 'naked', lacking the outward presence with which it was cloaked. But this inward presence, being now in the realm of the dead (*ibid.*), still has all the parts and functions it had when 'clothed', such as hands, feet and fingers (*ibid.*). The inward presence has shape and figure, and is able to think (*op. cit.*: 46). It awaits the resurrection, when it will again be clothed, only now with a new body (*ibid.*) for eternity.

The outward-inward presence of the human being is the main anthropological distinction Janse makes. It becomes alive when God's animating breath gives it spirit. Vollenhoven too accepted the distinction of inward and outward. But, unlike Janse, he refrained from giving this any distinct representation, preferring to confine his terminology to more philosophically loaded meaning.

For Vollenhoven, the body is, as is any individual thing, a 'unity of subjection', meaning that its (functional) acting and being acted upon takes place in a way that is coherently structured, 'unbroken' (Vollenhoven 2005d/e, **139**) inclusive of both so-called 'bodily and mental' functions. At death this structure of the 'outward human being' dissolves. Soul is the "direction determining" principle in virtue of which personal life is conducted "for good or evil", whereby the Self, as 'inward person', bears responsibility in the full diversity of bodily and mental functionality. To the extent that soul involves will, choice and resolve, it is something that is more or other than the bodily and mental function; in its influencing the functions it is itself "pre-functional" (*op. cit.*, **91-93**). While alive, the unity of body and soul is intrinsically dynamic. At death the soul parts from the body but is not thereby annihilated.

III. *The Dooyeweerd contact: from adequate concept to modally qualified law*
A. Introduction

The second person who is conspicuously present in Vollenhoven's life as his philosophical thought develops is Herman Dooyeweerd. The latter, born 7 October 1894, was almost two years Vollenhoven's junior . They went to the same high school in Amsterdam, and both registered with the Free University, Vollenhoven in the Faculty of Theology and the Faculty of Arts (which included the study of philosophy) in 1911, and Dooyeweerd in the Faculty of Law in 1912. Both wrote and published student essays, Vollenhoven on philosophical topics, while Dooyeweerd shows a particular interest in literature and music, in particular Richard Wagner.[66] On 2 July 1917 Dooyeweerd defended his Ph.D. thesis,

---

66 Vollenhoven was one of the editors of the student magazine *Opbouw*, a "monthly in the service of the Christian life- and worldview, of and for young people". It had a short existence—1914-1916—perhaps on account of its taking itself too seriously. He published well-formulated pieces, such as: "Abaelard en het scepticisme" [Abaelard and scepticism], (Vollenhoven 1914a); "Het persoonlijke in den oorlog" [The personal in the war], (Vollenhoven 1915b); "Henri Bergson", (Vollenhoven 1915a); "'Zijn' is 'denken' èn 'doen'" ['Being' is 'thinking' and 'doing'], (Vollenhoven 1916b). Of Dooyeweerd we mention: "Leekengedachten over Richard Wagner en zijn Tristan" [Layman thoughts concerning Richard Wagner and his Tristan], (Dooyeweerd 1914); "De troosteloosheid van het wagnerianisme" [The desolateness of wagnerianism], (Dooyeweerd 1915a); "Neo-mysticisme en Frederik van Eeden", (Dooyeweerd 1915b). This last piece has been translated by J. Glenn Friesen and placed on his internet site [www.members.shaw.ca/

entitled *De Ministerraad in het Nederlandse Staatsrecht* (The cabinet in Dutch constitutional law). Vollenhoven often preached during the time he worked on his dissertation, and in the final year he preached weekly to stem financial need (cf. Stellingwerff 1992: 23, 26). He defended his Ph.D. thesis somewhat later than Dooyeweerd, on 27 September 1918. On 10 October 1918 Vollenhoven married Dooyeweerd's older sister, Hermina Maria Dooyeweerd.

It is probably on account of their having become familial that important information about their contacts, especially early contacts, is so spotty. The one letter that is extant from Dooyeweerd to (the family) Vollenhoven is dated 7 December 1920. From its content one can surmise that it was part of a more extensive correspondence. But the letter, which will be discussed below, also shows the mixture of private family correspondence combined with academic 'shop talk'. We may assume that on account of their being, for an important part, private, these letters were not saved with other academic correspondence and were subsequently lost. An important part of their contact had to be by correspondence after Dooyeweerd moved from Amsterdam to Harlingen in Friesland, in December 1916, when his Ph.D. studies were near completion. Regular face-to-face discussion was resumed four and a half years later, in The Hague, as of late May 1921, when the Vollenhoven family moved there; Dooyeweerd himself had already moved to The Hague in 1919. The contact which then took place was direct and the discussions deep. Of this period Vollenhoven has said: "Both authors had a very searching contact".[67] During the five years in The Hague—both moved to Amsterdam in 1926 when they were simultaneously appointed to their chairs at the Free University—the foundation of their joint philosophical endeavour was laid. Vollenhoven being our main topic, we are especially interested in the contact of these men seen from his perspective.

Both Vollenhoven and Dooyeweerd have left reminiscences, late in life, of their early contact. These reminiscences are of uneven quality, some published, some private, and taken as a whole not entirely consistent. What complicated the memory are the motives and interests, that are not always explicit. There were philosophical differences that each recognized, but which were long kept private on both sides in the interest of maintaining a united front to avoid jeopardising the outreach

---

hermandooyeweerd/Curators.html].
67   The Dutch reads: "Beide auteurs hadden een zeer diepgaand contact"; Vollenhoven 1953o. The passage was deleted in the 5th edition.

of 'Reformational philosophy'.⁶⁸ Then there is also—one tends to think 'inevitably'—the matter of who, when partners are completely matched in knowledge, ability and qualification, is the leading man. There was a 'practical' allotment that long alleviated this 'problem'. Vollenhoven was the leading man in virtue of his being the first chairman of the Association of Reformational [formerly: Calvinistic] Philosophy from 1935 till 1963, while Dooyeweerd had the leading role as first editor of *Philosophia Reformata* and, particularly in his later years, also in virtue of the international recognition he gained.

But when both looked back at the roots of their movement, a peculiar sketch of the situation emerges. Vollenhoven pointed to features of his early thought that he had had to overcome, and, as we saw, he acknowledged Janse's influence in his coming to take a position that comported better with the neo-Calvinist strain of the Reformed tradition he wished to emphasize. Janse had no recognizable effect on Dooyeweerd whatsoever. Dooyeweerd, in his published tribute to Vollenhoven in 1973, honoured him as "cofounder of the reformational trend of thought" (Dooyeweerd 1973: 5). But he singled out an earlier "pre-reformational phase of his philosophical thought". What he especially had in mind was the constructive part of Vollenhoven's dissertation, which, in Dooyeweerd's characterization, was still "quite bound to the traditional metaphysics of realist scholasticism" (*ibid.*: 6). This characterization is somewhat broad and diffused,⁶⁹ but Dooyeweerd's implication of a change is essentially sound, as we saw. Regretfully, he mentions no date when *he* thought the change in Vollenhoven took place, nor what he considered to be distinctive about that change that supports his characterizing it as *co*-founding the Reformational trend of thought. As we shall see, Dooyeweerd began to have constructive philosophical contact with Vollenhoven as of 1919. On Vollenhoven's own evidence, we found that the important change in his thought begins to take place in late 1923, in the aftermath of his illness. But, because Dooyeweerd is silent about the details of the transformation in Vollenhoven, there is no indication how this change in Vollenhoven affected him, or even whether it affected him.

---

68   We stated this about Vollenhoven earlier. That Dooyeweerd was of like mind is attested to by M.E. Verburg, Verburg 1989: 88.

69   For example, one wonders whether Dooyeweerd means to say that there is also a metaphysics of 'non-realist scholasticism' or even a 'non-traditional metaphysics of realist scholasticism'. This is of some importance in connection with the characterization of Dooyeweerd's own early work. For Vollenhoven the problem is, as we saw, the 'scholastic harmony' between subjective and objective rationality. This is more specific than Dooyeweerd's locution.

Instead, in the said tribute, Dooyeweerd goes on to describe what his own 'founding role' had been, and it is from that perspective that he situates Vollenhoven.[70] Important in this connection is what Dooyeweerd says about Kuyper and about his own appointment to the position of deputy director of the Dr. Abraham Kuyper Foundation in October of 1922,[71] a position he held until 1926. (He says he needs to broach this, for "it throws light upon my cooperation with my brother in law [sic] during our stay in The Hague" (*op. cit*.: 7).) This appointment enabled him to give ample time, as he explains, to study philosophical theories of law and the state, social philosophies, and to delve "ever more deeply into the study of universal philosophical systems and their historical interrelatedness" (*ibid.*: 7)—all this being "necessary to come to an understanding of Kuyper's neo-calvinistic conception of anti-revolutionary politics in contrast with other political views" (*ibid.*, p. 7). Should the idea occur that this is a rather tortuous way to study politics, Dooyeweerd explains himself immediately. "Such a study alone, moreover, could clarify the nature of the conflict in Kuyper's thought" (*ibid.*, p. 7). Kuyper embraced a "philosophical *Wissenschaftslehre*", developed in the first volume of his *Encyclopedia of Sacred Theology*, that was not in line with Kuyper's "reformational basic conception of Calvinism as world and life view but, instead, opposed its consistent elaboration" (*op. cit*: 8). Dooyeweerd targeted as being truly Reformed the Kuyper who had said (on the occasion of the opening of the Free University in 1880): "There is not an inch in the whole of temporal life of which Christ, as Lord of all men, does not say 'mine'," (*op. cit*.: 7). It is also the Kuyper of the *Lectures on Calvinism* of 1898.[72]

It is this (supposed) conflict in Kuyper that set the agenda of the discussions with Vollenhoven, according to Dooyeweerd. He describes this in the following three sentences:

---

70   Dooyeweerd fills many pages of this tribute to Vollenhoven with an account of his own thinking and development. It is difficult to see why Dooyeweerd did not suppress this, as being inappropriate for the occasion. While Dooyeweerd throughout his career mostly used a terminology implying equality between himself and his brother-in-law—cf. Dooyeweerd 1935-1936, vol. I: viii—he sometimes lapsed into a different mode, as when, clearly implying Vollenhoven, he spoke of "some adherents of my philosophy"—Dooyeweerd 1953-1958, vol 1: 31 note 1—and when calling Vollenhoven "my first ally" (*mijn eerste medestander / mijn medewerker*) in discussion with a journalist, as reported in Verburg 1989: 89 (cf. also Dooyeweerd 1935-1936, vol. I: 33). Possibly Dooyeweerd said the latter in jest, though Verburg speaks of a "charming answer". But Dooyeweerd's speaking of "my philosophy" raises serious questions about the enterprise of the brothers-in-law being a joint venture, and also what "co-founding" means in this context.
71   Henderson 1994: 29.
72   Cf. Dooyeweerd 1939: 211.

> My brother in law [sic], *Vollenhoven*, had come to the same conclusion in his own way, as I was soon pleased to discover. Therefore our discussions in The Hague centred on the necessity of a reformational epistemology and ontology that would be able to match itself against both the neo-thomism dominant in reformed scholasticism and the Humanistic neo-kantianism which still dominated epistemological theories during the twenties. We were also agreed that a veritable reformation of philosophy would have to be understood in the spirit of Kuyper's basic conception of Calvinism as a world and life view that was to be clearly distinguishable from both the Roman Catholic and the Humanistic ones. (*Ibid.*: 8)

There is something seriously skewed in this account. When did these discussions take place? Dooyeweerd's explicit reference to his appointment to the Kuyper Foundation puts this between October 1922 and (mid-) 1926, the timespan of his deputy directorship of the Kuyper Foundation. Given the implication of the time he needed for the research, the said discussions could not have taken place immediately. But in January of 1923 Vollenhoven had his break-down, which incapacitated him for most of that year. So the discussions referred to by Dooyeweerd could have begun at the earliest towards the end of 1923. There is nothing said about the relevance of the prior contact from the time of May 1921, when Vollenhoven too moved to The Hague. Dooyeweerd does speak of "the close spiritual contact" they enjoyed during their joint residence in The Hague (*ibid.*, p. 5), and Vollenhoven's own statement of "very searching contact" supports this. But nothing is made explicit about this contact prior to Dooyeweerd's deputy directorship. This is odd, to say the least. If the discussions really did only get underway towards the end of 1923, then this takes place at a moment—as Henderson reports and we will confirm below[73]—when Dooyeweerd first begins using the terminology of "law-idea" and "law-spheres", a use that was to become standard. So Dooyeweerd already had some fundamentals of his thought in place when the said discussions with Vollenhoven proceeded.[74] But nothing is said about Vollenhoven's own thought here nor his possible role.

The fact that Dooyeweerd speaks of "discovering" that Vollenhoven had come to "the same conclusion" about a more radically Reformed trend of thought does not go well with the attestations of a prior "close contact", unless indeed that contact was interrupted. Now because there was the interruption of Vollenhoven's long illness, we would appear to

---

73 Henderson 1994: 30.
74 Indeed, Dooyeweerd reports that he "had been convinced already as early as 1922 [presumably in connection with his appointment to the Kuyper Foundation] that Kuyper's deepest intentions had been voiced in the statement referred to above", i.e. the Christo-centric statement. (Dooyeweerd 1973: 7.)

have a confirmation that the discussions Dooyeweerd has in mind were conducted after Vollenhoven's convalescence in late 1923. When we considered this from Vollenhoven's side, we found that from late 1923 on, Janse's influence and stimulus are having an effect. The academic contact between Vollenhoven and Dooyeweerd during Vollenhoven's convalescence (about which no information has been found to date) must have had to be subdued, if it existed at all, to spare the possible stress on Vollenhoven. When serious discussion did resume, Vollenhoven could report some changes in his thought.[75] These would quite likely have been novel for Dooyeweerd. And naturally Dooyeweerd could now report about the progress he made in 1923.

But let us return to the quotation above. Dooyeweerd states in the second sentence that it was consequential to the 'discovery' of their mutual Reformed intentions that discussions on epistemology and ontology took place. This statement suggests that it was the principled stance with respect to the "more radically Reformed trend of thought" that now occasioned the discussions on epistemology and ontology. Anyone familiar with the history of Reformational thought will tend to agree. But what the statement is silent about are the discussions prior to 1923. We will show below that such discussions did take place, with a focus on epistemology and methodology in the context of cosmology, were indeed conducted with vigour and are amply documented. If they took place before the Reformed stance was explicit, what were the initial motivations and leading ideas? Was there a break when the Reformed stance was consciously accepted, or were prior elements of epistemology and ontology taken up in the new stance? These questions are not without merit. For we found that Vollenhoven himself at first accepted a realist construal of (adequate) concept and (realist) idea, expressive of the scholastic harmony of subjective and objective reason, over against the idealist neo-Kantian understanding of this distinction and that he broke with this in the revision of his thought after 1923. But Dooyeweerd continued to use the terminology of concept and idea. Is he continuing Vollenhoven's earlier use, or does he have another meaning in mind? We need at least to look at these early discussions to get clarity on this important phase of the development of the two reformed thinkers.[76]

---

75 In his first letter to Janse after his recovery, 19 February 1924, Vollenhoven wrote that he agreed with the critique of "the dualistic metaphysics [of body and soul]" but not with Janse's argumentation, implying that he had made up his mind on this independently of Janse's sending him copies of his articles of 1923 in November 1923. Cf. the earlier discussion of the Vollenhoven-Janse contact.

76 M.E. Verburg, availing himself of private material belonging to the Dooyeweerd

The third sentence of the quote above asserts that both men agreed that the required reform of philosophy would have to be in the spirit of Kuyper's (Neo-)Calvinism, understood as worldview, and contrasting with that of Roman Catholicism and Humanism. This touches on the ideological context of their endeavour. On the face of it there seems little to broach. But there was a difference of implementation from the start that Dooyeweerd is silent about. Dooyeweerd emulated the Kuyper who spoke of the unity of consciousness as lying deep in the human heart, where a human being, in retreat from the diversity of life experience, discloses itself to God. Dooyeweerd called this the non-theoretical "religious centre", and he himself described it as "the full concrete unity of consciousness of Self and of God, the Selfhood of a human being. . . ."[77] It was in connection with such a consciousness that Dooyeweerd used and applied the term "law-idea" in the 1930s. (We return to this at the end of our discussion of Dooyeweerd below.) Vollenhoven, on the other hand, jettisoned the very notion of idea in the overhaul of his thought. The (to him) 'mystical' notion of a unity of consciousness of Self and God is incompatible with the 'boundary' to which the Self is subject in its awareness of God. The notion of a 'tasked subject' does not answer to an *idea* of law, but to law in its *actual impingement* that conditions 'standing in subjection'. Such impingement, one might now say, 'deconstructs' any supposed "unity of consciousness of Self and of God". At least, the alternative to such a 'mystical unity' would certainly be important for an

---

family, asserts that, as regards these discussions, Dooyeweerd explicitly stated that they had "not the least influence on the direction in which his philosophy developed." The source is a tape recording of what Dooyeweerd said in August 1964 while visiting his oldest daughter living in Vancouver, B.C., Canada. In the same context Dooyeweerd is taped as saying: "In the beginning I had these evenings with Uncle Dick [= Vollenhoven] that we talked together because we both found that such a philosophy [i.e. a Calvinistic one] was needed. But that was actually just beating the air somewhat [*eigenlijk een beetje gepraat in de ruimte*], about neo-Kantianism and so forth." Verburg situated this last remark in the time prior to Vollenhoven's illness, in other words at the time when Vollenhoven said "very searching contact" took place! (Verburg 1989: 88, 87 resp.) Dooyeweerd expresses a very selective memory here. Stellingwerff quotes from a letter of Dooyeweerd to Colijn (no date given, but written while Dooyeweerd was still with the Kuyper Foundation): "You might remember how he [Vollenhoven] and I worked together from the start and are completely of one mind. The evenings and nights that we talked together and inspired each other, are unforgettable for me"; Stellingwerff 2006: 33. For a larger part of this letter, see Puchinger 1994: 17-18.

77 The passage in Kuyper is in the first Stone Lecture on "Calvinism a life-system", *Lectures on Calvinism*, p. 20. H. Dooyeweerd, "Kuyper's wetenschapsleer", *Phil. Ref.* 4 (1939), p. 204. In this same article Dooyeweerd recommends, on page 211, that the passage in Kuyper be learned by heart!

'other way' of practising Reformational philosophy.[77a] Perhaps the tribute was not the place to enter into this kind of a discussion. But one might have expected Dooyeweerd to at least hint at some of the factors that embody Vollenhoven's "own way", deserving at least the respect as befits a "co-founder". Instead he is silent about the nature of Vollenhoven's own contribution.[78] Stellingwerff, when reviewing the general relations between Dooyeweerd and Vollenhoven, concludes: "One is forced to conclude that Dooyeweerd applied his own philosophy as measure in judging Vollenhoven."[79] In the above we have a case in point.

So, in the quoted reminiscences, Dooyeweerd is writing history, as seen from his perspective. He lets it start from the point where, for him, a Kuyper inspired religious motive becomes operative and gives urgency to a 'reformation' of philosophy. At that point in time he 'discovers' that Vollenhoven, in his own way, shares that concern. This common history could have begun only in late 1923. Thereby Dooyeweerd passes over the prior years of *actual* history, when the relation between Vollenhoven and Dooyeweerd was intense and consequential. We shall pause to review what that contact actually was.

B. The early contact

As already stated, the information about the early contact between Vollenhoven and Dooyeweerd is fragmentary. However we need not strive to be complete. We want to see something of the drift of this contact, and also to search for those points where the contact was influential and beneficial. We shall, in the main, limit our search to information that is

---

77a The qualification "mystical" first appeared in connection with Kuyper through Vollenhoven's introduction of the term "semi-mystical" in 1959 in the context of the problem-historical method. In that context, the term 'mystical' refers to the 'mystical bond' between the godhead and the universal mind or spirit, in which the higher part of the human being participates and with which it remains bonded at death, when the human body, being temporal, falls away. Cf. Vollenhoven 2005c: 377-381. Vollenhoven himself preferred to speak of "life-unity", in which the human being serves God by striving to live according to the whole law. Cf. Vollenhoven 1955i in Tol and Bril 1992: 122.

78 Dooyeweerd does comment on the work of 1933, *Het Calvinisme en de reformatie van de wijsbegeerte*, expressing appreciation of its historical part, and the first volume of Vollenhoven's *Geschiedenis der Wijsbegeerte* (1950), in which Dooyeweerd mistranslates Vollenhoven's characterization of that work as "consequent probleemhistorisch", viz. "*consistent* problem-historical method"—Vollenhoven means to say 'consequential problem-historical' i.e. tracing what historically changes and what remains constant in the conceptions (problems) of philosophers as history progresses—and then criticises Vollenhoven for "overestimating the part that logic is to play in historical research"; Dooyeweerd 1973: 6. There is no acknowledgement of Vollenhoven's own program.

79 Stellingwerff 1992: 57.

published, though occasionally we have had to turn to archival material.

The information about what appears to have been their first philosophical contact is from Vollenhoven. In preparation of G. Puchinger's interview with him, published in 1961, Vollenhoven gave him some autobiographical notes. Thus Puchinger could report: "Already in the beginning of the summer of the year 1919 Dr. Vollenhoven, in Oostkapelle, had received a letter from his brother-in-law, Dr. H. Dooyeweerd, who wrote that he too felt the need for a deeper foundation in the area of philosophy and science in general".[80] The letter is no longer extant, and there is no way to corroborate the date and the content reported. We have no option but to accept the information as it stands — but that has its implications.

As Verburg and Henderson report and discuss,[81] Dooyeweerd was very much aware of philosophy in his student days, but there was no planned interest in its study at the time. In his dissertation, which is focussed on Dutch jurisprudence and was published and defended in 1917, Dooyeweerd's Introduction evidences acquaintance with the theories of law of Grotius, Locke, De Montesquieu, Hegel, Puchta, Kant and Jellinek. Also, the question of the source of law in the face of parliamentary rules and practice is discussed at length in this work. However he refrains from subjecting the theories about this question to a critical discussion, claiming this to be inappropriate in the work at hand, but also because, in his judgment "the problem [as to the nature of parliamentary norms] cannot be resolved apart from any connection with the philosophy of law".[82] We cannot say whether this announces a plan of later study, or whether it is only meant to explain the absence of discussion in this work.

Between finalizing his Ph.D. dissertation and his appointment as deputy director of the Kuyper Foundation in October 1922, Dooyeweerd was practically employed, first in Harlingen, Friesland, where he worked for the national revenue, then in Leiden as of January 1918, where he served as legal adviser for the city authorities, finally in The

80 Puchinger 1961: 90.

81 Cf. Verburg 1989: 20-28; also Henderson 1994: 22-25. The biographical data related to Dooyeweerd in this and the following paragraph are taken from these works.

82 Dooyeweerd 1917: 31. It is not without interest to add, in light of Dooyeweerd's later thought in which law (norm) and subject (fact) play an important role, the following. Dooyeweerd states that with regard to the parliamentary system, which is distinctive for the modern government cabinet, two sides need to be carefully distinguished: a formal-normative side and a material-factual side. The formal-normative side is determined by written laws, supplemented by unwritten norms of the parliamentary system; the material-factual side has no rigorous determination but simply rests on the political structure of a country. (Cf. *op. cit.* : 25-26)

Hague, from the beginning of 1919, where he was appointed to a position in the Health Office of the Department of Labour. In a letter, dated 15 May 1922, written in connection with the possible appointment to the Kuyper Foundation, Dooyeweerd stated: "Since completing my doctorate in 1917 I have devoted my free time entirely to methodological studies and studies in the philosophy of law".[83] The generalization is perhaps a bit of an overstatement. In Harlingen Dooyeweerd was also active in the Literature and Art Society, and he gave a talk there on "Religion and Beauty" that was well received according to the local press. So initially study was tempered with organized relaxation. It is this 'free time study'[84] that needs a more careful perusal.

Dooyeweerd gives important information in the first lecture he gave to the students as the newly appointed professor of jurisprudence in the fall of 1926. He states: "When my interest first began to be focussed on the philosophy of law, I began to study one book after another quite haphazardly. First of all I wished to know what was actually understood by 'philosophy of law'. The result was a hopeless confusion in my mind".[85] We cannot be sure when this first focussing of his interest took place, perhaps already while in Harlingen. Anyways, it can only be after some period of (spare time) study that he discovers the confusion of his reading and comes to feel the need to bring more organization into it. So it would be reasonable to expect him at this point to shift his attention to foundations and, accordingly, to more explicitly philosophical topics, especially methodological matters. But when did this take place? And did Dooyeweerd make this shift entirely on his own?

I believe that at this point Vollenhoven's information concerning the letter he received from Dooyeweerd in mid-1919 is relevant. (Dooyeweerd had by now settled in The Hague, Vollenhoven is still in Oostkapelle, Zeeland.) Dooyeweerd is said to have indicated to Vollenhoven (as we quoted above) "that he too felt the need for a deeper foundation in the area of philosophy and science in general". This 'need' fits the experience of confusion Dooyeweerd confessed to. So with this first letter to Vollenhoven, Dooyeweerd would appear to be reaching out to his brother-in-

---

83   Letter to J.J.C. van Dijk, Minister of War and Secretary of the Kuyper Foundation, along with the "Nota" of Dooyeweerd's proposed work program and implementation, in Van Dijk 1961: 47-52. The quotation is on p. 48.

84   For what it's worth in connection with the 'scope' of this spare time, Dooyeweerd had full-time employment but was a bachelor until 19 September 1924. (Vollenhoven led the wedding service.)

85   Verburg 1989: 418. The entire lecture, which is in many ways illuminating (we return to it below), is reprinted in Verburg 1989: 415-427.

law for intellectual contact. Now why would Dooyeweerd have expected contact with Vollenhoven to be beneficial at this stage?

I want to enter an assumption into the discussion that was long never even entertained. It is the assumption that Dooyeweerd acquired (probably was given) a copy of Vollenhoven's dissertation on the philosophy of mathematics, and that Dooyeweerd actually read that book to his own benefit soon after receiving it.[86] We quoted Dooyeweerd in an earlier chapter, when, in his 1973 tribute to Vollenhoven, he referred to this dissertation as "an enormous achievement". The earliest reference to it found to date is from 1925, in Dooyeweerd's series on 'the struggle for a Christian policy of state' (started in 1924, cf. Dooyeweerd 1924, I), where he refers to it as "the excellent dissertation" (*het voortreffelijk proefschrift*).[87] Now this earliest reference does not link Vollenhoven to Dooyeweerd's need, expressed in mid-1919 towards investigating "deeper foundations". But at least it does put Dooyeweerd's reading of it at a fairly early date and, of more importance, that he thought highly of it.[88]

---

86   M.E. Verburg gives no indication that Dooyeweerd had any acquaintance with Vollenhoven's early work at all. He brings Vollenhoven into his biography of Dooyeweerd at the point when the brothers-in-law gain their academic appointments in 1926. This negligence is to his own detriment. He fails to see the mind of Vollenhoven behind Dooyeweerd's early work, thus he misinterprets the very texts he quotes extensively to indicate Dooyeweerd's own originality, and he even feels obliged to correct Dooyeweerd's statement about Vollenhoven being a co-founder of Reformational philosophy, preferring to emphasize Dooyeweerd's off-hand remark to a journalist about Vollenhoven being his first ally. Cf. M.E. Verburg, *Herman Dooyeweerd*, pp. 87-90. R.D. Henderson, in his *Illuminating Law*, is aware of the early contact between Vollenhoven and Dooyeweerd, but he fails to show acquaintance with Vollenhoven's early work. Cf. R.D. Henderson, *op. cit.*, pp. 29, 32-34. Both Verburg and Henderson failed to pick up the conjecture of A.M. Wolters: "On the basis of Vollenhoven's early publications, a good case can be made for the thesis that he in some significant ways shaped the developing systematic philosophy of Dooyeweerd,...", in "The intellectual milieu of Herman Dooyeweerd", in *The Legacy of Herman Dooyeweerd: Reflections on critical philosophy in the Christian tradition*, ed. by C.T. McIntire (Lanham: University of America Press, 1985), p. 16. J. Stellingwerff does more justice to the available data. He points to Vollenhovian insights present in Dooyeweerd's unpublished work at the time. He also gives a fine general assessment of their relations, early and later. However, on numerous points of detail and general philosophical evaluation, further discussion is in order. Cf. J. Stellingwerff, *D.H. Th. Vollenhoven*, pp. 55-56.

87   The reference in Dooyeweerd's tribute is in Dooyeweerd 1973: 5; for the 1925 reference, cf. Dooyeweerd 1924, VI: 235, n. 3 and 238, n. 2. Regrettably, the latter footnote references are only historical. The first note reference is in the context of a discussion of Pythagorean naive-mystical speculation, and the second in discussing Plato's relapse to number mysticism in the *Timaeus*.

88   We want to point to the timeframe here. Vollenhoven defended the dissertation on 27 September 1918, so his book would have become available some time during the

We find a further clue in Dooyeweerd's letter sent to the family Vollenhoven, dated 17 December 1920.[89] A main part of this letter is specifically for "Dik", about neo-Kantianism. This part of the letter continues their on-going critical discussion about neo-Kantian thought. (Dooyeweerd thanks Vollenhoven "for his last letter", which is no longer extant.) Dooyeweerd offers some philosophical thoughts, which we shall refer to presently. But he ends by saying: "in the meantime, I ought not to depend too much on my philosophical schooling [to date], maybe my view of the matter is entirely wrong. Write this to me sometime . . . ." Clearly, the less experienced Dooyeweerd is open to the guidance of the more experienced Vollenhoven. If Dooyeweerd is so open towards Vollenhoven about his own uncertainty at the end of 1920, then the letter to Vollenhoven of mid-1919 would very likely have expressed not only Dooyeweerd's need for insight in foundations in the area of philosophy and science, but also contained a request, perhaps stated explicitly or at least implied implicitly, to Vollenhoven to be willing to lend him that more experienced ear in discussion. In mid-1919, the only basis for approaching Vollenhoven in this way was the latter's dissertation. (Of course Vollenhoven and Dooyeweerd would have known in a general way what the one could expect from the other. But Dooyeweerd left for Harlingen already in December 1916,[90] so much of Vollenhoven's philosophical position, as developed in the dissertation, would not have been common knowledge.) When we now also find that Dooyeweerd freely avails himself of Vollenhoven's terminology in his early work, the conclusion can only be that Dooyeweerd consciously *aligned* himself to Vollenhoven and accepted the latter's more knowledgeable authority as context to develop his own thinking in the area of the philosophy of law.

One final remark about a peculiar feature of this early Dooyeweerd-Vollenhoven contact. Dooyeweerd had from the start his own interest, which was focussed on the area of the philosophy of law. Vollenhoven had, apart from his general interest in philosophy and its history, a partic-

---

summer of that year. Dooyeweerd changed his employment and residence (now moving to The Hague) in the beginning of 1919. Between his receiving the dissertation and his writing to Vollenhoven in mid-1919, Dooyeweerd would have been able to study Vollenhoven's book, which cannot be well-understood without careful study. Also it doesn't seem reasonable to expect Dooyeweerd to write to Vollenhoven about his interest in pursuing philosophical questions without being up-to-date about Vollenhoven's own thought and stance!

89   This letter is published in full in Stellingwerff 1992: 47-48.
90   Cf. Verburg 1989: 28.

ular interest in the philosophy of the natural sciences.[91] It is something of a surprise to see Vollenhoven also immerse himself in the literature of the philosophy of law. In 1920 and 1921 there is correspondence between Vollenhoven and the professor of jurisprudence at the Free University at the time, W. Zevenbergen, correspondence to which Dooyeweerd was privy.[92] The material in the Vollenhoven Archives related to this work is very incomplete. But one can make out that Vollenhoven subjected work on the philosophy of law of men like E. Lask, G. Radbruch and H. Kelsen to a close reading. In 1922 (perhaps already in 1921) Dooyeweerd himself (again?) picks up the works of these men, along with that of R. Stammler and others, and writes extensive studies on them.[93] No doubt Vollenhoven read these men to be personally up-to-date in this 'normative area'. But, viewed from the point of view of the contact with Dooyeweerd, Vollenhoven seems to have been prepared to go the extra mile in this contact, in taking the trouble to be knowledgeable in the current literature of Dooyeweerd's area of special interest at that time. Vollenhoven's coaching had general philosophical scope but it also had a relevance for the philosophy of law, enabling their contact to be close. Perhaps that is relevant to Vollenhoven's remembering so specifically: "From October 1921 till the fall of 1922 we often had these late evenings when we talked and exchanged ideas with each other".[94]

C. Dooyeweerd in Vollenhoven's world of thought

Dooyeweerd entered into Vollenhoven's world of thought prior to the latter's temporary collapse and the influence of Janse. So it should be beneficial to pause to see how Dooyeweerd is moving about in the world of the early Vollenhoven, a world which Dooyeweerd himself later claimed (as quoted earlier) to be "quite bound to the traditional metaphysics of realist scholasticism".[95] And of course it is of interest to see what happens

---

91   Vollenhoven to Janse, 19-02-1924: "Having dealt with mathematics and physics, I am now specifically occupied with the logical foundations of biology, and this first has to be completed before I can tackle psychology".

92   In the one extant letter to Vollenhoven, Dooyeweerd says that he finds Vollenhoven's correspondence with Zevenbergen "very interesting". Cf. Stellingwerff 1992: 47.

93   Cf. Stellingwerff 1992: 54. R.D. Henderson discusses this material of 1922 in "Chapter 3. Unpublished manuscripts" of his Henderson 1994. We discuss some of this material below.

94   Stellingwerff 1992: 52. It must be in this period that they realized they could stimulate each other, giving rise to discussions, then and later, that each valued. This is also why each, in print, expressed appreciation of the other's appointment when they were simultaneously appointed to chairs at the Free University in 1926; cf. chapter 1, footnote 2.

95   Dooyeweerd 1973: 6.

when Vollenhoven makes the definitive shift, after his illness in 1923, to his self-termed 'Calvinistic thought'. We propose offering a synopsis of Dooyeweerd's writings of most of the 1920's, the period in which he himself undergoes rapid development. We shall be especially on the lookout for tell-tale signs of affinity or distance between Dooyeweerd and Vollenhoven as they work on what is evidently a common cause.

1. "The problem of municipal monopolies in the interest of public health, considered mainly in the light of new views on free enterprise" (October 1920)[96]

This is Dooyeweerd's first publication after completing his dissertation. As Henderson reports, the work is related to Dooyeweerd's legislative work in the Health Office in The Hague.[97] There is little to discern of the contact between Dooyeweerd and Vollenhoven in this article, assuming that Vollenhoven is correct in stating that Dooyeweerd first sought contact in mid-1919. It is clear that Dooyeweerd is pursuing the topic of law of his own interest. But we do see something of philosophy in the background.

The leading question here, says Dooyeweerd, is not whether municipal authorities may interfere with a business' free enterprise, but what the extent of its interference should be, especially when matters of public health are involved (*op. cit.*: 126). The freedom of enterprise can no longer be construed on the basis of 'subjective right', expressive of an individualistic view of society. Society has become much more socialized, especially due to the effect of the first World War (*op. cit.*: 139). This calls for a new view of the freedom of enterprise. The out-dated 'subjective right' needs to be replaced by "the so-called *fact* that freedom of enterprise is nothing other than a *social function*" (*op. cit.*: 126). He adds the intriguing remark that this introduces "a new concept taken from the metaphysical world", something not generally recognized in the current positivistic, anti-metaphysical climate. However enticing it is, he states, to subject this new concept to a "critical evaluation" (*ibid.*), he feels he must refrain from this as falling outside of the scope of the article (cf. *op. cit.*: 127). The article indeed restricts itself in the main to practical matters of municipal interference in specific business enterprises.

However, at one point Dooyeweerd does stop to remark about the

---

[96] H. Dooyeweerd, "Het vraagstuk der gemeentemonopolies in het belang der volksgezondheid, hoofdzakelijk beschouwd in het licht van de nieuwe opvattingen in zake de bedrijfsvrijheid", in Dooyeweerd 1920. Cf. also Henderson 1994: 25-26, and the brief remark in Verburg 1989: 29.

[97] Henderson 1994: 26.

"philosophical impossibility" (*ibid.*) of maintaining the view of the subjective right in the context of the current freedom of enterprise. In recognition of the changed societal circumstances, one must ask which idea of justice offers the best interpretation. In the modern juridical consciousness, though not itself a source but certainly a touchstone of positive law, the doctrine of freedom of enterprise as subjective (individualistic) right is no longer relevant (*op. cit.*: 138-139). Current juridical practice no longer addresses malpractice in enterprises in terms of subjective right but sees it as a social function in light of the demand of the common interest.

The view of freedom of enterprise in terms of a social function is to be preferred over that of individualistic subjective rights. The idea of justice itself calls for a *social will*. When the ideal of this will is not ethically attainable, then the law must step in and offer protection in terms of objective right (*op. cit.*: 140). This does mean that the interpretation of the freedom of an enterprise in terms of its social function is one-sided, in being only concerned with matters juridical (*ibid.*). However this should not be seen as disqualifying the individual. Individual freedom ought itself to function in the light of the common interest, and the latter is an ethical notion. "The common interest, as ethical notion, is served by honouring individual freedom, so long as this individual freedom justifies itself through social functioning" (*op. cit.*: 141).

Dooyeweerd's dubbing this 'social function' in the strong realist terminology of a 'metaphysical concept' suggests a context of 'objective validity'. The latter also has meaning in Vollenhoven's early thought. But since Dooyeweerd does nothing here to substantiate or explain this characterization, it remains at best a tenuous thought. Telling is the subservience of juridical matters to ethics, something prominent in the neo-Kantian positions at that time, which Dooyeweerd will soon quite strenuously oppose. The relation of matters juridical and ethical is an important problem in Dooyeweerd's subsequent early work.

2. Letter to Vollenhoven, 17 December 1920[98]
About three quarters of this letter, directed to Vollenhoven and his wife in Oostkapelle, is concerned with philosophy. In it Dooyeweerd asks for

---

98   Published in Stellingwerff 1992: 47-48. Three small editorial corrections are in order: (i) 10th line from the bottom of the letter: read "beteekenissen scherp uit elkaar" instead of "beteekenissen uit elkaar; (ii) 9th line from bottom: read "van den kenvorm" instead of "van een kenvorm"; (iii) 6th line from bottom: read "niet te veel" instead of "niet veel". M.E. Verburg ignores this letter; R.D. Henderson mentions it in passing, *op. cit.* : 27-28.

a copy of Vollenhoven's lecture on Bergson,[99] and he finds the correspondence of Vollenhoven with Zevenbergen especially interesting. In other words, Dooyeweerd is privy to the academic work and correspondence Vollenhoven is putting out, as is to be expected when, as of mid-1919, there is a concerted interest in investigating (as quoted above) "a deeper foundation in the area of philosophy and science in general". Dooyeweerd also thanks Vollenhoven for his last letter. Thus there was an ongoing correspondence between them, of which only the present letter is extant.

Dooyeweerd is particularly interested in the 'human sciences,' which he refers to as 'value sciences,' and his first statement is of special interest. "To approach the value sciences in terms of transcendental realism is also in my opinion a must in order to save Calvinistic metaphysics".

To my knowledge, this is the earliest mention of 'Calvinistic metaphysics' in their contact to date. We note that Dooyeweerd here expresses his *agreement* with the concern to 'save' it, implying that Vollenhoven has already expressed that interest. (Recall that Dooyeweerd also sided with Vollenhoven earlier, when writing to him, in mid-1919, that "he *too* felt the need" [emphasis added] for a deeper foundation.) There is no hint as to what the term means here. But given Vollenhoven's context of thought at the time, it may be taken as at least referring to the ideational extramental realm. Whether this includes the monadological cosmology is uncertain.[100] Dooyeweerd proceeds to recount a feature of 'transcenden-

---

99   Vollenhoven had lectured on Bergson from notes on several occasions, in 1919 and 1920. The lecture was finally written up in 1921, but it was never published; cf. Vollenhoven 1921ms.

100   When both Dooyeweerd and Vollenhoven turn self-consciously to the work of John Calvin, they focus on what they see to be central in Calvin, namely the distinction between divine sovereignty—expressed in Calvin more usually as 'omnipotence' and applied as providence*—and the concomitant creaturely dependence. This is metaphysically secured in God's essence, which is *inter alia* infinite, implying finitude on the part of the creature. Thus Dooyeweerd says, in *Calvinism and Natural Law:* "Both systems [of Thomism and Stoicism] wrong the sovereignty of God, who does not tolerate any abating of the boundary between himself and the finite." There is a "*concept of boundary* between the infinite and the finite, the Absolute and the creature who is dependent on him in everything." H. Dooyeweerd, *Calvinisme en Natuurrecht* (Amersfoort: Wed. W. van Wijngen, 1924), p. 12. And Vollenhoven: when God reveals himself in his work, "then the Infinite grasps the finite, never the other way around: '*finitum non est capax infiniti*'." D.H.Th. Vollenhoven, *Logos en Ratio* (Kampen: Kok, 1926), p. 31. Thus the early understanding of 'Calvinistic metaphysics' may have focussed on this distinction between divine infinitude and creaturely finitude. That could then also serve as correction to Vollenhoven's use of the actual infinite in his dissertation, this being there a character-

tal realism' in connection with value sciences. And this account is vintage Vollenhoven.

Dooyeweerd raises the problem of the origin of norms. In idealistic systems (i.e. of neo-Kantianism) each norm "hangs in the air" (*in de lucht hangt*). For, one must accept spiritual realities from which, taken from the human side, norms proceed. Thus a formal function of faith is required, for which idealism has no place. In idealism norms become the object of theorizing, over against the theorizing subject. But this merely accentuates the problem of grounding the norm, thus making a thorough "fiasco of every critical idealistic theory of values".

What Dooyeweerd here expresses is entirely consistent with Vollenhoven's view of norms, as expressed in his dissertation, about God (the Holy Spirit) being their source (transcendent condition) and warrant (transcendental-immanent condition). Norms can never be the object of theorizing, for their 'reality', from the human side, is their impinging on the human subject, as transcendental condition. The transcendent origin of norms calls for "the formal function of faith", i.e. acceptance of the "spiritual reality" of the Holy Spirit. All told, this defines a form of transcendental realism, not a (neo-)Kantian transcendental idealism.

One can be more specific when compared with the Baden school of neo-Kantianism. In this school values are taken to be transcendent, and in relation to the human being or culture values 'hold' as norms. So here norms find their origin in values that subsist in and of themselves.[101] Values are formally in the position where the early Vollenhoven speaks of the Holy Spirit.

The second part of the letter's discussion with Vollenhoven is Dooyeweerd's response to a question Vollenhoven had posed: what in 'critical realism' (presumably an alternative for 'transcendental realism') would be the relation between the value of the knowing of being (say, in the natural sciences) and the values that are the object of the value sciences? Dooyeweerd says that we "need to clearly separate two meanings

---

istic also of the World. (Such a correction need not affect the acceptance of the potential infinite of select domains, such as the unending number series, spatial forms, etc.) Upon realizing that such a notion of the World is incompatible with a 'Calvinistic metaphysics' the motive to 'correct' it could come from a desire to 'save Calvinistic metaphysics'. This could have consequences for maintaining a monadology, but whether this would definitely count against it is difficult to say. If the above *guess* is anywhere near the mark, then it could explain why Vollenhoven said that "already quite soon" after 1918, an unchanged second printing of his dissertation was out of the question (cf. the quote in the Introduction to chapter 4).

* Cf. Calvin 1960, Book I, Chap. XIII, 1: 120-121, n. 1, and Book I, Chap. XVI, 3: 200.
101   Cf. Henderson 1994: 66, 77.

in the concept of value in the value sciences," *viz.* the values that the value sciences are about (i.e. investigate) on the one hand, and the value of value sciences as to their form of knowledge. It is only the latter meaning that can be compared with the sciences of being, for value is relevant here only in connection with their form of knowledge, the object here being material facts not values. This remark is sensible, though one suspects that it was not the final word in their continuing correspondence.

The fact that Dooyeweerd compares 'value sciences' and 'natural sciences' in a matter of course way, would appear to suggest that the difference in kind between these types of sciences does not affect the general reflection on the philosophy of science in Dooyeweerd and Vollenhoven's discussions. In other words, the 'value sciences' would also appear to belong to the 'organism of science' (whether or not in a distinct compartment). There is no textual backup for this assumption in Vollenhoven's dissertation—of course that work doesn't call for a discussion of the 'value sciences'—but the context of Vollenhoven's thought does permit their inclusion.[102] For, if the natural sciences conceptualize the phenomena of the *world* against the background of ideas of being ('thing-laws'), then the human sciences conceptualize *human normative/evaluative experience* (of cultural life), whether logical, aesthetic, juridical, ethical, etc. within the range of the Self, against the background of 'ideas' of values (i.e. objective values warranted by the Holy Spirit).[103] A value science may be seen as conceptualizing the norms that hold in human experience and society, doing so in a way that clarifies relevant objective value, a complete knowledge of which would be an 'adequate concept' of value. (In the next section there is an example of such a use of 'concept and idea' with respect to legality in Dooyeweerd.)

This inclusion of value sciences in no way strains Vollenhoven's context of thought. In a letter to F.W. Grosheide (16 November 1921) Vollenhoven explicitly compares and contrasts the natural sciences and the value sciences. He writes: "logic is, along with ethics, aesthetics etc. precisely as science of norms distinguished from the explicative [i.e. descriptive or natural] sciences (to which belong not only those that formulate causal laws, such as natural science, but also those that need to make do with the principle of causality, such as [the science of] history . . .)"[104]

---

102 One expects the correspondence between Vollenhoven and the professor of jurisprudence, W. Zevenbergen, threw light on this point.

103 We add that it is the Self's own practice (of description, valuation, etc.) that calls for norms, but through the Self's being itself cosmic, there will be ideas that secure this practice extra-mentally.

104 Vollenhoven to Grosheide, 16-11-1921.

Causal laws are part of the metaphysics of the world, while the value sciences are predicated on the validity of norms as holding for human life. (Vollenhoven includes a diagram in the same letter, showing the 'Reformed standpoint' to involve the *distinction* of causality and validity of norms [*gelden van normen*].) The Self-World distinction, so characteristic of Vollenhoven's early thought (cf. chapter 2), is clearly an operative assumption here. Scientific knowledge, being a 'reality' in its own right, includes not only the natural sciences but also the value sciences.[105] And *both* kinds of science presuppose 'the dualism of concept and idea', essential to maintaining a critical or transcendental realism.

Dooyeweerd ends with a question: "can one attribute reality to the value of a form of knowing?" This question goes in the direction of a metalogical consideration of validity. Valid knowledge no doubt has its value. But what is the status of that value? Can or should it too be reified in a way similar to cultural values studied in the value sciences? Dooyeweerd expresses "great interest" here, "because it is so fundamental for advancing reflection." But at this point he expresses little confidence in his philosophical advance to date.

By July of 1921 Vollenhoven has finished his "Hegel in our elementary schools?",[106] in which he outlines his metalogical reflections in the context of his own theism. He now puts more emphasis on the "epistemological dualism of concept and idea." (Cf. the metalogical discussion in section IX of chapter 2.) We find this emphasis also reflected in Dooyeweerd's subsequent writings.

3. Response to G. Scholten

On 8 April 1922 the Society for the Philosophy of Law held a meeting in The Hague in which the Dutch neo-Kantian legal scholar, dr. Gerben Scholten, presented a paper, entitled "Staatsbemoeiing en individueele vrijheid" (State interference and individual freedom). There were pre-

---

105   The 'scope' of the distinct sciences and the problem of what counts as a science were much discussed at the turn of the twentieth century. Freiburg neo-Kantians tended to group sciences in two classes, natural and cultural, with basic characteristic differences as to their methods, e.g. generalizing vs. individualizing, respectively, as in Rickert. W. Dilthey drew a basic distinction between the natural sciences and the '*Geisteswissenschaften*', the latter including human studies and the sciences of society (history, jurisprudence, sociology, economics, etc.). For him the natural sciences are explanatory, the *Geisteswissenschaften* interpretive, appealing to understanding, '*Verstehen*' . Cf. Makkreel 1975. In general, the attempt was to fit the sciences in a view of reality as a whole. Vollenhoven and Dooyeweerd also do this, not only with their (early) 'critical realism', but also their later definitive view of the plurality of methods.

106   Vollenhoven 1921c.

pared responses, one of which was Dooyeweerd's. This is the first time Dooyeweerd went public with his burgeoning ideas of legal philosophy and method. The paper and the responses were published in the Society's "*Handelingen*" (Acts).[107]

On reading Dooyeweerd's response to Scholten's paper, one finds considerable intellectual advance in Dooyeweerd's work, both as to content and philosophical expression. The response is sufficiently coherent to be understood without requiring explicit knowledge or explanation of Scholten's paper. The content of Dooyeweerd's response is in line with his own special interest in the philosophy of law (legality) and its broader context in connection with the methodology of the 'value sciences'. In philosophical expression we find him using the terminology of Vollenhoven's metalogical outline (July 1921). The substance of that outline would probably have formed an important topic of their discussion at the time. It cannot be a mere coincidence that the period that Vollenhoven recalls of intense, late evening discussions—October 1921 till the fall of 1922 (i.e. until Dooyeweerd becomes deputy director of the Kuyper Foundation)—commences when the metalogical reflections have just appeared. They can now stimulate each other and together wrestle with the dominant neo-Kantian climate of the time.

Dooyeweerd opens his response with a remark that he intends to focus primarily on questions of method. This is important to keep in mind when, in the course of the response, terms are used that recur in a later context of his philosophical development.

Scholten's topic of discussion is state interference and individual freedom, which comes down to a problem concerning the relation between legality and morality. Scholten, who is a representative of Freiburg neo-Kantianism in the philosophy of legality (1922a: 32), begins with a discussion of legality. In this school legality is taken to be a feature of culture, which is a "relation sphere" (1922a: 32), i.e. its meaning is gauged in relation to human valuation practice. Here a distinction is made with respect to legality between its *being, viz.* factual presence, psychical will, etc., and its *meaning (zin)*, namely as norm. Accordingly, the science of legality, as Scholten has it, avails itself of two methods: a causal psychological-sociological method, to account for the knowledge of the being

---

107 Cf. Dooyeweerd 1922a; also Verburg 1989: 29-31 and Henderson 1994: 40-46. *In this section* I shall refer to Dooyeweerd's text simply as '1922a'. For matters juridical in this text, Dooyeweerd uses the term 'recht'—as in 'recht en moraliteit', 'rechtsbegrip', 'rechtsidee'. To avoid confusion with 'law' (in Dutch 'wet') I shall, following Henderson, use the term 'legality' throughout as translation of 'recht', such as 'legality and morality', 'concept of legality' and 'idea of legality', respectively.

of legality from its factual, psychical-imperative side, and a teleological method, which deals with the knowledge of the meaning of legality, as norm.

This "dualism of method" (1922a: 33), or "two methods of ordering" (1922a: 32), elicits Dooyeweerd's first criticism. For him, the first condition of a science is that its object of knowledge conforms to 'the postulate of uniformity' (*postulaat van de Einheitlichkeit*). This precludes there being two juridical methods. To avoid the possible misunderstanding of taking Dooyeweerd's denial of a pluralism of method as favouring Marburg idealism (in view of the latter's monistic procedure of allowing for only one method for all of the sciences), he states this explicitly, and then immediately adds the remark that the postulate of uniformity retains its validity from "the standpoint of transcendental realism" (1922a: 32). This is the characterization of his own and Vollenhoven's position, as we saw. In "Hegel in our elementary schools?" (1921), Vollenhoven had replaced his initial (Marburg-like) view of a general unity of method for all the (natural) sciences, with a view that reckoned with "diverse domains of validity of logical norms" (*op. cit.*: 85). We interpreted this (cf. chapter 2) as underscoring a fundamental diversity of domains of science, most naturally secured by specifying a metalogical ideal for a science in regard to its specific domain, pursued by a fitting method. Dooyeweerd's mention of a 'postulate of uniformity', as requirement of a specific science, is precisely in line with this interpretation of Vollenhoven, even though Vollenhoven does not expressly speak of a 'postulate' in this connection.

Scholten's distinction between the two senses in which 'legality' is taken, *viz.* as *being* and as *meaning*, in correlation with his dualism of method, occasions another flat disagreement on the part of Dooyeweerd, who had forewarned that he would have "immanent criticism" (1922a: 32) to offer. Dooyeweerd states categorically: (i) when legality is taken to be at once fact and norm, this sins against the logical principle of identity; (ii) 'being' and 'meaning' (Dooyeweerd uses the term 'ought' (*behoren*) at this point, but the context suggests this is meant as a synonym for 'meaning') are "two exclusive forms of thought, which, in my opinion, correspond to two exclusive primal forms (*oervormen*) in the objective sphere of the divine Cosmos" (1922a: 33); and (iii) one needs to make a choice, "conditioned, in my opinion, by metaphysical objectivity", the choice being in favour of holding legality to be exclusively *norm* (1922a: 33). On each point a brief remark.

The first point, about the double meaning of 'legality' being contrary to the principle of identity, must be more than a merely semantic criticism. For that would hold for most words used in a language. Dooyeweerd voices the said objections in connection with the "weak spot" in working with two "juridical methods" (1922a: 33). In other words, a consequence of the methodological postulate of uniformity is that the characterization of *the domain in which the method is applied* calls for a basic unity of meaning. In that sense a dualism of methods, such as Scholten defends, undercuts the *logical* identity of 'legality'.[108]

The second disagreement raises two points. In the first place it proceeds from the difference between 'thought forms' and 'forms in the objective sphere' to which the former are correlated. This reminds one immediately of Vollenhoven's distinction between thought and being, whereby the former involves (psychical) thought processes calling for the guidance of norms, and the latter is the given that is foreign to thought, hence is extra-mental. In the second place, Dooyeweerd holds that the distinction in thought forms between 'being' and 'meaning' (or 'is' and 'ought'), corresponds to 'two primal forms in the objective sphere'. The fact of dealing with two 'thought forms', i.e. two *concepts*—or, more accurately, two forms of adequate concepts—has been argued in connection with the distinctness of the two methods of studying legality. The 'primal forms' to which these concepts correspond must be the relevant *extra-mental ideas* in the metaphysical world. The objective sphere, after all, is that of the "divine Cosmos" (1922a: 33). And this metaphysical world has an ideational part, involving the mind (or 'Counsel') of God

---

108   It may be useful to comment on the use of 'logic' here. Vollenhoven, from the start, correlates logical norms to psychical acts of knowing. In his long letter to F.W. Grosheide, 16 November 1921, he states: "*Logical* over against aesthetical, ethical etc. 'means' everything that *can* be examined according to the norms of our thought in the broad sense of consciousness . . . [according to truth and falsehood]." This is consistent with his early thought in general. Examination that takes place according to norms involves an essential factor of (formal) organization that is applied to content entertained in thought. But the examination is scientific only if the organization itself makes use of carefully chosen categories and forms of judgments, and the content is not psychically fleeting but consists of terms representing distinct meanings (mental material), such as Vollenhoven advanced by means of *Gegenstandstheorie*. The latter provides for terms and complexes (propositions). In logic norms hold for concept formation, the predication of judgment and the drawing of conclusions, and in its methical organization merges with scientific method. To illustrate: Christoph Sigwart's *Logik*, (cf. also footnote 110 below) consists of two volumes; the first is entitled "The doctrine of judgment, of concept and of conclusion", the second, "The doctrine of method". Given the contact between the brothers-in-law at the time, there is no reason to expect Dooyeweerd to have had a different understanding of logic. In the manuscript discussed in the next section Dooyeweerd states: "we limit genuine pure logic to the logical system of pure categories and pure forms of judgment." This locks *pure* logic into the formal side of knowledge.

and a factual cosmological part. Dooyeweerd's characterization suggests the ideational part, the *idea of legality*.

We will come across the term 'divine Cosmos'[109] in other early work of Dooyeweerd, in contexts that are not as explicit as is the case here. In speaking of "primal forms in the objective sphere" (1922a: 33) one is hard put to suggest an interpretation other than the metaphysical one that is also in the early Vollenhoven, especially since Dooyeweerd here also speaks of "metaphysical objectivity" (1922a: 33). There will be occasion below to remind ourselves of the metaphysics operative here, and also that besides this evidence of 'metaphysical realism', there is also a metalogical realism of knowledge in what Dooyeweerd will call 'the *Gegenstand*-sphere'. However, the latter term does not occur here in the discussion with Scholten.

The third point of disagreement is a follow-up of the other two, *viz.* to choose which of the two uses of 'legality' is appropriate. In Dooyeweerd's opinion that choice falls to *norm*. He appeals to the condition of metaphysical objectivity, without saying what that is. Again, if we follow a Vollenhovian train of thought we get a very viable interpretation. The alternative is between an understanding of legality as something factual as over against something normative. If the idea of legality controls something factual, then legality is naturalized, and the science of legality would be 'denatured' to be a natural science or a psychology (1922a: 33). This is "absolutely impossible" (1922a: 33) for Dooyeweerd. But if the idea of legality controls something normative, then it is relevant to the human agent, and hence to human culture. There is an alternative of choice here, and the choice falls to the human being, not to the non-human natural world. This hard 'metaphysical' difference is part and parcel of Vollenhoven's early thought.

A final remark is relevant in this connection. The phrase 'idea of legality' (that we used above) does not actually occur in this part of Dooyeweerd's text. So perhaps we are guilty of a biased reading. But further on, Dooyeweerd makes a puzzling statement. He states that he "*repeats again*, . . . that he acknowledges, without reservation, a valuation of legality according to the *idea of legality*" (1922a: 35; emphases added). Looking back, the only point in his response where the idea of legality could have been implied (since the phrase does not occur there) is where we have

---

109 The expression "divine Cosmos" is not unambiguous. The Reformed tradition precludes its being interpreted as holding that the cosmos is a divinity in its own right. Our 'Vollenhovian' interpretation takes it to mean the world's being upheld by the extramental ideas, which implicate the mind of God. But to my knowledge, the expression itself never occurs in Vollenhoven.

made it explicit in the above discussion in connection with metaphysics. Continuing his response, Dooyeweerd now pursues the choice made for legality as norm, whereby the teleological method is the appropriate method for the science of legality. This method makes essential use of the means-end schema, whereby legality as means serves ethics as end (cf. 1922a: 34). (This is how Scholten gets the part of ethics and freedom into his discussion.) The teleological method serves to explicate the *concept of legality*. But behind the logic of this method, "behind the whole Freiburg logic of legality" (1922a: 35), there is "the view of the concept of legality as being a relation concept" (*ibid.*). This is consistent with the Freiburg view of culture as being a "relation-sphere" (1922a: 32). An unsuspecting reader would probably pass this somewhat 'formal' topic by. But here the term *modal* also occurs for the first time. In light of later developments this term ought not to be ignored. So let us review Dooyeweerd's discussion here more carefully.

How does one attain a concept of legality when the term 'legality' is interpreted as a meaning, not a fact? Scholten advances, in line with the Freiburg approach, the relation of legality as being a 'modal relation'. The term is taken from Christoph Sigwart, says Dooyeweerd, whereby "the subject places legality as a value in relation to itself".[110] This view is, in

---

110 The work of Christoph Sigwart here meant is his *Logik*, 2 volumes, 4th edition edited by Heinrich Maier (cf. Sigwart 1922), which was popular at the time. Vollenhoven had quoted Sigwart in his dissertation to endorse his interpretation of the principles of logic as norms (cf. Vollenhoven 1918a: 15). Sigwart speaks of *modal relations* as follows. All predicates of modal relations are such as express a relation to one's knowing (*op. cit.*, I: 131). Modal relations themselves are unique, in being other than causal relations. "Mit keiner andern Relation vergleichbar ist diejenige, in der die *Objecte unseres subjektiven Tuns*, unseres Anschauens und Denkens wie unseres Begehrens und Wollens zu uns selbst, als dem Subjekte geistiger Tätigkeit stehen." (*ibid.*, 48) In other words, a modal relation concerns that relation in which the objects of our mental acts stand to us, i.e. objects of discerning, thought, desire etc. We see at once that this concerns intra-mental acts and their intra-mental objects. "Nennen wir diese Klasse von Relationen mit einer Erweiterung des kantischen Sprachgebrauchs die *modalen*: so fallen darunter alle Beziehungen, in welche wir Objecte zu uns setzen, sofern wir sie vorstellen, und als vorgestellte begehren, wünschen, in ihrem Werte für uns beurteilen" (*ibid.*, 49). So it is difficult to see any important difference between these 'modal relations' and the awareness (via the concrete and the analytical intuition) of *Gegenstände* that is so prominent in Vollenhoven's early thought (cf. the discussion in chapter 2). Though prominent, they are not exclusive. Vollenhoven's 'realism' does not deny a place to transcendent (extra-mental) objects that can be correlated to *Gegenstände*, though there are *Gegenstände* that lack such correlation (such as 'wooden irons', 'square circles', etc.). So if 'modal relations' are taken to be the end-all and be-all in any specific context, then one's standpoint is intra-mental, i.e. 'idealist' (in some sense), not realist. As long as the extra-mental is acknowledged, the intra-mental is not exclusive, and so the intra-mental 'modal relation' needs to reckon

Dooyeweerd's relentless judgment, "a subjective view of legality as relation" (1922a: 35)—in other words, difficult for a 'realist' to accept—but also logically untenable and even self-destructive for the science of legality. How does Dooyeweerd argue this?

To refer to the meaning of legality as being (essentially and exclusively) a 'modal relation' makes it rather tenuous. For then, indeed, it is only in relation to the subject in the context of culture that legality has value, with the character of norm, of 'holding for,' as valued. The 'subject' that is relevant here is the culturally valuing agent who intuits values. In line with this valuation, the concept—i.e. the adequate concept—of legality is then based on this 'modal relation' of agent and intra-mental content. If I may venture an illustration, traffic laws have meaning or status of legality only for the culture (the culturally valuing subject) that has a need for roads and vehicles. Do traffic laws then have validity/legality only as shared values in the specific situation in which they are relevant?

Dooyeweerd now argues: if I think of the relation of legality as holding between a 'subject of legality' and another 'subject of legality'[111] (in our illustration: two persons driving on the road) *or* if I think of the relation of legality as holding between 'objects of legality', such as a connection of goals (again in our illustration: traffic lights that signal when to stop and go) *or* if I think of the relation of legality as holding between a 'subject of legality' and an 'object of legality' (our driver, who is expected to behave on the road as indicated by the traffic lights), then "in each of these [three] forms the two terms [whether the subjects or objects] of the relation must lie outside of [the scope or meaning of] legality" (1922a: 35). Dooyeweerd now expects the reader to understand why this is so, for he does not say so explicitly. But it follows from the interpretation of legality being a 'modal [and hence intra-mental] relation'. For, then, only through the valuing of legality on the part of the meaning attributing subject (the valuing agent) is there an impinging norm here; in other words, the specific persons (car drivers) or the distinct goals (traffic lights) *as such* have nothing of legality about them. For Dooyeweerd this is tantamount to considering these specific persons and distinct goals as "terms of the relation that lie outside of [the modal relation of] legality" (*ibid.*). But if such participating persons and things cannot be considered terms of the relation of legality, then their characterization as 'subjects of

---

with something other than what is present in its own context. We will see, in subsequent discussion, that this is important to Vollenhoven and Dooyeweerd as they develop 'Reformed philosophy'.

111 These 'subjects' clearly cannot merely be the culturally valuing subjects, but must also be specific participants of culture.

legality' and 'objects of legality', respectively, goes by the board. It is in that sense that Dooyeweerd speaks of a 'logically untenable' situation.

Dooyeweerd also states that this destroys the science of legality. This science, he maintains, needs to be able to refer to the 'positivity of legality'. The science of legality does not exhaust itself in contemplating legality only as modal relation of valuing, which is metalogical in its focus on valuation. It needs to address cases ('positivities') of legality (like our example of traffic laws), so as to come to an (adequate) *concept* of legality. But then one needs subjects and/or objects of legality to embody the 'positivities' of legality. The view of legality as 'modal relation' does not adequately allow for this (cf. *ibid.*). The destruction of the positivity of legality is also to destroy "its logical independence, its sovereignty" (*ibid.*).

This logical independence or sovereignty of legality is also not explained directly. But when compared to ethics, it gains in meaning. Scholten links ethics to legality in the teleological approach of linking ends to means. The moral norm is freely posited, Kantian-wise, by the autonomous subject, but for Dooyeweerd this is tantamount to "destroying the objective character of the [moral] norm" (1922a: 36). Autonomy in this sense cannot be maintained (1922a: 37). Dooyeweerd concludes that there is an ethical standpoint and there is a standpoint of legality, but one cannot be positioned on both standpoints at once. "Both systems [*stelsels*] are each in itself sovereign, and can never be such simultaneously. For the moralist, who positions himself on an ethical standpoint, legality as a logically independent order does not exist, and vice versa" (*ibid.*).

The echo of a Kuyperian 'sphere sovereignty' should not be taken as leading clue here. Now I do believe that it would have been difficult *not* to think of Kuyper when the phrase 'sphere sovereignty' occurs, at least given Dooyeweerd's time and place. But it must have been accompanied, so I tend to think, by a sense of (remarkable) coincidence, *viz.* that Kuyper's phrase, itself used only in a practical and societal context, is usable in a scientific, methodological one. This 'coincidence' first came to expression in Vollenhoven, when, in developing his metalogical outline, he spoke (in 1921) of "the 'sovereignty (of regulation, not of creation) in its own sphere'."[112] He there defends a 'dualism of idea and concept'. An idea is an extra-mental essence, while a concept represents the knowledge of the idea, in process of becoming adequate with respect to it, and this 'becoming adequate' takes place in its own sphere according to an appropriate method. Thus, applying this to Dooyeweerd's discussion, when the idea of legality is acknowledged—as he explicitly does (cf. 1922a:

---

112   Vollenhoven 1921c: 80.

35)—one is in a position to develop conceptual knowledge of legality, being guided by the metalogical intuition of the adequate concept of *this* idea. But when the idea of morality is acknowledged, one is in a position to develop ethical knowledge, being in turn guided by the metalogical intuition of the adequate *moral* concept. Distinct ideas control, through the corresponding adequate concepts, distinct conceptual procedures of thought. These ideas are the warrant for the "metaphysical objectivity", spoken of earlier, "in the objective sphere of the divine Cosmos" (*op. cit.*: 33). Hence these procedures are sovereign only in the light of the relevant idea and adequate concept. Thus, while there is (as Vollenhoven expresses) a "*certain* autonomy in its own sphere",[113] this is not due to an activation or evaluation by an autonomous subject, nor is it here directly theistically grounded—as in Kuyper, in being divinely delegated—but it is in virtue of the transcendental realist acceptance of the heteronomy of idea and adequate concept. Dooyeweerd does not specifically mention any intuition (metalogical or metaphysical) in his response, but this would appear to be implicit in the use of 'concept and idea'. The agreement with Vollenhoven is hard to miss once one is aware of the main features of his early thought.[114]

The concluding point of Dooyeweerd's discussion merits mention. Over against Scholten's fear that legality (as represented by the state) and

---

113   Vollenhoven 1921c: 80 (emphasis added).

114   M.E. Verburg maintains: "It was in this response that Dooyeweerd for the first time put in the spotlight immanent criticism and modal sovereignty." Verburg is probably correct about Dooyeweerd's emphasizing immanent criticism (1922a: 32), but it comes as no surprise. Vollenhoven had applied it very explicitly in the historical parts of his dissertation. In its introduction Vollenhoven said: "history will have to render its always to be appreciated guidance" (Vollenhoven 1918a: 3) in connection with tracing the metaphysical roots of mathematical empiricism, formalism and intuitionism. Also Vollenhoven emphasized the lack of immanent criticism in T. Hoekstra's *Geschiedenis der Philosophie I* [History of Philosophy I] (cf. Hoekstra 1921) in his critical review of it, published in January 1922; cf. Vollenhoven 1922a: 293-301. Perhaps this review stimulated Dooyeweerd to make a statement of his own about immanent criticism (cf. Dooyeweerd 1922b1), such as is found in the first of the three unpublished manuscripts, referred to in the next section below, and published in Verburg 1989: 32-33. But Verburg's reference to "modal sovereignty" (here in its characteristic sense) in Dooyeweerd, is quite untenable: (i) the phrase as such does not occur; (ii) 'sovereignty' needs to be interpreted *within the present context and period*, which strongly suggests the limited meaning of: 'objectively founded scientific method'; (iii) 'modal' occurs in the phrase "modal relation" that is *criticised* by Dooyeweerd, as being too subjective and logically untenable as the provenance of norms, in the very quotation given by Verburg at this point (cf. Verburg 1989: 31); and (iv) as long as Dooyeweerd avers adherence to (transcendental or critical) realism, it is inconsistent to *privilege* anything 'modal'. Dooyeweerd's criticism of 'modal relation' returns in the next document discussed below.

morality might conflict, Dooyeweerd maintains quite strongly that "a conflict between legality and morality is impossible" (1922a: 37), at least as concerns the critical-logical problem of Scholten's paper. Dooyeweerd does allow for the possibility of a psychological conflict in the individual person regarding moral duty and legal duty. But this conflict can be 'eliminated' when a specific conflict is considered in the light of one's conscience, or perhaps by accepting a higher authority (such as "divine revelation"; 1922a: 38) and one makes a choice. One must not let psychology dictate a relation between legality and morality, for that would only 'naturalize' the whole area of norms. The personal-psychological choice must be kept distinct from metalogical-conceptual understanding. This distinction too is present in Vollenhoven, viz. between the Self and organism of science. Dooyeweerd concludes: the religious norm, namely, "One ought to obey God rather than men", has higher authority than either legality or morality. This reminds one of the religious (theistic) concern present in the background of the early common endeavour of Vollenhoven and Dooyeweerd.

The above discussion has, I believe, removed any reasonable doubt about the early intellectual relation between Vollenhoven and Dooyeweerd. Dooyeweerd is conditioning and testing his wings in the context provided by Vollenhoven. We emphasize again that Dooyeweerd has his own focus and pursues his own topical interests. This is what gives even this early work its distinct value. But the recognizable philosophical strategy is that of the early Vollenhoven. We shall continue to survey Dooyeweerd's remaining early work, only this will now be more selective. We shall highlight the relevant factors that bear upon the continuing intellectual relations between these men.

4. From the third of three unpublished manuscripts
In 1921 and 1922 Dooyeweerd conducted three studies in which he researched the works of prominent legal theorists of the time. This work was never published, though parts of the second and third study did find their way, where necessary adapted, into later publications. In the first study,[115] the work of Rudolf Stammler, a legal theorist of the Marburg neo-Kantian school, is the main focus of attention. In the second

---

115 This first study is entitled: "Een methodologische inleiding in de geschiedenis der rechtsphilosophie in het begin der XXe eeuw" [A methodological introduction to the history of legal philosophy in the beginning of the 20th century] (cf. Dooyeweerd 1922b). It is dated (presumably its completion date) 14 April 1922. Cf. Henderson 1994: 55-64; also Verburg 1989: 32-33.

study,[116] the attention shifts to the Freiburg or Baden school of neo-Kantianism. Mention is made of Wilhelm Windelband, Heinrich Rickert, Emil Lask, and finally Gustaf Radbruch, to whom the greater part of this second study is devoted. The third study[117] discusses (in the main) the work of the school of Hans Kelsen. Dooyeweerd's chief aim is to take a stand in the philosophy of legality by means of a critical discussion of the works of prominent theorists at the time. At the same time this entailed a confrontation with neo-Kantianism in general, which was the main philosophical influence in the Netherlands after the first World War.

The third of these three studies, "Normative legal doctrine", attained the most definitive form. It was stencilled, with intentions to publish (at least Dooyeweerd refers to it in his inaugural address as "not yet published"; cf. the last footnote above). Whatever its exact date (again, cf. the last note above) it falls close in time to the discussion with Scholten. For example, on pp. 53-54 we find a more explicit criticism of the view of norms as grounded in 'modal relations' (to which we will return below) and references to 'legal positivities', 'legal concept', 'legal idea', the '*Einheitlichkeit* [uniformity] of legality', etc., much in the spirit of the discussion with Scholten.

Now "Normative legal doctrine" contains an extensive section on epistemology, from which Verburg has selected and published a chief part in his biography of Dooyeweerd.[118] We shall pause to review this text fragment, to see what it implies as to the Vollenhoven-Dooyeweerd contact. We should also get a heightened sense of their use of "*Gegenstand*" in this period, especially when placing the cited passage in a larger context.

---

116 "De Badensche School" [The Baden school] (cf. Dooyeweerd 1922c). Parts or all of pages 33-34, 42-46, 88, 93-97 and 100 of this Baden manuscript were used, adapted, on pages 43-49 (discussion of details) and 101-104 (corresponding endnotes) of Dooyeweerd's inaugural address, *The Significance of the Law-idea for Jurisprudence and Legal Philosophy* (Dooyeweerd 1926d). Cf. Henderson 1994: 64-78.

117 "Normatieve rechtsleer. Een kritisch-methodologische onderzoeking naar Kelsen's normatieve rechtsbeschouwing" [Normative legal doctrine. A critical methodological investigation into Kelsen's normative view of legality] (stencilled; cf. Dooyeweerd 1922d). Cf. Henderson 1994: 78-86; Verburg 1989: 33-39. Henderson reports that this text was stencilled by the Kuyper Foundation, probably in 1923. The text also refers to a work by Felix Kaufmann that appeared in 1922 ("this year"; cf. this text: 43). Dooyeweerd mentions this third study in his inaugural address, and dates it 1921 (Dooyeweerd 1926d: 91, note 5). This same date occurs in the Dooyeweerd bibliography in Van Dijk 1961: 71. But Verburg dates the work 1922. (I take this to be essentially correct.) The pages 74-88 were used in Dooyeweerd 1926c, i.e. "Calvinisme contra Neo-Kantianisme", *Tijdschrift voor Wijsbegeerte* 20 (1926), 29-74 (namely pp. 34-59).

118 This is Dooyeweerd 1922d1; the passage translated here is on pp. 34-35; the original typescript, p. 45.

The first part of this passage can be quoted in full. It reads as follows (in my translation, with paragraph numbers added to facilitate reference).

(§1) It now remains to give an account of our view. The cosmic sphere of that which is foreign to thought is after all a postulate of realism itself, which, being a critical epistemological position, is grounded in a *view of life* [*levensbeschouwing*], that does not lend itself to further proof.

(§2) However, the assertion that the foreignness is controlled by *cosmic* categories is not commonly accepted in realism, as far as I know. It [the assertion] arises through a critical awareness, that in the so-called "metaphysical" sphere, logical distinctions are not to be accepted on pain of committing the old, naive mistake of the [inwardly] repeating [*verdubbelende*] "copy theory". The *Gegenstand*-sphere, defended above, is a different case. Contrary to the neo-Kantians, including Lask, the *Gegenstand*-sphere is taken to be a-logical, for we limit genuine pure logic to the logical system of pure categories and pure forms of judgment.

(§3) The psychologically oriented epistemology in the first place asks: "Why [posit] a *Gegenstand*-sphere?" We reply, in agreement with the Kantians: "Because we cannot and may not withdraw reality, with all of its problems, from the control of pure thought, [and] because we must find a foundation for the logically immanent meaning of judgments, which cannot lie in the psychology of experience.

(§4) But, the idealism that is oriented to Kant asks: "Why do you deny that the *Gegenstand*-sphere has a logical character? What other characteristic, other than a logical one, could the *Gegenstand*-sphere have, when you, rightly, pluck it away from the entanglement of psychology?"

(§5) Our reply is: The reason why we deny that the *Gegenstand*-sphere has a transcendental-logical character is because we reject the dogma of the autonomy of thought, because we attribute to Kant's Copernican turn not a universal but only a limited meaning, namely for the logic of relations.

(§6) Furthermore, [we deny that the *Gegenstand*-sphere has a transcendental-logical character] because the *Gegenstand*, taken up in thought in the system of the *logos* by means of the logical categories, would [then] have to be allotted—were it to lack an a-logical ideal origin—either to the creative power of thought itself (Marburgers), which we reject, or to *experience* (Hume, Locke, etc.), which would undermine the foundations of logic, or to metaphysics, which would rob logic of its transcendent meaning (Aristotle) and lead to naive realism.

(§7) The ideational *Gegenstand*-sphere is necessary for us as material for the judgment of logic, which [judgment] postulates a transcendent *Gegenstand* according to its immanent meaning, which cannot itself in turn be of a logical nature. We reject Kant's and Lask's distinction between *formal* and *transcendental* logic; not however to accede to logic, as do the Marburgers, a *Gegenstand* creating function, but only to grant the material of thought as non-psychological, a-logical and non-metaphysical, its place in a *metalogical Gegenstand-sphere*.

The first paragraph speaks of "our view" being that of *critical realism*, and we have found enough indications to know that this is how the early position of Vollenhoven, and Dooyeweerd who sides with it, is characterized by them. Intrinsic to the position is the thought-being polarity that was basic to Vollenhoven in his dissertation. Being is that which is other than thought, hence foreign to thought. It concerns the extra-mental reality that transcends consciousness, which any critical realism needs to accept, as grounded in concrete existence or a life-view.

The reference to a life-view is precisely to motivate the acceptance of a 'cosmic sphere'. There can hardly be a significant difference between Dooyeweerd's emphasis on life- and worldview and Vollenhoven's penchant for metaphysics, a term which Dooyeweerd too (as we found) does not eschew.[119] In the first of the three studies, mentioned above, Dooyeweerd also emphasized the fundamental position of a life-view, to which is correlated a worldview.

The foreignness to thought hangs together with the 'cosmic sphere', in connection with which 'cosmic categories' (§2) are accepted as entailed by the 'postulate of realism'. Dooyeweerd's meaning here is not immediately clear. How can foreignness be controlled by categories? But the sentence about the 'copy theory' throws light on the situation. One speaks of 'naïve realism' when, as in empiricism, knowledge is taken to be a direct reflection of the facts. But this simply duplicates content without being distinctive in terms of truth (predication). That is why in *critical* realism, as Vollenhoven had insisted in his dissertation, knowledge is taken to be a result of an assimilation or working over of the given, which means that the role of the knowing subject is more than merely being receptive. There must be an exercise of thought, but this is not to apply 'logical distinctions' to the cosmic or metaphysical sphere itself. Logical principles apply to and hold for the knowledge (judgments and concepts) that result from the working over of the given (as we found in chapter 2). They don't hold for the given as such. In its own cosmic or metaphysical sphere, the given (as that which is foreign or other) is *governed by ideas*.

Dooyeweerd's meaning here is 'Vollenhovian', all the more so when he says that realism is not commonly taken in a sense that includes foreignness or otherness. This echoes Vollenhoven's statement about the difficulty, in neo-Kantianism, of accepting ideas in the cosmically relevant

---

119   Cf. our earlier remark at the end of section III.C.2 above, and also the discussion with Scholten ['divine Cosmos'] in section III.C.3. For more on 'worldview' (to use the more standard expression) in Dooyeweerd, cf. Verburg 1989: 32-33.

sense, for doing so implies accepting "thoughts of God".[120]

The discussion then shifts to the topic of a '*Gegenstand*-sphere'. The *Gegenstand* concerns the 'material of thought' (§7), and this material is such that the *Gegenstand*-sphere is said to be of a 'metalogical' character (§7). We need hardly repeat that Vollenhoven from the start worked with a '*Gegenstandstheorie*', and that he outlined further metalogical developments with regard to it in his "Hegel-article" of July 1921. What needs discussion is grasping Dooyeweerd's meaning and comparing this to what we know of Vollenhoven at the time.

The discussion is considerably aided by having available a succinct overview of Vollenhoven's early position in the context of critical realism. We give the following overview, which is in close agreement, though in an adjusted format, with the last two figures given in chapter 2.

The chief parameters of critical realism[121]

	Holy Spirit	Logos	Counsel of God
Principles of validity	Ideal reality of norms or values	Source of rationality	Ideal reality of general ideas
Transcendental	Mentality, qualities of subject of obligated Self (real)	Organism of the sciences (metalogical)	Thing-laws controlling coherence and development (r.)
Empirical	Psycho-physical organization with forms of sensibility	Interaction of subject and object; knowledge; judgments and concepts (logical forms)	Things and forces, physical and psychical; abs. sp.-time
	Self (human beings)	Knowledge/Science	World (Metaphysics)

From the start Dooyeweerd takes the *Gegenstand*-sphere to be a-logical (§2), that is to say, the material content of thought is not itself of a logi-

---

120 Vollenhoven 1921c: 86. Of course Dooyeweerd's referring to 'cosmic categories' and Vollenhoven to 'ideas' (of distinctive being) may imply a difference in connotation. Vollenhoven's early use included both 'essences' (general ideas) and 'thing-laws' (individuated ideas). It may be that Dooyeweerd is especially thinking of the determination of 'domains' of reality or of culture, which could then be in terms of 'cosmic categories', in correlation with the adequate concepts of a science (whether this be natural or value science), as discerned by the metalogical intuition. But this of course does not constitute a difficulty for Vollenhoven.

121 The reader may wish to consult section III.G.1. below for a summary explanation of what the diagram intends to portray.

cal nature. Logic, at least 'genuine pure logic', is limited to "the logical system of the pure categories and pure forms of judgment" (§2). Logic is oriented to knowledge (concepts and judgments) to the extent that knowledge accords with logical principles. This does not as such determine the 'material of thought' that is 'worked into' knowledge, for that content is 'critically produced' in the merging of the (objective) factor of the given and its (subjective) organization by the knowing subject. Logic on the other hand deals with categories and forms of judgments. Now, though Vollenhoven does not use the term '*Gegenstand*-sphere', the latter's 'a-logical' character and its characterization as 'metalogical' by Dooyeweerd does place it where Vollenhoven speaks of the 'organism of the sciences'. As will become clear, the *Gegenstand*-sphere embodies the content of scientific knowledge.

Dooyeweerd then makes certain statements, in reaction to possible epistemological objections, which clarify his meaning. First, from the (imagined) side of psychologism (§3), the question is raised about the very need of a *Gegenstand*-sphere. Dooyeweerd's two-pronged response emphasizes the relevance of both the objective and the subjective sides that come together in knowledge. Psychologism is oriented to the experiencing subject. But such an approach does not allow thought to tackle problems of reality. On the other hand, the logically organized immanent meaning of a judgment, i.e. the objective content of knowledge, calls for a foundation that the psychology of experience cannot provide. In other words, the *Gegenstand*-sphere is required to account for a feature of knowledge that cannot be identified with the mere psychological presence of the subject nor with the mere cosmological presence of the given object (that is foreign to thought)—though both are present and 'come together' in the knowledge situation—nor is logic able to provide for this feature, for logic concerns the *form* of thought and does not directly affect the epistemic character of its content or material. Hence, in reference to the diagram above, the *Gegenstand*-sphere belongs neither to the side of the Self nor to that of the World. It is relevant to knowledge or science, but not to its logical side, which is formal, but to the content or material of knowledge.

The second imagined objection comes from Kantian idealism (§§4, 5 and 6). They are said to agree with the critique levelled at psychologism, but they object to denying that the character of the *Gegenstand*-sphere is logical. But what other character could it have? (§4)

Dooyeweerd's reply here is again two-pronged. In the first place, the characterization of the *Gegenstand*-sphere as being logical, is linked by

Dooyeweerd to Kant's so-called Copernican turn. Kant held that knowledge of the world is not acquired merely through the confrontation with the world, but knowledge is validated only in virtue of certain structures of the mind or of consciousness, which structures are grounded in the transcendental unity of apperception of the Self. This supports, or rather is the very expression of, the dogma of the autonomy of thought, and naturally, through it, the logical characterization of the *Gegenstand*-sphere is turned more specifically into a 'transcendental logical' one. Dooyeweerd does give the Copernican turn partial support, which is perhaps difficult to appreciate, for he is not explicit in his reasoning. But if we bring in Vollenhoven's characterization of the Self and thought, an explanation is forthcoming. The denial of the autonomy of thought lies in the denial of the Self being an autonomous source of knowledge. For, if the Self is to fulfil its role of embodying and executing thought, then it first needs to take on the quality of knowing subject, and that calls for submission to (transcendent) norms. (Recall Dooyeweerd's letter to Vollenhoven, discussed above.) Only then is the knowing process validated, when there is submission to norms. The limited meaning Dooyeweerd does however recognize for the Copernican turn has to do with the experiential basis of representations. Here representations are influenced in their formation by the forms of sensibility of the human psycho-physical organization. This is the level of Vollenhoven's 'acquaintance' (*kennen*), and the interaction of the organizing subject and the given object. Here a 'logic of relations' has a useful application, in which the Self, from its psycho-physical side, has a determining role (§5).

This reply (§5) to the objection from the side of Kantian idealism (§4) focussed on denying the supposed 'transcendental logical' characterization of the *Gegenstand*-sphere. It is followed up by a second reply (§6), which asks, where, when the *Gegenstand*-sphere is so characterized, it is to be allotted. Dooyeweerd discerns three options: (i) allotment to the creative power of thought itself (the option of the Marburgers); this is rejected when rejecting the autonomy of thought; (ii) allotment to experience (such as in Locke and Hume); but that undermines the foundations of logic, presumably (so we add) because it allows only for inductive logic, which lacks a priori principles; (iii) allotment to metaphysics. The latter is objected to, for it "rob[s] logic of its transcendent meaning (Aristotle) and lead[s] to naïve realism" (§6). I take Dooyeweerd to mean that this entails a copy-theory (of naïve realism) all over again, which is contrary to logic's own (transcendent) significance (in terms of a priori principles). And of course, à la Vollenhoven, the logical principles have no determining role in metaphysics (as opposed to ideas and/or 'cosmic categories').

So the *Gegenstand* as 'the material of thought' cannot be 'placed' either in direct rapport with the knowing subject and the forms of knowledge (it is *a-logical*) nor is it metaphysically given (it is *non-metaphysical*) and also it does not arise at the experiential level of empirical subject in contact with given phenomena (it is *non-psychological*; cf. §7). One glance at the overview of Vollenhoven's early thought, as given above, and we see immediately how Dooyeweerd's options dovetail with the three realities Vollenhoven identified, *viz.* in connection with the Self, in connection with the World, and in connection with the knowledge relation (of acquaintance) between these. The only remaining 'place' for a *Gegenstand*-sphere is in connection with the organization of knowledge, in terms of the *organism of the sciences*. It is precisely here that Dooyeweerd allots this sphere, for he brings in the '*logos*'.

The organism of the sciences is a 'reality' situated 'between' that of the Self and the World. It is the reality that Vollenhoven sees as warranted by the (divine) *Logos*.[122] Dooyeweerd also brings in the *Logos* when he turns to characterizing the *Gegenstand*'s 'a-logical ideal origin' (§6). Knowledge must clearly abide by logical categories and accord with logical principles. Hence knowledge content is *organized* by the logical categories. But the *content* is still other than the formal means by which it is organized, hence it calls for its own determining principle. That content, as *Gegenstand*, is "taken up in thought *in the system of the logos* by means of logical categories" (§6; emphasis added). Content, or material of thought, has a status that calls for its own recognition, not being 'produced' (whether logically, experientially or metaphysically). It has its own 'categories' by which knowledge content, as entertained in human cognition, is itself systematically organized. (This is specified more particularly below.) Thus the very material that logic organizes necessitates, 'according to its immanent meaning', the 'postulating' of a distinct (Dooyeweerd speaks of 'transcendent'; §7) *Gegenstand*. This is an 'ideational *Gegenstand*-sphere', a '*metalogical Gegenstand-sphere*' (§7), that stands in direct relation to the (divine) *Logos*. Presumably it is in virtue of the connection with the Logos that the *Gegenstand*-sphere is attributed, by postulation, its (own) 'transcendent' status.

So much for the quoted passage. The account of the '*Gegenstand*-

---

122 As has been our practice throughout, we emphasize again that 'Logos' with a capital L always refers to the divine Word-revelation, the second Person of the Trinity, in its specific meaning for knowledge. When written with a small l, 'logos' refers to human cognition or subjective rationality.

sphere' is what is most prominent here. The context that Dooyeweerd assumes for this account conforms to Vollenhoven's outline, which we also found to be relevant for the closely contemporaneous discussion with Scholten. To clinch the 'Vollenhoven connection' we give the following two-sentence quote.[123] This summarizes the main roles of the three-some: thought, *Gegenstand* and cosmos. The quotation also invites reviewing some matters in more detail.

> And so the categories of judgment do not appear [to be], contrary to what the Marburgers assert, a creation of pure autonomous thought, but rather the means by which the *Gegenstand* can enter into thought, although the *Gegenstand* itself, determined according to the categories of essential connection, finds its a-logical origin in the thought-foreign cosmos, which is itself ordered according to the *cosmic categories of thought-foreignness*.
>
> Thus, posed in this way, critical realism consciously adduces the cosmic thought-foreign (less correctly called 'metaphysical') form-material as substrate (*hypokeimenon*) of the ideal *Gegenstand* and the latter in turn as material of the categorial synthesis in the judgment of pure logic.

To summarize: logic (judgment) is required so as to enable the *Gegenstand*, as knowledge content, to be thought, while this knowledge content itself originates from the cosmos, which is itself other than or foreign to thought. Each of these three 'stations' has an input or efficacy, expressed in terms of or controlled by 'categories'. The (subjective) execution of thought is structured according to categories of concepts and judgments. Then, the *Gegenstand* is said to be determined by 'essential connections'. We will see immediately, in the more detailed discussion below, that Dooyeweerd appeals to the (metalogical) intuition by which essences, that enter into essential connections, are viewed (cf. *op. cit.*: 44). But the main presupposition of critical realism is the cosmos as foreign to thought. The categories here are those of "the cosmic unity of connection, wherein no *logical* distinguishing can enter" (*ibid.*). The cosmos, being 'foreign to thought' and thus to be accepted as given, is also Vollenhoven's way of characterizing it. Then we can safely assume that the 'unity of connection' here is that of the *idea*, although this term does not occur here. The categories of this unity, in turn, refer to the basic diversity that is controlled by the idea. The thought-foreign cosmos is the substrate of the *Gegenstand*, as grasped meaning, which is in turn worked over by thought in categories of concepts and judgments.

Dooyeweerd continues the longer text quoted above with the remark that he has some additional referential observations to make about logic in connection with "the system of the sciences" and "the doctrine

---

123   Dooyeweerd 1922d: 44.

of the logical categories".[124] Here we discover details that are taken up—sometimes only temporarily—in later published work of both Dooyeweerd and Vollenhoven. We will cull some relevant information from these observations. This may be material that is original to Dooyeweerd, or it may reflect what came up in the discussions of the brothers-in-law. In any case Dooyeweerd is the first to record it.

a. *Gegenstand*-theory and logic.
The 'critical realist view' that he has defended, says Dooyeweerd, allows for a sharp distinction between logic and theory of knowledge (Dooyeweerd 1922d1: 35). Having rejected the 'autonomy of thought' on the part of the Self, on the basis of which transcendental logic, i.e. (non-empirical) 'material logic' as over against 'formal logic', serves as foundation of the theory of knowledge, the latter needs to be accounted for in another way. 'Pure logic' is relevant to theory of knowledge only as regards its formal side (the form of judgments and concepts). The content of knowledge calls for '*Gegenstand*-theory' (*ibid.*). In the critical realist view, the *Gegenstand* is aligned not with the Self but with the Logos. Here, however, "the *Gegenstand* is not, and cannot be, an element of the Logos [which would have the effect of appealing to a 'higher logic', or perhaps even 'Logos speculation'?; A.T.], but only the in itself a-logical material of the Logos" (*ibid.*).[125]

So *form* and *content* are the two cardinal foci here. (Recall the two

---

124   Verburg 1989: 35. The continuation of the text discussed so far and directly quoted above is on pp. 35-38.

125   One may well note that Vollenhoven and Dooyeweerd will, in time, argue against the Logos doctrine they upheld in their early thought. Vollenhoven motivates a 'Christian logic' negatively through his *criticism* of 'logos-speculation'—cf. his *De Noodzakelijkheid eener Christelijke Logica* [The necessity of a Christian logic] (Vollenhoven 1932b: 1-2)—and Dooyeweerd criticises Kuyper's appeal to the Logos as this occurs in the latter's general view of scientific knowledge—cf. Dooyeweerd 1939. It was part of the climate of the times—encouraged by the scholastic strain in the Protestant Reformed tradition—to honour this scholastic understanding of the Logos. We find it in A. Kuyper, J. Woltjer, H. Bavinck, W. Geesink and V. Hepp, to name but the more prominent, though they did not always hold to nor formulate it uniformly among themselves. The appeal to the Logos in this tradition is clearly theological, against the background of metaphysics. But the term is also used in a more 'secular' or methodological sense, to denote *objective meaning* (or, to be more exact, the principle of rationality of objective meaning) as is evident in Vollenhoven and Dooyeweerd's use. Because their development includes an important feature of self-criticism, it seems more advised to focus on the details of their own understanding rather than on the scarce attestations of affiliation with the older generation. Besides, one would still need to understand their own use to be able to appreciate the relevant affiliation.

sides of the organism of the sciences, formal and material, in Vollenhoven.) Form concerns arrangement, which is achieved by means of categories of concepts and forms of judgments. Thinking is unthinkable without such a function of determinate arranging. Content, in turn, is what is understood, and what comes to be arranged by applications of categories and forms, but it has an 'a-logical' source. What then is the relation between form and content?

Dooyeweerd takes *logic* to be "the system of the categorical determinations of the *Gegenstand* in the judgment" (*ibid.*). This is applicable as long as there is content to determine. But there is also 'pure logic'. It adjudicates over the 'pure categories and pure forms of judgment' used in logic. In other words, the categories and forms of thought, pure (or formal) though they be, now serve in pure logic as content or *Gegenstand* of a higher consideration (*ibid.*). Pure logic treats of the forms of form. So: "Pure logic, as systematic science, needs to be preceded by a *Gegenstand*-theory of the categories and the forms of judgment themselves" (*ibid.*). Is (pure) logic then dependent on *Gegenstand*-theory so as to be provided with its own content of forms?

That would be a hasty conclusion. For *Gegenstand*-theory has a structure, calling for its own categories and judgments. But then logic would appear to precede *Gegenstand*-theory. We end up in a vicious circle of each preceding the other. We break the circle when taking into account the *aim* of *Gegenstand*-theory, as over against that of logic. The aim of pure logic is that of truth, and to that end one needs to retain distinction and difference in relation. But the aim of *Gegenstand*-theory is understanding "the factual [*zakelijke*] unity of the *Gegenstand*, [while] that of pure logic [is grasping] the formal unity of the truths about the *Gegenstand*" (*op. cit.*: 36). This factual unity of the *Gegenstand*, over against the formal unity of pure logic, would appear to emphasize connections in the *Gegenstände* that 'belong together' (so to speak), "essential connections". Thus Dooyeweerd says: "The *Gegenstand*-sphere is . . . the cosmic-form-material, in its ideality, that is predisposed to agitate thought. It is not the *relation*, the logical basis of the *system*, that dominates the structure in the *Gegenstand*-sphere, but the essential connection of the simple in each other" (Dooyeweerd 1922d: 50).[126]

Dooyeweerd offers (elsewhere in "Normatieve rechtsleer"; i.e. in 1922d) an example taken from Edmund Husserl. A triangle is a *Gegenstand*, which can enter into different (logical) judgments, such as "This

---

[126] The distinction of relation and connection is later consolidated in Vollenhoven in two different 'determinants', the 'individual' and the 'modal', respectively; cf. chapter 4.

triangle is equilateral" and "This triangle is equiangular" (Dooyeweerd 1922d: 43). There is logical diversity, but a single *Gegenstand*. Now the triangle, as *Gegenstand*, delineates an "essential connection", for "it marks off a gamut of synthetic judgments a priori" (Dooyeweerd 1922d: 49) in virtue of the togetherness of lines and angles in the triangle. The category of the *highest unity* that is relevant for the essential connection here is that of *space*. Space is an example of a *region category* or *modality*.

Having different aims, *Gegenstand*-theory and pure logic each operate according to a different method. In *Gegenstand*-theory one can only "become conscious of the factual unity of the highest categories of thought through viewing [*schouwen*; or: discerning by beholding intuitively]" (Dooyeweerd 1922d1: 36). This viewing is an apperceptive method of a fundamental kind of 'seeing' or 'discerning'. It should be taken as implying acknowledgment. One apperceives what one understands as belonging together, and so one is able to come to acknowledge the relevant factual unity in the highest categories of the *Gegenstand*-sphere. Following the Freiburger, Emil Lask,[127] Dooyeweerd calls these unities 'region categories', and, through the intuition of viewing, each such regional unity is acknowledged to be of distinct *modality*. In pure logic, on the other hand, the method is different. Here the unity of the categories only counts formally, and one will attempt to come to "the truths about the categories and forms of judgment in a system" (*ibid.*) by taking into account distinction, synthesis and the like.[128]

In the above account we again surmise Vollenhoven's metalogical outline in the background, though details here may be original with Dooyeweerd. At least there is a consistent interpretation if one takes the 'viewing' or 'discerning' (*schouwen*), in Vollenhoven's sense of the *metalogical intuition*, the apperceiving of an endpoint of thought—the 'adequate concept'—as focussing on the unity of a 'domain of validity' (alias 'region category'). M.E. Verburg ventures to guess that the use of "schouwen", that occurs here in Dooyeweerd ("for the first time", he states), was probably borrowed from Husserl. Now Husserl's name, as we saw, does occur here, but it is often in criticism (cf. *op. cit.*: 37). Would Dooyeweerd then attribute the same meaning to the term as found in Husserl?

Apart from the general unlikelihood, in view of Dooyeweerd's ad-

---

[127] Verburg makes note of the fact that Dooyeweerd felt an affinity towards the work of Emil Lask, who died in 1915 at the age of forty, a casualty of World War I; cf. Verburg 1989: 38.

[128] Elsewhere in this paper Dooyeweerd lists, as *formal categories:* identity, diversity, relation, continuity and system; as *pure forms of judgment* he lists: analysis, synthesis, affirmation and denial, hypothesis and categorical explanation; cf. Dooyeweerd 1922d1: 37.

herence to 'critical realism', there are at least two specific counts against this guess. In the first place, there is a much greater likelihood that its meaning is 'borrowed' from Vollenhoven, who introduced it explicitly as metalogical intuition in 1921. In the second place, Vollenhoven's introduction of the term includes a remark about a difference from Husserl's use. Husserl's *Wesensschau* is the viewing of an intended correlate of an act, a phenomenal content not requiring support of any transcendent object. When Husserl's thought took an idealist turn, as first became evident in his "Philosophy as rigorous science" (cf. Husserl 1911), his notion of a phenomenon merged appearance and representation. Now while there are 'fulfilled' phenomena, as over against 'unfulfilled' ones, there are no objects independent of consciousness. (In comparison to Sigwart, it is as if Sigwart's 'modal relation' has taken on primary significance in Husserl; Dooyeweerd, we will see presently, continues to criticize this use of 'modal relation'.) Thus Husserl's intuition is for Vollenhoven "purely formalistic".[129] Vollenhoven, contrary to Husserl, does recognize the transcendent object, considering it to be foreign to thought, warranted by ideas, and as a factor relevant to the content of thought. Dooyeweerd's being so forthright about 'cosmic categories' and 'foreignness', puts him in league with Vollenhoven, not Husserl.[130] (However, in Dooyeweerd's next paper we will indeed recognize a more distinct influence of transcendental phenomenology.)

b. Cosmic Selfhood; 'modal relation'
The emphasis on the Selfhood as being cosmic, as over against a transcendental or empirical subjectivity (or other qualities of subjectivity), is another point that underscores agreement with Vollenhoven. Dooyeweerd remarks that, from the realist standpoint, the intuitive viewing (apperception) needs to precede any logical thought or logical distinction, when acquiring systematic knowledge. This naturally needs to be

---

129   Vollenhoven 1921c: 81, note 1. As to Husserl, see De Boer 1966, especially his discussion of the transition in Husserl from descriptive psychology to transcendental phenomenology in the period 1901-1910, pp. 353 ff.

130   Dooyeweerd even makes a specific point of this in "Normatieve rechtsleer". Husserl, he says, "rejects the cosmically ordered foreignness" and "confuses the *Gegenstand*-sphere with pure logic" (Dooyeweerd 1922d: 44). The latter is particularly apposite in connection with the intuition, confirming the characterization given by Vollenhoven, namely of its being "purely formalistic" in Husserl. We add, what is stated explicitly in chapter 2, that the acknowledgment of the cosmos, as foreign to thought and warranted by the idea, itself calls for a 'metaphysical intuition'. In a critical remark about relativism's dynamism of thought, Dooyeweerd censures maintaining "that there does not exist a resting metaphysical and metalogical sphere" (*op. cit.* : 72).

actually carried out. Just as there needs to be a knowing subject in logic and knowledge, so there must also be a 'viewing subject', or a 'centre of viewing' relevant to the *Gegenstand*-sphere. "The unity of viewing, thinking and knowing is, in our view, rooted in the cosmic Selfhood [*kosmische ikheid*]" (Dooyeweerd 1922d1: 36). Dooyeweerd states he will not develop this thought. But even as it stands, one recognizes Vollenhoven's use of the Self, which is indeed a 'cosmic reality'. The Self 'becomes' a distinguishing subject or a knowing subject only upon submission to (logical) norms. In this way, a quality of being a subject has no independent or autonomous status. Dooyeweerd here adds the 'quality of viewing', something not expressly stated in Vollenhoven.

This is an appropriate place to add a remark about the term 'modal relation', first met with in the Scholten discussion. Dooyeweerd's interpretation of it, in "Normatieve rechtsleer" (1922d), is that it consolidates an autonomous status of subjectivity, and is on that account culpable. But first a formal remark. Dooyeweerd's positive use of 'modality' here (as synonym for 'region category') does not automatically signal acceptance of 'modal relation'. In fact, there is a choice for Dooyeweerd: in a general sense, *either* something is a relation *or* it concerns modality (cf. 1922d: 55, in connection with 'the ought'). When a relation is relevant, then there is intrinsic *diversity*, and logic has a relevant role to fulfil. But modality is different. When modality is appropriate, this concerns a *unitary* characterization that can only be *intuited* (viewed). So what is one to make of 'modal relation'?

Dooyeweerd here repeats Sigwart's characterization of the 'intramental' nature of the relation involved (being as indicated above in the discussion with Scholten). A modal relation is one whereby "we bring objects in relation to ourselves insofar as we represent them, and, as represented, desire or want them for their value as judged" (*op. cit.*: 53). Hence the modal relation is a "relation of valuation" (*waarde-relatie*), whereby thought evaluates according to a "value that is *accepted a priori as measure*" (*ibid.*; emphasis added). This a priori acceptance signals the autonomy of the evaluating subject. In the neo-Kantian context, the evaluation of values, as conducted by the evaluating subject, leads to the evaluated value's becoming a norm, to which one is subsequently subject. Here is "*autonomy*" (*ibid.*) in operation, and it is explained as predicated on the modal relation's role in valuation and norm acknowledgement. There are no norms for neo-Kantians apart from the evaluating subject.

Because Dooyeweerd does not discuss what he means by 'subject of viewing' we cannot be sure of his own meaning here. But clearly he

303

is sceptical of the term 'modal relation'. It could of course be used simply to factually indicate the intra-mental relation between the Self, in its subjective acts, and its representational content. As long as this relation is not privileged or taken to be authoritative (autonomous, as in the Freiburg context), there is little to object to. This intra-mental relation is close to what Vollenhoven originally called the 'concrete intuition', with the analytical intuition as allied to it. But with the increased attention accorded metalogical matters as of 1921, the concrete intuition has receded, in part due to the realignment of the analytical intuition (now as logical categories) to the metalogical intuition. So there is little reason for Dooyeweerd to honour the term 'modal relation' as being of special value for him at this point.

c. The system of the sciences
Dooyeweerd also remarks about the possibility of 'a science of the system of the sciences'. Each science has a formal and material side, calling for logic and *Gegenstand*-theory, respectively. Logic and *Gegenstand*-theory together form the context of the system of the sciences. The *Gegenstand*-sphere is the factual realization of the '*Encyclopedia* of the sciences', or what Vollenhoven called the 'organism of the sciences'. This 'system of the sciences' is an essential, if not central, topic in the philosophy of science. The main thought of the science of the system of the sciences is formulated succinctly by Dooyeweerd as follows (Dooyeweerd 1922d1: 36):

> The assumption of a factual *Gegenstand*-sphere leads moreover to the necessity for a science of the system of the sciences, to a "*Wissenschaftslehre*" of the "*Wissenschaftslehren*", in which the order of the distinct sciences, [each] with its appropriate logic, is systematically determined according to the degree of *Gegenständlichkeit* of its modalities or region categories, and whereby pure logic, with its simplest determination of *Gegenständlichkeit*, is given the ordinal position of first element in the well-ordered series [of the sciences]. We require some such systematics of the sciences before we are in a position to create the correct ordering in the doctrine of the categories.

This passage has historical importance. It contains elements that will find a permanent place in Reformed thought, be it after some whittling and refitting. In the first place, there is the occurrence of *modality*, used in a positive, constructive sense. Secondly, there is the statement that the sciences form a well-ordered series. And thirdly, there is the view that pure logic itself is in the position of being the first science in this series of the sciences. Let us take each point in turn.

The term modality, as we saw, is a synonym for Lask's term 'region category'. The term is used in *Gegenstand*-theory to indicate the characterization of the most basic 'factual unity of the *Gegenstand*' within a science, as determinative for its terrain. Lask's term 'region category' is suggestive in this regard. Dooyeweerd illustrates this as follows (*op. cit.*: 37): for arithmetic the modality is *quantity*; for geometry, *space*; for natural science, it is '*being* or *reality*' (*het zijn, het werkelijke*); for the normative sciences, it is '*so-ought*' (*het zo behoren*). The feature of modality fits in snugly with the intuitive viewing (*schouwen*, or metalogical intuition) spoken of earlier, when Dooyeweerd said: "The [Self involved in] *Gegenstand*-theory can only become conscious of the factual unity of the highest categories of thought through viewing" (*op. cit.*: 36). In this way, the Self as 'viewing subject', in discerning the modality of a science, grasps the most basic unitary feature of that science. In other words, this feature of modality focuses on (emphasizes, points to) the unitary feature of the adequate concept of a domain of thought.

We have indicated above that one should not confuse the intuitive nature of 'viewing the modality' with 'modal relation' as used in the Freiburg context (as indicated by Sigwart). That would privilege things intra-mental. The alternative of critical realism, as held to by Vollenhoven and Dooyeweerd here, is that behind the factual unity of a domain intuited (i.e. the modality that qualifies, in the adequate concept, the unitary feature of a science) there is the idea. Thus the 'subjective' moment in the viewing of the modality, as the unitary characteristic of a science's content, is indeed present, but it is hemmed in by 'realist factors', *viz.* the cosmic Self and the idea of being. In not privileging the adequate concept (just yet), the realist context prevents an 'idealist turn' to a possible 'modalism' that could otherwise (in theory) be prepared by it.[131]

The second point concerns the order of the sciences. This systematic feature of the sciences is also influenced by Lask, who suggested that the different sciences differ among other things by the 'degree of *Gegenständlichkeit*' of the modality of the science. Modalities do not only differ intrinsically, each also has a distinct measure of 'content opposition' that the science in question has to deals with. For that reason, each science will have its own 'applied logic' (*op. cit.*: 37) in conformity with its distinct

---

131   This is not just fanciful. To anticipate later developments, in the late 1920s Dooyeweerd relinquishes the realist moorings of his earlier thought. He accepts an ontology of meaning and the cosmic Self becomes a religious Self. The modalities of meaning then take on the role of serving as the horizon of experience, the 'sounding board' for all distinctions and references. We touch on this at the end of our current discussion of the early Dooyeweerd.

'grade of *Gegenständlichkeit*' (*ibid.*).[132] Dooyeweerd does not indicate what the order of the sciences is. In the one sequence he gives—which is: natural sciences, normative sciences, arithmetic, and geometry—it is hard to see any intrinsic order, and undoubtedly it was not meant to suggest this. But what the phrase "well-ordered series of the sciences" does mean to suggest is that "each of the basic modalities can *specify* itself [*zich specificeeren*] by adopting a higher grade of *Gegenständlichkeit*" (*ibid*; emphasis added). When a modality is encumbered with more *Gegenstand*, a more specific science results. When space (the modality of geometry) is encumbered with (the modal categories of) motion, force and matter, we have the science of motion (phoronomy); when being, as modality of natural science, is encumbered with (the modal categories of) quality and 'organity' (*organiteit*), we have biology; and in connection with the normative sciences, the basic modality of 'so-ought' can be encumbered to get the moral ought in ethics, the juridical ought in jurisprudence, the aesthetic ought in aesthetics, etc. (cf. *ibid.*).[133]

The notion of the order of the sciences will take on central significance in Reformed thought. In Vollenhoven the order of the sciences becomes the chief indication of the structure of cosmic reality. The determination of the order, as here suggested by the 'specification' of the basic modalities, will give way later to a more considered view of 'analogies and anticipations' between the modalities.[134] But the notion of specification

---

132   In Vollenhoven 1926d: 154, Vollenhoven opposes this suggestion of Lask about there being 'grades of *Gegenstand*' quite vigorously. "Number may be a *Gegenstand* [of arithmetic] that stands lower than energy [the *Gegenstand* of physics], [but] both are, despite the difference in ordinal position, nevertheless *Gegenstand*. This being-*Gegenstand* is incompatible with gradual difference." At this point there is the theory of the cosmic law-spheres, whereby each sphere is the context of a field of inquiry of a *Gegenstand*. This allows one to say that the *Gegenstände* of the sciences are gradated, i.e. placed in an order, without acknowledging 'grades of *Gegenstand*' in virtue of 'gradual difference'. Very likely Vollenhoven also has his former opinion in mind (cf. his 1918a: 434-437), when he did defend gradual differences within the organism of the sciences, due to the inverse ratio between the form and the content as characteristic of a science (cf. chapter 2, section VIII.C.3.c).

133   These are all rather inchoate ideas. The distinction between a 'basic modality' (*grondmodaliteit*) and 'specified modality' was short lived. The 'essential connections' are also 'categories' within a modality. They come to be worked into the analogical structure of the modalities.

134   This appears in the work of both Vollenhoven and Dooyeweerd in 1926—Vollenhoven in his "Kentheorie en natuurwetenschap" (1926d, as concerns analogy) and Dooyeweerd in his inaugural address, *De Beteekenis der Wetsidee voor Rechtswetenschap en Rechtsphilosophie* (1926d: 65, as concerns both analogy and anticipations).

attests to a realization that there is some measure of relevant coherence or connection between the domains of the sciences. In the discussion with Scholten, Dooyeweerd had emphasized that the standpoint of ethics and that of legality are mutually exclusive. Though their modalities are and remain distinct, we now see that Dooyeweerd recognizes a link between them via the notion of specification in the context of the normative sciences.

The third point concerns pure logic, in particular its place of 'first science' in the order of the sciences. This point may seem inconsequential in light of the later 'canonical' view of the (near) middle position of 'the logical' in the series of the modalities. But in Vollenhoven's work published in 1926—his first formulations of the more Reformed position—it is basic.[135] So what does this point involve?

Pure logic is the 'first science' because its *Gegenstand*, which concerns the general categories and forms of judgments themselves that are applied in the other sciences, is relevant to the whole terrain of the sciences. As Lask had it, pure logic centres on validity, and Dooyeweerd appears to agree. That would mean, though Dooyeweerd does not say so explicitly, that *validity* is the modality of pure logic (as science). At least one can then make sense of Dooyeweerd's critical remark regarding Lask, when he expresses his disagreement with Lask's attributing validity also to the other region categories of *being* (natural sciences) and *ought* (normative sciences). Dooyeweerd attributes validity only to pure logic as such, otherwise there would be a violation of the modalities involved— 'being' (as modality of natural science) would have to be 'being-validity' (or a 'specification' of the modality of 'validity'); and also 'so-ought' (of the normative sciences) would have to be 'so-ought-validity' (here too a 'specification' of 'validity') (cf. *ibid.*, p. 37). In fact this would define a 'logicism'—where each science is a specification of pure logic's validity[136]—but this is inconsistent with critical realism. For Dooyeweerd, validity is relevant in the sciences (other than pure logic) only to the extent that each science has a formal side, and thus each makes use of relevant

---

135 Vollenhoven changed this (as a visible correction) in his first lecture notes at the Free University in 1926-1927 (cf. Vollenhoven 1926msA). Dooyeweerd criticized the view of the 'created logos' being "the most simple law-sphere" in Dooyeweerd 1928a: 37.

136 An (at least partial) example of this is Bertrand Russell's early (naïve realist) logicism. In his *The Principles of Mathematics* (Russell 1903) terms and axioms are laid down (pure logical validity) from which he derives the truths of the main parts of logic, of pure mathematics and of physics (insofar as this is pure). It is through definitions, appropriately formulated, that content is brought within the sway of logic. One could interpret the latter (the definition of new terms on the basis of accepted terms) as specifying 'grades of *Gegenstand*'.

forms of judgment (*ibid.*, p. 37). But validity does not, and should not, dominate the non-logical modality as highest *material* characteristic of the *Gegenstand* of a science (apart from pure logic).

So pure logic, as the science of the sciences, itself has content and form. Its *content* (*Gegenstand*) is the primary forms that are applied in the logic of each science, as relevant to its categories and forms of judgment. The *form* of pure logic involves the "formal unity of the truths about the *Gegenstand*" (Dooyeweerd 1922d1: 36). This is the study of validity in connection with the degrees of encumbrance of the *Gegenstand*, and the requirement that a science needs to have an adequate applied logic in agreement with the degree of encumbrance involved. This essentially returns in Vollenhoven in 1926 when he speaks of the logical schema, as the simplest ('first') modality, the primary system of truth, and every encumbrance as defining the logical 'states of affairs' relevant to a science.

Dooyeweerd relates his own disagreement with Lask, as reported above, to his *realist position*, which Lask does not share. Lask has logic dictating to every science, so that he takes *being* and the *ought* (as modalities or region categories of the natural and the normative sciences respectively) to be forms (or 'specifications') of validity. "According to realist opinion, [however,] *validity* is also already encumbered with *Gegenständlichkeit* [this being logical forms]. And *being* is not a *validity* modality, but a basic modality as equally independent as is 'validity'.[137] Also the 'ought' is such an independent modality and not a modality of 'validity'" (*op. cit.*: 37). In Dooyeweerd's emphasizing the independent status of being (warranted by ideas) and the ought (grounded in norms) we have again an indication of the Vollenhovian context of Dooyeweerd's thought. The whole *Gegenstand*-sphere is neither grounded in the Self nor in the World, but, as these critical realists would have it, in "the in itself a-logical material of the Logos" (*op. cit.*: 35).

At the same time this underscores something the brothers-in-law soon come to feel as not being satisfactory. If a science's validity is only a matter of the adequate logical form of the judgments of a science, while a science's content is warranted by, or has a 'substrate' in, the cosmic reality as governed by the idea, what does this mean for the "a-logical material of the Logos"? Does it merely answer to the desire to know, to attain a pure and ideal rationality, under the aegis of the divine Logos, the principle of rationality? Such could be the motive behind the focus on modality,

---

137   The typescript (Dooyeweerd 1922d: 47) and the text as printed in Verburg (cf. Dooyeweerd 1922d1: 37) have "being" here. The sense of the passage clearly calls for "validity".

as the *basic unitary feature* of scientific content. But in his defence of the relevance of the *Gegenstands*-sphere, Dooyeweerd had referred to "reality" and "all of its problems" (*op. cit.*: 34), problems that should *not* be withdrawn from pure thought. But reality or the cosmos has remained a rather elusive, thought-foreign element in the discussion so far. The 'next move' in their discussions is to bring the *Gegenstand*-sphere and the cosmos into closer proximity of each other.

D. Interlude
The early work of Dooyeweerd that we have discussed so far is written prior to his joining the Kuyper Foundation on 1 October 1922. In this new position, he was expected to write advisory reports, based on research that related to practical political work relevant to the political party which Kuyper had formed, the 'Anti-Revolutionary Party' (in short: the ARP).[138] Hence Dooyeweerd's area of attention nominally shifted considerably. But he was able to put his prior research to good use. In a memorandum that he had written, when applying for the position of deputy director of the Kuyper Foundation, he sketched a program of work that coincided with his own interest and the expertise he had by then gained.[139] The advisory capacity of the Foundation, he held, needed to be more securely founded on systematic and principled research, i.e. "clear insight in the foundations of the so-called neo-Calvinistic life- and worldview in its application to legality, economics and politics" (Dooyeweerd 1922e: 49). To that end, he suggested, the *first* task was to develop the method by which the research would be conducted, and only *then* could attention be given to the "*fundamental problem* of the whole Calvinistic view of legality and society", namely the problem of sovereignty (*op. cit.*: 50).

Both counts relate to Dooyeweerd's prior research. The technical part of his research, as we saw above, had been focussed on methodology. The way he formulates the importance of method is interesting. He states: "This method cannot be neutral but must be guided by the prin-

---

138 The ARP was the first political party in the Dutch parliamentary system. It was founded in 1879 and was an independent political factor until 1980, when it merged with two other parties to form the 'Christen Democratisch Appèl' (CDA; Christian democratic appeal).

139 The memorandum, which consists of two parts, the program of work and the implementation, was an attachment to his letter of application, dated 15 May 1922, to the position of deputy director of the Kuyper Foundation, sent to J.J.C. van Dijk, who was Minister of War but also the secretary of the Kuyper Foundation; cf. Dooyeweerd 1922e.

ciples of the brilliantly erected epistemology of Dr. Kuyper. Beside this, in my opinion one ought to make critical use of the newer methodological researches, to the extent that they can contribute to conceptual clarity" (*op. cit*: 49). The latter—the newer methodological researches—no doubt involve the sort of suggestions Dooyeweerd found useful in Lask. But this is set off from the reference to Kuyper. Perhaps the context motivated the somewhat exuberant—and unexpected—reference to Kuyper; unexpected, for his name had not occurred in the epistemological discussions to date. Dooyeweerd must have had 'critical realism' uppermost in mind. Kuyper's epistemology is no doubt also a version of critical realism.[140] But it is Vollenhoven's template of critical realism that is more directly relevant for Dooyeweerd. The broadening of reference to include Kuyper was strategic.[141]

The reference to the problem of sovereignty reminds one of the discussion with G. Scholten, conducted in the prior month of April. In that discussion we found that the emphasis was on the difference between the standpoints of legality and ethics. They being mutually exclusive, each has its own sovereignty. Their sovereignty is defended on the basis of a prior methodological or value-scientific clarification of the relevant domains, i.e. adducing the distinct ideas and the corresponding (adequate) concepts of legality and ethics. So Dooyeweerd's suggestion that the discussion of scientific method be *prior* to the discussion of sovereignty, has in the background the notion of the *Gegenstand*-sphere (the part relevant for the value-sciences) and the divine Logos that is its warrant and principle. I believe that this puts a stamp on Dooyeweerd's statement in the memorandum that "from out of the Calvinistic doctrine of sovereignty lines need to be drawn for the relation of church and state, state and society, government and laity, and the [parts of] laity mutually" (*op. cit.*:

---

140 Dooyeweerd's later *negative* assessment of Kuyper's epistemology includes this realism. He finds in Kuyper, as well as in J. Woltjer and H. Bavinck, a philosophical influence that is "in part of scholastic, in part of modern epistemological origin", which is incompatible with the religious basic view (*religieuze grond-conceptie*) of Calvinism. He summarizes: "The scholastic line comes especially to expression in the traditional philosophical view of soul and body, in the doctrine of the logos and the realism of ideas, the modern [line] in different parts of Kuyper's philosophical epistemology, that have a so-called critical realist stamp"; Dooyeweerd 1939: 197.

141 This was before Dooyeweerd 'rediscovered' the importance of Kuyper when reading meditations by him, as reported by R. Henderson on the basis of information Dooyeweerd recorded late in life. The references in this report to 'offices of the Kuyper Foundation' and 'landlady responsible for meals' situate this rediscovery between 1 October 1922 (the beginning of his employment for the Foundation) and 19 September 1924 (his wedding day); cf. Henderson 1994: 113-114.

50). These areas need to be studied methodically, as domains of sciences, so as to clarify what does and what does not belong to each, before commencing with the study of the sovereignty relevant to each. The latter would no doubt involve practical applications and historical parameters of content assessment. To that end the works of Stahl, Groen and Kuyper are recommended for study, as well as those of Augustine and Calvin. But the encompassing approach is delineated by the critical realist scientific methodology.

Dooyeweerd was given the green light. The recommendation for study that he had formulated became his own study plan. Four very fruitful years ensued. Up to this point he had written quite extensively but published little. His first aim had been to achieve clarity with respect to problems in the philosophy of legality and to develop a viable position for himself. Vollenhoven, we saw, had provided the groundwork for this search.[142] Dooyeweerd could now apply himself full-time to academic work. He continued to develop, but he was now more his own man.[143]

It does not seem likely that Dooyeweerd and Vollenhoven continued their late evening contact during Dooyeweerd's new employment. Vollenhoven's specific remark, that their "searching contact" lasted till the fall of 1922, seems to suggest that it terminated at about the time when Dooyeweerd began working for the Foundation. The new employment did not involve a change of residence outside of The Hague. But Dooyeweerd (still unmarried for another two years) invested even his free time (evenings) in this unique opportunity of study and writing. But whatever contact there was, it was put on hold during Vollenhoven's long illness that suddenly set in in mid-January of 1923. Vollenhoven was institutionalized in Amsterdam till the end of June 1923. Contact between the brothers-in-law could not have been very frequent in light of the distance between The Hague and Amsterdam. Vollenhoven did not resume his pastoral duties till the end of 1923, but one tends to think that academic discussion could and would have resumed some time before the end of

---

142 Here too Dooyeweerd's recollection is problematic. He speaks of this period of contact with Vollenhoven as their "transitional period", between the completion of their academic training and their later university careers. Vollenhoven had completed formal studies in philosophy, so he "was philosophically better equipped than I was." Thus, continues Dooyeweerd, "I, after completing my studies in law, still needed to undertake my philosophical formation *on my own authority*. . ."; Dooyeweerd 1973: 5 (emphasis added). This is formally correct, but materially it holds only for Dooyeweerd's period at the Kuyper Foundation. It is not the whole truth as regards the period up to the fall of 1922.

143 Cf. Verburg 1989, chapter 2: 42-82, for a full discussion of the period of Dooyeweerd's employment at the Kuyper Foundation.

that year,[144] though now there would be much less time to invest in it.

We found that the period of Vollenhoven's illness forms a watershed in his contact with Janse. While recuperating, Vollenhoven subjected his previous position to serious scrutiny, being stimulated by Janse's anthropological questions and remarks. The contact with Dooyeweerd will also, as we shall see, lead not only to revisions in their common view but also to certain contrasts. But Vollenhoven does not begin to publish in philosophy until 1925/1926, and we lack other material evidence from his side. We get a much fuller picture from Dooyeweerd's side. In the latter part of 1923 we find in him the first occurrences of terminology that is more representative of 'Reformed thought' than had previously been the case, namely the terminology of 'law-spheres' and 'law-idea'. Vollenhoven fully shares in the use to the first term, but studiedly avoids the latter term.

But before continuing to discuss further work we pause to note Dooyeweerd's earliest recollections of his work prior to his becoming deputy director, and also to look for hints as to their mutual relations in late 1922 in light of a planned joint project.

1. Rudimentary conception and 'humanistic philosophy'
How did Dooyeweerd himself look back on the early work we have discussed when he had himself moved beyond it? He makes an autobiographical remark in the Foreword of his *De Wijsbegeerte der Wetsidee* (vol. 1, 1935) that is apropos here. He states that "the first, still very rudimentary conception of [the system of the philosophy of the law-idea] had already ripened with me before my arrival at the Kuyper Foundation in The Hague" (Dooyeweerd 1935-1936, I: v). This statement is difficult to interpret on account of the vagueness of "rudimentary conception". If Dooyeweerd's work prior to his period at the Foundation can be said to contain a conception, then it can be none other than a 'critical realist' one. But it is difficult to see how that could be interpreted as a rudimentary version of the later system. So perhaps we are not properly attuned to what Dooyeweerd means to say. Strictly speaking he only says that a rudimentary form *of his later system* was already present in his work prior to his joining the Foundation. For the rest he does not say anything distinct about that work.

Now there *is* something prescient or lasting (in a "very rudimentary" sort of way) about the domains of distinct modality—logic, nature,

---
144 Cf. Stellingwerff 1992: 63-65, for more information about Vollenhoven's period of illness.

culture, number, space—each of which invites a distinct methodological approach in view of the "(adequate) concept and idea (of distinctive being)" characterization. It is in virtue of this methodologically distinct feature that each domain is said to safeguard its own sovereignty, a sovereignty that is in fact a "sovereignty . . . in its own sphere", as Vollenhoven had emphasized (Vollenhoven 1921c: 80).[145] So perhaps it is this metalogical feature of the early work that falls within Dooyeweerd's meaning. Then it is "very rudimentary" not only in lacking the modal analysis that will lead to the distinction of more than a dozen modalities, but also in how the domains of appropriate modality are founded. As to the latter, there is nothing explicit about modal law as yet, and the role of the Logos retains a scholastic-dogmatic understanding of rationality.

In the above interpretation, we have had to surmise Dooyeweerd's meaning. But at one point, in 1928, Dooyeweerd makes a direct autobiographical statement related to his early work. An opponent of Dooyeweerd, Leo Polak, had said: "mixing things ethical, juridical, religious etc. is incorrect on any standpoint"; so why, he asks, should Calvinism be advanced as having a special priority here?[146] Dooyeweerd claims to understand the objection "very well, for there was a time, when I was myself of the opinion that the distinguished scientific terrains could be kept correctly separated without the help of a law-idea. Logical analysis . . . should alone be adequate here. But, this was exactly the postulate of humanistic philosophy, wherein its rationalistic character so strongly reveals itself."[147]

If we take Dooyeweerd at his word here (and it would be inappropriate not to) then he seems to be saying that his work of as recent as five years ago—'law-idea' is introduced in 1923—could not really be sufficiently distinguished from humanistic, rationalistic philosophy. By implication, this judgment devolves on Vollenhoven's efforts as well. It is difficult to know what to make of this. Certainly Vollenhoven's early theism has rationalistic traits; but this, being in a theological setting, is difficult to qualify as humanistic. And the critical realist setting of their common position also does not really evidence a patent humanism. The role of the Self would have to be more determinative than allowed in the critical realist setting. So perhaps Dooyeweerd has something more

---

145 As stated earlier, this is not "sphere-sovereignty" as later understood. Missing is the essential feature of law, including the role of 'modal laws'. Thus the use of 'modalities' here is still primarily that of indicating the highest material categories of scientific content.
146 As related by Dooyeweerd in Dooyeweerd 1928b: 422.
147 Dooyeweerd 1928b: 422-423.

specific in mind. In speaking of "distinguished scientific terrains" the attention shifts to methodology. We are reminded of Dooyeweerd's memorandum to the Kuyper Foundation, in which he had emphasized that the study of the methodology of the value sciences was to *precede* the research of the topic of (societal) sovereignty. There is something 'rationalistic' in this procedure, for it is the (meta-)logical analysis of the different scientific terrains that is expected to warrant the results. But that warrant is provided by the Logos, not the Self. So the humanistic provenance of this 'rationalism' is still difficult to confirm. And we should not forget Dooyeweerd's specifying the context of the "neo-Calvinistic life- and worldview" (Dooyeweerd 1922e: 49). The latter is not what a humanist would applaud. Hence Dooyeweerd's qualifications remain uncertain as regards his pre-1923 work.

Now when taking a closer look at the *function* of a life- and worldview, we do find a rather 'rationalistic' orientation, at least initially, though to my knowledge Dooyeweerd nowhere refers to this. Verburg has quoted an interesting passage from the manuscript, dated 14 April 1922 (just after the discussion with Scholten),[148] in which Dooyeweerd relates how life-view and worldview together are set to work in epistemology. Dooyeweerd emphasizes the importance of *immanent criticism*, namely following a line of argument in terms of its own "epistemological premises" to discover whether unsatisfactory conclusions follow. When this is the case, then this indicates that there is something unsatisfactory in the premises. One may then present one's own alternative premises and show that they lead to more satisfactory results. The use of premises, says Dooyeweerd, is "propelled by waves of life-view" (Dooyeweerd 1922b1: 32). A life-view cannot itself be demonstrated as to its logical correctness. But if one holds to the "objective validity of truth", then one should admit that "every objective error in the life-view" necessarily leads to an "objective error of thought" (an error of fact). Immanent criticism is the way to reveal the need to review life-view considerations when errors in the conclusions are made logically patent.

There is more than one problem with this account, not least of all how life-view related to argumentation. Dooyeweerd seems to take 'life-view' to denote a belief structure of statements in a hermeneutical context.[149] An unsatisfactory hermeneutical context will harbour ob-

---

148   The passage is from the first of the three unpublished manuscripts—Dooyeweerd 1922b, 1922c and 1922d—mentioned at the beginning of section III.C.4. above. Cf. Verburg 1989: 32.

149   At this point, as Verburg points out, Dooyeweerd distinguishes life-view and world-view; Verburg 1989: 33. Whatever the precise distinction is, the latter pertains to

jectively false statements. The recognition of this fact—which calls for logical analysis—legitimates proceeding from a life-view that is hermeneutically more satisfactory. This procedure depends in an important sense on 'logical analysis'. We will see shortly that the introduction of a 'law-idea' (in 1923) is meant to mediate between life- and worldview considerations and cosmology (the domain of facts), which at least indicates that Dooyeweerd too soon felt there was something unsatisfactory in this connection. The importance attributed to 'logical analysis' would appear to evidence the 'rationalism' of his early work that Dooyeweerd may perhaps have in mind here. But the characterization as 'humanistic' remains problematic.

2. Vollenhoven's due?
A question quite naturally arises at this point in the discussion concerning the contact between the early Vollenhoven and Dooyeweerd. Dooyeweerd provides more textual (manuscript) evidence of the intrinsic development of their thought during the period we have discussed than Vollenhoven does. So isn't Dooyeweerd already 'on his own', and shouldn't we simply credit the burgeoning theory of modalities and methodology of science, as discussed above, to him?

Now it may well be that there is material original to Dooyeweerd, though we shall probably never be in a position to be able to attribute to each his due. But it seems to be against the spirit of their early contact to make any such apportioning. As long as both see and interpret their work in a way that they characterize as 'critical (or transcendental) realism', then it is a project that Vollenhoven initiated. He gave it a sufficiently delineated outline in his dissertation, along with the metalogical adjustment of 1921, so as to make mutual discussion fruitful and promising. Other 'critical realists'—if we may so characterize the philosophical input of Kuyper, Bavinck or Woltjer—are simply not referred to in the written evidence of their discussions, neither in points of detail nor for doctrinal support. The brothers-in-law are working 'on their own' as it were, within the outline provided by Vollenhoven.

---

the context of content (facts and values), the former to the context of *thought*; that is why I interpret this as a "belief structure of statements in a hermeneutical context". A certain 'rationalism' is then intrinsic to 'life-view', which attaches itself directly to the believing human being. In Dooyeweerd's subsequent work the two terms are united in the way that is common in Dutch: "levens- en wereldbeschouwing". In my discussion of this early work, I retain the direct translation: "life- and worldview". The more current use of simply "worldview" could be interpreted as one-sided.

The fact that Dooyeweerd published so little of his early work[150] *could* be indicative of the acknowledgement (by common courtesy) that it was not original enough to be attributable to him in print. There is at least evidence, not hard and fast, but nevertheless telling when carefully considered, that can be interpreted as implicitly acknowledging Vollenhoven's leading role, namely in the plan of a publication. Dooyeweerd raised this plan, in which he, along with Vollenhoven and Josef Bohatec of Vienna (a Calvin scholar) were to contribute. But this plan ultimately failed, though there were two attempts to realize it, in 1922 and again in 1925.

In a memorandum to the board of the Kuyper Foundation, dated 16 September 1925, Dooyeweerd recommends "the annual publication of collections of essays entitled 'Calvinistic philosophy'".[151] The first volume was to contain essays by himself, Vollenhoven and Bohatec. He adds the detail that there had been a plan made several years ago "to publish on the significance of Calvinism for philosophy and epistemology" (*op. cit.*, p. 34), but that that plan had to be postponed on account of Vollenhoven's illness. The latter detail puts this initial plan prior to mid-January 1923 (when Vollenhoven became ill), probably late 1922, when Dooyeweerd had started his work for the Kuyper Foundation. In fact, this earlier '1922 plan' meshes with Dooyeweerd's proposal, raised in his memorandum to the Kuyper Foundation of May 1922, of initiating a continuing series of publications, the first of which was to deal "in basic contours with the question of method and the problem of sovereignty".[152] The proposal of May 1922, the plan of late-1922 and the plan of September 1925 all hang together. For in the 1925 memorandum Dooyeweerd adds: "From the beginning of my connection with the Kuyper Foundation . . . I have had a work plan in mind which included developing Calvinistic principles in the areas of philosophy, epistemology, jurisprudence, politics and history."[153]

From the start Dooyeweerd had had a *concerted* effort in mind. In his proposal of May 1922 he expressed the hope that the Kuyper Foundation would become a centre from which work initiated in which different

---

150   We pointed out earlier that material from the second and the third of the unpublished manuscripts were used (sometimes with adapted terminology) in later publications. The third, "Normatieve rechtsleer", was even stencilled in early 1923. The reference to it, in Dooyeweerd 1926d: 91, note 5, includes the remark "not yet published", raises the question why this was forestalled.
151   This information is in Henderson 1994: 34-35. I have not been able to see this memorandum.
152   Dooyeweerd 1922e: 50.
153   Henderson 1994: 35.

scholars would participate, particularly jurists of the Free University.[154] Thus it comes as no surprise that the first concrete proposal of late 1922 concerns a publication in which different authors participate.

It is uncertain what Bohatec would have contributed.[155] Vollenhoven's contribution was to be (in the wording of the 1925 memo) on "the general perimeters of an epistemology from a Calvinist standpoint". This description does not conflict with what we know of the early Vollenhoven. The 'Calvinist standpoint' is not likely to differ much from what Dooyeweerd, in his letter to Vollenhoven of 17 December 1920, had referred to as Vollenhoven's interest in 'saving Calvinistic metaphysics'. But to date no evidence has been found that throws light on what Vollenhoven's contribution in late 1922 might have been. We have only Dooyeweerd's description to go on, which, in speaking of "general perimeters", hints at it's being quite basic. Dooyeweerd gives as the title of his contribution (also in the wording of 1925), "The meaning of the Calvinistic law-idea and sphere sovereignty for epistemology and philosophy". This wording, we note, depends on his own development as of late 1923, so it cannot be representative, in a direct sense, for what Dooyeweerd had planned to contribute in the late 1922 initiative.[156]

The rather basic nature of Vollenhoven's planned contribution must reflect the actual situation of the time. That situation would appear to place Vollenhoven close to the heart of the enterprise. Dooyeweerd endorses this, for he here presents himself as the 'editor' of the project, knowing the nature of Vollenhoven's planned contribution. I believe that this reflects a certain authority enjoyed by Vollenhoven at that time, one which cannot be divorced from his role in connection with critical real-

---

154   Dooyeweerd 1922e: 50.

155   Josef Bohatec, an Austrian theologian and philosopher, was a frequent contributor to *Philosophia Reformata*, and from its inception in 1936 was on its editorial board. In 1950 he received an honorary doctorate from the Free University; cf. Berkelaar 2007: 45-47.

156   In 1923a, in what is probably Dooyeweerd's first study that he undertook at the Kuyper Foundation, he refers in a footnote to the epistemological ideas, discussed in its chapter two (entitled "Cosmos and Logos") of that study. These ideas, he says, are "explained very schematically" here. But, he continues, "they form the foundation for a study [*verhandeling*] to be brought out by the Kuyper Foundation within several months, in which the points raised will be elaborated more specifically." (1923a2: 37). On p. 42 he anticipates, "hopefully soon to appear", offering "a specimen of the theory of modalities" that he adumbrates in "Cosmos and Logos". One expects these two statements to refer to the same planned project. There is no mention of other authors, but this may possibly be, or be related to, what Dooyeweerd initially planned to contribute to the 'late 1922 initiative'. Cf. the discussion of "Cosmos and Logos" in section E below.

ism. So this volume, as planned in 1922, would, I believe, have given Vollenhoven his due had it materialized.

But Vollenhoven's illness placed the planned volume on the back burner. In 1925 (as we said) the project is resuscitated by Dooyeweerd, though it again fell through, now on account of Bohatec's having fallen ill! Dooyeweerd expected this plan to definitely materialize. For, in a footnote to his "Calvinisme contra Neo-Kantianisme" (Dooyeweerd 1926c: 29, note 1), he announced a publication—which must be the one in question—to appear "within some months" by the Kuyper Foundation, that would contain contributions of himself, Vollenhoven and Bohatec. Dooyeweerd also gives the title of his contribution, this being "The meaning for philosophy of the Calvinistic law-idea and of the principle of sphere-sovereignty that follows from it".[157] Nothing is said about Vollenhoven's or Bohatec's contributions. But, in Vollenhoven's case, the general wording of his expected contribution, as formulated in the memorandum of 1925, namely on the general perimeters of an epistemology from a Calvinist standpoint, comes very close to that of the first of Vollenhoven's three publications of 1926, entitled "Contours of the theory of knowledge" (*Enkele grondlijnen der kentheorie*) (April 1926). If this was indeed Vollenhoven's planned contribution to the volume announced by Dooyeweerd—it is difficult to doubt this—then (i) this volume's realization was postponed after Dooyeweerd had submitted his article "Calvinisme contra Neo-Kantianisme" with the quoted footnote, but before April 1926, when Vollenhoven's article appeared elsewhere, and (ii) Vollenhoven (and Dooyeweerd) evidently could not wait for Bohatec's convalescence, for Vollenhoven published his planned contribution separately almost immediately. Now why this sudden haste? After all, Dooyeweerd's own planned contribution was not yet in press.

Crucial for the argument here, I believe, is the fact that Dooyeweerd's "Calvinisme contra Neo-Kantianisme" (1926c) contains a sizable chunk of "Normatieve rechtsleer",[158] (1922d, stencilled in 1923), in par-

---

157   The Dutch title is "De beteekenis van de Calvinistische wetsidee en van het daaruit voortvloeiende beginsel der Souvereiniteit in eigen kring voor de Wijsbegeerte". To my knowledge, this text is no longer extant. But its content may well have been absorbed into other publications, such as Dooyeweerd's inaugural address of October 1926, entitled "De Beteekenis der Wetsidee voor Rechtswetenschap en Rechtsphilosophie" [The meaning of the law-idea for jurisprudence and the philosophy of law].

158   Pages 34-59 of the published article are from the stencilled typescript of "Normatieve rechtsleer", pp. 74-88. There are minimal adaptations of the long passage in order to be at least somewhat in step with post-1922 developments. The term 'region category', as synonym for 'modality', is retained even though the term 'field of vision' (cf. discussion below) is now the preferred description and also occurs in the more recently written parts

ticular an epistemological section dealing with the *Gegenstand*-sphere and its methodological relevance in terms of 'viewing' and thought, particularly in application to Marburg neo-Kantianism. (This is in tandem with the discussion of material from the same document in section III.C.4. above.) Vollenhoven gives a concomitant epistemological discussion in the said article, though with more attention to fundamentals. (He develops this more expansively in the other two publications of 1926: "Kentheorie en natuurwetenschap" [1926d] and *Logos en Ratio* [1926a].) One might well find nothing peculiar here, namely that Dooyeweerd is the first to publishing on epistemology in the critical realist vein of the brothers-in-law. Now the announcement in the first footnote of Dooyeweerd's article, 1926c, not only raised expectations about the joint publication and Vollenhoven's contribution to it, but also would have served (so I seriously believe) to justify Dooyeweerd's making public work that called for the recognition of Vollenhoven. In announcing (in 1926c) the imminent appearance of Vollenhoven's contribution on 'epistemological basics', Dooyeweerd would have felt he had given Vollenhoven his rightful due. But when that joint project was again delayed *after* Dooyeweerd had submitted his "Calvinisme contra-Neo-Kantianisme", the only alternative was—and no doubt Dooyeweerd would not have wanted it otherwise—for Vollenhoven to publish elsewhere as quickly as possible. So Vollenhoven offered his article to a journal.[159] This of course also signalled the termination of the planned joint publication.

It must have been frustrating for Dooyeweerd to have to hold back, when the initial plans for publication were made already in late 1922. In Dooyeweerd's *Calvinisme en Natuurrecht* (1923d; written in 1923/1924)[160] there are two paragraphs devoted to epistemology, constituting less than half a page. This short (and somewhat cryptic) discussion is entirely out of character with Dooyeweerd's otherwise expansive discussions in this booklet. He says that he can only "indicate in passing" (*op. cit.*: 13) what Calvinism can mean for epistemology. He ends the passage by saying: "We cannot say more on this topic here" (*op. cit.*: 14). While he does not explain his reticence, clearly Dooyeweerd felt that there were constraints with respect to his public handling of this topic. This accords with my assumption that he felt an obligation towards Vollenhoven. The latter, still convalescing in late 1923, would not have been able to plan his

---

of the article.
159   Vollenhoven 1926b.
160   Dooyeweerd 1923d. The publication is not dated. It was published in 1924; cf. footnote 187 below.

work as yet, hence further specifics had to go unmentioned.

Now looking ahead, there is still one unpublished study that deserves separate discussion before we turn to published material that is indicative of a distinct development in Dooyeweerd in the mid-1920s. When that has been discussed we can round off our discussion of Dooyeweerd's early thought. We reserve for the following chapter the discussion of Vollenhoven's thought, in which his own revisions will be highlighted.

E. Cosmos, *logos* and faith
An unpublished study of Dooyeweerd, entitled "Roman Catholic and Anti-revolutionary policy of state" (c. February 1923; our code: 1923a), has several important features that are worthy of mention in the present context. The introduction of this text (1923a1) is in Verburg 1989: 48-50. Chapter two has a section (folio-sized typescript 1923a2) on epistemology, entitled "Cosmos and Logos" (*Kosmos en Logos*) that calls for discussion; only its final section, "Transition to cosmology" (*De overgang tot de kosmologie*) (1923a3), is available in print (cf. Verburg 1989: 59-61). Verburg is not definitive about the date of this study, but he states that it represents Dooyeweerd's thought at the end of 1922 and beginning of 1923 (*op. cit.*: 48). On the basis of this information, this study is probably the first one undertaken by Dooyeweerd as deputy director of the Kuyper Foundation.

1. The Introduction
The introduction is entitled "Idealism, realism and life- and worldview" (cf. 1923a1: 48). It mentions two divergences. The first is the opposition between idealism and realism. Idealism in its modern variant is described as embodying "the haughty demand of the autonomy of thought" (*ibid.*), while realism seeks a foundation outside of thought. This divergence is briefly illustrated in mentioning mathematics and natural science. Idealism takes the fundamental notions (number, space, motion, energy, atom, etc.) to be creations of thought, while realism takes them to be founded on something outside of thought. Also in the normative sciences the difference between idealism and realism is an important factor. The second divergence mentioned by Dooyeweerd is one within the realist camp itself, where there is "a desperate confusion in problem and method" (*op. cit.*: 49). This confusion attests "in the main to a sad lack of insight in the correct boundaries and the correct methods of the special sciences" (*ibid.*).

As it stands, the situation as sketched is familiar, though Dooyeweerd has not been so explicit about a *divergence on the part of realism*. This takes on significance for his actual topic. He posits that "in the last analysis the conclusive stand also taken in the conflict of method is one of life- and worldview" (*ibid.*). Christianity, he says, "obviously sides unconditionally with the realists over against the idealists" (*op. cit.*: 49-50). A Christian maintains on the one hand the creation as fact and on the other hand the fundamental difference between creator and creature (*op. cit.*: 50). This is of itself a quite 'Calvinistic' statement of Christian realism, though Dooyeweerd does not describe it as such.[161] In fact, he gives the description of realism an even finer point in the following novel statement. Realism, he says, "accepts for the logos of thought a divine cosmos, of which thought constitutes only a part and out of which thought also derives both its typical logical forms and the ideal material to be worked over".[162] Several points call for separate mention here.

First of all, differences and divisions "everywhere in the domain of thought" (*op. cit.*: 48) are taken to be accountable in terms of life- and worldview issues. This holds for the two divergences mentioned above, namely between idealism and realism, but also the stated divergence within realism itself. The latter divergence brings the relevance of life- and worldview close to home. In "Normatieve rechtsleer" (1922d) Dooyeweerd had linked the "postulate of realism" to a view of life, one that one either accepts or rejects (Dooyeweerd 1923d1: 34). This is how the "thought-alien cosmic sphere" is broached, this being accepted as the postulate of realism that is concomitant to the view of life one proceeds from. Thus, a life- and worldview has direct relevance for metaphysics (as we have noted before; cf. footnote 55 above), and accordingly a Calvinistic life- and worldview may be expected to prescribe a relevant metaphysics or understanding of realism. (To anticipate: in the course of 1923

---

161 This may be taken to be in line with the "Calvinistic metaphysics" spoken of in Dooyeweerd's letter to Vollenhoven of 17 Dec. 1920, discussed above. But at this point there appears to be a greater sense of antithesis. Dooyeweerd's opening sentence of this introduction reads: "There is a deep philosophical meaning hidden in the slogan of Calvinism: the acknowledgment of Gods sovereignty on *all terrains* of life; it [Calvinism] proceeds from the only correct fundamental thought, namely that the difference in life- and worldview should be unconditionally determinative for both thought and action, and that a neutral zone can nowhere be selected in which belief and unbelief can cooperate (*elkander de hand kunnen reiken*) (Dooyeweerd 1923a1: 48).

162 The Dutch reads: "realisme, dat voor den logos van het denken een goddelijke kosmos aanvaardt, waarvan het denken slechts een onderdeel uitmaakt en waaruit het denken ook zoowel zijn eigenaardig logische vormen, als de ideëele stof ter bearbeiding put." Dooyeweerd 1923a1: 48.

Dooyeweerd introduces a notion—'law-idea'—that *mediates* between life- and worldview and cosmology or metaphysics. This turns the relation between the two into a topical problem.)

In the second place, in this study Dooyeweerd no longer used the phrase 'thought-alien cosmos'. Thought and cosmos are brought into a much closer proximity to each other than had previously been the case. Realism is now said to accept "a divine cosmos . . . for the logos of thought". The latter we may equate with what was previously termed the '*Gegenstand*-sphere'. The "logos" here is that of human rationality, not that of the warrant of the divine Logos, for "the logos of thought" spoken of is *a part of* the "divine cosmos", from which that logos draws both the logical forms and the ideal material, these being the two prime features of the *Gegenstand*-sphere, alias "the logos of thought". The *Gegenstand*-sphere was formerly said to be grounded neither in the Self nor the World (the cosmos), but rather, as critical realism then had it, in "the in itself a-logical material of the Logos" (Dooyeweerd 1922d1: 35). In the present document, however, the *Gegenstand*-sphere or the logos of thought does appear to be grounded in the world/cosmos. Not that the world is a construct of thought—it remains a presupposition, its existence accepted. But it is no longer 'thought-alien' (perhaps one could think of it now as 'thought-familiar'). If human rationality—which avails itself of "the logos of thought"—is now a "part of" the "divine cosmos", with the latter being the source of the former, then clearly human rationality is dependent on the "divine cosmos". This 'divine cosmos' is in a position of conditioning "the logos of thought" quite directly. (We will see below that this "logos of thought" is now itself said to have a 'cosmos character'; Dooyeweerd 1923a2: 37.)

Then, thirdly, there is the phrase "divine cosmos", also met with previously. This phrase no doubt can be read as meaning "God's creation", as Dooyeweerd himself does in this introduction (cf. Dooyeweerd 1923a1: 50). But Dooyeweerd's re-emphasizing that Christianity unconditionally takes the side of the realists, also suggests the continuity of the realist's understanding of the World/Cosmos as 'objective sphere' whose 'primal forms' are extra-mental ideas (in God's Counsel or the mind of God; cf. the discussion with Scholten in III.C.3 above). We find a substantiation of this interpretation in the present study, and there is no suggestion of any retraction or change of meaning. We will find it to be continued in later (published) texts as well (cf. III.F.5 below). Hence we may assume the continued presence of this metaphysical import in the use of 'divine cosmos' here.

It may be that the sense of continuity overrides the feeling of discontinuity that takes place in the shift towards the 'thought-familiar' cosmos. For Dooyeweerd gives no indication that his description of thought being a part of the cosmos is novel or unusual as compared to earlier statements.[163] He gives more forthright attention to the possibility of Christian realists still being able to wander with regard to questions of methodology. *Christianity itself* needs to be thought through more philosophically, and one needs to focus on the distinction among realists, of those who accept "the Christ of Scripture" and those who reject him (Dooyeweerd 1923a1: 50). It is this facet of the divergent life- and world-views of Calvinism and Roman Catholicism that is up for discussion in this paper. We shall return to this later. But we wish to emphasize that the current document is probably the first to contain an explicit 'Christocentric' statement.

It is the novel statement of realism, about the logos being part of the cosmos, that first calls for discussion. It is difficult to exaggerate its importance for Reformed thought. It is a characteristic feature of the latter to accord the logic (or rationality) of thought its own cosmic structure, a structure that itself is not logically organized,[164] and which is the source of the content of thought as well. Vollenhoven too endorsed it, as we said. It is a central feature of his work of 1926 and later, expressed as "knowing

---

163   There is an earlier statement in "Normatieve rechtsleer" (Dooyeweerd 1922d, p. 44) that seems to anticipate the idea of thought being a part of the cosmos, when Dooyeweerd announces that critical realism first of all assumes: "a thought-foreign cosmos, encompassing the whole of God's creation, thought included, organized according to categories." He immediately adds that these categories are not logical but cosmic, being that of "the cosmic unity of connection". Above we identified the latter as being of the order of *ideas*. The 'encompassing' character of God's creation does not, I believe, make thought a 'part of the cosmos' in a strict sense, for that would contradict the description of the cosmos as being 'thought-foreign'/'thought-alien'. There is the cosmic substrate that thought 'works over' and organizes in logical categories; also the 'cosmic Self' has the capacity of thought. These would appear to be the ways in which thought is here said to be 'encompassed' by God's creation, while its content is organized in the distinct *Gegenstand*-sphere.

164   Dooyeweerd writes: "de door God kosmisch – niet logisch geordende schepping" (Dooyeweerd 1923a1: 50); i.e. "the creation cosmically not logically arranged/organized by God". The meaning of the contrast between 'cosmic' and 'logic' is not immediately evident here. (We return later to a suggestion that occurs at the end of this section of Dooyeweerd's text.) Vollenhoven associated the term 'cosmic' with its aesthetic root, meaning that the creation is a work of the divine Artisan, a product of his will (cf. Vollenhoven to Janse 7-11-1922, section II.C. above; also Vollenhoven 1926msA, §1). Thus the cosmos is a "harmonious whole" in which logical understanding, knowing and methodological treatment are interwoven, and without which logic would lack context (order) and relevance (meaning).

'resorting' under being". (In fact, it is this feature that kept Vollenhoven's definitive thought congenial to realism.) This entails a rejection of the *polarity of thought and being*, at least in the way this has been worked into texts up to this point of time. Also, when viewed against the background of Vollenhoven's initial Trinitarian theism, there is a shift with respect to the role of the divine Logos. The role of warranting knowledge now comes to be allotted more in connection with the world. Perhaps this provides the opportunity of a more 'Christo-centric' and less theological-dogmatic emphasis of the *Logos*. In other words, there is a quite important revision of philosophical orientation involved here. So what does Dooyeweerd now make of '*cosmos* and *logos*? What does the reorientation involve?

2. *Logos* as the realm of meaning
'Cosmos' and '*logos*' are quite loosely referred to as two realms, areas, worlds; they interpenetrate, but need to be clearly distinguished. The *logos* "is the realm of meaning" (*het rijk van de zin*), and it is *included* in the cosmos: "The cosmos encompasses the whole well-ordered world of creation, including the logos, the realm of meaning" (Dooyeweerd 1923a2: 37). Accordingly, the *logos* has a "cosmic character".[165] But this must be understood as suppositional. All individual knowing takes place on the basis of the (cosmic) logos and thus presupposes it. Our consciousness is walled in by this *logos* and we can never transcend it and view its connection—"essential connection" (*wezensverband*; *ibid.*)—with the cosmos generally. All that the human being is able to know is the (essential) connection *within* this cosmic *logos*.[166] So Dooyeweerd discusses this first. At the end of this epistemological discussion he returns to the question of cosmology.

What is the 'essential connection' within the (cosmic) *logos*? And what are the 'essential connections' between this *logos* and the encompassing cosmos? Dooyeweerd now avails himself explicitly of a Husserlian idiom, more so than had previously been the case. Three factors stand in mutual opposition in the *logos*: "meaning-giving (*noèsis*), meaning-having object (*noèma*) and the meaning itself (*noumenon*), as the lawfully secured

---

165 This 'cosmic logos' is clearly not the 'divine Logos'. The latter can hardly be thought to be, given the Reformed tradition, a 'realm' that 'intersects the cosmos' and is included in it. As 'realm of meaning' this logos is a 'small-l logos', relevant to the *Gegenstand*-sphere. This cosmic or created logos will in time soon be transformed into 'the logical law-sphere'.

166 Dooyeweerd will however relativize this. Cf. the last part of our discussion of this document below.

referent prior to every individual meaning-giving".[167] This somewhat idiosyncratic terminology can be brought to intelligible proportions if we note the description of each of these three factors.

(i) *Meaning-giving* is said to be "nothing but consciousness" (*ibid.*). As such, it is not yet knowledge but the precondition of any knowledge. It is a "viewing of meaning" (*schouwing van den zin*; *ibid.*), in the sense of discerning intuitively a given or available meaning. This "given meaning" is also as viewed: the water we see on the road may be real but could also be a mirage. I believe we can use the term 'act' here. Mental acts signal an active consciousness, and this also accords with the phenomenological use of 'noèsis', which is active cognition, intelligence.

(ii) The *meaning-having object* is "the rough material of all our subjective experiences" (*ibid.*) that accrues in virtue of being individually conscious of it. This is the 'content', and it has an inseparable essential connection with acts within consciousness. It is, as the term 'noèma' also suggests, the content of the "individual activity of the viewing consciousness" (*ibid.*), the thought or what is intended upon and grasped in the viewing.

(iii) The *meaning itself* is what is presupposed throughout. In the correlation of act and content, the meaning is that which comes to consciousness, hence 'becoming conscious' has something ineluctably subjective about it (*ibid.*). But the act could not be a conscious viewing unless there is something given to view, something that is simply present and that is 'picked up' (so to speak)—or an aspect of it—in conscious acts. This "given meaning" (*gegeven zin*) is therefore the *objective-primary meaning*, which is presupposed by act and content alike. It is "noumenon" that becomes "phenomenon" in mental intellection. It is this noumenon that links *logos* to *cosmos* (*ibid.*)

This 'given meaning' (noumenon) itself is very nearly identical to, or strongly suggests, the term *Gegenstand* of former discussions. But it is not likely to be an accident that the latter term is practically absent in the current text. (It occurs once in the last section, in brackets, after, and as alternative to, "objective meaning"; Dooyeweerd 1923a3: 60). The occurrence of act and content calls up the mentality of the Self as used by Vollenhoven in his dissertation. It should also not escape us that act and

---

167 The Dutch reads: "Binnen den logos dan staan tegenover elkander zingeving (*noesis*) [sic], zinhebbend voorwerp (*noema*) [sic] en de zin zelve (*noemenon*) [sic] als de wettelijk vaststaande beduidenis voorafgaande aan iedere individueele zingeving" (1923a2: 37). The term 'meaning' would appear (to anticipate the discussion of this matter) to refer to anything that affects the conscious Self in a measure that is sufficient to allow it to be noticed and named, whether as act or as content.

content are 'intra-mental features', and that their relation falls within what Sigwart described as a 'modal relation'. But let us first stop to compare Dooyeweerd's discussion with that of the early Vollenhoven discussion (studied in chapter 2).

Vollenhoven made particular mention of three acts: sensation (or sense-awareness), memory and representation. To each act there is correlated a fitting content, *viz.* that which is psychically enjoyed—perhaps only fleetingly—as relevant to the act. All this occurs within the confines of the Self. Via the psycho-physical body, the mind is affected by outer experience in sensation, whereby it calls up sense-data. The mind uses these to form representations, or, accruing in memory, to recall this content as remembered. In order to be more profitable in connection with thought and cognition, the Self is able to turn this content into more definitive meanings, namely *Gegenstände*. But this requires that the Self take on the quality of distinguishing subject, which is achieved by a willing submission to the extra-mental norm of identity. In this attitude, as controlled by the norm of identity, the psychically enjoyed content can be compared and differentiated as to its own intrinsic identity. This is the process of *Gegenstand* formation, yielding objective meanings that can be communicated and applied in securing knowledge and scientific understanding.[168]

There is little difficulty in recognizing the similarities between this early Vollenhoven account and Dooyeweerd's use of act (meaning-giving) and content (meaning-having object) (in "Cosmos and Logos"; 1923a2). But Vollenhoven's '*Gegenstand* formation' is more difficult to place. This takes place through subjective submission to a norm, the result (a formed *Gegenstand*) having objectivity in virtue of the norm's being extra-mental. It all takes place on the part of the Self in *disjunction* from the World. For that reason there is the prior step of psycho-physical mediation, for the mind has nothing to enjoy unless data enter through the body. (There is also the metaphysical intuition, but that is the immediate awareness of otherness and identity, acknowledged in the idea, preventing sense-data from being interpreted as mere figments of the mind.)

Now if we exchange the 'Self-beside-World' model of the early Vollenhoven for a 'Self-attached to-World' model,[169] we see how the media-

---

168 These *Gegenstände* are Objects (terms) and Objectives (complexes or propositions). In the context of the *Gegenstand*-sphere, as discussed so far, they delineate the 'essential connections' that are themselves organized in modalities, or the domains of the highest material categories of thought.

169 This 'model' is suggested by Dooyeweerd's description of consciousness being "walled in by the (cosmic) logos" (*ons bewustzijn in den logos is ingemuurd*) (1923a2: 37).

tion of the psycho-physical body can be circumvented. An act can then be interpreted as taking place in rapport with something that is immediately present to the Self. We then have a purer cognition or intellection than is the case when representations first have to be shaped by the psycho-physical forms of sensibility. Act and its intentional content then bring to consciousness what is already there *for* consciousness, a noumenon. It is as if a *Gegenstand's* extra-mental determination (by the principle of identity in the early Vollenhoven), in virtue of which it is deemed 'mental material' as based on an available act and content, is now itself turned into and taken to be a precondition—"primary-objective meaning"—for consciousness, with act and content now being the (subjective) means of actually acquiring an (immediate) consciousness of it. The *Gegenstand* is then no longer 'formed', but is already there for the sake of consciousness and given with the world. It only needs to be *focussed on* (in an act) and *attended to* (as content). At the same time this primary meaning is the warrant for the 'essential connections' that the human being is able to know, namely those between act and content within the logos. Implicit, too, though Dooyeweerd does not state this as such, is that the primary-objective meaning has absorbed within it the (former) role of the 'norms' (warranted by the Spirit), so that the *Gegenstand*, now said to be given for consciousness, has a quality of norm- or law-impingement. This would appear to be implied in the expression that meaning itself—the noumenon—is the 'legally secured referent' (*wettelijk vaststaande beduidenis*) (Dooyeweerd 1923a2: 37; on p. 38 he speaks of 'legally secured meaning').

The foregoing makes clear that the terminology of a 'thought-alien cosmos' is no longer suitable. But we are left in the dark as to why the shift in understanding, reflected in the revised terminology, took place at all. Part of the reason could be the realization that acts and *Gegenstand* formation, on Vollenhoven's early view, were still too much 'quasi-autonomous' processes of thought, despite the appeal to extra-mental norms here, particularly in light of the Self's context as being separated from the World.[170] This had perhaps become an embarrassment in light of the

---

Of course, the Self is not identical to consciousness, so the Self is not thereby submerged in the world, though the Self's consciousness is.

170   What is here described as the shift to the 'Self-attached to-World' model is consonant with Vollenhoven's shift to a 'tasked subject', described in Vollenhoven's reaction to Janse's questioning; cf. the Janse discussion in the first half of this chapter. This does not mean to say that there could not have been a preparatory move in light of an enhanced awareness of Calvinism. Vollenhoven, looking back later, wrote about a "discovery" somewhere about the summer of 1922. We return to this at the end of this chapter

"slogan of Calvinism" with which Dooyeweerd opened (cf. footnote 96 at the beginning of this section E.). Consciousness is now taken—more phenomenologically—to depend on the very reality that one becomes conscious of. There are 'essential connections' involved. There is an intensification as to what consciousness is about, including a feature of demand on consciousness. Thus, it is not as if Dooyeweerd is simply 'switching models' regarding the Self and the World. There is an element of reformation, of reworking former (or accepted) work and reshaping this to answer to a view with more satisfactory worldview implications.

3. Modality – Field of vision – Region category
Distinctions and terms, such as 'modality', 'region category', 'viewing', etc., we came across earlier are now incorporated into this newly formulated view, a view that is predicated on certain 'essential connections'. Basic to the new view is the 'given meaning', as the 'objective-primary meaning'. Because this meaning is 'for consciousness', the first thing to expect is that it be 'accepted' and 'held'. When consciousness is essentially the accepting and holding of (given) meaning, then our subjective consciousness always involves both. One accepts in acts and one holds their content. Acts and content are always 'essentially connected' in consciousness. This is because the connection is one of (metalogical) intuition, of "viewing". "The meaning-having object [content] entirely hangs together with the meaning giving [acts] as individual activity of viewing" (1923a2: 37). Such viewing is the essential requisite for thought and knowledge. Therefore this viewing of content in an individual act is the 'essential connection' within 'the logos of thought': there is no act (meaning giving) without content (meaning-having object), and vice versa.

Consciousness is 'walled in' in the logos. This is not to deny it great diversity. One may always, in a new act, reflect on content that is held and grasp, and now seize on new content on the basis of it. (Dooyeweerd's example: in the twilight one might take a tree to be a person, and only on second thought does one recognize a tree; *ibid*. 37.) The initial act and content are subjective with respect to the 'objective-primary meaning' (noumenon) of person-like shape. The second act and content are also subjective. But, in being based on the former act and content connection, the latter is now part of the primary objective meaning of this second act and content. This 'intra-conscious viewing of viewing' needs to be secured, and this calls for 'essential connections' of the logos with the cosmos.

(cf. III.G. Overview).

Determinative for all or any viewing is that the act (meaning giving) of viewing has distinct *forms*, these being "primary functions of consciousness" (1923a2: 38). Dooyeweerd now uses the term 'modality' to denote a *primary function of consciousness* (*primaire bewustzijnsfunctie*). When in an act of consciousness we grasp one or more numbers or spatial figures or moments of time or consider physical objects, etc., such acts presuppose that we grasp number as meaning, space as meaning, time as meaning, 'reality' as meaning, respectively. In each case this is a form of consciousness, enabling one to grasp the relevant specific essences in concrete acts. This is said to be "an absolute prerequisite . . . for these concrete acts [*concrete zingevingen*]" (*ibid.*). So when viewing, one attends to concrete content, and thereby one presupposes the 'form' or 'modality' relevant for the viewing. "All these forms of viewing, without which concrete meaning giving would be impossible, must, in themselves, (as objective meaning) therefore stand in an essential connection to the viewed meaning itself [*den geschouwden zin zelve*]" (*ibid.*). In other words, any specific act of consciousness (meaning giving) cannot take place without answering to a prerequisite of meaning as such, namely the adequate form of the viewing. Modality is this 'form of viewing', and thus it is presupposed in or for any consciousness. It cannot be viewed as such, for any viewing requires its own adequate form of modality. In this sense modality represents an 'essential connection' between consciousness and (its) reality, that is, between the logos of thought and the cosmos. Because "viewing, the meaning giving, is the primary function of Self-consciousness [*ik-bewustzijn*]" (1923a2: 43), the cosmic reality here is that of the Self.

It should be evident that this use of 'modality' is different from its former use, in which it served as synonym for 'region category'. In that use, it denotes the highest material unity of the *Gegenstand* of a science. Of course, such a characteristic can only be grasped or acknowledged in an intuition or metalogical "viewing". But previously this did not call for fundamentally *different modes* of viewing, as is now argued in the text at hand (1923a2). In other words the term 'modality' has now acquired a more 'subjective' primary use.[171]

Dooyeweerd sets this 'subjective use' off by retaining the term 'region category' as analogue for this subjective use. There is undiminished need to acknowledge the highest material unity of content. Dooyeweerd's

---

171   The use of 'subjective' is not meant in a psychological sense. Dooyeweerd states: "Meaning-giving is often confused with psychological sensibility, representation, feeling etc. (1923a2: 40). Rather, it suggests a link with the Self.

own words are clear. "To the modality as primary form of the viewing consciousness [act], there must be something that answers in the world of the meaning viewed, other than the concrete character [*geaardheid*] of the meaningful essences themselves [content]; this analogue we call the *essential connection of the region* in the world of the meaning viewed, or simply *region category*" (1923a2: 38-39). Of course regions differ as to modality or the nature of the highest unity grasped. Here too, much as any viewing presupposes a form of viewing, so any content grasped presupposes a unity of characterization. The essential connection with respect to region categories is what links the content of the "the logos of thought" to the world. This too is a connection that cannot be brought to consciousness on account of its being presupposed in all consciousness.

In short: "The modality is [a] subjective form of the meaning giving, in objective sense [it is] a form of the essential connection of the region within the world of the meaning viewed" (p.39). So the term 'modality' is now used in both a subjective sense and an objective sense. If we focus on its relevance in the context of scientific methodology – which is its primary context – leaving out its ramifications in other areas, then I believe one can interpret the statement of modality as a defence of the *synthetic a priori*. Modality is intrinsic to objective necessity (within a region), and at the same time calls for (subjective) apodictic acknowledgement (within a form of viewing). The problem of the synthetic apriori was certainly on the minds of Dooyeweerd and Vollenhoven at the time. A solitary statement of Vollenhoven, after his recovery, at least points in this direction. In his letter to A. Janse of 19 February 1924, he writes that each science needs to have a distinct *field* that can be *viewed*, for "only in that way can we investigate what its categories and synthetic-aprioristic judgments are."[172]

There is yet a third term, itself new, that Dooyeweerd introduces. That is the term 'field of vision' (*gezichtsveld*; 1923a2: 38).[173] There is

---

172 The modalities that Dooyeweerd actually mentions in "Cosmos and Logos" (1923a: 38) are virtually the same as those of "Normative legal doctrine" (1922d), namely number, space, matter/energy, reality, the psychical, normativity and '(logical) system (or validity)' (cf. section III.C.4.c).

173 It is difficult to choose an adequate translation for all the intuitionist terms. In Dutch the terms 'gezichtspunt' and 'gezichtsveld' form a quite natural pair, i.e. 'point of view' and 'field of view', respectively. But the latter is not idiomatic English. Now as to their meaning, over against the meaning of 'point of view', which is a viewing from a particular position or angle, a 'field of view' is meant to express the range or scope within which viewing can or actually does take place. But, because the word "viewing" is already in use in translating "schouwen", I resort to 'field of vision' to translate "gezichtsveld" (the 'vision' being that of (in)sight, not of dreaming). John Kok translated the term, when this

need to keep the viewed content—Dooyeweerd speaks of "viewed meaning essences" (*geschouwde zinwezens*; *ibid.*)—together. It is relevant to keep specific content together only if they agree as to modal characteristic. They need to belong to the same (objective) region or to result from one and the same form of viewing. So in the term 'field of vision' we have the essential connection *within* the logos or consciousness itself, between act and content, as anticipated earlier. This term will acquire, at least in Vollenhoven, a permanent place among the furniture of his thought. In Dooyeweerd, later, it merges with (that much overworked term) 'aspect'.

We add the remark that the relation between modality as a form of viewing and the content of a field of vision falls within the scope of the relation that Sigwart calls a "modal relation". Dooyeweerd objected to this term (as we saw) on account of the autonomy of (evaluative) viewing it entails. The term does not occur in the current document. Were it to be used—after all the relation between act and content is explicit—then 'modal relation' would not be autonomous in Dooyeweerd's use, in virtue of the essential connections with the objective-primary meaning, as lawfully secured, in which the cosmos is there for consciousness. Dooyeweerd's realism would 'hold back' an explicit autonomy in this regard.

The *Gegenstand*-sphere, met with in former work, is redefined in the current work as a cosmic domain of rationality (cosmic *logos*). It is cosmic because the inner workings of this rationality presuppose consciousness as the medium that reflects essential connections with reality. At this primary level cosmic reality is present as intuit-able by the 'viewing consciousness'. In the diversity of its forms (modalities), the viewing consciousness draws objective meaning (content) into its fields of vision (1923a2: 42). The (created) *logos*, in its most general sense (= the former *Gegenstand*-sphere), is this world of objective meaning (*ibid.*).

Knowing and thought are now 'fitted into' this intuitive consciousness. The region categories organize intuited content according to each region's own essential connections and differences. Such an organizing of content is a prerequisite for knowing. For, in its relation to knowing, the *logos* "is the world of known meaning" only when "with respect to the knowing consciousness, the *logos* is constructed in the perspective of its region categories, that are encompassed by the viewing consciousness in its modalities" (1923a2: 42). Knowing presupposes intuitive viewing in the diversity of its modalities. Then, as to thought, 'logical thought'—this

---

occurs in Vollenhoven's work of 1926, as "intellectual horizon"; cf. Kok 1992: 248 ff. This opts for a term ('horizon') that gets a firm place in Dooyeweerd's (later) thought, but not in Vollenhoven.

taken in the sense of 'applied scientific methodology'—operates within the scope of both intuitive consciousness and knowing consciousness. It introduces *systems* into the regions that are distinguished in the knowing consciousness; e.g. the 'region' of nature is turned into the scientific system of nature (cf. the next section) in physics as science.

So, in summary, whereas the former *Gegenstand*-sphere has the two sides of content and logical structure, with content organized in region categories of distinct modality, and intuited as such, the current 'created logos' proceeds from a *broader intuitive base*. It introduces, as new element, the modes of viewing of intuitive consciousness, with attendant fields of vision. Another important difference is that, whereas the *Gegenstand*-sphere is warranted directly by the divine *Logos*, belonging to neither the Self nor the World, the created *logos* has essential ties with cosmic reality, both as regards the Self (to which the modal forms of viewing are linked) and the World (represented in region categories). This puts the role of the 'divine Logos' in a new light. The qualification of the cosmos as 'thought-alien' no longer applies. But the cosmos is still a 'divine cosmos' (cf. section 5 below).

In this document Dooyeweerd avails himself of a more phenomenological approach in visualizing how knowledge of the world can be accounted for, through an immediate contact with the world to the extent that the world can be intuited, the world as 'given meaning'. The world we can know is the world insofar as the world becomes the content of consciousness. This, however, is to be realistically understood, not idealistically, for it presupposes the existence of cosmic reality. This would appear to definitely place the world as a whole beyond the human rational reach. For meaning is the *"lawfully secured referent* prior to every individual meaning-giving [act]" (1923a2: 37; emphasis added). It turns out though that this is not the last word. But before continuing the discussion in connection with the transition to cosmology, we first need to review logical thought more specifically within the range of the created *logos*.

4. Logical thought
'Logical thought' warrants separate mention, for certain features of it recur in later writings of both Dooyeweerd and Vollenhoven. We will briefly make note of what Dooyeweerd asserts in the current text.

Dooyeweerd begins—in "Cosmos and *Logos*" (1923a2: 40)—by distinguishing arbitrary thought from systematic or logical thought. *Arbitrary thought* is given with the diversity of the modalities, in the sense that the diversity to which the 'viewing of meaning' is subject, attests to the different ways in which intellectual attention can be focussed. In other words, arbitrary thought is as broad as the intuited range of the cosmic *logos* itself. One is able to attend to what is psychically present in sense-experience, but equally one could turn one's attention to the theorem of Pythagoras, to the memory of yesterday's copious meal, or to one's duty or promises, etc. Each such attitude is a context of meaning in which one comes to formulate a judgment. "I direct my attention to a given meaning and form for myself a judgment about it" (*ibid.*). This is the context in which knowing takes place, its scope being as broad as that of 'arbitrary thought'. But *logical thought* is "entirely different". It is systematic thought, and that concerns being involved with the systematic logical connections between judgments within a field of vision of specific modality. These systematic logical connections define the *method* of thought (*ibid.*).

Systematic thought, as method of thought, is directed towards the content within a modally specific field of vision. Systematic thought involves its own acts of logical viewing. Logical viewing is itself a modality within the cosmic *logos*. To be more specific, logical viewing is viewing content with a view to the logical categories of *unity* and *diversity*. These categories impose fundamental conditions on the content viewed. They guarantee that everything that enters into logical thought, as belonging to the (logical) field of vision, has "identity with itself and diversity with everything else" (1923a2: 41; this reminds one of Vollenhoven's initial account of *Gegenstand* formation, though now transformed). When so defined, the systematic connections (between logical viewing and content viewed) become the subject of investigation. The imposition of the logical categories *secures* the content of a field of vision in such a way that the content becomes a "field of thought" (*denkveld*) (*ibid.*). (I shall refer to this as 'field of inquiry'.) What this says more plainly is that the logical viewing represents the intention of organizing the content viewed into a system. To that end the categories of unity and identity serve to mark this goal of arranging into a system. The systematic connections that become explicit are indicative of *validity*, the latter being itself the modality of logical thought, now applied to a specific field of inquiry. Thus "the fundamental modality of logical thought is the system as form of thought" (1923a2: 42), i.e. the discerning of validity as relevant for a field of inquiry.

In practice, the identity condition by which a field of inquiry is laid out, takes on the form of well-defined terms, concepts and judgments. In arranging these systematically, one arranges them methodically; say: one takes stock of which terms are general, which specific, which concepts are complex, which simple, which judgments follow from which other judgments, etc. The logical viewing this calls for, i.e. the viewing that has the mode of the *logical modality*, is, indeed, the *intention* of organizing terms, concepts and judgments into a *system* of thought.

So the relation between logical viewing and a field of inquiry also exemplifies, in a more restricted or controlled sense, the essential connection between act (meaning-giving) and content (meaning-having). The methodical-systematic intention of inquiry directs the logical viewing. At the same time the essential or cosmic connections between the *logos* (as meaning for consciousness) and what is beyond the *logos*, a connection always assumed but not knowable in itself, can still be studied methodologically in the measure that this is reflected in the content of a field of viewing and grasped in terms of region categories. The differences between the fields of viewing will call up different relevant categories within a field. The region categories make evident the boundaries between the fields of viewing and hence also between the fields of inquiry.[174]

Systematic thought is scientific thought, as over against the arbitrary thought of everyday knowing. The latter takes place through a directed (intended) viewing attitude. Scientific knowledge on the other hand is based on the *synthesis* of viewing and thought, for the viewing of a field of vision now needs to be transferred into a logically fixed content of a field of inquiry. The problem of synthesis will recur in Dooyeweerd's 'transcendental critique of theoretical thought'. In Vollenhoven, what is here termed 'arbitrary thought' versus 'logical thought', becomes the distinction between knowing and thinking. Dooyeweerd will attempt to validate the synthesis in terms of conditions that are of a religious character. However Vollenhoven offers an analysis of 'logical thought' that makes evident its multiple links with cosmic structure and human direction.

---

174 When executing systematic organization through logical thought, the content itself comes to be known as a system. Thus, thought that is focussed on the physically real field of vision, results in our acquiring a knowledge of physical reality as a *system of nature* (cf. p. 41). Dooyeweerd adds that, as regards logical thought, not only does it consider non-logical content, but it can also focus on logical thought itself as well, i.e. thought in its organizing activity (as logical meaning-giving) within diverse fields of inquiry. One then becomes aware of the different methods required to do justice to the differences between fields of inquiry. In other words, in the context of logical thought one gains an encyclopaedic knowledge of the sciences; thus logic itself is also the science of the encyclopaedia of the sciences.

5. Transition to cosmology

In order to bring the theme of the cosmos into the discussion, Dooyeweerd first discussed two applications of logical thought as encumbered by the content of a field of vision. In the first place there is the science of physical reality. Here it is typical (for it involves an 'essential connection') to treat the content (phenomena) of the physical field of vision in terms of the relation of causality, with its own necessity. Every effect has a cause, but not every effect need have only one cause. But an effect without a cause, or a cause without an effect, has no place here. Thus, in connection with physical reality, "it is foolishness to speak of a first cause or a last effect". Objectively seen, causality is a necessary connection, and in a subjective sense, it is an ordering of a modally encumbered form of thought. In other words, because the category of causality cannot be applied outside of physics—this is because physics *is* the science of the essential connection of causality, to the extent human beings can be aware of it—questions as to whether God is the first cause of the world, or how mind can affect matter, are logically absurd (cf. 1923a2: 43-44).

The second application is that of the teleological relation of means and goal. This relation occurs in biology and in the sciences of culture (or normative sciences). Biology is the field of inquiry of which the modal field of vision is that of organic reality. The logical relation here is the 'essential connection' of means functionally connected to ends in an organically relevant sense. In the normative sciences the 'essential connection' is that of accountability, which is a normative way in which means are related to ends in a way practically relevant to active, willing persons. (Here too the sciences in question are erected on the basis of these connections, as experienced in terms of data for consciousness.) The conclusions drawn are similar to those concerning causality: (i) the applications of the teleological relation are limited; (ii) one should not confuse organic teleology and practical teleology, nor pass from one to the other; (iii) there is no first means nor final goal, hence the teleological connection is a modally encumbered relation (cf. 1923a2: 44-45).[175]

The final section on the transition to cosmology (cf. 1923a3) is brief

---

175   Causality and teleology, being necessary connections, allow for and actually require, an infinite series of phenomena, so as to forestall the 'absurdity' of a first or a last member. This means that the fields of inquiry presuppose an infinite complexity in the modally qualified fields of vision they are based on (cf. 1923a2: 44, 45). We may add that this holds for arithmetic and geometry too, *viz.* the unending series of the natural numbers and the unending variations in spatial forms. One suspects, what was also stated in section 3 above, that the 'essential connections' are the basis for formulating synthetic a priori's for the sciences involved.

but rich in content. It is immediately made clear why the applications of causality and teleology preceded. Traditional cosmological thought seems to have the ineradicable urge of placing everything in connection with a final goal or a first cause.[176] Kant subjected this thought to a critique that exposed the cosmological antinomies. Since then, everything is placed in a relation, idealistically, to human reason, the latter taken to be autonomous. The Marburgers see in thought the origin, out of which arise both the problems of thought and the categories with which to think them. In reaction to this, various forms of 'life philosophy' (Henri Bergson, Georg Simmel) jettison, rather naïvely, along with the autonomy of thought, "the independent right of thought, the forms themselves" (1923a3: 59). In other words, though he finds the autonomy of thought to be untenable, Dooyeweerd is not rejecting the legitimate right of distinct forms of thought.

The thought forms he does take to be legitimate are those that are connected to intuitive viewing. Edmund Husserl and Emil Lask are mentioned as examples of a similar trend, despite their adherence to idealism, namely of those "who award a primary value to objective meaning (to the *Gegenstand*) over against formal thought" (1923a3: 60). This inspires Dooyeweerd to summarize his own position as follows (1923a3: 60-61):

> He who posits objective meaning as primary must assign to consciousness, as its chief task, that of viewing. Proud thought must surrender its throne to the humble viewing of objective meaning. Viewing and thinking themselves become objective meaning, standing in an essential connection to the whole world of objective meaning.
>
> Everything that exists lies bound to its objective meaning, that determines its essence. Viewing is bound to its fields of vision, thought [is bound] to its categories.
>
> In this connection of viewing and thought lies their objective meaning. Now where consciousness no longer *posits* anything as autonomous, but has received everything, *is posited* in everything, as objective meaning, — now that the *law of heteronomy* comes to rule unlimited in all that exists, also in the meaning-giving consciousness, [there] the question arises of its own accord concerning the law-giver, the arranger [*de ordenaar*], the creator. . . .
>
> When everything that exists is *determinate meaning* [*vaststaande zin*], such

---

176   The typescript reads: "laatste doel, resp. laatste oorzaak", (1923a2: 45), which may be a slip of the pen in light of what Dooyeweerd means to say. On page 47 of the typescript Dooyeweerd speaks of the view of God being "laatste doel en eerst *bewegende* oorzaak" [reading '*bewegende*' for '*bewezende*' here, hence: final goal and first moving cause]. In any case Dooyeweerd refers to the dual context of teleology ("means to end") and causality ("cause and consequence"); cf. 1923a2: 48.

is the case only in virtue of *divine meaning-giving*. Nothing exists in itself, nothing exists 'apo-state', disconnected from the divine meaning-giving, everything exists *in* and *through* this divine noesis [sic]. Between all that exists there is the divine cosmic essential connection.

Our subjective logos is intercalated in this essential connection, and thus is also essentially connected to the meaning viewed, known, willed. We cannot however comprehend the essential connection with our thought, for it lies outside of our fields of vision themselves. We cannot express the connection between the fields of vision in logical relations, for the [logical] relation only has meaning within the field of vision that is attentively fixed [*ingeklemde gezichtsveld*]. Likewise we are incapable of specifying in relations the connection between our meaning-giving and the meaning viewed. We can only *know logically* the essential connection *within* the field of vision. Both our meaning-giving and our thought are discontinuous. But that this essential connection between all that exists and our Self-consciousness is an unassailable reality, and that the whole cosmos, including our logos, is 'given' by the Divine Noesis [sic], by the Divine word, must be the alpha and the omega of every veritable epistemology.

Sin makes our thought, our viewing and our willing apostate, unfaithful. We no longer view the world of objective meaning in the divine meaning-giving. And whoever relinquishes this divine noesis [sic] relapses in a series of antinomies and heresies: consciousness, thought, will, feeling becomes '*Ding an sich*' disconnected from God, autonomous, sovereign. With that the cosmos falls and [also] the world of objective meaning, in which our Self-consciousness is only a link.

By the special grace of redemption through Christ Jesus, our viewing and thought are again directed towards the divine meaning-giving, and we again view the world "*sub specie aeternitatis*", "in the light of eternity".

This interesting statement calls for several comments. In the first place, the priority of 'humble' intuitive viewing to 'proud' thinking is motivated by the anti-humanistic drive to undercut autonomy, the latter including the urge to 'create God in the human image' (cf. 1923a3, p. 59). Here is an effect of the Calvinistic life- and worldview position becoming explicit, that Dooyeweerd had announced in the introduction (1923a1; cf. E.1 above). Dooyeweerd implements this by maintaining that the *logos* (subjective reason) is cosmos-embedded. Any individual expression on the part of the human being is first of all a matter of 'becoming conscious through viewing', which in turn is an acceptance of meaning (i.e. anything one can become conscious of, as being intuit-able or 'view-able'), and applying this in subsequent acts of thinking, willing, feeling, etc. and their respective content.[177] The perspective of intuition

---

177   Dooyeweerd states: "Viewing, the meaning-giving [i.e. act], is the primary function of Self-consciousness. We could characterize this function as region category of Self-consciousness (as objective meaning). Thinking, willing, feeling, empathy etc. are

encompassing knowledge, and the latter in turn encompassing thought, is motivated by the Calvinistic life- and worldview, as here understood.

That worldview understanding, secondly, advances notions that affect the whole context of understanding. In speaking of "the divine cosmic essential connection", the recurrence of the implicated 'divine cosmos' here reminds one of the metaphysics still in operation, namely of a realism of being, as warranted by the idea in the divine Counsel. This is not spelled out here, but the reference to "essential connection between all that exists . . . an unassailable reality" *at this level* makes it hard to interpret the phrase other than in the metaphysical-scholastic sense we found in the prior documents.

New, and not continuous with prior work, is the reference to the divine *Logos* here. It is referred to in the idiom of meaning and meaning-giving, divine meaning-giving, divine *noèsis* (thinking, intelligence), etc. Here is the principle of divine rationality. Familiar is the appeal to the divine Logos, as independent divine Person and as warrant for knowledge (the *Gegenstand*-sphere). But the divine Logos is now given the role of warranting the primary objective meaning. Objective meaning is "posited", which suggests the metaphor of 'giving', but in a way that is lawful, securing, holding. This turns the primary human role into one of passively receiving, submitting, of grasping the objective-primary meaning *for* human consciousness. So the divine meaning-giving is what makes the cosmos intuit-able for human consciousness. The divine Logos here 'acts' *within* the context of the (divine) cosmos, making the cosmos intelligible for human beings—recognizing essential connections—to the extent that this falls within the scope of the created logos' capacity in terms of human intuitive consciousness.

Thirdly, unless the human being can relate to the divine *Logos*, there will not be a proper awareness of the source of the objective-primary meaning for human consciousness. This leads to and is attested to by the endless difficulties by way of antinomies, heresies, etc. One needs to accept on faith and as special grace (for no other option is viable) that everything exists in and through this *Logos*—the link to Self-consciousness makes this an "unassailable reality". Our limited subjective *logos*, by means of the "redemption through Christ", can then again be directed

---

secondary functions of consciousness, in *that* sense that they presuppose the viewing of the meaning willed, the meaning felt, the meaning empathized with. They are as it were the modal categories of Self-consciousness" (1923a2: 43). Dooyeweerd here suggests that self-consciousness might be approached as being a modality in its own right, with a region of its own. Little became of this proposal, but it does emphasize the Self-attached to-World position that Dooyeweerd now defends.

to the divine meaning-giving and thereby gain access to a viewing of the world from the point of view of eternity (*sub specie aeternitatis*).

It is difficult to avoid the conclusion that Dooyeweerd is here taking over a feature of Catholicism, that he otherwise critically reviews in this study. If the term 'faith' is taken generically to stand for accepted belief, special grace, redemption, and the like, then it is such faith that is needed to *supplement* the limitation of human reason. The limitation of human reason intuiting meaning is, of course, not itself due to human fallacy; only the lack of orientation to the divine *Logos* is religiously culpable. But redemption, which relieves the human being of this censure, is also thought of as putting the limited human *logos* in a right relation to the divine *Logos*, permitting the human *logos* to overcome its inherent limitation and see the world as God sees it, *viz.* in the light of eternity. This makes sense only when the divine *Logos* and the human *logos* are significantly congruent or in harmony, otherwise faith's orientating us to the divine *Logos* would not have the effect of supplementing our human viewing. This is, of course, a variant of the scholastic view of the relation between subjective and objective reason we also found in the early Vollenhoven, and it is now still in effect in what is new in the current document.

We add the remark that it is not clear how faith effects this, unless this supplementing is within and part of faith's own function. We quoted Dooyeweerd as stating: "Thinking, willing, feeling, empathy etc. are secondary functions of consciousness . . ." (cf. footnote 112 above). Faith is not mentioned as a 'function'. But in light of "the special grace of redemption through Christ Jesus" (1923a3: 61), faith would appear to be more directly relevant for the connection of the Self and the divine *Logos* (in Christ).[178]

---

178 In the typescript of the current text (1923a), Dooyeweerd has a summary statement near its end that is worthy of quote.

> Calvinistic cosmology takes a stand when confessing that the whole world of objective meaning exists only in and through the divine meaning-giving (*noèsis*), and that everywhere essential connections exist, which we however can only know within the fields of vision. Thought ought to subject itself to the divine revelation, but [it] cannot bridge a gap between our fields of vision by introducing a relation which can only be applied within particular fields of vision.
>
> Nature and grace remain divided, in Calvinistic thought, by a deep chasm of the different fields of vision and can only be reconciled in the divine *noèsis* (the divine meaning-giving) of regeneration, rebirth. (*op. cit.* : 52)

The redemptive moment of life experience (in Christ) is essential to appreciate the Logos'

One might wonder whether this text does not announce Dooyeweerd's later explicit view of meaning as ontological principle, found in *De Wijsbegeerte der Wetsidee* (1935-1936). Meaning is there stated to be 'the *being* of all *creaturely reality*'.[179] Thus understood, it undercuts the question as to what has or carries meaning. That meaning is channelled through the diversity of the modalities—'meaning' here too is 'meaning for consciousness'—but it takes on definiteness in terms of the coherence, totality and unity of meaning.[180] I believe it would be a mistake to read this 1935 view into the current text. For the current text has its locus in the philosophy of science. The essential connections between the fields of vision (that limit the scientific consciousness) would appear to presuppose a foundation in a cosmology. The text, which speaks of the transition to cosmology, does not actually indicate what that cosmology is. But when, in connection with the (religious) fall, he speaks of "the [divine] cosmos *and* the world of objective meaning, in which our Self-consciousness is only a link" (1923a3: 60; emphasis added), this assumes a cosmos apart from "the world of objective meaning"—the latter (the intuit-able cosmos) is in fact an alternative formulation of what was formerly termed 'the *Gegenstand*-sphere'. This agrees with the characterization of the creator as "the arranger" ["*de ordenaar*"] (1923a3: 60) and the Christian's "holding to the fact of creation" (1923a1: 50). Meaning is here taken as portraying the arrangement inherent in the cosmos. Our being participants of the cosmos—through participation we are a *part* of the cosmos, not a pole of thought over against being—secures the law of heteronomy, on which depends the primary viewing of consciousness. And, as emphasized in the introduction (section E.1), Dooyeweerd holds that the Christian chooses resolutely for realism over against idealism in that viewing. Realism is not relinquished (as yet).[181]

---

cosmological role of meaning-giving.
179   Dooyeweerd 1935-1936, I: 6. The Dutch reads: "De *zin* is het *zijn* van alle *creatuurlijk zijnde*. . . ."
180   The terms 'totality of meaning' and 'unity of meaning' are given religious determinations in *De Wijsbegeerte der Wetsidee* (1935-1936). Thus it is not a priori certain that the 'scholastic problem', signalled in the current text, does not continue to have an effect in Dooyeweerd's later work. Also the metaphor of the 'lookout tower' (*uitzichttoren*) from which, as 'Archimedean point' for philosophy, a standpoint can be taken above the temporal diversity and coherence of meaning (*op. cit.* , I: 10, 14-15), retains something of the 'seeing in the light of eternity'. Naturally, all this deserves careful discussion of its own, which is out of place here, though we will return to this at the end of this chapter. Cf. the parallel reference in Dooyeweerd 1953-1958, I: 8, 12.
181   Note that in this document of Dooyeweerd the Self is not explicitly said to be 'cosmic'. There is too little textual evidence to be clear on the anthropology here. But

Important features of this text recur in Vollenhoven's work of 1926. Central is the *resorting* of knowing under being. With him too the cosmic connections between what are then called "law-spheres" are not open to inspection. But the analogies (once they are seen) between the fields of inquiry are themselves indicative of the cosmic structure. The Self's connection to the activity of thought is also one that cannot be brought entirely to consciousness. But there is no hint in Vollenhoven's work of the introduction of 'faith' as somehow warranting a view of the world '*sub specie aeternitatis*'. That had not been part of his 'qualified scholasticism'[182] in his early work either.

F. Law-idea

We have now reached a point where we can begin to round off the discussion of Dooyeweerd's early work. The signal for this is the appearance of the term 'wetsidee'—law-idea—in (about mid-)1923, a term central to Dooyeweerd, which Vollenhoven hardly ever used.[183] We can bring together numerous writings of Dooyeweerd that all centre on this theme. In fact, we now reach a point where Dooyeweerd does indeed publish work, meaning that he considers it suitable to be published and for which he accepts responsibility. The theme of law-idea focuses on a cluster of

---

Dooyeweerd does say that viewing is the primary function of Self-consciousness, with thinking, willing, feeling, empathy, etc. as secondary functions (1923a3: 43). What is thought, willed, etc. first needs to be intuited through viewing (*ibid.*). Thus, while for example thinking takes place in direct rapport with the cosmic primary meaning, the viewing subject has a 'deeper' basis in Self-consciousness. If we include the relevance of the *sub specie aeternitatis* then the Self could already here appear to have 'supra-temporal' significance.

182   Vollenhoven's early 'qualified scholasticism' is the view that, though there is a harmony between subjective and objective reason, this harmony is not sufficient to act as foundation of knowledge. A (metalogical) intuition that supports 'synthetic a priori's' is also required; cf. chapter two.

183   It is only in the late 1930s and early 1940s that Vollenhoven temporarily used the term "philosophy of the law-idea" in application to his own thought; cf. Vollenhoven 1939k: 5; also Vollenhoven 1942m, in which he switches between "philosophy of the law-idea" and "Calvinistic philosophy". I can't help thinking that part of the reason is the opposition that Vollenhoven and Dooyeweerd were subject to in the 1930s, which was then coming to a head. A united front was strategically essential. But 1938-1941 also evidences development. For from that time the law, as boundary between God and cosmos, is no longer simply taken by Vollenhoven to be predicated on their difference, but also includes its own moment of connection, and as something knowable in its own right. This change is worked into the text of *Isagôgè Philosophiae* in the editions of 1939 and later, though without using the term '*wetsidee*'; cf. chapter 4 and also my "Algemene inleiding" [General introduction] to the text-critical edition of *Isagôgè Philosophiae*, i.e. Vollenhoven 2010.

notions that help characterize the distinct position that Dooyeweerd and Vollenhoven have sought within the tradition of Calvinism and is also indicative of a distinguishing feature of philosophical understanding.[184]

In a study (unpublished, 1923b), dated October 1923, entitled "The doctrine of the sovereignty of legality and of state sovereignty in its consequences for the relation of government and laity", there is mention of notions that are identified as being explicitly Calvinistic. They are: "the absolute sovereignty of God over the whole terrain of his creation" and "between God and his creation [Calvinism] posits everywhere the law as boundary concept, that human reason cannot transcend".[185] Dooyeweerd is now, more explicitly than before, reflecting on the roots of the Reformed tradition so as to give more security to his basic life- and worldview stance from which he operates. The very term 'Calvinism', as he (again) emphasizes—as had Abraham Kuyper in his *Lectures on Calvinism*—is used "not merely as a theological system, but rather as a view that encompasses all the terrains of life" (Dooyeweerd 1923c: 63).

---

184   There are numerous works of Dooyeweerd relevant to the discussion. To facilitate reference, the following system of bibliographical codes is used.
- 1923d: *Calvinisme en Natuurrecht*. Referaat voor de Calvinistische Juristen Vereeniging. Amersfoort: Wed. W. van Wijnen, [not dated, but published in 1924]; 32 pages.
- 1923e1-5: "Het Calvinistisch beginsel der souvereiniteit in eigen kring als staatkundig beginsel." *Nederland en Oranje* 4, (1. October 1923; 2. March 1924; 3. April 1924; 4. May 1924; 5. August 1924.
- 1924, I: "In den strijd om een Christelijke Staatkunde. Proeve van een fundering der Calvinistische levens- en wereldbeschouwing in hare wetsidee." *Antirevolutionaire Staatkunde* 1 (no. 1, Oct. 1924), 7-25 (Introduction and first of fifteen instalments).
- 1924, VI: "In den strijd om een Christelijke Staatkunde; VI", *Antirevolutionaire Staatkunde* 1 (no. 6, March 1925), 228-244.
- 1925: "Leugen en waarheid over het Calvinisme." *Nederland en Oranje* 6, 81-90.
- 1926a: "Tweeërlei kritiek. Om de principieele zijde van het vraagstuk der medezeggenschap." *Antirevolutionaire Staatkunde* 2 (no. 1, Jan. 1926), 1-21.
- 1926b: "Het oude probleem der Christelijke staatkunde." *Antirevolutionaire Staatkunde* 2 (no. 2, Feb. 1926), 63-84. (Summary of the instalments I-XII of 1924)
- 1926c: "Calvinisme contra neo-Kantianisme. Naar aanleiding van de vraag betreffende de kenbaarheid der goddelijke rechtsorde." *Tijdschrift voor Wijsbegeerte* 20, 29-74. (Note: pp. 34-59 are from the typescript "Normatieve Rechtsleer", 1922d.)
- 1926d: *De beteekenis der wetsidee voor Rechtswetenschap en Rechtsphilosophie*. Kampen: Kok. Inaugural lecture, 15 October 1926.
- 1928a: "Het juridisch causaliteitsprobleem in 't licht der wetsidee", *Antirevolutionaire Staatkunde* n.s. 2 (no. 1, 1928), pp. 21-121.
- 1928b: "Naschrift. Inzake het recht der Calvinistische wetenschapsbeschouwing, en het misverstand eener 'neutraal-wetenschappelijke' kritiek"; "Beroepsmisdaad en strafvergelding in 't licht der wetsidee" *Antirevolutionaire Staatkunde* n.s. 2 (no. 4, 1928), pp. 419-436.

185   Cf. Verburg 1989: 62; a quote from 1923b.

In securing this, he now speaks of a 'law-idea' that is typical of Calvinism, a term he found in the German theologian, Matthias Schneckenburger, who used it to typify Calvinism's Christology and ethics, but which Dooyeweerd now generalizes to cover all terrains of life.[186] But the most explicit statement of "Calvinism" is in a booklet, entitled "Calvinism and Natural Law".[187] It includes a discussion in which the term 'law-idea' is introduced and defended. It would appear to be the first statement on Calvinistic thought that was actually published.

In setting the tone of his discussion, and in confirming Kuyper's view of Calvinism as embodying a unitary view of life and the world, Dooyeweerd claims that Calvinism "contains in itself a deep philosophical view of life, offers the contours for a distinct [*eigen*] epistemology, a distinct philosophy of science, a distinct psychology, a distinct view of history, a distinct doctrine of legality, a distinct state policy [*staatkunde*]" (Dooyeweerd 1923d: 3). The root of this vitality lies not in Calvin but in the "unfathomable word of God "[*Gods woord*]", in Calvin's acknowledging of divine sovereignty in the very distinct and pregnant sense over the whole of creation" (*ibid.*). In other words, Dooyeweerd now takes Calvinism to be more pregnant in meaning than had been the case before, though ever since his letter to Vollenhoven (17 December 1920) there has been an appeal to Calvinism in a positive and (depending on how 'metaphysical' is used there in this letter) broad sense.

1. Law-idea as '*organon*'
In order to get a handle on this richer meaning, Dooyeweerd turns to history in search of how classic thinkers brought a synthesis to bear in their life- and world view. One then discovers, as "'the organon'[188] of every self-

---

186   Cf. Dooyeweerd 1924, I: 9, note 1.
187   1923d. The text is a presentation Dooyeweerd planned for the first annual meeting of the Association of Calvinistic Jurists on 3 June 1924. Lack of time led to Dooyeweerd's presentation being postponed to the next annual meeting a year later. But the text was already in print in 1924, for Dooyeweerd refers to it in the fourth instalment of a popular series on Calvinism, in *Nederland en Oranje*, August 1924 (1923e4, 72). Cf. also Verburg 1989: 70. Henderson states, without offering any support, that the text was written in 1923; cf. Henderson 1994: 117, n. 209. Evidence supporting this early composition is Dooyeweerd's letter to J. Ridderbos of Kampen, dated 16 January 1924. About half of this letter is an explanation of the "Reformed law-idea" (*gereformeerde wetsidee*), and it reads as a direct summary of the relevant part of *Calvinism and Natural law* (prior to the parts about natural law).
188   John Kraay used this term to characterize Dooyeweerd's early thought (1924-1926). Because he limits himself to the published work, no connections are laid with Dooyeweerd's prior texts, for which this term is less suitable. Kraay interprets shifts in

contained system of life- and worldview a leading cosmological principle that one can call the *idea of law* [or "law-idea", *wetsidee*] (1923d: 4). In ancient philosophy one finds a *lex naturalis* (natural law), which serves as a principle of arrangement (*ordeningsprinciep*), an architectural "design plan" for the whole of creation. It is variously expressed, being *idealistic* in Plato, *entelechistic* in Aristotle, *materialistic* in the Stoa, etc. In each case there is a distinct way in which the main features of life and the world come together, features of nature, of the human being, of natural life, or social life, of politics, ethics, cultic life, etc. And in that coming together a *cosmological* principle serves as blue print. In the Stoa everything is causally determined; hence a '*prima causa*' is the principle of determination, operating through the cause-effect connection. In Aristotle, everything is oriented to ends, hence here the '*ultima finis*' is the privileged principle, operating through the means-end relation. (Plato, perhaps tellingly, is not mentioned further.) Important for Dooyeweerd is that these two different connections also serve as models of rationality. Via a cause-effect structure reason attempts to understand how everything comes to be, via a means-end relation reason asks why.

In Christianity it is "Augustine who, in a vigorous attempt, ventured to formulate a law-idea from out of the Christian life- and worldview" (1923d: 7). With him the law-idea is expressed as a *lex aeterna* ('eternal law'; the "lawful plan of God"; 1923d: 9) not a natural law (the latter is implicated in the former). This eternal law is predicated on "the absolute sovereignty of God and the boundary division between the finite and the infinite" (1923d: 8) Augustine availed himself of elements of Philo's 'Logos doctrine' and the Neoplatonic layered arrangement of hypostases of being to fill-out his law-idea. In Neoplatonism's vertical arrangement, God is the highest unity, from which emanate intellect (*nous*), which includes the (Platonic) Ideas, then the Soul and finally Nature or matter in its infinite forms. Augustine replaced the emanation with creation and the Neoplatonic *nous* with the Philonic *Logos*, and there we have "in rough form the content of Augustine's law-idea" (1923d: 8).

But this *lex aeterna* of Augustine does not completely satisfy. In emphasizing creation, there is the "Christian-theistic strain" in which the will of the personal God is central, the creator of Heaven and Earth, as predicated on the boundary division between the infinite creator and the finite creature. (This is central to the theological doctrine of providence and predestination; see below.) But there is also the "Neoplatonic strain"

Dooyeweerd's terms, and in their meanings, to be indicative of "successive conceptions" in his development; cf. Kraay 1979.

in which this boundary is relativized. The hierarchical structure of being makes it possible to descend and lose oneself in the lower diversity, but also to ascend to the highest region and gain mystical union with the Godhead. But this "identifies the eternal law with God's essence, whereby that law is made to be binding on God" (1923d: 8). So this "Augustinian-Platonic law-idea" (1923d: 9) is idealistic, in the sense that "it posits the dominance of the spiritual over the material, the soul over matter, the idea over its concretization" (1923d: 8). The net effect is that the Christian-theistic boundary distinction between the infinite God and the finite creature was accommodated to support cosmological interpretations of the Neoplatonic descent and ascent, namely in application of either a *'prima causa'* doctrine or a *'ultima finis'* one, respectively. Thomas Aquinas, by working an Aristotelian entelechism into a nature-grace doctrine, offered Catholicism such a 'synthesized' (mediated) law-idea.

Luther broke with the Thomistic arrangement of nature and grace. He rejected the view of the church as the warrant and dispenser of grace, replacing this with a more personal, soteriologically oriented life- and worldview. But this still entailed a split view, for it lacked a unifying cosmological law-idea. It was Calvin who came with a clear and unifying law-idea, that Dooyeweerd characterizes as a divine "uniform providential world-plan", which could serve as instrument (*organon*) for the Protestant-Calvinistic life- and worldview. In basing himself on providence and predestination, Calvin conceived of this "providential world-plan" as differing *toto caelo* from Stoic and Thomistic-Aristotelian ones (cf. 1923d: 11). The Stoic law-idea being causally deterministic, it induces a (blind) fatalism, dominated by reason. In Stoicism, reason is a divine, active principle that holds sway in the world and acts as a model for human reason to follow. The Thomistic-Aristotelian view allows human reason to understand the natural world, as the 'natural component' (*lex naturalis*) of Gods world-plan—in other words, subjective and objective reason are here in harmony—and only for the higher region of grace is the supplement of faith required (cf. 1923d: 12).

Calvin breaks with both views. They are speculative in the sense of being uncritical as to the use of reason—causality and teleology are applied far beyond their proper reach—and they "wrong the sovereignty of God, who does not tolerate the slackening of boundaries between himself and the finite" (1923d: 12). The cosmological sense of the boundary between the infinite and the finite is expressed by Calvin in the *notion of law*. God has ordained everything according to fixed rules (1923d: 12).

At this point Dooyeweerd's discussion broaches three topics: that of Calvin's law-idea, said to be a religious law-idea, its meaning for epistemology and philosophy, and the principle of sphere sovereignty that follows from it. On each point we offer some discussion.

2. Calvin's law-idea

The sovereignty of God is basic to the Christian confession. But, according to Dooyeweerd, it is only in Calvin that this sovereignty gains a religious meaning that is free from speculative elements. God's sovereignty is attested to by the notion of law, defined as "the universal boundary line between the [infinite] essence of God and the [finite] essence of creation" (1923d: 13). This is said to be a "formal" moment of Calvin's law-idea. Indeed, it is formal in that this condition draws upon such a stark polarity between God and creation, so that a difference of nature or essence follows by definition (so to speak). That difference generates a boundary line. At the same time, as such, it says nothing about the relation between God and creation. Hence material conditions need to be specifically added.

Dooyeweerd sees in Calvin's law-idea also two material conditions. The first is, as content, "that of an arrangement/regulation [*ordening*], flowing forth from God's wisdom in his providential world-plan, in which it [the plan] finds its unity, which is beyond [our] understanding, also for [our] reason" (1923d: 13). Providence, as usually understood, involves both foreseeing and providing. Providence takes place through regulation, i.e. through rules that express God's will and that impinge in the sense that they 'call for submission'. This application of rules or ordinances would appear to emphasize the *foreseeing* of providence. Its locus, theologically expressed, involves the Counsel of God (1923d: 14). In the early Vollenhoven, as we saw, this is given a Platonist twist, in his adhering to a realism of ideas, when, in God's Counsel, ideas are individuated, thereby being able to function as 'thing-laws', regulating the coherence and development of what is thus determined. At this point it is more difficult to assume a background of ideas in Dooyeweerd—though that will soon be resolved—for here God's *will* is central, not his cognition. We appear to simply fall back on a 'God would have it so', which cannot be questioned because of its being beyond our understanding. Indeed, "no creature, nothing in heaven or on earth, can call Him to account for His deeds, but everything outside of Him is bound to His law" (1923d: 12). But Dooyeweerd also explicitly denies divine arbitrariness, such as found in nominalism (he points to Occam and Occamists). God would act arbitrarily if the arranging of the world, according to his will, were independent of the "divine reason and divine wisdom". That would be an assault, says Dooyeweerd, of the very essence of Calvin's law-idea (1923d: 13). But, so I surmise, if will is to hang together with reason and wisdom in God, one would expect a Trinitarian embedding, with the Logos being the warrant for divine reason and the Spirit divine wisdom. But Dooyeweerd is not explicit on this point.

The second material condition of Calvin's law-idea is said to be its "positing, also in the Augustinian sense, a continual relation of dependence between the creator and the creature. (God's maintaining of the creation is a continual creation.)" (1923d: 13). It would appear that Dooyeweerd here expresses the specific moment of *providing*. At least the addition in parentheses emphasizes the *theistic* immanence of God. This is stated over against *deism* which, "also posits a boundary of essence between God and creature, but denies . . . the relation of dependence of creature on God" (1923d: 13).[189]

So the two material conditions together appear to say, first, that the arranging involves ordinances, which God in his infinite wisdom—hence

---

189   There is a point that remains in the dark here concerning how predestination fits in. Dooyeweerd takes providence and predestination as belonging together in Calvin, in fact he says that predestination "falls under" providence (1923d: 12, 13), and he laments their being so often misunderstood. In his letter to J. Ridderbos (16 January 1924) he states that the material condition of the Reformed law-idea is "predestination (this taken in its inclusive cosmic sense) being the expression of the Reformed view of God's sovereignty over everything created." In 1926c: 69, Dooyeweerd states: "In the Calvinistic sense, this law-idea coincides with the divine providence or predestination (in its most broadest sense)". Dooyeweerd's two material conditions would appear to cover providence, but without touching on predestination in its specific sense of election and reprobation. But what does predestination in an "inclusive cosmic sense" mean? Dooyeweerd appears to suggest that everything is predestined, and that this is the presupposition of the two material conditions of providence (foreseeing and providing). (We have added reason to interpret it this way, when we look at the law-idea more closely, in its realist interpretation, below.) It may be that a difference in the editions of Calvin's *Institutes of the Christian Religion* (Calvin 1960) is a source of confusion. In the editions of 1539-1554, Calvin treated providence and predestination in the same chapter. But in the final edition of 1559 the two topics are separated. Providence belongs to Book I (chapters 16-18) on the knowledge of God the Creator, while predestination is treated in Book III (chapters 21-24) on the redemptive work of the Holy Spirit; cf. Calvin 1960: 197, note 1. But whatever the case, Calvin saw both doctrines, namely that of foreknowledge (providence) and that of God's foreordaining human beings either to eternal life or to eternal damnation (predestination), as being *independent* of each other (*op. cit.* : 926: "subjecting one to the other is absurd"). The foreordaining is not based on worthiness of the person nor merit of works, thus foresight plays no role. Evidently, on Calvin's view (irrespective of what Calvinism has made of it) the eternal destiny of the human soul, as governed by predestination, is independent of the events of the world and the human being's role in them, that God governs by his providence.

unfathomable for human reason—imposes upon the finite creatures of his creation, and that, secondly, the creatures are so provided for that they are continually maintained as (capable of) responding to the arranging. Formulated in this way, we can see that neither causality nor entelechism are suitable models to use here. God's imposing rules or ordinances, which hold sway over things, is not a (top-down) causality, nor is subjecting things to an order a (bottom-up) meeting of ends. We have a condition of ordinances holding for creatures, and one of creatures held fit to respond to ordinances. These three conditions, one 'formal' (a line of essential difference) and two 'material' (foreseeing via ordinances, and providing for as response) are the conditions of the Calvinistic law-idea.

Dooyeweerd qualifies this Calvinistic law-idea—God's worldplan—as religious (cf. also 1926c: 65). The fact that God's providence, as foresight and provision, is central here no doubt suggests this, in a *prima facie* sort of way. But in a generic sense, a law-idea is a *cosmological* principle, be it of theistic signature, and in that guise it serves as the *organon* of a life- and worldview.[190] More needs to be said in this connection. But we best first continue with the discussion of epistemology and sphere sovereignty.

3. Calvinistic epistemology

What Dooyeweerd has to say here he states in a short statement (in two paragraphs) about the consequences of the Calvinistic law-idea for epistemology.[191] It is essentially a summary—and a very brief not to say cryptic one at that—of what he wrote in 'Cosmos and Logos', discussed in section E above. Calvin's cosmological law-idea—that notion, of course, was not yet in the picture in "Cosmos and Logos", which speaks of 'divine cosmos'—Dooyeweerd now applies "as transcendental, boundary separator" (1923d: 13). The law as boundary holds especially for human reason. Thereby any *speculative* metaphysics is rejected out of hand, for such a metaphysics "would always be founded on a speculative law-idea" (1923d: 13). The discussion of Stoic and Aristotelian examples of metaphysics have been cases in point. Here reason avails itself either of a universal causality (Stoicism) or a universal entelechy (Aristotelianism). But Dooyeweerd does allow metaphysics to have a role. Indeed, that is im-

---

190 It is significant that Dooyeweerd speaks of a life- and worldview having to be 'self-contained' (1923d: 4) or 'closed' (1926b: 64; 1926c: 69; 1926e: 425) before a 'law-idea' can be identified that fits it. A law-idea, as cosmological principle, needs to be all-encompassing.

191 We discussed the possible reason for this brevity in the Interlude above; cf. section III.D.3.

plied in the very notion of the law-idea, in its being a leading *cosmological* principle serving as '*organon*' of a well-rounded life- and worldview (cf. 1923d: 4). It is *speculative* metaphysics that is countered by the Calvinistic law-idea, in the formal condition of the boundary, not metaphysics as such.

So what use of reason is justified? To start with, human consciousness needs to proceed from the *given*. (Is the giving in this context a factor of providence, or divine giving?) And given are "lawful fields of vision", each of which includes a domain of formal categories and essential properties. It is through intuition not reason that the 'giving' takes place: "viewing brings them to consciousness" (1923d: 14). (Dooyeweerd does not use the terminology of "Cosmos and Logos" (1923a2), of 'meaning-giving', 'meaning-having' etc., at this point.) But speaking of "lawful fields of vision" *would appear* to imply that, whereas in "Cosmos and Logos" the modality is a mode of viewing intuitively, as focussed on a corresponding field of vision, now the 'be-holding', that takes place through intuition, also makes way for the acknowledgement of the factor that *holds* with respect to the field of vision. What holds is *the factor of law*. Hence the 'modal viewing', namely the active viewing of the Self, now includes more explicitly the acknowledgement of the factor of law or regulation that is relevant for the content of the '*lawful* field of vision' viewed.[192]

The fact that Dooyeweerd does not emphasize this acknowledgement could be related to the greater interest he places in the discussion of 'law-idea'. 'Modal law', as the 'lawful factor' of a field of vision, is a 'metalogical' notion. But given the cosmic moorings of the metalogical, the foundation of law-acknowledgement in the cosmos is of greater interest here. That 'mooring' is what the notion of 'law-idea' sets out to achieve in its being a principle of cosmology.

Dooyeweerd leaves no doubt about the *realist* nature of his view. The "world of creation" stands (as in "Cosmos and Logos") in two kinds of connection. There is first the absolute dependence upon the creator, a connection that is not that of reason. Reason is part of the creation that stands in the relation of dependence. ('Reason' is here a synonym for 'created logos' of "Cosmos and Logos'.) The creation is the terrain of the *cosmos* (which, for intuitive viewing, is what is intuit-able in its own lawfulness, i.e. what in 1923a2 was dubbed "primary given meaning".) The

---

192 It seems ad hoc to speak of 'law' or 'lawful'. But the thought here is that grasped meaning presupposes a norm that warrants the grasping. We found this in "Cosmos en Logos", in which it reflects Vollenhoven's original account of *Gegenstand*-formation, as calling for the law of identity.

second connection is within the cosmos, namely between reason and its objects. This connection is the terrain of the (cosmic/created) *logos*. Thus there is the same positioning of the (human) *logos* within the cosmos as met with previously. When a field of vision, that comes to consciousness in being viewed, is made the object of thought (which occurs through the viewing that is modified logically, a viewing of unity, difference and relation), then that field becomes a field of inquiry, and the *Gegenstand* that was viewed as belonging to the field of vision now becomes the object or assignment of thought in so far as systemic relations can be determined here (such as nature as a system) (1923d: 14). The discussion is so brief, that its novelty can barely be noticed, and one is hard put to grasp it without a knowledge of "Cosmos and Logos", with its distinction between the 'divine Logos (*noèsis*) and the 'created logos'. Yet it is the first published statement of 'Calvinistic epistemology'.

Calvinistic epistemology holds its own, Dooyeweerd concludes, between on the one hand the Thomistic-Aristotelian position, which assumes a common essence of reason between God and the reasonable creature, and on the other the critical idealism of Kant, who proceeds from the sovereignty of the *logos* or reason and thus makes the *Gegenstand* to be dependent on the creative function of thought. Clearly, the Thomistic-Aristotelian position sins against the stipulation of the cosmos being a creation, thus distinct from God the creator. The Kantian position sins against the given character of reason as being dependent on the intuitive relation of modal viewing and its *Gegenstand*. Dooyeweerd qualifies the epistemology which he outlines, in line with previous work, as "*transcendental* realist" (1923d: 14).

4. Sovereignty in its own sphere
The notion of a 'sovereignty in its own sphere' is not new to our discussion. We found it to occur for the first time in Vollenhoven's metalogical outline of July 1921 (1921c). It was a notion that was put to work in epistemology, in particular in the philosophy of science. Here in Dooyeweerd the term again recurs, but now for the first time (I believe, at least in print) in a way that is recognizably an assimilation of a meaning that stands close to Kuyper's original societal use, although the name of Kuyper does not occur. There is now a 'sovereignty in its own sphere', said to be a philosophical consequence of, or resulting from (*wijsgeerig uitvloeisel*; 1923d: 14), Calvin's law-idea. This puts sphere-sovereignty in direct rapport with divine sovereignty, as is the case in Kuyper, and it provides the context for the human viewing of lawfulness. But Dooyeweerd's

discussion remains rather brief and not everything is explicit.

Having stated that the law is the boundary holding for the whole of creation, when one now considers created reality, the boundary does not provide a handle for considering this reality to be a unity. Such would be a move of reason,[193] but a move in which reason overreaches itself. One can only *intuitively view* the cosmos, in which case one is confronted with a diversity. "Under the notion of law as boundary the cosmos unfolds in a multiplicity of sovereign spheres" (1923d: 14), each of which has its own ordinances. All these ordinances are "grounded only and exclusively in the divine sovereignty" (1923d: 14), and reason has no authority to construe these into a speculative unity. The 'spheres' Dooyeweerd mentions are (in line with earlier work) nature, history, the normative field of legality and morality. This is no doubt only a *prima facie* indication.[194] Dooyeweerd's chief point is to argue that, given subjective reason's limitations (it being itself part of the cosmos, capable of operating only within its limits) what is apperceived, apart from reason, is given by way of a transcendental-realist viewing of reality, a reality subject to ordinances. Sphere sovereignty involves accepting the right of each sphere of self-regulation according to its own ordinances. The sovereignty pertains to the different spheres mutually, not to persons who participate in these spheres. "Divine sovereignty radiates in the sovereignty of his ordinances" (1923d: 15). If the essential factor of the Calvinistic law-idea is divine sovereignty, then sphere-sovereignty is indeed a direct derivative of it. Hence this law-idea is characterized as being *theonomic*, and in undercutting all human autonomy it is *heteronomic* as well. It does not invite, let alone is it based on, any community of will or of reason between God and the creature (1923d: 15).

5. Discussion and assessment

The Calvinistic law-idea is a complex notion. It combines a concept of law (as boundary) and the conditions of the law's implementation (a cosmological plan that stands in relation to a life- and worldview). Its

193   Reason is here identified, without explanation or apology, with the role of establishing unity. This seems to suggest that Dooyeweerd takes reason's essence to be that of establishing connection and synthesis, 'synthetic a priori'. This is an idealist view of reason, in which difference and the drawing of distinctions is considered to be of a lower, or at least a different, order.

194   Here too we notice that the discussion is provisional. Had Dooyeweerd explicitly tied the spheres in question in with the fields of vision, that are intuited in modal viewing in epistemology—a step no doubt implicitly taken—then the summary indication of the spheres could have been suggested by the primary sciences as well. But Dooyeweerd kept epistemology here to an absolute minimum. For a possible reason, cf. III.D.2. above.

introduction, as discussed above, assumes a realist setting (cf. the discussion below). This needs to be said at once, for in the early 1930s (perhaps already as of 1928) Dooyeweerd reinterprets the notion of the law-idea to be that of a *transcendental limiting concept*, whereby the realist-cosmological context has itself given way to a context that only appeals to objective meaning (as modal horizon of experience, with a discernible structure of diversity, totality and unity). But this more metalogical emphasis of 'law-idea' is of later date. Originally it is conceived in a realist setting, from where our discussion must make its start. In its realist setting, the chief characteristics of the law-idea are its being *theonomic, heteronomic* and *cosmological*, these being predicated on the three listed conditions of the law-idea, the formal condition and the two material conditions of foresight and providing. We need to establish this more closely. But first a preliminary remark is in order.

Those familiar with the later emphases in Reformational philosophy will know that the view of law as boundary was more exclusively underscored by Vollenhoven than by Dooyeweerd. One tends to think that the very thought must have come from Vollenhoven. He saw it as essential to Reformed thought. In fact, in 1968 he states that the relation of the creature to God, expressed in the creature's standing in subjection to law, is non-negotiable, "otherwise the basis of all our work crumbles."[195] Now the notion of the law as boundary is as such not new in 1923. But the way Dooyeweerd implements it in 1923, in terms of a law-idea that mediates between cosmology and life- and worldview, is striking. And what one cannot fail to notice is the energy Dooyeweerd invests in it, namely in his early publications after 1923. There is nothing of the reticence (in going public) we found in connection with epistemology and scientific methodology. So here one tends to think that, whatever Vollenhoven's role might have been, Dooyeweerd feels no constraints in developing this idea in his own way. And he has every right to this freedom. For, as already pointed out, Vollenhoven fully accepted the notion of the law as boundary, and with it the notion of law-spheres. But he studiedly avoided the notion of law-idea. Sometime during or just after his recuperation, Vollenhoven was no longer satisfied with his former metaphysics of ideas (though he did not abandon realism). Dooyeweerd, so we shall point out, retains a metaphysics of ideas for some time. The best attestation for that is his very use of the notion of the law-idea as originally conceived.[196]

---

195 Vollenhoven 1968b: 200.
196 When putting this development in a time perspective, we notice that 'law-idea' is first used by Dooyeweerd in late 1923. This is the time when Vollenhoven is in the last

a. Law as boundary
However much the formulation of the law as boundary between God and the creature is ontologically loaded, *viz.* in speaking of an infinite and absolute essence on the one hand and a finite and dependent essence on the other (cf. also Dooyeweerd 1923e5: 72), its 'theonomic' implication points to the concern here for authority and power, which in turn assumes a volitional context of willing. The Calvinistic life- and world-view is given its full effect here. "Calvinism maintains, with its rigorous defence . . . the absolute right of God, which may not be relativized" (1923e3: 15). And, in Calvinism the human being has no right to question God's authority, thus it "rejects all theodicy, which places itself as judge over God's world governance" (1926d: 63). Hence, prominent on the side of the finite and dependent creature is the human being, for only the human being makes conscious use of the will. This will may therefore appear to be free, but the human being needs a context to implement will. Also the human use of reason is restricted, for it cannot of itself fathom the mystery of existence. Both will and reason, while not lacking in their own legitimate relevance, are held in check by divine authority, which expresses itself as sovereignty over all that there is. Sometimes Dooyeweerd expresses the theme of the boundary entirely in terms of the divine and human agents: Calvinism sees "the law as a posed, ultimate

---

stage of convalescence. One assumes that there must have been some exchange between the brothers-in-law by then, so some influence from Vollenhoven cannot be excluded a priori. Now the notion of law-idea is essentially a notion of *coherence* (as unity of diverse spheres). It is predicated on the God-creature difference and constitutes the "lawful plan of God" as to how the main features of life and the world hang together (cf. III.F.1 above). In former work, the notion of sovereignty tended to emphasize the distinct natures of the spheres or domains in question. The concern for coherence, as advanced by the law-idea, will lead to what Dooyeweerd later describes as "the modal aspects of the horizon of experience". This is the phrase he used to describe what he remembers as having suddenly realized, while on a walk in the sand dunes on a warm summer evening while living in The Hague. Clearly, the realization was important to him, and the notion itself dear. The insight, as described, is formulated in a later terminology than when he lived in The Hague. So it may initially have been the insight of the 'law-idea', which lies at the basis of Dooyeweerd's descriptive phrase. Whether Dooyeweerd was alone on that walk or accompanied by Vollenhoven (as has been attested; cf. Stellingwerff 2006: 33), is not really important if, indeed, the insight in question is that of the law-idea, for Vollenhoven never accepted it. On the basis of this guess, the most likely year of this warm summer evening walk is 1923; cf. Dooyeweerd 1977: 37. Vollenhoven's reference to a 'find' by the brothers-in-law about the summer of 1922, concerns "the beginning of a more Scriptural way of thinking" and should, I believe, not be confused with what happened during the walk in the dunes. (Contra Henderson 1994: 186, also p. 38; cf. the discussion of 'Developments in 1922' below.) Stellingwerff puts the walk in the dunes in "1921 or 1922", but his reasoning is unclear; Stellingwerff 1992: 53.

boundary between on the one hand human reason and will, on the other hand divine reason and will" (1926c: 65; cf. also 1926d: 63, 64). There is no question of a "community of will or reason" between the Creator and the rational creature (cf. 1923e5: 72)

It is in virtue of this bare difference in essence that a boundary line comes into view. It is the line of the difference in will power, the difference of capacity in acting and being; it is a line marking the difference between sovereignty and subjection. One can understand how ordinances come into view here, as being the will of the 'sovereign' with respect to the 'subject'. Ordinances are 'law-markers' that certify the difference between and the duality of God and the human being. Divine sovereignty is confessed to be the origin of all laws (cf. 1926b: 68). The "Thou shalt..." marks the *divide*, it does not act as a bridge. "Only God, who is Eternal, Unbegotten and Infinite, stands above the law, [and is] not determined by the law" (1923e5: 72).

Yet there is a difficulty here. To the extent that law is founded in the divine will, law has a transcendent origin. But for the human being, who is subject to this will, the law's impingement is a transcendental condition. Accordingly, this calls for recognition on the part of the human subject, which recognition includes awareness of the context in which laws are to hold. No doubt something like a teaching of different 'spheres' or 'domains' is called for—like Dooyeweerd's tentative domains of nature, history, morality, legality, etc. (1923e4: 31)—to enable laws or ordinances to be recognized by the human being as (possibly) relevant laws and how they are to be applied. But Dooyeweerd does not allow for interpretation, which indeed is difficult to fit in when the law as boundary is taken to be a *formal* condition based on essence. The sovereignty of God and the standing-in-subjection of creatures (particularly human beings) is then directly synonymous with authority and submission respectively. In this synonymy, the transcendence and immanence of God are not adequately accounted for. The transcendence of God calls for a careful account of religion—the covenantal meeting of the 'infinite' and the 'finite', which is quite other (as Vollenhoven will emphasize) than a 'unity of consciousness between the Self and God' (see below)—and the immanence of God is 'his present providing' (of giving, forgiving and fulfilling) in the context of the human realities, through which the human being is able to respond.

By working authority and submission so markedly into the law-idea, Dooyeweerd short-changes its basic meaning. In fact it adds to the portrait of Calvinism being authoritarian and rigid, precisely in ascribing absolute status to laws in virtue of the divine origin of authority. The deficiency here is that the transcendental significance of a domain of (human) response is taken as a channel or medium of absolute authority (cf. 1925a: 88). Dooyeweerd will, in time, significantly nuance his view by the introduction of the central law of love. But in the meantime, the initial introduction of the law-idea implies a theonomic absolute.

This is especially noticeable in Dooyeweerd's discussion of morality and legality. Each is a sphere with its own ordinances. For morality there is the *Decalogue* (*zedewet*) (1923e3: 28-29), and for legality the rules relate to *retribution*. In practice, the 'divine origin' of these ordinances lies in Scripture. But so long as hermeneutics is not given leeway, an authoritarian use cannot be challenged. (But one then privileges one's own historically bound thought and action, by exempting them from any call to account.) Consider: "The doctrine of retribution . . . is the stronghold of the principle of sovereignty in its own sphere, as applied to the sphere of legality and the state. Here there is no confusion with the sphere of morality. Legality must be maintained for the sake of the holiness of the divine ordinances of legality themselves and not for any reason that lies in the moral personality of the human being or in human society. He who maintains the doctrine of retribution, confesses the sovereignty of God also in the affairs of legality (*rechtsleven*). He who relinquishes it, assaults the sovereignty of God" (1923e4: 31). This is theocracy in a blatant form.[197]

b. Law-idea as world-plan
The formal condition of the Calvinist law-idea emphasizes the boundary condition between infinite essence and finite essence. This provides for the 'concept of law', this being the understanding of the authority by which sovereignty and subjection (of will and reason) are determined. This concept of law is clearly theonomic. But there is also diversity of law to be accounted for, a diversity calling for recognition, whereby the recognition is not itself determinative for the diversity. The laws are heteronymous and cosmological. This involves the context of law in the *realist setting* in which the diversity and unity of law is accounted for in a cosmological sense. It is here that the law-idea as *organon* is emphasized,

---

197 In this respect Vollenhoven was much more careful. I believe that, in his whole oeuvre, there are only two law-spheres for which he hazarded to formulate their law: the logical law-sphere and the pistical law-sphere. There 'having to be a law' for a law-sphere is 'formally accepted' as intuitively valid, and calling for responsible response. This leaves the actual formulation of a modal law an open question, calling for reflection that includes a law's application.

enabling it to serve to defend the Calvinist life- and worldview of sphere sovereignty.

The material condition of the Calvinist law-idea is that it is the "uniform providential world-plan'. It holds for cosmic life, and as we saw it is 'situated' and 'secured' in the Counsel of God. It is in the Counsel of God that divine providence and predestination takes place in the divine governance of the cosmos. It is likewise the locus of the ideational realm of ideas in the realist metaphysics of the early Vollenhoven. Is this relevant in Dooyeweerd's use of law-*idea*?

It is part and parcel of the realist metaphysics to accept ideas as principles of distinctive being.[198] The distinctive being that is relevant at this point concerns the cosmos in the way it unfolds according to the providential world-plan of God's wisdom. In God's wisdom it has a unity (1st material condition; 1923d: 13), but it also encompasses the main features of reality—as to nature, culture, society, history, etc.—hence there is also specification in the world-plan that effects a diversification of the law into a diversity of ordinances. In that way there can be a transcendental effect on cosmic life. Thus, formally, what we have here is analogous to the individuation of ideas in God's Counsel in the early Vollenhoven, which is also beyond human reason. Hence, this unity and diversity is such that human reason has no alternative but to accept it as condition of its own rationality.

An explicit and significant statement in this regard is the following. "God's providential world-plan forms a harmonious unity, but that unity cannot be grasped by human reason. Under the boundary of the law the unity of the plan of creation unfolds in a plurality, in an *endless diversity* and in that endless diversity only the law, the ordinance of God, creates order. But that law itself is not a rigid unity of kind (*star enerlei*), but it unfolds itself according to God's unending wisdom itself in a *plurality of law-spheres*. Only in that way is the distinctness, what is typical, of diversity preserved" (1923e5: 72-73; emphases added).

There is a double unfolding here. There is that of the unity of the law unfolding in a diversity of law-spheres. This connects the unity of divine authority to the plurality of ordinances, warranting the heteronomy

---

198   Contra Henderson 1994: 117, which, in reference to Dooyeweerd's early use of 'realist' and 'critical realism', states: "Realism represents an assertion of the existence of things as apart from ideas, which presupposes that the two are not part of one and the same reality." Realism, in the entire context of the early Vollenhoven and Dooyeweerd, *concerns* ideas, in their Platonic interpretation. After 1922, Vollenhoven has no use for the term, and warns: "in Greek thought ideas are said to be true being", and this is what is accepted in critical realist thought; Vollenhoven 1952k: 86.

of sphere sovereignty. But there is also the *endless* cosmological unfolding of cosmic reality itself, according to "the plan of creation". Here we have more than an echo of what in Vollenhoven was general essence that individuates ('unfolds') in a diversity of thing-laws. The law-idea is the providential world-plan, as entertained by God in his Counsel.

The "Christian law-idea" warrants unity, a unity "not found by fading the boundaries between divergent arrangements, but by acknowledging an ultimate final law, an eternal divine world-order, wherein all diversity of essence is reconciled into a divine harmony, a world-plan posed from eternity" (1924, I: 18-19).[199] The emphasis on eternity here makes the 'providential world-plan' hard to distinguish from a 'predestined world-program'.[200]

In case the realist interpretation of ideas, that is here said to be supporting the understanding and use of 'law-idea', needs extra support, there is the following example of the 'idea of legality' that occurs in "Calvinism and Natural Law" (1923d, 28). When summarizing his view of "political natural legality" (*politisch natuurrecht*), Dooyeweerd states: "We posit on the basis of God's law itself, with great emphasis, that the only normative directive of the government is political natural legality, summarized in the idea of legality; and that this idea of legality is absolute, *raised above human evaluation*. . . . [For] in God's ordinance of legality, every human being has been endowed with an independent goal and an infinite value, in the context of which the idea of society must be realized" (*loc. cit.*; emphasis added, for the significance of which, see the end of the next section c.). Dooyeweerd 'officially' limits the human use of reason to the context

---

199   I believe that it is not unfair to say that Dooyeweerd's later distinction in the law, between modal laws of sphere sovereignty and thing-laws as individuality structures, is prefigured in the original realist understanding of his use of 'law-idea'. He will drop the realist context of his early understanding in favour of an ontology of meaning, but the two meanings of lawfulness remain.

200   Vollenhoven was very disquieted by speculative influences of pagan thought in the Jewish-Christian tradition, among which was predestination speculation. This was an important motive of his later problem-historical work. On the theological influence of Aristotle's *Metaphysics Lambda* he states: "In that work this theology accepted an all-determining divine activity, and in this acceptance this theology lapsed into a deterministic semi-mysticism, that would in time also enter into Christian circles: for example think in this connection inter alia of the view of predestination as evident in, say, Augustine in his last period and by his followers in later centuries, also within Reformed circles". Kuyper too evidences this influence: "the cross of Golgotha, the suffering, the resurrection has contributed nothing to our salvation [*heil*] . . . That we are saved lies prior to our birth in the Counsel of God, but for our consciousness this only becomes real when we are justified *in foro conscientiae* [before the tribunal of conscience]"; Kuyper 1910: 71. Both citations are in Vollenhoven 2000: 368-369.

of the cosmos, but it is more than evident that, in the meantime, a metaphysical understanding is in effect about the limitations themselves.

c. Law-idea and the 'central lookout tower'
The Calvinist law-idea is, as cosmological principle of God's providence, the *organon* of the Christian life- and worldview. So just what sort of an 'instrument' is the law-idea?

In the Christian life- and worldview the moment of religious belief predominates, in particular the moment of Christian religious belief. As such there is no necessity in this. For example, in his *Weltanschauungslehre*, Wilhelm Dilthey qualified worldviews in different ways. He distinguished as basic and irreducible three types: besides the religious types, there are also "poetic", i.e. aesthetic, types and "metaphysical" types (whether as favouring naturalism, freedom idealism or objective idealism).[201] The choice for the religious type in Dooyeweerd may seem obvious, given the Calvinist context in which he moves. But Calvinism is initially a theological system, and only through Kuyper's transformation did it take on the general significance of a life- and worldview orientation. More to the point regarding the choice for the religious type is that the choice itself involved a principled limitation of will and reason in virtue of divine sovereignty. In the Calvinistic life- and worldview, the will needs to accept and submit to an authority that is higher or greater than itself, and in that limitation reason too is restricted to the human reach, a reach that is short of postulating unity. This is not to deny there being a unity of experience, or of thought and action. But that unity is for Dooyeweerd given as the divine providential world-plan, with which one cannot be in rapport apart from *a confessional stance*. In other words, the law-idea is operative and relevant (for the human being) in the unity of its meaning only through an active function of faith on the part of the human being.

The following selected quotes give an indication of this function of faith. "[The different ordinances] all work together in that one unfathomable divine world-plan, the unity of which cannot be grasped by the limited human reason, but yet is as secure as the divine wisdom itself. The Christian ought to accept that unity on faith . . ." (1925a: 87-88). "The divine honour is served according to Calvinistic confession . . . by propagating, in the world, the unity of the divine world-plan as an incisive word of faith [*slagwoord des geloofs*]" (1925a: 88). "Calvinism acknowledges the sovereignty of the law-spheres in the sovereignty of the eternal

---
201   Dilthey 1931: esp. pp. 87 ff.

Creator and seeks worshipfully the highest unity in God's unfathomable providence . . ." (1926a: 6). "There is an *irrational connection in cosmic, hence a-logical, sense* between the different law-spheres, a connection that for the believing consciousness is grounded in the *law-idea* . . ." (1926c: 69). Finally: "The law-idea that is foundational for the Calvinistic life- and worldview is rooted in the two foundations of all Christian thought: in the confession of the divine creator's sovereignty and in the confession of the divine providential world-plan" (1926d: 63; cf. also p. 61).

Now, while statements such as these can be read as indicative of an attitude or motivation, there is an additional significance in that this faith function is not only *expressive* of something, it also serves as means that *sights* on something. The unity of the world-plan that it confesses to is made to be effective in and through that active confession. This is the role of the law-idea as "central lookout tower", a term Dooyeweerd first used in 1924 (1924, I: 18; *centrale uitzichttoren*).[202] It is from such a 'lookout point' of faith that the law-idea is seized and understood in its capacity of providing perspective and orientation. The Christian law-idea is "the central lookout tower, from which one can gain an orientation encompassing all the terrains of the life- and worldview in terms of a fixed point" (1924, I: 18). We see at once that this in fact repeats what Dooyeweerd had expressed in the unpublished study "Cosmos and Logos" (1923a2-3) (cf. section III.E.5) about faith enabling one to view the world "*sub specie aeternitatis*", from the point of view of eternity. There is a fideism here, in that to faith is attributed the unique capacity of sighting the reality of the unity of the cosmos, as expressed in the law-idea. The realist interpretation of an idea warrants that there is a 'distinctive reality' capable of being acknowledged. This acknowledgement is not forthcoming from the (free) will, nor from reason, for the latter would have to speculatively

---

[202] We note here, and return to it later, that the term "uitzichttoren" also occurs in H. Dooyeweerd, *De Wijsbegeerte der Wetsidee*, vol. 1 (1935), p. 10. There it is linked to the notion of an 'Archimedean point' of philosophy (*ibid*, pp. 14-15), a term first occurring in 1928, in a "Postscript" to "Beroepsmisdaad en strafvergelding in 't licht der Wetsidee" [Professional crime and penalty retribution in the light of the law-idea]. We quote: "Regarding the question [how the connection and the boundaries of the law-spheres are to be determined] the answer is alone forthcoming from the law-idea, for here a transcendent standpoint needs to be taken in, [i.e.] an Archimedean point above all the specific law-spheres of psyche, logos, ethos, legality, beauty, history, etc." (1928b: 425). Along with the Archimedean point, Dooyeweerd then (in 1928) also speaks of a "time transcending kernel of the human spirit" (*ibid.*) (also 'heart' or 'Self') that occupies this point and commits itself. Though it makes a difference whether one speaks of faith or of the human heart (cf. our later discussion), the common construal of a 'lookout tower' provides for the continuity of the problem at hand.

construct the unity. But the denial of a community of will and of reason between Creator and creature does not mean that there is no community for Dooyeweerd. This is the ambience (in light of the faith function, as cited above) in which "the full concrete unity of consciousness of Self and of God" arises.[203] That community, implied by that unity, is what the function of faith effects, or at least for which the function of faith is a precondition. If the law as boundary is particularly relevant as drawn between the human reason and will on the one hand and the divine reason and will on the other, then in faith this boundary is bridged.

Accordingly, faith supplements reason. Naturally the content of faith needs to be given. This is channelled through the Scriptures; in other words, what faith sights on becomes insight of knowledge through the revelation of the Logos. We can now only voice the same conclusion we came to earlier in connection with "Cosmos and Logos". There is a scholastic effect on Dooyeweerd when he maintains that human insight comes into harmony with the structure of the cosmos in virtue of the supplement provided by faith's receptivity to the divine Logos (cf. III.E.5. above). The law-idea has given this situation extra point, it has not corrected or eradicated it.

In the meantime we can point to the lingering early Vollenhovian format, of 'concept and idea', in the publications of Dooyeweerd of the mid-1920s. The *concept* is the adequate concept that can only be approached in a rightly oriented metalogical process of reason's use. Reason becomes rightly directed through the supplement of the Logos provided through faith. The *idea* is what governs the reality that there is. Dooyeweerd's former use of 'divine cosmos' takes on a more developed form in his 'Calvinistic law-idea' as cosmological principle. Its acknowledgement calls for a faith stance. The novelty of "Cosmos and Logos" had been that the metalogical viewing (of the adequate concept), whereby the intuition of content or 'meaning-having objects' answers to modally distinct 'fields of vision', no longer takes place in its own (*Gegenstand-*)sphere. What is viewed is the objective meaning of the cosmos itself to the extent that this is 'intuit-able' and given with the reality of the cosmos. This puts extra emphasis on the intuitive viewing itself, whereby the modal forms

---

203 The phrase is from Dooyeweerd's discussion of Kuyper's doctrine of science (Dooyeweerd 1939: 204), and is there descriptive of the 'non-theoretical religious centre'. By then, Dooyeweerd has distinguished the function of faith from the significance of the 'heart'. But the citations on the function of faith, given above, lay emphasis on faith's grasping the unity that remains out of reach of reason. Its realization through the pistical relation is clearly a precursor for the later role attributed to the heart. Thus a 'unity of consciousness of Self and of God' is what is in fact broached here.

of viewing, that establish a relation between acts and content, become *possibly autonomous* evaluative 'modal relations' (recall Sigwart's use and Dooyeweerd's initial criticism of it). This possibility is 'blocked' when taking into account the *factor of law* as part and parcel of the very reality of the cosmos one acknowledges in the realist mode. So with the introduction of the Calvinistic law-idea, one understands that the given cosmos—indeed a 'divine cosmos'—is given 'under God's law', within law-bound spheres. What one intuits via the metalogical intuition is law-bound meaning in 'fields of vision', or "lawful [*wetmatige*] transcendental essence of that given which God has assigned/prearranged [*toegeordend*] to our knowing function" (1926c: 68). The epistemological outline is now clearly fitted into the *organon* of the law-idea via the doctrine of sphere sovereignty.[204]

G. Overview: from critical realism to transcendental criticism
Our discussion has sufficiently demonstrated that there was close contact between Vollenhoven and Dooyeweerd in the years prior to their appointment to chairs at the Free University in 1926. Dooyeweerd approached Vollenhoven and aligned himself to his project of critical or transcendental realism. Dooyeweerd sought clarity with regards to topics of his interest, which centred in the main on the philosophy of legality. The texts he wrote in his 'free time study', prior to his appointment as deputy

---

204   In Dooyeweerd's first lecture, as newly appointed professor of jurisprudence (fall of 1926), he summarized the 'foundation' of his approach as follows:

> I wish to place before you . . . the central point, the point of departure of all legal scientific and legal philosophical thought. All specific regions have their own laws. Above these specific region laws there must be a universal law-order, in which all the specific region laws are founded, from which they derive their specific validity and also wherein each law-sphere's own area of competence is delimited. Each law-sphere has its own concept of law; together they equally appeal to a law-idea, a unity of all specific law-spheres, to a cosmic world-order, a world-plan.
>
> In that way, from the start of our philosophical orientation, we distinguish the law-concept, as the concept of all specific region laws, and the law-idea, as the higher unity of all specific laws. . . .
>
> Thus, in that way, the foundation of our philosophical thought is the law-idea, the notion of the deepest ground of validity and mutual coherence of all region laws. In referring to the law-idea, we have far superseded the narrow scientific terrain and we have placed ourselves in the middle of the region, very inadequately called metaphysics. We prefer to replace this word with the term cosmology, associating with this expression the meaning of the doctrine of the harmonious coherence of the creation in all of its existence-spheres and validity-spheres. (1926e: 423-425)

director of the Kuyper Foundation, were studies in neo-Kantian works on the philosophy of legality. The writers of these works were rationalists, in the sense that they held that the philosophy of legality defends the advance of reason in the interest of underscoring the validity of legality. That meant that the methodological context of reason's use is paramount towards acquiring generally valid ends. These 'ends' are insights of validity as gained through pursuing the 'value sciences', and such insights have important influence in the cultural practices of politics, jurisprudence, ethics, economics, etc. Insights acquired through reason hold promise, when applied to culture, to help make cultural practice itself more rational. This 'making culture more rational' was expressed as living according to the sovereignty or autonomy of reason, against the alternatives of religious bigotry, that enslaves, or irrational power, that seeks domination.

But for Dooyeweerd this use of reason, by which norms are merely applied values, reduces norms to the human measure. The differences in insight and even in the methodological accounts of reason—especially Marburg neo-Kantianism versus Freiburg neo-Kantianism—were indicative of differences of a different order, at the level of worldview (context, aim, interpretation, etc.) and which differences were not being made explicit. Through immanent criticism Dooyeweerd aimed to expose inconsistencies and difficulties that are indicative of problems with the principles from which one proceeds. In the meantime, the brothers-in-law were in close contact until the time of Dooyeweerd's appointment to the Kuyper Foundation (October 1922). Dooyeweerd wrote up their burgeoning views in which the methodological side of their critical realism was further explored and clarified.

1. Vollenhoven's early thought in review[205]
In Vollenhoven's critical realism the subjective rationality of the Self interacts with the objective rationality inherent in the World. Through this interaction knowledge arises through the synthesis of judgments. Both on the part of the Self and on that of the World there are factual and ideal factors. The Self gains factual data that are organized in *forms of sensibility*, and it needs to submit to (extra-mental) *norms* in the rational procedure of knowledge acquisition. The World has a factual side that is embedded in the *matrix of absolute time and space*. But the things of the World are governed by (extra-mental) *ideas* of distinctive being, that regulate the structure of things in their appearances, their interactions

---

[205] The reader may wish to consult the diagram in III.C.4 above, for a schematic outline of this early thought.

and their species development.

Knowing takes place by means of the said interaction in judgments: representations, had by the Self, are predicated to appearances of the things of the World; knowing takes place in a *process* of understanding that becomes progressively more adequate. But there is also the *intuitive awareness* that something takes place in the mind when the mind is affected, and also an intuitive grasp of identity in differences of appearances and differences between individuals as to species (or kind). This intuitive awareness is *immediate* and takes place in the Self in three ways: as principle of consciousness (*concrete* intuition), as awareness of difference of content (*analytical* intuition) and the awareness of the identity of the given as appearance and (general and individualized) idea (*metaphysical* intuition). There is a priority of being that is acknowledged in knowing, which is dependent on the given as given, i.e. as foreign to thought. But in intuition, the concrete intuition of self-consciousness has precedence.

Now knowledge or science has its own 'reality' (as: logically organized truth content). It is not just produced by the Self, nor is it merely a direct reading of the World. It needs to comply to truth, as warranted by norms of thought (the principles of logic), and there is the content, acquired by working over the givens of the World, that is in principle shared, inter-subjective. Content is warranted in terms of a (Meinong-inspired) *Gegenstandstheorie*, by which impressions and representations, enjoyed by the Self, are fixed in their meaning according to the principle of identity. This yields objective meanings that serve as terms ('Objects') and relational complexes ('Objectives") in reference to given phenomena. Science has a formal and a material side, namely of logic (truth) and content (*Gegenstand*) respectively. In an ultimate sense, the reality of World and Self, with that of knowledge/science distinguished from both, find support in a Trinitarian theism: the Father concerns the World, as supported by ideas, the Spirit addresses the Self, imposing norms, and the Son or Logos warrants knowledge in being the principle of the harmony of objective and subjective rationality.

In mid-1921 Vollenhoven formulated a more 'metalogical' variant of rationality. The sciences, so he had initially held (more Marburg-like) in his dissertation, form an organism, in that the sciences partake of one method in which the distinction of the sciences are delineated by quantitatively distinct ratios of the formal and the material sides of knowledge. But now he comes to recognize (more Freiburg-like) distinct domains of validity, each with its own typical content. Within each domain, science is conducted in a way that guides the genesis of thought peculiar to that domain. Thus each domain aims to achieve the *adequate concept* of the reality it investigates, a reality that is itself upheld by its *idea*. Thus, the *logic* of the genesis of knowledge is guided by the *metalogical* awareness of the adequate concept as ideal, which would, if actually had, be the full knowledge of the relevant *idea*. Hence the entire domain of science constitutes a '*Gegenstand*-sphere' with a complex structure of domains or regions. But the distinction of '(adequate) concept and idea (of being)' aligns the subjective rationality, which aims to increase knowledge, to the objective rationality, as warranted by the idea. The analytical intuition, which initially took its cue from the concrete intuition, is now more attentive to the side of the idea. It now serves as the 'metalogical intuition', that determines methodical direction through 'viewing' (*schouwen*) the adequate concept as ideal end.

This viewing is notable, so we may conclude, in that it calls for a distinct quality of the Self as 'viewing subject'. The Self that views grasps, i.e. evaluates, that which is viewed in relation to itself, this being what C. Sigwart referred to as a 'modal relation' of evaluation. So long as the adequate concept operates in a realist context, the possibility of this evaluation becoming autonomous, is kept in check. The function of this metalogical viewing is discerning the highest unitary material feature of the adequate concept of a science. This unitary feature is the *modality* (or 'region category') of the content of a science, which unity can only be grasped intuitively and not by logic (which is dependent on diversity). This 'metalogical standpoint' is the starting point for new developments.

2. Developments in 1922

Considering the nature of the evidence, the new developments are easier to trace in Dooyeweerd than in Vollenhoven. Initially, in his work of 1921-1922, Dooyeweerd focuses on this 'metalogical variant' of Vollenhoven's critical realism. He moves searchingly in this context and adopts notions that he finds useable in developing a critical realist methodology. If Vollenhoven took metaphysics as the anchor of his thought—for Vollenhoven at the time metaphysics included an empirical moment— Dooyeweerd (considering his orientation to the human sciences) placed the methodology of the sciences more explicitly in a context of life- and worldview. But at this point this hardly counts as an essential difference.

The main novelty of 1922 is found in Dooyeweerd's work. He begins his employment with the Kuyper Foundation in October 1922, and among the first things he writes is the text entitled "Cosmos and Logos". With this document he clearly continues his prior research on methodology. But it also evidences an influence, not formerly noticed, from the side of *phenomenology*. He proceeds from the premise that is entirely new, *viz.* of a 'created *logos*', here understood to be human rationality, as being *a part of* the cosmos.

This 'created logos' embodies the presuppositions required to maintain the *Gegenstand*-sphere but in a changed setting. Whereas formerly the *Gegenstand*-sphere was distinct from Self and World in its having its own security in the (divine) Logos, it is now taken as presupposing connections to the Self and the World. Without these connections there could not be any *Gegenstand*. For, as to the World, it is now said to present an intuitable 'objective-primary meaning' which, when focused on in *acts* and selected as to *content*, yields the constituents (*Gegenstände*) of the *Gegenstand*-sphere (alias the 'created logos'). The 'objective-primary meaning' is *for* consciousness directly. (Dooyeweerd here makes use of an explicit phenomenological terminology; cf. section III.E.2.) This 'giving' of objective-primary meaning makes the more circuitous route via the forms of sensibility redundant. The former acknowledgement of different 'region categories', each with a highest material characterization of distinct modality is retained, as well as the acceptance of basic 'necessary connections' between the constituents of a region as being lawful for the region in question. Any knowledge of the World presupposes intuitive acknowledgment of what the World presents for it to be knowable.

As for the Self, the intuiting of the region categories and of the necessary connections they include needs to be supplemented by subjective 'forms of viewing', themselves too of distinct modality. This is another presupposition, namely of the 'connection' of the Self and the *Gegenstand* or 'created logos'. There is not simply 'a viewing subject', performing distinct acts, but the viewing (and thus intellectual understanding) itself presupposes a diversity of modal forms, in step with the diversity of the region categories. A region, as modally viewed, in a 'field of vision'.

In virtue of these presupposed connections of the Self and the World to the *Gegenstand*-sphere, the latter is drawn more closely into a cosmic context, which is to say that the *Gegenstand*-sphere has structured features in virtue of creation. The human exercise of rationality, i.e. the *human logos* active in acquiring knowledge and spending thought, is now taken to be confined to—"walled in" by—the 'created logos'. This exercise of human rationality focuses on connections between act and content within a region that is viewed in a modally relevant way. The knowledge enterprise takes place against the background of intuited conditions.

Knowledge is not a reading of the world, but arises by assimilating the content, made available through the prior intuitive intelligence and organized in fields of vision according to region categories. Thought—scientific thought—is a further working over of knowledge. It is a logical viewing, in which unity and diversity are imposed on a 'field of vision', thereby turning the latter into a 'field of inquiry'. Scientific thought seeks a *synthesis* of logical viewing and a field of inquiry, resulting in scientific knowledge of the field as system. Knowledge arises through 'arbitrary thought', while scientific knowledge is thought guided by the methodical treatment of the content of a field on inquiry. Thought and knowledge are not free creations of reason but are enclosed within an intuitive intelligence, "the humble viewing of given objective meaning" (1923a3: 60). Self and World being presupposed here, realism is not relinquished.

A puzzling feature of this writing of Dooyeweerd is that there is no apology or explanation for the important difference noticeable here as compared to his former work. Of course, that former work was not published, so there was no external incentive for explanation or account. But if Dooyeweerd felt a certain 'ownership' or primary responsibility with respect to this development, one might expect a word of motivation for the present view over against the former view.

This raises the possibility of the relevance of Vollenhoven's presence, though there is little known of this directly at this point. In his first publications Dooyeweerd's references to epistemology, in the trend of the development of 1922, are very brief and guarded. On the other hand, Vollenhoven's first important publication on epistemology, on "Contours of the theory of knowledge" (April 1926), with its view of 'knowing resorting under being'—which was Vollenhoven's way of expressing that the 'created logos' is part of the created world—is one of its main props. Despite the late date (related to the contingency of Vollenhoven's illness), if we are correct in our surmise of Dooyeweerd's having been deferent to Vollenhoven in this connection (cf. the discussion in III.D.2), then that would increase the likelihood that this input of renewal comes from Vollenhoven.

Although the noticeable change, as found in Dooyeweerd's writing, seems to be a rather technical point of methodology, there are also broader ramifications. The theisms of critical realism would appear to be directly affected. The three-some 'World, Science/Knowledge and Self', stands in direct correlation to Father, *Logos* and Spirit, respectively. But with science/knowledge now meshing in with the cosmos, and with the Self's viewing as a presupposed condition, that must imply that the (divine) *Logos* is no longer seen—at least in the current role regarding rationality—as being so distinct from the World as was formerly the case, and that the Logos also has more direct cognitive relevance for the Self. The *Logos* appears now to be more 'operative' in the World, the guardian of the meaning-for-consciousness that the World reveals insofar as this is intuit-able. We also notice in the same text of Dooyeweerd, as relevant for the Self, a more pronounced expression of the role of faith. Sin affects our viewing adversely. What we know begins with what we 'see' in the attentive perspective of our subjective *logos*. If we see wrongly, we cannot appeal to facts, for there is no separate world available to us that is not itself channelled through the *logos*. This calls for a relevance of the divine Logos that is additional to that of guardian of rationality. One needs to stand right in a more inclusive sense with the divine *Logos*, meaning not merely rational correctness in terms of categories and method, but also a more personal rectitude in terms of an existential attitude that affects the viewing, with 'faith' implications. This role of the Logos is more dependent on "the special grace of redemption through Christ Jesus". But the two meanings need to be taken together, for only then can we see "*sub specie aeternitatis*", from the view of eternity.

This reference to eternity would appear to be typical to Dooyeweerd. At least it occurs nowhere in Vollenhoven. We said above that his emphasis on 'knowing resorting under being' is relevant to Vollenhoven's way of expressing the way human rationality is structured by cosmic features and thus operates in the context of the 'created logos'. In other words, Vollenhoven formulates an analogous shift. The human Self also undergoes a 'change in position' in Vollenhoven, namely from a position of being 'beside the World' to a position of always already standing in subjection (to law) in the pluralist context of the World. (We referred to this change in the discussion of Vollenhoven's response to Janse's ideas.)

Now there is a remark made by Vollenhoven that would appear to have a bearing on this new development. In a letter to Cornelius Van Til, dated 4 February 1936, Vollenhoven recalls his early contact with Dooyeweerd and their dissatisfaction with Christian scholarship. He continues: "The intentions were in many cases excellent, but one continually ran aground for not daring to think in a consequential Scriptural way, also in the area of philosophy. We then began to seek (from about 1920) and, God be praised, initially found (about the summer of 1922) [a more Scriptural way of thinking]. In 1926 we were appointed on the same day by the Free University. . .".[206] If we can trust Vollenhoven's memory of

---

206   Quoted with permission. The archivist of the Westminster Theological Seminary

more than a dozen years, then he at least signals something significant in connection with his contact with Dooyeweerd, which took place around the summer of 1922, that had implications for their philosophical work. As being the *beginning* ('initially') of a more consequential way of thinking scripturally, it may be that Vollenhoven signals a realization of the relevance of a more direct faith stance, without wishing to be understood as implying this to have been definitive. The new development, discussed above, is at least consistent with this report of memory. Regretfully, Vollenhoven is not more specific, so we cannot be sure that what was 'found' is relevant to the change to which Dooyeweerd's text attests. But in the light of that change, it would appear to involve the view of "knowing resorting under being", itself a lasting insight of Vollenhoven's definitive thought.

We add to this a more challenging memory of half a century later on Dooyeweerd's part. In his tribute to Vollenhoven in 1973 he mentions: "I had been convinced already as early as 1922 that Kuyper's deepest intentions had been voiced in the statement referred to above", i.e. the statement "There is not an inch in the whole of temporal life of which Christ, as Lord of all men, does not say 'mine'."[207] Dooyeweerd would appear to imply that he came to this realization from Kuyper in 1922. His "Cosmos en Logos" (1923a2) does evidence a new awareness of the possible relevance of a faith stance in philosophy. It is in light of that evidence that this memory could bear upon this change in Vollenhoven and Dooyeweerd.[208]

One might ask whether Vollenhoven's correspondence with Janse throws any light on the change of 1922. On this point that evidence (as found to date) is disappointing. The crucial correspondence with Janse towards the end of 1922 focuses on anthropology, so in that sense a change in philosophical methodology would not be an expected topic of discussion with Janse. What we do have, as mentioned in the discussion of Vollenhoven's letter of 7 November 1922 in the earlier part of this

library, Ms. Grace Mullen, kindly provided me with a copy of this letter from the Van Til collection. The translation of the quoted passage is mine. (The second sentence of the quote echoes the "seek and you will find" of Matthew 7: 7.)

207   Dooyeweerd 1973: 7.

208   In autobiographical remembrances Vollenhoven recalls having had an influence on Dooyeweerd in a way that he had come to regret. The influence concerns Vollenhoven's view of time and number, as defended in the dissertation (Vollenhoven 1918a); cf. Vollenhoven 1963c: 173-177 and 1968b: 202-205. Prima facie this is distinct from the development of 1922. But there are numerous inconsistencies in these remembrances, and a consistent interpretation of all the known facts points to a possible relevance of 1922 after all. This is discussed in the addendum to chapter 4.

chapter, is that Vollenhoven, in speaking of the "relations of the one soul to the distinguished terrains" (cf. Stellingwerff 1992: 62) or worlds (of validity, of values, of physical nature), states that the connection of the soul to these terrains is determined "by the nature of the relations" (*den aard der relaties*) (*ibid.*). Viewed formally, this understanding of a relation does not agree with the preferred monadic view of a relation, as found in Vollenhoven's dissertation, but—again considered formally—it does agree with the way 'essential connections' are discussed in Dooyeweerd's text. But without Dooyeweerd's text, it is difficult to put one's finger on Vollenhoven's meaning, as indeed our own discussion of this letter attests (cf. section II.D. above). Thus, as supporting evidence, this is very tenuous.

3. Developments in 1923

In 1923 Vollenhoven is out of reach most of that year due to his illness. He is institutionalized in Amsterdam until the end of June. He resumes his full pastoral work at the beginning of December. One assumes that in the second half of that year, when back in The Hague, there would have been time and occasion for discussions between the brothers-in-law, though probably this had to be subdued at first. In any case the next step worthy of mention is the occurrence of 'law-idea' in Dooyeweerd in late 1923 (cf. section III.F.). Here, for the first time, we have a notion that can be fully attributed to him, for Vollenhoven did not take to it. Needless to say, it is not the Lockean 'idea' that figures here, as mental representation, but in this case as the representation of law. (Dooyeweerd calls the representation of law as boundary "the concept of law"; Dooyeweerd 1923d: 12.) The term 'idea' is still in line with Vollenhoven's metaphysical use of a distinctive being, a use that the recuperated Vollenhoven no longer underscored. The fuller picture is as follows.

Dooyeweerd has given new (or renewed) attention to Calvin, probably in conjunction with a more self-conscious reading of Kuyper.[209] Calvinistic metaphysics proceeds from the difference between the Creator, who is infinite and sovereign, and the creature, who is finite and stands in subjection. The boundary between the infinite and the finite is now said to be the law, namely, as that which is posited by sovereignty and that to which the creature stands subjected. Sovereignty is empowered by God's will, a will that the creature is not in a position to question. But God does not reign by fiat. *His* wisdom and *His* reason support *His* will, so that what God wills can be expected to be good and in application

---

209 Cf. Henderson 1994: 113-114; also footnote 76.

wise.²¹⁰ So God has a 'providential world-plan' that governs the course of creation. Essential to this plan is that the law, which is a unitary boundary between God and the creation, itself unfolds in a diversity of manifestations (things) and of spheres, each with their own sovereignty. The law-idea is itself the providential world-plan; hence it involves, as formal condition, the law as boundary between the infinite and the finite as well as two material conditions, namely the foresight of law, understood as ordinances, and the providing for the creature in such a way as to be fitting to respond to ordinances. In other words, the law-idea, as providential world-plan, is a Calvinistic cosmology in a nutshell, useable as *organon* in life's practice in the context of a life- and worldview.

There is no evidence of a similar development in Vollenhoven. He did fully accept the law-as-boundary understanding, but he did not encapsulate this in an idea. In fact, his very understanding of law-as-boundary *arrested* the continued use of that notion. From his first statements in 1926 till late in his career, Vollenhoven limits his basic statement about the cosmos to a two-fold confession, without implying that there is any 'cosmic unity' or 'providential world-plan' to 'sight on'.²¹¹ (i) "God created the cosmos" – a biblical given, but without making anyone privy to the 'mechanism' of creation. It is at the level of Leibniz's statement "why is there something rather than nothing?".²¹² Analysis cannot account for all (finite) presences and their determinations; for at some point one accepts what there is, as a 'this', that is not capable of further analysis.²¹³ (ii) "God imposed on the cosmos his law". This is the theistic, providential factor—God's "carrying everything by the word of his power" (cf. Heb. 1:3)—by which Vollenhoven means the presence of ordinances, of laws of modally different law-spheres. While creation as such is 'beyond our

---

210   We would appear to have a full Trinitarian relevance of divinity in connection with the law-idea. Because the law-idea is a cosmological principle, its Trinitarian feature holds (so to speak) 'intra-cosmically'. This supports the predestinarian connotation in Dooyeweerd's references to the law-idea.

211   There is the problem of 'the whole', discussed in the Janse section of this chapter. It too is approached as a condition one abides by, without being able to acknowledge it as idea. Taking 'cosmos' in its aesthetic connotation, Vollenhoven did entertain the metaphor of the cosmos as a work of art, with God as "the architect and the artisan of the cosmos"; cf. Vollenhoven 1930b: 13. In that vein, the thought of cosmic unity would point in the direction of a harmony. But even this aesthetic metaphor is dropped in the early 1930s.

212   Leibniz 1976a: 639

213   Cf. "the method of resolution and composition" in section II.E. of chapter 1 and section III.B.3.e and f of chapter 4.

ken', laws or ordinances are intuit-able as conditions to be met.[214] "These laws are not hidden: they resort under the revealed part of [God's] will of decision. . . . To be more precise, these laws differ modally, as do the functions that are subject to them."[215] Modal laws govern the functioning of things, not their make-up, the latter being in virtue of creation. In the realist use of 'idea', the emphasis lies with the make-up of a thing, and through that make-up one attempts to account for the thing's lawful functioning. Here the two factors of creation and law-subjection are merged: the make-up of things is constitutive for their functioning. The provenance of 'modal law' in Vollenhoven is what he had previously referred to as the 'extra-mental norms' that determine qualities of subjection. These 'norms' are now re-interpreted to qualify as the laws/norms of all functioning.

By denying the relevance of ideas as principles of distinctive being, there is in Vollenhoven no longer an operative controlling unity of creation that is within human reach or for the human being to sight on. This underscores the human being's being a finite creature, hence a creature that is completely under the law. Also God's dealing with the cosmos is itself not delimited by any knowable 'definite unity of the cosmos'.[216] The prime cosmological feature that Vollenhoven does allow is what might be called the 'intersection principle'. It assumes created things, and it accepts their functioning in law-spheres according to modal laws. The prime datum for philosophy here is the acknowledgement that things

---

214   An early reference is in Vollenhoven 1926d: 190; a later statement is in Vollenhoven 1951h: 55. Also, throughout the years 1930-1945, Vollenhoven 2010, section **13**; also Vollenhoven 1933a: 24.

215   Vollenhoven 1930b: 17.

216   The net effect is that, in the context of cosmology, Vollenhoven only acknowledged the so-called "modal laws", these being the "ordinances" that regulate, norm-like, cosmic life. Vollenhoven's former "thing-laws" seem to be continued in Dooyeweerd's later "individuality-structures", for which Vollenhoven had no use. The only question that remains concerns the kingdoms. Formally, the latter occur where Vollenhoven spoke of general ideas. Vollenhoven always maintained that the things of the cosmos are 'kingdom bound' in virtue of creation. In his cosmology (cf. Vollenhoven 2005d/e, **26**), distinct things and their general context in kingdoms form an *ultimate cosmic contrast*. If ideas lose their relevance in connection with distinct things (as 'thing-laws') then one may expect an analogous redundancy with respect to general ideas (as 'general essences'), and the notions of 'individual' and 'kingdom' need to be accepted as primitive terms. Individuation would appear to be synonymous with the process of genesis, a process that Vollenhoven sees as guided by the Spirit (cf. Vollenhoven 2005d/e, **22**). However, the whole theme of law is not thereby settled, for Vollenhoven also distinguishes the law of love, and in 1953 he speaks of three kinds of law. But there is no recurrence to ideas after their rejection (probably as of 1923).

and law-spheres always intersect. This needs to be discussed in its own right (cf. the next chapter). But this 'intersection principle' does not support a 'cosmic unity' such as is promoted by Dooyeweerd's law-idea.

So what does the absence (or rejection) of Vollenhoven's former 'idea' imply in a more general sense? 'Idea' in Vollenhoven's early thought served as thing-laws for things and persons. For persons, that idea is the thing-law of the person as complete substance, controlling its appearances and functioning (in body and mind), its interactions with other human beings or things, and also its development over time, all of course under the auspices of the human essence. By virtue of this thing-law, each human being has a controlling unity throughout its states, features and changes. In other words, were one to know the idea of this human being, then one would know all that will happen to that person, since it is 'programmed' (as it were) into the person's substance (idea). The substance is not just the sum-total of states and features; its controlling power is something in its own right. The future is predestined. Denying the relevance of idea in this case implies at least a rejection of this view of cosmic necessity.

Dooyeweerd placed a strong emphasis on providence when he launched the notion of 'law-idea'. It is uncertain what he means to say exactly when he links the terms 'providence' with 'predestination'. Sometimes he speaks of predestination falling under providence, sometimes he equates the two. In any case, providence as such includes the two meanings of 'foresee' and 'provide'. In Calvin this is how God regulates events and occurrences. Predestination in Calvin is the Augustinian notion of each human being's state of eternity, as saved or damned, being predestined and fixed, completely apart from any merit of works or the worthiness of the person. When Dooyeweerd speaks of predestination "in the general sense", he seems to say that predestination holds not only with respect to persons, but for everything within creation, of everything under the law. Then indeed it is fitting, in line with Vollenhoven's early metaphysics, to continue to speak of 'law-idea', if the law of the cosmos is thought to be such that it acts as a 'thing-law' for the cosmos, i.e. as the governing unity in which everything is predestined that takes place in the course of the cosmos' existence. All that occurs is then 'intra-cosmic' (so to speak), its destiny predetermined.

When Vollenhoven jettisons 'ideas' he rejects this (classical and frightening) [217] doctrine of double predestination. He allows for election,

---

217   For example, Calvin himself said of predestination (of election *and* damnation): "The decree is dreadful indeed, I confess." Calvin 1960: 955. Not being able to break

which is the basis of the church, but is silent about reprobation. We can understand that his rejection of a 'cosmological law-idea' includes an 'analytical' view of development and history. What develops is not already completely self-contained. There are concrete and contingent influences too; there is nature and there is nurture. Later in his career Vollenhoven explicitly claims that God 'goes along with history', but the thought was not new.[218] The cosmic context is a context for development, and this takes place under the divine influence that reveals direction, together with the guidance towards satisfying ends. The directing and the guiding are attributed to the Logos and the Spirit, respectively.[219] These roles are not merely intra-cosmic, though naturally they are not disjoint from the cosmos either. The cosmos is open-ended, which is why every wrong turn of evil is a catastrophe, and every return to good praiseworthy. Direction is not in virtue of creation—that would make it an intra-cosmic entelechy, and encourage seeing good and evil as a balance of opposing forces—but the reality of the lived present of creation life, in its unceasing appeal to choose: to oppose and undo evil and to promote and sustain good.[220]

4. Concept and idea

Dooyeweerd writes in the 'Foreword' to his *De Wijsbegeerte der Wetsidee* (1935-1936, I: v): "initially under the strong influence first of neo-Kantian philosophy, later of Husserl's phenomenology, the great turning point in my thought was marked by the discovery of the religious root of thought itself, whereby a new light was shed on the continuous failure of all attempts, including my own, of bringing about a synthesis between the Christian faith and a philosophy that is rooted in faith in the self-sufficiency of human reason."

---

away from his Augustinian reading of Scripture, Calvin took the doctrine to be biblically sanctioned. Recall Vollenhoven's disquietude in connection with predestination speculation as quoted in footnote 200 above.

218   There was from the start the 'immanence of God'. In 1968 Vollenhoven spoke explicitly of God's presence in history; cf. Vollenhoven 1968b: 209-210. In 1942 Vollenhoven had stated: "Hence God goes along in the deployment of his world plan, a '*concursus Dei*'." Vollenhoven 1942m: 1. Obviously, the use of 'world plan' here should not be confused with 'world program'. The very effect of his 'going along' is to be relevant 'in the present', now.

219   Cf. in this regard the first version of *Isagôgè Philosophiae*, of 1930/1931, sections 71 ff. in Vollenhoven 2010.

220   Cf. Vollenhoven 2005d/e, **85** ff. , or 2010, **85** ff. I have attempted to express this relevance of direction more fully, in a 'Vollenhovian way', in my "Time and change in Vollenhoven"; Tol 1995, esp. "Time and its meaning", pp. 117-120.

We have indeed found evidence of the neo-Kantian and the phenomenological influences. The first was especially noticeable prior to his employment at the Kuyper Foundation. The latter comes more particularly to the fore in late 1922, when the notions of the *Gegenstand* and the cosmos become more closely wedded together and the *Gegenstand* arises from the objective meaning for consciousness, phenomenologically elicited from the cosmos. But the great turning point of which he speaks is not noticeable until 1928. If that is the point in time when "his" philosophy begins—if that is what he means to say here—then he leaves in the dark the decade of work and effort that preceded it. Or rather, he characterizes it as a specimen of the attempt to bring about a synthesis between the Christian faith and philosophy based on the self-sufficiency of human reason.

But this characterization may be questioned. The sovereignty of God *over against* the self-sufficiency of human reason is a recognizable concern from the start. Self-sufficiency is *challenged* when the methodological use of reason is channelled in domains of validity; and when Dooyeweerd formulated his 'law-idea', there is the explicit motive to *undo* human reason of any pretended self-sufficient authority as concerns the unity of insight or knowledge regarding the cosmos. It may be that Dooyeweerd means to point to the 'critical realist' context of his early work, which he now looks back on as having been a failure. But then his formulation is infelicitous. Critical realism depends on the realism of ideas. This realism is not grounded in human reason, but in divine reason, in tandem with the interpretation of the *Logos* as principle of rationality as embedded in knowledge. This reminds one of the problem of scholasticism. Vollenhoven and Dooyeweerd were initially more affected by *this* problem than by adherence—never a matter of principle—to neo-Kantianism or Husserlian phenomenology.

Dooyeweerd did indeed relinquish (somewhat later than Vollenhoven) the realism of ideas.[221] The year 1928 seems to be the watershed in this regard. Be that as it may, the important question is what he replaced it with. A summary indication will have to suffice at this point.

To start with, there is a telling passage in his inaugural lecture where he describes the epistemology he—and by implication, also Vol-

---

221 Vollenhoven's realism became a realism of law-spheres. The emphasis on the importance of realism increased. In a letter to A. Janse, 24 October 1924, Vollenhoven states: "In addition, in my epistemological reflections . . . a sharper turn towards realism has taken place." Also relevant is a statement to Janse in a letter of 25 October 1926: "In my inaugural [*Logos en Ratio*] . . . you will find a sharper struggle against rationalism, a total break with all psychologism." Cf. Vollenhoven to Janse 24-10-1924 and 25-10-1926.

lenhoven—has worked with to date but which he now finds wanting (cf. Dooyeweerd 1926d: 64). There is too much emphasis, he claims, on the *difference* between the law-spheres in the metalogical viewing, and insufficient recognition of the "organic thought of unity", which is more appropriate to the "organic law-idea". (The qualification 'organic' is new here.) The law-idea (i.e. the cosmological principle of totality or world-plan) should *penetrate* the sovereignty of the spheres, so that *in each sphere* a coherence of *all the spheres*, as warranted by the law-idea, becomes evident. He offers examples of this. In a cosmological sense there is the connection of a sphere to the spheres that are simpler that it, which constitute its *substrate*; in an epistemological sense there are the *analogies* of substrate law-spheres in the sphere of which they are the substrate. Such analogies are reflected in the modality of the sphere in question. Likewise there are *anticipations* in the modality of a law-sphere to the spheres that are more complex than it is (1926d: 65). In these ways the cosmic continuity of the order of the law-spheres is reflected in each law-sphere in its own way. This is what Dooyeweerd calls the universality in its own sphere.[222]

There is something remarkable about this universality in Dooyeweerd. If one takes, say, the logical law-sphere, then in this law-sphere is reflected the whole cosmic order. In other words, one can immediately assert a 'harmony' between 'subjective' reason—the logical law-sphere that channels subjective functional thought—and 'objective' reason, *viz.* the structure of the cosmic whole. One should seriously ask whether this is not a reaffirmation of a view that is at least 'scholastic-like' all over again. One generally does not ask this question because *each* law-sphere, and not just the logical sphere, displays the harmony with the whole. One might be more inclined to think of a 'perspectivism' in this regard. But when considering each law-sphere as the context of a fundamental science, then the method of development of a science in each case follows—or at least ideally ought to follow—the pattern of the cosmic whole. Compared to critical realism, the structure of a modality provides the 'ideal adequate concept', intuited by the metalogical intuition of 'modal viewing', while the pattern of the cosmic whole is what the

[222] It is not superfluous to note that Vollenhoven never accepted this view of modal universality. Vollenhoven recognizes a necessary relation of a law-spheres to the spheres that constitute its substrate spheres, which is reflected in the analogies (or retrocipations). But the anticipations call for mediation in cosmic creatures. For Vollenhoven there is no cosmic structure or order apart from the cosmic creatures that are structured in that way and exemplify it. (This is related to the 'intersection principle' of Vollenhoven's revised metaphysics.) What Vollenhoven referred to as the "universality of the law-sphere" is the cross-sectional participation of every subject or object in a law-sphere. Cf. Vollenhoven 2005d/e, **65**, or 2010, **65**.

law-idea, as 'world-plan', captures. The sure path of a science is *warranted* to the degree that it is in step with the cosmos as a whole, as reflected within the law-sphere of a science. Hence this reformulates rather than undercuts a 'harmony model.' In 1926 the distinction of concept and idea still serves in the basic way that is prevalent in critical realism; there is only some adjusted terminology:

> All specific regions have their own laws. Above these specific region laws there must be a universal law-order, in which all the specific region laws are founded, from which they derive their specific validity and also wherein each law-sphere's own area of competence is delimited. Each law-sphere has its own *concept* of law; together they equally appeal to a *law-idea*, a unity of all specific law-spheres, to a cosmic world-order, a world-plan.[223]

But the 'organic' feature, both within the law-spheres and the world-plan, continues to hold Dooyeweerd's attention. In 1928 Dooyeweerd speaks of the whole cosmic order as being a "law-organism", whereby each law-sphere is in itself a modality of the whole cosmic order (cf. Dooyeweerd 1928a: 24). (Note: this signals an increased relativizing of the diversity of the law-spheres; diversity that Vollenhoven so prized! Also the term 'aspect' now finds use.) What we have now is that the part (a law-sphere) reflects the whole (cosmic order) and the whole is reflected in each part. When taking this as a hermeneutical circle—since Dooyeweerd concentrates on meaning, the circle can hardly be anything else—one can understand how a certain 'cosmic realism' can be taken as having become redundant. For each part (law-sphere), as a modality of 'the whole', allows the participating (modally viewing) Self to represent the whole from the perspective of the modality in question. This is possible for every modality. But then the (modally viewing) Self is a constant factor in connection with the modally changing perspectives in which the whole is viewed. So the Self can become the metalogical locus of convergence for all the law-spheres. The cosmic whole can be represented in the Self through the 'modal relation' (Sigwart) in which the Self stands to this represented content.

The question that arises at this point is: what serves as warrant for the 'proper understanding' of this (metalogical) modal relation? Considered against the background of critical realism, there would appear to be the alternative of *either* securing the presence of the representations in a cosmic realism—one takes into consciousness what, realistically, there is for consciousness (via the metaphysical intuition)—*or* critically guarding the understanding of this content in terms of conditions to which the

---

223   Dooyeweerd 1926e: 423 (emphases added). Cf. the larger quote, of which this is a part, in footnote 204 above.

Self must comply (norms). Critical realism accepted both, but Dooyeweerd now feels that calling on a 'realist metaphysics' is more problematic than increasing the emphasis on the conditions that guard criticism.[224] Can a choice for the Self suffice if properly instructed?

It is of cardinal importance that the Self understands itself in a way that does not privilege any one law-sphere. Thus a 'law-idea' is called for that focuses on coherence, in which the modal diversity is taken up, a coherence that reflects the unity of the "law-organism" of the whole. The Self can operate with this understanding of 'law-idea' only when its own position transcends the law-spheres. (Even the law-sphere of faith must be transcended.) This suggests the need for an "Archimedean point", *viz*. a standpoint that transcends the order of the law-spheres. The Self can choose this transcendent standpoint only in being self-critical, in the sense of not privileging one particular law-sphere or modal function. When taking the position in the Archimedean point—which is tantamount to being self-critical (in the sense of being truly modally unprejudiced)—the Self finds itself in the open vista of being able to overview and understand the whole or the totality, i.e. understand it in terms of the Self's own deepest participation in this totality. This participation must be 'supra-temporal"—time is for Dooyeweerd a 'diversifier' (the way a prism breaks up light, so time breaks the unity of meaning). What the participation leads one to understand is the religious determination—at the 'supra-temporal' level, this is the only *kind* of determination that remains—of both the totality and the diversity of cosmic experience.

In this connection Dooyeweerd refers to the "discovery" of the human "heart" (first [?] clearly implicated in 1928),[225] in its religious meaning, as spiritual principle, and taken as relevant for philosophy. "Well

---

224   One can see how Dooyeweerd is tending in this direction in 1926. In 1926e: 425 (already quoted in footnote 204) he states: "the foundation of our philosophical thought is the law-idea [as world-plan], the notion of the deepest ground of validity and mutual coherence of all region laws. In referring to the law-idea, we have far superseded the narrow scientific terrain and we have placed ourselves in the middle of the region, very inadequately[!] called metaphysics. We prefer to replace this word with the term cosmology[!], associating with this expression the meaning of the doctrine of the harmonious coherence of the creation in all of its existence-spheres and validity-spheres." The latter reference to "existence-spheres and validity-spheres" is the distinction between cosmic reality and the *Gegenstand*-sphere respectively, in continuation of critical realism.

225   Verburg 1989: 121 ff., signals 1930 as an important year of new developments in Dooyeweerd's work. Verburg points in this regard to Dooyeweerd's first indication of the appreciation of the notion of 'cosmic time'. Of course, cosmic time presupposes the interpretation of the human heart as supra-temporal. Henderson states, in Henderson 1994: 115, that there is "only sporadic mention of 'the heart' in [Dooyeweerd's] writings in the period 1923-1927".

now, only in its deepest kernel does the human spirit transcend the temporal [i.e. cosmic] coherence of law, only *the religious kernel of personality is the eternal in the human being*, not its moral, logical, psychical or aesthetic subject-functions, that are rather entirely fitted into the temporal coherence of law" (Dooyeweerd 1928b: 425; emphasis added). This "deepest kernel . . . [of] the human spirit" is what is new here, but not the characterization of the human being as having eternity in its make-up. The latter is the "*sub specie aeternitatis*" we found in the text on 'Cosmos and Logos' (1923a3: 61). In that text the 'point of view of eternity' put us in a position to accept the meaning given for consciousness as being the work of the "Divine Noèsis" (i.e. the divine Logos), a position realized though our faith function. This sets our otherwise distorted understanding of the cosmos, as due to sin, aright. But in 1928 the focus is not on understanding the cosmos as such aright, but—a deeper focus—on being self-critical with respect to cosmic reality when participating in its totality. The eternity in the human being offers the opportunity for the Self to realize that "the view of the meaning-totality is not possible without a view of the origin, the *archè* of both the totality and the diversity of meaning" (Dooyeweerd 1935-1936, I: 10). The way through the Self in self-criticism has taken priority over the way via the cosmos, when the latter is 'uncritically' assumed (merely) to be subject to law.

That Dooyeweerd made a choice for the Self as over against the World is clear in *De Wijsbegeerte der Wetsidee* (1935-1936). There we find a definitive cancellation of realism by accepting an *ontology of meaning*: "The *meaning* is the *being* of all *creaturely beings*, the mode being also of our selfhood, and has a *religious root* and divine origin" (*op. cit.*, I: 6) If a modal relation is again taken in its original meaning of "a relation of valuation to a knowing subject" (Sigwart), then the transcendent Self is able to capture, via the distinct modalities of experience, the structure of the whole of what is thus experienced by means of the meaning experienced.[226] Rather than having to assume a reality behind the phenomena, even a reality for consciousness, the Self, once properly situated in the Archimedean point, is able to account for the totality of meaning; that is to say, when taking into account the status of the Self and the totality

---

226 The acceptance of cosmic reality becomes redundant when meaning (formerly the *Gegenstand*-sphere) is given a status that is no longer dependent on that of reality. This leads to Dooyeweerd's tortuous use of *meaning*: 'meaning-diversity', 'meaning-totality', 'meaning-structure', 'meaning-aspects', 'meaning-individual structure differences', 'meaning-systasis', etc. This is evident already in Dooyeweerd 1931—e.g. "the meaning-structure of cosmic reality" (*op. cit.* : 84)—when "De wijsbegeerte der wetsidee" was in an advanced stage of composition.

of meaning as dependent on the origin of meaning, which is God. This is how there can be "the full concrete unity of consciousness of Self and of God", which is the fulfilment of self-critical understanding.[227] But at the same time this community not only relativizes the boundary between Creator and creatures, but also blurs the difference of autonomy and heteronomy between them.

An ontology of meaning is deemed to be adequate to delineate the full complexity of human experience, without having to assume what it is that bears meaning. This puts an end to any scholastic "objective rationality",[228] as warranted by ideas that regulate things and their coherence, interactions and development, such as is part of critical realism and such as was captured in Dooyeweerd's original use of 'law-idea' as world plan. But there is still need for the guidance of 'subjective rationality', i.e. the human involvement in the diversity of the modal meaning aspects. In that light, the term 'idea' needs to be recast. Dooyeweerd predicates a new meaning of the tandem 'concept and idea' on the Self in the interest of criticism. There is the moment of self-criticism, in which one recognizes (meaning-)diversity, but without prejudicing or 'absolutizing' any feature of this. The concept is at home in understanding this meaning-diversity in the distinctness of its modalities. It seizes on modal retrocipations, substrate-spheres, object-functions, and the like to understand how this diversity coheres. But to warrant the proper view of the very context of this diversity, there needs to be an appeal to the Self's participation in the totality of meaning. That view (or metalogical intuition) of the totality yields the ideal insight, wrought in the light of the "religious root and divine origin", that is able to orientate conceptual understanding, in the sense of providing direction to conceptual understanding. In the idea, conceptual understanding seizes on the anticipatory moments of a modal aspect. In its anticipatory structure, a modal aspect reflects the totality of meaning, as progressively won when viewed from that aspect. Thus the new, non-realist meaning of 'law-idea' is now that of a 'limiting concept'. It is direction determining in light of the Self's participation in

---

227 Dooyeweerd 1939: 204.

228 Perhaps this is stated too bluntly. The Self, as viewed up to this point, was always taken to be itself cosmic (though this is uncertain in Dooyeweerd's "Cosmos en Logos"). Thus an appeal to the Self can still have metaphysical overtones. Dooyeweerd's predicating 'eternity' in the human being has such an overtone, making one wonder whether this isn't an anthropology of mortal (body) and immortal (soul) all over again, though not with the difference falling between lower and higher functions, but between functions over against a higher spiritual centre of the functions. One sees the latter duality reflected in the new use of concept and idea.

the totality of meaning.[229]

But in taking this step, one wonders whether Dooyeweerd was himself sufficiently self-critical. This use of idea is the very use that Vollenhoven had indicated, in 1921, as being typical of neo-Kantian thought. He states: "The 'idea' is used here [in formalism or idealism] exclusively to indicate a direction, not to determine a final goal".[230] In Dooyeweerd, concept and idea continue to serve as critical tandem. A concept concerns a restricted meaning, seizing on retrocipations and substrates; an idea involves conceptual insight in a progressively transcendental course towards fuller meaning, i.e. the totality of meaning, ideally towards the full potential of the limiting concept. In the meantime we are left to wonder why this use of concept and idea does not, despite the Christian context in which it is addressed, in fact reaffirm an essentially neo-Kantian construal of rationality.

---

229   Cf. Dooyeweerd 1935-1936, I: 10; parallel passage in Dooyeweerd 1953-1958, I: 8. This (recast) use of concept and idea in Dooyeweerd is subject to historical and critical study in Strauss 1973.

230   Cf. Chapter two, section IX above. The full quote is: "The 'idea' is used here [in formalism or idealism] exclusively to indicate a direction, not to determine a final goal; . . . . 'The Ideal' of which I spoke . . . includes in the first place the final goal as point of rest, and only in the second place [does it include] the connection of this point of rest with moving thought [i.e. inferential thinking], whereby it acquires a direction determining meaning. *This second meaning is more or less equivalent to the whole meaning of 'idea' with the neo-Kantians.*" Vollenhoven 1921c: 85-86, footnote 4 (emphasis added).

4

Embarking Within Bounds of Law: The Initial Definitive Platform

"When, in our work, we on the contrary clearly acknowledge its historical background with its dual dangers [of dualism and monism], then we won't founder on account of the oppositions that divided an earlier generation, but together overcome them."

D.H.Th. Vollenhoven (1970)

I. *INTRODUCTION*
In an unpublished text fragment, written at the end of 1926 (or very early in 1927) Vollenhoven sketched a plan of writing a series of articles on the philosophy of mathematics. The immediate occasion was an article on the foundations of mathematics by the well-known mathematician, Hermann Weyl (1885-1955), in the first issue of the new journal, *Symposion. Philosophische Zeitschrift für Forschung und Aussprache* (1926). There was also a more personal reason for renewed attention to this topic. An illuminating paragraph of Vollenhoven's plan is the following:

> It is now about eight years ago that I received my doctorate on the basis of the dissertation, entitled "De Wijsbegeerte der Wiskunde van Theïstisch Standpunt". It has been sold out for several years, so I could have considered a new printing; but I could not find the time for its preparation. For it was evident to me, already quite soon, that an unchanged second edition was impossible; my view as to what is characteristic of Calvinism had changed rather drastically, and through that change the possibility first dawned on me of making the basic thoughts of a Calvinistic epistemology also fruitful in the area [of the philosophy of mathematics] that I had previously set foot on with only the wavering glimmer [*weifelend schijnsel*] of theism.[1]

---
1   Vollenhoven 1926msC: 2-3; translation mine. D.H.Th. Vollenhoven, "De wijsbegeerte der arithmetiek en der chorologie van Calvinistisch standpunt" [The philosophy of arithmetic and of space from a Calvinistic standpoint] (1926/1927). The document is a manuscript of three pages, plus seven pages of notes on Weyl and two pages of bibliography. Nothing became of the plan, unless Vollenhoven's "Problemen en richtingen in de wijsbegeerte der wiskunde" [Problems and approaches in the philosophy of mathemat-

Important for our purposes is Vollenhoven's report of a recent change in his outlook. He is not specific as to details, but the motive for the change is a new awareness of what is characteristic of Calvinism. This led to "a Calvinistic epistemology", the basic thoughts of which have ramifications for the philosophy of mathematics. His strong wording underscores the felt significance of the reorientation: an unchanged reprint of the dissertation is "impossible" (*onmogelijk*) because his view had "changed rather drastically" (*tamelijk sterk veranderde*). His new understanding of Calvinism contrasts so favourably with his earlier theism that the latter pales to a "wavering glimmer".

In chapter three we found that, shortly after completing his dissertation in 1918, Vollenhoven's thought was indeed 'on the move'. There is evidence from Vollenhoven (as we saw) that, already in mid-1919, there was a felt need to look "for a deeper foundation in the area of philosophy and the sciences in general" (cf. above, chapter three, section III.B.). Then in December 1920 there is mention of the challenge to "save Calvinistic metaphysics" (cf. chapter three, section III.C.2.). We cannot be sure how the latter relates to the search for deeper foundations, but both factors are mentioned in the paragraph above. In a letter to A. Janse, of 21 March 1924, Vollenhoven expresses his growing conviction. He writes: "But that with sufficient effort and available time one can achieve the goal of a Calvinistic [understanding of] science that can withstand [neo-]Kantianism and not [merely] avoid it—of that I am no longer in doubt. . . . I now see more [clearly] its possibility".[2] Certainly from that point of time, an unchanged reprint of the dissertation could not be entertained.[3]

---

ics], (Vollenhoven 1936hh) is the (much reduced) fulfilment of it.

2   *Janse Archives* 157, Box 8, Folder 32. Amsterdam: Historisch Documentatiecentrum, Free University.

3   Vollenhoven says in the quoted passage that it was already rather soon after its appearing that an unchanged reprint had become unfeasible. On the basis of the material researched in chapters two and three, we can hazard to detail the changes or shifts mentioned above more closely. The shift mentioned in mid-1919 probably pertains to the move from a Marburg-like unity of methodology orientation to a more Freiburg-like pluralist orientation. Published evidence is in Vollenhoven 1921c. Then there is the urge to "save Calvinistic metaphysics", mentioned by Dooyeweerd in his letter to Vollenhoven, 17 December 1920. In that letter it sounds like a fresh topic in their contact. This probably focussed on the distinction between the infinite essence of God and the finite nature of everything creaturely. This affects Vollenhoven's dissertation directly, for he maintained the actual infinity of the world in that work. This is probably what Vollenhoven initially looked upon as requiring revision (cf. above, in chapter three, footnote 100). Critical realist metaphysics as such need not be implicated, apart from an adjustment within the bounds of the potential infinite. Only in the aftermath of his illness (in the course

Vollenhoven's words here, regarding his new understanding of Calvinism, intimate changes in scientific methodology and philosophy, but also suggest his rejecting what had proven to be a hindrance, namely his earlier theism. Then, in the quoted passage of the letter to Janse, there is the reference to [neo-]Kantianism, which Vollenhoven now feels he can confront head-on. Hence in reference to the *same context of change* regarding a Calvinistic epistemology and/or understanding of science Vollenhoven mentions theism (in his quoted plan) and [neo-]Kantianism (in his letter to Janse). The unsuspecting reader will not immediately connect theism and neo-Kantianism in this regard. Yet there is a connection.

Availing ourselves of the research discussed in earlier chapters, the broad connection between theism and neo-Kantianism would appear to imply the following. We found that the neo-Kantian influence pertains particularly in the use of 'concept and idea'. The 'concept' represents the growth of knowledge, as empowered by 'logic' and guided by the 'adequate concept'. Neo-Kantianism tends to treat the adequate concept as 'limit concept', this being the 'idea', i.e. the anticipation of the systematic completeness of the knowledge in question. Accordingly, when the 'growth of knowledge' is guided by the idea, the (subjective) rationality of the knowledge gained becomes increasingly more adequate to, or in harmony with, the (objective) rationality of the systematic idea. The harmony of the two forms of rationality is warranted in neo-Kantianism in various ways, e.g. by the transcendental structure of logic, transcendental consciousness, dialectic of reason, etc., but it is secured in the human personality in its primal rectitude of autonomy.

In their 'critical realism', Vollenhoven and Dooyeweerd had rejected this warrant and security of rationality. They attributed metaphysical import to the idea. Thus the 'adequate concept' is not equivalent to the idea, but the adequate concept reflects the ideal of complete knowledge of the idea, as a knowledge of reality. The idea's objective rationality is expressive of the structure of the world and is not as such merely secured in the Self. But that calls for a different kind of warrant for the harmony of subjective and objective rationality than is accepted in neo-Kantianism. Vollenhoven and Dooyeweerd had looked to the (divine) Logos as warrant of knowledge; for knowledge has an objective reference

of 1923) does Vollenhoven reject the 'dualistic metaphysics' (of substance and phenomenon), along with the substantialistic interpretation of the 'immortal soul', as is evident in his letter to Janse, 19 February 1924. Only when Vollenhoven's revised understanding of Calvinism includes these shifts in metaphysics and anthropology would there appear to be a sufficient motive on his part to combat his earlier theism.

to the world while expressive of subjectively acquired meaning, organized logically. In this 'critical realism' a (traditional) scholastic understanding of the Logos, as the warrant of rationality, is operative, over against the humanistic warrant of neo-Kantianism.[4] This theism of the Logos is, of course, not what neo-Kantianism supports. But theism and neo-Kantianism do share the distinction between subjective and objective rationality and the ideal of their agreement. In fact, the common trait of their rationalism is such as to relegate the said difference to the status of a secondary problem, namely that of a humanistic versus a metaphysical interpretation of the idea.

Vollenhoven's revised understanding of Calvinism needs to be seen against the background of this problem, in particular in the way scholastic rationalism and the realist interpretation of the idea are implicated. For these 'now' stand accused. The timeframe—to gauge this from the letter to Janse cited above—is that of the mid-1920s. Vollenhoven's convalescence in 1923 stimulated intellectual renewal as well as health. In the meantime Dooyeweerd has also (as we saw) taken a very pro-Calvinist stance in positing his notion of the 'law-idea' in the latter part of 1923. But we found that in him this is combined, initially at least, with the continued critical realist understanding of idea. At some point—difficult to pinpoint, but in any case related to the novel emphasis on the Self, as the central, spiritual personality, that positions itself in the Archimedean point (cf. Dooyeweerd 1928b)—the realist-metaphysical understanding of idea makes way in him for an ontology of meaning and a shift towards a use of 'concept and idea' with a *more direct* neo-Kantian connotation (as we concluded). How Dooyeweerd deals with the problem of rationality at this point is not our current topic. But we need to mention this, not only to be reminded of the problem at hand but also to be prepared to look at Vollenhoven afresh. The term 'Calvinism' is now (as of late 1923) used, in a refined sense, to denote a position from which philosophy is to be practised. Both Vollenhoven and Dooyeweerd wave the same banner, but in their practice of 'Calvinistic philosophy' Dooyeweerd remains sensitive to a neo-Kantian pull, while Vollenhoven (as will appear below) retains a—reformed—theistic stance.

4　At this point we leave unmentioned the role of the intuition. From the start Vollenhoven had denied that the harmony of subjective and objective rationality is itself an adequate basis for knowledge, insisting on the inclusion of an intuition to account for 'synthetic a priori's'. This complicates the problem but does not essentially change it. We add that the distinction between the two forms of rationality led to the prominent distinction in the philosophy of science in the second half of the twentieth century, namely between context of discovery and context of justification.

In this chapter we will discuss Vollenhoven's revised platform and the main contours of what he called 'Calvinistic philosophy', as initially formulated by him. I shall refer to this as his 'initial definitive platform'. It includes the development from the mid-1920s till the early 1930s. The first published documentation of this reform is from 1926. It was preceded, in 1925, by a short article, entitled "A plant of our own soil".[5] The article is nominally a recommendation of a work of elementary teaching material in arithmetic, called *Book of Arithmetic* [*Rekenboek*] by A. Jager and A. Janse. However Vollenhoven takes the opportunity to make a brief statement about his own "Calvinistic arrangement theory" (Calvinistische ordeningsleer), which he maintains is presupposed in the background of this teaching material of Jager and Janse. A much fuller statement of Vollenhoven's renewed thought is contained in the three publications of 1926, written prior to his inauguration as professor of philosophy and theoretical psychology at the Free University on 26 October 1926. They are two articles, (i) "Contours of the theory of knowledge" and (ii) "Epistemology and natural science", and the monograph on which the inaugural lecture was based, entitled (iii) "*Logos and Ratio*: their relation in the history of western epistemology".[6]

This work of 1925-1926 focuses on epistemology, with consequences for the philosophy of science and matters metalogical. Vollenhoven also mentions ontological presuppositions, but these are not discussed explicitly. We need to include material from his lecture notes in systematic philosophy of his first few years as professor to get a glimpse of his more explicit ontological reflections. These lecture notes, preserved in the Vollenhoven archives, are important in their own right (cf. Vollenhoven 1926msA, 1927ms, 1928ms). They also offer a background sketch for the introductory course in philosophy, for which *Isagôgè Philosophiae* is the syllabus. The latter text is in development in the late 1920s. The first complete version of the syllabus for that course is available for student use in October 1930 (with a corrected version in January 1931). This is

---

5   Vollenhoven 1925c: 391-394.

6   The cited order is their (approximate) order of appearing: (i) "Enkele grondlijnen der kentheorie" (Vollenhoven 1926b); (ii) "Kentheorie en natuurwetenschap" (Vollenhoven 1926d); and *Logos en Ratio, beider verhouding in de geschiedenis der westersche kentheorie* (Vollenhoven 1926a). The second instalment of the second article appeared after *Logos en Ratio*. Vollenhoven expected this instalment to appear in the third issue of *Orgaan*—cf. 1926a: 73, footnote 72—but it became the fourth. The extra time allowed him to add a couple of footnote references to *Logos en Ratio* in the second instalment, including a proposed change of terminology; cf. 1926d: 178, note 1; 179, note 2; 188, note 1. This material of 1926 is discussed in Kok 1992, Chapter 7: "Logos, states of affairs, and knowledge".

our point of termination of this chapter, though we will also glance at some later developments.

This point of termination is somewhat arbitrary, but not entirely so. Vollenhoven revised the text of *Isagôgè Philosophiae* for 1932 rather drastically, though the main themes of the initial definitive platform are continued. New at this point in time, among other things, is his introduction of the body-soul distinction in tandem with a shift in the understanding of the relevance of the moral antithesis of good and evil. The developments that the entire series of versions of *Isagôgè Philosophiae* evidences are discussed in the general introduction to the text-critical edition of that work.[7] This gives us added reason to focus on the initial definitive platform in this concluding chapter.

Perhaps the best point of departure for this chapter is Vollenhoven's criticism of the use of the term 'theism'. He no longer finds this term serviceable in expressing his own position. What does this criticism involve and where does it lead to?

II. THEISM'S "WAVERING GLIMMER"

We should clarify at once that Vollenhoven's criticism of theism was not due to any 'falling from faith'. In his dissertation he had stated his conviction that "being a Christian and a thinker could be combined" (Vollenhoven 1918a: 2). This remained unchanged throughout his life and career. But it is how the combination is implemented in philosophy that calls for consideration. He was convinced that the combination should result in the development of a specific 'Christian philosophy' (or, in his more specific terminology, 'Calvinistic philosophy').

We found in chapter two that Vollenhoven's understanding of theism is complicated and nuanced. He has a (sequential) Trinitarian understanding of God, who creates and sustains life by his Counsel (the Father), his Word/Logos and his Spirit. There is relevance for philosophy in that this doctrine of God permits the specification of transcendent and immanent conditions regarding prime features of the world and the human being. This is expressed explicitly for the first and third Persons: there are general essences that God (the Father) individuates into 'thing-laws', and there are divine norms (of the Spirit) the validity of which is maintained for human knowing. This double pair of transcendence and immanence delineates the context of objective and subjective rationality, respectively. The second Person (the Logos) is the warrant of knowledge, in that it is the warrant for the harmony between the

---
7   Cf. Tol 2010a.

subjective rationality of the human being's answering to norms and the objective rationality of the world's law-like features and development.[8] This scholastic understanding of rationality was part and parcel of Vollenhoven's understanding of theism at the time. But his *own adherence* to this theism was on condition that the Logos' warrant of knowledge be *supplemented* by intuitively accepted synthetic a priori's of science. For, so he held, the scholastic harmony, though necessary, is not sufficient to secure the sense of validity of the synthesis that is characteristic of the judgments of scientific knowledge.

Theism's importance for philosophy, as seen by the early Vollenhoven, is theism as *ideal*. Theistic philosophy pursues the ideal of acquiring "the philosophy that God wills that we should have" (Vollenhoven 1918a: 2; also p. 443 which adds: "of all the given"). The pursuit of this ideal was for him from the start *not* that of 'thinking God's thoughts'. For the latter effaces the difference between divine thought and human thought, which would in turn invite 'Logos speculation'. It is Vollenhoven's emphasis on the role of intuition, which is secured anthropologically in the dissertation, which keeps the human limitation centre stage. The way God wills that we should think is a way in which the data (controlled by ideas; objective rationality) are worked over in submission to the logical norms, divinely given to thought (subjective rationality). In that way the theistic ideal is itself an "ideal epistemic system", bringing subjective and objective rationality into harmony. Were it to be realized, it would validate the 'adequate concept', which would then be the complete knowledge of the world (cf. Vollenhoven 1918a: 443).

But the pursuit of the theistic ideal meets with hindrances, in particular the ever present tendencies of deism and pantheism. Though each expresses a valid moment of truth, namely transcendence and immanence respectively, each is also one-sided and thus culpable. Deism refers to God but at the expense of his immanence; pantheism too refers to God but at the expense of his transcendence (cf. Vollenhoven 1918a: 443). A popular misconception is to take theism as the saving alternative to this opposition. Vollenhoven exclaims: "How often does one not place deism and pantheism in polar opposition, and then consider one's own

---

8 We found that it remains uncertain whether the metalogical notions of knowledge *progress* (directed thought) and *rest* (the intuition of the adequate concept) are meant to indicate immanent and transcendent conditions, respectively, of the Logos; cf. in chapter 2, the discussion of 'metalogic' (section IX). Such does appear to be suggested in the fact that 'critical realism' is also referred to as 'transcendental realism', which pertains to the transcendental significance that the immanent conditions of divinity have with respect to human awareness.

position as 'theistic' [alternative]!"[9] Thus theism, in its early 1918 meaning as "ideal epistemic system," needs constantly to keep the assumptions about divinity in balance, if the Logos' warranting this ideal is not to be thwarted.

Now why question this theism?

A. Theism reconsidered

Vollenhoven states that it was a critical remark in Abraham Kuyper's *E Voto Dordraceno* that stimulated him to reconsider his use of the term 'theism'. Kuyper's basic complaint is that the term 'theism' is too vague to serve as antidote against misguided alternatives. The term arose, he claims, in reaction to English deism. Deism is a consequence of exchanging the confession of God for a "God in case of need".[10] This reduces the understanding of God to a minimal "doctrine of God" that only reckons with the acceptance of his existence. Germans, finding this superficial, responded with a deeper "theistic" concept of God. But both are obnoxious to Kuyper, for each takes God as object of inquiry instead of confessing to God's presence in the believer's experience of creation, salvation and sanctification. Besides, there is also the drawback that 'theism', even when used in a primarily confessional sense, need not entail a Trinitarian understanding, as indeed is often the case.[11]

Now it is not immediately clear what set Vollenhoven thinking here. The stimulus to reconsider the use of 'theism' must have taken place before 1926, as the first quote of this chapter attests (where he speaks of theism as a "wavering glimmer"). But already in his dissertation

---

9 Vollenhoven 1931a: 194 [= 1931g1: 399]; same passage in Vollenhoven 1933a: 49.

10 "God voor het geval van nood"; Kuyper 1892, I: 177. *E Voto Dordraceno* is Kuyper's commentary on the *Heidelberg Catechism*. The current discussion is in chapter six of his discussion of "Sunday 8; Question and answer 25" about the "one unique Essence of God" and the three divine Persons.

11 Vollenhoven quotes directly from Kuyper in Vollenhoven 1931a: 194, footnote 6 [= 1931g1: 400, note 1.] The quote reads (slightly adapted): "And with [the disappearance of] this 'doctrine of God' [by re-emphasizing confession] the fencing with the equally Greek-philosophical concept of Theistic [*begrip van Theïstisch*] will disappear by itself. But this says nothing. At best it entails a denial of Deism and Polytheism, but it does not hinder in the least the intrusion of Pantheism, and the Unitarians, such as our Groningers, who reject the holy Trinity on point of principle, even prefer using the word Theistic." Vollenhoven repeats the quote in Vollenhoven 1933a: 49, footnote 45. The quote is from Kuyper 1892, I: 178. The "Groningers" were 19th century liberal evangelicals, who issued the journal "Waarheid in Liefde" [Truth in love], edited by J.F. van Oordt, P. Hofstede de Groot en L.G. Pareau of the University of Groningen. Cf. Algra 1966, chapter 6: "De Groninger Richting" [The Groningen movement]. Kuyper had for a while been sympathetic towards the Groningers; cf. Sweetman 2007b: 3 ff.

Vollenhoven had agreed to the objection of making God an object of inquiry. He even quoted Kuyper in support of this: "[for] the thinking human being to think itself as *subject* over against God as *object* is a contradiction in terms" (Vollenhoven 1918a: 442). The contradiction results, in Vollenhoven's context, when the finite human subject attempts, in the progressive steps of thought, to grasp an actually infinite being, such as God is presupposed to be. Hence the theological study of God needs to focus on the evidences that God has placed of himself in "monuments and documents" (i.e. Nature and Scripture; cf. *op. cit.*: 442-443).[12] Such evidences, being finite, do permit the thinking subject to come to a (partial and provisional) conceptual understanding, but never apart from acknowledging God's infinite being. In short, at this point there is nothing for Vollenhoven to regret or retract.

The second point, about 'theism' being too vague to discriminate between different understandings of divinity, is closer to home. Vollenhoven was aware from the start in 1918 (as we saw) of the dangers of deism and pantheism in the pursuit of the theistic ideal. In 1926, when he characterizes theism as a "wavering glimmer", he has more to look back on and reflect upon. For theism, as 'ideal epistemic system', had in the meantime shifted. The Logos, as understood in 1918, is the warrant of knowledge, for it activates the disposition for subject and object to come together. Now, in the dissertation, the prime examples or basic forms of synthesis are the synthetic a priori's of arithmetic and geometry. These are founded in the human being, namely in the mind and the psycho-physical body respectively. The importance attributed to the concrete intuition (or inner awareness) 'pulls' the analytical intuition— and with it the Logos' synthesis disposition—towards the human subject.[13] But when Vollenhoven formulates the metalogical variant of

---

12 Vollenhoven refers to and quotes from Kuyper 1909, II: 165, 168. (The same quote recurs later, in a similar critical context, in Vollenhoven 1938p: 5.) We note that the emphasis upon the confessional context does not restrain Kuyper in his speaking ontologically of God (JHWH) as "eternal Essence" (*eeuwige Wezen*). Basing himself on Ex. 3: 14—where God's name is said to be "I am who I am"—the description 'eternal Essence' is even a preferred expression in Kuyper. God's is, was and will be are unchanging, while all creatures miss this constancy and are subject to becoming and change. Between God and his creatures there is "a gap, a separation, a boundary line". Cf. Kuyper 1892, I: 150. Vollenhoven too (still) used the word "Essence" [Wezen] in reference to God in his 1926a: 28; cf. also Vollenhoven 1918a: 134. And around 1930 he spoke of God as "substance/ hypostasis"; cf. footnote 33, in section III.A.1 below. We add that the term 'essence/being' also occurs in the "*Belgic Confession*" (cf. Article 8) and the "*Heidelberg Catechism*" (cf. Question 25).

13 In this connection the adequate concept and the metaphysical intuition are more

his thought, the metalogical intuition of sighting the adequate concept comes to play a more central role. In the critical realist understanding, the metalogical intuition presupposes the idea, as principle of being. In the acknowledgement of the idea (by the metaphysical intuition), the adequate concept is divided into various 'regions', each of which has, as its modality, a highest factual unity of content. In the light of these unities, one discerns 'essential connections' that are characteristic of the regions' content in question. Thus the principle of synthesis, as predisposed by the Logos, now leans towards the World instead of the human Self.[14] Considered together, the Logos' role of warrant of knowledge synthesis has 'wavered' between a subjective and an objective fulfilment.

Admittedly, the above interpretation picks up on the trend in Vollenhoven's early work, not on a direct statement in his text. But the 'wavering' in his pursuit of the 'ideal epistemic system' is evident. Telling in this regard is the *new* step Vollenhoven takes in his work of 1925-1926. Synthesis, as somehow answering to the Logos' disposition for subject and object to come together, is entirely reinterpreted. In its new meaning synthesis (to anticipate this briefly here) is taken to be either a psychological feature of knowledge—which feature is now said to *lack* direct epistemic relevance—or as subsidiary to a more 'structured togetherness', one that Vollenhoven calls 'systasis'.[15] Knowing is then interpreted to be a *state* of mind and not an *act* of synthesis (cf. Vollenhoven 1926a: 11). This entails an overhaul of Vollenhoven's former position, in favour of a more externalist-realist stance. For he now postulates, metalogically, a 'region of truth', of truth in itself (cf. *op. cit.*: 22, 29). Knowledge entails 'possessing' truth, and is no longer seen as 'forming' truth through synthesis. Thus the divine Logos no longer has the role of 'disposing' synthesis. Clearly, this puts an end to any 'wavering' as to which way the synthesis might go.

Whether Vollenhoven's earlier wavering attests to a prior pantheistic tendency followed by a deistic influence, is, I believe, secondary. There

---

directly relevant to—over against the immediate certitude of the concrete intuition—the progressive acquisition of knowledge (by acquaintance), the content of which is subsequently secured by *Gegenstände*. The latter are formed by the concrete and analytical intuitions in compliance with the principle of identity. Cf. chapter 2, VI.A.

14   The most insistent attempt to express this alternative is in Dooyeweerd, "Cosmos and Logos" (Dooyeweerd 1923a2 and 1923a3; cf. our discussion in chapter 3, section III.E). There the 'Divine *noèsis*' (= Logos) is the principle of 'meaning-giving for consciousness', and it enables the human being to know the world through its being put, via the (metalogical) intuition, in a direct rapport with it.

15   This term is not new. It also occurs in Vollenhoven 1921c, when Vollenhoven came to place more weight on metalogical features in response, among other things, to H. Rickert's work.

was, of course, never an expressed partiality to either. Yet Vollenhoven did feel that there was something to confront in line with Kuyper's remark. For the term 'theism', he claims, is not decisive enough over against deism and pantheism.

B. '*Theos*' and '*kosmos*'

Vollenhoven felt challenged to clarify the vagueness of 'theism' in a definitive way, with an appeal to fundamentals. The relevance to himself—or perhaps we should say to his former 'critical realism'— becomes more evident if we include the features of divine immanence and transcendence. His own initial tandem of the concrete and analytical intuitions may not have been pantheistic, but it did emphasize 'immanent validity' of divine norms; also the subsequent weight put on the duality of metalogical intuition (viewing) and the idea is not typically of deistic design, but there is something here of a dogmatic antenna that pretends to gain 'transcendent insight' regarding God's Counsel. These are tendencies to which critical realism was prone. In each of these cases (of immanence and transcendence respectively) there is a 'boundary problem' between divinity and the creature. For, when duly considered, divine immanence is what conditions in a transcendental-like way; it is not a presence within human control. Similarly divine transcendence calls for the most primordial sense in which reality deserves respect; it is not a means for a human being towards acquiring a higher or privileged knowledge.

Vollenhoven continued to honour the distinction between the divine transcendence and immanence as such. It is the relevance to the human condition that needs to be carefully reassessed. Vollenhoven's continued commitment is evident from the following quote of later years. In 1942 he emphasized:

> The highness of the Lord involves two things: He stands, far exalted above the world, [but also] in continual contact with it, so that on the one hand every creature *is in Him* and can neither turn nor move outside of Him, and on the other hand *He operates in* the world and *lives in* His people. Thus Scripture teaches both: the transcendence and the immanence of God.[16]

---

16 Vollenhoven 1942m: 1 (emphases added). The article is unsigned, but tell-tale signs—terms and turns of phrases—point to Vollenhoven as the author. Vollenhoven's reason for (re)emphasizing the topic of the title lay in the misunderstanding that had arisen in consequence of Vollenhoven's and Dooyeweerd's work. Their criticism directed against "immanence philosophy", meant as a criticism of the principle of the autonomy of thought, was taken as suggesting a denial of God's immanence (*ibid.*). Vollenhoven had probably agreed to write also on behalf of Dooyeweerd—is that why the article is unsigned?—for he alternates the use of "Calvinistic thought" and "Philosophy of the

We see how close this statement is to Augustine's expression of God's "Excellency of an ever-present eternity", quoted earlier (cf. Vollenhoven 1918a: 134; also chapter 2, section VIII.B. above), an "Excellency" that does not forfeit but bears upon the more specific forms of transcendence and immanence with respect to the creation. When 'theism' is understood as acknowledging deity, in the sense quoted (which I take to be more in line with common usage),[17] then obviously Vollenhoven is and remained an ardent theist. It is the meaning of theism as "ideal epistemic system" that is up for critical discussion. It is in this connection that deism and pantheism need to be reviewed.

1. A boundary problem
The way Vollenhoven chose to make headway was to clarify the situation of the use of "deism" and "pantheism" in terms of fundamentals. Accordingly (now back to the 1920s), Vollenhoven takes the basic problem to be that of "the boundary is between God and that which is created".[18] He considers this to be the question that "dominates all other questions". I believe that in light of our account of critical realism, one can see why this question is put in the centre of attention, in any case as calling for a fundamental overhaul of critical realism. But Vollenhoven hoped to achieve more. The stimulus from reading Kuyper's *E Voto Dordraceno* got Vollenhoven to think about "rubricating the basic themes of opponents, considered from one's own standpoint" (*ibid.*). He devised a terminology that, he says, served him well "the last few years" (*ibid.*). (This last remark puts the development of this point in the second half of the 1920s, hence in the timeframe of Vollenhoven's initial definitive platform.)

Vollenhoven himself favours a position in which there is a clear boundary between God and the creature. In section III of this chapter we will see what this standpoint involves. The general thesis of a boundary also serves to characterize positions Vollenhoven criticizes. We shall first mention the rubrics he chooses to characterize the positions he *opposes*. These are chosen in such a way as to include 'theism' in an ideal epistemic context, hence making the latter term no longer serviceable in reference to his own position. So here we shall come across his philosophical rejection of this term.

Law-idea".
17 *Webster's New Collegiate Dictionary* offers, under "theism": "Belief in the existence of one God, transcending, yet immanent in, the universe".
18 Vollenhoven 1931a: 194 [= 1931g1: 400].

To avoid confusing the censurable use of 'theism' with the more latitudinarian (common sense) use, meaning 'belief in God', both in his transcendence and immanence, let us state Vollenhoven's boundary problem. The boundary problem is that of determining the line between '*theos*' and '*kosmos*'. In resorting to Greek terms we can emphasize that neither the existence of God (*theos*) nor that of the world (*kosmos*) is in question here for Vollenhoven. What the boundary problem is about is how the *features* of divinity and of the cosmos are mutually apportioned, in the sense of what may properly be attributed to what, in the light of their primary meaning.

The boundary problem can 'swing' two ways. On the one hand, there is the possibility of attributing to *kosmos* what properly belongs to *theos*. There is then (so to speak) 'too much divinity' (or too much taken as divine-like). This is said to be 'theistic' and to engender the*ism*. Similarly, on the other hand, one may attribute to *theos* what properly belongs to *kosmos*, in which case there is 'too much world' (or too much taken to be world-like). This, in turn, is said to be 'cosmistic' (*kosmistisch*) and to engender cosm*ism*. So, in both cases, Vollenhoven takes the suffix '-ism' as suggesting excess or exaggeration. The word 'cosmism' in itself suggests this, but the word 'theism' would not normally be taken in this way. Yet that is how Vollenhoven now uses this term in the present context.

2. Monism and dualism
So far the discussion is formal. What, now, are the actual positions of opponents that Vollenhoven distinguishes?[19] There is, to start with, the preliminary question about the boundary itself. Is its presence (or relevance) denied or is it acknowledged? The first alternative leads to *monism*, the second to *dualism*. Let us look at monism first.

Monism's denial of the boundary may be based on either *negation* or *subsumption*. The boundary is negated when either the existence of God or that of the cosmos is denied, giving rise to *a-theism* and *a-cosmism* respectively. Accordingly, this negation of the boundary takes place by default. Also, the term 'monism', as here used, denotes a whole in which nothing basic is set off from anything else basic. But of course, 'atheism' and 'acosmism', as negative rubrics, disclose nothing about the actual prime features of the positions in question, i.e. they don't indicate how the whole is characterized. Hence Vollenhoven does not consider these to

---

19 The following discussion is based on Vollenhoven 1931a: 194-195 [= 1931g1: 400-401]. It recurs in more expanded form in Vollenhoven 1933a and also in *Isagôgè Philosophiae* of 1932. The latter two versions are taken up in Appendix IIb of Vollenhoven 2010.

be genuine rubrics in their own right. He leaves these forms of negating monism aside from further discussion.[20]

'Subsuming monism' (the second form of monism) denies the boundary between *theos* and *kosmos*, not through denying the existence of what either term refers to, but in subsuming one entirely under the other, whereby their effects mutually interfere. This also gives rise to two possibilities. When the cosmos is subsumed under God, we have *pantheism*; when God is subsumed under the cosmos, *pankosmism*. The pantheism Vollenhoven has in mind here is the view that everything in or of the cosmos displays the trait of deity. What comes to mind is, say, Nietzsche's 'will to power', where all life-activity is a striving for self-sovereignty by the continual overcoming of obstacles in the environment. Pancosmism, on the other hand, is the view (as here meant) of the 'block universe' (as, say, in Parmenides) in which everything is determined, and even divinity is subject to the necessitating conditions of the cosmic whole to which it belongs.[21]

Vollenhoven did not give these positions of pantheism and pancosmism much specific attention in his published work. For the denial of any boundary between God and the cosmos removes them from the direct line of his interest, which is the boundary acknowledged. Accordingly, Vollenhoven is more interested in dualism and the alternatives it offers. Dualism as such comes closer to home, for he thinks of the Calvinistic position as being *properly* dualistic, a 'biblical dualism'. The improper (or 'non-scriptural') dualisms call for attention first.[22]

Dualism, as understood by Vollenhoven at the time, is the view that the acknowledged existence of *theos* and *kosmos* entails a boundary that is effective *by virtue of* their difference. Vollenhoven takes the chief characteristics of these existences to be *sovereignty* and *subservience*

---

20   Vollenhoven 1933a: 55; also Vollenhoven 2010, Appendix IIb, 150*.

21   A case in point is the view defended by Alvin Plantinga in his Aquinas Lecture of 1980, *Does God have a Nature*, in which God is taken to be "the first being of the universe" (Plantinga 1980: 1, 9); reprinted in Plantinga 1998: 225, 228.

22   Vollenhoven seldom uses the term "biblical/scriptural dualism", but the meaning is clearly implied when speaking of dualism as "accepting a boundary between God and cosmos" and that "non-scriptural dualism . . . assumes the boundary to be other than as the Holy Scripture directs" (Vollenhoven 2010, Appendix IIb, §150). We add that this use of 'dualism' focuses on the correlation of God and world and does not *as such* include an anthropological dualism of, say, immortal soul and mortal body—Vollenhoven had expressed his agreement with Janse's criticism of this anthropological view in his letter to him, dated 19 February 1924. Also it does not entail an antithesis of good and evil (as in Gnosticism, Catharism, etc.). John Kok referred me to one use of "scriptural dualism" that is in print, namely in Vollenhoven 1934a, instalment VI (27-11-1934).

respectively. The boundary problem is how these characteristics are implemented when appealing to *theos* and *kosmos*. If something of *kosmos* is thought to be intrinsically *sovereign*, though without taking this to hold for the whole cosmos, then there is not a full pantheism. But there is still too much taken as sharing in sovereignty. Vollenhoven refers to this as '*partial theism*'. Examples are: a spiritual kernel in the human being, taken to be holy, autonomous, etc.; Caesar worship; the starry heavens taken to be divine; etc. On the other hand, if something of *theos* is taken to be *subservient*—something of divinity is taken to be creaturely-like— but without this being a full pancosmism, then we still have too much that is subservient. This is '*partial cosmism*'; e.g. the position of the Holy Spirit as subservient to the other Persons; the denial of the divinity of Christ, etc.

These forms of 'improper dualism' are not just 'metaphysical'. They can inform and are reflected in worldviews. When anything of the cosmos is given *privileged status*, such as *fideism* in honouring an unfettered belief function, or *spiritualism*, that attributes autonomous authority to matters ethical or juridical, or *aesthetic modernism*, with its ideal of an ever-continual creativity, etc., then such 'partial theistic' views give prominence in particular to humanistic views of life and the world. They 'divide the world' in a way that can lead to forms of totalitarianism and forced submission within the contours of human life (the church not excluded). Such divisions of the world threaten freedom.[23] On the other hand, 'partial cosmistic' views have an element of fatalism. In the heart of the matter, life cannot be redeemed; it lacks meaning or purpose over which divine sovereignty has no control. Such worldviews tend to be ineluctably tragic, though not always without poignancy, as when the divine is touchingly described as "the fellow-sufferer who understands" (Whitehead).[24] Vollenhoven however does not himself expand on these worldview features, so we limit our remark here to an indication of their presence.

All told, Vollenhoven reduced the fundamental positions of 'opponents' to four. There are two forms of (subsuming) monism, namely pantheism and pancosmism, and there are two forms of (improper) dualism: partial theism and partial cosmism. In this phraseology, the positions indicated, if set to work in philosophy towards delineating an 'ideal epistemic system', would bring about a distorted general understanding, evidenced (as we will see) by antinomies. Both 'cosmism'

---

23   Cf. Vollenhoven 1933a: 26.
24   Whitehead 1978: 351.

and 'theism', in whatever shade of meaning, are found to be, formally at least, wanting and in that light unsuitable for 'Calvinistic' use. They are indicative of the required 'reformation' of philosophy.[25]

Of the four positions of 'opponents', as here distinguished, only partial theism was significantly ventilated. In the important work of 1933, *Het Calvinisme en de Reformatie van de Wijsbegeerte*, the second main part is devoted to an historical study of the influence of partial theism in the West from the time of early Greek culture and philosophy up to and including the time of the Reformation and John Calvin (1509-1564).[26] The choice for the discussion of partial theism, in its historical relevance, is motivated by its importance towards critically understanding the partial theistic nature of humanism and the autonomy of thought in modern times, in particular in Vollenhoven's own day. The current terminology of philosophers, he says, is so drenched with humanism as to make the attempt to sift this out futile (cf. *op. cit.*: 16). Thus philosophy that strives to reckon with the Christian faith, through advancing a properly dualistic position, must take a stand against any accommodation with (this kind of) "prevailing philosophy" (*gangbare wijsbegeerte*).

Vollenhoven's critical use of the terms 'theism' and 'cosmism', and their derivatives, was actually short-lived. In a note published in 1941, Vollenhoven explains that, though the distinctions of the two forms of monism and dualism were clarifying, their application led to difficulties, particularly when an author is not explicit about "the most encompassing relation" between God and the world, on the basis of which a 'position', as here meant, can be ascertained. Hence he comes to a reassessment, already begun in 1938,[27] as to what the chief characteristic of "prevailing philosophy" is. He turns to characterizing this in light of the conflict between realism and nominalism/antirealism.[28]

---

25   When 'theism' is taken to mean 'too much deity', then 'atheism' could ('formally', so I note) be taken to imply "the rejection of too much deity". This could be looked upon, by a 'Calvinist', as a positive recommendation! Because Vollenhoven simply bypasses atheism, this suggestion nowhere surfaces. The same holds for 'acosmism'. We also note that Vollenhoven takes 'deism', somewhat surprisingly, to be a form of 'pancosmism', for it looks upon God, he says, as a machine designer (*machinebouwkundige*), which implies that God is part of the cosmos. However, there is something to say for deism being 'partial cosmistic', in that God is reduced to the role of 'first cause' of the cosmos, without the follow-up of revelation and guidance. Cf. Vollenhoven 1933a: 52, note 47; Vollenhoven 2010, Appendix IIb, §150, note 10.

26   Vollenhoven 1933a: 69-301.

27   Vollenhoven 1938v.

28   Vollenhoven 1941k: 65-66, note 2 (first instalment); cf. also Tol 2010a. The approach in terms of realism and nominalism was, in turn, replaced in the early 1940s

This shift in his approach to prevailing philosophy in fact reflects a new change in his own understanding of the encompassing relation between God and the cosmos. It is time we turn to the discussion of what that position is and why it was itself, in time, superseded.

III. BOUNDARY AND LAW

The problem of the boundary had Vollenhoven's attention throughout his career. In this section we will discuss Vollenhoven's approach and formulation of it. The very concept of a boundary, this being crucial when speaking of God and the world, was for him nonnegotiable. The world or cosmos, being a creation, calls for determining or delimiting conditions; it is intrinsically not self-sufficient; it is *subservient*. These conditions, which hold for the world, have their source in God. This source, however conceived, has a determining and sustaining efficacy; it is intrinsically *sovereign*. God and world, being mutually different, when taken together delineate a boundary, as called up by their different natures. 'Formally' a boundary exists by default, being called up by the necessary difference between God and cosmos; 'materially' the boundary serves to mark off the difference between sovereignty and subservience. Hence it has the character of *law*. In introducing this notion, Vollenhoven used the (not so fortunate) monarchical metaphor of the 'absolute prince'. The metaphor was chosen also to emphasize an important measure of voluntarism involved here, and that the chief connotation of law is that it is ordinance-like.[29] Law, of course, may be cognitively contemplated. But contemplation should bring to the fore the source of law in God's *will*, hence that law is something to be followed up and not primarily studied and admired. The first and foremost effect of law is its being a dynamic factor in life practice. In this regard, the basics presuppose a context of activity, whereby cognition is checked by the law-constrained will. So the theme of 'boundary and law' calls for careful discussion.

For the duration of his career, marked by the inaugural lecture (26 October 1926) and the valedictory lecture (26 October 1963), there is

by the development of the 'problem-historical method'. In the context of that method the terms monism and dualism acquire their definitive meanings for Vollenhoven. They then denote a basic feature of the cosmos as such (no longer the God-world correlation): *monism*, when a unitary feature presides, *dualism* when two (or more) principles are postulated. Vollenhoven's *own* understanding of the correlation of law and cosmos now precludes his own position (from the early 1940s on) from being either monistic or dualistic; cf. section III.V.C. below. Of course, Vollenhoven did continue to point to types of thought, in the context of his problem-historical work, that proceed from the God-world correlation.

29   Vollenhoven acknowledged this specifically in his 1933a: 23-24.

explicit continuity regarding the law as boundary. In the former lecture, discussing the question as to where the principal boundary (*hoofdgrens*) is to be drawn, Vollenhoven opts for "the pure dualism, namely that between God, who institutes his ordinances and the cosmos which stands under these laws" (Vollenhoven 1926a: 7, also 18, 20-21). In his farewell address, in which he discusses Plato's realism, he states: "Hence Calvinistic philosophy—contrary to Greek-Hellenistic thought and the synthesis thought dependent on it—sees the law as the boundary between God and the cosmos."[30] However, a telling difference appears in the very next sentence. "Whereby at the same time the dualism that is unacceptable for a Christian, but still finding acceptance, of God and world is replaced by the view that is neither dualistic nor monistic, of a law posed by God that is correlate with a world created by him." So the initial "pure dualism" of the correlation of God and the world has been replaced by the correlation of law and the world, itself included in a complex of God-law-cosmos that is neither dualistic nor monistic.[31]

In order to make headway in the ensuing discussion we shall first carefully toe the line of 'pure dualism'.

A. The boundary properly determined

Continuing the discussion of monism and dualism, as initially defined by Vollenhoven, the main points of contention of the positions Vollenhoven opposes concern, formally, (i) there being a boundary between God and the world—monism failing to acknowledge such, but dualism ceding—as well as (ii) when ceded, where the boundary runs. The criterion for determining the properly situated boundary is a 'Christian' or 'Scriptural' criterion. The God of the Scriptures cannot, part or whole,

30   Vollenhoven 1963a: 128; also in Tol and Bril: 155-156.
31   In chapter three we made mention of the fact that Dooyeweerd was the first to put the theme of 'law as boundary' (as 'sphere sovereignty') in writing (cf. Dooyeweerd 1923d) and to publish forceful defences of it (cf. work of 1924 and later). Little is known of his contact with Vollenhoven at the time, who, in late 1923, was in the advanced stage of convalescence. How this topic arose in their contact remains in the dark. For Dooyeweerd 'law as boundary' was integral to what he called the 'law-idea', which posed boundaries to the use of reason and expressions of the will, but not to the role of faith, later replaced by the spiritual selfhood. For Vollenhoven, law as boundary holds across the board. As our discussion will indicate, Vollenhoven never accepted the context, and also rejected the notion, of a 'law-idea'. In their later careers, the 'law as boundary' theme appeared to be more characteristic of Vollenhoven than of Dooyeweerd. Dooyeweerd's relinquishing realism (in the late 1920s) was no doubt a factor. This is in step with his formulation, particularly when the ontology of meaning is presupposed, of the boundary problem as 'sides' ("law-side and subject-side") of "the structure of *reality in the diversity of meaning*"; Dooyeweerd (1935-1936), vol. 2: 3.

share features with the cosmos, which is his creation. Thus Vollenhoven takes the 'Scriptural position' to be formally dualistic, as involving the acknowledged existence of God and of the cosmos, as well as their complete difference. The existence of the cosmos being dependent on that of God, the distinction of their prime characteristics of sovereignty and subservience is itself predicated on this difference. The alternative forms of dualism are objectionable, 'by definition' as it were, merely in applying the prime characteristics in a way that is not congruent with the difference between God and cosmos.

If this were the whole account, it would be very unsatisfactory. Theists and cosmists (as defined by Vollenhoven) could complain that the 'biblical criterion' simply does not agree with their view of reality. Also, as we mentioned, there are worldviews that inform life in ways that reflect versions of 'theism' and 'cosmism' (as defined). So alternatives to 'biblical dualism' are not just speculative construals, to be waved away on account of their being speculative. One needs to argue more pointedly if conclusions proper to philosophy are to be drawn in favour or disfavour of any of these positions.

This, in fact, is as Vollenhoven would have it. His choice of doing philosophy in a way that reckons with Scripture is motivated and conditioned from out of the (Protestant) Christian religion. But this is not to replace or side-step philosophy. It orientates one with respect to the questions asked, questions that then need to be responded to— formulated and critically discussed—*within the possibilities of philosophy*. A statement of Vollenhoven from 1942 is apposite and is characteristic of Vollenhoven in general.

> Truly, Calvinistic thought does not take the view of Holy Scripture being a work of philosophy, from which one simply reads a philosophy. If one is to do philosophy, then one ought to instigate a serious and fundamental inquiry into the structure of the whole cosmos. Don't think that the Scripture exists to spare us the difficulty that will come our way when conducting such research.[32]

But in Vollenhoven's initial definitive work, he was apt to reformulate the complex of God and the cosmos almost directly into the mode of critical philosophy. This was done not to call special attention to God—that could initiate an 'inquiry' into God's existence, the sort Vollenhoven, citing Kuyper (as we saw), had explicitly rejected as being speculative—but to draw out the main implication about the nature of the law, as based on the difference between God and the cosmos. Thought

---

32   Vollenhoven 1942m: 1.

cannot start from nowhere with no means. It is what the acceptance of the existence of God and the cosmos entails that calls for consideration. Two terms in particular are favoured: substance and infinity.

1. Substance and antinomy
When the existence of God and the cosmos is spoken of in a religious context, the focus is more on the *meaning* of that existence than on the bare acceptance of existence. The religious confession of God's relation to the cosmos expresses the conviction that God, in being the source (*archè*) of the cosmos, is also its essential support, its "firm ground". Vollenhoven did not hesitate to use the term 'substance' or 'hypostasis' in this connection.[33] (This use however ceases after 1932). In this capacity as 'firm ground' God is the bearer or maintainer of the cosmos that is itself dependent, non-self-sufficient.[34] This characterization, which is itself religious, takes on critical meaning when considering the situation in which the import of this confession is *not* honoured. Such a situation occurs when the 'firm ground' of the cosmos is sought within the cosmos itself. But then the cosmos has to provide its own foundation. This, now, results ineluctably in *antinomies*; for in that case the substance of the cosmos, which in bearing the cosmos also conditions it, is sought within that which is conditioned. In this way the former discussion concerning the 'boundary' between God and the cosmos has an immediate relevance for the problem of such antinomies.

This 'Kantian' theme of antinomies in fact becomes integral to Calvinistic philosophy in its *critical* sense. For antinomies—*prima facie* 'clashes' of boundaries—cannot be tolerated in the world that the human being seeks to know and to live in. Thus the principle that antinomies are to be excluded—the '*principium exclusae antinomiae*'—is written across the face of Calvinistic philosophy, for, as Vollenhoven states: "this principle . . . is none other than the corollary or effect of the confession of God's sovereignty over all things, on whatever terrain."[35]

33   Vollenhoven 1932d: 397-398; also Vollenhoven 2010, Appendix IIb, §151. This ontological characterization was not taken over into the (reworked) parallel text of Vollenhoven 1933a. This temporary use at the time may simply reflect the use within the Reformed tradition—until thinking better of it—as also in Kuyper, where God is spoken of as '(eternal) Essence' (cf. footnote 12 above).

34   The confessional statement given philosophical attention here is: "God has created everything and still carries this by the word of his power", which echoes Heb. 1:3; cf. Vollenhoven 1926d: 190. In Hebrews 11:1 the term 'hypostasis' occurs in the sense that Vollenhoven wished to advance: "Now faith is the hypostasis of things hoped for . . .", presuming that it is the *import* of faith that is taken as 'hypostasis', not the act.

35   Vollenhoven 1931a: 190 [= 1931g: 396]; also in Vollenhoven 1933a: 29.

We need to review this theme of antinomies more closely. In Kant, antinomies signal a conflict of reason in conjunction with the understanding, namely when 'concepts of reason' (ideas) are treated as objects of the understanding. For Kant, too, the problem arises in a misuse of 'condition and the conditioned', in particular the way the understanding is conditioned or determined by conditions of reason.[36] Vollenhoven formulates this more directly as a conflict of boundary arrangement, in particular in connection with what is determined by boundaries in terms of what they regulate.

To state this formally and generally, the context of boundaries will be free from antinomies only if (i) that which conditions is not itself conditioned, at least is not dependent on a higher condition for itself to be a condition, for that would introduce an *infinite regress*, and (ii) that which is conditioned, is such not by virtue of something that is self-imposed, for then it would be *in itself* self-determined. In other words, the first alternative says that there must be a principal boundary, the second says that that boundary cannot itself be part of what it bounds. The first is needed in connection with the cosmos, the second can only be rightly attributed to God.

Perhaps unexpectedly, Vollenhoven is reluctant to say much about the principal boundary. For, to delve into it could invite an 'inquiry' into the Counsel of God, and that would be speculative. But an effect of that boundary is its delineating the unity or the whole of the cosmos. On that point Vollenhoven says:

> We should proceed from the creation by God. Hence the cosmos stands under the law of God. Here there is no objection to acknowledging unity: on the contrary, one who draws the principal boundary accurately has no alternative but to take all that is 'not-God' together. This [gathered] unity has more than just a negative logical meaning. For in the Scriptures the creation is called 'cosmos' = 'elegantly ordered whole'. Thus the unity is that of God's work of art.[37]

---

36   In Kant, an antinomy results when a concept of reason is used in a way that assumes that it is capable of illustration in a 'possible experience', as is fitting for or a criterion of the understanding. However, reason and its ideas condition the understanding, for they answer to the desire for completeness of insight with regard to the Self, the World and God. These being 'totalities', they cannot themselves be thought via the categories of the understanding, and the attempt to do so yields (among other things) antinomies. As Kant states it, the difficulty arises when "reason, rather, in continuous progression of the empirical synthesis has been led to [ideas] necessarily when it tries to liberate from every condition, and to grasp in its unconditioned totality, that which can always be determined only conditionally in accordance with rules of experience." Kant 1998, A462/B490.

37   Vollenhoven 1926msA, section 19, also section 1.

The unity of the cosmos is taken to be of an aesthetic nature. This provides little opportunity to get a firm grip on antinomies. At best an antinomy could be signalled by the 'disharmony' it engenders. Vollenhoven retains this aesthetic characterization of the whole only in the period of his initial definitive thought.³⁸ It drops out of sight in the early 1930s when Vollenhoven's anthropology becomes more pronounced and, with it, a new emphasis on the antithesis of good and evil. We return to this below.

For Vollenhoven, antinomies are especially evident in connection with what is bounded, i.e. what is subject to law. When the principal boundary is not drawn right, the resulting disharmony entails conditions being entangled. The principle of the exclusion of antinomies, as corollary to the confession of God's sovereignty, has an important distinguishing effect that is of direct philosophical relevance, as the following passage clarifies.

> When, in a strict sense, we maintain 'subject' to mean 'subject to law' then that excludes the acceptance of any anti-nomic subject. The discovery of an anti-nomic subject demands that we differentiate it into as many subjects and, parallel to this, accept as many laws as is found to be necessary to resolve the antinomy. It would be the simplest to call this principle: *'principium exclusae antinomiae'* (or better: *'principium exclusi subjecti antinomici'*), the principle that states: the sustained acceptance of an antinomy is excluded. And when its application leads to the discovery of more than one law-sphere, then that plurality of law-spheres is now secured, namely in the correlation: law-subject.³⁹

An 'anti-nomic subject' is a subject that lets itself be determined by different, i.e. mutually exclusive laws or ordinances in terms of which its own activity is deemed warranted or 'lawful'. It is essential not to confuse 'subject' in 'subject to law' with 'subject' as 'determining subject'. (In Dutch this is "subjèct" as over against "súbject", respectively.) The latter—a humanistic alternative—*merges* the individual agent and its role of subjecting. In that case, an "anti-nomic" subject involves the trait of a person stubbornly attempting to harmonize different perspectives, in an attitude that maintains that the error is chiefly one of not properly using intrinsic determining capacities, such as reason and understanding. But the former alternative—'subject' as 'subject to law'—*distinguishes* the

---

38 In Vollenhoven 1930b: 13, Vollenhoven continued to speak of "God the architect and artist of the cosmos" (p. 13). The phrase is deleted in later reprints. In this same work there is mention of 'good and evil', but, characteristic of Vollenhoven's initial platform, this is treated in a wholly religious context. In 1932 the 'antithesis of good and evil' is re-interpreted and introduced as a more distinct determination of the human condition. Cf. the discussion in section V.B. below, or Tol 2010a.
39 Vollenhoven 1927ms, section 64.

individual from its qualities of 'standing in subjection'. When standing in subjection, the individual agent is aware not only of his/her own attitude but also of the context of activity and the kind of regulation it requires to make sense of that activity. E.g. at a cocktail party the context is *social*, at the market it is *economic*, in court it is *juridical*, etc. (Recognition of context and characteristic is of course more than just personal belief or merely subjective assessment.) Now, if one can agree that justice should not be bought (doing such is to subject matters juridical to economic norms) nor ought the market to privilege social contacts (which invites societal corruption) etc., then one acknowledges, and accepts on point of principle, that different contexts of activity call for different kinds of regulation to which one ought to submit in kind. This is how Vollenhoven avoids the subject's becoming 'anti-nomic': the person is called on to answer only to such norms as are suited to the situation. This is to acknowledge a diversity of 'qualities of subjection'. The radius in which such a quality is exercised may (provisionally) be called a 'law-sphere'.

So the principle that antinomies be excluded has the effect of calling attention to and requiring a *pluralism* of laws, or rather, a *diversity* of (general) situations—law-spheres—calling for regulation in terms of relevant ordinances or laws. Nothing is said about the extent of this diversity, nor does Vollenhoven offer the possibility of a 'derivation' from out of a unity of law. Again, his explicit wording is quite clear.

> This absolute unity [of the aesthetic whole of the cosmos] can only be reconciled with a multiplicity if this multiplicity is ranked under it, hence despite all the difference of the many, nothing of this many falls beyond the boundary of the unity, i.e. outside of the boundary of being creaturely and hence subject to God's will. That is why, if this multiplicity exists, we have to speak of *law*-spheres.[40]

Hence, Vollenhoven holds that however much the avoidance of antinomies calls for the acknowledgement of a diversity of law-spheres "under" the unity of the principal boundary (of God's will)—in other words, the distinct law of a law-sphere is a *case* of the principal boundary—this does not *prove* that there is such a plurality. The last quotation continues with the statement:

> That there is a multiplicity of law-spheres, in other words that there is more than one law-sphere, is here presupposed. It can only be proven in connection with the law by way of knowledge, proven by way of the logic that knowledge presupposes. (*ibid*)

This statement appears to say that one needs to appeal to a 'law of logic'—

---

40   *Op. cit.* , section 19.

in connection with a 'logical law-sphere'?—to prove that there is more than one law-sphere. Wouldn't the one 'law-sphere'—wouldn't that be the cosmos as a whole under the principal boundary?—from which the 'proof' proceeds then be of a logical character? That would constitute a fundamental denial of the cosmic character of created reality, in favour of a 'logical' or cognitive characterization. This cannot be a correct reading.

When Vollenhoven speaks of the logic that knowledge presupposes, he is appealing to a *metalogical* situation of the order of knowledge, its logic being the 'order' found to hold in that situation. Relevant epistemological remarks will be made in an ensuing section. At this point we can appeal to Dooyeweerd's prior work for clarification, at least in its broad outline, to which Vollenhoven concurred (if not being its initiator).

The metalogical situation, as documented in the early 1920s, is that of critical realism, in which rationality and scientific research is channelled in a multiplicity of 'region categories'. These 'regions' differ as to modality, which is to say that they differ in the unity of the highest material characterization of each region. Within a distinct modal region 'essential connections' are found in conjunction with the 'logic' or rationality that is fitting for that region. So the "logic that knowledge presupposes" is a logic that proceeds from a multiplicity of regions, mutually distinct as to the characterizing modality of each, which together delineate the metalogical situation of a *pluralist rationality*, not reducible to a unity. The regions are distinguished by means of the *metalogical intuition*. The intuition's viewing focuses on the 'adequate concept' of a region by which the rational operations of knowledge acquisition in a region is guided, while at the same time the viewing, as executed by the viewing subject, is itself of the appropriate kind of modality for the region involved.

If, for the moment, we may take 'region category' to be the ancestor of 'law-sphere'—Vollenhoven's understanding of a law-sphere is certainly very much like a 'region' category, but we can't clinch the correlation just yet—then the 'proof' of a multiplicity of law-spheres appeals to the current methodological situation in scientific practice and to the need of acknowledging a diversity of (kinds of) science, requiring a diversity of methods. A dominant unity of method, such as maintained by the Marburg neo-Kantians, was definitely passé for Vollenhoven as of 1921, this being inconsistent with the prime role performed by the metalogical intuition in discerning *Gegenstand* regions of different modality. In later work Vollenhoven retained this close link between philosophy as general science and the special or the fundamental sciences, through the correlation of the fields of investigation (of the primary sciences) with the law-spheres. The theme of modality, of the highest material characterization as discerned by intuition, plays a decisive role here.

We can now see how the critical realist background is fit into the current 'law as boundary' discussion. The principle of antinomies (that antinomies be excluded) not only holds for the subject in its qualities of subjection; it is also relevant for the 'regions' in which the qualities of subjection are implemented. Such regions constitute the domains of inquiry of a science, each of which is the context of a specific method. Should a domain of inquiry be 'worked over' with an unsuited method, or a combination of methods, then that would make it liable to harbouring antinomies.[41] So the principle that antinomies be excluded is relevant for the methodology of science as well, in the role of a 'metalogical' principle in the 'order of knowledge'. At this metalogical level, antinomies are avoided by the recognition of an adequate diversity of domains, whereby each domain has a method that is suitable to working its content. This was acknowledged in critical realism as well. But at that time the metalogical intuition's viewing had to suffice in making and securing the adequate distinctions. (At the same time, there is the metaphysical intuition in the background, but up to that point in time the 'presence of reality' and its ideas had not been made explicit.) Now, however, with the diversity of 'qualities of subjection' worked into the methodological context, each such quality requires a 'sphere' of implementation, a proper 'law-sphere'. The regulation of this implementation is attributed to a 'law' (norm or ordinance) suitable for a specific sphere. Thus the 'order of knowledge' offers an argument for *requiring* a diversity of law-spheres, in line with the diversity of methods that are 'materially' in operation in the fundamental sciences.

This 'order of knowledge'—whose pedigree is *Gegenstand* theory and the metalogical intuition—is a permanent element of Vollenhoven's thought. Later he refers to it as 'the noetic' (*het gnotische*), meaning knowing and learning to know as part of and belonging to cosmic life (cf. Vollenhoven 1948p: 16; this should not be confused with Gnosticism nor the autonomous inner 'spark of knowing'). Because knowing resorts under being, this order of knowledge does not have an autonomous status. (As we will see, this also affects the distinction between the metalogical and the metaphysical intuition.) 'The noetic' is the reality of our knowing life, involving the acquisition of everyday knowledge and

---

41 An antinomy is not a logical mistake within an argument, but a clash between lines of arguments, each of which is logically valid. This gives the principle of antinomy methodological relevance.

scientific knowledge.[42]

Having an argument that calls for a diversity of law-spheres, we now need to properly assess its status in reality. To that end we need to pursue the topic of the 'cosmic order'.

2. The Infinite and cosmic being

The link to the order of reality is prepared by way of the distinction between the infinite and the finite. This distinction is worked into the boundary problem on the basis of God's being infinite and the cosmos finite. This is not a sudden, novel element. In Vollenhoven's earlier work he had worked with the same characteristics.[43] The finite cannot encompass the infinite. The finite is delimited in a way that the infinite is not. Finitude is a characteristic that calls for a superior or supporting principle. To be finite is to be vulnerable in a way that the infinite seems to supersede. So when God is said to be infinite and the cosmos finite, these traits of infinitude and finitude have meaning for the the cosmos as well. God is superior, and the cosmos, being finite, requires the support of God as superior principle. Hence, with respect to the cosmos, one needs to presuppose an upholding principle, as coming from God, for the cosmos' own existence. In other words, God's being infinite is an *ontological* characterization on a par with the confession of God's sovereignty, and the cosmos' being finite is on a par with its status of subservience. Vollenhoven finds this in Calvin, though without any suggestion that the characterization derives from him. In *Logos en Ratio* (1926a) Vollenhoven paraphrases Calvin as holding that God is of everything the creator according to his will and can treat it as he wants.[44] In that way "the Infinite seizes the finite and the reverse is never the case: *finitum non est capax infiniti* [the finite is not able to grasp the infinite]" (*op. cit.*: 31). He adds (significantly, as we will see) that this thesis (*stelling*) dominates Calvin's Christology and his doctrine of the sacraments and of grace (i.e. the understanding of the work of the Spirit) as well.

---

42   Cf. Vollenhoven 1948p: 16.
43   Cf. chapter 2, section VIII.A. In the dissertation (1918a) Vollenhoven accepted both God and the world, as given, to be actually infinite. It seems he changed his mind about the world in this regard soon after; cf. also footnote 3 above.
44   Vollenhoven subscribes to Calvin's voluntarism. "For Calvin's way of thinking [over against Luther's anthropological point of departure], God stands at the beginning. He is the creator of everything through his will. That is why the cosmos is merely his artefact. He can do with it as he favours, reveal himself in a special way" (Vollenhoven 1926a: 31). We see how the 'aesthetic' characterization of the cosmos itself evidences divine voluntarism.

The pair 'infinite-finite' throws light on the boundary problem, for it calls attention to God's transcendence and immanence. One needs to avoid confusing an ontological and a cosmological interpretation. The duality induced by the boundary (as described) seems to put God 'above' the cosmos and the cosmos simply 'below' this boundary. Hence the boundary could be thought to act as a separator between God and cosmos. Vollenhoven is often interpreted that way. Yet his own wording in *Het Calvinisme en de Reformatie van de Wijsbegeerte* (1933a) is explicit in countering such a reading: "Whoever is of the opinion that God stood *outside* of the cosmos, does not do justice to the confession of His immanence".[45] God's infinitude *includes* his presence in the world, and it is through that inclusion that his presence warrants the cases of the law's obtaining for the world. At the same time one must also acknowledge God's transcendence. Thus Vollenhoven states:

> This limit [i.e. law as boundary; A.T.] marks off that which is created from God, *but not God from that which is created*. To accept the latter position would be incompatible with the acknowledgement of the infinity of God, who is always and everywhere acting *in* and *upon*—and certainly *not only from within*—the cosmos.[46]

So when speaking of the dualism between God and the cosmos, Vollenhoven does not mean to assert God's separation from the cosmos. This is what a primarily cosmological reading suggests. But this makes havoc with God's immanence. God's infinity is a warrant for both his transcendence and his immanence. To put it simply, God's being infinite entails his presence everywhere (omnipresence). It is when coming to the *chief characteristics* of God and the cosmos that the 'dualism' makes itself felt. It is primarily the pair 'sovereignty and subservience', in the guise of infinite and finite, that calls for an apportioning of terms above and below

---

45 *Op. cit.* : 24. Vollenhoven here argues against taking the 'boundary' terminology, with its spatial connotation, as having actual spatial import.

46 Vollenhoven 2005d/e, **13**, comment 2; emphases added. The addition in dashes appears to suggest that at this point for Vollenhoven it is the transcendence, rather than the immanence, that needs the reminding! A recent reaffirmation of the misunderstanding is in Friesen 2005; Friesen states: "Vollenhoven's basic idea is the triad God-law-cosmos. God is not in the cosmos. Nor is God's law in the cosmos; law stands outside, and governs and structures the cosmos. Law is the boundary between God and cosmos" (p. 110). The first and last sentences are correct, those in between are not. Not only does Vollenhoven take God to be immanent in the cosmos, but he also holds that the cosmos has an immanent structure as well (with the two cases of immanence taken in different senses), a structure that needs to be duly distinguished from ordinance-like laws that impinge upon the cosmos. This misunderstanding, being at a fundamental level, sends confusing reverberations throughout his discussion.

the law as boundary. But this is not meant as a cosmological separation. It is an ontological matter, a characteristic of being, a *difference in being*. In his lecture notes of 1927-1928 Vollenhoven states explicitly:

> And also one who speaks of the being of God, without being conscious that this being is a being *above* the law and hence has nothing in common with being *under* the law [uses language lacking in meaning]. The one is the *archè* [= controlling principle] of the other, and whoever wants to subsume them under a common denominator will transgress, consciously or unconsciously, the boundary that God has posited upon him as creature.[47]

We need to keep in mind that Vollenhoven does not mean to conduct inquiry into God, otherwise his stricture on taking the stated problem as inviting a (monistic) search for a being that is common to God and cosmos is difficult to follow. It may also help to read the word "being" as an infinitive "to be". The voluntaristic context of Vollenhoven's thought emphasizes the reality of activity. God's being is a "to be sovereign", and that of the cosmos a "to be subservient". In any case the existence of God and cosmos are never in question. (We may add that when existence is taken without the recognition of sovereignty and subservience, one overlooks the very reality that makes it dynamic.) It is how their prime features are mutually apportioned. What the pair infinite-finite adds is the understanding that the infinite 'includes' the finite, but at the same time the infinite is 'other' than the finite. The infinite has a priority over the finite, not just in being transcendent, elevated 'above' it, but in also having an immanent governing and regulating effect upon it.

The 'duality' we came across earlier, of speaking on the one hand of the principal boundary in the correlation of God and the cosmos and on the other hand of the diversity of law-spheres within (the aesthetic unity of) the cosmos, can now be understood better. It evidences the distinction between God in his transcendence and God in his immanence. So, while we *confess* the principal boundary to be the law, as the expressed will of God, the law that we can *know*, in becoming aware of it, needs to take into account our human condition or cosmic situation, which is that of obtaining law in the context of law-spheres. The latter is no less a matter of 'divine imperative', but tailored to human possibilities, guided by the avoidance of antinomies. Were one to ignore the confession here, one would not be motivated to acknowledge the laws that hold within the unity of the cosmos to be of divine or 'external' origin, i.e. expressive of the divine will. The option for the humanistic variant of claiming validity to originate in the human Self or some spiritual-mental feature

---

47   Vollenhoven 1927ms, section *8; translation mine.

of it would be more enticing. But in Vollenhoven the confession of God's sovereignty/infinity is consonant with the philosophical acceptance of a strong externalist-realist perspective regarding the law. The following quote brings it together.

> Whoever honours the [law-]boundary between God and cosmos, abandons the humanistic concept of subject (= active substance) and accepts the Calvinistic concept of subject (= being subject to the law), thereby [also accepting] a difference in different qualities of subjection, in correlation with the difference of the law-spheres, [that person] is more and more cured of the illusion as if from one or other classification of the old psychology [= consciousness as substance with well-defined or distinct qualities/faculties] a criterion to distinguish law-spheres could be adopted. And all these law-spheres *belong*—together with the matching qualities of subjection—*to being* [*behoren . . . tot het zijn*].[48]

So we now see that the metalogical exclusion of antinomies is not the last word. The threat of antinomies calls for the acceptance of different 'qualities of subjection', whereby to each quality a 'region' or 'law-sphere' belongs to operate within. The last step is to accept that a law-sphere, as region of a quality of subjection, is controlled by an *externalist-realist factor of law*. Law (as injunction), law-sphere and quality of subjection pertain to 'cosmic being'. Law in general—in terms of its transcendent source—is the defining or delimiting condition of the cosmos in its unity, but its immanent effect as injunction within the cosmic and its finite unity is the law's obtaining in *cases* of law-spheres. Therefore the qualities of subjection that match the law-spheres are determined, not by criteria of consciousness—that appeals to a humanistic priority of consciousness—but by the reality of the law's holding, which also 'guards' the chief features of a law-sphere.

The metalogical intuition of discerning the *modality* of a 'region category', in correlation with the 'form of viewing' of the viewing subject—this was the 'principal' feature within 'critical realism', as written up by Dooyeweerd (cf. "Cosmos and Logos", 1923a)—we now see to be superseded. There is too much of a 'subjectivist' criterion operative here, so long as the modality as *form of viewing* is decisive.[49] True, region categories were also grounded in the cosmos, but at that point all that can be known of the cosmos is what is 'given for consciousness' as recognized

---

48   Vollenhoven 1926msA, section 18; emphasis added.
49   This is a feature taken over from Ch. Sigwart, from whom Dooyeweerd and Vollenhoven first borrowed the term 'modal', in 'modal relation', which is 'intra-mental content in an evaluative relation to the Self'; cf. chapter 3, footnote 110, also in chapter 3, section III.C.4.b. The term 'modality' is also used as synonym for E. Lask's 'region category'.

by the viewing subject. Hence the focus remained metalogical. Now that the quality of subjection is linked to the awareness of regulation of a law-sphere, as context of subjection, one can understand that the awareness itself is an intuitive discerning of the *appropriate regulation*, fitting for the law-sphere (region and its modality) in question. This is now said to be at the *level of being*, hence the intuitive discerning is not merely a metalogical matter, but more importantly a realist acknowledgement of being as requiring concurrence. The modality of the region category/law-sphere and the intuitive acknowledgement of its character, are secured in the realist validity of what holds here, which is a law regulative for a sphere of law, a case of 'law as boundary' for the cosmos.

Another way to put this is to say that consciousness is 'affected' in the sense that the presence (being) of a *law-sphere* and of its *law* is itself determinative for the awareness that takes place in the attendant *quality of subjection*. The latter too is being, namely the being of the quality that the Self takes on when standing in subjection to a sphere's law. This awareness of standing in subjection is intuitive, and it is primal as regards consciousness. It yields "judgments of discernment", whereby the law-spheres are discerned in their typical differences as pertaining to terrains of reality.[50] This is in step with the discussion of antinomies. An 'anti-nomic subject' is a person (Self) who is confused in the judgments of discerning, one who does not properly discern the modality relevant to a quality of subjection as regulated by its law. It is the awareness of law and its proper discerning that marks the quality of subjection; it is this awareness of being that is presupposed when coming to know it. *Knowing resorts under being.* This was already stated by Dooyeweerd in his "Cosmos and Logos" (1923a). But now it has been secured more firmly in connection with the laws of appropriate modality, laws of being, proper to the cosmos itself. Only by virtue of that resorting is human acquisition of knowledge regarding the cosmos possible.

So the (former) role of the 'metalogical intuition' is now taken over by a more fundamental intuition that discerns the being in terms of law-reality. Here too, the term intuition retains its former quality of 'viewing or seeing', though this is now a discerning of cosmic presence, resulting in "judgments of existence or of discerning" (*existentie- of ontwaringsoordeel*) (Vollenhoven 1926a: 8). A judgment of existence is also said to be a "judgment of the intuition concerning modality" (*op. cit.*: 28, 63). There

---

50   Judgments of discerning arise entirely through the intuition. It is not a form of perception (Vollenhoven 1926a: 10, 14) for the latter yields representations. The judgment of discerning is preparatory for "possessing truth", i.e. coming to know; cf. further discussion below.

is no resuscitation of the initial 'concrete intuition' of 1918, which is an inner certitude of being affected—'that I am affected'—when affected. To the extent that such an effect takes place, it is psychological and subsidiary to knowledge. The heart of the intuitive discerning of existence or of presence is that it presents to the mind the cognitive challenge of truth, that is to say, it presents reality in the guise of its ability to be cognitively known in predicates, concepts and judgments.

Once Vollenhoven brought about this change in his realism in the mid-1920s, he never relinquished the realism of creaturely being, as warranted by law and knowable by virtue of intuitive discernment. However Dooyeweerd, in time (probably from about 1928), did relinquish it in favour of an ontology of meaning, when the Self, in its supra-temporal position, is turned away from "the diversity of meaning of the cosmos" and towards the (divine) totality of meaning and its source. This is to favour a supra-temporal condition of the Self (with metaphysical overtones), that secures the metalogical level of discourse in an ontology of meaning.[51]

This divergence between Vollenhoven and Dooyeweerd should not be reduced to a matter of interpretation. From the side of Dooyeweerd there is clear evidence as to his position. The ontology of meaning is central to his *De Wijsbegeerte der Wetsidee* of 1935-1936. In 1931 he speaks of his "theory of knowledge and cosmology" as "extensively discussed in my *De Wijsbegeerte der Wetsidee*, which has not yet appeared".[52] This suggests that a significant portion of this text was in existence in 1931 (at least in a draft version). Because 1928 appears to be the year of "the discovery of the religious root of thought itself" (Dooyeweerd 1935-1936, I: v), Dooyeweerd must have begun writing it shortly after this discovery in 1928. *De Crisis* itself advances the ontology of meaning: "but the *whole of reality*, high to low, is *meaning*, which has its origin in the religious fullness of meaning" (Dooyeweerd 1931: 94). The following passage has more than just an 'anti-realist' ring to it:

> Our thesis: 'There does not exist any religiously neutral experience of reality' asserts a truth that everyone will admit to who mutually compares the

---

51   Cf. chapter 3, section III.G.4 where the effect of the 'ontology of meaning' in Dooyeweerd is discussed. Dooyeweerd introduced a 'second way' of transcendental criticism when acknowledging that the 'first way' depended too much on the transcendent character of the Self. In the second way Dooyeweerd attempts to make do with transcendental subjectivity. Cf. Dooyeweerd 1953-1958, I: 34 ff.
52   "Voorwoord" to Dooyeweerd 1931: 3. For other anticipating references to "De wijsbegeerte der wetsidee" in *De Crisis*, cf. p. 99, note 1, and p. 125, note 1 (with thanks to K.A. Bril).

pre-theoretical experience of reality of a simple Christian and that of a simple citizen. One may also express it as follows: In an apostate attitude of self-consciousness one does not penetrate to one's true transcendent Selfhood. That self-consciousness *adheres* in idolatrous fashion to the temporal, it is *dispersed* in the diversity of meaning of the cosmos, and it *lacks the true concentration in the focus of existence*: the service of God! (Dooyeweerd 1931: 86, note; translation mine)

Philosophy is here made to undergird confession in formulating an 'upward trend' counteracting diversity. Vollenhoven, however, cherished diversity, as being indicative of the richness of creation, the acknowledgement of which entails 'praising God'.[53]

At some point near the end of the initial definitive period Vollenhoven refers to the quality of subjection as the 'function of subjection' (*subjèctsfunctie*). I believe that the main motive for the switch in terminology is the more favourable connotation of the latter phrase. The phrase "quality of subjection" reminds one (too much) of the former "quality of being a subject" in critical realism, in which the Self takes on a quality by choice. The phrase "function of subjection" more fittingly suggests the Self's stance in existence as always already being a 'tasked subject', that conditions the Self's functioning. The functioning evinces the subjection, calling for validity of law as its warrant. As trait of being, a function of subjection as such cannot be subject to choice. What is subject to choice is the attitude of response—willing or unwilling—and the nature and degree of actual response. On that understanding, the two phrases can be taken as synonymous. The limited degree to which there is choice in this connection is important in distinguishing laws and norms, which also calls for a discussion of the 'cosmic order', to which we now turn.

3. The cosmic order

A quality of subjection/function of subjection is delimited by a distinct law of relevant modality. The laws that govern the law-spheres are cases of the 'law as boundary' between God and the cosmos, and their 'holding for' the cosmos attests to God's immanence.[54] So a law-sphere is the region

---

53   I believe that it is historically accurate to say that, if 'reformed philosophy' began in 1923—Vollenhoven accepting 'tasked subject' and rejecting realism of ideas; Dooyeweerd working with 'law-idea' but in the context of the realism of ideas—then Dooyeweerd re-founded it in 1928, in light of his 'ontology of meaning'. In other words, with the 'philosophy of the law-idea' of 1928 and thereafter, Dooyeweerd 'cofounded' reformed philosophy 'in his own way'.

54   In the context of religion and worldview, God's immanence will be referred to in a different idiom, involving "inspiration", "salvation", "renewal", etc. Cf. Vollenhoven

of a modally distinct quality of subjection as governed by an appropriate law (as ordinance).

The need for a plurality of law-spheres, as argued for metalogically (as we saw) in order to avoid antinomies, raises the question as to their arrangement. The question arises in accordance with Vollenhoven's methodological maxim (freely stated): where there is a difference one can ask about a relevant relationship (cf. Vollenhoven 2005d/e, **10**). The diversity of the law-spheres is warranted by the difference in the laws that hold for them. The expectation of a relationship between the law-spheres points to an assumption of a 'cosmic order',[55] an order that delineates cosmic being and is grounded in an inner complexity of cosmic being (of the functions of subjection, as we will see). The assumption—indeed, it is an assumption, an ontological assumption—is that the plurality of law-spheres is not a haphazard collection but an organized arrangement. For Vollenhoven the law-spheres form a *linear order*, an order he portrays as a *vertical order of being*. The vertical order is due to a certain *necessity* that holds between law-spheres mutually: of any two, one is necessarily presupposed by the other. The law-sphere that is presupposed by the other law-sphere is portrayed as lying 'under' the latter. (The 'metaphysics' of this cosmic order is discussed later.)

Examples of this 'underlying' are the following. The physical sphere of energy interactions presupposes the sphere of motion, which in turn presupposes space and number; psychical sensitivity, in turn, cannot take place without an organic basis, which itself presupposes energy relays, etc.; juridical functioning of right and wrong presupposes the economics of property and ownership, which presupposes social interaction, and this in turn linguistic interaction and logical analysis and discernment, etc.

The number of law-spheres presupposed by any one law-sphere is a measure of the complexity of being of that law-sphere. So in the

---

1942m. In 1918a Vollenhoven stated that the norms of logic call for God's immanence to account for their being "maintained for our knowing" (1918a: 438). I cannot see any reason why Vollenhoven might have changed his mind about this in the overhaul of his thought in the mid 1920s. If the law as boundary does not separate God off from the cosmos (Vollenhoven 2005d/e, **13**), then it makes sense to expect God's immanence to be relevant in connection with the law as boundary.

55   The term 'cosmic order', though not its meaning, was short lived. It occurs prominently in the work of 1926: in *Logos en Ratio* as "cosmic order of the distinct spheres" (1926a: 11; cf. also pp. 36, 46, 49, 63); also in "Contours of the theory of knowledge" (1926b: 392, 393, 397, 399); and "Epistemology and Natural science" (1926d: 153). In the first version of *Isagôgè Philosophiae* (1930d, §42) Vollenhoven simply speaks of "natural order", an expression that is retained in later editions; cf. Vollenhoven 2010, **54** ff.

vertical arrangement there is an increase in complexity of being as one passes from the bottom to the top. During Vollenhoven's initial definitive period, the portrayal of this cosmic order was still subject to discussion and experimentation. But the assumption that there is a cosmic order to the modes of being subject itself became a fixed element of Vollenhoven's thought, as 'natural order', the main feature of cosmic (earthly) being. He put it to work in the context of the 'intersection principle' of his cosmology (cf. the next main section). The cosmic order, as ontological order, is the 'backbone' of his thought. But as assumption, its being an *hypothesis*, it is of course not a validated truth but an operating platform (though its etymology might entice one to treat a particularly useful hypothesis as a true 'underlying thesis'). The assumption of the cosmic order of being is so vital to Vollenhoven that, practically speaking, he treats it as a cosmic truth. (In the section on truth below this point is given more proper attention; cf. III.B.3.d.-e.) Confessionally, Vollenhoven thought of the cosmic order as a reality by virtue of creation, but this does not change its status in philosophy as an assumption. It is, of course, also the main guard against the pitfall of antinomies.

In the early work of Dooyeweerd (cf. his 1922d1, 1923a2), we came across a 'proto-version' of distinguished region categories or modalities, namely quantity, space, (physical) being, so-being, (logical) validity, etc. (cf. chapter 3, section III.C.4.c). By the mid-1920s the listing had become nuanced and more definitive. In 1926 Vollenhoven listed the lower law-spheres as: the logical, number, space, time, motion, energy, the biotic and the psychic; of the higher spheres mention is made of the economic, the aesthetic, the juridical/legality and the ethical, but not yet in a definitive order.[56] In the lecture notes of a course on epistemology given in 1926-1927 the position of 'the logical' is moved from the lowest rank to an approximate middle position, next above the psychical. In 1930(b: 17), in "The first questions of psychology", the partial listing is: "arithmetical, spatial, mechanical, physical or energetic, organic, psychical, analytical, social, etc." and subsequently continued (on p. 18): "analytical, social, historical, linguistic, economic, juridical, ethical, and pistical." (The 'aesthetic', about which there was still uncertainty, is left out.) The order in the first version of *Isagôgè Philosophiae* (1930d, §23) is: arithmetical, spatial, mechanical, physical, organic, psychical, analytical, historical, linguistic, social, economic, aesthetic, juridical, ethical and

---

56 Vollenhoven 1926d: 154; in Vollenhoven 1926a: 55; also "legality and economic life are law-spheres" (1926a: 57); 'ethics' i.e. "moral life" (1926a: 46, 54, 57); "aesthetics region" (1926a: 54).

pistical, which (later) became the 'standard' listing.⁵⁷

The assumption of this order gives rise in Vollenhoven to a rather recondite discourse, that is intelligible only when keeping the assumption of the cosmic order firmly in mind. The one or more law-spheres presupposed by a law-sphere—hence those 'below' it, of less complex being—constitute its 'substrate spheres' (or just its 'substrate'); the one or more law-spheres not presupposed by a law-sphere—hence those 'above' it, being more complex—are its 'superstrate spheres' (or just 'superstrate'). Two prefixes are introduced to denote what, from a chosen law-sphere, belongs either to its substrate—indicated with 'sub-'— or to its superstrate—indicated with 'supra-'. E.g. the arithmetical law-sphere being the first in the cosmic order, every other sphere belongs to its superstrate and is 'supra-arithmetical'. (This is not to say that they embody some kind of recondite arithmetic. It would be better to speak of the numerical law-sphere throughout.) Or in the case of the pistical law-sphere, which is the highest and last in the order, the other spheres all belong to its substrate and are 'sub-pistical' (which is not meant to suggest unworthiness of belief). The law-spheres that are neither lowest nor highest may have either prefix; e.g. at the physical level, its substrate spheres are 'sub-physical' and its superstrate spheres are 'supra-physical'; at the lingual level, every sphere of its substrate is 'sub-lingual', those of its superstrate 'supra-lingual'; etc. In use, this terminology allows for very trimmed expressions; e.g. Vollenhoven recommends that "the term *cause* . . . be reserved for certain supra-spatial relationships" (*Is.Ph.* sec. **68**). What this says is: (i) in the cosmic order being assumed here,

---

57   The most noteworthy shifts in these listings are: the logical (to be referred to below, cf. footnote 103 below); time as law-sphere, that soon is simply deleted; the social, which indicates an early view of the distinction between individual (up to and including the analytical) and community (above the individual, hence beginning with the social law-sphere), and the position of the aesthetic. In a 'provisional listing' in lecture notes of 1928-1929 (Vollenhoven 1928ms; section 38) the position of the aesthetic is said to be uncertain. Perhaps the uncertainty relates to the viewing of the unity of the cosmos as being aesthetic, making it difficult to consider it a law-sphere. In the same provisional listing there is no mention of the physical, probably an oversight or a typing error, for the distinction of the mechanical and the physical is an important point of discussion in Vollenhoven 1929d. However, in 1931 and later, this distinction is annulled, with the mechanical and the energetic both merged into 'the physical'. (This is standard in *Isagôgè Philosophiae* from 1931 on.) Dooyeweerd reintroduced the distinction between the mechanical and the physical/energetic in the early 1950s, with which Vollenhoven then agreed. Naturally, in connection with these shifts, one expects to find discussions that focus on threatening antinomies that necessitate the making of these distinctions. But this is, disappointingly, hardly ever the case; the intuition's role of discerning difference of modality is usually taken to be sufficient as a telling indication.

the term 'cause' is limited to an (intra-) cosmic use (this excludes the use, say, of treating God as the 'first cause' of the cosmos); (ii) 'cause' is furthermore meaningful in each of the superstrate spheres of the spatial sphere, meaning it is deemed to be relevant in all the law-spheres from the physical upwards (hence not just in the physical); (iii) the spatial and the arithmetical spheres, in being excluded from the superstrate in question, are not deemed relevant contexts of causality; finally, (iv) in being called a 'relationship', causality is among the 'horizontal connections' of the supra-spatial law-spheres, not the 'analogies of being' (cf., for this distinction, the discussion of cosmology below).

4. Laws of being
There are, in Vollenhoven's thought, some peculiar features regarding law and function of subjection. First, as to laws, it should be clear that they are taken as being the most general determinators, in the sense of regulators, of cosmic life. They are themselves of distinct modality. Their effects are intuited by the human being in the most general 'spheres' of cosmic life. Despite the importance of this intuition, Vollenhoven was very hesitant, throughout his career, to actually hazard a formulation of the law for a law-sphere. There are two exceptions. One is the pistical law-sphere, the law for which is simply said to be the Word of God ("as to its faith aspect")[58] as regulator of pistical life; the other is the analytical law-sphere, where the formulation of the law focuses on distinction and identity.[59]

Vollenhoven's reticence probably reflects his wanting to avoid the pretension of being able to read God's mind. We are better off in describing what the main traits of such laws are. First of all, they are *injunctions*, formulated as prescriptions or ordinances (cf. the last footnote above, where the formulation of the law of the analytical law-sphere begins with 'distinguish'), and they have a regulating effect. Then, in holding for or regulating 'cosmic life', they hold for the creatures that populate the cosmos or universe. Here the realist character of these laws is important, for it says that the *creaturely condition of being* is to be subject to (a multiplicity of) law(s), without a choice in so standing, within the cosmic order of law-spheres. Thus the creaturely condition includes the

---

58   Vollenhoven 1950d: 74.
59   *In his* Hoofdlijnen der Logica (Vollenhoven 1948p: 30), Vollenhoven formulates this as follows: "distinguish what is distinguishable, whatever that be, well", or, in a broader formulation: "distinguish what is distinguishable, A, whatever that be, as analysable A from everything else that is analysable, the latter being non-A, for only in what is analysable is A A."

impulse to answer/respond to injunctions. But the creaturely response to laws (see the next point) can never be identified with those laws: there is an *ontological difference* between impinging injunction (as condition) and the function of subjection as context of response. "Law and function [of subjection] are correlate. This can only be the case when they differ mutually."[60] It is by virtue of this (ontological) difference that the actual response to the impingement of law can be submissive or dismissive, with many shades of variation between these extremes. For law, in the sense here meant, is essentially norm-like.

Lastly, law as injunction should not be confused with patterns, plans, templates, structures, regularities, trends, etc., namely all that can be *de*scribed within cosmic parameters, rather than (in a fundamental sense) *pre*scribed. All such 'described structures' fall *within* the compass of the law-spheres and do not dictate *to* the law-spheres. For the laws which hold *for* cosmic life—injunctions—are cases of the 'law as boundary'; structures, patterns, regularities, and the like, that are discernable *within* cosmic life, are descriptions of that life in its functioning. A possible confusion might be felt in that both injunctions and descriptions are in a sense 'universal', and both may be said to 'hold'. But this does not negate the radical difference between them. Injunctions *enjoin and address* the functions of subjection (the factor of willing, impulse, tendency, etc. being relevant here); descriptions *denote and pertain to* states of affairs that are met with within the conscious experience of standing in subjection (calling for intra-cosmic recognition). Thus the former pertains to the law as boundary, the latter to what is under or within the scope of the law as boundary, i.e. within law-spheres. Cosmology concerns the reality within the law boundaries, and in that context Vollenhoven fully recognizes, indeed proceeds from, the fundamental distinction between (cosmic) individuality and (cosmic) universality of describable states in the order of the law-spheres (cf. the discussion of cosmology below). In 1950(e: 40) he summarized this succinctly as: "(1) All that is subject to the law . . . is both universal and individual. (2) The mutual relation of the universal and the individual in the creation is this, that both are of equal value and always and everywhere occur together." But cosmology/creation as such presupposes the order of being that is set by the order of law.[61]

---

60 Vollenhoven 1930d/1931f, §115 [= 2010, Appendix I, §115]; cf. also Vollenhoven 1950d: 73.

61 This has particular relevance for so-called 'abstract objects': sets, states of affairs, propositions, etc. Vollenhoven takes these as falling within the scope of the (created) cosmos and its law-spheres. Within the cosmic order there are, besides individual creatures,

On first hearing, one might be willing to grant the relevance of injunctions as regulating human life. After all, life without norms ("Thou shalt . . ."; "Do not . . ."; "So act that the maxim . . .") would leave life in chaos. But is this relevant for the spheres the human being shares with other creatures? Here too Vollenhoven never specified the 'laws' that might be relevant, though he certainly maintained that there are such laws for the lower law-spheres. On the basis of the general features that such laws should have (and leaving wide margins for further consideration), one expects such formulations to (i) be injunction-like, (ii) be distinct as to modality, (iii) be broad enough to impinge upon all the relevant functioning, and (iv) act as boundaries within which detailed functioning takes place.

A very tentative attempt to address the 'sub-analytical' law-spheres in the interest of a first indication might (Vollenhoven-wise) go as follows. The psychical law, mindful of the sensibility and sensitivity that is relevant not only to human beings but also (the higher species of) animals, might be: "abstain from harming and denigrating psychic creatures, promote rather their happiness and wellbeing". For the organic law-sphere there is the drive of life to sustain itself and to multiply, as if in response to: "live and multiply". At the physical level there is the peculiar character of the second law of thermodynamics and the conservation laws. The former says that, for the whole physical universe, entropy (the measure of randomness) increases. The conservation laws say that basic physical quantities are conserved in all physical processes: the conservation of energy, of (linear and angular) momentum, of charge, of baryon number, and of leptons.[62] As for space and number, considered in disjunction from the physical world, there would appear to be the 'control' over mathematical infinity: the inward spatial continuity of position or situation, and the unending series of the natural numbers.

---

also universal features, the most prominent of which are 'analogies of being' (whereby one law-sphere is partially reflected in another) and 'relations between beings' (connections between creatures). When these abstract objects are said to hold or to obtain, this is more of a fixed 'keeping together' of denoted form ('5+7=12' holds eternally) than an injunction to abide by. So, for Vollenhoven, this 'holding' of abstract objects is also by virtue of creation.

62   The second law of thermodynamics is time–asymmetrical, meaning that the time-parameter cannot be reversed (from +t to –t), whereas the usual laws of physics (Newton's laws, Maxwell's laws, Hamilton's equations, Einstein's general relativity, etc.) are symmetrical in time and are of a structural nature. Cf. Penrose 1989: 392; also Penrose 2005: 696-697. The conservation laws hold irrespective of the type of processes and of time and space location. The renown physicist, Richard P. Feynman, states: "In the last analysis, we do not understand the conservation laws deeply", Feynman 1998: 84.

The cosmic order is by virtue of creation. In the above we have not touched on its 'metaphysical' status. We do so at the appropriate place below.

5. Qualities of subjection / functions of subjection
We also wish to note a peculiarity of the cosmic order in connection with human beings. All beings—'creatures'—participate in law-spheres. Every creature is an individual being—Vollenhoven initially spoke of a "cosmic unity", a term he soon dropped in favour of "individual". Each acts as a "substance, the bearer of different qualities of subjection".[63] As discussed earlier, the distinction between individual thing/person and qualities of subjection, enables the one thing/person to 'have' (or be the bearer of) a multiplicity of such qualities of subjection—later called "functions of (standing in) subjection",[64] as traits of its being. Creatures (cosmic unities) display differences of being in that not all participate in the same law-spheres. All participate in the lowest spheres. In fact, the natural numbers, these being the 'simplest' of beings, have only the numerical function of subjection. Spatial figures have both the numerical and spatial functions. Then minerals, chemicals, inorganic material, physical objects, etc. reach (in the cosmic order) up to and include the physical law-sphere/quality of subjection. Plants reach higher to include the organic, and animals include the psychical. Only the human being participates in the entire cosmic order, in the sense of having/bearing all the functions/qualities of subjection.

Now, given that 'knowing resorts under being', the possibility of knowing relates to the human being's participation in the (full) cosmic order. Each quality of subjection involves a subjection to law, for there is always the ontological difference between law and the function of subjection. The human being, Vollenhoven now maintains, is aware of this difference, and this is clearly so at the point in the cosmic order where the consciousness of difference and connection becomes explicit. This occurs at the level of participation in the analytical law-sphere, the injunction of which is (to paraphrase somewhat) "to distinguish what there is to distinguish as different" (cf. footnote 59 above). "For that matter, it lies in the nature of the analytical function that also this difference [of law and function] is [given the cosmic order] first discerned

---

63 Vollenhoven 1926msA, section 12.
64 It may be that the phrase "quality of subjection", which reflects Vollenhoven's early use of "quality of being a subject" (when the Self complies to norms), is too limited in Vollenhoven revised context in which every creature "stands in subjection to laws". The phrase "function of subjection" is broader and gained preferential use in Vollenhoven.

here."[65] Because the analytical law-sphere lies in the substrate of every 'supra-analytical' law-sphere, this consciousness of law and function is relevant in all the supra-analytical spheres as well.

Intrinsic to this consciousness of the difference between law and function is the awareness of the law's 'holding for' the function. Now the difference of law and function brings with it the possibility of functional compliance or non-compliance to the respective law, at least at the level (from the analytical function and higher) where one is aware of this difference. This is not to say that the person, who is functioning at that level, is capable of annulling the standing in subjection. There is only the 'measure of freedom' for a person to comply either in a positive sense or a negative sense to the relevant law. (E.g. 'anti-social' is still to be social, but in a negative sense, while 'non-social' is to lack the social function; a rebellious youth is anti-social, never non-social, as animals are.) In this way, the laws of the analytical law-sphere and of the 'supra-analytical' spheres take on the role of *norms*, in light of which a human being can realize different directions of response, depending on his/her meeting or flouting the laws as norms.

It may seem that the introduction of norms induces a difference in the order of the laws themselves, between those that hold 'as laws' and those (at the typically human level) that hold 'as norms'. But Vollenhoven does not mean to 'split' the cosmic order in a (higher) part, governed by norms, and a (lower) part, governed by laws. (That might serve as incentive to deny or at least overlook the difference between law and function in the law-function correlation in that lower part.) It is the kind and degree of *complexity of the functioning*, in correlation with laws, that motivates the distinction. What remains constant is that law and function nowhere coalesce, and that the cosmic order is governed by one order of laws (injunctions).

But the awareness of the difference between law and function of subjection is not 'suddenly' felt at the analytical level. At this level it is clear and marked. (When attentive we soon spot a contradiction, i.e. realize a logical norm is not being respected.) In the 'sub-analytical' regions, from the psychical law-sphere and down, something of this difference is 'felt', though with progressively diminishing consciousness, including the contrast that reflects the difference of direction of response. One can, through wanton living—a misplaced exercise of 'personal freedom'—overburden one's psychical life (through instinctual disrespect of oneself?), resulting in shame, guilt or mental disturbance, and the like;

---

65   Vollenhoven 1930d/1931f, §115 [= 2010, Appendix I, §115].

on the positive side one can 'feel good' when sensitivities are in balance. Similarly for organic health: abnormal attention to or neglect of organic well-being can lead to illness, while a more relaxed and subconscious 'listening to one's body' would be wiser. Then, at a more physical level, there is a vague fluctuating physical awareness/non-awareness, such as fatigue in bearing one's weight, or in behaving so as not to occasion the reprimand "you don't know your own strength". As to space, there is the 'field awareness' of requiring space and the effect of having too little or too much of it (claustrophobia, agoraphobia, etc.). Finally, there is a sense of personal unity—as assumed in "one man one vote"—and its damaged form in schizophrenia.[66] In all these cases, it is not the awareness, vague or clear, that constitutes the standing in subjection; the awareness is an effect of so standing.

We add the remark that consciousness for Vollenhoven is intrinsic to the functioning human being, i.e. awareness as correlated to functions of subjection. Hence this awareness is modally diverse. Once, late in his career, he stated: "consciousness is in the body".[67] (This is not 'body' as *soma*, but as 'unity of subjection'; cf. section IV below.) There is no longer the independent concrete intuition, as formulated in his earliest work. As to animals and plants, the former are admitted to be sensitive creatures, having awareness, but indications of the ontological difference of law and function are limited to variations within instinctual boundaries. Individually, plants are even more limited in their variability (response to the environment). Contrary to his position in his earliest work, Vollenhoven is no longer a proponent of a 'plant psychology'.[68] In the course of time Vollenhoven raised the possibility of distinguishing more functions of subjection in living creatures than the traditional organic

---

66   In mentioning these 'sub-analytical' cases I go beyond Vollenhoven's own discussion. In Vollenhoven 1930b: 20. Vollenhoven speaks of "law-spheres whose laws are norms"—cf. also Vollenhoven 1930d/1931f, §81 (= 2010, Appendix I, §81)—and then proceeds to mention that there is relevance for the law-spheres beneath the analytical law-sphere. "Here too lies the difference [in direction of response] in [organic] health and illness, [psychical] guilty and innocent, etc." Surprisingly, this discussion of 'laws as norms' was suppressed in the versions of *Isagôgè Philosophiae* of 1932 and later, although the topic remained fully valid for Vollenhoven. The topic is central in Vollenhoven 1951h (i.e. "Norm and natural law"), and explicitly discussed in Vollenhoven 1963c: 188 (i.e. "Problems in connection with time"). The distinction of law and norm is first discussed in lecture notes of 1926-1927; cf. Vollenhoven 1926msA, section 11.

67   Vollenhoven 1963c: 191.

68   Cf. Vollenhoven 1930b: 24; in this connection he speaks of "confused premises" that don't lead to "dependable conclusions". On 'plant psychology' in the early Vollenhoven, cf. chapter 3, footnotes 21 and 31.

and psychical functions.[69]

B. The boundary threefold
So far the boundary concept has found an application as a concept of law, where law is taken in the sense of principle of governance, formulated prescriptively as injunction. This is consonant with the religious interpretation of the principal boundary as law, this being the expressed will of God. We will return to this interpretation below. But first a further point about the boundary is in order concerning its application. The application of the boundary is in fact broader than as discussed so far, namely in connection with law, though this remains the dominant (or most explicit) application.

The boundary, in Vollenhoven, has a full Trinitarian scope. Above we quoted Vollenhoven as saying, about Calvin's use of the distinction between the Infinite (God) and the finite (creature), that this holds not only in a cosmological sense, but that it is also relevant for Christology and towards understanding the work of the Spirit (Vollenhoven 1926a: 31). This clearly suggests a relevance, religiously, of the boundary as holding in connection with the three Persons of the Trinity. Otherwise he would not have followed this up immediately with the comment: "this clear seeing of the boundary between Him who poses laws and those who are subject to them" (*ibid.*). Vollenhoven made this explicit in the first format of *Isagôgè Philosophiae* (1930-1931). But we should add at once that Vollenhoven maintained a low profile in this matter. The relevant passages were reworked in the next version of 1932, with the Trinitarian understanding now being more suggested implicitly than stated explicitly; as a result, this topic is not common knowledge.[70] Nevertheless it is a central feature of Vollenhoven's thought, so much so that one may continue to qualify Vollenhoven's position as being Trinitarian theistic.

---

69   Vollenhoven proposed a 'biotic function' relevant for unicellular creatures, a 'sensory function' of creatures (plants) that respond to stimuli, a 'vital function' of creatures with urge and impulse, and a 'feeling function' of creatures that feel pleasure and pain. Cf. Vollenhoven 1963c: 183-184. J. Klapwijk, in his recent *Purpose in the Living World? Creation and Emergent Evolution* (2008) explores new avenues in this regard against the background of the Reformed tradition.

70   One of the first (if not the first) to discuss the Trinitarian framework in the early Vollenhoven was Albert M. Wolters, in "Vollenhoven on 'Word of God'" (Wolters 1979b). His prime reference is to *Isagôgè Philosophiae* of January 1931, which (for the topic in question) is slightly revised as compared to the first version of October 1930; cf. Vollenhoven 2010.

1. The Trinitarian theistic position
In the 1930-1931 text,[71] mentioned above, Vollenhoven, when speaking of the connection between the sovereign God and the creature, provisionally calls this "the religious" (*op. cit.*, §71), which is a vague term (as he himself admits; *ibid.*), but it allows for a broad account of divine activities. He then refers to the three basic activities of God, activities in which each of the three Persons has a distinct or at least leading role. There is first the *creating* of God the Father, then the *revealing* of God the Son/Logos, and finally the *guiding* of God the Holy Spirit (*op. cit.*, §§72, 73). There is a sequence here, in that the Logos-revelation presupposes the creating work of the Father, and the guidance of the Spirit presupposes the work of both the Father and the Son/Logos. This reflects their positions within the (transcendent) Godhead of the Trinity. Furthermore, each Person also effectuates its own characteristic conditioning in connection with the cosmos. From the Father there is *the imposition of law*, the Son/Logos effectuates 'word-revelation' in that he *commands by way of indicating direction* (*op. cit.*, §75), and the Spirit, in turn, *guides in the light of determined direction* (*op. cit.*, §76).

These effects of divine immanence also accord with the sequential character of the Persons in their transcendent roles. For *laws*, being laws for being, maintain and sustain creaturely life in the most basic sense of its dynamism. But, given the difference between law and subject/creature, this maintaining and sustaining of law does not preclude the possibility of different directions of activity. Hence in Scripture one finds many instances in which God 'speaks' by way of *commanding* that this or that take place, from the "let there be light" (in the Genesis 1 creation account) to the "thou shalt love . . .", of the 'love command' directed specifically to human beings. In connection with this speaking God is said to be the *Logos* (*op. cit.*, §74). This 'speaking' of the Logos presupposes the work of the Father. Thus "every command—the result of commanding—presupposes a law, and a command of the Logos presupposes a law of the Creator." Also "every command entails a law, while not every law entails a command" (*op. cit.*, §75). The commanding of the Logos has a relevance that is additional to the imposing of law in connection with the creation.

Then there is also God's relation to the creature in which he is the guiding Spirit. This is specifically relevant in connection with *genesis and development*. This too is an 'additional' feature not accountable in terms of the (prior) work of the Father and the Logos. In the Genesis 1 account there is the "Spirit of God brooding over the waters" (Gen. 1:

---
71 Vollenhoven 1930d/1931f; also Vollenhoven 2010.

2) and the subsequent guiding of the Spirit in "the unfolding of specific creatures that are mutually diverse from out of the earth as pre-different [*praedifferente aarde*] to this diversity" (*op. cit.*, §76).[72] This topic of genesis and development, as guided by the Spirit, remained a prominent feature of *Isagôgè Philosophiae* (cf. Vollenhoven 2010, 22). Vollenhoven sees the earth as initially enveloping or enclosing a motley diversity, and takes development to be the evolving out or disclosing of this enveloped state into an openness and a sustaining of mutual connections. The Spirit's guiding is towards *determined* direction—I read this as being goal guiding—while the presupposed command (only) *points* in a direction (Vollenhoven 1930d/1931f, §77).

The above account of the three divine Persons, relevant at the time of Vollenhoven's initial platform, is I believe sufficient to warrant the conclusion that Vollenhoven retained a 'theistic position'. In using this term, which Vollenhoven himself did not use for himself apart from his earliest work, we must hasten to add two qualifications. First, this theist position is typically Trinitarian. The distinct relevance of each of the Persons of the Trinity not only allows for separate reference to each but also requires this. Creaturely cosmic life is never without the relation to the triune God. In his immanence God 'goes along' with creaturely life, sustaining, directing and guiding it. But, also in connection with this immanence, there is always the ontological difference between God's sovereignty and the cosmic life's subservience, a difference by virtue of which cosmic life is meaningful and challenging, centring on direction. Vollenhoven's retaining this position is most clearly evidenced by a lecture he gave in 1955, entitled "Life-unity" (Vollenhoven 1955i). Here he again speaks of "threefold law" and "threefold standing in subjection" (*ibid*, p. 122), in direct correlation with the three Persons of the Trinity. (We note though that the term 'law' here is itself used in a threefold sense, but the meanings agree with the uses denoted by the earlier 'law', 'command' and 'guidance'.)[73]

---

72 Evidently, with "pre-different earth", Vollenhoven means to indicate an early stage of created reality. Mindful of his use of "earth", as synonym for "universe", he would appear to have an early stage of the universe in mind. In this connection he also refers to Psalm 104, a hymn to the Creator in the form of a meditation on the creation.

73 Vollenhoven re-emphasizes 'threefold law' from 1953 on, as creation law, law of love and positive law (cf. my discussion of its first re-appearance in Tol and Bril 1992: 107-111). However Vollenhoven's explicit Trinitarian statements are in work he left unpublished. In published statements he mentioned the threefold law without making the correlation with the Persons of the Trinity explicit; cf. his 1953l, 1959d and 1963a, reprinted in Tol and Bril 1992: 104, 138 and 155-156 respectively. Then, in his lectures on time, i.e. 1963c, he states that over the years, "there was a gradual consolidation of

Secondly, Vollenhoven's critique of 'theism', when that term is used in connection with an 'ideal epistemic system', in the sense of attributing, partially or completely, sovereignty to the cosmos, remains in full effect. The cosmos is bounded by, thus dependent upon, sustaining laws, direction determining commands and guidance towards goals. Broadly speaking, Vollenhoven's position is teleological. Not that the teleology is 'built-in', as in Aristotle or in Hans Driesch.[74] For Vollenhoven, cosmic life does indeed tend towards 'last things' on account of God's immanent 'goading'. But this is meant to include the human being, who, when responding to God in a positive sense, hastens the Coming, but when responding negatively, thwarts it. There is no predicting the wayward course of actual life in reaching the *eschaton*. This implies that life is neither rigidly set nor unboundedly free. Response, and thus responsibility, are vital.

At this point we may look back to see what is changed in connection with Vollenhoven's former 'theism' and his 'critical realist' position in philosophy. At the same time, his initial definitive position was not the last word on many a topic, though it is the platform for all later changes. In our discussion we will be particularly interested in surmising 'what happens' to the scholastic problem of the harmony of subjective and objective rationality. That problem is interwoven quite typically with theistic themes. When that is clarified we will give an outline of Vollenhoven's cosmology, and then touch on how he overcame the 'dualism' of his initial definitive position.

Changes with respect to Vollenhoven's former early position are perhaps easiest to gauge by taking the formulations of the roles of the Persons of the Trinity as guiding thread. We begin with that of the Spirit.

2. The work of the Spirit reviewed
There is a major shift in the way Vollenhoven formulates the relevance of the work of the Spirit. In critical realism the Spirit's work is taken to include that of warranting norms, not only the norms of thought (logical norms) but also norms of aesthetics, ethics, religion etc. These norms are distinct from laws, as the term was then used in the usual sense of 'laws of

---

[my] own view of years ago in the *Isagoge*", and he then lists the "*threefold law* requiring a threefold *being subject*"; cf. Tol and Bril 1992: 171-172. The only versions of *Isagôgè Philosophiae* that fit the bill in this regard are those of the first setup of 1930-1931. Cf. also in my "Algemene inleiding" to the text-critical edition of *Isagôgè Philosophiae*, in particular the discussion of the first setup of this text (Tol 2010a).

74   Vollenhoven had criticised the latter on this score in his 1920a; cf. chapter 3, note 21 above.

nature'. A characteristic feature of the early view is that the human being, as a Self, has the independence of submitting or not submitting to these norms as based on its own prior intuition of self-certainties. Only when submitting does the Self gain the 'quality of being a subject', this being a 'distinguishing subject' in light of the norm of identity, a 'thinking subject' in light of the principle (as norm) of contradiction, an aesthetic or ethical subject, etc. in the face of aesthetic or ethical norms, etc. In that sense the 'normative effect' of norms is dependent on the voluntary submissive attitude of the Self. (In the background we have the 'objective values' of neo-Kantianism, whereby values have an evaluating effect only when taken in [the modal] relation to the valuing subject; though from the start Vollenhoven clearly distinguished the Self and its qualities of being a subject, something that is lacking in neo-Kantianism). But the independence of the Self's intuition, relevant to the 'concrete intuition', Vollenhoven comes to see—Janse's criticisms had a role here—as being subjective, possibly with undesired humanistic implications.

In the revision, Vollenhoven retains the distinction between Self and 'quality of being a subject', but he re-interprets the context in which this is implemented. The intuitive self-certainties are now taken to be merely psychological, so that these self-certainties no longer attest to the independence of the Self. Related to this is Vollenhoven's rejection of the soul being an immortal substance, which takes away any firm basis in the Self. Then there is also the undercutting of the thought-being polarity, whereby the pole of thought had been firmly planted in the Self. All this, taken together, in effect removes the basis from which knowledge can be formed with the authority of subjective rationality. Knowing now resorts under being.

The Self is brought into a much closer rapport with the World (cosmos), expressed as the Self being 'tasked' or always already 'standing in subjection'. Vollenhoven retains the view that the Self, in its qualities of subjection (or 'functions of subjection'), is subject to norms. But he now re-interprets norms as 'laws of injunction' and takes the latter to be of a *cosmic* character. The usual cosmic 'laws of nature' thereby become subsidiary to the 'cosmic' laws of injunction.

This last step, which involves taking norms to be a species of laws (of injunction) and interpreting the latter as 'laws for cosmic life', seems a big and perhaps arbitrary step. To Vollenhoven it was probably less so. From the start he spoke of the Holy Spirit as 'law-giver', as when speaking of truth as a "norm, posited by God the Holy Spirit as law-giver . . ." (Vollenhoven 1918a: 391). In critical realism the Self is spoken of as "cosmic Self"—even as "microcosm" (Vollenhoven 1918a: 442)—which perhaps explains Vollenhoven's terminology at this point. When 'norm' and 'law-giving' are themselves put in a cosmic context, in that of the cosmos as world-in-the-large—this is the chief shift that takes place here!—then that consolidates the cancellation of the relative independence of the Self vis-à-vis the World. This is in agreement with Vollenhoven's initial definitive platform.

Given the stated change, with the Spirit no longer seen as functioning as the warrant for the norm's holding capacity, the Spirit's role now calls for reconsideration. From the time of Vollenhoven's initial definitive platform, the emphasis falls on guidance. Regretfully, Vollenhoven never gave an explicit account of this guidance. What complicates and to some extent confuses matters is the status of the 'spiritual world' (heaven) that Vollenhoven brings into the picture. (The latter goes virtually unmentioned in Vollenhoven's earlier work.) Janse's emphasis on the presence of the spiritual world has a follow-up in Vollenhoven.[75] There are heavenly creatures, said to influence the lives of earthly creatures (Vollenhoven 2005d/e, **138**; also 2010, **138**),[76] though Vollenhoven never elaborated on this influence. In any case the influence is for good or evil, for there are 'upright' and 'fallen' spirits (angels and demons).[77] But the work of the (Holy) Spirit cannot be identified with these forms of spiritual influence, for the latter are an influence of (heavenly) creature upon (earthly) creature, in other words, this influence is 'inter-creaturely'.

The Spirit, as divine Person, transcends the creaturely, though there is also the effect of the Spirit's immanence as well. A prominent effect of the Spirit is, as we saw, that of guiding development and disclosing the potential of earthly life. This is a role in the context of creation. In later work Vollenhoven also emphasizes the effect upon office-holders in

---

75   One finds a clear reminder of Janse in Vollenhoven's understanding of 'spirit'. On the one hand spirits are "powers" under God's command, on the other hand spirit is like "wind, which controls the creatures in their growth and movement and, correlate to this, [it is] the capacity of animal and human being—contrary to plants—to move about on the earth" Vollenhoven 1930b: 13. In Vollenhoven 2005d/e, **139** and 2010, **139** (from 1932 on), the biblical meaning of 'spirit' is, according to Vollenhoven, 'principle of direction'.

76   Vollenhoven 1930b: 13, heaven and earth are said to be "in continual connection with each other . . .".

77   In 2005d/e, also 2010, Part III on the connection between heaven and earth, Vollenhoven comments: "As far as angelic influence 'for worse' [is concerned], being 'possessed' is its most abnormal form" (section **138**). Heaven (the spiritual world) and earth (the universe) are the two main realities that make up the cosmos, both of which are characterised as 'being subject' or 'standing in subjection' (section **19**).

societal spheres of responsibility. The sense of responsibility, relevant to the societal tasks of the office in question, attests to the presence of the Spirit.[78] Societal office, as such, is not 'man-made'. In light of the Trinity's sequential arrangement, the offices of societal spheres presuppose norms (perhaps now concentrated in norm-principles) and directing commands. But when considering the actual human response on the part of office-holders we must (I take it) *also* allow for the influence of the spiritual world, for good or evil, which influence might be noted empirically as 'strength of character' or 'bending to corruption', respectively. But even Vollenhoven's later notes were incomplete in this respect.[79]

3. The work of the Logos and role of the human logos reconsidered
The understanding of the work of the second person, the Son or the Logos, also undergoes change. The initial, predominantly metalogical role of warranting the harmony of subjective and objective rationality makes way for a fuller but also thoroughly transformed account. The former 'harmony' was taken to be an agreement between on the one hand the *adequate concept*, which directs the subjective discovery and growth of knowledge, and on the other hand cosmic reality, as acknowledged in the *idea*, itself the warrant for the rational structure of the cosmos. The scholastic harmony is undercut (or at least seriously thwarted) when either the pole of the Self or that of the World is sufficiently refashioned. The revision (as described above) of the understanding of the Self, and with it that of the Spirit, has removed the basis for an independent acceptance of subjective rationality supporting an adequate concept. We have seen that the idea (of objective rationality) also goes by the board. But that still leaves the Logos' role of 'disposing the synthesis of subject and object' to consider in its own right.

a. Why an intuition?
Vollenhoven, we found, when defending the scholastic harmony, held that the harmony, though necessary, is not itself a sufficient cognitive basis for knowledge. The harmony is necessary, for the subjective and the object must agree in the end. But this can only be deemed sufficient in light of a *means* that includes essential features of the subjective and the objective. In his dissertation Vollenhoven saw subjective rationality as

---
78   Vollenhoven 1950n, in Tol and Bril 1992, esp. p. 44.
79   The clearest statement is in "Levenseenheid" (Life-unity), Vollenhoven 1955i. Vollenhoven's lectures on time, Vollenhoven 1963c: 194-195, announced, but did not actually treat, the topic of societal offices.

contingent and factual; objective rationality as necessary but formal. The 'synthetic a priori' is able to bridge this divide; it has content but at the same time is necessary.[80]

Vollenhoven's prime reason for appealing to intuition in his earliest work was to justify the synthetic a priori. The intuition must offer immediate certainty, not derived, but it still needs to be understood as properly situated so as to be justified. The analytical intuition, which is the immediate grasp of similarity and difference of data (Vollenhoven 1918a: 350), has a decisive role here. In Vollenhoven's earliest work it is brought into rapport with the cosmic reality of the Self (as 'microcosm'), whereby the mind and the body provide the focus for the primary synthetic a priori's, namely that of arithmetic (in connection with the mind and the concrete intuition) and of spatial localization (as concerns the body and the forms of sensibility). Then (as confirmed in 1921) there is the shift towards the World (cosmos, the idea, and the metaphysical intuition), which is now itself seen as basis for distinguishing distinct regions of scientific endeavour, each of which has a distinct modal character and is the context of 'essential connections'. The analytical (= metalogical) intuition picks up these essential connections (as synthetic a priori's, of which the mathematical are now some among others) as means of adjudicating between on the one hand the pluralist subjective discovery and growth of knowledge and on the other hand the ideal of systematic complete knowledge of a region, grounded in the idea, as represented by the adequate concept of a region. Whether the analytical intuition operates in league with the Self or with the World, it is as a (human) 'small-*l* logos' that it complements, in the sense of making sufficient, what the (divine) 'large-*L* Logos' disposes as ground pattern of harmony. An awareness of the *logos*' standing with the *Logos*, would appear to be assumed here, for the Logos' role of *disposing* subject and object to come together needs to be answered to if the harmony of subject and object is to become an accomplished fact. This awareness no doubt is, or at least involves, a moment of faith. But it is a faith that complements and completes reason's aim of achieving an (objectively) true and (subjectively) adequate understanding. Now what happens to this scholastic cognitive schema in Vollenhoven's revision? We find that he gives a much more careful account of that which falls under the aegis of the Logos.

b. The 'Logos-logos' difference
In Vollenhoven's reconsideration, he retains the use of the 'Logos-

---

[80]   Vollenhoven 1918a: 9; cf. also chapter 2, section IV.A.

logos' pair, in the primary meaning of the second Person of divinity and the human context of rationality, respectively. So *prima facie* the reconsideration does not seem to be radical. But the human context of rationality is now said to involve "the created logos",[81] situated in the cosmic order. This created logos is the logical or analytical law-sphere. This says that rationality is now contextualized. Furthermore, the latter is subjected to a notion of "truth in itself".[82] This realist indication of truth takes the place of the former disposed harmony of subject and object. The 'disposing', formerly a divine effect, is now of cosmic alloy. All this is quite new. Thus the meaning of the 'Logos-logos' pair needs to be looked at more carefully in the context of the new discussion that replaces the former use.

In the revised context of the mid-1920s, the meaning of the term 'Logos' is, before anything else, fixed in its primary biblical use in portraying God's 'speaking' or his 'revelation' to the creature, as second Person of the Trinity. Thus 'Son' denotes the second Person in its transcendence, while 'Logos' refers more to its immanence—"the light . . . coming into the world" (John 1:9; cf. also Vollenhoven 1926a: 18). This divine speaking usually takes the form of commanding (as we saw; cf. Vollenhoven 1930d/1931f, §75; also 2010, Appendix I, §75). The commanding is such that, as regards knowledge, it directs by way of promoting relevant knowledge acquisition and warning against error, i.e. avoiding "going astray" (*dwalen*). (Vollenhoven often uses the pair "*kennen* en dwalen", "knowing and straying", as being on a par.)[83] The commanding directs in that it aims at a judicious 'handling' or assessing of the epistemic situation, which is more than just being in the know. A prime example of a command of the Logos is the (biblical) central love command, which is (in essence) 'to love God above all and one's neighbour as oneself' (cf. Mark 12: 30-31). This enjoins piety and righteousness, and when applied to the epistemic situation, advances a 'good or loving' handling of rationality and truth. "The logical function needs to be controlled by love."[84] Knowledge acquired and used calls for

---

81 This term is used almost exclusively in Vollenhoven 1926b and 1926d; in Vollenhoven 1926a it is gradually replaced by "logical law-sphere" as the text proceeds.

82 Vollenhoven 1926b: 385. It is completely indifferent to truth whether it be known. It is only when known that it has 'validity' (*op. cit.* : 384). Vollenhoven finds a rapprochement with Bernard Bolzano, who also spoke of "*Wahrheiten an sich*"; cf. 1926a: 51-52.

83 Vollenhoven 2010, **11, 13**.

84 Vollenhoven 1963c: 189. The love command does not make the logical norms, to which the logical function is subject in a direct sense, redundant. It directs only on

a context of wisdom.

We see at once that the understanding of the primary role of the Logos is now quite removed from any 'disposing of subject and object to come together'. The main role of the Logos is to provide aim. It orientates cognition, i.e. the operating of the analytical function, in such a way as to warrant a satisfactory outcome of the knowledge endeavour. At its own level the divine Logos is 'above' knowledge synthesis. To acquire a satisfactory outcome of the knowledge endeavour, the human exercise of rationality (= the logical function in use) needs not only to submit to norms—this is what was required in Vollenhoven's former view as well—but also to practise rationality in a way that edifies. This is not a '(subjective) reason + faith' construction, but the 'right/proper rational use of a function'. The analytical function is (1) itself the basis for the possibility of understanding through distinguishing differences and establishing connections; (2) this possibility becomes rationally actual in compliance to logical norms; (3) the function's rational actuality is right, proper or justified when exercised in light of contributing to advancing life 'for good', which 'light' is provided by the Logos. Of course, 'beliefs' as moments of awareness are present throughout, but this is not 'faith' as meant in a scholastic context, namely as superadded truth.

In Vollenhoven's former view, the knowledge situation itself was one in which the merging of subject and object was taken to be the primary feature, in what was described as 'knowledge by acquaintance' (cf. chapter 2, section V.D.). In that situation the knowledge synthesis is one in which the Self, in its quality of being a knowing subject, assimilates, processes or works over (the Dutch verb is 'verwerken') the object, making it answer to or serve human ends. In other words, the former model of knowledge is one in which *control* is central, being a model of subject dominating object, as end in itself. The new view calls for an orientation of the entire knowledge endeavour, so that, whatever possibility of control knowledge provides, this is itself situated to serve towards *enhancing* life in which it is had and put to use.

c. Values and assessment

Now how is the knowledge endeavour described that *stands subject* to the orienting (commanding) aim of the Logos? It seems that Vollenhoven initially (in the late 1920s) wished to emphasize the contextualization of

---

the assumption that the logical function is used validly. Love is no warrant to cover up mistakes! Cf. also, Vollenhoven 1948p: 25, i.e. "section 10: The meaning of this law [for the analytical function] qua modal law [/norm]."

knowledge in terms of *values*. In somewhat neo-Kantian, Freiburg-like fashion, he held values to be objective and "ubiquitous in the cosmos". When the epistemic situation is "assessed"—he distinguishes 'assessment' (*beoordelen*) and 'judgment' (*oordelen*) in this connection—that involves the recognition of value. On the other hand, the value that knowledge has "for us" "can only be properly assessed when acknowledged as anchored in the Logos."[85] Thus there is an intriguing connection suggested as holding between the Logos and the knowledge situation (within the cosmos), as relevant to the topic of values. The text that discusses this is a section in the first version of *Isagôgè Philosophiae* (1930-1931; sec. 124). However, the whole context is reworked in the next version of 1932 and the topic of values appears simply to drop out of sight, apart from an isolated memory of it.[86] But the topic itself fits the 'aesthetic' characterization of the cosmos we find to be prevalent till the early 1930s, when it too simply falls away, and appears to be replaced (as of Vollenhoven 1932e) by a more 'moral' qualification (about which more later).

I believe we should interpret Vollenhoven's view of values at the time to be the most encompassing *metalogical* feature of the cosmos. Values appear to delineate (what might be called) 'objects of attention'; they are such as to serve to make human awareness take notice. If we may assume this to be correct—textual support is very limited—then "value" appears to be a synonym for what Dooyeweerd, in "Cosmos and Logos" (1923a2), referred to as "objective meaning", understanding this to be: "meaning as 'given for consciousness'."[87] The way objective meaning (in Dooyeweerd at the time) involves awareness of reality as given for consciousness, in a similar way value (here in Vollenhoven) appears to invite awareness of reality in its being given for discernment. Basically there is the same thought expressed in two different idioms.

---

85   Vollenhoven 1930d/1931f, §124; also 2010, Appendix I, §124. A work that discusses these matters is N. Maxwell, *From Knowledge to Wisdom. A revolution in the aims and methods of science* (1984). The author wished to go beyond the 'philosophy of knowledge' towards a more inclusive 'philosophy of wisdom'. The view proposed is based on "an objectivist, realist view of value" (p. 248).

86   In Vollenhoven 1932e and later versions, there is a classification of judgments, arranged according to the way that the structure of the cosmos is presented. Between the class of religious judgments and that of the kingdoms, there is the class of judgments about values, and the example given is: "It is good to speak truth." Strangely enough, there is no longer any direct textual support about values in the main body of the text. But the 'position' of this class of judgments (between that of religion and cosmic kingdoms) matches the 'high ranking' that is attributed to values in the earlier version. Note also that the example of the value given here is itself 'moral', namely 'good'.

87   Cf. the discussion in chapter 3, section III.E.

Each supports the thesis of 'knowing resorting under being'.
But the current discussion is post-1923, hence the assumption of the presence of cosmic being, as law-spheres and their laws, is relevant. Value brings the relevance of being 'to light' (as it were). The awareness of cosmic being takes place as the intuitive valuing of what is given, an awareness yielding "judgments of discerning or of existence". These judgments—in 1930, as we stated, they are referred to as "assessments"—affirm a presence (existence) of distinct modality (discerned).[88] We see immediately that this intuition of the value of being combines in one what was formerly distributed over the metaphysical intuition (identity of distinctive being) and the metalogical intuition (of the adequate understanding of being). Combined, they allow one to transform a given of being into a presupposition for knowledge. Because the discerned pertains fundamentally to law-spheres and their modal characterization, this 'assessment' turns the law-sphere as assessed into a "gezichtsveld", a "field of vision" or "region",[89] which serves to meet the ends of knowledge. These fields are fundamental towards delineating the epistemic situation: on the one hand the valued presence is now attended to as something *knowable* (object of attention or of discerning) in a context that is subject to law, on the other hand the focus of the valuing embodies the *interest in knowing* in the acknowledgment of value (hence: striving to know, reflecting a 'prepared' situation that the knowing agent finds him-/herself in). Thus the order of the law-spheres supports an 'order of associated fields of vision', which is the order of the cosmos as knowable.[90] So the former 'metalogical intuition' loses its distinct sense, at least it cannot be used to denote an involvement in a *'Gegenstand* sphere' that is separate from an acknowledged order of reality, as in critical realism. Knowing resorts *under* being, thus 'the metalogical' has an ineluctable 'metaphysical' facet as well. Later (as we said) Vollenhoven calls this order of knowledge, or general epistemic situation, 'the noetic' (*het gnotische*), this being the

---

88   The 'judgments of existence or of discerning', these being based in the intuition of modality (Vollenhoven 1926a: 9, 28) and themselves the basis of concept formation (*op. cit.* : 25, 28, 63), do not have a subject-predicate form. Vollenhoven represents an existence judgment as 'A is'; hence a subject-predicate judgment, having the form 'S is P', is built up from 'S is' and 'P is' (*op. cit.* : 14, 60). Vollenhoven would appear to be following Brentano in this analysis of a complex judgment (*op. cit.* : 60). For a study of Brentano's logic, cf. "Chapter 3. Brentano's reform of logic" of Simons 1992: 41-69.

89   On this terminology, cf. chapter 3, section III.E.3, especially footnote 173.

90   In Vollenhoven's epistemological writings of 1926, the notion of 'field of vision' is sometimes used as a synonym for 'law-sphere'. But officially there is the difference brought on by the intuitive discerning or "assessing" of value.

reality of our everyday and scientific knowing.[91]

On consideration, the interplay of value and being seems problematic. All being is subject to law, but discerned value is dependent upon given attention, which might be haphazard and flighty or concentrated and serious. The 'meeting' of being and value seems difficult to grasp. But when considering that the being, which is subject to law, needs to be a knowable something, and that the attention given it is to yield something that is discerned about it, then the context of values gives a foothold for the distinction of the basic components of a judgment: 'subject' (as the object of attention) and 'predicate' (what is discerned). It would appear that the interplay between value and being is the concern of, and controlled by, *truth*.

d. Truth 'in itself'

The weight Vollenhoven places on truth in his writings of 1926 appears almost overdone. It is over-illuminated, making it difficult to grasp his meaning. Truth is taken to be 'in itself' (Vollenhoven 1926b: 385; 1926a: 51). It is irrelevant to the essence of truth that it is known; validity is an effect of truth when subjectively grasped (1926b: 384). But the main feature of truth is that it is the kernel of knowledge. Because knowledge calls for an agent and an object known, the knowledge situation is, in general, that of 'an agent possessing truth about something' (1926b: 381; 1926d: 54). The heart of this '(agent) possessing truth about (something)' is that truth signals the *state* of connection, a '*systasis*' between agent and something; it does not (i.e. no longer) signal(s) a process of synthesis, of coming together, involving only agent and object.[92] It is a genuine 'third factor', beside agent (subject) and something (object) (1926b: 395; 1926d: 56). So knowledge, as truth possessed about something, might be loosely described as 'understood cosmic connections', or 'cosmic connections rightly grasped'. In any case, cognition is *threesome*, no longer assumed to involve only subject (agent) and object.[93]

We will not go into a detailed discussion of Vollenhoven's epistemological views at this point, preferring to focus on the broader

---

91   Vollenhoven 1948p: 16.

92   1926a: 11: "But knowing is truth possession: it is *systasis*, not synthesis, certainly a state of affairs, least of all act."

93   There is an intriguingly similar analysis of *volition* in René Girard, in his distinguishing, besides subject (agent who desires) and object (what is desired), also the required presence of a 'third factor', namely the model who mediates the desire. Desire is analysed as being 'triangular'; cf. Girard 1965. In Girard's later work he also emphasizes the biblical 'logos of love'.

epistemic context and its basic set-up.[94] What calls for clarification is the distinction between knowing and thinking. Only then do we get to see what the 'small-*l* logos' amounts to in the revisions Vollenhoven introduces.

e. Truth known
Knowledge's resorting under being implies, among other things, that the knowing agent and the object known are embedded in valued being, i.e. they are embedded in discerned law-spheres and as such stand in subjection to the laws/norms of law-spheres. Thus the most primitive judgments (in the sense of being 'prime') are judgments (or assessments, as we saw) of discerning the general modal characterization of things and of one's own involvement. The knowing agent knows itself to be 'instated' in reality in such a way as to involve, among other things, the 'task' (or 'interest') of understanding appropriately (Vollenhoven 1926b: 382). The human agent is not a collector of impressions, though impressions are involved at a psychical-perceptual level. Understanding does not take place by forming a synthesis of sense-data. This is evident when considering our everyday knowledge.

Much of what we know is *conveyed* to us, accepted on trust, the truth assumed. Knowledge that is conveyed brings us in the know (when true) about something of being. One might be told that an earthquake has set up a tsunami, that the neighbour broke his arm, that a niece got the highest marks in the exams, that this or that political party won the elections and will now form the next government, etc., etc. We assume without question the relevance of the levels of reality involved in such cases: geological, physiological-organic, educational, political-juridical, etc. Of course, one can throw doubt on such claims and set about to investigate their truth. But not everything can be investigated, certainly not all at once, nor even in series. Very many claims are, practically speaking, never doubted, relying as we do on the truthfulness of the conveyer. Knowledge is embedded in reality as lived, and truth partakes of its structure. We apportion knowledge in accordance with the (modal) level of subjection (of the 'field of vision') that is relevant to the statements made.[95]

---

94   For a more detailed discussion, cf. "Chapter 7: Logos, states of affairs, and knowledge" of Kok 1992: 233-290.
95   From 1932 on, Vollenhoven stated in 2005d/e, **154**, that "in the nature of the case, coming to know differs modally according to the law-sphere within which it takes place". He restricts (as he states) his discussion of the "knowing connection" to the analytical law-sphere, but this connection is present and relevant in the 'supra-analytical' law-

f. Truth acquired: thought

Now knowledge may also be *acquired*, as well as being conveyed. When acquired, one proceeds from an absence of the appropriate knowledge and sets out to seek the truth.[96] One then calls upon *thought* in a more direct or focussed way than is the case when knowledge is conveyed. For one must now make the necessary distinctions in light of relevant differences and place things in relations that evidently belong together. This 'more focussed way' of proceeding involves a choice on the part of the knowing agent to subject itself to typically logical or analytical norms. Here the 'logical law-sphere'—the 'created, little-*l* logos'—is brought to bear. The 'logical function of subjection' is that of making distinctions and connections, subject to logical norms (i.e. the principle of identity, the principle of contradiction, etc.). But the 'thinking agent' brings this analytical functioning to bear on the content that is thought about. What we have is a situation in which the knowing subject, by using the logical function, focuses on a knowable topic that is now investigated as to intrinsic differences and connections. In the attempt to discover truth, the knowing agent *participates* in the search for truth by means of the logical functioning, and the known object is treated as *represented* by the differences and connections being searched. For representation to be possible, one must assume that the relevant context of the known object has 'an analogy' of the logical sphere, in being analysable.

The logical law-sphere itself concerns the business of analysing and connecting. This matches the primary functions of distinguishing and relating. Hence the "logical essence *par excellence*" is "the 'relation'."[97]

In his epistemological work of 1926 this "logical essence" is applied in such a way that the logical law-sphere lays bare its two sides: the formal or schematic side and a material or content side.[98] Relation, in its 'logical essence', is then described as the 'logical schema'[99] of "a system

spheres as well. One needs to keep this broad modal setting in mind, for the context in which this is stated is the discussion of 'everyday knowledge', not the scientific knowledge of the specific sciences.

96   For the distinction between conveyed and acquired, cf. Vollenhoven 1926b: 382-383; 1926d: 58.

97   Vollenhoven 1925c: 393.

98   Every law-sphere has, as will be pointed out later, a general and a particular 'side', as relevant for its standing in subjection to the law/norm. The ancestor of this view is the '*Gegenstand* sphere', with its two sides of form and content.

99   Vollenhoven first spoke of "contentless truth" (i.e. formal truth) in 1926b and in the first instalment of 1926d; in the second instalment of the latter article he switched to using "logical schema"; cf. 1926d: 178, footnote 1; 179, footnote 2, and 188 footnote 1; also cf. footnote 6 above.

of a relation with (in the simplest case) two moments, which moments become relata by virtue of the relation".[100] It is the instrument for *drawing distinctions* (by virtue of the difference between moments) and *laying connections* via the relation. But this is formal or general. It needs to be met with content that particularizes the logical schema. Vollenhoven draws up the following correlations:[101]

General logical schema:		Particular state of affairs:
- system	(is modulated by)	- the modality
- the relation	(is modulated by)	- the essential connection
- the moments	(are modulated by)	- the *Gegenstände*

At this particular point, the states of affairs are particularized content *in the logical law-sphere* as representative *of what is real* or at least of what is outside of the logical law-sphere. To illustrate, the logical schema might be indicated as 'a-R-b', i.e. the simplest case of two moments, *a* and *b*, that stand in the relation R. Then this can be 'particularized' in a host of ways, say: psychically as 'Anne kisses Bob', arithmetically as '5 exceeds 2', in a juridical sense as 'Judge Jackson convicts criminal Carl', etc. Each case is qualified in a modally distinct sense, but in each there are (two) terms (*Gegenstände*) taken as standing in a relation that fits the modality in question. Each of these statements is a much reduced sketch of a broader reality, whereby the reduction focuses on the 'relational facet' by means of which the reality can be represented in the logical law-sphere.

We add the remark that each law-sphere has a characteristic 'essential connection', appropriate to the modality in question, which forms the basis of a 'general truth' for that law-sphere. This puts the concern about the synthetic a priori to rest. Also, concepts are forthcoming when considering that different *Gegenstände* can be placed in the position of relatum of a relation, yielding cases of 'the so-being of this or that' (Vollenhoven 1926b: 393). Setting up the represented content in the relational schema—encumbering the logical schema (1926d: 58)—is an essential part of the logic of inquiry, being the way basic concepts and judgments get to be formulated. This is how the truth is gained as mediated by the logical law-sphere.

---

100 Vollenhoven 1926b: 397, cf. also 1926d: 57. In this formulation the relation is no longer a factor dependent upon the (particularised) relata, taken as being prior to the relation, as is the case in the monadological understanding of a relation in Vollenhoven earliest work. As discussed in chapter 2, the basic relations are now taken to be 'external'; cf. chapter 2, V.B.

101 Vollenhoven 1926b: 397; also 1926d: 57.

g. Method
But besides gaining (*verwerven*) knowledge there is also its "*verwerken*", its processing. This is a matter of methodology and no longer the direct concern of logic (Vollenhoven 1926d: 59-60). Each encumbrance of the logical schema that represents a different modality gives rise to different concepts and judgments. When intermixing concepts and judgments of different modality, a confusion of method arises, which can in turn give rise to antinomies. Modally different encumbrances form the basis of different sciences. But in each modally distinct science, one can investigate its states of affairs in either of two ways, or two 'directions': (i) one may *resolve* a term by taking it itself to be a unity of system of terms standing in a relation; in this way one proceeds in the *way of analysis*; (ii) one may *compose* a term by merging given terms via a relation to form a new (systematic) unity; in this way one proceeds in the *way of synthesis*.[102]

The fact that matters of non-logical law-spheres can be represented in the logical law-sphere as states of affairs is due to a certain 'connection'— itself a '*systasis*', a 'standing together', not a synthesis—between the logical and the other law-spheres. This is evidenced by each of the non-logical law-spheres' having an analogy of the logical system-of-related-terms. This makes it possible to meet the content of the non-logical law-sphere in a logical way.[103] This connection of analogy (*systasis*) between law-

---

102   In 1926d: 158) and in 1926a: 58) Vollenhoven spoke of "*simplicerende* [sic] en complicerende richtingen", i.e. 'simplicating [thus] and complicating directions. In *Isagôgè Philosophiae* this became resolution and complication. In the methodology of science there are various ways in which the dual method of analysis and synthesis is applied, a classical application being that used in geometry by the ancient Greeks; cf. Hintikka and Remes 1974. Vollenhoven's application is 'dialectical' in that it moves between unity and diversity, not with a view of cancelling either but towards showing complexity in unity and connectedness in diversity. I shall refer to the route of "complicering" as that of composition.

103   I make mention of the fact that, in a fuller discussion, the differences in the order of the law-spheres would need to be taken into account. In the work of 1926, the logical law-sphere is the lowest in the cosmic order. Every non-logical law-sphere has an analogy by virtue of the fact that the lowest law-sphere is presupposed by every other law-sphere. About early 1927, the logical law-sphere is moved to its position immediately above the psychical law-sphere. The law-spheres that are then 'sub-logical' no longer contain an analogy of the logical sphere. They do have so-called 'anticipations' of the logical law-sphere. But, in Vollenhoven, anticipations are actual only when mediated by creatures who function in the anticipated law-sphere. In this case (of the logical law-sphere) only human beings can fulfil this mediating role. How we have to see this role in connection with the natural sciences remains uncertain (cf. Vollenhoven 1926msA, section 22b). There is also, more or less simultaneous with the shift in position of the logical law-sphere, a change in the view of states of affairs. In the work of 1926, states of affairs are representations, in the logical sphere, of the logical analogy in the non-logical spheres.

spheres cannot be investigated or derived, for it is presupposed in any investigation that involves thought, i.e. that involves the distinguishing of difference and the relating of what is connected.

h. Concluding summary

The general conclusion of this (all too brief) discussion is that the former role of the analytical intuition, namely of helping to provide the connection between subjective and objective rationality, is completely redefined. The divine Logos' role itself is no longer seen as disposing the harmony of subject and object. It is now taken as 'revealing' (or focussing on) the fundamental difference between knowing and straying, in 'commanding' that knowledge be pursued in love and error abated. This places the 'problem of the synthesis of subject and object' entirely in the human-creaturely context of that which is subject to the divine Logos, whereby this 'standing in subjection' is evident in the *value that being has for knowing*. It is first and foremost a matter of the *intuition of discerning* to pick up on this value, which results in an explicit awareness of the modal diversity that is grounded in the cosmos.

Within the awareness of this modal diversity, knowledge and thought have their distinct roles. Knowledge is a matter of possessing truth. Truth attests to the connection of knowing agent and known object. Truth is not itself a confluence of agent and object, but a genuine 'third factor'. Thought, in turn, operates explicitly with the possibility that is provided by the 'created logos', this being itself a 'logical law-sphere' in the cosmic order of the law-spheres. This 'created logos' contains the logical schema with which one explicitly distinguishes and connects. The logical schema becomes operational when encumbered with content from another law-sphere, as represented in (or through) the logical law-sphere. This 'small-*l* logos' indeed provides or supports a connection between subject and object. But the subject is the thinking agent, i.e. the Self as bearing the *logical quality of subjection*, and the object is the *something knowable*, as represented by means of the logical relevance of content. Both the subjective and the objective are contextualized in the cosmic order. Thus the model of an order of thought coming into agreement with an order of being is entirely superseded.

So truth, when possessed as knowledge, sits (so to speak) in between

But this is changed so that each law-sphere is considered to have its own states of affairs in a primary way. Cf. Vollenhoven 2005d/e, **173**; also 2010, **173**, and also the cosmological discussion below. In any case, this development at the 'philosophy of science' level takes notions from the prior context of critical realism and incorporates them in the burgeoning cosmological insights; cf. also chapter 3, section II.C.4.c.

thought and intuition; it is presupposed by the former and contextualized by the latter. Truth connects, in the cosmic order, the human being's *discerning* on the one hand with the *value of being* when known on the other. In that sense, truth assumes one's getting the cosmic connections right, if the ordering of one's concepts are to be dependable. In that light, the 'boundary of the cosmos', which delineates the latter's scope, is relevant to truth. The following citation of a text of 1932 brings the essentials together:

> The principle according to which concepts are ordered, then, is no longer that of the genetic order in which they came to the knower at the time but another one entirely. The significance of the arenas [i.e. law-spheres/fields of view; A.T.] involved depends on the extension they have according to the knower. As a result, it is crucial that when ordering these concepts one sees their extensions and their mutual relations correctly. For example, if you take the area of that which is created too narrowly, you will end up deifying that part of the cosmos that, as you see it, falls outside it [i.e. 'partial theism'; A.T.] and you will begin to ask all kinds of questions about the relationship between the parts of the one cosmos, which in this way have been thrown asunder, and so on. That makes it clear why whether one bows to the Word revelation [Logos] helps to decide about the value [and disvalue/non-value; "*waarde en onwaarde*"] of such an ordering. One who obeys God's Word can certainly still err when it comes to details, but one who does not arrives at concepts that are false in their basic structure.[104]

4. Creator and creation

A subtle but decisive change also occurs in Vollenhoven's 'Trinitarian theistic' position in connection with the creation, the prime work of the Father, as governed by the divine Counsel. The basis or 'metaphysics' of Vollenhoven's cosmology has so far remained in the background. Naturally, this topic was essential to (critical) realism, for cosmology was also the main prop in the earlier work. But the attention given it was primarily focussed on its supporting role in the metalogical discussions of epistemology and philosophy of science. (We found this to be the case in the early work of both Vollenhoven and Dooyeweerd, as discussed in chapters 2 and 3.) But enough came through to be able to at least discern its main outline.

a. The metaphysics of ideas

Vollenhoven initially viewed the cosmos, as we saw, as secured metaphysically in ideas, realistically understood. Ideas are the principles of distinctive being, of general and particularized essences. As general

---

104 Vollenhoven 2005d/e, **182**. The text stems from 1932, with small changes introduced in subsequent editions, for which cf. 2010, **182**.

essences they govern the species of creatures. When individuated, they serve as the 'thing-laws' of individual beings, controlling a thing's appearances and development and the connections to other things. Ideas are metaphysically present in the divine predestining Counsel, which makes them primarily subject to the will of God the Father or Creator. Cosmology studies the whole terrain in which individual things play-out their predestined roles, in seeming interaction with each other. Vollenhoven referred to this cosmology as a monadology (cf. chapter 2), which was apt. The name most famously associated with a monadology is that of G.W. Leibniz (1646-1716). He (Leibniz) was himself aware of standing in the tradition of an Aristotelian-based theory of substance, which combined "a prominent strand of Platonic, Neoplatonic, and Augustinian teaching, particularly the thesis (shared in a long line of Christian thinkers) that the ideas of things in the mind of God functioned as archetypes of God's creation."[105]

But Vollenhoven did not have to have a special inclination towards Leibniz (indeed, he didn't) when formulating his early view of the cosmos and its security in metaphysical ideas. The Reformed tradition itself is no stranger to the view in question, it being in essence a scholastic view. The principal proponents of the Free University in its early years—Abraham Kuyper, Jan Woltjer, Herman Bavinck, etc.—were later targeted by Vollenhoven and Dooyeweerd as having been too accommodating towards scholasticism.[106] Thus, Vollenhoven, who attended the grammar school of which Woltjer was also rector, imbibed this influence already in his secondary education and through his university training. The Free University itself expressed an understanding of the "Reformed principles", referred to in "Article 2" of its statutes, in a way that presupposes the distinction of subjective and objective rationality. The Senate of the university once explained: "under 'principles' is to be understood, not those points of departure which lie in the facts and in the essence of things, but such principles as control, in consciousness, the world of thought."[107]

In terms of immediate influence, the person who was most noticeably

---

105 Antognazzi 2009: 52.

106 Recall Dooyeweerd's criticism in this regard, as formulated in his "Kuyper's wetenschapsleer" (1939); cf. footnote 140 in chapter 3.

107 *Publicatie van den Senaat der Vrije Universiteit, in zake het onderzoek ter bepaling van den weg die tot de kennis der Gereformeerde beginselen leidt* (Publication of the senate of the Free University regarding the inquiry towards determining the way that leads to knowledge of the Reformed principles), J. Woltjer, rector, A. Kuyper, abactis (Woltjer and Kuyper 1895: 8). Cf. the discussion of this document in chapter 1.

present in Vollenhoven's early life was, undoubtedly, the classicist, Jan Woltjer (1849-1917).[108] Kuyper was no longer teaching at the Free University when Vollenhoven entered its halls, and Woltjer had impressed Vollenhoven already in his high school years, before Bavinck came into the picture. Woltjer became Vollenhoven's university mentor. His death prevented him from guiding Vollenhoven in the actual completion of his dissertation, a role which then fell, more or less perfunctorily, to Wilhelm Geesink, who did most of the teaching in philosophy at the time.

In Woltjer we find a strong and explicit defence of the harmony between subjective and objective rationality. He speaks of "an agreement between our minds and nature". To paraphrase his wording: He states that, because we find that our deducing of concepts and ideas from other concepts and ideas in the mind traces the same path as the things of nature, we are obliged to conclude (i) that there are ideas in nature, which are also realized in nature, and (ii) that because ideas in our minds result from a thinking subject, this must also be the case with the ideas in nature.[109] Ideas play a central role. "The idea, expressed in the things, is the unity in the plurality of relations, given with each thing, the whole in the parts" (Woltjer, J. 1896: 214). That ideas also serve as 'thing-laws' is evident from a statement such as: "More real than the perceptible world is the world of ideas, of imperceptible things, that control the perceptible [things]" (Woltjer, J. 1901: 152). This has full cosmic implications. "But the idea also controls the connections and relations of things mutually, each time in wider circles climbing up to *the idea of the whole of the cosmos*, which encloses the harmonious whole of all relations in what is creaturely. In that way, through ideas, that which is viewed becomes knowledge, and the knowledge elevates itself to science and science to wisdom" (Woltjer, J. 1896: 214; emphasis added).

Woltjer summarizes, by way of conclusion, his basic thoughts about the ideal and the real in the following way.

> The ideal exists, in the first place, as the eternal thoughts of God, His specifications [*bestek*] and His Counsel [ideas; archetypes], according to which He has brought forth all that is created in its being and becoming and in their countless relations, both as to being and as to consciousness. — The ideal exists, in the second place, objectified, as ectype, in the cosmos and in the human being, to the extent that both, in their resemblance as well as in their opposition, are the effect of the one plan of creation. This objecti-

---

108   On J. Woltjer, cf. the book length study of H. van der Laan (Van der Laan 2000); also Vollenhoven's short article under "Woltjer, Jan", with the addendum by K.A. Bril, in Vollenhoven 2005c: 441-442. Cf also footnote 110 below.

109   Woltjer, J. 1896: 211. All translations of the Woltjer citations are mine.

fication or positing can be called—over against the ideas themselves—the real, but then from this it immediately follows that the ideal cannot be of less value in connection with *being* than the real, but is the ground on which this real exists. [—] Finally, the ideal exists in the mind of the human being or humankind, for, being created according to God's image, by virtue of this spiritual capacity, he can know, from out of the cosmos, the ideas that are objectified in the cosmos, and in that way he carries in himself a distinct world of ideas which, to the extent that they are rooted in the essence, connection and the order of God's creation, form his science. (Woltjer, J. 1896: 218)

These citations, selected to be sure to indicate their close proximity to the early Vollenhoven and Dooyeweerd in their 'critical realism', do not touch on Woltjer's defence and argument, on his analysis of thought and language, nor on the hermeneutical principles he maintained in his orientation to classical antiquity. The more precise similarity and difference with Woltjer need not be pursued here.[110] However, a noticeable difference is Vollenhoven's appeal to the intuition, which is not evident in Woltjer, as the means of acquiring certainty about the harmony of the subjective and the objective orders. Thus Vollenhoven was creative in working within his mentor's framework. The influence on Vollenhoven was effective through the high respect and admiration he felt towards Woltjer, as Christian scholar and thinker. But however sustained and positive Vollenhoven's feelings were in this regard, this attitude did not detract from his realizing, in time, that this '*logos*-tradition' needed reforming.[111]

b. 'Substance-phenomenon' philosophy
The criticism that Vollenhoven directs against the metaphysics of the *logos*-tradition is aimed, not at Woltjer in any direct sense, but at essential features of his *own* implementation of that tradition, as monadology.

---

110   For a balanced and exploratory discussion of J. Woltjer's thought, cf. Kok 2007: 41-64, in Sweetman 2007a. Dooyeweerd offers a critical discussion of J. Woltjer's thought in Dooyeweerd 1939. The knowledge that Dooyeweerd himself, up to about 1928, held to ideas, in the sense that he later criticized in Woltjer, throws a new light on that discussion.
111   In Vollenhoven 1926d: 191, Vollenhoven responds to a paper, entitled "Over de beteekenis der natuurwetten" (On the meaning of laws of nature) by R.H. Woltjer, a son of J. Woltjer (Woltjer, R.H. 1925). He refers to "the so highly esteemed father, also by me" in the context of which he criticizes Woltjer senior's "Ideëel en reëel". He mentions in particular J. Woltjer's acceptance of "the subject-object schema" of knowledge, which does not allow for 'truth' as distinct factor; "its terrain then has to be spread over subject and object, and in semi-idealism is attributed [entirely] to the subject. This results in the doctrine of the logos being immanent in the subject."

He characterizes this as 'substance-phenomenon' philosophy.[112] The substance of things lies in their ideas, their principle of unity, while what we know of a thing comes by way of the interaction with what the phenomena reveal. This 'knowledge by acquaintance' (cf. chapter 2, section V.D.) is supplemented by the metaphysical intuition, through which one attains a direct grasp of a being's identity, despite the change of motion and the variety of species among individuals (Vollenhoven 1918a: 351). In other words, the metaphysical intuition offers a grasp of the idea of a thing, as its substance or 'thing-law' (inner principle), thereby supplementing what is not come by via the outer approach of knowledge by acquaintance. Taken together there is knowledge of the complete whole of substance and phenomena. What gives critical point to this philosophy is its anthropological application. There is body and soul, each an 'incomplete' substance—incomplete in that each is (only) a part of the human being: the psycho-physical body being animal-like, and the mental soul, "angelic-like"—that together constitute the whole of the human being (the Self). As 'complete' substance, the Self combines the two incomplete substances, making a human person to be a unique complex being. The soul, in being an immortal substance, is controlled by an idea with implications as to its predestination in eternity.[113] Isn't the notion of substance just what Christian thought would embrace?

i. The 'substance-phenomenon schema' deconstructed
Vollenhoven has two critical discussions of substance-phenomenon philosophy. The first is in *Logos en Ratio*, in the part where he discusses ancient philosophy (cf. 1926a: 8-11). Here he sees the rise of the notion of substance as idea. The gist of the matter is that the discovery of cognition in ancient philosophy is predicated on a limited, perceptual schema. Vollenhoven finds it to be inadequate. The Sophists, Socrates and Plato are influential in its formation.

---

112 As described by Vollenhoven, Leibniz's monads or 'atoms' "have a kernel . . . called 'soul'; the body is the visible circumference or appearing, from which two forms, space and time, can be abstracted" (Vollenhoven 1926a: 41). Should one fail to notice an autobiographical undercurrent here, then the next sentence has added significance. "Not the sphere [of sphere sovereignty] with its laws is the point of departure here, but the animated [literally: "besouled"] individual substance." The new point of departure of sphere sovereignty is integral to the intersection principle (cf. discussion below).

113 In connection with the human being one should not confuse the concrete and the metaphysical intuitions in the early Vollenhoven. The metaphysical intuition is an immediate awareness of being or presence in its identity, while the concrete intuition is the awareness of experience, namely of being affected when affected (e.g. when remembering, the awareness that I remember).

The Sophists introduce the subject-object distinction, but they implement this in the context of the human being, who seeks to dominate the environment by means of *logos* (thought expressed in speech). This striving for control is looked on as an exclusive and privileged form of humanism, for the human being is the measure of all things.

Socrates, in looking for a more objective ground of judgments, turns to defining concepts in terms of representations that are more 'general' than those of normal perception, the latter being particular. The perceptual context induces the demand that the general and particular awareness on the part of the human subject be objectively secured in a similar distinction on the part of the (perceived) object in the environment. The feature of generality controls something in the object that is of 'greater scope' than the feature of particularity. Thus the former is correlated to a concept, the latter to representations of perception.

Plato advances on Socrates' work. He proceeds from a more anthropologically secured notion of the human subject. The human being has an inner and an outer reality. The outer is bodily, and through its sense-organs, perception takes place. The inner being is intellectual, where cognition, and hence concept formation, takes place. Now, because Plato also accepts the subject-object context of the human subject and its environment, with its emphasis on control, a primary difference on the side of the human being calls for a corresponding difference on the side of the object or environment. "This is then modelled on an anthropology, so that, as in a human being, there is an inner and an outer side; the outer is the appearing, which addressed the sense-organs, the inner is the essence, which is known by means of concepts" (*op. cit.*, p. 10).[114] What Socrates termed 'general' is in Plato 'essential', and the former's 'particular' has in Plato become—Vollenhoven says "degraded to the rank of"—'appearance'. We have in fact a glorification of the intelligible. Concepts are honoured as being "the key enabling one to unlock the secrets hidden behind the appearance".[115] In Platonism cognition "is

---

114 One recognizes readily that Vollenhoven is referring to the image of the proportions of the divided line in Plato's *Republic* VI 509. There is first of all the difference in the human knowing and the reality known. In each, Plato draws a line and makes an analogous division between perception and cognition in human knowing and the perceptual and the intelligible on the part of reality. For his discussion here, Vollenhoven does not need the further division Plato makes in each line segment. On the human side, perception is divided into imagining (*eikasia*) and belief (*pistis*), and cognition into thinking (*dianoia*) and intelligence/knowledge (*noesis/episteme*); on the side of reality, in analogous proportion, Plato has images, visible things, mathematical objects and forms/ideas. Cf. Plato 1977: 221-223.

115 *Ibid.* The (classical, Platonic) low ranking of knowing (as a knowing about, as

exalted into a magic wand that forced the 'inner side of nature' to disclose its treasures" (*op. cit.*, p. 11). This inner nature is the essence, which Plato calls 'forms or ideas'.

However much cognition is venerated in Platonism, it cannot be denied that cognition is looked upon as a kind of 'higher perception'. One starts with things in their environment, as phenomena to be explained. Essences, as 'higher objects', retain a link with the perceived objects in that the latter are taken to be exemplifications of the higher objects. This enables the higher objects (as forms or ideas) to operate as the controlling principle of things, their 'thing-law'. The mind enables the human being to conceive ideas, much as the sense-organs allow the human being to perceive empirical things.

Vollenhoven now takes distance from this view. He insists that perception and knowing/cognition are of different orders.[116] Each involves the "whole human being" but in different ways, without the one being in the extension of the other (Vollenhoven 1926a: 37). When perceiving, "the soul is directed by the sense-organs towards the material that is within and outside of the body" giving rise to representations (data). Representations evidence that something is 'known about' the perceived object in the human environment. That is of value to science, as means of verification. But this is not a knowing that implicates truth; it is psychological (*op. cit.*: 11). In perception the duality of subject and object suffices, but for cognition one needs the threesome: subject, object and truth.[117] We readily see that this separation of perception

---

belief) over against the exalted position of concepts is continued in modern philosophy via Descartes. In a letter to Marin Mersenne (27 May 1630), Descartes states that one can know without comprehending. "[I]t is possible to know that God is infinite and all-powerful although our soul, being finite, cannot comprehend or conceive Him. . . . To comprehend something is to embrace it in one's thought; to know something it is sufficient to touch it with one's thought" (Descartes 1970: 15). This tradition is behind the use of 'adequate concept', as the aim of progressing towards the complete knowledge (comprehension) of the idea.

116   Vollenhoven 1926d: 178: "Knowing is something other than perceiving. On both terrains, one deals with at least two subjects [i.e. agent and object] that stand in a relationship. The nature of the relationship is determined by the terrain. The relation of knowing is a *different* one from that of perceiving." Also: "Concept and representation differ *toto caelo*. . . . [T]he human being who perceives [i.e. represents] creates the more or less, individually different, free reproduction of a perceived figure; whereas understanding [i.e. forming a concept] is bringing together a form [logical schema] and a content [state of affairs]. . ." (1926a: 9).

117   The full quotation is: "For indeed the whole human being is active, both when knowing and when perceiving, but that is not to say that both of these activities lie in each other's extension: when perceiving, the soul is directed by the sense-organs towards

and cognition undercuts Vollenhoven's former view of knowledge by acquaintance. That too is a perceptual procedure. But it was taken as involving a synthesis of subject and object, whereby the knowing subject processes and works over the data, yielding truth. Such a synthesis, so we found, is now rejected by Vollenhoven, and this has direct implications for the epistemic status of perception/acquaintance.[118]

The chief criticism levelled at the view of cognition being in the 'extension' of perception is the confusion concerning cognition. As Vollenhoven has it, the kind of rapport that the "whole human being" has in the cognitive contact with reality has to do with truth. To that end one must grasp the being of what is conceived. In cognition, one is focussed on what is present to mind, resulting in an 'assessments of existence', that brings the modality of being to the fore. This is not itself any 'higher object', but it is a making explicit the basic characterization of what is conceived. But when the perceptual schema controls cognition, the relevance of discerning the mode of being threatens to be overlooked in favour of assuming that one is focussing on an (inner or higher) 'object'.[119] In fact, such an object is the result of hypostatization. What should be taken as the awareness of modality becomes the awareness of an essence.

Thus the substance-phenomenon schema is now unserviceable. The substance (essence) is a pseudo-object, while the phenomena are merely the appearances of things as perceived. The 'substance' that the phenomena 'reveal' is just the concrete thing as bearer of the appearances. When it comes to truths about the thing, one needs to focus on its modalities of being, the law-spheres relevant to it.[120] These are not controlled by

the material that is within and outside of the body, when knowing, it is directed towards truth..." (1926a: 37).

118 The representations of perception are said to act as 'truth-marks', analogous to the way a trademark is relevant for the product it marks. The distinction of perception and cognition is also important in connection with concept formation. Concepts do not derive from representation, but arise within the application of the relational 'logical schema'. However, representations can be organized into a system that provides orientation for perception. Aristotle took abstract representations for concepts, which long "hindered insight in the essence of concept formation" (Vollenhoven 1926d: 149).

119 Cf. the quote in footnote 116 above. Cf. also Vollenhoven 1926a: 9.

120 Consider: "Indeed, in the human being the function[s] of perceiving and knowing go hand in hand. To these are correlated objects of perception and truths [respectively]. But these two do not stand to each other as appearance and essence. The essence is a cosmic unity [= individual], and some truths, namely the metaphysical ones, are indeed truths about them. But there are many truths that don't deal with essences but concern their intersections, namely [truths] about essences to the extent that they lie in a distinct law-sphere" (Vollenhoven 1926a: 10).

the thing's essence, but they are governed by the laws/norms (modal injunctions) that hold for the modalities in question. In deconstructing this substance-phenomenon schema, Vollenhoven also rejects the subject-object context it presupposes, as well as rejecting the kind of domination or control that is deemed suitable for that context. Ideas that control a thing's appearances and development dominate in *a different way* from the way injunctions govern in connection with functions. Injunctions presuppose 'room' (the ontological difference) for response, something which is not entailed by ideas that control a thing.

ii. Contra the dualist anthropology
The second discussion of substance-phenomenon philosophy is an anthropological application in the lecture "The first questions of psychology" (Vollenhoven 1930b: 14-15). In this discussion, which is not geared to give a careful analysis but is more intent on sketching a trend of religious thought, Vollenhoven offers the mind-set, outside of the biblical tradition, that supports a dualistic anthropology.

Vollenhoven proceeds from the assumption that there has always been some sense of a cosmic order. Human beings function in more complex ways than animals, and these in turn are more complex than plants. When placed in one context we have the view of a primal self-contained unity, a substance, on which everything else depends and is thought to be appearance (*op. cit.*: 14). I believe we can interpret this as the common background of views that can subsequently be developed in monistic or dualistic ways. It will be pantheistic (monistic) when there is no definitive difference between the substantial unity and the appearances. But when difference is taken into account, we may have either partial theistic or partial cosmistic schemata (cf. section II.B. above for discussion of these terms).

This common background suggests that God and cosmos are thought to be arranged in a vertical order. The expression made famous by Arthur Lovejoy, in his "The great chain of being", readily comes to mind.[121] Plato's elevation of ideas and intelligence found a classical and elaborate application in Neoplatonism's order of being. Augustine's accommodation of this in a Christian context influenced Christian scholars to find this acceptable. The whole medieval period felt the pull of this accommodation. A scholastic notion of objective rationality resulted, in which there are in God governing ideas of being that are realized in the order of the cosmos.

---

121   Lovejoy 1960.

Vollenhoven does not object to the acceptance of a (vertical) 'cosmic order'. Indeed, ever since 1926 (as we saw) this is the backbone of his work.[122] What he objects to is taking the relation between God and the world as an application of the schema of substance and appearance. In that application, God is, as substance, the highest point of security, on which the cosmos depends, in the sense of its being phenomena or appearances (emanations) of this substance. This gives rise to a 'centre-periphery' effect, inducing a scale of worth: whatever is closest to the centre is more 'worthy', in its having more intrinsic merit than what is farther away and inexorably deficient, "more ephemeral, a thicker cloak, more chance contingency, etc." (1930b: 14). This can be made more definitive when an actual division is made, as in partial theism, between what is of positive value, as sharing in the (higher) Godhead, and what negative, disdained, being 'lower' or 'peripheral'.

This sort of a worldview finds a most ready application in anthropology. The mental-intellectual capacities of the human being, taken to be higher than those of the body, are brought in direct conjunction with the divine substance. In that way, substantial value is attributed to the higher functions of the human being, such as immortality, over against the dubious value of the lower functions (mortality).[123] It is against this sort of a background that a dualist anthropology commends itself. "I know that those in our circle, who speak of the metaphysical substance in the human being, usually don't mean to harm. But still this use of substantial thought is not so innocent. . . . It isn't just [innocently] 'self-evident', but it's what [the apostle] Paul calls a really 'natural' [way of thought], . . . of not understanding the things that are of the Spirit of God. Hence it appears to me to be the first demand of Christian thought that we *totally break* with this substance-phenomenon philosophy" (1930b: 15; emphasis added). Vollenhoven concludes that a half-way view of '*substantia incompleta*' does nothing to rectify this context of thought. It appeals to a higher functional or substantial bond with God.

The alternative to all this, according to Vollenhoven, is that of the biblical version. It now becomes clear that when he defends the dualism

---

122 Cf. 1926a: 11, 36, 46, 49, 63.

123 Consider: "Religion is then . . . an *unio substantialis* [substantial union] or *unio functionalis* [functional union]. The way to please God is . . . to retreat from the so-called lesser contingencies on the periphery; [e.g.] one fasted—not out of love of neighbour nor from sorrow, in shame confessing . . . sins, but—from pride, seeking rest in thought. When not letting the sense organs function, and ignoring the consciousness of pain and representation, the provisional ideal is reached, for nothing remains to be distinguished . . . by the analytical function after having turned inward to the Self" (Vollenhoven 1930b: 14-15).

of God and cosmos, he does not mean to suggest a vertical arrangement. At issue is a difference-in-being. The religious understanding of this is religion as a *unio foederalis*, a federate union, instead of a functional or substantial one. God and humanity enter into a covenant in which humanity is accorded responsibility in its whole life and interaction with the cosmos, a total 'walk with God'. Here the 'centre-periphery' model has no place, for there is no 'part' of life or of the human being that is intrinsically nearer to God over against other 'parts' that lie farther removed. Here there is no incentive to introduce a higher-lower split into the human being's self-understanding nor in the human being's life in the world. In other words, though there is a 'vertical' cosmic order, this order is based not on 'worthiness' but on a gradated complexity of law and function. Higher functions of subjection are more complex than lower ones. But each has a boundary, which is an instance of the pervasive boundary between God and the World.[124]

c. Order and law

What, now, is the order of reality according to Vollenhoven? To start with, the basis of order lies in the order of laws. Correlate to this order is the analogous order of the law-spheres. Between the order of laws and the order of the law-spheres there is an ontological difference: the order of laws is grounded in the will of God, the order of the law-spheres delineates the cosmos. God's being is being sovereign, as evidenced by the law-order; that of the cosmos is being subservient in the context of law-spheres. Vollenhoven denies that this correlated order is a rational order, an order that can be viewed as an objective model of rationality by the human being. "The difference between these functions [within law-spheres] is not analytic in nature" (1930b: 17), for the analytical function is itself one within the order. Neither can any other function/law-sphere be the origin of the whole order.

The law-order as boundary between God and the cosmos is an order by virtue of creation. In taking it to be an order, one assumes that differentiation is involved; at the same time it could not be an order without unity. We remarked earlier that in the late 1920s Vollenhoven

---

124 We add two remarks. (i) The difference between laws that are norms and those that are not norms does not define a 'kink' or 'break' in the cosmic order. This difference depends (as we saw) on the degree of consciousness that functions involve. (ii) In some work around 1930 Vollenhoven did use the term 'substance' to indicate the Godhead in its religious role of 'secure ground'. But he did not mean to suggest that he looked on the cosmos as 'appearance'. This use could confuse, thus it is fortunate that it was short-lived. Cf. Vollenhoven 1932d: 397-398.

took the unity of the cosmos to be aesthetic-like. I believe his motive was to avoid referring to some fixed characteristic; hence, the unity there is, is by way of the harmony or concord of the diversity involved. He does not mean to say that each law-sphere has an aesthetic qualification and warns, in any case, against confusing order and law. "For there is an order *of* laws, in the same way that there is an order of the functions [of subjection in law-spheres]. If one identifies order and law, then all kinds of confusion threatens" (Vollenhoven 1933a: 31). Vollenhoven lists three alternatives: either the one order is interpreted as entailing that there is only one 'functional law' (this would immediately invite antinomies); or the multiplicity of functional laws makes one conclude to a multiplicity of arrangements or orders, thereby losing sight of the order of laws; or one functional law is taken as determining the entire cosmic order, with the result that beyond the scope of this functional law there is no order.

To seek a law for the law-order itself is in fact to deny the ultimate boundary character of the law-order. Important to Vollenhoven is what we can and cannot know of this order. In 1930 he expressed it as follows. Functions of subjection are grounded "in an act of creation of God. And because he has created everything and maintains it subject to his will, all things stand under his *laws*, in other words are 'subject to God'. These laws are not hidden: they resort under the revealed part of the will of decision [*wil des besluits*]. Though they are knowable in that which is subject to them, they are not identical to our formulations of them and therefore are not 'wavering'. More specifically, these laws are modally diverse, analogous to the functions that are subject to them" (Vollenhoven 1930b: 17)

I believe that the long and the short of the problem of the 'metaphysics' of the cosmos is given with the phrase "the revealed part of the will of decision". The reference to the will of decision appeals (so I take it) to the divine Counsel that subjects everything to laws. But about that Counsel, only a part is revealed, namely that part that can be surmised by considering what is subject to these laws. In other words, here too the distinction of God, in his transcendence and immanence, is in effect. We can know the immanence of God through the maintaining effect, via law, to which created things are subject. These laws are *modal* laws, they are not 'thing-laws'. In fact, maintenance through modal laws *assumes* that there are creatures that are subject to them, sustained in their being by them. But creatures themselves come forth through the act of creation. This is totally beyond the human ken, for it is grounded in God's transcendence. Creation as such belongs to the 'hidden' part of the will of decision. This hidden part is precisely that part of God's Counsel in which the (platonic) ideas are thought to reside, the ideas that govern the order or set-up of anything creaturely. After 1923 Vollenhoven ceased appealing to such ideas.[125] It makes no sense to appeal to something that is in point of principle hidden from human purview. Obviously, Vollenhoven's very intuitional approach is readjusted.

Vollenhoven's deletion of ideas is not just on account of a theological qualm about the degree to which the mind of God can be known. There is also the matter of the 'metaphysical intuition'. In Vollenhoven's former view, this intuition is the means of acquiring an immediate awareness of the identity of things. But this presupposed a substance-phenomenon schema, in which the principles of distinctive being are thought of in terms of an ideal schema governing the appearances of things. Ideas are controls of order and organization, i.e. 'laws of individuality'. But Vollenhoven has come to understand the being of the cosmos to be a matter of subservience, of being sustained, law-bound, addressed to respond. The being of the cosmos is not a deterministic, predestining principle that includes all that will happen to the cosmos as a whole and to things in particular. The being is its being maintained and sustained by modal laws, allowing the future of the cosmos to be open.[126] The intuition of this being is an awareness of the modal diversity of subjection to law, the foundation of the realist correlation to law. It is no longer fitting to call this a 'metaphysical intuition'. The intuition in question involves the *assessment of distinct modality*. This means that the terms '(modal) law' and 'individual' need to be accepted as *primitive* (in a cognitive sense). This is indeed the case, as our discussion of Vollenhoven's cosmology will show.

Terms that are primitive in a systematic sense still call for motivational discussion. One of the more prominent indicators of 'reckoning with Scripture' is Vollenhoven's statement: God created

---

125   The term 'idea' remained, in light of its Greek ancestry, metaphysically loaded for Vollenhoven in an objectionable sense. In a later context he states, in passing: "in Greek thought ideas are said to be true being" (1952k; Tol and Bril 1992: 86), which shows that the meaning of "idea" remained objectionable to him. Hence he boycotted the very use of the term.

126   This should not be taken as a denial of predestination, which Vollenhoven certainly did not deny. But Vollenhoven's understanding of predestination is predicated on 'God's going along' with the world and his interaction with it in terms of creation, revelation and fulfilment. This is essential to redemptive history, a discussion of which is a fixed topic in *Isagôgè Philosophiae* from the start (in the versions of 1930 and 1931: §§81-94). Cf. the different versions in the text-critical edition, Vollenhoven 2010.

the cosmos and subjected it to his law.[127] One should not overlook the *duality* of being created and standing in subjection. "For a law without something for which it holds is as meaningless as a subject without law."[128] The created cosmos cannot be without law. But that does not mean that created things arise or unfold by means of 'thing-laws'. The ontological difference between law(s) and creaturely function(s) prevents the order of the functions and, more generally, the order of the law-spheres of the cosmos, from being controlled by any 'law of unfolding' or 'law of organization'. Were that the case, then one has not really taken distance from a metaphysical construction in the order of Platonic (thing-)ideas.

d. Creationism?
Creation, and with it the cosmic order and the order of (modal) laws, is accorded a primary status. Is Vollenhoven then a creationist? Taking this in a philosophical sense, the answer is, I believe, "no". For a creationist, the creation is the be-all and end-all of life. The future then has nothing new in store. The 'fall' (traditionally seen) brought about evil, which called for redemption and spirit guidance. In a creationist context, redemption and guidance constitute a return to the original intentions of creation.[129] Wouldn't that introduce a new attempt for human, subjective striving to be in harmony with a (God-)given order?

Vollenhoven's Trinitarian theist position opens to another view. Naturally (speaking theologically) everything starts with creation, and one need not (as indeed Vollenhoven never did) deny that God has a 'plan' with the world. The divine 'will of decision' does not annihilate the ontological difference between the Creator and the world. It is that difference that welcomes further orientation, as offered by divine revelation, prior to any fall, so as to be more properly guided towards God-intended fulfilment. The appearance of evil intensifies revelation and guidance, but the 'fall' did not occasion the first appearance of redemption and guidance. Beside the 'will of decision' there is the 'will

---

127   The wording varies somewhat at different places, but the thought remains constant; cf. Vollenhoven 1926d: 190; 1926a: 7; 1931a: 186 [= 1931g: 392]; 1933a: 23, 24; 2005d/e, **13B**; also in later work, in Tol and Bril 1992: 55, 98, 104-105, 113-114, 123, 138, 156, etc.
128   Vollenhoven 1953l: 104.
129   This I believe includes "the intuition that grace restores nature" said to be central to Herman Bavinck. Cf. Veenhof 2006: 3. In a similar spirit Albert Wolters wrote *Creation Regained. Biblical Basics for a Reformational Worldview* (Wolters 2005). The title chosen for the Dutch translation, *Schepping zonder grens* (Creation without bounds) is even more telling.

of command'. Vollenhoven associates this will with the second Person, the most central command being the love command.[130] And to clinch 'the good life', there is the Spirit that motivates and calls to responsibility. The human being is a 'tasked subject'. However much this comes to be marked by the fall, it is of prelapsarian vintage. Vollenhoven's discussion of good and evil cannot be understood without such a context.

When taking the human condition as a whole, Vollenhoven's understanding of 'covenant religion', as a 'walk with God', does not mean a return to creation, let alone a spiritualist kind of attempt to escape from creation; it assumes all along a *concursus Dei*, of God, in his immanence, going along with 'his work'. Being aware of how prone these thoughts are to speculation, Vollenhoven kept a low profile. But he did once say, as to the present, that among its possibilities God continually chooses one to be realized.[131] Possibility evidences the present's unpredictable openness to the future. To neglect this is to mistake the understanding of the creation in its openness of possibility and its aim of fulfilment. "What are the demands of a Calvinistic philosophy and a Calvinistic logic other than [being] consequences of the confession that the Spirit[!] lives and works in the world of his making?"[132]

The world of his making—what are its chief parameters and features? Vollenhoven's cosmology follows up on the conditions that he has placed the cosmos under. We review this as a distinct topic.

IV. *The cosmological 'intersection principle'*

In light of the rejection of a 'substance-phenomenon' metaphysics, it is fitting to ask what its alternative might be. What view of the cosmos does Vollenhoven now defend? We indicated above that two terms are given 'primitive status': *individual*, i.e. distinct things, such as Aristotle called 'primary substances', and *law-sphere*, i.e. a sphere of response to law that is of distinct modality. In use, these terms never occur separately from each other. "[God] created cosmic unities [= individuals] in such a way that

---

130   This is the "wil des bevels" (will of command), which puts the 'will of decision' in a broader, or at least more practical context. For Christians do not seek rest in a particular function "but only in the functioning of everything, to the extent that this takes place out of love towards God, according to the will of command" (Vollenhoven 1930b: 18). The precise interplay between the love command and the creation order (of modal laws) is subject to some subtle shifts in step with Vollenhoven's placing the moral antithesis of good and evil in a more central position, as of 1932; cf. section V.B. below.

131   In Vollenhoven 1948p: 36, Vollenhoven states: "For the present implies diverse possibilities, from which God each time chooses one to become reality."

132   Vollenhoven 1942m: 2.

they are intersected by diverse law-spheres".[133] This view of intersection, often repeated in *Logos en Ratio* (1926a), is not given a name, but the thought of intersection is fundamental. In his *Hoofdlijnen der Logica* (1948p: 83) Vollenhoven repeats: "These fields of inquiry [= law-spheres in a scientific context] are modal intersections of reality, extending over the whole breadth of the cosmos and they have a universal character." This intersection also plays a central role in *Isagôgè Philosophiae*, from the time of its first version in 1930. There he adds the thought that the order in which the topics of individuality and law-spheres are taken is "immaterial, for they never occur separately" (Vollenhoven 2005d/e, **29**). I believe it is legitimate to call this fundamental role of intersection, the 'intersection principle', though Vollenhoven does not call it a principle.

The intersection principle focuses, as the citation from *Hoofdlijnen der Logica* (1948p) indicates, on the contrast between individuality and universality (both taken in a broad sense). This is the main contrast *within* the cosmos, thus it belongs entirely on 'one side' of the ontological difference between law and what is subject to law, *viz.* the latter side. The order of law is, as ontological given, the backbone for the cosmological intersection principle. The order of the law-spheres are correlated to its order, and individuals, as things, are governed by the order of law through participation—which is what the intersection is—in the order of the law-spheres. The fact that Vollenhoven first spoke of "cosmic order" in connection with the law order—he intended to emphasize the correlation with the law-spheres—in no way cancels the ontological difference. But "intersection principle" is used entirely on the 'cosmos side' of the ontological difference.

The intersection principle postulates that individuality and universality never occur separately. In order to catch the import of this "togetherness", we need to expand on what these basic terms entail. Each is said to represent a *determinant* (*bepaaldheid*). Now a determinant is a configuration (to be specified immediately) that centres on states of affairs. Initially (in 1926a, 1926b, 1926d; cf. the earlier discussion in section III.B.3.f.) a state of affairs is taken to be logical content that answers to (or is organized by) the 'logical schema' of the unity of system, relation and moments. So long as the logical law-sphere is taken to be the first law-sphere, its analogy occurs in every other law-sphere, by virtue of the logical law-sphere being in the substrate of every other sphere. In that

---

133   Vollenhoven 1926a: 43; cf. also pp. 10, 13, 35, 39, 41, 42, 57. The term 'cosmic unity' occurs in the writings of the second half of the 1920s, but is soon replaced by 'individual'. I shall use the latter term in the current discussion.

way all content could be distinguished as to modality (system), essential connection (relation) and *Gegenstände* (moments). In other words, a state of affairs is a relational fact of two or more terms standing in some relation, itself of distinct modality. But soon Vollenhoven generalized this, *viz.* from a logical setting to a cosmological one. Wherever one is confronted with a difference (of terms) calling for a distinction, one can also inquire as to their connection (i.e. their relation). This is first stated explicitly in *Isagôgè Philosophiae* of 1931, but without any explanation.[134] When tracing its use, it is clear that this serves as the basic *methodological* stipulation that guides cosmological understanding. Thus, judging from Vollenhoven's practice, a determinant is a configuration involving the schema of 'difference and connection'.

A determinant need not be limited to a basic cosmological use. Wherever there is difference and connection Vollenhoven speaks of a determinant. Thus there is the determinant consisting of the difference and connection between heaven and earth, and the moral determinant of good and evil, etc.[135] But the determinants essential for cosmological analysis pertain particularly to individuality and universality. This says that there is diversity and connection within each category. The determinant of individuality concerns all the *different* individual things there are and the *relationships* in which they stand. The determinant of universality, in turn, concerns the *diversity* of law-spheres and the *connections* between them.[136] In depicting these two determinants, Vollenhoven applies a spatial metaphor: the relationships between individual things is portrayed horizontally, while the connections between the law-spheres are indicated using vertical (upward or downward pointing) arrows in a law-sphere. So the intersection principle is not just the assumption of universality and individuality never occurring separately. It has the more complex form of their determinants never occurring separately, each with a complexity of

---

134   The statement is retained in subsequent versions, but never with an added comment. It reads: "In every case where two things are different, we can ask about the relationship between the two" (2005d/e, **10**; 2010, **10**). The term 'thing', that occurs here, needs to be taken very liberally, for its very first application, in the very next sentence, is in connection with the difference between philosophical and non-philosophical knowing: what their difference and their connection entail.

135   2005d/e, **19**, **85** respectively; also 2010, **19**, **85**.

136   Vollenhoven speaks of individual things as standing in "samenhangen"—literally: hanging together—and of law-spheres in "onderling verband"—mutual connection. I shall use "relationship" to translate "samenhang", thereby diverging slightly from the translation of *Isagôgè Philosophiae* (2005d/e), where "interrelation" is used. The latter is somewhat cumbrous when translating "inter-individuele samenhang" and "intra-individuele samenhang".

difference and connection.

Cosmological inquiry (as in fact any scientific inquiry) needs to proceed methodically. When Vollenhoven first applied the *relational schema* in its *logical* context (the 'logical schema' of 1926), he applied this schema in either of two directions: *resolution* or *composition*. In the broader cosmological context, there is a similar application in two possible routes. When going in the direction of resolution one attempts to arrive at the point where a determinant resists further analysis, a point where the determinant is resolved into an abstract framework that is incapable of further analysis. The direction of composition "cloths the framework" (as it were), showing how the more complex situations are manifold complications of, and within, the determinant in question. Mindful of the cosmic context or cosmic boundary, and in line with what is said about cosmic being's being knowable, the way of resolution does not lead to ideas in the mind of God but rather to the fundamentals (not being further analysable) of that which stands in subjection. Their surfacing in the way of resolution makes them appear distinctly. On the other hand, the way of composition is not an erecting of a human construction based on privileged representations. The way of composition makes it possible to see how specifications and additions can be introduced to the fundamentals, as revealed by analysis, in our coming to understand better the complex reality we live in. The links laid in the way of composition are not random steps, but laid in the interest of truth.

For reasons of expediency, Vollenhoven invested much more effort in *Isagôgè Philosophiae* in discussing the way of composition than the way of resolution. The way of resolution is only given a scant indication. He mentions the cosmos as a whole and then refers to the kingdoms and species, ending with individual persons and things and their features.[137] For dearth of material we will have to follow suit in limiting our discussion to the way of composition.

The way of composition begins where the two primary determinants are at their most abstract or elementary. (Vollenhoven dubs these the 'individual determinant' and the 'modal determinant'.) Because the intersection principle stipulates that neither can be seen as separate from the other, one might expect first a description of each, in the complexity of the difference and connection of each, and then a follow-up as to what is involved in their intersection. But that is not the sequence Vollenhoven follows. His discussion is much more circuitous. His strategy is (I) first to take the feature of *difference* in each of the two determinants and

---

137   Cf. 2010, **22**.

discuss these separately (Ia and Ib), followed by a discussion of their combination as differences (Ia+Ib). Then (II) the same is done with the feature of *connection* of the two determinants: first the separate discussion of relation (IIa) and modal connection (IIb), and then their occurring combined (IIa+IIb). This allows for the step-by-step introduction of cosmologically relevant notions.[138]

A summary discussion of the notions that Vollenhoven introduces will have to suffice. The starting-point is, as we said, the beginning of the way of composition, where the 'materials' are most abstract or elementary. In fact, Vollenhoven lets it begin with the most elementary form of the intersection principle itself, in a 'this-such' combination. A 'this' is some distinct, referable feature understood to be (modally or characteristically) 'such'. A combination of this kind is a state of affairs. One might think of a specific ethical act, or a specific physical event, or a specific uneven number, or a specific economic windfall, etc. Each case is a 'this' or 'that' that is *such* and *such*. (One can represent this with a '+'-sign: the vertical bar stands for the 'this', the horizontal bar represents the 'such'.)

From this elementary beginning the two kinds of differences (I) can be introduced. First the 'individual difference' (Ia). This is achieved by keeping the modal characteristic of a state of affairs constant and to group with it other states of affairs of similar modality. E.g. to this physical event is grouped other physical events; to this economic windfall is placed other economic events, to a specific natural number is grouped other numbers. This 'individual difference' may be represented as

$$\{\ldots, +_{a,1}, +_{a,2}, +_{a,3}, +_{a,4}, \ldots\}$$

(whereby the scope is potentially infinite; the 'a' represents the chosen modality). All the 'this's' of the same modal characteristic form the (scope of the) *law-sphere* of that modality. To warrant such a grouping in a law-sphere, one needs to secure a law-sphere in what typifies the one modal grouping over against another grouping of different modality. This is secured by the *law* for such a law-sphere. The states of affairs of a law-sphere answer to the modal characteristic for which the corresponding law holds.

But the 'modal difference'(Ib) can also be grouped. Events of different modality can also be combined if they 'lodge' within or occur in the 'same individual'. The specific economic windfall can be together

---

138   The ensuing summary discussion is based on the following sections of *Isagôgè Philosophiae* (2005d/e or 2010): I: **30-49**; Ia: **36-40**; Ib: **30-35**; Ia+Ib: **41-49**; II: **50-84**; IIa: **50-53**; IIb: **54-66**; IIa+IIb: **67-84**.

with an ethical act of pledging troth and having a physical accident, etc. if this all involves the same person. Not only persons but also animals, plants and specific things (mountain, river, chemical element, etc.) can be involved in a diversity of modally distinct states of affairs. We may represent this as:

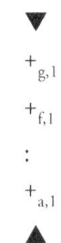

(The vertical scope of modal differentiation is indicated by the two triangles and is finite; '1' represents the individual.)

The grouping is a 'coming together' of modally different characterizations to which one is susceptible only when being that way. (An animal can be specifically aware—a dog recognizes his master—a stone cannot.) Thus the grouping brings together the features to which something can be subject. As a grouping it denotes a *unity of subjection*, the warrant of which is the *individual* said to bear these 'qualities of subjection'.

The two types of differences that are organized in law-spheres and unities of subjection can also be combined (Ia+Ib). *Individual* and *law* are the presupposed realities that warrant the groupings. The existence of an individual is, in an ultimate sense, by virtue of creation, and creation stands subject to law. In the course of an individual's conforming to law, its specific quality of subjection can pass from one state of affairs to another within the law-sphere for which the law holds. Thus a unity of subjection always participates in the law-sphere in which its qualities of subjection are present. In this way a unity of subjection maintains itself in the law-spheres to which its qualities belong. This 'maintaining itself' is a *functioning*, which itself attests to the combined presence of unity of subjection and law-sphere. Thus an individual's subjection to law involves functioning within the scope of validity of law, and the individual is said to have 'functions of subjection'.

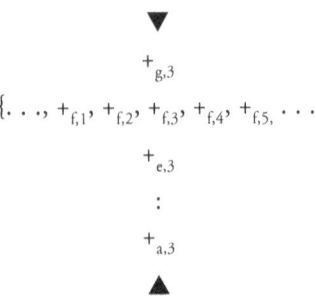

(A function at modal level 'f' of an individual '3', within the law-sphere of modality f.)

In this approach, the problem of substance and phenomenon, being that of hidden essence and public appearance respectively, has been thoroughly transformed. An individual is still a 'substance', the bearer of qualities. But the substance is not run (as it were) by a hidden motor (idea). Its dynamics is by virtue of being law-bound in its functioning. Its 'essence' is not a schema that holds the appearances together; rather, the 'essence' is the unity of subjection, which attests to the reality of being law-bound. It is the 'externalism' of the law-order, in its ontological difference with the cosmos, that undercuts the substance's so-called "hidden working" from within and allows its being the bearer of properties (proper to it) as over against mere appearances.

And then there are the features of connection (II) in each of the two cosmological determinants. Vollenhoven first mentions the feature of connection in the 'individual determinant' (IIa). This discussion is, from its first formulation in *Isagôgè Philosophiae* of 1930, very brief. But it concerns *relations*. Individual things, or even modally distinct 'this's' and 'that's', can, and very often do, 'hang or cling together'. (Vollenhoven's term is "samenhang".) If this is not to be a mere coincidence, one needs to assume the reality of relations. Relations can be of any modal level, for there are relations between numbers, between moving bodies, there are relations at a psychical level of influence, ethical relations, etc. The relations meant at this point are external relations (cf. chapter 2, section V.B.), the reality behind the 'essential connections', spoken of in the context of critical realism. Typical for these relations is that "terms become relata by virtue of the relation", not the other way around, as in the case with relations monadically understood.[139] A relationship is a case

---

139   Vollenhoven does not state this as explicitly as I do. The quoted phrase is from Vollenhoven 1926d: 57, where the logical schema and states of affairs are discussed. Be-

(a "samenhang") of terms bound by a relation. Because the relation is itself of a distinct modal level, the relationship is too.

$$[+_{b,1} \rule{1cm}{0.4pt} +_{b,2}]$$

$$[+_{a,1} \rule{1cm}{0.4pt} +_{a,2}]$$

(A relation between the individuals '1' and '2' is indicated with a bold line, at the modal levels 'a' and 'b'; the relationship is the whole within square brackets.)

There are also features of connection in the modal determinant (IIb). The basic thought is that of connection between 'modal levels' (i.e. either between law-spheres or between the functions of subjection in an individual). What 'relation' is to relationships, the 'natural order' is to the connections to be described here. In an earlier discussion we made reference to the distinction between the substrate and the superstrate of a law-sphere. This distinction reflects a 'natural order' (what Vollenhoven called the 'cosmic order' in 1926), an order that arises by virtue of a primary 'dependence' of a law-sphere on one or more other law-spheres, whereby this/these other law-sphere(s) are presupposed by the law-sphere in question. The presupposed law-spheres are its substrate, those not presupposed its superstrate.

Against the background of this given order, Vollenhoven points to evidences of this order in the occurrence of functioning. E.g. the life functions in an organism cannot take place without energy interaction (metabolism), transport of materials, spatial arrangements and quantitative balances. These are 'retrocipations' *in* the organic function and controlled by organic law, but they express, not directly but *analogically*, features of the life's substrate functions. On the other hand, one can also make separate study of biochemical processes, as answering to physical-chemical laws, or separate study of the transport of materials and its complex mechanisms, or study the spatial shapes of proteins and the quantitative relations. In these cases, the studies are conducted at the physical, mechanical, spatial and numerical levels respectively, as belonging to these law-spheres and their respective regularities. But for these studies one needs to proceed from the overriding assumption that

---

cause the current cosmological discussion proceeds from a generalization of this logical schema and states of affairs, the assertion of the externality of these relations is, I believe, justified. This is not to say that all relations are external; more monadic-like relations are referred to below.

they 'anticipate' the life function or life context in order to be able to understand their very existence.

So in general, when considering the actuality of a function—not just its existence as function of subjection, answering to modal law, but an effective or 'subject(ing) function'—its operating can be visualized as passing through a series of states of affairs at the relevant modal level. Such functioning also depends on the presence of the substrate levels, said to be *retrocipations*. But this functioning will refer to superstrate levels, as *anticipations*, only on condition that what performs the functioning itself actually has a function at the anticipated level. E.g. the difference between animals and human beings as to the organic material each has is of essential importance for performing the more complex (higher) functions. In a human being this material is of more complex organization than is the case in animals. In human beings this supports the higher functions and behaviour a human being evinces (say speech, aesthetic appreciation, etc.) as over animal behaviour that lacks the higher functions.

▼

$$\downarrow^c — \downarrow^b — \downarrow^a — +_{d,1} —$$
$$\downarrow^b — \downarrow^a — +_{c,1} — \uparrow^d$$
$$\downarrow^a — +_{b,1} — \uparrow^d — \uparrow^c$$
$$— +_{a,1} — \uparrow^d — \uparrow^c — \uparrow^b$$

▲

(Note. The arrows pointing downward are retrocipations at a specific modal level, analogically referring to the modal levels below that level; the arrows pointing upward are anticipations at a specific modal level, analogically referring to the modal levels above that level. These analogical references are predicated on an individual '1', subject to four functional levels: a, b, c, and d. The horizontal lines are not relations; they merely indicate the function level. Were one to place another individual '2' beside individual '1', then the basic relations would apply at the modal levels. There are also relations that reckon with the relevant anticipations or retrocipations. These relations are more like 'monadic relations', in being dependent on these anticipations and retrocipations as 'predicates' or particularizations of the terms.)[140]

---

140   The fact that the anticipations (upward arrows) are on the right side of the individual (between the triangles) and the retrocipations on the left side (downward arrows) is of no significance. Vollenhoven was in the habit of repeating the anticipations and the retrocipations, mirror-image, on both sides. This was to emphasize that these analogies concern structure, which remains the same, whether on the right side—indicative of the morally good direction—or the left—the morally evil direction.

In the first setup of *Isagôgè Philosophiae* (1930-1931), the above-mentioned retrocipations and anticipations are the only indications of connection within the modal determinant. From 1931 on, Vollenhoven included the account of 'object functions' which, in the first setup, was discussed in the subsequent topic of the combination of the two kinds of connection. The later account puts the emphasis on the 'inter-modal' meaning of an object function. E.g. gold, being a physical metal, does not itself have an ethical function. But it can be made to serve an ethical end when, in the shape of a ring, it is used to certify wedding vows. The metal ring then has an ethical 'object function'. Thus, things, plants and animals can have relevance at modal levels where they do not of themselves have qualities of subjection.

In Vollenhoven's first account of object functions, the emphasis is more on the relational facet (e.g. the relationship between wedded pair and the ring). This fit the topic of the combination of the two kinds of connections of the individual and modal determinants (IIa+IIb). This topic was still in flux in the late 1920s and early 1930s, and we need not review its development here. The main point of the combination of the two kinds of connection is two-pronged. In the first place, the introduction of retrocipations and anticipations serves to pull a unity of subjection together (as it were). Its qualities of subjection are, when actually functioning, interconnected (as analogies of being). In other words, a unity of subjection is in fact 'structured throughout' (*doorgestructureerd*). This opens the door to the treatment of 'individuals', now as concrete things and persons, in all their complexity. Secondly, the relationships between things and persons can now also be more properly respected in their complexity and nuance. In this connection Vollenhoven introduces distinctions between inter- and intra-individual relationships, between inner and outer relationships, between successive and simultaneous relationships, etc. These are all predicated on the basic (external) relations, but now, additionally, taking into account qualities of the individuals concerned.

This completes the review of the intersection principle, which governs the intersection of the modal and the individual determinants. Taken from its most primitive point, namely the starting point of the way of composition, this starting point presupposes the reality indicated by four terms: (modal) law, individual, (modal) relation and natural order.[141]

---

141   It is tempting to call these terms 'transcendentals', though Vollenhoven does not do so. As assumed or acknowledged realities, they are instrumental in the acceptance by thought of notions that defy analysis, namely "law-sphere', 'unity of subjection', 'relationship' and 'analogy' respectively.

(i) *Law* warrants the grouping of states of affairs of similar modality, taken together in one *law-sphere*. (ii) The *individual* warrants the grouping of states of affairs in a *unity of subjection*, when the qualities of subjection involved are borne by a specific individual. A *function of subjection* attests to the combined presence of a law-sphere and a unity of subjection. (iii) The reality of *relations* is the ground for *relationships*, of whatever modal level, between states of affairs and, in their extension, between individuals. (iv) The *natural order*, indicated by substrate and superstrate functions of subjection/law-spheres, is the basis for the *analogies of being* (retrocipations and anticipations) between functions of subjection or law-spheres. When taking relations and the analogies together, a complex *relational network* results.

The effect of the intersection principle begins (in the order of composition) from its simplest exemplification with the two cosmic determinants, namely in states of affairs: (distinct) 'this's' and 'that's' which are (modally) *thus* or *so*. The full intersection of the two determinants (at the end opposite to the simplest exemplification) involves the conjunction of *functions of subjection* operative within a *relational network*. Taken together, the above summary presentation presents Vollenhoven's schematic model of the framework of our complex world, offered to enable us to help analyse and understand it better.[142]

A point of detail that is found only in *Isagôgè Philosophiae* of 1930 (1930d, §§64-69) is worthy of mention because it helps to explain a peculiarity in the theory of knowledge that is retained in all the later versions of the text, but without the explanation. It concerns the forerunner of the account of object functions. Vollenhoven applies two sets of terms: "potential and actual" and "latent and patent". Two steps are required in accounting for an object (e.g. the golden wedding ring, mentioned above). First, something must be present that is suitable for becoming an object; secondly, someone must actually realize the object in question. The first step involves the assessment of suitability, which is the step from potential to actual. Gold is found to be suitable for a role between married couples by virtue of its lustre, endurance, economic value, etc.; but then this actualization of choice (of gold) must be transformed into an actual ring (meaningful object). In gold as (chosen) material, the ring is only latent; it becomes patent when made concrete (what Vollenhoven calls "the cancellation of latency"). Meaningful

---

142   It is of some interest to compare this schematic model with the one sketched and discussed by Hendrik Hart, himself a former student of Vollenhoven, in Hart 1984. A certain kinship of approach and in the content is evident.

objects of the sort here meant are not just culture-bound. They occur in nature too. A bird selects twigs (actualization), which it uses to build a nest (cancellation of latency). A wall gives protection from the north wind (actualizing protective surroundings) enabling plants to grow more abundantly (*op. cit.*, §67).

Vollenhoven applies this to memory and perception as well (adding expectation in 1932). A human being doesn't just remember or perceive. The attention needs to be triggered or set to focus on a past or present event. That means that, of all the events that could, potentially, be remembered by an agent, a particular event becomes the actual choice (potential to actual). Then, through the actual remembering, one recalls what that event involved, i.e. the latency of its content becomes patent content. The same holds for perception: a present event that can be perceived—this is perceivable—discloses, when actually perceived, its content patently. The choice that actualizes the remember-*able* and the perceiv*able* (and later the expect*able*) places the event in a relation to the knowing subject, who subsequently 'now remembers', 'now perceives' and 'now expects' what the event involves.[143]

The actual event remembered, perceived or expected may be dynamic or dull, weighty or of no consequence, etc., but in the relation to a knowing agent it is passive, a know*able* event. Its being knowable is not, as such, the object function. An object function needs the active or actualizing initiative of the agent in connection with which anything fulfils an object function. Being knowable is prior to anything actual, whether as a subject(ing) function or an object function. The knowable is "noetically passive" (*gnotisch-passief*),[144] i.e. is epistemically passive, a phrase that we found was relevant in connection with the 'ubiquity of value' in the cosmos (Vollenhoven 1930d/1931f, §124). Despite the brevity of the text about values (as mentioned earlier), the reference to value would appear to give epistemological relevance to 'actualization'. Something needs to trigger or set the focus on an *actual knowable* event in the context of what is *potentially knowable*. A candidate could be *value*, realistically conceived. Values could then mediate, as already surmised, the difference between reality and content of consciousness, in that value is operative in that 'selection process' (or 'assessment'; *ibid.*) to which consciousness is subject. Value is the warranty for being's being knowable. In that sense it is directly relevant in undergirding the view that knowing

---

143   Cf. 2005d/e [or 2010], **160**B, **160**C, **161**D, **164**C, **168**C.
144   Vollenhoven 2005d/e, **201**; in 1930d/1931f, §140; both references in Vollenhoven 2010.

resorts under being.

V. REVIEW OF VOLLENHOVEN'S INITIAL DEFINITIVE PLATFORM AND NEW DEVELOPMENTS

In the early 1930s Vollenhoven ceased speaking openly of values. This was simultaneous with his ceasing to characterise the cosmos in aesthetic terms and the Creator in the metaphor of an artisan. Also he revised his account of knowledge and objectification. More important, there is the appearance of the moral antithesis of good and evil coming more into the foreground than had been the case so far. This new emphasis on good and evil has everything to do with the new discussion of the human being, as soul and body, but now in the terminology of "direction determining centre" and "direction determined periphery."[145] We shall now attempt to give a unifying sketch of Vollenhoven's initial definitive platform, despite the fragmentary character of the sources, and then discuss its two most important developments: anthropology and the overcoming of dualism.

A. Cosmic life and knowing

Vollenhoven once defined 'cosmos' as "created reality and hence the reality dependent on God's will" (Vollenhoven 1926d: 56). He then immediately mentions a primary distinction within the cosmos. All reality is real (*realiteit*), but only a part of reality is factual as well (*werkelijkheid*). Factual reality is "that part of the cosmos that is spatio-temporal in nature and acts upon our organism as environment, in other words [the part which constitutes] the humanistic reduction of reality" (*ibid.*). To non-factual reality belongs, for example, (any) truth (*op. cit.*: 57).

In this reference to factual reality one sees a development of what was initially described as the level of the "the psycho-physical organization" in Vollenhoven's dissertation (cf. chapter 2). Sensibility absorbs sense-data through the spatial and temporal forms of sensibility. The data themselves derive from the outer world, localized in the absolute context of space and time. This 'realm of appearances' has in the meantime made way for a view that focuses on the relational network that the human being shares with nature. Vollenhoven now also recognizes organic functioning as a non-reductive reality.[146] In the work of 1926 he speaks of the environment of an organism, which he refers to as (following Hans

---

145   Vollenhoven 1932e, §64; also in 2010, **93**.
146   Vollenhoven had expressed a tendency towards attributing more independence to the biological world, than had been his wont, in the letter to A. Janse, 7 November 1922; cf. chapter 3, section II.C. In his letter to Janse of 19 February 1924 he states that he is working on "the logical foundations of biology".

Driesch) an organism's 'absolute medium',[147] a term that evinces the transformation of the earlier work.

This absolute medium is the context of perception. The "whole human being" is active in perception, for "the soul is aimed at the content within and outside of the body by means of the sense-organs" (Vollenhoven 1926a: 37). Perception yields representations of things, gleaned in the subject-object relation of organism and environment. To the extent that this has epistemic relevance, it is a 'knowing about', but it does not appeal to an awareness of truth. (The 'knowing about' was the former knowledge by acquaintance, which was thought to involve truth through the synthesis of subject and object. The latter is now rejected.) Truth is central when 'knowing that'. Knowing, in the sense of 'knowing that' also takes place through the activity of "the whole human being", but this activity is "aimed at the truth" (*ibid.*), or "the grasping of truth-content" (1926a: 13-14).

So we see how 'the whole human being', active in perception and knowing, matches the 'whole cosmos', in the reality of its 'factual part' and its 'ideal part'. Again, as in Vollenhoven's earlier position (cf. chapter 2), there is at least an analogy between the Self and the World, provided we can interpret the expression "whole human being" as synonym for 'Self', and "cosmos" for 'World'. Depicted schematically, we have:

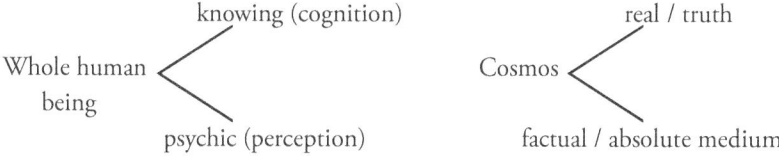

While this analogy between the human being and the world reminds us of the earlier setup of 'occasionalism', Vollenhoven is now not simply repeating himself. In the human being the main distinction is no longer that between psycho-physical body and conscious mind. We had noted that the human being (or the Self) was portrayed as a psychical creature: the psyche being a factor of the psycho-physical body, but also relevant for the immortal soul and its support of the mind. But in the current view, *knowing* is taken as common factor: perception provides the representation by which we 'know about' inner and outer reality, while cognition is focussed on grasping truth, in 'knowing that'. In both

---

147 Cf. Vollenhoven 1926b: 394; 1926d: 54, 155, 193. It is in 1926a: 13 that he indicates that the phrase "the biotic absolute medium" comes from Hans Driesch. The term was soon dropped, but the meaning, insofar useable, is preserved in speaking of the environment as relational network.

cases there is an "activity of the soul", a dynamic principle common to both, but with a difference: the "grasping [on the part of cognition] does not *arise* through perception" (*ibid.*), and "concept [of knowing] and representation [of perception] differ *toto caelo*" (Vollenhoven 1926a: 9). If, in Vollenhoven's earlier work, 'psychical growth' was taken to be of cardinal importance—you might say "the point of it all"—this now seems to be replaced by 'coming to know' and the quality of 'rest' that achieved knowing brings with it. The weight now placed on knowing, and the context in which this takes place (as indicated very roughly in the schema), gives this view a certain consonance with what Vollenhoven, in his later terminology of the problem-historical method, referred to as "ennoetism" (literally an 'in-the-mind-ism'). We will discuss this more thoroughly in the addendum to this chapter.

Now the cosmos too has diversity, but not as separate parts. Vollenhoven is clear in his terminology, namely that the entire cosmos has the reality (*realiteit*) of standing in subjection to God. But factual reality (*werkelijkheid*) is a subpart (*onderdeel*) of reality, being the reality that is essentially spatial and temporal. Thus reality is the encompassing category, of which factual reality is only a (sub)part (1926d: 56-57). An important feature of non-factual reality is truth. It is on a par with knowing that, which is important to Vollenhoven, for now "it is possible to secure knowing in the real" (*op. cit.*: 57). And the intersection principle ensures that the factual (as individual determinant) and the non-factual (as modal determinant) are always taken together.

One may ask whether this contrast of the factual and the real remained in effect. In Vollenhoven's theory of knowledge there is the peculiar but not properly explained two-step feature of first selecting a content for the mind and then asserting or affirming it (cf. the end of the section on the intersection principle). The first step is a 'making now knowable' (perceivable, remember-able, expectable). It is difficult to maintain that this is not a moment of perception that yields 'noetically passive' content for the mind. The mind's subsequent affirmation underscores its truth. This view remained unchanged throughout the editions of *Isagôgè Philosophiae*.

Now we can take the next step and consider the distinction between Self or 'whole human being' and World or 'cosmos'. We portrayed this above as it occurs in Vollenhoven's earlier thought, *viz.* side-by-side. But then it was secured in what Vollenhoven at the time took to be a cardinal difference, i.e. between thought and being. The Self embodies the qualities and properties needed for thought, while the World is the context of cosmic being. In the meantime any independent status of the Self has been annulled in favour of the view of the Self as essentially that of a 'tasked subject'. It stands subject to laws/norms that serve as cases of boundaries for the World. This says that the former difference between Self and World has essentially collapsed. The Self still has its part to play, but this is no longer taken to be executed on the basis of a solipsistic self-conscious thought, predicated on the individual. The Self is 'wedded to the World' (as it were), in the sense that it is itself a creature that belongs to the cosmos as created. Vollenhoven has shifted in his thought towards a 'holism' or 'universalism'. Four independent lines of consideration point in this direction.

In the first place, there is the shift that is indicated by "knowing resorting under being". This would appear to be the advance made about mid-1922. It at least says that knowing should not be taken as taking place in independence from the World. But it does not directly call for a dependent Self.

Secondly, there is the evidence in connection with the critical apparatus that Vollenhoven developed in the second half of the 1920s, when he aimed to understand philosophical views as variants of theism or of cosmism. God and cosmos are taken in one arrangement, and the prime question is *where* the line of difference is drawn and *what* that difference entails. He expressed his own stance at the time in terms of the same question. But he eventually, certainly before 1941, found this approach to be dissatisfactory.[148] He characterizes this approach as implementing a 'whole-part schema'. In our discussion of this approach above (section II.B.2), one observes that there is no (direct) concern for a possible fundamental distinction between a 'cosmos-in-the-small' and a 'cosmos-in-the-large', despite the focus on the cosmos. If Vollenhoven's earliest context still held sway, in which the thought-being polarity did find cosmic expression in the *non-holistic* distinction of microcosm and macrocosm, then he certainly would have reckoned with it when setting up his critical apparatus (of the forms of theism and of cosmism). Now an argument from silence is, of course, always somewhat tendentious. But his own (later) qualification, of 'whole and part' in this regard, breaks the silence. His own view of the late 1920s falls under the same qualification, which therefore indicates holism or universalism.

---

148 Vollenhoven expresses his dissatisfaction with this approach in "Richtlijnen ter oriëntatie in de gangbare wijsbegeerte" (Orientating directives in connection with current philosophy); 1941k: 65-66, footnote 2). The 'whole-part' qualification first occurs in comment 4, section **13** of *Isagôgè Philosophiae* of 1941, the revised version of that year. Cf. Vollenhoven 2005d/e, **13** or Vollenhoven 2010, **13**.

Then thirdly, there is a statement of Vollenhoven in 1926 which, at face value, sounds extreme, but which, on consideration, fits the context of a universalism. "A human being is not only not an individual that is suddenly mature; he is not in any sense (*in het geheel niet*) an individual, but he has a historical place in the whole of humankind, which for many centuries is executing—regrettably continually with failures—its task *viz.* exercising the office of being subject" (1926b: 382). The individual is nothing outside of humankind, and that humanity as such stands in subjection. There is now no separate or distinct status of the individual in a cosmic sense.

Finally, there is the epistemological evidence. The former distinction of Self and World served as the poles on which knowledge acquisition took place. The Self receives data from the World, which it assimilates in terms of its own structures (forms of sensibility and *Gegenstände*). Knowledge is a synthesis, first in the form of judgments, then, in a constructive sense, also in the form of concepts. But we found that Vollenhoven now clearly rejects this account of knowledge. The synthesis there is, involves representations, which are psychical. Hence the synthesis of representations is also psychical, put together and lacking in truth-value. Genuine knowledge is a *systasis*, i.e. a structure in which truth is grasped, as a 'knowing that'. In that case, 'coming to know' does not proceed from an activity of the Self, but it takes place in the context of law-spheres, whereby the first concern is the *intuitive discerning* of modal qualification of the relevant truth (1926a: 14) .

I believe that the above evidence is sufficient to assert that Vollenhoven's initial definitive position is committed to a universalism. Let us attempt to bring this 'holism' more sharply into focus. But we can state at once that, in its original understanding, it was short-lived. In 1932 Vollenhoven brought the human being more explicitly in the picture again, when he made the theme of 'body and soul' more pronounced. This did not eradicate the theme of the whole, but it did put it in a different light (as we will see).

How is 'the whole' initially characterized? The best way to discover this is to focus on the situation in which Self and World are together, which is the situation of knowledge.

Vollenhoven's paradigm of knowledge is indicated as 'I know something', which, translated into the idiom of a *systasis*, is 'I *have* knowledge *about* something'. Because 'having' knowledge comes down to 'possessing truth', and 'I' being a knowing Self, the paradigm statement becomes 'Self possesses truth about something'. This is a tripartite schema of knower, truth and the knowable, with two relations: one of possessing—best described as 'participating'—and one of representation.

Now truth is 'in itself', in the sense that it is not dependent on the subject or knowing agent, nor is it dependent on language, nor the facts.[149] (I believe we can say that for Vollenhoven truth, in the present context, is based on given connections which, when acknowledged (or seized) are true, as seized, of reality.) What calls for consideration are the knower and the knowable in connection with truth.

In the situation of everyday knowledge, truth is conveyed as information or as a truth content . For any understanding of information to take place, the first prerequisite is that the knower intuits the modal characteristic of information conveyed. For the Self this means discerning the relevant modal quality of subjection and its modal law. Likewise, the something that is knowable—this need not be a simple object, but could be an event, or a situation, or itself a state of affairs, etc.—needs also to have the relevant qualification. Vollenhoven does not make this explicit, though it is clear that there needs to be a modal qualification of the same modality as that of the quality of subjection. The link that indicated the modal qualification of something of reality is, I believe, *value*. Here 'value' needs to be taken in the manner of our earlier discussion, namely the value that signals being's being knowable. The 'something' is not merely part of a blanket being. Cosmic being displays diversity, so that one 'part'—a facet, moment, event, situation, occasion, etc.—can be picked out and be known. The take-off point of perception and memory is (as was said above) that that which is perceived or remembered is 'picked out' as being knowable.[150]

The Self 'bears' its qualities of subjection, it does not freely form them from its own activity. In the same way, a 'something' 'bears' its value', in the sense that it can be deemed relevant in a multiplicity of ways. This calls for a deeper level of account.

Vollenhoven now turns to religious categories. The knowledge enterprise is taken to be part and parcel of fulfilling (as discussed earlier)

---

149   In 1926a: 51-52, Vollenhoven expresses rapport with Bolzano's distinctions between independent propositions (*Sätze an sich*), independent truths (*Wahrheiten an sich*) and independent representations (*Vorstellungen an sich*). The truths-in-themselves are prior to, and independent of, language (propositions) and human thought (representations); cf. Bar-Hillel 1972.

150   I repeat that linking value to this actualization is not supported explicitly in Vollenhoven's text. But it helps to make sense of what Vollenhoven's all too brief text in this connection fails to explain, while being in accordance with what he does say; cf. section III.B.3.c. above.

the *prophetic office*.[151] This 'office' is relevant not just for an individual knowledge seeker. It includes the knowledge seeker, and, with him or her, the cosmos in the sense of that about which knowledge is sought. In speaking of office here, Vollenhoven means to point to a 'post', with a 'task' or obligation to be met. It is communal in involving all humankind, but it is not a 'community-idea', as if it guarantees the possibility of achieving shared knowledge. It is more like the call that awakes the knowledge interest, making one receptive to the 'noetic' value of being's being knowable.

In speaking of office or task, Vollenhoven is at the point where the Self stands subject to the law. The Self is at the boundary, and it is at the boundary that religious categories hold. Here we find the final characterization of 'the whole'.[152] Vollenhoven speaks of "the religious" at this point.[153] It is where the *concreteness* of cosmic life becomes definitive, over against the *abstract framework* of where cosmology began. We have found that Vollenhoven had spoken of the aesthetic characterization of the whole, underlying the use of 'cosmos'. But that does not go beyond a general or abstract characterization. When speaking of office, its fulfilment can be none other than concrete. And that fits the knowledge enterprise. Human beings come to particular truths, and each individual knower invests his or her own measure of interest of acquiring knowledge in line with the possibilities offered by the context towards acquiring knowledge.

Religion is not merely about having a belief about God. For Vollenhoven, religion is much more encompassing. It is about fundamental life-attitudes, about taking a stance in the face of the exigencies of life. Here the 'standing in subjection' of an office is understood to involve a position of responsibility. The category of 'the religious' links the anthropology of responsibility to the divinity from whom responsibility derives. In that sense, concrete existence reflects divinity. Ideally, the image of the triune God reflected in the human being is also threesome. "The human being, being created with all his functions by the living God

---

151   There are also the priestly and the kingly offices. The three offices are relevant for anthropology, but only the prophetic office is directly relevant for epistemology.

152   The cosmos, being knowable through the mediation of values, also has religious relevance for Vollenhoven. For (as quoted in an earlier context) "value can be adequately seen only when taken as anchored in the Logos" (Vollenhoven 1930d/1931f, §124; also 2010, Appendix I).

153   Vollenhoven 1930d/1931f, §71; 2010, Appendix I. He admits the expression to be vague, which is probably why, or at least part of the reason why, it was written out of later versions of *Isagôgè Philosophiae*.

out of the earth, addressed by him and guided, is in this triune structure of *created*, *addressed* and *guided*, the subject on the side of that which is subject, the correlate of the triune God."[154] So we find that Vollenhoven continues to have a theistic understanding of the characterization of the whole of reality. The three cases of God's immanence, where the divine will expresses laws, commands and directives, provide the 'points of contact' with cosmic life.[155]

But Vollenhoven must have sensed that this formulation was not entirely satisfactory. For he speaks of the *structure* of the human being at the very point where the concern is that of *direction*, i.e. response to norms, commands and directives. It does not help to encourage taking the *right* direction by only emphasizing that there is the capacity of choice. In the next version of *Isagôgè Philosophiae* (1932) there is progress in terms of a renewed anthropology.

B. Renewed anthropology
Of the numerous changes Vollenhoven introduced into the text of *Isagôgè Philosophiae* in 1932, a significant one was no doubt that concerning the human being. With this change came an increased emphasis on the theme of the 'moral' antithesis of good and evil, a theme that is directly relevant to the distinction between structure and direction.

In the work of 1926 Vollenhoven appears to use the word 'soul' as synonym for 'the whole human being', that is, when the whole human being is active, as in perception and in knowing (cf. Vollenhoven 1926a: 37). In "The first questions of psychology" (1930b), the thought is repeated, with emphasis on its biblical use, where 'soul' is associated with the 'breathing' of animals and human beings,[156] itself a metaphor for being concretely alive. In the Bible there is also a link, says Vollenhoven, between the soul and that which influences life, for good or evil (*ibid*). The latter is given more scope in *Isagôgè Philosophiae* of 1930-1931.

The context of the discussion in the first setup of *Isagôgè Philosophiae* is religious (or redemptive) history. The fall of humankind (in Adam and Eve) makes good and evil a reality or actual in human life. (Vollenhoven

---

154   Vollenhoven 1930d/1931f, §79; also 2010, Appendix I.

155   The understanding of the roles of the Persons of divinity is not the same as initially formulated in Vollenhoven's dissertation (1918a). The change is discussed in III.B. above.

156   *Op. cit.* : 12-13. The discussion of this topic is in line with work of A. Janse. In the renewal that Vollenhoven introduces in 1932, he places more of his own stamp on the handling of this theme. For a recent discussion of Vollenhoven's more considered view, cf. Van der Walt 2010a.

follows the text of Genesis explicitly; cf. 1930d/1931f, §§83-84). The reality of good and evil invites a systematic discussion of it, which Vollenhoven offers in four short sections (§§85-88). In the revised versions of 1932 and 1939 these sections are lifted out of the context of redemptive history and placed in a position adjacent to the discussion of cosmology (the intersection principle). The justification for this move is Vollenhoven's revised view, that the antithesis of good and evil constitutes a determinant in its own right, a 'third determinant', in addition to the modal and the individual determinants. The content of these four sections, while undergoing expansion, is not essentially changed. What is changed is the anthropological consequence drawn from the change of the position of these sections.

The essential point of the systematic discussion of good and evil is, from the start, to demonstrate that this antithetical relation does not fit into the cosmos, i.e. cannot be reduced to or is fundamentally different than the two primary determinants of the cosmos, individuality and modality. While each of these two determinants involves difference—the 'this-that' difference between individuals and the modal differences between the law-spheres—nowhere can these differences legitimately offer a foothold to secure the difference of good and evil: of anything in the cosmos, never can we say that 'this' is exclusively good or evil, nor is this the case for any one mode of being subject. What also stands in the way of any merging of good and evil with these two determinants of the cosmos is that any difference with respect to these determinants can be 'relativized', for wherever there is a difference one can ask about the connection (2005d/e, **10**). But good and evil cannot, and certainly should not, be connected or 'relativized'. We all know that rationalizing our missteps doesn't get us off the hook—which is why Vollenhoven speaks of an *antithesis*. The concepts of good and evil differ in their own right, but there is no connection that overrides this difference, hence in reality good and evil are antithetic.

This means that this 'third determinant' cannot be integrated into the two cosmic determinants, despite its being listed as third. In other words, it does not itself 'intersect' with the other two determinants. This accords with the biblical evidence that the antithesis of good and evil does not obtain by virtue of creation.[157] Whatever its exact

---

157   Vollenhoven 2005d/e, **85**, or 2010, **85**. One should not confuse this with the biblical indication of the creation being 'good', even 'very good', in the opening pericope of Genesis. The original Hebrew has 'tov', which means 'in good order, pleasing, satisfying'. This is closer to 'good' as in 'good versus bad' than to 'good' as in 'good versus evil'. E.A. Speiser, the translator and editor of the Genesis volume in the Anchor Bible series,

origin',[158] good and evil became evident in human life owing to what is termed 'the fall'. That is why Vollenhoven initially placed its discussion in the context of redemptive (covenant) history, and spoke of "religious direction", good and evil being two different directions in human life, for or against God.[159] But from 1932 on, the antithesis of good and evil is listed along with the other two determinants of creation. Why is that? I believe the answer is that, by appealing to this antithesis, Vollenhoven saw a way of introducing the distinction between body and soul, all the while staying clear of the dualistic substantialist view of a human being. (The prior religious context of the discussion of good and evil did not include this anthropological distinction.) But the distinction, as introduced in 1932, did induce a peculiar tension in Vollenhoven's thought.

One cannot of course merely juxtapose the antithesis of good and evil *beside* the cosmic determinants—this in itself constitutes a difference or contrast in its own right—without expecting a connection. The connection is not, as we said, an 'intersecting' of good and evil with the two cosmic determinants, but they need at least in some sense to be related. Vollenhoven now has the *soul* mediate the connection between the cosmic determinants and that of good and evil. Take the two cosmic determinants in turn. In the modal determinant, law and function (of subjection) never coalesce. In the 'supra-psychical' law-spheres the human being is aware of this ontological difference, which is why law is then said to be a norm. At this level the human being is able to consciously function or act contrary to the norm. Here a factor of *direction*, *viz.*, that of compliance or defiance with respect to a (supra-psychical) norm, presents itself. In each of the law-spheres, from the analytical upwards, this possibility is present. But it can't be that the compliance or defiance is itself merely a 'modal phenomenon', distinct in each of these law-spheres. After all, the same human being participates in all these law-spheres, and it is the human being who is held accountable. It is more likely that an *attitude in the person* contributes towards inclining either way in the context of a law-sphere. This attitude is not peculiar or partial to any one particular function, hence it must already lodge in the human being 'prior' to the specific expression of functioning in the face of a modal

Genesis, translates the divine expressions in chapter 1 (with slight variations) as: "And God was pleased with what he saw"; Speiser 1964: 3-5.

158 Vollenhoven adduces the biblical evidence of a prior 'fall in heaven', whereby "the most important angels did not remain standing in the truth, that is to say, in the constancy, safety and faithfulness of God" (2005d/e, **21**, or 2010, **21**.)
159 Vollenhoven 1930d/1931f, §88.

law. (In 1941 Vollenhoven referred to this as 'pre-functional', but the thought is present in 1932.) The *seat* of this attitude in the person is then the *soul* or *hart*.[160] It is relevant *for* functional life, in the law-spheres being the channel for compliance or defiance, but it cannot be identified *with* anything in functional life, say, one specific function or a group of functions. The latter is contrary to the traditional view of the soul as mental/spiritual 'substance' controlling higher functional expression.[161]

Now this soul is related to the body. This is specified in connection with the individual determinant. The soul or heart is localized in the individual human being. Now the functions of an individual being form a connected unity, which in itself does not encourage privileging one or more of these functions to act as seat for the soul. But what about the unity of subjection itself? This is 'the body' in the full sense of the word. (Vollenhoven includes all the supra-psychical functions in what he refers to as the body.) The body is structured throughout.[162] But this holds for animals, plants and even ordinary things, though these have progressively less functions than the human being has.[163] The unity of subjection is warranted by individuality, hence one speaks not only of *this* person, but also of *this* plant, *this* animal, etc. The cardinal difference between a human being and the non-human creatures is not just the latter's lack of the higher functions—which should not occasion grouping these as 'soul', for then we again 'break' the human body's unity of subjection— but (more importantly) the lack of any evidence that the non-human creatures can in any way be held accountable for their behaviour. There is no determination of choice in their 'compliance or defiance'. They are too integrated in their surrounding world for that, though there are limited

---

160   Vollenhoven 1932e, §63****; also 2010, **92**. Vollenhoven uses synonymously the two pairs: "soul and body", "heart and "function mantle". The latter pair is suggested by the expression used by the apostle Paul, in 2 Corinthians 5: 1, where he speaks of the body as an "earthly tent".

161   Consider: "When in my work I speak of *the* dichotomy in an averse sense, then this always pertains to the dichotomy in the functionalistic-substantialistic sense as proposed in pagan and humanistic philosophy. But I do myself maintain the dichotomy of soul and body. . . ." D.H.Th. Vollenhoven, letter 4 April 1939 to the Curators of the Free University. Website J.G. Friesen, www.members.shaw.ca/hermandooyeweerd/Curators.html.

162   In *Isagôgè Philosophiae* Vollenhoven uses the term "unbroken unity of subjection", in later work he speaks of "doorgestructureerd", i.e. 'structured throughout'. Cf. 1932e, §94***, or 2010, **139**. For the second term, cf. the index to Tol and Bril 1992.

163   Consider: "Although the structure of a human being, if we overlook the heart, corresponds, as was seen, with that of things in that it, too, is functional . . ." 2005d/e, **92**, or 2010, **92**.

'measures' of freedom. But human beings are accountable for their doings (which is not to deny that there are dispositional factors to take into account). Thus the soul, as seat of the direction determining attitude, is 'something' that is distinct from the body (as unity of subjection), but it does stand in an intrinsic (intra-individual) relationship to the (whole) body. Thus Vollenhoven calls the soul the 'direction determining centre' of the body,[164] the functions of which, in consequence of the soul, are inclined in a direction either for good or evil.

Now what determines the inclinations of the heart or soul in its pre-functional significance? We naturally think of a 'law' criterion. But this cannot be a law in the sense of a norm. Norms control the (higher) functions. Also, one may functionally act in accordance with norms, yet use this to cover over evil intentions of the heart. (Consider the discussion of knowledge and its 'good or loving' handling; cf. section III.B.3.b.) Commands, as we saw, give more pointed orientation as compared to norms. The prime command for Vollenhoven is the (biblical) love command. This is what serves as criterion for determining the good direction as over against the one evil (2005d/e, **114**, or 2010, **114**).

But the status of the soul was never made completely clear. In line with A. Janse's use, Vollenhoven refers to the soul as the 'inward human being' while the body is the 'outward human being'.[165] Inward and outward belong together, and in that sense they are part of the structure of the human being. Yet each is attuned to different impositions: the soul or inward man is subject to the love command, the body or outward man to the laws/norms of the cosmic order. Vollenhoven once called the soul our 'centre of willing'.[166] In that sense, the soul is sensitive to good and evil. But it is not a build-in teleology, for then the moral obligation loses its point, in confrontation with the (external) love command. It is

---

164 In 1941 Vollenhoven dropped the terms "centre" and "periphery", and spoke merely of "direction determining" and "in direction determined" (cf. 2010, **93**). In 1939 he also re-introduced the qualification "religious direction" (1939h, §63****; or 2010, **92**). Vollenhoven never favoured the term 'moral' (cf. *op. cit.* , **114**). But if one agrees to distinguish this term from 'ethical', as in 'ethical function', and not presuppose an autonomous practical reason, the term is, I believe, useful. After all, the antithesis of good and evil is moral, it's the context and account given to it by Vollenhoven that calls for the predicate 'religious', as over against Kant's account that turns it into an autonomous feature of practical reason.

165 Cf. Vollenhoven 1952k: 78 ff., 86. The terms "inward man" and "outward man" also occur in the Pauline corpus; cf. Rom.7: 22; Eph. 3: 16; 2 Cor. 4: 16.

166 He speaks of "centre of willing in the Scriptural sense"; letter to the Curators of the Free University, 4 April 1939; cf. website J.G. Friesen: www.members.shaw.ca/hermandooyeweerd/Curators.html .

a case of the correlation of law-as-command and subjection-as-direction-determining, which is *sui generis*.[167] It is at death that the distinction between soul and body becomes an evident difference. The soul goes through death,[168] it is the (functional) body that is annihilated when dying. However, this separated state is characteristic of death. When alive the soul is the heart from which the issues of (functional) life proceed.

Upon comparing Vollenhoven's original 1918 view with the revised view, we find that, whereas formerly there was the Self, as higher synthesis of the two incomplete substances of (psycho-physical) body and (mental) soul, the term 'soul' is now used (as complete human being) in the position of the Self. Vollenhoven's statement about dying calls for reinterpretation. In 1918 he stated: "Dying is the dissolution of a complete substance [*viz.* the Self] on account of the soul's organ becoming unserviceable" (25th statement appended to the dissertation, 1918a). The organ or instrument of the soul here is, as John Kok has pointed out, the body (Kok 1992: 38). In itself this (so-called 'scholastic') view is rather remarkable. For the Self, which is said to dissolve on account of the body's corruptibility, is (in Vollenhoven 1918a) the invariant principle that regulates the connection between body and soul. One might expect *this* to be the seat of personality, or whatever affects *both* body and mind together, yet this is what is said to dissolve when dying. In Vollenhoven's revised view, which never went completely public, it is this seat of the whole human being that "goes through death" but is not annihilated. What is now taken to be dissolved at death is the coherence of 'body and mind', or what Vollenhoven came to call the entire "bodily structure of functions", which includes 'mental functions'.[169]

167   Vollenhoven did also illustrate the relation of body and soul as modelled on that of modal laws and the love command. E.g. in 1951h: 55-56, he states: "Thus, one readily notices, analogous to the difference between soul and body in connection with the human being—taken in the Scriptural sense of heart and function mantle—the difference between the principle intent [*hoofdsom*] and differentiation in connection with the law. The former summarizes the kernel of the law as the demand of love to God and to the fellow human being, whom he has placed beside us. However, this one law [of love] is differentiated in a diversity of laws for functional life." The two pairs: body/modal laws and soul/love command are clear enough. But it is how the former pair is a 'differentiation' of the latter pair (respectively) that remains in the dark.

168   Cf. Vollenhoven 1933a: 44; also consider: "The continued existence of the soul after death is not in discussion for Calvinistic philosophy;" first proposition of the list of propositions written at the request of the Curators of the Free University (probable date 19 March 1938; my translation). Website J.G. Friesen: www.members.shaw.ca/hermandooyeweerd/Curators.html .

169   It is of interest to compare (noting similarities and differences) the above "scholastic" view with Aristotle's view of the instrumental body of the soul in the (re)interpreta-

Vollenhoven wishes to avoid speculation. And that severely restricts any 'thorough' treatment of this topic. If we resort to the routes of Vollenhoven's method, then the 'way of resolution' (the way of analysis) calls for the distinction of soul and body, a distinction of inward centre of willing and outward functional-directional effect, a distinction that also requires us to recognize a peculiar relational, 'intra-individual' component. But when retreating on the way of composition (the way of synthesis), one does not merely 'reassemble the parts'; there is also the recognition of a more concrete or existential reality that is 'better understood' as a whole on account of having distinguished the parts. In the light of that more concrete reality, the soul (the "inward" person) represents the 'whole person' (as is to be expected of an *intra*-individual relationship of soul and body), while the body (the "outward person"), when taken by itself, is merely an abstraction. For body without soul is not a concrete human reality. In that sense an anthropological analysis needs to presuppose, and cannot completely account for, the unique worth of the human person that each one is.

C. Dualism overcome

In his early years Vollenhoven used the term 'dualism' to portray a primary or essential contrast. This is how it occurred in his dissertation (as we found in chapter 2), where it referred to the duality of norm and fact and, in extension, God and the world. In his work of the late 1920s there is the similar use, to again indicate the primary distinction between God and the world. The distinction is called upon in connection with the practice of philosophy, as helping to delineate philosophical methodology. It does not necessary imply an ontological dualism in the strict sense of the word. The methodological distinction *could* be based on a strict ontological dualism, but it can equally be the primary contrasts of a unity, as we found is the case in Vollenhoven's dissertation.

Now, when speaking of the practice of philosophy one can readily distinguish a constructive and a critical part. The constructive part concerns, in Vollenhoven's phraseology, "the complex of statements expressive of the knowledge acquired in the human being's striving to know" (*Is.Ph.*: **1**). Vollenhoven restricts this to the cosmos, to what is within human reach to inquire into. But the critical part concerns the discussion of philosophy's "place and task" (*Is.Ph.*: **10, 14-17**). If the constructive part is philosophy proper, then the critical part is meta-philosophical. In meta-philosophy there is the discussion of the

---

tion of A.P. Bos; cf. Bos 1999.

presuppositions of philosophy, which serves to clarify the conditions that hold of the practice of philosophy; cf. chapter 1, section IV.B. Philosophy and meta-philosophy should be carefully distinguished. Should this be neglected, two kinds of problems may arise. One might be tempted to treat a meta-philosophical factor as belonging to philosophy in the constructive sense. In that case one induces an element of *dogmatism* in philosophy. On the other hand, a philosophical construal might be deemed to represent reality so convincingly as to be raised to a condition of philosophy. This introduces *speculation* in the meta-philosophical understanding of philosophy.

Nowhere does the problem between the meta-philosophical and the philosophical in Vollenhoven become more evident than in the first setup of *Isagôgè Philosophiae* of 1930-1931. Vollenhoven proceeds from the correlation—the "dualism"—of God and cosmos. Vollenhoven always accepted the existence of God and of the world, not on the basis of argument, but from out of his understanding of religion and worldview, as informed by biblical religion and the Reformed historical tradition. As such this is meta-philosophical, depending as it does on choices made within an understanding of the discourses of religion and worldview. But how does this meta-philosophical discourse affect philosophy in Vollenhoven's initial definitive position? We need to consider this from the point of view of epistemology, ontology and cosmology.

As to epistemology, an element of dogmatism is, I believe, initially evident. Vollenhoven would appear to maintain that the meta-philosophical discourses justifies taking the existence of God and the World (cosmos, nature) as being realities that are *knowable*. The important factor is how the knowable comes to the attention of the knower. There are two "sources of knowledge" or "means of knowing", according to Vollenhoven, *viz.* Scripture and Nature.[170] Each source reveals the knowable—namely God and the World—in its own way. Therefore Vollenhoven organizes his epistemological discussion by first focussing on the knowledge of the cosmos, thereby appealing, in sequence to Nature (as source) and Scripture (as source). Then he turns to discussing the knowledge of God, by appealing (in the opposite order) to Scripture and Nature.

The crosswise treatment of the knowledge of God and the cosmos

---

170   In the revised version of *Isagôgè Philosophiae* of 1932 Vollenhoven replaces the term "source of knowledge" with "means of knowing", this being part of a thorough overhaul of the whole epistemological discussion; cf. Vollenhoven 1932e, §118; or 2010, **173**. The two means of knowing God are written into the *Belgic Confession*, Article 2, *viz.* through nature or creation and Scripture; cf. Zwanepol 2004: 168.

through Nature and Scripture turns this epistemological complex into one network. Where the source of Scripture is central, there the discussion is surely meta-philosophical; but where nature is central, the discussion is philosophical. In terms of the current setup these are placed entirely on a par. But in the actual execution of the discussion there is a difference. The first category (knowledge of the cosmos by means of Nature) has *priority of place* in terms of the extent of its treatment (§§104-127). The discussion of the other three categories is much briefer (§§128-130; 132-134; 135-136 respectively),[171] to the point of hardly exceeding the format of outlines. The imbalance in the treatment might attest to a certain misgiving by Vollenhoven from the start. In any case, he thoroughly revised his whole epistemological discussion in the edition of 1932 which, apart from internal adjustment brought to bear in later versions, remained essentially intact. From that point, the discussion of knowledge focuses *only* on human knowledge concerning the cosmos, in both of its variants, everyday knowledge and scientific knowledge.[172] This at least brings greater consistency in the execution of Vollenhoven's own professed intentions.

Beside the duality in sources of knowledge, there is also the dualism of God and cosmos. We found that Vollenhoven secures this ontologically in terms of the difference in the natures of each. God is an infinite being, who is sovereign; the cosmos is a finite creation that stands in subservience. The two are correlated through the 'law as boundary'. This boundary is, as far as ontology is concerned, by default by virtue of the difference in their natures: infinite versus finite. This difference is law insofar as it expresses sovereign will and delineates creaturely subservience.

Here too one might wish for a clearer distinction of the philosophical and the meta-philosophical. When Vollenhoven maintains that the principle of the exclusion of antinomies in philosophy is the correlate of the confession of God's sovereignty, then we have a clear difference between the philosophical and the meta-philosophical. Also, when Vollenhoven is more forthright about the cases of 'law as boundary' for

---

171 The text, with the indicated sections, is in Vollenhoven 2010, Appendix I.

172 The account of scientific knowledge—the treatment ought to be compared with Vollenhoven 1926d—is brief and incomplete. After 1932 the text underwent only superficial changes. The setup is in two chapters: the first, on the special sciences, is a short account of (in the main) scientific method (Vollenhoven 2005d/e, 200-205); or 2010, **200-205**), the second only announces the topic of the general sciences, which would have to include philosophy. Vollenhoven deferred the discussion (cf. *op. cit.*, **206**) to which, as it turned out, he never returned.

the distinct law-spheres, as over against an assertion about the unity of the cosmos, then he respects the limitations of philosophy. But when God's infinity becomes a virtual synonym for God's sovereignty, it is hard to avoid dogmatic and speculative moments, at least if these descriptions are taken to be philosophical. Philosophy has good reasons to adduce a notion of 'source' on which the world depends. But is that source to be understood as being sovereign through dominance (imposed will)? And its having an infinite essence, isn't that a speculative suggestion adduced from the experience of finitude of our world?

But Vollenhoven does maintain the difference between the philosophical and the meta-philosophical. Is he then at times confused, or must the reader apply the distinction more explicitly when interpreting Vollenhoven's text? The latter is relevant when we remind ourselves that Vollenhoven introduced the 'being of God' in a way that has nothing in common with the being of the cosmos (cf. section II.B.1. above). The fact that this should not be read as an ontological dualism is attested to by the following quote from lecture notes (Vollenhoven 1927ms, section 35), entitled "The *archè* as philosophical":

> God is sovereign. Hence he is not to be investigated by us, but [on the contrary] he investigates us. . . . That is why philosophy cannot concern itself with Him. We stand in connection with Him through religion, and only through it; a connection in the prime sense of God being its author and we its receivers, who are urged to reciprocate in love.
>
> Does that not make philosophy a-theistic? On the contrary: it will serve God so long as it remains within the boundaries set by Him. And whoever serves can never negate the one who is served.
>
> But then God and God's relation to the created world can never become an object of philosophical inquiry.

In cosmology the same problem recurs. When Vollenhoven characterizes his standpoint concerning God and cosmos as 'properly dualistic', and finds the alternative dualisms maintaining a schema of God and the Cosmos in one vertical arrangement but with incorrectly placed boundary, then one follows suit by interpreting 'proper dualism' also vertically. But then the higher that one is in the cosmic order, the closer one is to God. But that occasions misunderstanding. Every law-sphere of the cosmic order involves a case of 'law as boundary'. There is no difference in proximity to God within the cosmos (cf. Vollenhoven 1930b: 14). In other words, the vertical schema should not be applied, though Vollenhoven's terminology does not always avoid its connotation.

If *Isagôgè Philosophiae* of 1930-1931 attests to Vollenhoven's

"Scriptural dualism" at its boldest and, I might add, its most vulnerable and contestable, then the revision of the text did not at once affect the dualism, despite the changes in the account of knowledge. The 1932 version incorporated other changes that are predicated on the same dualism. The most prominent change is the discussion of the antithesis of good and evil (cf. discussion above), and its anthropological relevance in terms of the characterization of the soul. Vollenhoven also brings this to bear in his discussion of religion.

The section on religion has also undergone revision. He no longer speaks of "the religious". He now defines religion as "the connection between God and humankind that is inclusive of the whole cosmic order" (Vollenhoven 1932e: §72; 2010, Appendix IIa). This expresses the covenant understanding of religion. Now the follow-up of this quoted passage is remarkable. It continues: (religion is the connection) "that not only points over and above the cosmos [*boven den kosmos uitwijst*], but it also enables us to see the cosmos as it is" (*ibid*; cf. also §18). In *Het Calvinisme en de Reformatie van de Wijsbegeerte* (1933a) there is a similar description. There, speaking of the covenant relation as a relation between God, who does not belong to the cosmos, and the human being who does, it follows, says Vollenhoven, that this relation "does not lie within the cosmos, but, because the cosmos is taken up in this relation, it refers beyond it" (*op. cit.*, pp. 40-41). This puts the reader in a quandary. Is this description meta-philosophical (as one would expect)? But if the cosmos refers beyond itself, that trait must be of relevance for philosophy, which investigates the cosmos.

The systematics of this 'trans-cosmic' relation is that it is a connection between God and the cosmos, the latter more particularly in and through humankind. Humankind belongs to the cosmos, but it is through humankind that there is a 'referring beyond' to God. On the other hand, God places himself in relation to the cosmos/humankind via the expression of his will, which is the law. The dualism of God and cosmos/humankind is 'bridged' (as it were), not through any 'third factor' that would warrant the link, but through a 'meeting' of the two. If the 'referring beyond' on the part of humankind is to enable the relation to be laid, it must be capable of answering in a positive sense to the law, as expressed will of God. The description of the *human soul* (as of 1932) meets this demand. It being a 'direction determining centre', its direction is determined in the face of the law of God. Thus it is through the soul that the 'referring beyond' takes place. The soul is not merely an existential condition, but also an ontological one: the condition of being referential.[173] Taking into account the distinction of body and soul, one will readily see that the law that enters into this relationship between God and humankind is not modal law—at least not in a direct sense, for modal laws govern the functions of the body—but the central love command.

One cannot but think of Dooyeweerd in this connection, who in the meantime spoke of the supra-temporal heart and its position in a privileged Archimedean point. Vollenhoven I believe is trying to meet Dooyeweerd 'half way' as it were, at least to the extent that his own discourse allowed for this. However the characterizations 'supra-temporal' and 'Archimedean point' are absent in Vollenhoven here, although the privileged viewing—seeing the cosmos "as it is"—on the part of the human being/soul, who stands in the covenant relation, does come through in Vollenhoven at this point.

Vollenhoven's revised view of religion at this point still fits his 'biblical dualism'. But this revision itself turned out to be only provisional. In the *Isagôgè Philosophiae* version of 1939 Vollenhoven introduces, almost unawares, a change that will become more explicit through the further changes introduced in 1941. In 1939 the law is said to be *knowable*. The significance of this addition is easy to miss if one does not realize that this implies attributing to the law its own status of being. In the 1939 text this is not made explicit, though some implications are drawn in connection with concepts and judgments. Also there is some discussion about the use of 'boundary', when speaking of the law as boundary.[174]

---

173 In Vollenhoven 1963c: 186, Vollenhoven explicitly advises against using the term "referring beyond", though for himself he had long rejected the term, it being "too onto-logical". He prefers to speak of a Christian's "reaching out", which is existential and does more justice to the religious context of the term's use. He explains: "the human being is more than all those other creatures, because he can respond to the revelation, and this responding on the part of the human being now is the same as the 'reaching above' all the other creatures."

174 This 'boundary' discussion is in Vollenhoven 2005d/e, **13**; 2010, **13** (the 1939 edition, 1939h, the section is §12), which is about God, the cosmos and the boundary between the two. Vollenhoven now adds three Comments (in 1939h these are numbered 1, 2 and 3; in the revision of 1941 they are numbered 2, 3 and 5; cf. 2010, **13**). These three remarks attempt to clarify, without actually addressing the status of the law. The first says that God is not separated from the cosmos through the law; he is both within and beyond the cosmos. In other words, this reaffirms Gods immanence and transcendence. Comment 3 emphasizes that the term 'boundary', as spatial metaphor, is not itself meant to be a boundary in a spatial sense. This too is not a new element. The last Comment (no. 5), separates 'difference' and 'boundary'. The term 'law as boundary', Vollenhoven now states, does not adequate touch on the whole difference between God and cosmos. Vollenhoven does not explain, but he probably refers to the limitation to the creation, as over

The bigger change comes in the course of 1941.

Isagôgè Philosophiae of 1941 has new passages (e.g. on society) and revisions, particularly the discussion of religion. The phrase "referring beyond" is deleted, nor is there any mention of 'privileged seeing'. But the most important change lies in four additional Comments to section **13**—numbered 1, 4, 6 and 7 (cf. 2005d/e or 2010)—about God, law and cosmos.

Taking the *Comments 6 and 7* together, the first focuses directly on the mode of being of the law, which is said to be a "holding for". The law is always distinct from that for which it holds, *viz.* the cosmos. This is of course clear from the start. But the reference to its own mode of being emphasizes that the law is now taken to be something distinct from God. (It is of course God who is said to posit it, but this is like the cosmos which, though said to be created by God, is still distinct from him.) God's being is to 'be sovereign', the law's being is to 'hold for', and that of the cosmos is to 'be subject'. *Comment 7* says that this 'holding for' is not a matter of human choice. E.g. normative laws remain valid, also when they are transgressed.

So law is taken to be a 'domain', a realm of being in its own right. Does this 'realist emphasis' of the law not constitute a regress towards neo-Kantianism (of the Freiburg school)? In a superficial sense Vollenhoven is 'in their vicinity'. If laws were taken to be objective values, then there would be a similarity. But the neo-Kantians held that values become empowered as norms—hence gain an authority of 'holding for'—only through the evaluating subject. That takes validity to be a subjective feature; then value, in the status prior to gaining its validity, is merely a kind of intellectual objective concept. For Vollenhoven laws/norms are above the distinction of subject and object (cf. *Comment 6*). If value serves to make being knowable (cf. our discussion above), then laws—these now claimed to be knowable—no doubt also have value, but that serves to recognize and acknowledge them, not to empower them with validity. So there is not really a rapprochement with neo-Kantianism.

But what does it benefit to 'add' a distinct domain of being? We will see presently that it enables Vollenhoven to express a deeper sense of the relevance of law for cosmic life. But its more immediate effect is to *undercut* the dualism of God and cosmos, as favoured by Vollenhoven up to this point, but without falling back into a monism which, superficially,

---

against revelation and fulfilment. Then he adds that 'difference', as relevant in contrasts such as Creator-creature, infinite-finite, etc., does not actually act as boundary. This last remark affects biblical dualism directly and adversely (as becomes clear in the 1941 edition).

might be thought to be the only alternative.

Comment 1 addresses this.[175] This remark is important in that Vollenhoven takes distance from both a dualist understanding of the God-cosmos relationship and a monistic one. In the dualist understanding the relationship is determined by relevant qualities of its terms. This is clear from Vollenhoven's own prior dualism. The law, as 'expressed will' of God, is volitional, not ontological, and the cosmic/human side 'stands in subjection' through the soul. Law-consciousness—divine expression and human response—remains enclosed in a religious consciousness of difference. We add that, given the volitional characteristic of law, this consciousness could take on an authoritarian air, particularly when nothing modulates sovereignty and subservience. So when sovereignty and subjection are 'defined' merely by appealing to their difference, there is an 'automatic' dominance on the part of sovereignty, empowering the 'Thou shalt'. In the early Dooyeweerd there is evidence (as we saw) of an authoritarianism, which in his case was reinforced by his 'intra-cosmic' view of providence (cf. chapter 3, section III.F.5.a.). But in Vollenhoven, the cosmos is, from the start, more open, not merely intra-cosmic. He allows for 'commands' that offer orientation within the difference between the expressed divine law and the cosmos, particularly the love command that is answered to in the moral choice of good and evil. And there are the further directives that guide, though Vollenhoven is silent about this after 1931.

What the acknowledgement of the distinct being of the law directly affects is that it serves as warrant for the *connection* between God and cosmos/human being. There is still their difference, of course, but this difference is bridged not merely through the qualities of the terms, i.e. God's being sovereign and the cosmos' being subservient. The law mediates the connection. This is no longer adequately described as the boundary of difference, it is the basic bridge of the difference. The law that connects is indeed 'posited' by God. But at the same time, in order

---

175   The comment reads as follows: "This means [i.e. upon focussing on the relationship between God and cosmos] that we reject the following: a. The attempt to understand the basic relationship between God and cosmos purely in terms of their similarity. This happens when God and cosmos are seen as manifestations of phases of a 'being' or 'process': In this way, God as well as cosmos are subordinated, for example, as *coincidentia oppositorum* ([the coincidence of opposites] Nicholas of Cusa and Hegel), to something that stands above both and hence are coordinated with one another. b. The attempt to understand the basic relationship between God and cosmos purely in terms of their difference. This happens when people set God and cosmos over against each other as the divine and the non-divine and consequently call God *das ganz Andere* ([the "wholly Other"] K. Barth); in this way, the relationship becomes a contradictory one."

for the law to connect with the cosmos/human being, the law must actually serve to *support and secure* cosmic life. This makes any 'referring beyond' of the cosmos/human being, via the soul, redundant. For the law's support and security is no longer primarily 'for (or through) the soul' but for the 'whole human being', body and soul. (Cf. the attestation of this in the next paragraph.) The law is posited by God so as to be *in correlation with the cosmos*.[176] With this understanding of law, whatever authoritarian tone may continue to cling to 'law', 'sovereignty', 'will', and the like, it is now abated in favour of the law's entailing the divine concern that life be good. Up to this point God and the world had been in correlation, in 1941 Vollenhoven emphasizes the correlation of the law and the world.

Vollenhoven did not immediately make this explicit in print. But in Vollenhoven 1951h: 55-56, there is the explicit statement (repeated here as relevant in the present context):

> While it may be so that the law's diversity is not as extensive as that of the cosmos, [diversity] is certainly not absent regarding the law. Thus, one readily notices, analogous to the difference between soul and body in connection with the human being—taken in the Scriptural sense of heart and function mantle—the difference between the principle intent [*hoofdsom*] and differentiation in connection with the law. The former summarizes the kernel of the law as the demand of love to God and to the fellow human being, whom he has placed beside us. However, this one law [of love] is differentiated in a multiplicity of laws for functional life.

The modal laws and the central love command together now reflect the schema of the bodily modal functions and the soul or heart, in a way that brings what is central and what is modal/functional more closely together than was formulated before. The term 'differentiation' remains vague

---

[176] A passage from Vollenhoven valedictory address, "Plato's realisme", quoted earlier, is apposite here. "Hence Calvinistic philosophy—contrary to Greek-Hellenistic thought and the synthesis thought dependent on it—sees the law as the boundary between God and the cosmos. Whereby at the same time the dualism, that is unacceptable for a Christian but still finding acceptance, of the correlation of God and world is replaced by the view which is neither dualistic nor monistic, of a law posed by God that is correlate with a world created by him." Vollenhoven 1963a: 128; in Tol and Bril 1992: 155-156. The qualification, expressed in the second sentence, is first put into effect in 1941. I add, as formal comment, that a correlation would appear to involve a duality of two 'things', that nevertheless belong together without being 'bonded'. When Vollenhoven spoke of the "Biblical dualism" of God and the world, this was taken as the most encompassing correlation, even if not explicitly express that way. The correlation of law and world assumes the acknowledged being of the law (something formerly wrapped up on the acknowledgement of God's will), and it allows God to be more primary than both law and world, say a ground of being that sustains all. In any case the attention given to 'correlations' is more pronounced in the later Vollenhoven.

here, but it does suggest that the concern of love is not divorced from the conditions of law that regulate the universe. Anthropology represents this, because the whole human being is co-terminus with the whole of cosmic life.

The threesome 'God-law-cosmos'—*Comment 1* continues—should not be interpreted monistically either. For then God and cosmos are both subsumed under some common feature (process, qualification) they share or that applies to each. If the law is taken to be such a common factor between God and the human being, then God is subservient to the law. In that guise the law would act as a factor of fate for both God and the human being.[177] It is clear that Vollenhoven's new view avoids this monistic alternative as well.

Then there is also *Comment 4*. It has two parts. The first part expresses a criticism of realism, that is, realism when understood as the doctrine that maintains that the law also holds for God. This is a case of the point just made. But this comment's criticism is also in line with Vollenhoven's earlier work. Realism, in the sense meant, i.e. God being subservient to the law, is a version of partial (or pan-) cosmism, which was never an option for Vollenhoven.

The second part of this Comment expresses Vollenhoven's rejection of "the attempt to understand the basic relation between God and cosmos as that between whole and part." Vollenhoven states that this is consistently applied in pantheism and pancosmism, inconsistently applied in partial theism and partial cosmism. In other words, this second part of the Comment refers to the critical apparatus Vollenhoven had developed in the late 1920s. The rejection of the positions mentioned (of cosmisms and theisms) is in line with Vollenhoven's earlier critical stance. One wonders whether this part of Comment 4 is merely meant to make the rejection explicit.

In a footnote to an article of 1941 (the same year that Comment 4 appears), Vollenhoven states that he "has abandoned" the attempt to characterize "non-scriptural conceptions" in terms of "the most encompassing relation, namely between God and cosmos", and he then lists the options of the various theisms and cosmisms, in the way he had

---

177   Viewed from the point of view of the logic of relations, the dualistic context in fact encourages a monadistic understanding of relations, whereby the relationship depends upon the predicates of the terms. The revised view accords better with the external view of the relational element, a view that was already accepted for the primary relations within each law-sphere in the context of the intersection principle. Of course, the relation between God and the cosmos cannot be decided merely on the grounds of the formal understanding of what a relation is.

distinguished these.[178] Naturally, the stated positions are still objected to. But his point is to clarify that he now prefers to characterize conceptions differently. He now takes the most pressing problem to be that of realism and nominalism. He takes realism as entailing the acceptance of the distinction between being and becoming, whereby being serves as the law of becoming, while nominalism denies emphasizing being at all (*op. cit.*: 67). We see at once that this approach to 'non-scriptural philosophy' directly reflects Vollenhoven's own new emphasis on the being of the law. Vollenhoven's abandoning of his former versions of 'theisms' and 'cosmisms' in fact entails a rejection of his own 'scriptural dualism' to the extent that that dualism shares the framework of that approach, i.e. within the characterization (as Comment 4 now has it) of the *God-cosmos relation* as that of *whole and part*. The whole is indeed represented in that vague term (as first used by Vollenhoven), namely 'the religious', of which the cosmos is a part. The threesome, God-law-cosmos, whereby the law has its own being, now definitely supersedes that understanding.

So the terms 'God', 'law' and 'cosmos', that together came to serve as a kind of logo to signify Vollenhoven's position, in fact came into its own only from 1941 on. About at the same time—the early WWII years—Vollenhoven makes another switch in his approach to the study of the history of philosophy. The approach via the theme of realism and nominalism was in fact short-lived and in 1943 it is itself definitely abandoned.[179] In *Isagôgè Philosophiae* of 1941 one finds a prescient clue, that will soon be picked up by Vollenhoven and developed into a full method.[180] The conceptions, says Vollenhoven in this last public revision of *Isagôgè Philosophiae*, that one has reasons to oppose, should not simply be rejected. One must, on the contrary, make every attempt to understand such conceptions and thus also be clear as to why they are subject to criticism. However, *Isagôgè Philosophiae* is not the place for such discussions, he adds, for that text attempts to give a connected account of the position Vollenhoven himself deems worthy of defence. The critical discussion should be conducted "in the survey of the history of philosophy; for it is there that the different schools of thought are

---

178   Vollenhoven 1941k: 65-66, footnote 2 (first instalment).

179   Vollenhoven 1941k. This text was broken off after three instalments had appeared. This series is an emended and expanded version of approximately the first half of Vollenhoven 1941j, a separately published, 162 page text with the same title.

180   From the mid-1940s on, Vollenhoven published many articles related to the problem-historical method in the three media of the Association for Calvinistic Philosophy: *Philosophia Reformata, Mededelingen van de Vereniging voor Calvinistische Wijsbegeerte and Correspondentiebladen*.

outlined within *the framework of their basic thoughts* and in *the context of their historic period*" (Vollenhoven 2010, 4; emphases added; the passage first appeared in 1941b.)

This proposed critical discussion has two parameters: the framework of a school's basic thoughts and the context of its historical period. These parameters become the 'type' and 'current' distinction respectively of Vollenhoven's so-called "consequential problem-historical method". *Types* focus on distinguishable cosmological schemata, which are often found to essentially recur in time in the history of philosophy. Each such schema reflects a conceptualization of the modal law-order/law-spheres. *Currents* on the other hand signal the main features of the subsequent ages in which philosophy is practiced, in which schools wax and wane or renew themselves. A current proceeds from a sense of urgency as to what needs to be thought, which problems call for solution. In other words, a current reflects the sense of being addressed in the practice of philosophy; what Christian thought would bring in relation to the love command. Currents occur uniquely, types recur repeatedly.[181] The development of this method, and its application in outlining the main thoughts of the different schools in the history of philosophy, occupied Vollenhoven in the last three decades of his career, affecting everything that he wrote in his later years. Little can be fully appreciated of this 'later Vollenhoven' without an orientation in this problem-historical method.[182]

We have anticipated two of the more important changes—in anthropology and in the conception of the law—that Vollenhoven incorporated into his work, after he had formulated his initial definitive position. Our emphasis is on Vollenhoven's part in the *emergence* of Reformed thought, not on his proposals in connection with its later (historical) consolidations. That later history needs at least a firm basis in the material that has been discussed so far. Having reviewed and analysed the main contours of this early work (apart from a reflection on the past reserved for an addendum) this would appear to be a suitable moment to break off the constructive

181 For an exploratory discussion of the problem-historical method, cf. Bril 2005. For a discussion of the method against the background of Vollenhoven's systematic thought, cf. Tol 1993. For a discussion of the method's application to Ancient philosophy, cf. Tol 2007

182 The schematic charts associated with this method, explanations of terminology, and very many useful observations related to the content of the history of philosophy are to be found in Vollenhoven 2000, thanks to the extensive editorial work of K.A. Bril. Vollenhoven's articles, written for the *Oosthoeks Encyclopedie*, are predicated on the problem-historical method. They have been collected in Vollenhoven 2005c, with many comments added by the editor, Bril.

part of our discussion.

VI. ADDENDUM. VOLLENHOVEN'S RETROSPECTIVE ACCOUNT OF THE EARLY YEARS
In later years of his career, Vollenhoven occasionally looked back on his early work. He felt that there was something to learn from the past. He was aware of having come a long way from the intellectual position he defended in his dissertation. How does he formulate what he now sees of that earlier work? How does he assess its influence within the circle of his influence?

There are four autobiographical passages in print, two of which were published/approved in his lifetime, the other two appeared posthumously. One (which he published) relates to the time when Reformed philosophy emerged, the other three occur in the context of the discussion of current problems, the most prominent of which is the problem of time.[183] For Vollenhoven, part of that problem is how it came about that the numerical and the spatial law-spheres came to be seen as temporal, something he himself, in his later years, came to reject. He feels that his dissertation played a role here, in particular that it exercised an influence on Dooyeweerd in connection with the questions surrounding the understanding of number and time.

We note in passing that there is no doubt in Vollenhoven's mind about Dooyeweerd's acquaintance with the dissertation. Thus Vollenhoven feels that he "too is to blame for the difficulties in this regard" (IV; 1968b: 202). It is while discussing this problem that he characterizes the philosophical conception he was partial to in his dissertation as being 'ennoetistic'. This characterization calls for discussion. (We met with this term above, in section V.A.) But we will first pause to look at an earlier statement about himself and Dooyeweerd, regarding the period when Reformed philosophy emerged, for this fits the timeframe of our study. Then we will discuss Vollenhoven's characterization of his dissertation as

---

183   The four sources are numbered I-IV + date to facilitate reference:
(I; 1953p), i.e. D.H.Th. Vollenhoven, "Divergentierapport I" (April/May 1953), in Tol and Bril 1992: 107-117. (This is a posthumous publication.)
(II; 1953o), i.e. D.H.Th. Vollenhoven, "Wijsbegeerte, Calvinistisch", *Oosthoek' Encyclopedie*, 4th edition, volume 15, 1953; reprinted in Vollenhoven 2005c: 78-79. In the 5th edition the autobiographical passage in question is deleted in the article, now titled "Calvinistische wijsbegeerte"; this version is also reprinted in *op. cit.* : 76-77.
(III; 1963c), i.e. D.H.Th. Vollenhoven, "Problemen rondom de tijd" (1963); first published (posthumously) in Tol and Bril 1992, especially pp. 173-174.
(IV; 1968b), i.e. D.H.Th. Vollenhoven, "Problemen van de tijd in onze kring" (1968), text approved by Vollenhoven; first published in Tol and Bril 1992, especially pp. 202-203.

remembered, and follow this up by a discussion of the possible influence of the dissertation on Dooyeweerd. We end by taking a closer look at 'ennoetism' in Vollenhoven.

A. The early years in a nutshell

The autobiographical passage in source II (1953o) reads as follows (my translation, with the numbering of the sentences added for purposes of reference):

> (i) In connection with the mutual connection between intuition and thought, Vollenhoven, in his dissertation (1918), came close to the conception of [Henri] Poincaré, who combined life philosophy with ennoetism. (ii) This led, shortly afterwards, to undertaking a more focussed study of these two elements and the possibility of combining them with Calvinism, whereby the latter implied the ontic correlation of moral law and moral subject, that already [G.H.J.W.J.] Geesink had taken to be ethical. (iii) This was when Dooyeweerd too began to see the necessity of philosophical reflection. (iv) Both authors had a very searching contact. (v) In the following years the theory of knowledge was definitely subordinated to ontology, (vi) and Dooyeweerd demonstrated that the life- and worldview is always rooted in a specific law-idea. (vii) In 1926 both authors were simultaneously appointed to chairs at the Vrije Universiteit. (viii) Shortly thereupon, the distinction was drawn in anthropology between religion and the function of faith, and, related to this, heart (soul) and function mantel (including the psychical function); (ix) also the theory of the aspects, of the retro- and anticipations, and that of subject and object functions were further elaborated. (x) In 1931 and following, some characteristic publications appeared in short succession [by both Dooyeweerd (1931, 1935-36) and Vollenhoven (1932b, 1933a)].[184]

Re (i). Vollenhoven indicates the conception of Poincaré by naming its time current—life philosophy—and type—ennoetism. As to Poincaré's time current, in source IV (1968b) this is said to be pragmatism. In light of Poincaré's conventionalism, I believe that 'pragmatism' is more suitable than 'life philosophy'. But the characterization 'life philosophy' is better suitable to Vollenhoven himself at the time, when we take into account his stated dependence on Henri Bergson, who was definitely a proponent of life philosophy. (Vollenhoven gleaned the three forms of intuition, concrete, analytical and metaphysical, from a reading of his work; cf.

---

184 An edited version of this article is in the Vollenhoven archives, that was presumably initially destined for the 5th edition, but the article was subsequently rewritten. In this edited version sentence (iv) reads: "As of 1921, these authors, both having now settled in The Hague, had a very searching contact." Sentence (v) reads: "In the following years Vollenhoven learned to distinguish the psychical [function] from the soul, [and] the theory of knowledge was definitely subordinated to ontology." Finally, in sentence (ix), there is added: "also the theory of the modal aspects, . . .".

Vollenhoven 1918a: 348-351). About the "mutual connection between intuition and thought", I believe we may interpret this as "intuition and knowledge". The intuition is based on intra-mental awareness, knowledge on the forms of sensibility. The term 'thought' applies, in the dissertation, to both intuition and knowledge, namely in representing the 'subjective pole' in the contrast between 'thought and being'. Poincaré too distinguished intuition (the awareness of the mind's power of being able to repeat unendingly whatever can once be repeated) and forms of sensibility (cf. chapter 2, section III.A. and III.B.).

Re (ii). This sentence is a teaser. First of all, the "elements" that came up for closer study must be intuition and thought, not life philosophy and ennoetism. This would appear to be the natural reading. Also, while 'life philosophy' was a going term, 'ennoetism' (of Vollenhoven's own later making) was nowhere in the vicinity at the time. This "more focussed study" refers, in all likelihood, to Vollenhoven's study leave, from the end of May till the end of September, 1920, in Leipzig, to study under Felix Krüger. His theme was, as he explained in a letter to Krüger,[185] "the relation of emotion and intellect in Bergson, tested genetically and socio-psychologically". He hoped to acquire results that would confirm that "neither intuition (emotional knowledge) nor intellect can do without the other, and [both] are in and of themselves abstractions of psychical occurrence [*aus dem psychischen Geschehen*]." The teaser is to know what Vollenhoven means when he mentions his attempt to combine intuition and thought with Calvinism. The letter to Krüger has nothing about this. It may be that Vollenhoven refers to a renewed sense of Calvinism, in which Geesink had a role at that time. Wilhelm Geesink (1854-1929), who is Vollenhoven's mentor after the death of Jan Woltjer in 1917, did emphasize Calvinism's moral implications. I know of no source that illuminates specifically what Vollenhoven has in mind here.[186]

Re (iii). The mention of Dooyeweerd's becoming interested in

---

185 Letter to F. Krüger, 19 May 1920. For more about this trip and its disappointing results, cf. Stellingwerff 1992: 42-46.

186 There is a commemorative article by Vollenhoven on the occasion of Geesink's retirement from the Free University in 1926, whom Vollenhoven succeeded. In it he mentions the distinction Geesink often applied, between general human morality and Christian morality. When this threatened to become a rigid principle of division Geesink switched, says Vollenhoven, somewhere around 1910, to "the distinction between norm, subject and activity, which fit the content far better." Vollenhoven 1927a: 92. There is no evidence that Vollenhoven may have taken this distinction to heart at about the time that he is himself referring to, i.e. shortly after 1918. After all, he already worked with the distinction of 'norm and subject' in his dissertation, applying this in logic and the humanities.

philosophical reflection presents a slight problem of timing. Vollenhoven's "at this time" would appear to refer to the time of his own study leave (in 1920), and one then thinks of Dooyeweerd's (only extant) letter to Vollenhoven, 17 December 1920. But in that letter Dooyeweerd is already actively involved in philosophy. Vollenhoven's description (of Dooyeweerd's becoming interested) applies more aptly to his later memory of a letter from Dooyeweerd in mid-1919 (cf. chapter 3, section III.B.), although this is stretching "at this time" somewhat.

Re (iv). The contact that Vollenhoven refers to took place, according to the emended version (cf. footnote 184), when both Dooyeweerd and Vollenhoven were in The Hague, which is as of May 1921. Vollenhoven noted elsewhere the fruitful contact between October 1921 and the fall of 1922 (cf. chapter 3, section III.B.).

Re (v). In the "following years" (in other words as of 1922) the theme of 'knowing resorting under being' is relevant. This accords with what we found in Dooyeweerd's work of late 1922–early 1923 ("Cosmos en Logos"). This accords also with our own observation that the prior *polarity* of thought and being is still defended in Vollenhoven 1921c (which is dated July 1921). Vollenhoven's memory, expressed in 1963, of having broached this resorting theme already during a Hardenbroek conference in 1919, is not consistent with what he states here.[187] The emended version (cf. footnote 184) includes the remarkable admission about 'learning to distinguish the psychical function from the soul'. This can hardly be other than a reference to the influence of Antheunis Janse. The learning experience began with Janse's letters to Vollenhoven, late 1922, and took effect after Vollenhoven's breakdown, as Vollenhoven's own memory here evidences (cf. chapter 3, section II.C.).

Re (vi). Dooyeweerd's demonstrating that a life- and worldview is rooted in a law-idea is the development in Dooyeweerd that is first evident in the latter part of 1923 (cf. chapter 3, section III.F.). In this article Vollenhoven represents both Dooyeweerd and himself in this report of the emergence of Calvinistic philosophy. Thus his mention of 'law-idea' should not be taken as implying that he himself at first agreed to this term.

Re (vii). The appointments to the chairs at the Free University in 1926 need no comment.

Re (viii). The distinction between the faith function and religion is rather obvious in Dooyeweerd as of 1928, when he speaks of "the religious kernel of personality", where previously he referred to the unique role

---

187 Cf. chapter 2, footnote 153.

of the faith function (cf. chapter 3, section III.F.5.c.). Given the (more or less) chronological sequence in Vollenhoven's report, it would appear that he probably has Dooyeweerd in mind here. But in that case he short-changes himself. In his *Logos en Ratio* (1926a) the distinction is also evident, e.g. when he says that regeneration is presupposed by faith (*op. cit.*: 30) or "[t]he three offices [of priest, prophet and king] belong to the terrain of religion" (*op. cit.*: 32). The distinction he mentions next, between heart or soul and function mantle (i.e. the body and its functions), is certainly due to him, this being his typical wording. This distinction is first evident in *Isagôgè Philosophiae* of 1932.

Re (ix). The mention of the theory of the modal aspects, of the modal retrocipations and anticipations and that of subject and object functions reflects the developments of the details of Calvinistic philosophy in the second half of the 1920s. These theories were being tested at the time before they took on a definitive form.

Re (x). By the early 1930s Vollenhoven and Dooyeweerd have found their metier, Vollenhoven with his *Het Calvinisme en de Reformatie in de Wijsbegeerte* (1933a) and Dooyeweerd with *De Wijsbegeerte der Wetsidee*, three volumes (1935-1936). Dooyeweerd refers to the latter text in *De Crisis in de Humanistische Staatsleer* (1931) as a work that is evidently in an advanced stage (*op. cit.*: 3, 99, 125).

The above autobiographical note of Vollenhoven, written in 1953, is the closest to the events and the history remembered of all the statements of memory. As thumbnail sketch it is essentially accurate in light of the evidence found to date. Why this statement was deleted for the 5th edition of the *Oosthoeks Encyclopedie* is difficult to say. Perhaps Vollenhoven felt that at least some of the details mentioned require more discussion to be illuminating. At the time there was no archival material generally available. It is certainly true that, without the backup of research, at least some of the points mentioned are difficult to appreciate in what they entail.

B. The dissertation as remembered

A point that deserves fuller discussion is Vollenhoven's characterization of his early work as being ennoetistic. It is a term of Vollenhoven's own making, it being the 'type'-characterization of a philosophical conception. Types are the general 'schemata' of 'views as to the structure of the cosmos' that find adherence throughout the history of western philosophy. But ennoetism is mentioned also with a view to a problem Vollenhoven raises, *viz.* that of a difference between himself and Dooyeweerd, in connection with which the name of Henri Poincaré occurs and also the correlation of number and time. In this section we focus on the characterization of the dissertation; in the next section Vollenhoven's reference to Dooyeweerd will be discussed.

We begin by selecting relevant passages from the sources listed above in footnote 183:

> Listing I; 1953p: 115: "In his dissertation Vollenhoven accepted, with Poincaré, that the succession of number is correlate to time. In this connection Vollenhoven did not speak of time in space."

> Listing II; 1953o: 78: "In connection with the mutual connection between intuition and thought, Vollenhoven, in his dissertation (1918), came close to the conception of [Henri] Poincaré, who combined life philosophy with ennoetism."

> Listing III; 1963c: 174: "Where is time first introduced? In the arithmetical function, and through it (later) to all the [modal] functions. In Dooyeweerd [time] is exclusively in the functions." [The schematic portrayal of ennoetism occurring here in the text is repeated in listing IV.]

> Listing IV; 1968b: 202-203: "In my dissertation, which appeared in 1918 (. . .), I was still too dependent on Henri Poincaré, an influential French philosopher at the time, who was an ennoetist. He was an adherent of Kant's conception, but . . . with an irrationalist feature of a moderate pragmatism. I don't need to discuss Poincaré now, at least with respect to the question as to where precisely he stood, for the question that interests me particularly is that of number and space.
>
> The schema of ennoetism is:
>
>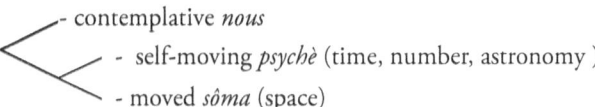
>
> - contemplative *nous*
> - self-moving *psychè* (time, number, astronomy)
> - moved *sôma* (space)
>
> Time pertains to motion; which is why it is considered to be correlate to number. Matter is what is moved, taken to be primarily correlate to space. In that way number comes to be above space, and is the correlate of the psychical, with the world-*psychè*. Hence, according to Poincaré, the succession of numbers is connected with, or secured in, the succession of time. This proposition [about the succession of numbers and that of time] is thanks (owing) to Poincaré, insofar as it finds adherence in our circle [i.e. in Dooyeweerd], and it stems from the time of my dissertation."

In our own discussion of Vollenhoven's dissertation (cf. chapter 2) we found clear evidence of the influence of Poincaré. Numbers are constructions of the mind, as Poincaré averred, being based on repetition of successive recurrence of a mental act (cumulatively adding 1 to 1, to 1+1, etc.). The intuition of this possibility is the basis for accepting the arithmetical principle of complete induction. Vollenhoven speaks of first order arithmetic, this being the account of the number concept, that arises through counting, and second order arithmetic, which is the science of arithmetic. (Cf. chapter 2, section III.A.) Geometry, in turn, is based on the 'group' concept, which is a specific set of conditions to which the transformations of spatial figures are subject. For Poincaré the group concept "pre-exists in our minds, at least potentially" (Poincaré, 1902), while experience presents an opportunity to apply a specific group. The one that is actually chosen for that purpose is based on convention, being whatever suits the psycho-physical makeup of the body best. Vollenhoven, while accepting this, takes a stricter line. Convenience in light of the psycho-physical makeup of the human body is not itself an explanation, but calls for one. The 'forms of sensibility' of the body provide the a priori possibility of localizing things spatially and temporally. This dictates a preferred spatial structure (first order Euclidean three-dimensional geometry), while the science of geometry (second order geometry) studies all the possible 'spaces' as based on the different group conditions. (Cf. chapter 2, section III.B.)

Essential to Vollenhoven's recollection of his own dissertation is the Kant-Poincaré precedence. Kant made an essential distinction between sensibility and understanding. Sensibility, through which one undergoes the outer and inner experience of data, is controlled by *forms* of sensibility, these forms being ordering schemata that allow us to experience sense-data either in sequence (time-wise) or contemporaneously (space-wise). The data, as organized by these forms, constitute the 'material' for the mind (understanding) to work on in terms of its own spontaneity and categories. The human awareness of the forms of sensibility is intuitive, which is why, in Kant, intuition is always related to (possible) sense-experience. He does not acknowledge a 'mental' or 'intellectual intuition'. Here the schema of ennoetism emerges, with its basic distinction between mind and sensibility (or the body), and at the bodily level, the distinction between *psychè* and *sôma*, in correlation with number and space, respectively.

Kant accounted for arithmetic and geometry by appealing to the forms of sensibility. As Vollenhoven has it, Poincaré's view of number and space is geared to the same schema. We (with Vollenhoven) need not ask whether this is persuasive, for Poincaré is not so explicit about the ontological (as over against the epistemological) foundations of number and space.[188] But what we do need to ask is whether Vollenhoven does justice to himself, *viz.* regarding the position he claims he took in the dissertation. We do find a similar sort of schema, in that there is a primary distinction between mentality and the psycho-physical, and in the latter, the temporal and spatial forms of sensibility. But in linking number and space to this schema, Vollenhoven is entirely clear (in 1918a) in insisting that *number* is correlated to a *mental intuition*, not to the temporal form of sensibility, while space and geometry is associated with the *psycho-physical body*. The two ranks of the synthetic a priori are linked to this distinction. The synthetic a priori of arithmetic appeals to the mental intuition, while the geometrical a priori (of localization) is based on the spatial form of sensibility. The *temporal form of sensibility* is correlated, not to number, but to *kinematics*! One statement sets it all in perspective: "the apriority of arithmetic is of higher rank than that of geometry and kinematics; we can distinguish them as intuition and form of sensibility" (Vollenhoven 1918a: 417) (Cf. chapter 2, section III.C.)

I don't believe it is possible to make the wording of the dissertation match with what Vollenhoven remembers. Even a not-so-close reading of the dissertation does not provide sufficient scope for an alternative reading. The difficulty is two-pronged: there is the matter of intuition as over against forms of sensibility, and there is the problem of where time and number fit.

To take the second difficulty first, it could be that a statement of L.E.J. Brouwer hung in the background of Vollenhoven's memory. In his inaugural address (Brouwer 1912), Brouwer states: "However weak the position of intuitionism seemed to be after this period of mathematical development [since the time of Kant], it has recovered by abandoning Kant's apriority of space but adhering the more resolutely to the apriority of time" (*op. cit.*: 69). This, to be sure, is not a rehabilitation of Kant, but it does put the emphasis on the intuition, as relevant to number, at a point in Kant's conception where, in Kant, the temporal form of sensibility is addressed. This is the 'place' where Vollenhoven thought he had himself positioned number and time. But in the dissertation Vollenhoven has two views of time. There is time as sequence and as succession. Time as form of sensibility is time as *sequence*. It is a *schema of organization* of one-after-the-other. This is relevant to motion and kinematics, e.g. in tracing the path of motion of a moving object. The 'number line' is relevant here,

---

188   Vollenhoven's characterization of Henri Poincaré (1854-1912) being an "influential French philosopher" is somewhat misleading. He was the leading mathematician of his day, whose writings on the philosophy of mathematics and science were influential.

the (as Bergson called it) spatialization of time. On the other hand, time as *succession* is the *actual undergoing*, in a cumulative way, of experienced changes of state. This is a matter of mental awareness that is quite distinct from any sensitivity of the body. The natural numbers are 'constructed' through counting, and counting is predicated on this intuitive awareness of succession. That awareness is the essential support of the a priori principle of complete induction. In this sense number (in counting) is correlated to time (as succession).

The other difficulty of intuition and form of sensibility also cannot be bridged. In a superficial sense one might appeal to Kant's use of the word "intuition", which he limits to sensibility (pure and applied). But if this is seized on to put number and time in Vollenhoven back in their 'Kantian place', then that creates havoc with Vollenhoven's epistemology. He distinguished (at the time) between 'knowing' and 'knowing that'. The former is essentially a matter of *acquaintance*, which involves a process. One can increasingly get to know an object better, and even the Self, in an approaching, or a Self-approaching process (as the case may be). The forms of sensibility mediate this process. But there is also the immediate awareness of knowing *that* I undergo seeing or feeling or willing or distinguishing, etc. This is an *intuitive awareness* of the state I am in (this is the 'concrete intuition') when and as I stand in relation to other things or persons. I can only know my states 'occurrently', i.e. when they really occur (subject oriented), whereas I can (progressive) know things so long as they are in my presence (object oriented). So quite apart from choice or use of terminology, there are two 'scenes' in the early Vollenhoven calling for recognition: 'becoming acquainted with' and 'being immediately aware of'. The one may (and does) reinforce the other, but neither can be subsumed under the other. The succession that is relevant to counting, and to grasping number that results from this,[189] is based on the primal two-oneness of intuition in self-awareness; this succession is *not* a species of sequence in a Self-approaching process of temporal localization.

Is it possible to characterize Vollenhoven's position more adequately? We found in chapter 2 that Vollenhoven's early work does at least hint at evincing 'a position'. The term 'occasionalism' arose in that context. How does occasionalism compare to ennoetism? We will need to define these terms first. We have, however, found a use for the latter term in the context of characterizing Vollenhoven initial definitive position. I believe

---
189   There is also the additional factor of the analytical intuition, needed to consolidate difference and similarity in the intuited content; cf. chapter 2, section VI.F.

that the significance of 'ennoetism' lies, not in the dissertation itself, but in the move away from the dissertation.

But before turning to this 'problem in Vollenhoven' there is still the question of the relevance in Vollenhoven's addressing Dooyeweerd about 'ennoetism'. If Vollenhoven appears to misinterpret the very work he claims influenced Dooyeweerd, what was that influence, if any? After all, Dooyeweerd nowhere seems to admit this. Is Vollenhoven's feeling of regret in this connection then misplaced? We need to take a closer look at Dooyeweerd's understanding of time and how it compares to Vollenhoven's view in the dissertation.

C. Dooyeweerd's 'modalization' of time

Let us summarize Vollenhoven's position on time as evidenced in the dissertation. Time and number 'lodge' in the intra-mental, concrete intuition. There is first the intuitive awareness or occurrent experience (Dutch: *"beleven"*) of awareness taking place. Secondly, its taking place gives rise to an accrual of content, in step with the acts of intuition. If there were no *succession*, there could be no accrual at all, thus time as succession is essential here. Then, thirdly, the addition of the analytical intuition reinforces the awareness of similarity and difference in the content accrued. Here is where the grasp of number takes place, *viz.* through the successive grasping of the addition of different 'this's', as this accrues in succession. This is prior to any concept formation; for grasping content is fixing on meaning (a prerequisite for any concept-formation). This grasping is of the essence of *Gegenstand* formation, which takes place by means of the analytical intuition, in submission to the principle of identity. In light of this principle, mental content is 'identified' (posited) as a fixed, objective meaning. The analytical intuition is not itself original, but it *presupposes* experience as needed for any content to be able to accrue. In other words, the analytical intuition presupposes the concrete intuition and the reality of succession, i.e. time. The intuition itself is a bi-unity that always involves the Self, in the sense that the intuition is the awareness of a state of the Self by virtue of the Self's participating in relations to things or other persons.

If we now take a representative text of Dooyeweerd on the topic of the problem of time, say, "The problem of time in the philosophy of the law-idea" (Dooyeweerd 1940), the reader soon discovers a (close) similarity in argumentation.

First, the sense of time, says Dooyeweerd, is deeply rooted in human experience; it is at a depth of *occurrent experience* [*beleven*] that is beyond the reach of the theoretical [or analytical] consciousness (*op. cit.*, p. 160-161). "Only in the "*beleven*" does the knowledge of reality become *our own*, and the awareness of *our own being* is the first condition of genuine knowledge" (p. 161). These statements place time in the centre of what in Vollenhoven was the concrete intuition and its link to self-consciousness.

Now, continues Dooyeweerd, whatever remains foreign to our Selfhood cannot be known (*op. cit.*: 161). It is in non-theoretical or naïve experience that one experiences full reality, in its 'in-one'-ness (*op. cit.*: 162). (This is much like Vollenhoven's 'bi-unity'.) Implicit in this cohering experience is the modal structure, which is 'how' reality reveals itself to us (*op. cit.*: 164). Thus human experience, in the deep sense of occurrent experience, and the experience of time this involves, is channelled in modes of being, that are at once modes of experience and a cadre in which reality appears. "Temporal reality *functions* in a diversity of modal aspects, which are not themselves subject to change in time, but rather form a constant and fundamental modal *cadre*, within which the individual changing things, events, activity, acts and societal forms have their variable *functions*, and which first *makes possible* that variable functioning" (*op. cit.*: 163-164). Given this modal cadre at the (depth) level of the Self's experience, a level where time is a real factor, it comes as no surprise that the modal cadre is a framework of time, in the sense that, in each modality, time comes to expression in a distinct way (*op. cit.*: 164). Dooyeweerd proceeds to list and describe the distinct ways in which time is modally expressed (*op. cit.*: 167-174), beginning with the arithmetical aspect. In this aspect, the series of the natural numbers, from small to large, is interpreted as evincing a temporal order of earlier and later.

I believe that this account, with its focus on the Self, its intuitive experience, and the factor of time that is involved (and its modal cadre), is too similar to Vollenhoven's early work to be merely coincidental. The only significant point of difference is the modal cadre. But that, of course, came into the picture in the work of 1922-1923, when the modalities are taken to be the *primary forms of consciousness* (modalities of viewing) beside their being region categories (cf. in particular Dooyeweerd 1923a; also chapter 3, section III.E.3). That modal cadre arose in the context of the *Gegenstand*-sphere and its organization in regions of distinct modality. It is presented as a (metalogical, intuitive) presupposition of the theoretical consciousness. Thus it 'fits' at the level where the 'modalization of time' takes place, given that time is the real succession of occurrent experience. Strictly speaking, Vollenhoven's observation (about the influence on

Dooyeweerd) points to this modalization. It was, as such, subsequent to the dissertation, but its introduction fits within the schema of the dissertation, which is that of critical realism. Dooyeweerd's account is predicated on the account of the Self as prevalent in critical realism.

Vollenhoven's point of criticism assumes, naturally, his regretting this modalization of time.[190] This only makes sense from the perspective of his having abandoned the appeal to the subjectivity of the concrete intuition, and everything that is part of that. In fact, he took that step when he re-gauged subjectivity from a *self-certain* subject to a *tasked* subject, a subject standing in a (prophetic) office. The recognition of modal diversity is then no longer dependent on the intuitive awareness of primary forms of consciousness. (Recall Vollenhoven's dubbing this an "illusion" in the quotation referred to in footnote 48 above.) That recognition takes place in the execution of the task of understanding, to the extent that this task involves acknowledgement of adequate regulating rules (ordinances) and the avoidance of antinomies. This is an externalist criterion, over against the former internalist, intra-mental criterion. Dooyeweerd, it would appear, continued to give pride of place to the Self's need of security of self-certainty, and when he accepted the ontology of meaning (in the late 1920s) the Self's self-centredness became essential to him as supra-temporal privileged participation in meaning (the *Gegenstand*-sphere of meaning of critical realism thereby becoming the modal cadre in *De Wijsbegeerte der Wetsidee*). Vollenhoven recognized something of his own former position in this, and so, whether rightly or not, felt responsible.

There is double irony here. Dooyeweerd spoke of the problem of time in the "Wijsbegeerte der Wetsidee", whereas we are now forced to acknowledge that the problem is that of the 'concrete intuition', as an inheritance of Vollenhoven's initial critical realism. Vollenhoven, in turn, assumed and regretted what was, indeed, an influence on Dooyeweerd. But in formulating this influence as an accommodation to 'ennoetism', Dooyeweerd probably could not catch his meaning. At least he never

---

190 It would be a mistake to assume that Vollenhoven denied the relevance of time in the first two law-spheres already at an early date. In 2005d/e, **48**, he states that we find time "in all the modalities of a unity of subjection", continuing immediately with "in the arithmetic as succession, in the spatial as simultaneity . . .". But he began by saying that "time is neither an individual nor a modal difference", which leaves us wondering what Vollenhoven's unspoken thoughts are here. The first evidence of Vollenhoven's questioning the 'modalization of time' is in "Divergentierapport I", (1953p); cf. my introduction to this report in Tol and Bril 1992: 108-111. Dooyeweerd's initial response to this would appear to be (as I stated in the said introduction) the long footnote in Dooyeweerd 1953-1958 I: 31-32, in which he (rather vigorously) defends the 'modalization'.

confirmed the influence.

D. From 'occasionalism' to 'ennoetism'
Now, finally, what about that enigmatic term 'ennoetism'? It stems from Vollenhoven's problem-historical method and is not a current term in philosophy. This is not the place for a close historical discussion,[191] but a general description is required in order to detect what relevance this might have towards understanding Vollenhoven in the present context.

1. The theory of priority
Ennoetism is a type of thought that belongs to a group of four types that Vollenhoven classed as the *theory of priority*.[192] This theory focussed on the threesome 'mind-*psyche-soma*', whereby 'mind', as higher principle, has priority over *soma* (matter), the lower principle, without there being a significant reverse effect. The *psyche*, which is traditionally the principle of motion, relativizes the duality of mind and matter in mediating, from out of a primary unity, the contact by which the higher principle affects the lower principle.

The sketch of ennoetism (given in listing IV [1968b], section B.) indicates that the *psyche* here belongs entirely to the lower principle, meaning that the psycho-somatic reality is entirely self-dynamic and self-guided. The chief role of mind, as higher principle, is to contemplate this reality which, in doing so, makes it the content of its knowing and affects it through knowing it. This is what suggested the term 'ennoetism' to Vollenhoven, which literally means: 'in-the-mind-ism'. Considered from the perspective of the human being, perception focuses on the psycho-somatic reality, while cognition characterizes the mind's own contemplation.

Ennoetism has, within the family of priority theory, a close cousin, in what Vollenhoven calls "occasionalism". In the latter the psycho-somatic principle is also self-dynamic, but it is not self-guided. Depending on the occasion, there is guidance, as called for, which is provided by the higher

---

191 Vollenhoven published a detailed study on the arise of ennoetism in his "Ennoëtisme en '*ahoristos duas*' in het praeplatonische denken" (Ennoetism and ahoristos duas [indefinite two-ness] in pre-Platonic thought) (1954c). But the article in no way hints that the topic might, in some way, be relevant to Vollenhoven himself.
192 In the late 1960s Vollenhoven re-interpreted priority theory in a way that affected occasionalism. I leave this aside, for it complicates the discussion without throwing new light on the problem at hand. Besides, the former interpretation was prevalent when the differences between Vollenhoven and Dooyeweerd were in discussion. Cf. Vollenhoven 2000: 17-19.

principle of mind. The higher principle is not just noetic, but psycho-noetic. Thus, in occasionalism there is a double (or at least a diverging) *psyche*, one (part) belonging to the psycho-somatic body (this accounts for self-movement) and one to the psycho-noetic mind (a teleological effect). In occasionalism the lower principle of individual existence is limited to the animus of the body, with psychical mental activity rising above this.[193]

The two other types that belong to the theory of priority are a vitalistic type and a type called "instrumentism". In "vitalism", the lower principle is bio-somatic; only a vegetative force is relevant here. All motion, in the sense of change of place and direction, is accorded to the *psyche*, that is part of the higher principle. Finally, in instrumentism, the lower principle only concerns physical matter, with the higher principle being the full source of growth, direction and thought.

Vollenhoven, it would appear, developed a preference for priority theory through the double influence of Bergson and his understanding of the Christian tradition. As a student, Vollenhoven wrote appreciatively on Bergson, though, as a later lecture on Bergson attests (cf. Vollenhoven 1921ms), he was critical of Bergson as well (e.g. there is too much change in Bergson, not enough stability). Bergson's *élan vital* is the principle of life that impels reality into an upward development, while matter is life spent, the dead precipitate of life—"life being the skyrocket bursting in air, and matter being the dead ashes falling down".[194] This suggests the instrumentistic version of priority theory, which indeed does justice to essential features of Bergson's thought.[195]

---

193 In illustrating occasionalism, Vollenhoven often used the example of a horse and its rider to portray the lower and the higher *psyche* respectively. Confusingly, J. Stellingwerff refers to this example as illustrating ennoetism; cf. Stellingwerff 2006: 28. Occasionalism is not without its own contemplative moment, in the context of the psycho-noetic higher principle. (Cf. Vollenhoven 2005c, "occasionalism": "the higher principle is not merely mind . . .", p. 298.) I believe we may interpret this as follows. This psycho-noetic principle contemplates what accrues in the psyche and, through contemplating it, turns it into 'inner objects' or 'mental material' in the process of *Gegenstand* formation. In other words, occasionalism includes a theory of mental objects.

194 Edman 1944: xvii.

195 Cf. Vollenhoven 2000, chart 43; also the article on Bergson in Vollenhoven 2005c: 63-64. Within the range of the *elan vital*, Bergson distinguished knowledge and intuition. Knowledge, particularly that of the natural sciences, is focussed on the inert, spatially extensive reality, while the intuition is an intra-mental intellectual sympathy, in empathy with life. The distinction of knowledge and intuition recurs in Vollenhoven, but with a difference. For Vollenhoven, the object-orientation of knowledge includes psycho-physical reality, as positioned in space and time. Also the intuition is not so much in empathy with life as being the psycho-noetic awareness of the Self's unity with whatever

The part that can be accorded to the Christian tradition is the doctrine of God's sovereignty, when interpreted as 'priority'. Strictly speaking this is philosophically relevant only 'on the boundary' between divinity and the creature, in other words, only where the immanence of God affects the creature, as constituting the effect of the 'priority', i.e. as transcendental condition. Vollenhoven recognized that in the history of Christianity there are many instances of how Christian thought is conceptualized in terms of traditions that are pre-Christian, priority theory being a case in point. He acknowledged that one cannot avoid these traditions, but one ought (very much) to be aware of them, in the broad spectrum of their historical presence, and be mindful of whether a specific accommodation helps or hinders philosophical understanding. In that sense, Vollenhoven, in time, moved away from priority theory.

The four arrangements (ontology) of mind-*psyche-soma* of priority theory also find applications in cosmology. The arrangements can be taken as characterizing the world in the large, with plants, animals and human beings integral to it—a kind of universalism—or as characterizing the individual creature, whether plant, animal or human being, depending on the chosen type, whereby the world acts as substrate to that choice—a kind of individualism. But it is also possible, for each of the four types of priority theory, to maintain both side by side, as *macrocosm and microcosm*, analogously structured. In that case the lower principle of the macrocosm acts as an 'Umwelt' or context for the creatures, whose own bodily nature fits that context.

2. Ennoetist metaphysic

We shall now attempt to pull the various loose strands of our analysis of Vollenhoven's thought together. I believe we can affirm, with a reasonable degree of confidence, that the type of priority theory to which Vollenhoven first felt affiliated is that of occasionalism, including its cosmological side-by-side arrangement of macrocosm and microcosm. The shift that is evident in Vollenhoven after his breakdown is more difficult to pinpoint, mainly because of the lack of a unifying text. But it has features that are consonant with what Vollenhoven later saw to be characteristic of ennoetism. The point, of course, is not to impose a schema on Vollenhoven's thought, but to do justice to how he understood

---

affects it mentally. But, despite this difference, Vollenhoven acknowledged the influence of Bergson in his dissertation, especially as regards the doctrine of intuition (cf. 1918a: 348). We add that this intuition, in being predicated on the psyche in its being relevant to the higher principle, can occur (leaving adjustments of context aside) not only in instrumentism but also in vitalism and occasionalism.

and formulated his primary distinctions.

For the evidence of an initial occasionalism we may point, first of all, to the last section of the discussion of metaphysics of chapter 2, where we indicated the primary theme of dynamic reconciliation in the occurrence of dualities in the early Vollenhoven, namely of duality becoming one by virtue of belonging together. Such occurrences are "occasions of experience" (to use Whitehead's phrase). This is intimately associated with the role of the intuition of positing bi-unities, which in fact becomes the model for all the main dualities. In that sense the term 'occasionalism' is a fitting characterization.[196]

Then, secondly, in the provisional summary offered in connection with Vollenhoven's Christian theism (cf. chapter 2, section VIII.B.3), the relevance of the arrangement of macrocosm and microcosm is discussed. This arrangement provides the context for the objective and the subjective orders, which themselves seek reconciliation through the harmony predisposed by the Logos. These two orders are given cosmic relevance in an interpretation of the world order and the human being in a way that matches the type of priority theory Vollenhoven calls "occasionalism". I shall not repeat here what is said there. But the illustration (in section VIII.B.3. of chapter 2) indicates an 'occasionalistic' arrangement of mind-*psyche-soma*.

The metaphysics of Vollenhoven's early work is that of a monadology of substances and their changing appearances.[197] The appearances occur in space and time, which form the context of nature and the human body. But these appearances are controlled by ideas, the substances of the appearing things. In the macrocosm (the World), the thing-laws are like 'psychic principles', themselves the individuation of general essences. In other words, they are 'psycho-noetic', and in that capacity they *regulate* or *guide* empirical things. On the part of the microcosm (the Self), there are the 'qualities of being a subject', themselves determined by objective norms, which are 'psycho-noetic' (relevant to the immortal soul, or will governed by recognized norms) and hold sway over the waywardness of

---

196 The features of occasionalism prominent in modern thought, such as 'seeing all things in God' (Malebranche) or 'linking thought to bodily reaction' (Geulincx), etc. are select features of this conception, which has roots in ancient philosophy (e.g. Philistion, Ekphantos). Cf. Vollenhoven 2005c, the articles: "Geulincx" (p. 158), "Malebranche" (p. 245), "Occasionalism" (pp. 297-198).

197 In the article on "occasionalism" in Vollenhoven 2005c: 298, Vollenhoven mentions, presumable without recalling its relevance to his own early work, that the macrocosm-microcosm variant of occasionalism in general harbours a monadology!

the human body (perishable body).[198]

When comparing Vollenhoven's changed position in the second half of the 1920s with the occasionalism of his early position, several things are readily noticed. First of all the micro- and macrocosm arrangement is dissolved. This is most pronounced in the denial of a 'principle of individuality'. A human being is part of humankind, and the individuals that we are need to be seen in the context of our 'standing in subjection'. The individual's subjectivity is not that of the certainty of self-awareness, but—in its being a 'tasked' subjectivity—that of being ineluctably in a position of responsibility.

This new understanding has important consequences. In the first place, there is no longer any basis for the distinction between thought and being. Thought belongs to being, which means that it cannot intelligibly be distinguished from it. This means that the concrete intuition has lost its earlier importance. It is no longer the prime witness of self-consciousness but a psychological phenomenon, useful but not to be elevated to a prime principle. The analytical intuition in turn shifts away from the concrete intuition and becomes involved in the role of assessing the value of being in its being knowable.

In the second place, the way Vollenhoven's theistic understanding is combined with the initial cosmological arrangement is also reworked. No longer is the Spirit the warrant of norms that impinge upon the Self's qualities of being a subject. Norms are now understood as being part of an integral 'creation order'. This means that the Logos also no longer has the role of disposing subject and object to form a synthesis. This signals the fundamental change in the scholastic framework of the harmony of subjective and objective rationality. The subjective order is itself directed from out of the cosmic order. The task is not to imitate or become adequate to that order, but to comply to it so as to effect fulfilment. The Self's general lack of independence (or autonomy) makes it possible to

---

198   There is further unexpected convergence on occasionalism in this respect, namely in the limited but sympathetic influence of R.H. Lotze and Ch. Sigwart. Vollenhoven appeals to Lotze, where the latter argues for the *reality of succession* in the world, that helps to certify the distinction between God and the world (cf. chapter 2, section VIII.B.1.). Of Sigwart, who emphasized the normative character of the principles of logic, Vollenhoven says: "In his meritorious *Logik*, thought resides in his opinion under the higher psyche, but at the same time is norm-controlled: logic is . . . not the physics but the ethics of thought" (Vollenhoven 2005c, "Sigwart": 383). Vollenhoven expressed a similar opinion in his early years: "logic is the ethics of psychical thought" (Vollenhoven 1921c: 82). The influence of each of these authors is where the higher principle affects the lower one, in the macrocosm and the microcosm respectively. Vollenhoven characterizes the type of thought of both authors as being occasionalistic; cf. Vollenhoven 2005c: 298, 383.

consider the Self and the World more as a whole.

This 'cosmological shift' does not as such evidence an ennoetism. For that we need to see what the main arrangement is of the whole. We saw already that the former psycho-physical realm (within occasionalism), with its ideals of absolute space and absolute time and met by the forms of sensibility of the human psycho-physical structure, has been worked into a fuller environment, now called an 'absolute medium' (Vollenhoven 1926a: 13; 1926b: 394; 1926d: 54, 155, 193). When, after 1926, the cosmological intersection principle is more fully developed, the environment becomes the full relational network of inter/intra-individual relationships (cf. section IV on the cosmological intersection principle). This is consistent with a shift, within priority theory, from occasionalism to ennoetism.[199]

The environment is also the object of perception. If one were to limit the cosmos to this feature, it would be a cosmos reduced to factual reality. But there are also non-factual features of the cosmos, as disclosed in knowing. The intersection principle ensures that it is one cosmos. But one can detect two emphases here: the environment that is perceived, and a distinguishable 'realm' above it, that is more typical of cognition. What does this 'higher realm' of non-factual reality look like?

In occasionalism, this higher realm is the domain of the ideas (of distinctive being). There are general essences, that are noetic, and they individuate into 'thing-laws' that govern the structure, coherence and development of finite things. As thing-laws they are principles of control or direction, in other works, they have a *psycho-noetic meaning*. They define the substance of things, which reveal themselves in the factual world via their phenomena. This is the 'metaphysics' of occasionalism, being essentially that of a monadology. We saw the effort Vollenhoven applied to undercut this metaphysics, as being unsuited for a more 'reformed philosophy', when realizing the liability of that metaphysics.

So what is the alternative? To start, Vollenhoven quite rigorously rejects the construal of 'thing-laws'. Ideas that are thought to have a controlling or determining role in factual reality are speculative and deterministic. They leave no freedom for consideration in what in Vollenhoven is the ontological difference between law and subject.

---

199 When comparing the four views of priority theory, *viz.* instrumentism, vitalism, occasionalism and ennoetism, one observes (in the given order) a progressively fuller understanding of the 'somatic' principle: from bare inert matter, whereby all change and activity is due to the higher psycho-noetic principle of development, direction and cognition in instrumentism, to a self-directing active soma, taken up in cognition by the higher noetic principle in ennoetism.

By rejecting ideas in the sense of thing-laws, Vollenhoven removes the 'psychic-dynamic factor' at the level of the psycho-noetic realm of occasionalism. In other words, that level has become more exclusively 'noetic', matching a more exclusive cognitive meaning. This step is at least consonant with the setup of ennoetism.

But isn't cognition just a function? Shouldn't we expect an alternative 'metaphysics' if the monadology of occasionalism is really being rejected? Cognition is indeed a function. But we need to see its broader use. It is called upon in the context of knowledge. Now knowledge can be conveyed or sought. But either way, there is an essential kernel to knowledge, and that is that knowledge attests to 'possessing truth'. Now we found a certain difficulty in understanding what truth is in this connection. The difficulty is caused not in the last place by the realist-metaphysical qualification Vollenhoven gives to this notion. It is entirely 'in itself', it has no need of a knower to be, and it is entirely indifferent to being known (Vollenhoven 1926b: 385). No doubt there are anti-psychological motives at work here, also anti-Kantian ones, such as opposing the view that truth 'holds' by virtue of the active knower (*op. cit.*: 384). But Vollenhoven is not merely being critical. At the same time he is asserting a position. He commits himself to truth as noetic principle, and in doing so he attests to accepting a 'metaphysic' of truth.

But to qualify as a metaphysic of ennoetism, it is not sufficient merely to assert truth as ontological principle. The 'facts' of reality must in some sense stand in relation to it. There must be a link between the higher (noetic) principle and the lower (somatic) principles. Now we find that this is indeed the case. There is truth, and there is 'a truth'. Truth in general is the schema in which knower and the knowable come together, not synthetically but 'systatically'. Any state of affairs that does not violate the structure of this *systasis* can be taken up into truth. In other words, everything that is structured according to the intersection principle of cosmology can become the content of thought. This is how the facts or the states of affairs can be dealt with, *viz.* in being cognized or in becoming known, which is to come to possess their 'systatic' truth. This trait is quite essential for the view of ennoetism: the lower principle is affected by mind in being known, i.e. through becoming the content of mind.

But don't we still need a connecting factor between knowledge and object and also to the subject who knows the object? If truth in ennoetism is on a par with substance in occasionalism, what is the correlate of 'phenomena'? And what is the correlate of their being revealed? We found that knowledge needs, on the one hand, to presuppose a prior intuition of assessment. The intuition of assessment views the most basic characteristic of what can be known, which is the modal characteristic. The intuition of modality is intrinsic to every cognition. On the other hand, there is also the factor by virtue of which any being is knowable. That is the factor of *value*. Value is "ubiquitous in the cosmos" (Vollenhoven 1930d/1931f: §124). However rudimentary Vollenhoven's view of value remains, it may nevertheless be understood as being the warrant for being's being knowable. It answers to what the intuiting subject assesses when attending to a being in the interest of knowledge. So if the metaphysic of occasionalism is the monadological schema of substance (thing-law) and (revealing) phenomena, then the analogous metaphysic of ennoetism in Vollenhoven is *truth* (in itself) and (intuited) *value*.[200]

Difficult questions arise in the wake of this assertion. The emphasis on values is consonant with the aesthetic qualification Vollenhoven gave the cosmos in his initial definitive period. But both values and this cosmic aesthetics retreat when, in the early 1930s, the moral antithesis of good and evil is introduced as determinate beside the two standard cosmic determinants. Is this a continuation of ennoetism, or does this development involve another shift? I believe that there is continuation,[201] but there is an important change in that the individual human being regains a relative independence, as effected by the introduction of the moral determinant. And what about the reinterpretation of the law as boundary in the early 1940s, whereby both monism and dualism have become problematic for Vollenhoven? Here I believe there is a shift away from ennoetism, for the re-interpretation of the law as supporting correlate of the cosmos, as over against the earlier view of law as revealed will, is difficult to rhyme with the 'priority' attributed to the higher principle of reality, that also ennoetism evidences. All these conjectures require careful discussion in their own right. But if our analysis of Vollenhoven's early work and his initial definitive position is not seriously in error, it should be possible to extend our approach to the later years in a way that

200   I restrict the formulation of this metaphysic to the terminology that Vollenhoven provides at this point. One would have to compare other proponents of ennoetism, in the period of late neo-Kantianism or life-philosophy, in order to investigate whether a more general mode of expression might be more suitable. In Vollenhoven's later problem-historical work he never, to my knowledge, formulated the metaphysic of ennoetism explicitly.

201   In personal correspondence (email, 27 February 2010) dr. K.A. Bril pointed out that, in connection with ennoetism, Vollenhoven distinguished an aesthetic and an ethical variant in the history of philosophy. Regretfully, he seldom refers to this, and never made the distinction explicit.

does justice to the nuance of his thought and to the historical sensitivity with which he executed it.

Bibliography

Alexander, P. (1971), *An Introduction to Logic. The Criticism of Arguments*. London: Allen and Unwin; second corrected impression.
Algra, H. (1966), *Het wonder van de 19e eeuw*. Franeker: Wever (6th printing 1979).
Antognazzi, M.R. (2009), *Leibniz. An Intellectual Biography*. Cambridge: University Press.
Aristotle (1941), *Metaphysics A*, in *The Basic Works of Aristotle*, edited and with an introduction by R. McKeon. New York: Random House.
Augustine, A. (1994) [397], The *Confessions*, in *Nicene and Post-Nicene Fathers*, ed. by P. Schaff, first series, volume 1: *The Confessions and Letters of St. Augustin*. Edinburgh: Clark; Grand Rapids: Eerdmens, 27-207.
Bar-Hillel, Y. (1972), "Bolzano", in *Encyclopedia of Philosophy*, volume 1. New York: Macmillan, 337-338.
Bergson, H. (1944) [1911], *Creative Evolution*, trans. by A. Mitchell. New York: Modern Library.
— (1983) [1946], *An Introduction to Metaphysics. The Creative Mind*, trans. by M.L. Andison. Totowa, New Jersey: Rowman & Allanheld.
Berkelaar, W. (2007), *'Het is ons een eer en een genoegen.' Eredoctoraten aan de Vrije Universiteit sinds 1930*. Zoetermeer: Meinema.
Beth, E.W. (1940), *Inleiding tot de wijsbegeerte der wiskunde*. Nijmegen-Utrecht: Dekker & Van de Vegt.
— (1950), *Wijsgerige ruimteleer*. Nijmegen: Dekker & Van de Vegt.
— (1964), *Door wetenschap tot wijsheid*. Assen: Van Gorcum.
Blauwendraat, H. (2004), *Worsteling naar waarheid. De opkomst van Wiskunde en Informatica aan de VU*. Zoetermeer: Meinema.
Bos, A.P. (1999), *De ziel en haar voertuig. Aristoteles' psychologie geherinterpreteerd en de eenheid van zijn oeuvre gedemonstreerd*. Leende: Damon.
Bouman, P.J. and J.C. van Zelm (1918), *De rekenkundige denkbaarheden in logische samenhang, met – als proeve van toegepaste logica – een rekenmethode voor de lagere school*. Amsterdam: W. Versluis.
Bradley, F.H. (1969) [1893], Appearance *and Reality*. Oxford: University Press.
Bratt, J.D., ed. (1998), *Abraham Kuyper: A Centennial Reader*. Grand Rapids: Eerdmans.
Bril, K.A. (1982), *Vollenhoven's laatste werk, 1970-1975*. Amsterdam: VU Boekhandel.
— (1986), *Westerse denkstructuren. Een probleemhistorisch onderzoek*. Amsterdam: VU Uitgeverij.
— (2005), *Vollenhoven's Problem-Historical Method. Introduction and Explanations*, trans. and augmented by R.W. Vunderink. Sioux Center,

Iowa: Dordt College Press.
Brouwer, L.E.J. (1905), *Leven, Kunst en Mystiek*. Delft: Waltman Jr.
— (1907), *Over de grondslagen der wiskunde*. Amsterdam and Leipzig.
— (1912), "Intuitionism and Formalism", trans. by A. Dresden, in *Philosophy of Mathematics. Selected Readings*, ed. by P. Benacerraf and H. Putnam. Englewood Cliffs, New Jersey: Prentice-Hall, 1964, 66-77.
Calvin, J. (1960) [1559], *Institutes of the Christian Religion*, ed. by John T. McNeill and trans. by F.L. Battles. Philadelphia: Westminster Press.
Comte, A. (1975), *Auguste Comte and Positivism. The Essential Writings*, edited and with an introduction by G. Lenzer. New York: Harper and Row.
De Boer, Th. (1966), *De Ontwikkelingsgang in het Denken van Husserl*. Assen: Van Gorcum, n.d.
— (1973), "Beyond being, ontology and eschatology in the philosophy of Emmanuel Levinas", *Philosophia Reformata* 38, 17-29.
— (1990), "Inleiding" to E. Levinas, *God en de filosofie*, vertaald, ingeleid en van aantekeningen voorzien door dr. Th. de Boer. Den Haag: Meinema, 6-8.
De Jong, W.R. (1993), Boekbespreking. "J.H. Kok, *Vollenhoven. His Early Development*, (Sioux Center, Iowa: Dordt College Press, 1992)", *Gereformeerd Theologisch Tijdschrift* 93, 265.
Descartes, R. (1972) [1637], *Discourse on Method*, Part VI , in *The Philosophical Works of Descartes*, vol. 1, trans. by E.S. Haldane and G.R.T. Ross. Cambridge: University Press.
— (1970), *Descartes. Philosophical Letters*, trans. and ed. by Anthony Kenny. Oxford: Blackwell.
Dilthey, W. (1931), "Die Typen der Weltanschauung und ihre Ausbildung in den metaphysischen Systemen", in *Gesammelte Schriften*, VIII. Band (Leipzig und Berlin: Teubner), 75-118.
Dooyeweerd, H. (1914), "Leekengedachten over Richard Wagner en zijn Tristan", *Opbouw* 1, 5-10, 37-42, 66-68.
— (1915a), "De troosteloosheid van het Wagnerianisme", *Opbouw* 2, 97-112.
— (1915b), "Neo-mysticisme en Frederik van Eeden", in *Almanak van het Studentencorps van de Vrije Universiteit*.
— (1917), *De Ministerraad in het Nederlandsche Staatsrecht*. Amsterdam: Van Soest.
— (1920), "Het vraagstuk der gemeentemonopolies in het belang der volksgezondheid, hoofdzakelijk beschouwd in het licht van de nieuwe opvattingen in zake de bedrijfsvrijheid", *Themis* 81 (oktober), 126-151.
— (1922a), (Response to G. Scholten, 8 April 1922), *Handelingen van de Vereeniging voor Wijsbegeerte des Rechts, VII. Staatsbemoeiing en individueele vrijheid*, 31-38.
— (1922b), "Een methodologische inleiding in de geschiedenis der rechtsphilosophie in het begin der XXe eeuw" (14 April 1922; manuscript). *Dooyeweerd Archives* 77, Box VN 38, Folder 190/VIN 190. Amsterdam: Historisch Documentatiecentrum voor het Nederlands

Protestantisme (1800-heden), Free University.
— (1922b1), text fragment from (1922b), in Verburg (1989), 32.
— (1922c), "De Badensche School" (manuscript). *Dooyeweerd Archives* 77, Box VN 38, Folder VIN 134. Amsterdam: Historisch Documentatiecentrum, Free University.
— (1922d), "Normatieve rechtsleer. Een kritisch-methodologische onderzoeking naar Kelsen's normatieve rechtsbeschouwing" (typescript). *Dooyeweerd Archives* 77, Box VN 38, Folder VIN 122. Amsterdam: Historisch Documentatiecentrum, Free University.
— (1922d1), Text fragment from (1922d), in Verburg (1989), 34-38.
— (1922e), "Nota", attachment to the letter of Dooyeweerd to J.J.C. van Dijk (15-05-1922), in Van Dijk 1961, 49-52.
— (1923a), "Roomsch-katholieke en Anti-revolutionaire Staatkunde" (c. February 1923; 57 pages, incomplete); *Dooyeweerd Archives* 77, Box VN 20, Folder 343. Amsterdam: Historisch Documentatiecentrum, Free University.
— (1923a1), "Inleiding: 'Idealisme, realisme en levens- en wereldbeschouwing'", part of (1923a); cf. also in Verburg (1989), 48-50.
— (1923a2), "Chapter 2, section A: 'Kosmos en Logos'", part of Dooyeweerd (1923a), 37-45 (typescript without the final section entitled "De overgang tot de kosmologie").
— (1923a3), "Chapter 2, section A's final part: 'De overgang tot de kosmologie'", part of (1923a), cf. also in Verburg (1989), 59-61.
— (1923b), "De leer der rechtssoevereiniteit en die der staatssoevereiniteit in haar consequencies voor de verhouding van Overheid en onderdanen" (October 1923; typescript, 9 pages). *Dooyeweerd Archives* 77, Box VN 20, Folder 342. Amsterdam: Historisch Documentatiecentrum, Free University.
— (1923c), "Het Calvinisme", third part of "De staatkundige tegenstelling tusschen Christelijk-Historische en Antirevolutionaire partij " (December 1923). *Dooyeweerd Archives* 77. Amsterdam: Historisch Documentatiecentrum, Free University. Fragments quoted in Verburg (1989), 62-66.
— (1923d), *Calvinisme en Natuurrecht*. Amersfoort: Wed. W. van Wijngen, [n.d.; written late 1923 or early 1924, published 1924].
— (1923e1-5), "Het Calvinistisch beginsel der souvereiniteit in eigen kring als staatkundig beginsel", *Nederland en Oranje* 4; (1) October 1923, 98-99; (2) March 1924, 185-189; (3) April 1924, 8-15; (4) May 1924, 27-31; (5) August 1924, 71-76.
— (1924; I), "In den strijd om een Christelijke staatkunde. Proeve van een fundeering der Calvinistische levens- en wereldbeschouwing in hare wetsidee" (Introduction and first of fifteen instalments), *Antirevolutionaire Staatkunde* 1 (no. 1, October 1924), 7-25.
— (1924; VI), "In den strijd om een Christelijke staatkunde; VI ",

Antirevolutionaire Staatkunde 1 (no. 6, March 1925), 228-244.
— (1925), "Leugen en waarheid over het Calvinisme", *Nederland en Oranje* 6, 81-90.
— (1926a), "Tweeërlei kritiek. Om de principieele zijde van het vraagstuk der medezeggenschap." *Antirevolutionare Staatkunde* 2 (no. 1, January 1926), 1-21.
— (1926b), "Het oude probleem der Christelijke staatkunde." *Antirevolutionaire Staatkunde* 2 (no. 2, Feb. 1926), 63-84. (Summary of 1924, instalments I-XII)
— (1926c), "Calvinisme contra Neo-Kantianisme. Naar aanleiding van de vraag betreffende de kenbaarheid der goddelijke rechtsorde". *Tijdschrift voor Wijsbegeerte* 20, 29-74.
— (1926d), *De Beteekenis der Wetsidee voor Rechtswetenschap en Rechtsphilosophie*. Kampen: Kok.
— (1926e), "Openingscollege van Herman Dooyeweerd, gehouden in 1926", in Verburg (1989), 415-427.
— (1928a), "Het juridisch causaliteitsprobleem in 't licht der wetsidee", *Antirevolutionaire Staatkunde* [new series] 2, 21-121.
— (1928b), "Naschrift. Inzake het recht der Calvinistische wetenschapsbeschouwing, en het misverstand eener 'neutraal-wetenschappelijke' kritiek", *Antirevolutionaire Staatkunde* [new series] 2 (no. 4), 419-436. (Hoofdartikel: "Beroepsmisdaad en strafvergelding in 't licht der wets-idee"; *op. cit.*, 389-436.)
— (1931), *De crisis der humanistische staatsleer in het licht eener Calvinistische kosmologie en kennistheorie*. Amsterdam: Ten Have.
— (1935-1936), *De Wijsbegeerte der Wetsidee*, 3 volumes. Amsterdam: H.J. Paris.
— (1935a), "De wetsidee als grondlegging der wijsbegeerte", volume 1 of Dooyeweerd (1935-1936).
— (1939), "Kuyper's wetenschapsleer", *Philosophia Reformata* 4 (no. 4), 193-232.
— (1940), "Het tijdsprobleem in de wijsbegeerte der wetsidee", *Philosophia Reformata* 5, 160-182, 193-234.
— (1942), "De leer van den mensch in de wijsbegeerte der wetsidee", *Correspondentiebladen van de Vereeniging voor Calvinistische Wijsbegeerte* 7 (no. 5, December), 134-143.
— (1949), *Reformatie en Scholastiek in de Wijsbegeerte*, Boek 1: *Het Grieksche Voorspel*. Franeker: Wever.
— (1953-1958), *A New Critique of Theoretical Thought*, 3 volumes + index volume, trans. by D.H. Freeman and W.S. Young. Amsterdam: H.J. Paris; Philadelphia: Presbyterian and Reformed Publishing Co.
— (1953a), "The necessary presuppositions of philosophy", volume 1 of Dooyeweerd (1953-1958).
— (1966), "Het oecumenisch-reformatorisch grondmotief van de wijsbegeerte der wetsidee en de grondslag van de Vrije Universiteit", *Philosophia*

Reformata 31, 3-15.
— (1973), "Introduction by the editor in chief, prof. Herman Dooyeweerd", *Philosophia Reformata* 38, 5–16.
— (1977), "Herman Dooyeweerd", in *Acht civilisten in burger*, ed. by J.M. van Dunné *et al.* Zwolle: Tjeenk Willink, 36-67, 280-282 (authorized interview).
Driesch, H. (1917), *Wirklichkeitslehre. Ein metaphysischer Versuch*. Leipzig: E. Reinicke.
Edman, I. (1944), "Foreword" to Bergson (1944), ix-xviii.
Feynman, R.P. (1998), *Six Easy Pieces*. London: Penguin.
Flipse, A. (2005), *'Hier leert de natuur ons zelf de weg': een Geschiedenis van Natuurkunde en Sterrenkunde aan de VU*. Zoetermeer: Meinema.
Foucault, M. (1972), "The discourse on language" in *The Archeology of Knowledge and the Discourse on Language*, trans. by A.M. Sheridan Smith. New York: Pantheon Books.
Friesen, J.G. (2005), "Dooyeweerd versus Vollenhoven: the religious dialectic within reformational philosophy", *Philosophia Reformata* 70, 102-132.
Girard, R. (1965), *Deceit, Desire, and the Novel. Self and Other in Literary Structure*, trans. by Y. Freccero. Baltimore and London: Johns Hopkins University Press.
— (1986), *The Scapegoat*. Baltimore: Johns Hopkins University Press.
— (1987), *Things Hidden since the Foundation of the World*, trans. by S. Bann and M. Metteer. London: Athlone.
Goheen, M.W. and C.G. Bartholomew (2008), *Living at the Crossroads. An Introduction to Christian Worldview*. Grand Rapids, Michigan: Baker Academic.
Görland, G.A. (1921), "Die Urhypothese des kritischen Idealismus", *Tijdschrift voor Wijsbegeerte* 15, 121-136.
Gregory Nazianzen (1989) [381], "Theological orations", *Nicene and Post-Nicene Fathers*, second series, ed. by P. Schaff and H. Wace; vol. vii: *S. Cyril of Jerusalem and S. Gregory Nazianzen*. Edinburgh: T&T Clark; Grand Rapids: Eerdmans, 1989), 280-328.
Griffioen, S. (1991), "The metaphor of the covenant in Habermas", *Faith and Philosophy* 8 (no. 4, October), 524-540.
Grossmann, R. (1974), *Meinong*. London and Boston: Routledge and Kegan Paul.
Hart, H. (1984), *Understanding our World: An Integral Ontology*. Lanham: University Press of America.
Hart, H., J. van der Hoeven and N. Wolterstorff (1983), *Rationality and the Calvinian Tradition*. Lanham: University Press of America.
Heath, T.L. (1956), "Introduction" to *The Thirteen Books of Euclid's Elements*, trans. with introduction and commentary by T.L. Heath, second edition. New York: Dover.
Hegel, G.W.F. (1975) [1830], *Hegel's Logic, Being Part One of the Encyclopaedia*

of the Philosophical Sciences (1830), trans. by W. Wallace, with a Foreword by J.N. Findley. Oxford: At the Clarendon Press.

Henderson, R.D. (1994), *Illuminating Law. The Construction of Herman Dooyeweerd's Philosophy 1918-1928*. Dissertation, Free University of Amsterdam.

Hepp, V. (1937a), *Dreigende Deformatie II: symptomen; Het voortbestaan, de onsterfelijkheid en de substantialiteit van de ziel*. Kampen: Kok.

— (1937b), *De basis van de eenheid der wetenschap*. Referaat voor de twee-entwintigste *wetenschap*pelijke samenkomst der Vrije Universiteit op 30 juni 1937. Assen: Hummelen's Boekhandel.

Hintikka, J. and U. Remes (1974), *The Method of Analysis. Its Geometrical Origin and Its Geometrical Significance*. Dordrecht/Boston: Reidel.

Hoekstra, T. (1921), *Geschiedenis der Philosophie* I. Kampen: Kok.

Høffding, H. (1916), *La philosophie de Bergson: exposé et critique*. Paris: Alcan.

Horkheimer, M. (1974), *The Eclipse of Reason*. New York: Seabury.

Horkheimer, M. and T. Adorno (1972), *Dialectic of Enlightenment*, trans. by J. Cumming. New York: Herder and Herder.

Husserl, E. (1911), "Philosophy as rigorous science", reprinted in Husserl 1965, 71-147.

— (1965), *Phenomenology and the Crisis of Philosophy*, transl. with an Introduction by Q. Lauer. New York: Harper and Row.

— (1970a) [1935], *The Crisis of European Sciences and Transcendental Phenomenology*, trans. by D. Carr. Evanston: Northwestern Univ. Press.

— (1970b) [1935], "Philosophy and the Crisis of European Humanity", Appendix I of Husserl (1970a), 269-299.

Jager, A. and A. Janse (1924), *Rekenboek*. Utrecht: Kemink en Zoon.

James, W. (1992) [1907], "Pragmatism", in *Pragmatism in focus*, ed. by D. Olin. London and New York: Routledge.

Janse, A. (1921a), "'Een rekenmethode voor de lagere school – door P.J. Bouman en J.C. van Zelm, – als proeve van toegepaste logica'", *Paedagogisch Tijdschrift voor het Christelijk Onderwijs* 14 (1921-1922), 137-149.

— (1921b), "Schetsen voor paedagogische studieclubs en voor 'zelfstudie'. Sketch III: Dr. Maria Montessori ", *Paedagogisch Tijdschrift voor het Christelijk Onderwijs* 14 (1921-1922), 329-341, 370-378; 15 (1922-1923), 17-26. [The three instalments are coded as: 1921b1, 1921b2, and 1921b3, resp.]

— (1923a), "Correctie 'liefhebben met het verstand'", *Paedagogisch Tijdschrift voor het Christelijk Onderwijs* 15 (January 1923) (1922-1923), 353-363.

— (1923b), "Levende wezens", *Paedagogisch Tijdschrift voor het Christelijk Onderwijs* 16 (February 1923) (1923-1924), 117-121.

— (1923c), "Tweeërlei levenshouding tegenover 'de levende ziel'", *Paedagogisch Tijdschrift voor het Christelijk Onderwijs* 16 (February 1923) (1923-1924), 140-144.

— (1923d), "Oostersche opvattingen over het levende wezen", *Paedagogisch Tijdschrift voor het Christelijk Onderwijs* 16 (March 1923) (1923-1924),

145-148.
— (1923e), "Indo-Germanen contra Semieten over de levende ziel", *Paedagogisch Tijdschrift voor het Christelijk Onderwijs* 16 (March 1923) (1923-1924), 149-152.
— (1923f), "Liefde voor – of heerschappij over de levende zielen (Indo-Germanen contra Semieten)", *Paedagogisch Tijdschrift voor het Christelijk Onderwijs* 16 (March 1923) (1923-1924), 173-180.
— (1923g), "Waar gaat het om in de artikelen over 'de levende ziel'?", *Paedagogisch Tijdschrift voor het Christelijk Onderwijs* 16 (December 1923) (1923-1924), 225-233.
— (1934a), *De mensch als 'levende ziel'*. Amsterdam: Holland; 2e printing 1937.
— (1934b), *Ikke*. Hoenderloo: Bibliotheek voor Bijbelse Opvoedkunde.
— (1938), *Van idolen en schepselen*. Kampen: Kok.
— (1940), *Om 'de levende ziel'*. Goes: Oosterbaan & Le Cointre, undated but c. 1940.
— (1982) [1938-1939], *Inleiding tot de calvinistische filosofie*. Amsterdam: Buijten & Schipperheijn (first published serially, 1938-1939).
— [1929-1946], "Dagboekaantekeningen 1929-1946", *Janse Archives* 157, Box 1, Folder 1. Amsterdam: Historisch Documentatiecentrum, Free University.
Janse, W. (2001), "Antheunis Janse (1890-1960)" in *Biografisch Lexicon voor de geschiedenis van het Nederlandse Protestantisme* 5, ed. by D. Nauta, et al., Kampen, 285-288.
Kant, I. (1998) [1781/1788], Critique *of Pure Reason*, trans. and ed. by P. Guyer and A.W. Wood. Cambridge: University Press.
— (1977) [1783], *Prolegomena to Any Future Metaphysics*, Paul Carus translation revised by J.W. Ellington. Indianapolis: Hackett.
— (1997) [1788], *Critique of Practical Reason*, trans. and edited by Mary Gregor. Cambridge: University Press.
Klapwijk, J. (1980), "Honderd jaar filosofie aan de Vrije Universiteit" in *Wetenschap en Rekenschap 1880-1980. Een eeuw wetenschapsbeoefening en wetenschapsbeschouwing aan de Vrije Universiteit*, ed. by M. van Os and W.J. Wieringa. Kampen: Kok, 528-593.
— (2008), *Purpose in the Living World? Creation and Emergent Evolution*. Cambridge: University Press.
Koch, J. (2006), *Abraham Kuyper: een biografie*. Amsterdam: Boom.
Kok, J.H. (1988), "Vollenhoven and 'Scriptural philosophy'", *Philosophia Reformata* 53, 101-142.
— (1992), *Vollenhoven. His Early Development*. Sioux Center, Iowa: Dordt College Press.
— (1998), *Patterns of the Western Mind*. Sioux Center, Iowa: Dordt College Press (2nd revised edition).
— (2007), "Woltjer on classical antiquity", in Sweetman (2007a), 41-64.
Kraay, J.N. (1979), "Successive conceptions in the development of the Christian

philosophy of Herman Dooyeweerd," *Philosophia Reformata* 44 (1979), 137-149; 45 (1980), 1-46.
Kraay, J.N. and A. Tol, eds. (1979), *Hearing and Doing. Philosophical Essays Dedicated to H. Evan Runner*. Toronto: Wedge.
Krijnen, C. (2001), *Nachmetaphysischer Sinn. Eine problemgeschichtliche und systematische Studie zu den Prinzipien der Wertphilosophie Heinrich Rickerts*. Würzburg: Königshausen & Neumann.
Kuhn, T. (1970), Structure *of Scientific Revolutions*, with a *Postscript*. Chicago: University Press; second edition.
Kuyper, A. (1892), *E Voto Dordraceno. Toelichting op den Heidelbergschen Catechismus*, I-IV. Amsterdam: Höveker en Wormser, 1892-1895); reprint Kampen: Kok; (not dated; Foreword in Volume I is dated 1 June 1892).
— (1909), *Encyclopaedie der Heilige Godgeleerdheid*, II. Kampen: Kok.
— (1910), *Dictaten Dogmatiek* III. Kampen, Kok (2nd printing).
— (1930) [1880], *Souvereiniteit in eigen kring* (1880). Kampen: Kok; English translation in Bratt 1998.
— (1931)[1898], *Lectures on Calvinism*, fifth printing 1961. Grand Rapids, Mich.: Eerdmans.
— (2002)[1898], *Het Calvinisme. Zes Stone-lezingen in oktober 1898 te Princeton (N.J.) gehouden*, ed. and with an introduction by G. Harinck. Soesterberg: Aspekt.
Leenders, H. (1999a), *Montessori en fascistisch Italië. Een receptiegeschiedenis*. Dissertation, University of Utrecht.
— (1999b), "Onderwijs", *Dagblad Trouw*, 22 September.
Leibniz, G.W. (1976a), "The principles of nature and of grace, based on reason" (1714), in *G.W. Leibniz, Philosophical Papers and Letters*, a selection translated and edited, with an introduction by L.E. Loemker. Dordrecht: D. Reidel, (2nd ed.), 636-642
— (1976b), "Monadology" (1714), in *G.W. Leibniz. Philosophical Papers and Letters*, a selection translated and edited, with an introduction by L.E. Loemker. Dordrecht: Reidel, 643-653.
Levinas, E. (1985), *Ethics and Infinity*, trans. R.A. Cohen. Pittsburgh, PA: Duquesne University Press.
Loemker, L.E. (1967), "Paul Deussen", *The Encyclopedia of Philosophy*, ed. by Paul Edwards, vol. 2, 378-379.
— (1972), *Struggle for Synthesis. The Seventeenth Century Background of Leibniz's Synthesis of Order and Freedom*. Cambridge, Mass.: Harvard.
Lovejoy, A.O. (1960) [1936], *The Great Chain of Being. A Study of the History of an Idea*. New York: Harper and Row.
MacCulloch, D. (2003), *Reformation. Europe's House Divided 1490-1700*. London: Penguin.
Makkreel, R.A. (1975), *Dilthey. Philosopher of the Human Studies*. Princeton: University Press.

Maxwell, N. (1984), *From Knowledge to Wisdom. A revolution in the aims and methods of science*. Oxford: Basal Blackwell.
McIntire, C.T., ed. (1985), *The Legacy of Herman Dooyeweerd: Reflections on critical philosophy in the Christian tradition*. Lanham: University of America Press.
Miller, A. and C. Wright, eds. (2002), *Rule-Following and Meaning*. Chesham: Acumen.
Montessori, M. (1916), *De Methode Montessori*, trans. by T. Bruyn. Zwolle: Ploegsma.
Moore, G.E. (1899), "The nature of judgment", *Mind*, n.s. 8, 176-193.
Newton, I. (1969) [1687], *Mathematical Principles of Natural Philosophy*, trans. by F. Cajori. New York: Greenwood.
Nietzsche, F. (1969), *Basic Writings of Nietzsche*, trans. and ed., with commentaries, by Walter Kaufmann. New York: Random House.
O'Shea, D. (2007), *The Poincaré Conjecture. In Search of the Shape of the Universe*. London: Allen Lane, Penguin Group.
Penrose, R. (1989), *The Emperor's New Mind*. Oxford: University Press.
— (2005), *The Road to Reality*. London: Vintage.
Plantinga, A. (1980), *Does God have a Nature?* Milwaukee: Marquette University Press.
— (1998), *The Analytic Theist. An Alvin Plantinga Reader*, ed. by J.F. Sennett. Grand Rapids, Mich: Eerdmans; Cambridge, U.K.
Plato (1961), *Theaetetus*, in *Plato: The Collected Dialogues Including the Letters*, edited by E. Hamilton and H. Cairns. New York: Bollingen Foundation.
— (1977), *The Republic of Plato*, trans. with introduction and notes by F.M. Cornford. Oxford: University Press.
Poincaré, H. (1902), *Science and Hypothesis*, trans. by W.J.G., New York: Dover, 1952 reprint.
Puchinger, G. (1961), "Dr. D.H.Th. Vollenhoven", in W.K. van Dijk (1961), 87-112.
— (1994), "Prof. dr. Herman Dooyeweerd (1894-1977)", in *Herman Dooyeweerd 1894-1977. Breedte en actualiteit van zijn denken*, edited by H.G. Geertsema et al. Kampen: Uitgeverij Kok, 11-27.
Ranschburg, P. (1916), "Die Leseschwäche (Legasthenie) und Rechenschwäche (Arithmasthenie) der Schulkinder im Lichte des Experiments", in *Zwanglose Abhandlungen aus den Grenzgebieten der Pädagogik und Medizin*, herausgegeben von Th. Heller-Wien und G. Leibuscher-Meiningen. Berlin: Julius Springer.
Rentsch, Th. (1980), "Metalogik" in *Historisches Wörterbuch der Philosophie*. Basel: Schwabe, vol. 5, col. 1174.
Rickert, H. (1892), *Der Gegenstand der Erkenntnis*. Freiburg.
Rorty, R. (1967), "Introduction. Metaphilosophical Difficulties of Linguistic Philosophy", in *The Linguistic Turn. Recent Essays in Philosophical Method*, ed. and with an introduction by R. Rorty. Chicago and London:

University of Chicago Press, 1-39.
Rullmann, J.C. et al (1929), *De Vrije Universiteit – Voorttrekken*. Amsterdam: Holland.
Russell, B. (1900), *A Critical Exposition of the Philosophy of Leibniz*. London: Allen and Unwin, 2nd edition 1937, 8th impression 1971.
— (1903), *The Principles of Mathematics*. London: Allen and Unwin, 2nd edition 1937.
— (1904), "Meinong's theory of complexes and assumptions", *The Collected Papers of Bertrand Russell*, volume 4: *Foundations of Logic 1903-05*, ed. by A. Urquhart with the assistance of A.C. Lewis. London and New York: Routledge, 1994, 431-474.
— (1905), "On denoting", *The Collected Papers of Bertrand Russell*, volume 4: *Foundations of Logic 1903-1905*, ed. by A. Urquhart with the assistance of A.C. Lewis. London and New York: Routledge, 1994, 414-427.
— (1911), "Knowledge by acquaintance and knowledge by description", *The Collected Papers of Bertrand Russell*, volume 6: *Logical and Philosophical Papers 1909-1913*, ed. by J.G. Slater with the assistance of B. Frohmann. London and New York: Routledge, 1992, 147-161.
— (1919), *Introduction to Mathematical Philosophy*. London: Allen and Unwin (many reprints).
— (1926), *Our Knowledge of the External World*. London: Allen & Unwin; 2nd edition.
— (1959) [1912], *The Problems of Philosophy*. Oxford: University Press.
— (1966) [1910], *Philosophical Essays*. London: Allen & Unwin.
— (1947), *A History of Western Philosophy*. London: Allen and Unwin, 1946; seventh impression second edition.
— (2001) [1931], *The Scientific Outlook*. London and New York: Routledge.
Ryle, G. (1949), *The Concept of Mind*. Harmondsworth: Penguin.
Santayana, G. (1980), *Reason in Common Sense*, vol. 1 of *The Life of Reason*. Charles Schribner's Sons, 1905; unabridged reprint, New York: Dover.
Sigwart, Ch. (1911), *Logik*, 2 Bände, 4th edition edited by Heinrich Maier. Tübingen: Verlag von J.C.B. Mohr.
Simons, P. (1992), *Philosophy and Logic in Central Europe from Bolzano to Tarski*. Dordrecht, etc.: Kluwer.
Spade, P.V. ed. (1994), *Five Texts on the Medieval Problem of Universals: Porphyry, Boethius, Abelard, Duns Scotus, Ockham*, translated and edited by P.V. Spade. Indianapolis: Hackett.
Speiser, E.A. (1964), *Genesis*, trans., with introduction and commentary by E.A. Speiser; Anchor Bible series. New York: Doubleday.
Stellingwerff, J. (1990), *De VU na Kuyper*. Kampen: Kok (erroneous copyright date 1987).
— (1992), *D.H. Th. Vollenhoven (1892-1978). Reformator der Wijsbegeerte*. Baarn: Ten Have.
— (2006), *Geschiedenis van de Reformatorische Wijsbegeerte*. Stichting voor

Reformatorische Wijsbegeerte.
Strauss, D.F.M. (1973), *Begrip en Idee*. Assen: Van Gorcum.
Sweetman, R., ed. (2007a), *In the Phrygian Mode. Neo-Calvinism, Antiquity and the Lamentations of Reformed Philosophy*. Toronto: Institute for Christian Studies; Lanham: University Press of America..
— (2007b), "A General Overview", in Sweetman (2007a), 1-12
Tol, A. (1993), "Vollenhoven's probleemhistorische methode tegen de achtergrond van zijn systematisch denken", *Philosophia Reformata* 58, 2-27.
— (1995), "Time and change in Vollenhoven", *Philosophia Reformata* 60, 99-120.
— (1998), "'Waarborg' als kentheoretische notie", in Van Woudenberg and Cusveller 1998, 83-97.
— (2003), "Vollenhoven en de wijsbegeerte van de wiskunde", *Beweging* 67 (nr. 2), 42-43.
— (2004), "Wijsgerige vorming" in *Het Nut van Filosofie*, ed. by R. van Woudenberg, M. Willemsen and G. Buijs. Budel: Damon, 61-66.
— (2005a), "Wetenschap en zinvragen: een historische terugblik", in *Ongekend nieuwsgierig. Zinvragen en wetenschap*, ed. by B. Voorsluis. Zoetermeer: Meinema, 16-33.
— (2005b), "Foreword" to Vollenhoven 2005d and 2005e, iii-xxxii.
— (2007), "Vollenhoven and philosophy in early classical antiquity: a critical review", in Sweetman (2007a), 127-160.
— (2010a), "Algemene inleiding", in Vollenhoven 2010, 11-56.
— (2010b), "Tekstverantwoording", in Vollenhoven 2010, 407-438.
Tol, A. and K.A. Bril (1992), *Vollenhoven als wijsgeer. Inleidingen en Teksten*. Amsterdam: Buijten & Schipperheijn.
Van Dalen, D. (1999), *Mystic, Geometer, and Intuitionist. The Life of L.E.J. Brouwer*, volume 1: *The Dawning Revolution*. Oxford: Clarendon Press.
Van der Heiden, G.J. and R. Muis (2003), "Vollenhoven en de kerstening van de wiskunde", *Beweging* 67 (nr.1), 38-41.
Van der Hoeven, J. (1976), *Karl Marx: The Roots of his Thought*. Assen/Amsterdam: Van Gorcum.
Van der Laan, H. (2000), *Jan Woltjer (1849-1917). Filosoof, Classicus, Pedagoog*. Amsterdam: VU Uitgeverij.
Van der Walt, B.J. (1989), *Antheunis Janse van Biggekerke*. Potchefstroom: Potchefstroom Universiteit.
— (2006), "The philosophy of D.H.Th. Vollenhoven (1892-1978) with special reference to his historiography of philosophy", *Tydskrif vir Christelike Wetenskap / Journal for Christian Scholarship* 42 (no. 1 and 2), 35-59; also chapter 5 of Van der Walt 2010, renamed "A new paradigm for doing Christian philosophy: D.H.Th. Vollenhoven (1892-1978), 152-182.
— (2008), "Antheunis Janse van Biggekerke (1890-1960): morning star of a Reformational worldview" in B.J. Van der Walt, *The eye is the lamp of the*

body. Worldviews and their Impact. Potchefstroom, 189-229.
— (2010), *At Home in God's World. A transforming paradigm for being human and for social involvement.* Potchefstroom: The Institute for Contemporary Christianity in Africa.
— (2010a), "The human heart rediscovered in the anthropology of D.H.Th. Vollenhoven", in Van der Walt 2010, chapter 9, 290-324.
Van Deursen, A.Th. (2005), *Een hoeksteen in het verzuild bestel.* Amsterdam: Bakker.
Van Dijk, W.K. (ed., *et al.*) (1961), *Perspectief. Feestbundel van de jongeren bij het vijfentwintig jarig bestaan van de Vereniging voor Calvinistische Wijsbegeerte.* Kampen: Kok.
Van Dyke, H. and A.M. Wolters (1979), "Interview with Dr. Evan Runner", in Kraay and Tol 1979, 333-361.
Van Woudenberg, R. and B. Cusveller, eds. (1998), *De kentheory van Alvin Plantinga.* Zoetermeer: Boekencentrum.
Veenhof, J. (2006), *Nature and Grace in Herman Bavinck,* trans. by A.M. Wolters. Sioux Center, Iowa: Dordt College Press.
Verburg, M.E. (1989), *Herman Dooyeweerd. Leven en werk van een Nederlands christen-wijsgeer.* Baarn: Ten Have.
Vermooten, W.H. (1923), "Ingezonden" (20 October 1923), *Paedagogisch Tijdschrift voor het Christelijk Onderwijs* 16 (1923-1924), 222-224.
Vollenhoven, D.H.Th. (N.B. The code here is in step with the "Vollenhoven Biography" of John H. Kok (1992): 363-382. Items not listed in that biography have been added.)
— (1914a), "Abaelard en het scepticisme", *Opbouw* 1, 102-126.
— (1915a), "Henri Bergson", *Opbouw* 2, 145-155, 175-185, 217-223.
— (1915b), "Het persoonlijke in den oorlog", *Opbouw* 2, 25-35, 54-66.
— (1916b), "'Zijn' is 'denken' èn 'doen'", *Opbouw* 3, 145-159.
— (1918a), *De Wijsbegeerte der Wiskunde van Theïstisch Standpunt.* Amsterdam: Van Soest.
— (1918c), bespreking van Vollenhoven (1918a), *Wiskundig Tijdschrift* 15 (aflevering 4), 208-212.
— (1919b), Press release, "Iets over het stelsel van Bergson", in *Zeeuwsche Kerkbode* 33 (no. 27, 4 July 1919), 2-3.
— (1919ms), "Paedagogiek en Paedagogie", *Vollenhoven Archives* 405, Box 3. Amsterdam: Historisch Documentatiecentrum, Free University.
— (1920a), "Iets over de logica in het vitalisme van Driesch", *Orgaan van de Christelijke Vereeniging van Natuur- en Geneeskundigen in Nederland,* 1-30.
— (1921b), "Einiges über die Logik in dem Vitalismus von Driesch", *Biologischen Zentralblatt* 41 (no. 8, August), 337-358.
— (1921c), "Hegel op onze lagere scholen?", *Paedagogisch Tijdschrift voor het Christelijk Onderwijs* 14 (1921-1922), 77-87, 99-106.
— (1921ms), "Iets over het stelsel van Bergson", *Vollenhoven Archives* 405, Box

3. Amsterdam: Historisch Documentatiecentrum, Free University.
— (1922a), "Eenige methodologische opmerkingen aangaande Dr. T. Hoekstra's *Geschiedenis der Philosophie I*", *Stemmen des Tijds* 11 (1921-1922), 293-301.
— (1925c), "Een plant van eigen bodem", *Paedagogisch Tijdschrift voor het Christelijk Onderwijs* 18, 391-394.
— (1926a), *Logos en Ratio, beider verhouding in de geschiedenis der westersche kentheorie*. Kampen: Kok.
— (1926b), "Enkele grondlijnen der kentheorie", *Stemmen des Tijds* 15 (April), 380-401.
— (1926d), "Kentheorie en natuurwetenschap", *Orgaan der Christelijke Vereeniging van Natuur- en Geneeskundigen in Nederland* (no. 2 en 4), 53-64, 147-197.
— (1926msA), "Philosophica Systematica I (Kentheorie) 1926-1927", *Vollenhoven Archives* 405, Box 5. Amsterdam: Historisch Documentatiecentrum, Vrije Universiteit.
— (1926msC), "De wijsbegeerte der arithmetiek en der chorologie van Calvinistisch standpunt" (1926/1927), *Vollenhoven Archives* 405, Box 5. Amsterdam: Historisch Documentatiecentrum, Vrije Universiteit.
— (1927a), "Prof. Dr. G.H.J.W.J. Geesink", *Jaarboek der Vrije Universiteit*. Amsterdam: VU, 89-93.
— (1927ms), "Philosophica Systematica II, 1927-1928", *Vollenhoven Archives* 405, Box 37. Amsterdam: Historisch Documentatiecentrum, Vrije Universiteit, Amsterdam.
— (1928ms), "Philosophica Systematica II [1928-1929]" (updated version of 1927-1928), *Vollenhoven Archives* 405, Box 5, 37. Amsterdam: Historisch Documentatiecentrum, Vrije Universiteit.
— (1929d), "De wis- en natuurkundige faculteit en de principia", in J.C. Rullman *et al.*, *De Vrije Universiteit – Voorttrekker*. Amsterdam: Holland, 52-64.
— (1930b), *De eerste vragen der psychologie*. Loosduinen: Kleywegt.
— (1930c), "Het nominalisme van Zeno de Stoïcijn", in *Wetenschappelijke bijdragen door hoogleraren der Vrije Universiteit, aangeboden ter gelegenheid van haar 50-jarig bestaan*. Amsterdam: Dagblad Drukkerij, 177-204.
— (1930d), *Isagôgè Philosophiae*. Course syllabus; taken up in the text-critical edition Vollenhoven (2010).
— (1931a), "De beteekenis van het Calvinisme voor de reformatie van de wijsbegeerte", *Antirevolutionaire Staatkunde* 5, 180-198, 266-334.
— (1931f), *Isagôgè Philosophiae*. Course syllabus; taken up in the text-critical edition Vollenhoven (2010).
— (1931g), "The Significance of Calvinism for the Reformation of Philosophy"; translation of Vollenhoven (1931a); *The Evangelical Quarterly* 3, 387-403; 4 (1932), 128-160, 398-427. [The year difference of the instalments is indicated as 1931g1 and 1931g2 resp.]

— (1932b), *De Noodzakelijkheid eener Christelijke Logica*. Amsterdam: H.J. Paris.
— (1932d), "Plaats en taak der wijsbegeerte aan de Vrije Universiteit", *Antirevolutionaire Staatkunde* 9, 395-411.
— (1932e), *Isagôgè Philosophiae*. Course syllabus; taken up in the text-critical edition Vollenhoven (2010).
— (1933a), *Het Calvinisme en de Reformatie van de Wijsbegeerte*. Amsterdam: H.J. Paris.
— (1934a), "Hedendaagsche wijsbegeerte", *De Standaard*; 27 instalments between 26 June 1934 and 27 January 1937.
— (1936hh), "Problemen en richtingen in de wijsbegeerte der wiskunde", *Philosophia Reformata* 1, 162-187.
— (1938m), "Is de ruimte euclidisch of niet-euclidisch?", *Correspondentiebladen* 3, no. 3 and 4, 72-75.
— (1938p), "Objectief", in *Mededeelingen van de Vereeniging voor Calvinistische Wijsbegeerte* (no. 1, May), 4-5.
— (1938v), "Realisme en nominalisme", *Philosophia Reformata* 3, 65-83, 150-165 (not continued).
— (1939h), *Isagôgè Philosophiae*. Course syllabus; taken up in the text-critical edition Vollenhoven (2010).
— (1939k), *Proeve eener ordening van wijsgeerige consepties* [sic]. Assen: Hummelen's Boekhandel.
— (1940n), *Theoretische psychologie*. Amsterdam: Theja; (syllabus n.d.; a somewhat shortened revision of 1930b).
— (1941f), *Isagôgè Philosophiae*. Course syllabus; taken up in the text-critical edition Vollenhoven (2010).
— (1941j), *Richtlijnen ter oriëntatie in de gangbare wijsbegeerte*. Vrije Universiteit: Publicatie van de Reünisten-Organisatie van N.D.D.D., no. 13.
— (1941k), "Richtlijnen ter oriëntatie in de gangbare wijsbegeerte", *Philosophia Reformata* 6, 65-86; 7 (1942), 9-46; 8 (1943), 1-33 (not continued).
— (1942l), "De waarheid in de godsdienst-wijsbegeerte", *Vox Theologica* 13 (nr. 6, July), 113-123.
— (1942m), "Belijdenis van de immanentie Gods contra immanentiephilosophie", *Mededeelingen van de Vereeniging voor Calvinistische Wijsbegeerte* (June), 1-2.
— (1945i), *Isagôgè Philosophiae* (Vollenhoven's private copy). Reference text of the text-critical edition Vollenhoven (2010).
— (1948h), "Instruction in philosophy at the Vrije Universiteit of Amsterdam", *The Philosopher*, Xth International Congress of Philosophy (August 11, 1948), 1 (translation of 1948k).
— (1948k), "Het onderwijs in de wijsbegeerte aan de Vrije Universiteit", *Mededeelingen van de Vereeniging voor Calvinistische Wijsbegeerte* (December), 5-6.
— (1948p), *Hoofdlijnen der Logica*. Kampen: Kok.

BIBLIOGRAPHY

— (1950d), "Het geloof, zijn aard, zijn structuur en zijn waarde voor de wetenschap", *Levensbeschouwing en levenshouding van de academicus.* Utrecht-Nijmegen: Dekker en Van de Vegt, 71-77.
— (1950e), *Geschiedenis der Wijsbegeerte* I. Franeker: T. Wever.
— (1950n), "De soevereiniteit in eigen kring bij Kuyper en ons", *Mededeelingen van de Vereeniging voor Calvinistische Wijsbegeerte* (December), 4-7; reprinted in Tol and Bril (1992), 39-46.
— (1951h), "Norm en natuurwet", *Mededeelingen van de Vereeniging voor Calvinistische Wijsbegeerte* (July), 3-6; reprinted in Tol and Bril (1992), 55-65.
— (1952k), "De visie op den Middelaar bij Kuyper en bij ons", *Mededeelingen van de Vereeniging voor Calvinistische Wijsbegeerte* (September), 3-9; reprinted in Tol and Bril (1992), 75-92.
— (1953l), "Schriftgebruik en wijsbegeerte", *Mededeelingen van de Vereeniging voor Calvinistische Wijsbegeerte* (September), 6-9; reprinted in Tol and Bril (1992), 93-106.
— (1953o) "Wijsbegeerte, Calvinistische", *Oosthoek's Encyclopedie*, 4th edition, volume 15; cf. also Vollenhoven (1960h), reprinted in Vollenhoven (2005c), 78-79.
— (1953p), "Divergentierapport I" (April/May), first published in Tol and Bril (1992), 111-117, simultaneous in Stellingwerff (1992), 207-212.
— (1954c), "Ennoëtisme en 'ahoristos duas' in het praeplatonische denken", *Philosophia Reformata* 19, 58-86, 145-168.
— (1955i), "Levenseenheid", first published in Tol and Bril 1992, 121-133.
— (1956b), *Kort Overzicht van de geschiedenis van de wijsbegeerte.* Amsterdam: Theja (syllabus); reprinted in Vollenhoven (2005a), 21-93; translated "Short Survey of the History of Philosophy" in Vollenhoven (2005b), 21-88.
— (1957a), *Inleiding tot de wijsgerige anthropologie.* Amsterdam: Theja; (retitled text of 1940n and 1930b).
— (1959a), "Conservatisme en progressiviteit in de wijsbegeerte" in *Conservatisme en progressiviteit in de wetenschap.* Kampen: Kok, 35-48; reprinted in Vollenhoven (2005a), 11-19; translated "Conservatism and Progressiveness in Philosophy", in Vollenhoven (2005b), 11-19.
— (1959d), "Getuigen in de wetenschap", *Sola Fide* (February) 12, 1-13; reprinted in Tol and Bril (1992), 137-151.
— (1959-1964), "Bergson, H.", "Ennoëtisme", "Geulincx. A.", "Malebranche, N.", "Occasionalisme", "Sigwart, C.", "Woltjer, Jan", *Oosthoeks Encyclopedie*, 5^e druk; reprinted in Vollenhoven (2005c), 63-64, 130, 158, 245, 297-298, 383, 441-442 resp.
— (1960d), "In memoriam Antheunis Janse", *Mededelingen van de Vereniging voor Calvinistische Wijsbegeerte* (May), 1-2.
— (1960h), "Calvinistische wijsbegeerte", in *Oosthoeks Encyclopedie*, 5th edition, volume 3; cf. also Vollenhoven (1953o), reprinted in Vollenhoven

(2005c), 76-77.
— (1961c), "De consequent probleemhistorische methode", *Philosophia Reformata* 26, 1-34; reprint in Vollenhoven (2005a), 95-140; translated "The Consequential Problem-Historical Method" in Vollenhoven (2005b), 89-135.
— (1963a), "Plato's realisme", *Philosophia Reformata* 28, 97-133; fragment pp. 127-130 reprinted in Tol and Bril (1992), 155-159.
— (1963c), "Problemen rondom de tijd", first published in Tol and Bril 1992, 160-198.
— (1968b), *Problemen van de tijd in onze kring*. Amsterdam: Filosofisch Instituut der Vrije Universiteit; reprinted in Tol and Bril (1992), 199-211.
— (1970a), "Historische achtergrond en toekomst", in *Mededelingen van de Vereniging voor Calvinistische Wijsbegeerte* (December), 2-3.
— (2000), *Schematische kaarten. Filosofische concepties in probleemhistorisch verband*, bewerkt door K.A. Bril en P.J. Boonstra. Amstelveen: De Zaak Haes.
— (2005a), *De Probleemhistorische Methode en de Geschiedenis van de Wijsbegeerte*, ed. by K.A. Bril. Amstelveen: De Zaak Haes.
— (2005b), *The Problem-Historical Method and the History of Philosophy*, ed. by K.A. Bril, trans. by J. de Kievit, S. Francke, J.G. Friesen and R. Sweetman. Amstelveen: De Zaak Haes.
— (2005c), *Wijsgerig Woordenboek*, ed. by K.A. Bril. Amstelveen: De Zaak Haes.
— (2005d) [1945], *Isagôgè Philosophiae / Introduction to Philosophy*, ed. by John H. Kok and Anthony Tol, trans. by John H. Kok with a preface by Calvin Seerveld and a foreword by Anthony Tol. Sioux Center: Dordt College Press. (Bilingual Dutch-English edition)
— (2005e), *Introduction to Philosophy*; separate English translation of Vollenhoven (2005d), with same preface and foreword.
— (2010), *Isagôgè Philosophiae 1930-1945 Tekstkritische uitgave. Filosofie in de Traditie van de Reformatie*, ed. by A. Tol. Amsterdam: Free University Press.
Vollenhoven, D.H.Th. and A. Janse (1919), "De activiteit der ziel in het rekenonderwijs", *Paedagogisch Tijdschrift voor het Christelijk Onderwijs* 12 (1919-1920), 97-109.
Weyl, H. (1925), "Die heutige Erkenntnislage in der Mathematik", *Symposion. Philosophische Zeitschrift für Forschung und Aussprache* 1, 1-32; *Gesammelte Abhandlungen*, vol. 2. Berlin etc.: Springer, 1968, 511-542.
— (1940), "The mathematical way of thinking", *Science* 92, 437-446; *Gesammelte Abhandlungen*, vol. 3. Berlin etc.: Springer, 1968, 710-718.
Whitehead, A.N. (1938), *Modes of Thought*. Toronto: Macmillan.
— (1978), *Process and Reality. Corrected Edition*, ed. by D.R. Griffin and D.W. Sherburne. New York: Macmillan.
Wittgenstein, L. (1976), *Philosophical Investigations*, trans. by G.E.M. Anscombe. Oxford: Blackwell.

Wolters, A.M. (1979a), "On Vollenhoven's Problem-Historical Method", in Kraay and Tol (1979), 231-262.
— (1979b), "Vollenhoven on 'Word of God'", *Anakainosis* 1 (no. 2, January), 5-9.
— (1985), "The intellectual milieu of Herman Dooyeweerd", in McIntire (1985), 1-19.
— (1988), *Schepping zonder grens. Bouwstenen voor een bijbelse wereldbeschouwing*, trans. and ed. by R. Kooistra. Amsterdam: Buijten en Schipperheijn, in samenwerking met Stichting voor Reformatorische Wijsbegeerte.
— (2005), *Creation Regained. Biblical Basics for a Reformational Worldview*, 2nd edition. Grand Rapids, Mich,: Eerdmans (1st edition 1984).
Wolterstorff, N. (1983), 'Introduction', in Hart *et al* (1983), v-vii.
Woltjer, R.H. (1925), "Over de beteekenis der natuurwetten" (off-print), *Orgaan der Christelijke Vereeniging van Natuur- en Geneeskundigen in Nederland*, 14 pgs.
Woltjer, J. (1891), "De wetenschap van den Logos", in *Verzamelde Redevoeringen en Verhandelingen*, ed. by Woltjer-comité. Amsterdam: De Standaard, 1931, 1-46.
— (1896), "Ideëel en reëel", in *Verzamelde Redevoeringen en Verhandelingen*, ed. by Woltjer-comité. Amsterdam: De Standaard, 1931, 178-235.
— (1901), "Beginsel en norm in de literatuur", in *Verzamelde Redevoeringen en Verhandelingen*, ed. by Woltjer-comité. Amsterdam: De Standaard, 1931, 147-177.
— (1914), "Het wezen der materie", private publication; reprinted in *Verzamelde Redevoeringen en Verhandelingen*, ed. by Woltjer-comité. Amsterdam: N.V. Dagblad en Drukkerij De Standaard, 1931, 236-257.
Woltjer, J. and A. Kuyper (1895), *Publicatie van den Senaat der Vrije Universiteit, in zake het onderzoek ter bepaling van den weg die tot de kennis der Gereformeerde beginselen leidt*, J. Woltjer, rector, A. Kuyper, abactis. Amsterdam: Wormser.
Zuidema, S.U. (1963), "Vollenhoven en de reformatie van de wijsbegeerte", *Philosophia Reformata* 28, 134-146.
Zwanepol, K. ed. with introductions by, (2004), *Belijdenisgeschriften voor de Protestantse Kerk in Nederland*. Zoetermeer: Boekencentrum; Heerenveen: Protestantse Pers; includes *Nederlandse Geloofsbelijdenis* (1561), *Catechismus van Heidelberg* (1563) and *Dortse Leerregels* (1618-1619); translations: *Confession of Faith* (also: *Belgic Confession*), *Heidelberg Catechism* and *Canons of Dort* (resp.), in *Psalter Hymnal of the Christian Reformed Church*. Grand Rapids, Mich.,1959.

Reviews of Vollenhoven's dissertation:
De Heraut, (1918), Sunday, 6 October 1918, p. 2.
Lasson, G. (1925), "Besprechung D.H.Th. Vollenhoven, *De Wijsbegeerte der Wiskunde van theïstisch Standpunt*", *Kant-Studien* 30, 198.

Mannoury, G. (1918), "Bespreking van D.H.Th. Vollenhove [sic] *De wijsbegeerte der wiskunde van theïstisch standpunt*", *Nieuw Archief voor Wiskunde* 2, (no. 12), 474-477.
— (1919a), "De wijsbegeerte der wiskunde van theïstisch standpunt", *De Beweging. Algemeen tijdschrift voor letteren, kunst, wetenschap en staatskunde*, 15, 371-378.
— (1919b), "Boekbeoordeling: D.H.Th. Vollenhoven. *De wijsbegeerte der wiskunde van theïstisch standpunt*", *Nieuw Tijdschrift voor Wiskunde* 6, 411-412.
Pos, H.J. (1919), "Philosophie aan de VU", *Fraternitas* 6, 25-31.
Van der Vaart Smit, H.W. (1918), "Recensie. D.H.Th. Vollenhoven. *De Wijsbegeerte der Wiskunde van theïstisch Standpunt*", *Gereformeerd Theologisch Tijdschrift* 19, 292-300.
Vollenhoven, D.H.Th. (1918c), bespreking: D.H.Th. Vollenhoven, *De Wijsbegeerte der Wiskunde van theïstisch Standpunt*, 1918, *Wiskundig Tijdschrift* 15, afl. 4, 208-212.

Correspondence
H. Dooyeweerd (17 December 1920) to (family) D.H.Th. Vollenhoven, letter, in Stellingwerff (1992), 47-48.
— (15 May 1922) to J.J.C. van Dijk, letter and memorandum, in W.K. van Dijk (1961), 47-52.
— (16 January 1924) to J. Ridderbos, letter, *Dooyeweerd Archives* 77, Box VN 26, Folder 429. Amsterdam: Historisch Documentatiecentrum, Free University.
— (16 September 1925) to the Kuyper Foundation, "Memorandum. Aan de leden van het Dagelijksch Bestuur der Dr. A. Kuyperstichting, 's-Gravenhage". Archives of the Kuyper Foundation. Amsterdam: Historisch Documentatiecentrum, Free University.
F.W. Grosheide (30 October 1921) to D.H.Th. Vollenhoven, letter, *Vollenhoven Archives* 405, Box 4, Folder 1921.
A. Janse (1 November 1922) to D.H.Th. Vollenhoven, letter fragment, in Kok (1992): 41.
D.H.Th. Vollenhoven (19 May 1920) to F. Krüger, letter, *Vollenhoven Archives* 405, Box 4. Amsterdam: Historisch Documentatiecentrum, Free University.
— (16 November 1921) to F.W. Grosheide, letter, *Vollenhoven Archives* 405, Box 4, Folder 1921. Amsterdam: Historisch Documentatiecentrum, Free University.
— (7 November 1922) to A. Janse, letter, *Janse Archives* 157, Box 8, Folder 32. Amsterdam: Historisch Documentatiecentrum, Free University; also in Stellingwerff (1992): 61-62.
— (19 February 1924) to A. Janse, letter, *Janse Archives* 157, Box 8, Folder 32. Amsterdam: Historisch Documentatiecentrum, Free University.

BIBLIOGRAPHY

— (21 March 1924) to A. Janse, letter, *Janse Archives* 157, Box 8, Folder 32. Amsterdam: Historisch Documentatiecentrum, Free University.
— (24 October 1924) to A. Janse, letter, *Janse Archives* 157, Box 8, Folder 32. Amsterdam: Historisch Documentatiecentrum, Free University.
— (25 October 1926) to A. Janse, letter, *Janse Archives* 157, Box 8, Folder 32. Amsterdam: Historisch Documentatiecentrum, Free University.
— (4 February 1936) to C. Van Til, letter, *Westminster Theological Seminary*; C. Van Til collection.
— (19 March 1938 [presumed date]) to the Curators of the Free University, list of propositions, website J.G. Friesen, www.members.shaw.ca/hermandooyeweerd/Curators.html
— (4 April 1939) to the Curators of the Free University, letter, website J.G. Friesen, www.members.shaw.ca/hermandooyeweerd/Curators.html
J. de Zwaan (9/10 February 1922) to D.H.Th. Vollenhoven, letter, *Vollenhoven Archives* 405, Box 4. Amsterdam: Historisch Documentatiecentrum, Free University.

Internet links

J. Glenn Friesen, www.members.shaw.ca/hermandooyeweerd/Curators.html .

Index

Abaelard, P. 263n, 524
Abnormalists vs. Normalists 53-54
absolute medium 467, 508
absolute space and time 90n, 121-122, 148ff., 158, 169ff., 179, 362, 508
abstract 39
acts 91, 93, 101n, 125ff., 135n, 155-156, 180, 232, 286n, 325-329, 333, 337, 361, 365
actual infinity 83, 97n, 109, 167-170, 278n, 382n, 406
d'Alembert, J. 97
Alexander, P. 115n, 513
Algra, H. 44n, 388n, 513
Althusius, J. 73n
analogy, between Self and world 119, 158ff., 178, 199, 213, 467
analogy, of functions 306n, 436, 438, 455, 461ff.
analytical intuition 84n, 124n, 128ff., 134, 138ff., 150ff., 161ff., 208n, 210, 213, 268n, 363ff., 429, 439, 500
anthropology 13, 101, 223, 227ff., 237n, 242, 245, 253ff., 257ff., 261ff., 340, 379n, 383n, 445, 448-450, 473-479, 492
anticipations 306, 375, 379, 438, 462, 492
anti-nomic subject 402ff.
antinomies 11, 56ff., 65, 336, 395, 400-405, 409, 414, 481
anti-psychologism 82, 106n, 202, 250, 374, 509
Antognazzi, M.R. 441n, 513
appearing and being knowable 91, 94, 104, 108, 110-119, 130, 142, 159, 161, 174, 177ff., 186, 189, 195, 249n, 260, 302, 362-363, 445ff., 449, 450n, 466
a priori's (in mathematics) of first and second rank 88, 89, 91, 101n, 139, 140, 169, 220, 498
archè 36, 63, 256, 378, 400, 408, 482

Archimedean point 11, 340n, 359, 377ff., 384, 484
Aristotle 20n, 21, 29n, 97n, 234, 249n, 292, 296, 344, 357n, 425, 447n, 454, 478n, 513
arithmetic, first order (cf. also counting) 81ff., 90ff, 137ff., 169, 220
arithmetic, second order (as science) 81ff., 90, 121, 169, 305ff.
arithmetical modality/law-sphere 305ff., 381, 414ff., 496ff., 501
assessment (of distinct modality) 37, 432ff., 447, 452, 465, 510
Augustine, A. 90, 97n, 171, 311, 344, 357n, 392, 448, 513

Bacon, F. 97n
Bar-Hillel, Y. 471n, 513
Barth, K. 486n
Bartholomew, C.G. 67n, 517
Bavinck, H. 19, 20, 47, 50n, 54, 231, 299n, 310n, 315, 441, 442, 453n, 524
being, difference in 408ff.
being-ought-can 73
Bergson, H. 90, 98n, 112n, 124, 126, 142n, 152n, 163n, 184, 206, 263n, 278, 336, 492, 493, 499, 504, 505n, 513, 517, 518, 524, 527
Berkelaar, W. 317n, 513
Berkeley, G. 97n
Beth, E.W. 79n, 198n, 513
biblical dualism 394, 487n
biblical religion 62
Bisterfeld, J. 73n
Blauwendraat, H. 43n, 79n, 80n, 513
body and soul 38, 88, 99ff., 102n, 154ff., 161, 229ff, 245, 310n, 379n, 466, 473-479
Bohatec, J. 316-318
Bolland, G.J.P.J. 225
Bolzano, B. 98n, 203n, 430n, 471n, 513
Bos, A.P. 479n, 513

533

Bouman, P.J.   210n, 225n, 226, 513
boundary and antinomies (cf. also antinomies)   398ff.
boundary problem   392ff., 417
boundary threefold   422ff
Bradley, F.H.   106, 109, 513
Brentano, F.   433n
Bril, K.A.   5, 19n, 21n, 66n, 69, 70n, 71n, 168n, 242n, 270n, 398n, 411n, 424n, 425n, 428n, 442n, 452n, 453n, 476n, 487n, 490n, 491n, 502n, 510n, 513, 523, 528
Brouwer, L.E.J.   79n, 82-84, 86, 88, 89, 95, 97, 98n, 128n, 162n, 168, 169, 177, 186n, 212, 498, 514, 523
Buijs, G.J.   523
Bullinger, H.   55n

Calvin, J.   47, 48, 55n, 157n, 250, 278n, 279n, 311, 316, 343, 345-348, 350, 369, 372, 373n, 396, 406, 422, 514
Calvinism   3, 16, 18, 43, 47ff., 161n, 343, 381ff.
Calvinistic cosmology   339n, 370
Calvinistic epistemology   319, 348ff., 381ff.
Calvinistic law-idea   318, 343, 348, 351ff, 358ff.
Calvinistic metaphysics   221, 278ff., 321, 382
Calvinistic philosophy   3n, 41, 18n, 55ff., 70, 76, 236, 241, 257, 326, 341, 385
Calvinistic principle   51ff.
Calvinistic worldview   5, 46, 221, 266ff., 321
Cantor, G.   79n, 83, 168n, 198n
causa occasionalis   114, 130n, 143n, 165
causality   280, 286n, 335ff., 344ff., 416
central lookout tower   358ff.
child development in Montessori   226-231
Christ   9, 181n, 266, 323, 337, 338, 339, 367, 368, 395
Christian psychology   148n, 240n, 243n
Christian realism   9, 212
Christian thought   260n
cognition   69-73
Colijn, H.   269n
commands   423
complete induction, cf. principle of
complexes   108-110
composition   38, 457ff.
Comte, A.   51, 52n, 63n, 97n, 514
concept, adequate   112, 118, 196, 383
concept, proleptic   111-112, 118
concept and idea   8-9, 10, 196, 284, 288-289, 313, 360, 373-380, 383
concrete   24, 39, 239, 242, 258, 262, 360, 379, 464, 472, 479
concrete intuition   84n, 124n, 126ff., 139, 151, 161, 208n, 250, 426, 500ff.
concursus Dei   373n, 452n, 454
consciousness and function   420, 421
content   125ff., 326ff.
correlation of God and world   398, 483
correlation of law and world   398, 487
cosmic categories   293ff.
cosmic order of law-spheres (cf. also "natural order")   412ff.
cosmic/created logos   321ff., 324ff., 333, 337, 350, 365ff.
cosmism, kinds of   391-397
cosmos as work of art   370n, 401
Counsel of God   172, 181ff.
counting (=1st order arithmetic)   81ff., 84n, 127n, 137ff., 225, 497ff.
creationism   453
critical realism   9, 11, 206n, 222, 293, 310
critical realism, review of   211-216, 294, 362-364
current philosophy   57-59
Cusveller, B.   61n, 524

De Boer, T.   302n, 514
Dedekind, R.   86
deism   170, 389

Democritus 97n
De Savorin-Lohman, A.F. 47
Descartes, R. 33, 34, 86, 97n, 99, 100, 194, 238n, 446n, 514
determinant 23, 38, 456ff.
Deussen, P. 246, 249, 520
development 423ff.
De Zwaan, J. 236n, 531
Dilthey, W. 67, 70, 281n, 358, 514, 520
direction 11, 59, 77, 88n, 105, 206, 207n, 237n, 243n, 259, 261, 373, 379ff., 423ff., 438, 457, 466, 473-479
diversity 24, 31, 37
divine cosmos 183, 285, 321-322, 332, 360
divine meaning-giving 337, 339n
divine word 337
domain of truth 248ff.
domains of validity 209, 210n
Dooyeweerd, H. 3-5, 8-14, 18, 19n, 52n, 53n, 54n, 55n, 61n, 76, 78, 79, 136, 166, 193n, 206n, 209, 210n, 217, 218, 221, 222, 223, 224n, 234n, 237n, 244, 245n, 261, 263-380, 382n, 383, 384, 390n, 391n, 398n, 404, 409-412, 414, 415n, 432, 440, 441, 443, 484, 486, 491, 492, 493, 494, 495, 496, 500-503, 514-517, 518, 520, 521, 524, 529, 530
Driesch, H. 25n, 124, 179n, 219, 231, 232, 235, 238, 242n, 243n, 425, 467, 517, 524
dualism 77, 80, 98-102, 141, 165, 211ff., 228ff., 281ff., 393-397, 398ff., 479-490

Eckhart (Meister) 168n
Edman, I. 504n, 517
Einstein, A. 148n, 418n
Ekphantos 506n
empiricism 95-97, 197
ennoetism 166, 468, 491, 495ff.
ennoetist metaphysic 505ff.
Epicurus 97n
Erdmann, B. 203n

essence 117, 145
essential connections 192, 300, 306n, 324ff., 335ff., 460
Euclid 84, 88n, 97n, 517
evaluating subject 251
Excellency of divinity 171
external relations 107, 460
extra-mental 130, 133, 145

Fabius, D.P.D. 47
faith and philosophy 373
faith function 279, 339, 358-360, 367, 368, 416
Feynman, R.P. 418n, 517
Fichte, J.G. 31n
field of inquiry 333
field of vision 328ff.
finite 382n, 406ff.
finitude 371
Flipse, A. 43n, 517
form of sensibility 88, 121, 148
formalism 95-97, 197
Free University 43
freedom-responsibility 67
Frege, G. 98n
Friesen, J.G. 18n, 224n, 263n, 407n, 476n, 477n, 478n, 517, 531
function of subjection 412, 417, 419ff., 426, 459
functional/functioning/functions 10, 18n, 34, 38, 49n, 59, 68, 88n, 94n, 127n, 142n, 145, 176, 199, 242n, 245ff., 249, 259, 262ff., 276, 329, 335, 339, 358ff., 371, 378ff., 418ff., 449ff., 454n, 460ff., 472, 476-479, 487

Galilei, G. 97n
Gassendi, P. 97n
Gauss, C.F. 98n
Geesink, W. 19, 20, 50n, 299n, 442, 492, 493, 525
Gegenstand 125ff., 326ff.
Gegenstände and concepts 131ff., 191
Gegenstände and judgments 131ff., 191
Gegenstand-sphere 9, 221, 285,

294ff.
Gegenstandstheorie 13, 131, 136, 208, 304
genesis 423ff
geometry 84-89
Geulincx, A. 506n, 527
Girard, R. 434n, 517
God and creation 346
God, the Father 181-183, 423, 440ff
God, the Logos 8, 9, 41, 185ff., 189ff., 198-201, 201ff., 207n, 253-257, 260ff., 297, 299, 308, 338ff., 350, 386, 390, 432, 439
God, the Spirit 47, 174ff., 177, 181ff., 183-185, 186, 188, 196, 200ff., 234, 248, 279, 294, 371n, 386, 423ff, 425-428, 454
Goheen, M.W. 67n, 517
good and evil 11, 63, 259, 263, 373, 386, 402n, 427ff., 454n, 462n, 473-479
Görland, G.A. 242n, 517
grade of Gegenständlichkeit 306
Groen van Prinsterer, G. 44, 311
Grosheide, F.W. 93n, 145n, 184n, 192n, 197n, 201, 202n, 210, 280, 284n, 530
Grossmann, R. 109n, 517
Grotius, H. 271
ground schema of philosophy 73-74
group of transformations 85
guidance 423

Hamilton, W.R. 418n
Harinck, G. 45n, 520
harmony (of two orders of rationality) 177, 186-187, 220-221, 375, 428-429
Hart, H. 464n, 517
Hartmann, N. 203n
heart 377ff.
heavenly reality 39-41, 259, 427
Hegel, G.W.F. 25, 31, 32, 196n, 202n, 203, 207n, 208, 226n, 271, 281, 283, 294, 486n, 517, 524
Henderson, R.D. 4, 236n, 266n, 267, 271, 273n, 275n, 276, 277n, 279n, 282n, 290n, 291n, 310n, 316n,
343n, 353n, 356n, 369n, 377n, 518
Hepp, V. 54, 241n, 261, 299n, 518
Heraclitus 97n
heterologic-heterothesis 203ff.
Hintikka, J. 438n, 518
historicism 70
Hobbes, T. 97n
Hoedemaker, Ph.J. 19, 20
Hoekstra, T. 289n, 518, 525
Höffding, H. 124n, 518
Hofstede de Groot, P. 388n
holism 469ff.
Holy Spirit; cf. God, the Spirit
human being, outward and inward 229, 262ff., 477, 479
human being, whole 444, 467, 479
humanism/-istic 45, 58, 162, 167, 195, 209n, 212, 250, 267ff., 312ff., 315, 384, 396, 402, 408, 409, 426, 445, 466, 476n
Hume, D. 97n, 292, 296
Husserl, E. 25n, 70, 195n, 206, 300-302, 336, 373, 514, 518

idealism and realism 321
ideas 112-113, 143n, 144ff., 181ff., 205-206, 293, 322, 360, 380, 384
identity, norm of 140n
identity-in-difference 149ff.
image of God 49, 473
immanence of God 373n
immanent criticism 289n
immortal soul 9ff., 13, 33, 180n, 219ff., 230, 233, 236, 242ff., 252, 383n
individual 419
individual as primitive notion 452
individuality as determinant 455ff.
individuality structures 357n, 452
Indo-German 246-247
infinite 278n, 382n, 406ff.
infinity 167ff.
inner perception 122
intersection principle 14, 371, 375n, 454-466
intuition 8, 13, 83, 122-130, 429
intuition vs. form of sensibility 89ff., 91n, 101, 137, 139, 141n,

155, 169, 493, 499
intuitionism 95-97, 99
Isagógè Philosophiae 6-7, 19-42
Ive, J.G.A. 178n

Jager, A. 385, 518
James, W. 24n, 35n, 518
Janse, A. 9, 10, 13, 14, 75n, 76, 128n, 179n, 217, 219, 220, 223, 224-263, 268, 275, 312, 323n, 327n, 330, 367, 368, 369, 370n, 374n, 382, 383, 384, 385, 394n, 426, 427, 466n, 473n, 477, 494, 518-519, 523, 527, 528, 530, 531
Janse, W. 519
Jellinek, G. 271
judgment 22, 24, 91, 94ff., 101, 110-113, 118-122, 123, 128n, 133ff., 135n, 186, 189, 193, 203, 296
judgments of discerning 37, 333, 364, 409, 410ff., 433, 439

Kant, I. 49, 68n, 84, 88, 89, 90, 91n, 95, 97n, 105, 115n, 174, 211, 255, 271, 292, 296, 336, 350, 401, 477n, 496, 497, 498, 499, 519
Kaufmann, F. 291n
Kelsen, H. 275, 291, 515
kingdoms 371n
Klapwijk, J. 4n, 20n, 50n, 61n, 422n, 519
knowable 465, 468
knowing 24, 33, 103
knowing and rest 468
knowing and straying 430
knowing resorts under being 9, 14, 28, 33, 199, 254, 322-324, 410, 494
knowing subject 40, 49, 57, 71, 93ff., 110, 114ff., 121ff., 141, 156, 186ff., 212ff., 293, 378, 431, 436, 465
knowing subject as office 248, 251
knowing-knowable 9, 33ff., 57, 71ff., 119, 433, 439, 465, 510
knowledge and intuition 13, 117
knowledge by acquaintance 72, 102, 103-104, 188ff.
Koch, J. 44n, 46n, 519

Kok, J.H. 4, 6n, 50n, 79n, 80, 93n, 98n, 102n, 112n, 143n, 145n, 152n, 170n, 178n, 232n, 233n, 236, 247n, 330, 331n, 385n, 394n, 435n, 443n, 478, 514, 519, 524, 528, 530
Kraay, J.N. 343n, 519, 520
Krijnen, C. 203n, 208n, 520
Kronecker, L. 86
Krüger, F. 203n, 493, 530
Kuhn, T. 197n, 520
Kuyper, A. 42-55, 59n, 67, 69n, 76, 181-183, 218, 266, 267, 269, 270, 288, 289, 299n, 309, 310, 311, 315, 342, 343, 350, 357, 358, 360n, 368, 369, 388, 389, 391, 392, 399, 400n, 441, 442, 513, 516, 519, 520, 522, 527, 529

Land, J.P.N. 148n
Lask, E. 203n, 275, 291, 292, 301, 304, 305, 306n, 307, 308, 310, 336, 409n
latent-patent 464ff.
law 36, 65
law as boundary 10, 14, 342
law as knowable 484ff.
law in externalist-realist sense 409
law in realist mode 361
law of logical law-sphere 416n
law threefold 424
lawful field of vision 349
law-giving 184
law-idea 10-11, 222, 312ff., 322, 341ff., 369
law-idea as cosmological world-plan 355-358
law-idea as organon 343ff.
law-idea as theonomic absolute 354-355
law-organism 376
laws of being 416ff.
law-spheres 68, 73, 218, 312, 356, 403ff., 458
Leenders, H. 228n, 229n, 520
Leibniz, G.W. 74n, 97n, 105, 107, 117n, 143, 161, 370, 441, 444n, 513, 520, 522

life- and worldview 314-315, 320ff.
limiting concept 11, 379-380
living soul 231ff., 236-240, 241, 245ff., 258
Lobachevski, P.I. 98n
localization 88
Locke, J. 97n, 271, 292, 296
Lockean idea 136, 369
Loemker, L.E. 74n, 246n, 520
logic 284n, 299ff.
logical function 430ff., 436
logical schema 437
logical thought 332ff.
Logos; cf. God, the Logos
Logos and analytical function 431
logos speculation 70ff., 76, 187n, 197, 387
Los, S.O. 231
Lotze, R.H. 98n, 105, 145, 171-172, 181, 182, 188, 507n
love command 477ff.
Lovejoy, A. 448, 520
Lullus, R. 97n
Luther, M. 55n, 345, 406n

MacCulloch, D. 55n, 520
macrocosm and microcosm 157ff., 178
Maier, H. 127n, 286n
Makkreel, R.A. 281n, 520
Malebranche, N. 97n, 167, 506n, 527
Mannoury, G. 78n, 79n, 98n, 530
Marburg neo-Kantianism 70n, 196n
Marx, K. 63n, 523
Maxwell, J.C. 418n
Maxwell, N. 432n, 521
McIntire, C.T. 5, 273n, 521
meaning for consciousness 327, 365, 432
meaning itself 325ff.
meaning ontologized 11, 340
meaning-giving 325ff
meaning-having object 325ff.
means of knowing 40, 480ff.
Meinong, A. 13, 78, 106n, 108, 109, 126, 127, 128n, 131, 133, 135n, 137, 139, 140n, 147n, 167, 202n, 250, 363, 517, 522

Mersenne, M. 446n
metalogic 13, 201ff., 203n
metalogical intuition 205-206, 208n, 301
metalogical reality of knowledge 116, 285
metalogical sphere (cf. also Gegenstand-sphere) 8, 204, 302n
meta-philosophical discourse 56ff., 69, 256, 480ff.
metaphysical intuition 129ff., 146-154, 161-164, 205, 452
metaphysics and Gegenstandstheorie 136, 139
metaphysics, directions in 77
metaphysics of ideas (cf. also ideas) 352, 440ff.
metaphysics of substance 13, 142ff.
'method of knowledge organization' 22-23, 28, 32-37, 57
method of resolution and composition 23, 29, 37-39, 438
method in Vollenhoven 12, 25
methodology 382n
Mill, J.S. 97n
Miller, A. 67n, 521
modal law 349
modal law vs. thing-law 451ff.
modal relation 286, 302ff., 376, 409n
modal sovereignty 289n
modality 221, 301, 328ff.
modernism 45n, 70n
monad 143, 177, 444n
monadic relations 106-108, 115, 460, 462
monadology 117, 143, 177
monism and dualism 80, 98, 102, 393ff.
Montesquieu, C. de S. 271
Montessori, M. 219, 226-232, 234, 240n, 244n, 246, 518, 520, 521
Moore, G.E. 133, 147n, 521
moral antithesis of good and evil 466, 477n
moral antithesis of good and evil as determinant 474ff.
Muis, R. 79n, 523

Mullen, G. 368n
mystical 157, 168, 242, 270n, 345
mystical unity 269

natural order (of law-spheres) 461ff.
neo-Calvinist (cf. also Calvinistic) 12, 42ff., 45ff., 53, 61n
neo-Idealism 3, 206
neo-Kantian(ism) 9, 11, 206, 373ff.
neo-Kantian rationality 362, 379-380
Newton, I. 90n, 97n, 148, 418n, 521
Nicholas of Cusa 486n
Nietzsche, F. 65, 394, 521
noetic, the 405, 433, 465, 468, 472, 504ff.
norm, 'ratio' and 'empirie' 93-97
norms and ideals 184, 186
norms and law 420
norms and values 93n, 209n, 251, 279, 281, 303, 426, 433, 485
norms, logical 93, 114n, 115n, 166-167
number 137-139

Object and Objective 131, 133n, 147, 208
object function 463
Occam, W. of 346
occasion of experience 165
occasionalism 165, 213, 499, 503ff.
Olevian, Caspar 73n
ontological difference 417, 453
ontology of meaning 378, 411ff
organic law-idea 375ff.
organism of science 122, 193ff., 207
O'Shea, D. 85n, 148n, 521

pantheism 170, 389
Pareau, L.G. 388n
Parmenides 394
Pascal, B. 91, 97n
Pasch, M. 98n
Paul (the Apostle) 260n, 449, 476n
Pauline 181n, 183n, 477n
Peano, G. 82, 139n
perception 120ff.
phenomenology 70, 373ff.
Philistion 506n

Philo 344
philosophy, place and task 12, 37, 59, 70
plant psychology 179n, 231n, 235, 421
Plantinga, A. 178n, 394n, 521, 524
Plato 21, 29n, 97n, 175, 188n, 249n, 260n, 273n, 344, 398, 444, 445, 446, 448, 187n, 521, 528
pluralism of methods 245
Poincaré, H. 79, 82-89, 95, 97, 98n, 167, 168, 181, 212, 220, 492, 493, 496, 497, 498n, 521
point of orientation 35
Polak, L. 313
Porphyry 20n, 522
Pos, H.J. 19, 20n, 50n, 79n, 530
postmodernism 199n
postulate of uniformity 283ff.
potential-actual 464ff.
praedicatum inest subjecto 143ff.
predestination 181, 347n, 372
predestination speculation 357n, 373n
predication 35
prefunctional 263, 476ff.
principle of complete induction 81ff., 138ff., 168n, 169, 497ff.
principle of substance 100, 142ff., 151ff., 154, 163, 177, 400ff.
problem-historical method 5
prophetic office 249
providence 346ff.
providential world-plan 345, 370
provisional result 26-28, 30
psychical 114, 242n, 467
psychical acts 93, 101n
psychical content 127
psychical growth 101, 126, 138, 162, 174, 190, 468
psychical synthesis 100, 101n, 139, 154ff., 162, 179, 235n
psychology, two-faculty 235n
psycho-physical organization 87-89, 100ff., 113ff., 122, 148ff., 154ff., 169, 170, 179, 200, 220, 235n, 326ff., 444, 466ff., 497ff.
Ptolemaeus 253

Puchinger, G.   269n, 271, 521
Puchta,   271
Pythagoras   333

quality of being a subject   247
quality of subjection (cf. also
   function of subjection)   403, 412,
   419ff.

Radbruch, G.   275, 291
Ralfs, G.   203n
Ranschburg, P.   225n, 521
rationality, subjective and objective
   8, 10, 13, 48, 76, 115, 158, 185ff.,
   195, 211, 220, 383-384, 441ff
realist scholasticism   265, 275
reality of science   159, 167, 180, 185,
   199
reason in neo-Kantianism   362
referent and relatum   113
Reformational philosophy   242n
'Reformed epistemology'   61n
Reformed foundation   50-55
Reformed philosophy   3, 18, 60
Reformed principles   46-50
reforming philosophy   61-73
region category   301, 328ff., 404
Reid, T.   61n
relation   102, 460ff
relation, nature of   105-108, 234, 369
relationship   460
religion and faith   18n
religion as trans-cosmic relation   483
religious attitude   256
religious, the   472
Remes, U.   438n, 518
Rentsch, T.   203n, 521
resolution   38, 457
retrocipations   462
Rickert, H.   202, 203, 208n, 209,
   281n, 291, 390n, 520, 521
Ridderbos, J.   343n, 347n, 530
Riemann, G.F.B.   98n
rule following   62, 67, 72
Rullmann, J.C.   43n, 522
Runner, H.E.   42n, 520, 524
Russell, B.   66n, 71n, 82n, 98n,104,
   106, 107, 109, 112, 133n, 143, 144,
   145, 147n, 173n, 307n, 522
Ryle, G.   238, 522

Santayana, G.   3, 522
Scheler, M.   219, 231
Schneckenburger, M.   343
Scholastic/-ticism   8ff., 48, 54, 58,
   69ff., 76, 79n, 187ff., 194n, 211,
   218ff., 221, 230, 238, 241, 261,
   265, 268, 299n, 310n, 313, 338ff.,
   341, 360, 375, 384, 428, 441ff., 507
Scholten, G.   281-290, 291, 293n,
   298, 303, 307, 310, 314, 322, 514
Schopenhauer, A.   246
Schröder, E.   98n
scientific outlook   66n, 71n
Scriptural philosophy   41, 253
Self   11, 100, 154ff., 179-180, 376
Self-awareness and Self-approaching
   process   123, 160ff.
self-certainty   250ff.
self-consciousness   52, 122ff., 160ff.
Semitic realism   239, 246-247
Sigwart, C.   127n, 284n, 286, 302,
   303, 305, 326, 331, 361, 364, 376,
   378, 409n, 507n, 522, 527
Simmel, G.   336
Simons, P.   433n, 522
sin   337
Skinner, B.F.   229n
Socrates   97n, 444, 445
solipsism   125
soul   233ff., 241n, 242n, 244n, 253,
   483ff.
soul and direction   475ff.
soul and spirit   239ff.
soul as substance   155, 219, 232n
sovereignty-subservience   63ff.
space, nature of,   120-122
specification of a modality   306
Speiser, E.A.   474n, 522
sphere-sovereignty   44, 66ff., 207,
   210n, 218, 288, 350ff.
Spinoza, B.   97n
spirit   144, 158, 177, 229ff., 232, 253,
   259, 261ff., 359n, 378ff., 427
spirit, life-giving   233, 235, 236-241
Stahl, F.J.   311

Stammler, R.   275, 290
standing in subjection   36, 64, 219
standpoint   35
states of affairs   437
Stellingwerff, J.   5, 18n, 20n, 54n, 55n, 75n, 77n, 81n, 204n, 224n, 232n, 233n, 235, 236, 242n, 253n, 264, 269n, 270, 273n, 274n, 275n, 277n, 312n, 353n, 369, 493n, 504n, 522
Strauss, D.F.M.   380n, 523
structure and direction (cf. also direction)   473
sub specie aeternitatis   337, 359, 378
substance and phenomenon   260n, 383n, 443-448, 449
substances   141ff.
substantia incompleta   13, 100, 232n, 238
succession (real)   90, 138, 149ff., 161-162, 169, 172
Sweetman, R.S.   388n, 443n, 523
synthetic a priori   8, 54n, 63, 68, 72, 84, 87ff., 89, 91ff., 94, 95, 97, 98, 121, 140ff., 164, 170, 193, 195, 198, 220ff., 245n, 301, 330, 335, 341n, 351n, 384n, 387, 429, 437
systasis   203ff., 390, 470
systematic philosophy   18n, 24

Tacitus, C.   156
tasked subject/ivity   10, 220, 248ff.
teleology   335
theism   166-201, 388ff.
theism, kinds of   391-397
theistic epistemic ideal   41, 166, 387, 390
theistic intuitionism   75, 77-78, 94
thetical-critical method   22, 28, 30-32, 56, 59
thing-laws   112, 145, 177, 181ff., 372
Thomas Aquinas   345
time   139
time and number   496, 500
Tol, A.   6n, 19n, 20n, 45n, 61n, 66n, 69, 70n, 71n, 79n, 199n, 270n, 373n, 386n, 396n, 398n, 402n, 424n, 425n, 428n, 452n, 453n,

476n, 487n, 490n, 491n, 502n, 520, 523, 528
Toletus, F.   97n
transcendence and immanence   175-177, 188, 200, 201, 386-387, 391, 407
transcendence of God   170ff.
transcendent world/things   136, 140, 147, 191n
transcendental criticism   11
transcendental critique   54n, 61n
transcendental realism   206, 278-279, 283
transcendentals   463n
Trinitarian theistic position   10, 11, 14, 180-201, 423ff.
truth   33, 72, 167, 188-189, 390
truth acquired   436
truth in itself   434, 471
truth known   435

unity of consciousness   269, 354, 360, 379
unity of subjection   459, 476, 421
universalism (cf. also "holism")   470
universality as determinant   455ff.
universality of a sphere   375

validity   201ff., 307
value   251, 279ff, 432, 471
value and assessment   432
value sciences   280, 282
Van Dalen, D.   168n, 523
Van der Heiden, G.J.   79n, 523
Van der Hoeven, J.   63n, 517, 523
Van der Laan, H.   50n, 442n, 523
Van der Vaart Smit, H,W.   79n, 530
Van der Walt, B.J.   6n, 75n, 224n, 473n, 523
Van Deursen, A.Th.   20n, 44, 46n, 47n, 51n, 55n, 524
Van Dijk, J.J.C.   272n, 309n, 515, 530
Van Dijk, W.K.   272n, 291n, 515, 521, 524, 530
Van Dyke, A.J.   42n, 524
Van Eeden, F.   263n, 514
Van Oordt, J.F.   388n
Van Til, C.   367, 531

Van Woudenberg, R.   61n, 523, 524
Van Zelm, J.C.   210n, 225, 226, 513
Veenhof, J.   453n, 524
Verburg, M.E.   4, 237n, 265n, 266n, 268n, 269n, 271, 272n, 273n, 274n, 276n, 277n, 282n, 289n, 290n, 291, 293n, 299n, 301, 308n, 311n, 314, 320, 342n, 343n, 377n, 524
Vermooten, W.H.   240n, 524
viewing   310ff., 325, 328ff., 336ff.
Vollenhoven, D.H.Th. (personal)   3-14, 17-22, 50n, 55n, 61n, 70, 75-80, 204n, 217-225, 241-244, 263-276, 315-320, 353n, 363-374, 441-442, 491-503
Vollenhoven, H.M. (nee Dooyeweerd)   3n, 236n, 243, 264
Von Hartmann, E.   203n
Von Helmholtz, H.   98n

Wagner, R.   263, 514
Weierstrass, K.   86
Wesensschau   206, 302
Weyl, H.   381, 528
Whitehead, A.N.   104n, 165n, 395, 506, 528
whole   245, 253ff.
will of decision   451, 453
will to know   156
Willemsen, M.   523
Windelband, W.   203n, 291
Wittgenstein, L.   66, 528
Wolters, A.M.   5, 30n, 42n, 79n, 273n, 422n, 453n, 524, 529
Wolterstorff, N.   61n, 517, 529
Woltjer, J.   19, 20, 47-50, 55n, 59n, 117n, 118n, 299n, 310n, 315, 441, 442, 443, 493, 519, 523, 527, 529
Woltjer, R.H.   443n, 529
Word revelation   60n, 70
world as idea   174-175
world order   178-180
worldview   66ff., 238ff., 256
Wright, C.   67n, 521

Zeno   65n, 97n
Zevenbergen, W.   275, 278, 280n

Zuidema, S.U.   80n, 529
Zwingli, H.   55n

www.ingramcontent.com/pod-product-compliance
Lightning Source LLC
Chambersburg PA
CBHW021823220426

43663CB00005B/116